ESSENTIAL WORLD ATLAS

CONTENTS

WORLD

8-9   **World: Northern part**
10-11   **World: Southern part**

12-13   **Arctic**
14-15   **Antarctic**

EUROPE

16-17   **Europe: Physical**
18-19   **Europe: Political**

20-21   **British Isles: South**
22-23   **British Isles: North**
24-25   **Southern England**
26-27   **Wales and South West England**
28-29   **Northern England**
30-31   **Southern Scotland**
32-33   **Northern Scotland**
34-35   **Ireland**

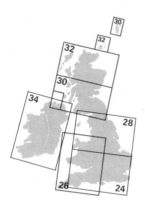

First published in Great Britain in 1993
by George Philip Limited,
an imprint of Reed Consumer Books Limited,
Michelin House, 81 Fulham Road, London SW3 6RB
and Auckland, Melbourne, Singapore and Toronto

Copyright © 1993 Reed International Books Limited

ISBN 0 540 05727 4

A CIP catalogue record for this book is available
from the British Library

Printed in Hong Kong

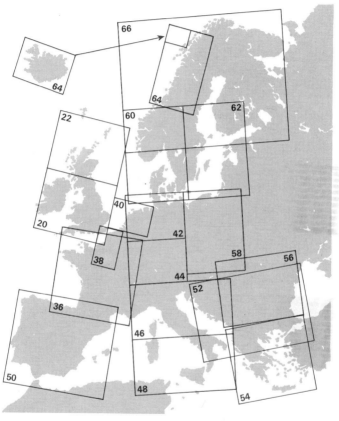

ASIA

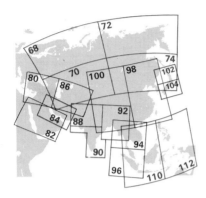

76-77   **Asia: Physical**
78-79   **Asia: Political**

80-81   **Turkey and the Middle East**
82-83   **Arabian Peninsula**
84-85   **The Gulf**
86-87   **Central Asia and Afghanistan**
88-89   **Pakistan and North West India**
90-91   **Central and Southern India, Sri Lanka**
92-93   **Eastern India, Bangladesh and Burma**
94-95   **Mainland South East Asia**
96-97   **The Malay Peninsula**
98-99   **China: East**
100-101   **China: West**

68-69   **Eastern Europe**
70-71   **Kazakhstan and Central Asia**
72-73   **North East Russia**
74-75   **South East Russia and Mongolia**

102-103   **Japan: North**
104-105   **Japan: South**
106-107   **Japan: Tokyo, Kyoto, Osaka**
108-109   **Japan: Kyushu, West Honshu and Shikoku**

110-111   **Indonesia: West**
112-113   **Indonesia: East**

AUSTRALASIA

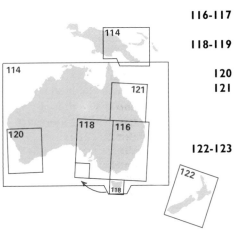

114-115 Australia, New Zealand and Papua New Guinea

116-117 Australia: Brisbane, Sydney and Melbourne

118-119 Australia: Adelaide, Melbourne and Tasmania

120 Australia: Perth

121 Australia: North East Queensland

122-123 New Zealand, Central and South West Pacific

AFRICA

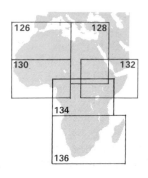

124 Africa: Physical

125 Africa: Political

126-127 Africa: North West

128-129 Africa: North East

130-131 Africa: West

132-133 Africa: East

134-135 Africa: Central

136-137 Africa: South

North America

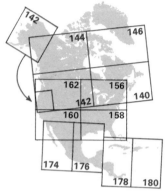

138 North America: Physical
139 North America: Political

140-141 Canada: South East
142-143 Canada: South West and Alaska
144-145 Canada: North West
146-147 Canada: North East
148-149 Canada: Saint Lawrence Estuary
150-151 Canada: The Great Lakes
152-153 Canada: Southern Saskatchewan and Manitoba
154-155 Canada: Southern British Columbia and Alberta

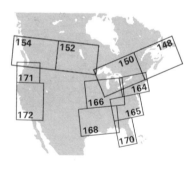

156-157 USA: North East
158-159 USA: South East
160-161 USA: South West
162-163 USA: North West
164 USA: Boston, New York, Washington
165 USA: Washington, Atlanta
166-167 USA: Upper Mississippi
168-169 USA: Lower Mississippi and Gulf Coast
170 USA: Florida
171 USA: Columbia Basin
172-173 USA: California

174-175 Mexico: West
176-177 Mexico: East
178-179 Caribbean: West
180-181 Caribbean: East

SOUTH AMERICA

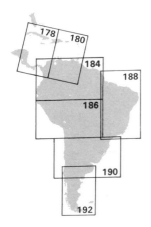

182 **South America: Physical**

183 **South America: Political**

184-185 **South America: North West**

186-187 **South America: West**

188-189 **South America: East**

190-191 **South America: Central**

192 **South America: South**

INDEX

MAP SYMBOLS

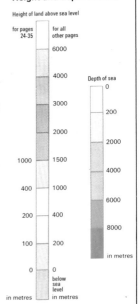

Height and depth colours

Settlement symbols in order of size

⬡ ⬡ ■ ◉ ◎ ○ ○ ○

——— International boundary

·········· Internal boundary

——— Principal railway

——— Principal road

┴┴┴┴┴ Canal

✿✈ Principal airport

⊣---⊢ Tunnel

〰 Permanent river

~~~~ Intermittent river

⬭ Permanent lake

⬭ Intermittent lake

⁙⁙⁙ Marsh

▲ 8 848 Altitude above sea level

▼ 10 497 Depth below sea level

263 Level of lake

⑱ Indicates the adjoining map

As far as possible the de facto situation of international boundaries is shown

Scale note
To the right of each map title there is a number representing the scale of the map for example, 1 : 2 000 000. This means that one centimetre on the map represents 2 million centimetres or 20 kilometres on the ground. Or, if the number is 1 : 40 000 000, one centimetre represents 40 million centimetres or 400 kilometres.

Height of land above sea level

for pages 24-35	for all other pages
	6000
	4000
	3000
1000	1500
400	1000
200	400
100	200
0	0
in metres	below sea level
	in metres

Depth of sea
0
200
2000
4000
6000
8000
in metres
~~~~

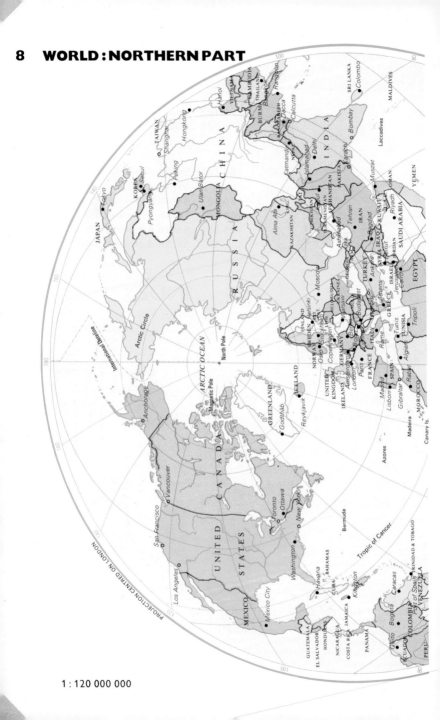

1 : 120 000 000

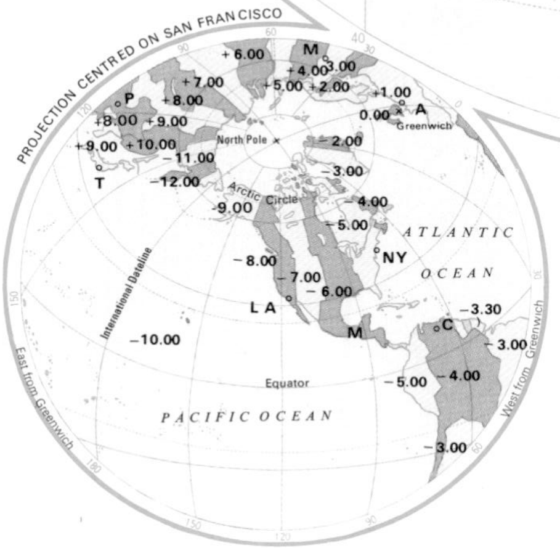

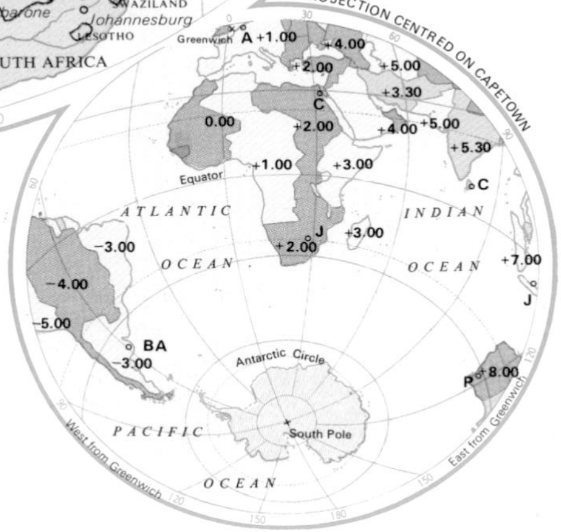

Chagos Arch.

PROJECTION CENTRED ON CAPETOWN

+7.00 J

+8.00 P

+5.30 C

+5.00
+4.30
+4.00
+3.30
+3.00

INDIAN   OCEAN

+2.00 +1.00 A
C
+2.00 J
+1.00
0.00
Greenwich
Equator

South Pole
Antarctic Circle

ATLANTIC   OCEAN

PACIFIC   OCEAN

−3.00 BA
−4.00
−5.00

West from Greenwich
East from Greenwich

MAURITIUS
Reunion
Antananarivo
MADAGASCAR
SEYCHELLES
Aden
Sana
Djibouti
SOMALIA
Mogadishu
ETHIOPIA
Addis Ababa
Khartoum
SUDAN
UGANDA KENYA
Kampala Nairobi
Dar es Salaam
TANZANIA
Lilongwe
MALAWI
Lusaka Harare
ZAMBIA ZIMBABWE
Maputo
MOZAMBIQUE
Pretoria SWAZILAND
Johannesburg
LESOTHO
SOUTH AFRICA
Gaborone
BOTSWANA
NAMIBIA
Windhoek
ANGOLA
Luanda
ZAIRE
Kinshasa
Brazzaville
CONGO
GABON
Libreville
EQUAT. GUINEA
CAMEROON
Yaoundé
Bangui
CENTRAL AFRICAN REP.
CHAD
Ndjamena
NIGER
NIGERIA
Abuja
BENIN
TOGO
GHANA Lomé
Accra
IVORY COAST
LIBERIA
Monrovia
SIERRA LEONE
Freetown
GUINEA
Conakry
GUINEA BISSAU
Banjul
SENEGAL
Dakar
MAURITANIA
MALI
ALGERIA
LIBYA
NIGER
BURKINA
Niamey
CAPE VERDE IS.

Cape Town

St Helena

Tropic of Capricorn

Ascension

Equator

West from Greenwich

East from Greenwich

BRAZIL
Brasília
Rio de Janeiro
São Paulo
BOLIVIA
Georgetown
GUYANA
Paramaribo
SURINAM
FRENCH GUIANA

TIME ZONES

• Capital Cities

9.00 6.00   Time Zone in hours fast (+) or slow (−) of Greenwich Mean Time

Standard Time not the Zone hour

No Official Time

All distances measured through the centre of the map are correct for scale

PROJECTION CENTRED ON SAN FRANCISCO

West from Greenwich
East from Greenwich

ATLANTIC   OCEAN
PACIFIC   OCEAN

−3.00
−3.00
−4.00
−5.00 NY
−5.00 M
−6.00
−7.00 LA
−8.00
−9.00
−10.00
International Dateline

Greenwich
+1.00 A
+2.00
+3.00
+4.00
+5.00
+6.00 M
+7.00
+8.00 P
+9.00
+10.00
−11.00
−12.00 T
North Pole
Arctic Circle
Equator

COPYRIGHT GEORGE PHILIP & SON LTD

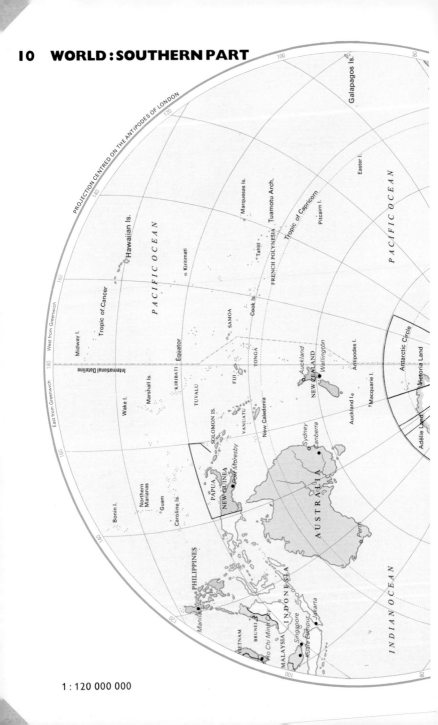

PROJECTION CENTRED ON THE ANTIPODES OF LONDON

Galapagos Is.

PACIFIC OCEAN

Easter I.

Marquesas Is.

Tuamotu Arch.

Tropic of Capricorn

Pitcairn I.

FRENCH POLYNESIA

Tahiti

Hawaiian Is.

PACIFIC OCEAN

Kiritimati

Tropic of Cancer

Cook Is.

SAMOA

Midway I.

Equator

International Dateline

Antipodes I.

Antarctic Circle

Victoria Land

Auckland

Wellington

NEW ZEALAND

TONGA

FIJI

Auckland I.

Macquarie I.

Adélie Land

Marshall Is.

KIRIBATI

Wake I.

TUVALU

VANUATU

SOLOMON IS.

New Caledonia

Sydney

Canberra

Bonin I.

Northern Marianas

Guam

Caroline Is.

PAPUA

NEW GUINEA

Port Moresby

AUSTRALIA

Perth

INDIAN OCEAN

PHILIPPINES

Manila

VIETNAM

Ho Chi Minh City

BRUNEI

MALAYSIA

INDONESIA

Singapore

Kuala Lumpur

Jakarta

East from Greenwich

West from Greenwich

1 : 120 000 000

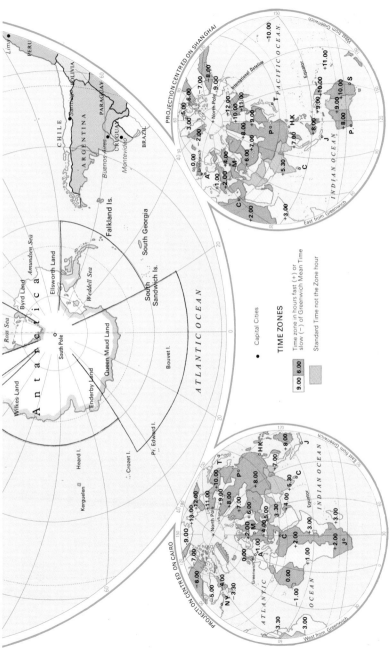

PERU
Lima

BOLIVIA
PARAGUAY
CHILE
ARGENTINA
URUGUAY
Buenos Aires
Montevideo
BRAZIL

Falkland Is.
South Georgia
South Sandwich Is.

Antarctica
Ross Sea
Amundsen Sea
Byrd Land
Ellsworth Land
Weddell Sea
Wilkes Land
South Pole
Enderby Land
Queen Maud Land
Bouvet I.

ATLANTIC OCEAN

Heard I.
Kerguelen
Crozet I.
Pr. Edward I.

• Capital Cities

TIME ZONES

Time zone in hours fast (+) or
slow (−) of Greenwich Mean Time

| 9.00 | 6.00 |

Standard Time not the Zone hour

PROJECTION CENTRED ON SHANGHAI

PACIFIC OCEAN
International Dateline
West from Greenwich
−10.00
−7.00
−6.00
−5.00
−9.00
−12.00
−11.00
−10.00
+9.00
+11.00
+3.00
−2.00
North Pole
+10.00
+8.00
+7.00
+6.00
+9.00
+10.00
HK
+8.00
+7.00
Greenwich
0.00
+4.00
+2.00
+1.00
+5.30
M
C
J
Equator
+2.00
+3.00
A
C
P°
T°
S°
P°
INDIAN OCEAN
East from Greenwich

PROJECTION CENTRED ON CAIRO

ATLANTIC OCEAN
West from Greenwich
East from Greenwich
HK
+8.00
−7.00
+13.00
+12.00
+11.00
+10.00
+9.00
+8.00
+7.00
+6.00
+5.00
+4.00
+3.00
+2.00
+1.00
0.00
−1.00
−2.00
+3.30
−3.00
+2.00
+3.00
+4.00
+5.30
−6.00
−5.00
−9.00
−3.30
N.Y.
North Pole
Greenwich
Equator
M
C
C
J°
P°
T°
INDIAN OCEAN

COPYRIGHT GEORGE PHILIP & SON LTD

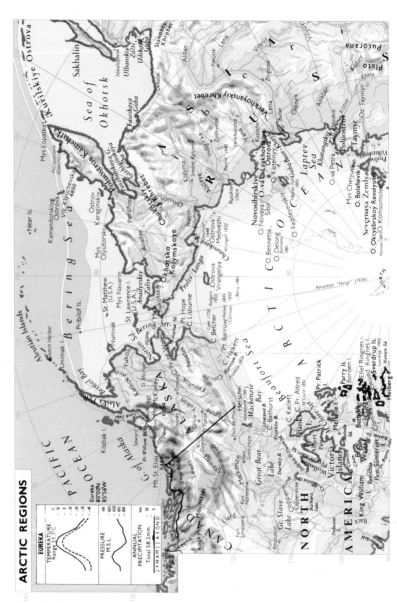

ARCTIC REGIONS

EUREKA
80°00N
85°56W

TEMPERATURE
Range 51°C

PRESSURE
M.S.L.

ANNUAL
PRECIPITATION
Total 58.2mm.
J F M A M J J A S O N D

1 : 42 000 000

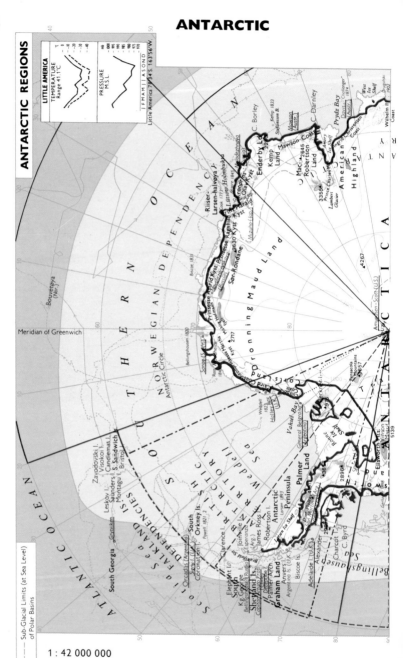

ANTARCTIC REGIONS

LITTLE AMERICA
TEMPERATURE
Range 41.1°C

PRESSURE
M.S.L.

Little America 78°34′S. 163°56′W.

J F M A M J J A S O N D

ATLANTIC OCEAN

Bouvetøya (Nor.)

Meridian of Greenwich

SOUTHERN OCEAN

NORWEGIAN DEPENDENCY

Antarctic Circle

Dronning Maud Land

Enderby Ld.

Kemp Land

Mac. Robertson Land

American Highland

ANTARCTICA

Amundsen-Scott (U.S.)

Weddell Sea

Ronne Ice Shelf

Filchner Ice Shelf

Palmer Land

Antarctic Peninsula

Graham Land

Bellingshausen Sea

South Georgia

Falkland Islands Dependencies

South Orkney Is.

South Shetland Is.

South Sandwich Is.

British Antarctic Territory

Ross Sea

1 : 42 000 000

---- Sub-Glacial Limits (at Sea Level) of Polar Basins

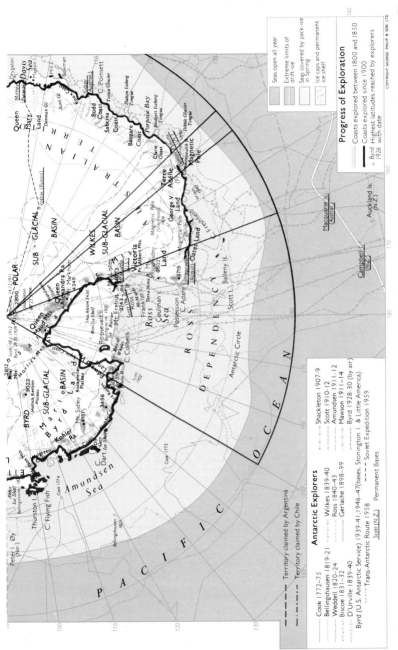

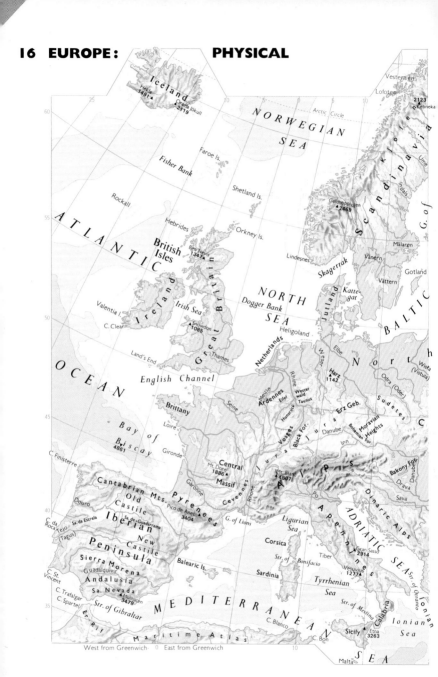

Iceland
Hekla 1491
Oraefa Jökull 2119

NORWEGIAN SEA

Arctic Circle

Vesterålen
Lofoten
2123 Kebneka

Scandinavia

G. of

Faroe Is.

Fisher Bank

Shetland Is.

Galdhøppigen 2469

Rockall

Hebrides

Orkney Is.

Mälaren

British Isles
Ben Nevis 1347

Lindesnes

Skagerrak

Vänern

Gotland

Kattegat

Vättern

ATLANTIC

Valentia I.

C. Clear

Ireland

Irish Sea

Jutland

BALTIC

NORTH SEA
Dogger Bank

Snowdon 1085

Heligoland

North

Odra (Oder)

Wisła (Vistula)

Land's End

Great Britain

Thames

Elbe

Weser

OCEAN

English Channel

Netherlands

Rhine

Harz 1142

Sudetes

Brittany

Seine

Meuse
Ardennes
Eifel
Westerwald
Taunus

Bohemian For.

Hunsrück

Erz Geb.

C. Finisterre

Loire

Vosges

Black For.

Jura

Moravian Heights

Bay of Biscay 4861

Gironde

Mt. Dore 1886

Central Massif

Danube

Inn

Bakony For.

Cantabrian Mts.
Old Castile
Pico de Aneto 3404

Pyrenees

Cévennes

Mt. Blanc 4807

ALPS

Po

Apennines

Dinaric Alps

Drava

Danube

C. da Roca

Douro

Tejo (Tagus)

Sa. da Estrela

Sa. de Guadarrama

Iberian

New Castile

Garonne

G. of Lions

Ligurian Sea

Gran Sasso 2914

ADRIATIC SEA

Sava

Str. of Otranto

C. St. Vincent

Peninsula

Sierra Morena

Guadalquivir

Andalusia

Balearic Is.

Corsica

Sardinia

Tiber

Vesuvius 1277

Str. of Bonifacio

Tyrrhenian Sea

Ionian

C. Trafalgar
C. Spartel

Sa. Nevada
Mulhacén 3478

Str. of Gibraltar

MEDITERRANEAN

C. Blanco

Str. of Messina

Sicily

Calabria

Ionian Sea

Er Rif

Maritime Atlas

Etna 3263

C. Bon

SEA

Malta

1 : 24 000 000

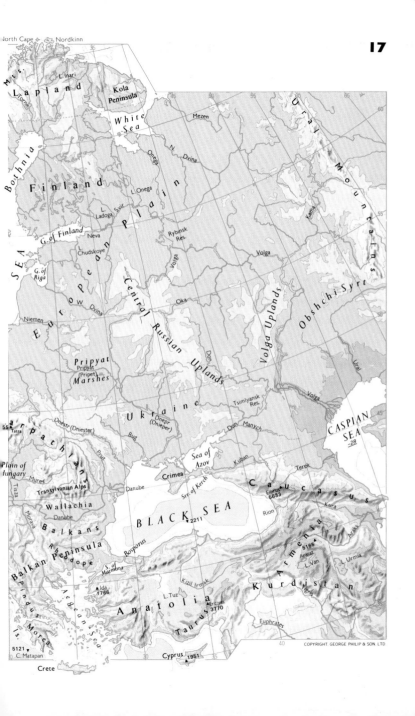

North Cape Nordkinn

Mts.
Lapland
L. Inari
Torne
Kola
Peninsula

White
Sea
Mezen

Bothnia
Finland
Onega
N. Dvina

L. Onega
L.
Ladoga Svir
Rybinsk
Res.

G. of Finland
Neva
Volga
Volga
Kama

SEA
Chudskoye
Volga

G. of
Riga
European Plain
Central Russian
Oka

Niemen
ow Dvina
Volga Uplands
ObshchiSyrt

Pripyat
Pripyat
(Pripet)
Marshes
Don
Ural

Ukraine
Tsimlyansk
Res.
Volga

Onestr (Dniester)
Dnepr
(Dnieper)
Don Manych
CASPIAN
SEA
-28

58
Tatra
Bug
Sea of
Azov
Kuban

arpathians
Prut
Crimea
Str. of Kerch
Terek
Caucasus
Elbrus
5633
Kura

Plain of
Hungary
Mures
Danube
BLACK SEA
2211
Rion
Araks

Tisza
Transylvanian Alps
Armenia
5165

Wallachia
Danube
Bosporus
L. Van
Urmia

Morava
Balkans
S. of
Marmara

Rhodope
Kizil Irmak
Kurdistan

Balkan Peninsula
Ida
1766

Pindus
Aegean Sea
L. Tuz
Anatolia
Ercyas
3770

Is.
Morea
Taurus
Euphrates

5121
C. Matapan
Cyprus 1951

Crete

COPYRIGHT GEORGE PHILIP & SON LTD

1 : 24 000 000

ammerfest

Pechenga
Murmansk

Galivara

Luleå

Kuopio

Vaasa

Tampere

Helsinki

Kronstadt

Vyborg

Tallinn
ESTONIA

Chudskoye
Ozero

Pskov

LATVIA
Liepaja   Riga

Kloipeda

LITHUANIA
Kaunas

Kaliningrad

Vilnius

ARSZAWA

BELORUSSIA
Minsk

Bialystok

Brest

Lublin

N D

Pripyat

Kraków

REP

Lvov

Chernovtsy

Miskolc

Debrecen

Cluj-Napoca

RY

Timişoara   Braşov

ROMANIA

rad   BUCUREŞTI

SERBIA

Slavi

Niš

Sofiya

Skopje

MACEDONIA

GREECE

Thessaloníki

Pátrai   Piraiévs   ATHÍNAI

Kríti   Iráklion

Beloye
More

Arkhangelsk

Mezen

Onezhskoye
Ozero

Sev. Dvina

Kotlas

R   U   S   S   I   A

St. Peterburg

Novgorod

Rybinskoye
Vdkhr

Vologda

Kostroma

Vyatka

Perm

Nizhniy Tagil

Yekaterinburg

Zlatoust

Chelyabinsk

Ladozhskoye
Ozero

Yaroslavl

Ivanovo

Nizhniy Novgorod

Izhevsk

Kazan

Ufa

Magnitogorsk

MOSKVA

Volga

Vitebsk

Smolensk

Tula

Orel

Penza

Syzran

Samara

Volga

Orenburg

Uralsk

Ork

Minsk

Mogilev

Gomel

Chernigov

Kiyev

Dnepr

Kursk

Don

Voronezh

Saratov

KAZAKHSTAN

Tambov

Volgograd

Guryev

Astrakhan

CASPIAN
SEA

Zhitomir

Berdichev

UKRAINE

Yelizavetgrad

Dnepropetrovsk

Krivoy Rog

Nikolayev

Zaporozhye

Kharkov

Lugansk

Donetsk

Don

Rostov

Volga

Ural

Makhachkala

Derbent

Dnestr

MOLDOVA

Kishinev

Odessa

Kherson

Azovskoye
More

Tagan rog

Stavropol

Krasnodar

Iaşi

Galaţi

Ploieşti

Constanţa

Sevastopol

Kerch

Novorossiysk

BLACK   SEA

GEORGIA

Tbilisi

Baku

AZERBAIJAN

Dunărea

Olteniya

Pleven

Ruse

Vurnup

BULGARIA

Plovdiv   Edirne

Sliven

Burgas

Sinop

Samsun

Kastamonu

Trabzon

Batumi

ARMENIA

Yerevan

Erzurum

Tabriz

İSTANBUL   Üsküdar

Bursa

Ankara

T   U   R   K   E   Y

Kayseri

Malatya

Diyarbakır

İzmir

Balikesir

Konya

Adana

Antalya

İskenderun

Al Mawsil

IRAN

SYRIA

IRAQ

Halab

CYPRUS   Nicosia
Limassol

SEA

Bothnia

FINLAND

SEA

Daugavpils

Neman

Oka

Zap. Dvina

Nyatka

Syr

COPYRIGHT GEORGE PHILIP & SON. LTD

C. Malin
I. Tory
North Channel
Aran I.
Derryveagh Mts.
Letterkenny
Coleraine
Londonderry
Antrim Mts.
Larne
Stranraer
Wigtown
Lifford
Ballymena
Donegal
NORTHERN IRELAND
Antrim
L. Neagh
Bangor
Mull of Galloway
Donegal Bay
Erne
Omagh
Belfast
Lisburn
Erris Hd.
Killala Bay
Bundoran
Blackwater
Downpatrick
ISLE OF MAN
Sligo
Enniskillen
Armagh
Dundrum
Ballina
Upper
L. Erne
Clones
Monaghan
Newry
Mourne Mts.
Douglas
Achill I.
L. Conn
Leitrim
Carrick-on-Shannon
Cavan
Greenore
Clare I.
Castlebar
Dundalk
Westport
Ceanannus
Mor
An Uaimh
IRISH S
L. Mask
Roscommon
Longford
Drogheda
Connemara
L. Corrib
Ree
Mullingar
Boyne
Balbriggan
Galway
Athlone
IRELAND
Athenry
Tullamore
Liffey
Dublin
(Baile Atha Cliath)
Anglesey
Galway Bay
Naas
Bray
Dun Laoghaire
Holyhead
Birr
Port Laoise
Kildare
Wicklow Mts.
Caernarfon Bay
Llangef
Ennis
L. Derg
Nenagh
Athy
Wicklow
Pwllheli
Loop Hd.
Kilrush
Limerick
Carlow
Arklow
Cardigan
Shannon
Listowel
Golden Vale
Thurles
Kilkenny
Bay
Tralee
Rath Luirc
Tipperary
Clonmel
Carrick-on-Suir
Enniscorthy
New Ross
Macgillicuddy's
Reeks
Cahirciveen 1040
Killarney
Mallow
Blackwater
Fermoy
Dungarvan
Wexford
Waterford
Rosslare
Fishguard
Cardigan
Castletown
Bere
Blarney
Lee
Cork
Youghal
Carnsore Pt.
St. David's
Hd.
Twi
Bantry
Bandon
Kinsale
Cobh
Cork Harbour
St. George's Channel
Haverfordwest
Carmarthe
C. Clear
Milford Haven
Pembroke
Llanell
Bristol C
Lundy I.
Hartland Point
Bude
St. Austell
Devonport
Truro
Camborne
Penzance
Falmouth
Lizard
Land's End
Scilly Is.

1 : 4 000 000

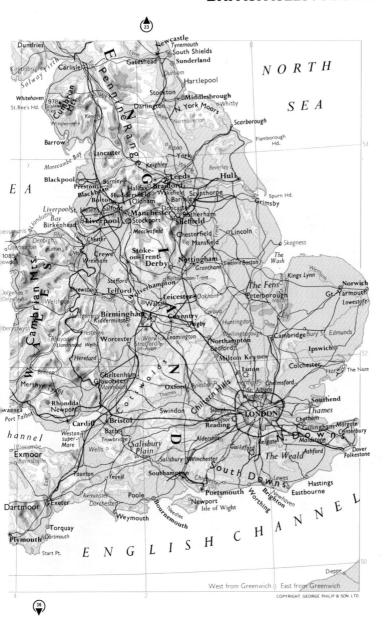

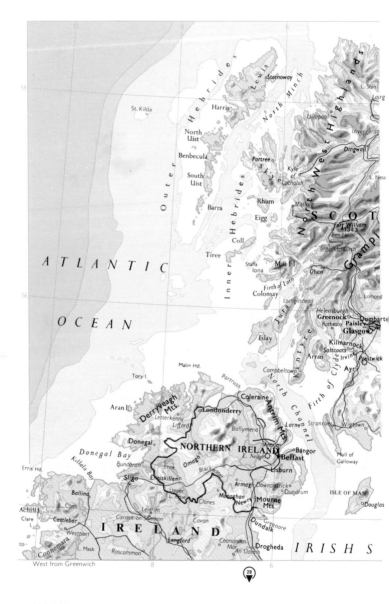

1 : 4 000 000

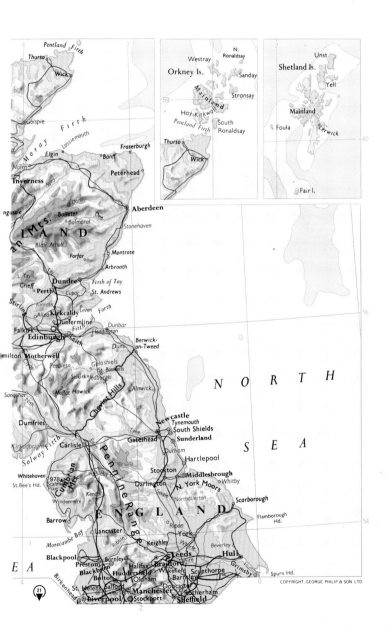

1 : 2 000 000

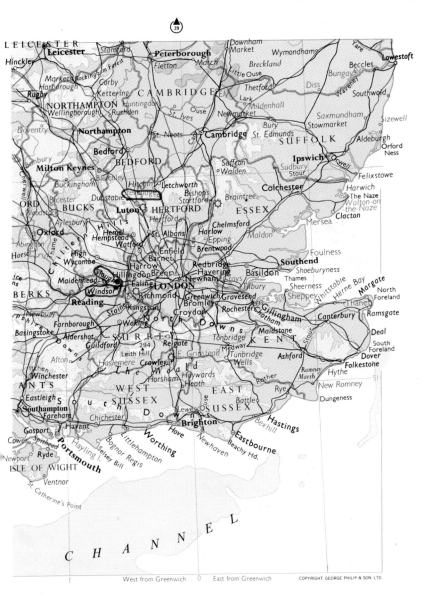

29

LEICESTER Leicester Stamford Peterborough Downham Market Wymondham Yare Lowestoft

Hinckley Fletton March Breckland Beccles

Rugby Market Harborough Rockingham Forest Corby Kettering CAMBRIDGE Little Ouse Thetford Diss Bungay Waveney Southwold

Daventry NORTHAMPTON Wellingborough Rushden Huntingdon St. Ives Ouse Lark Mildenhall Newmarket Bury St. Edmunds Saxmundham Stowmarket Sizewell

Northampton St. Neots Cambridge SUFFOLK Aldeburgh Orford Ness

Bedford Ipswich Orwell Felixstowe

Milton Keynes BEDFORD Bletchley Saffron Walden Sudbury Stour Harwich The Naze Walton-on-the-Naze

Buckingham Hitchin Letchworth Bishop's Stortford Braintree Colchester Clacton

Bicester Dunstable Stevenage HERTFORD ESSEX Mersea

Oxford Aylesbury BUCKS Luton Hertford Chelmsford

Woodstock Hemel Hempstead St. Albans Harlow Epping Maldon

Abingdon High Wycombe Watford Enfield Barnet Brentwood Foulness

BERKS Maidenhead Harrow HILLINGDON Brentford LONDON Redbridge Havering Southend Shoeburyness

Windsor Slough Ealing Newham Basildon Thames

Newbury Reading Staines Richmond Greenwich Gravesend Sheppey Sheerness Whitstable Herne Bay Margate North Foreland

Farnborough Woking Kingston Croydon Bromley Rochester Gillingham Chatham Thanet Ramsgate

Basingstoke Aldershot SURREY North Downs Maidstone KENT Canterbury Deal

Alton Guildford 294 Reigate Tonbridge Medway Ashford South Foreland Dover

Winchester Haslemere Leith Hill Crawley E. Grinstead Tunbridge Wells Rother Romney Marsh Folkestone Hythe

HANTS Horsham Haywards Heath The Weald EAST Rye New Romney

Eastleigh WEST SUSSEX South Downs Lewes SUSSEX Battle Hastings Dungeness

Southampton Fareham Chichester Brighton Eastbourne Bexhill

Gosport Havant Worthing Hove Newhaven Beachy Hd.

Cowes Spithead Hayling I. Littlehampton Bognor Regis Selsey Bill

Newport Ryde Portsmouth

ISLE OF WIGHT

Ventnor

St. Catherine's Point

C H A N N E L

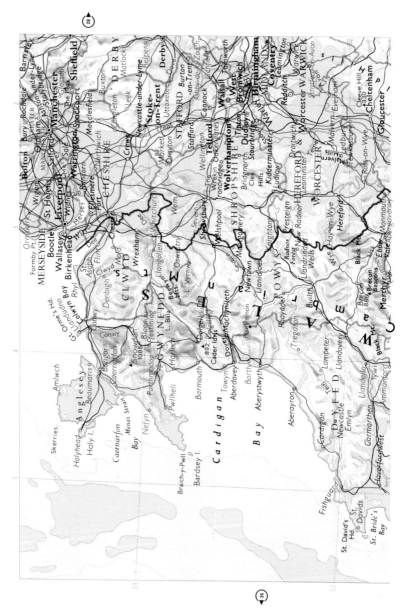

1 : 2 000 000

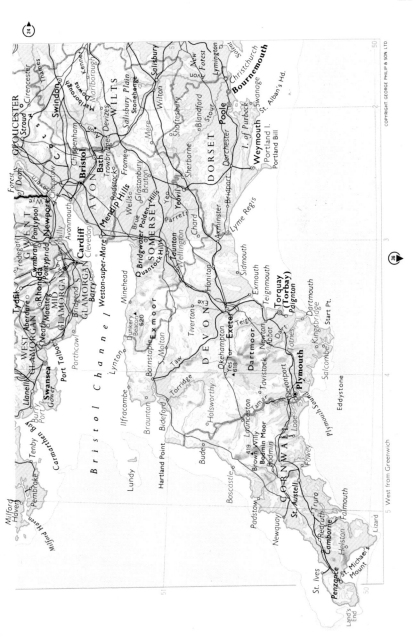

5 West from Greenwich

NORTHUMBERLAND

Ashington
Morpeth
Blyth
N. Tyne
Tyne-mouth
Dumfries
Annan
Gretna Green
Wall
Newcastle
Blaydon
Tyne
So Shi
Newton Stewart
Dalbeattie
Castle Douglas
Hexham
Gateshead
TYNE
W
Wigtown
Kirkcudbright
Carlisle
Consett
Sunderland
Houghton
le-Sprin
Wigtown Bay
Solway Firth
Silloth
Eden
Alston
Durham
Whithorn
Maryport
Derwent
Skiddaw
931
Penrith
Cross Fell
893
Wear
DURHAM
Bishop Auckland
Workington
Derwentwater
CUMBRIA
Appleby
Barnard Castle
Whitehaven
St. Bee's Hd.
Keswick
Helvellyn
950
Ullswater
Shap
Brough
Darlington
Sca Fell
978
Cumbrian Mts.
Richmond
Northallerton
Seascale
Ambleside
Kendal
Wensleydale
Ure
Pt. of Ayre
Ramsey
Windermere
Windermere
Whernside
737
Pen-y-Ghent
693
NORTH
Ripon
Peel
Snaefell
620
ISLE OF MAN
Millom
Ulverston
Ingleborough
723
704
Gt. Whernside
YORKSH
Port Erin
Douglas
Barrow-in-Furness
Furness
Bay
Walney I.
Morecambe
Heysham
Lancaster
Settle
Knaresborough
Harrogate
Castletown
IRISH
Morecambe Bay
Fleetwood
Forest of Bowland
Ribble
Skipton
Keighley
Leeds
SEA
Cleveleys
Blackpool
Fylde
LANCASHIRE
Nelson
Colne
Bradford
W. YORKSHIRE
Lytham-St. Annes
Preston
Burnley
Accrington
Halifax
Dewsbury
Wakefield
Southport
Ribble
Blackburn
Chorley
Rochdale
Huddersfield
Bolton
Bury
Oldham
Ashton-under-Lyne
Barnsley
SOU
YORK
Formby Pt.
Wigan
GR
MANCHESTER
Stalybridge
Skerries
Amlwch
MERSEYSIDE
St. Helens
Salford
Manchester
Glossop
Gt. Orme's Hd.
Bootle
Wallasey
Liverpool
Sale
Stockport
836
Sheffield
Holyhead
Llandudno
Colwyn Bay
Birkenhead
Widnes
Warrington
The Peak
Holy I.
Anglesey
Rhyl
Mersey
Runcorn
Macclesfield
Chesterfield
Beaumaris
Conwy
St. Asaph
Flint
Ellesmere Port
Northwich
CHESHIRE
Buxton
DERBY
Bangor
Caernarfon
Denbigh
Chester
Congleton
Leek
Matlock
Caernarfon
Menai Strait
Bay
Mold
CLWYD
Crewe
Newcastle-under-Lyme
Belper
Nefyn
Snowdon
1085
Wrexham
Stoke-on-Trent
Derby
Porthmadog
Blaenau Ffestiniog
Llangollen
Whitchurch
GWYNEDD
Llanfyllin
Berwyn Mts.
Oswestry
Wem
Market Drayton
Uttoxeter
Pwllheli
Harlech
L. Bala
L. Vyrnwy
STAFFORD
Burton-on-Trent
Ashby-de-la-Zouc
Bardsey I.
Barmouth
892
Cader Idris
Dolgellau
Severn
Shrewsbury
Wellington
Stafford
Cannock
Lichfield
Towyn
Aberdovey
Dovey
Machynlleth
The Wrekin
Telford
Oakengates
Walsall
Tamworth
Nuneaton
Montgomery
Newtown
SHROPSHIRE
Welshpool
Ironbridge
Wolverhampton
Tipton
West Bromwich
Severn
Bridgnorth
Dudley
Stourbridge
Warl
MIDLANDS
Birmingham
Coventry

West from Greenwich

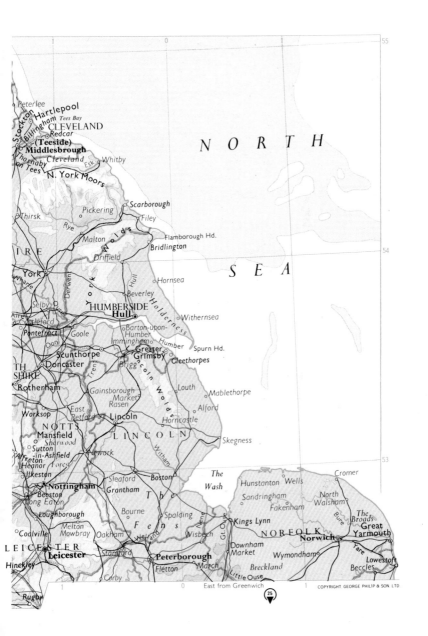

N O R T H

Peterlee
Hartlepool
Stockton *Tees Bay*
Billingham
Redcar
CLEVELAND
(Teeside)
Middlesbrough
Thornaby
Cleveland Esk *Whitby*
on Tees
N. York Moors

Thirsk

Pickering
Scarborough
Rye
Filey
Malton
Wolds
Flamborough Hd.
Driffield
Bridlington

IRE

York
Derwent
Wharfe
Hornsea

Hull
Beverley

Selby
HUMBERSIDE
Holderness
Aire
Hull
Withernsea
Castleford
Pontefract
Goole
Barton-upon-
Humber
Don
Immingham
Humber
Scunthorpe
Greater
Spurn Hd.
Doncaster
Brigg
Grimsby
TH
Trent
Cleethorpes
SHIRE
Rotherham

S E A

Gainsborough
Louth
Market
Mablethorpe
Rasen
Worksop
East
Lincoln Wolds
Alford
Retford
Lincoln
Horncastle
N O T T S
Mansfield
L I N C O L N
Sherwood
Skegness
Sutton
-in-Ashfield
Alfreton
Forest
Heanor
Newark
Witham
Ilkeston
Cromer
Sleaford
Boston
The
Wells
Nottingham
Grantham
Wash
Hunstanton
Beeston
Sandringham
North
Long Eaton
The
Walsham
Loughborough
Bourne
Spalding
Fens
Fakenham
The
Nene
Broads
Melton
*Great
Codville
Mowbray
Oakham
Welland
Kings Lynn
NORFOLK
Yarmouth
LEICESTER
Wisbech
Norwich
Leicester
Stamford
Downham
Wymondham
Hinckley
Peterborough
Market
Lowestoft
Fletton
March
Breckland
Yare
Beccles
Corby
Little Ouse

Rugby

East from Greenwich

25

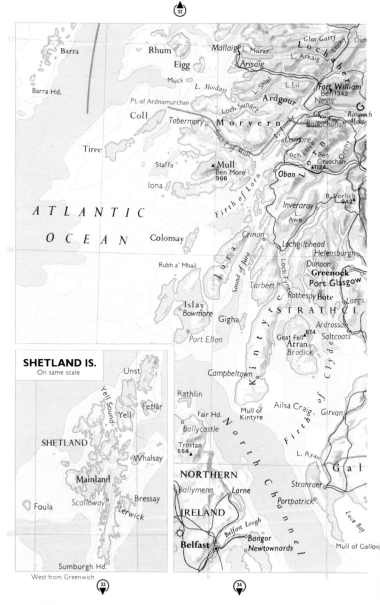

SHETLAND IS.
On same scale

SHETLAND

Foula

Scalloway

Mainland

Yell Sound

Unst

Fetlar

Yell

Whalsay

Bressay

Lerwick

Sumburgh Hd.

West from Greenwich

Barra

Barra Hd.

Rhum

Eigg

Muck

Coll

Tiree

Staffa

Iona

Colonsay

Rubh a' Mhail

Islay

Bowmore

Port Ellen

Gigha

Tobermory

Mull
Ben More
966

Mallaig L. Morar

Arisaig

L. Moidart

Pt. of Ardnamurchan

Loch Sunart

M o r v e r n

Sound of Mull

Glen Garry

L. Arkaig

L. Shiel

L.Eil

Fort William
Ben 1343
Nevis

Ardgour

Glen
Gov

Ballachulish

Rannoch
Moor

L.Linnhe

Lismore

Loch Etive

Ben
Cruachan
1124

Oban

B. Vorlich
943

Inveraray

L.
Awe

Crinan

Lochgilphead

Helensburgh

Dunoon

Greenock
Port Glasgow

Tarbert

Rothesay Bute

Largs

S T R A T H C L

Ardrossan

Goat Fell 874
Arran
Brodick

Saltcoats

Firth of Lorn

J u r a

Sound of Jura

Loch Fyne

K i n t y r e

Firth of Clyde

Campbeltown

Rathlin

Fair Hd.

Mull of
Kintyre

Ballycastle

Trostan
554

Ailsa Craig

Girvan

N o r t h
C h a n n e l

L. Ryan

G a l

NORTHERN

IRELAND

Ballymena

Larne

Portpatrick

Stranraer

Luce Bay

Belfast

Belfast Lough

Bangor
Newtownards

Mull of Gallo

A T L A N T I C

O C E A N

57

56

60

1 : 2 000 000

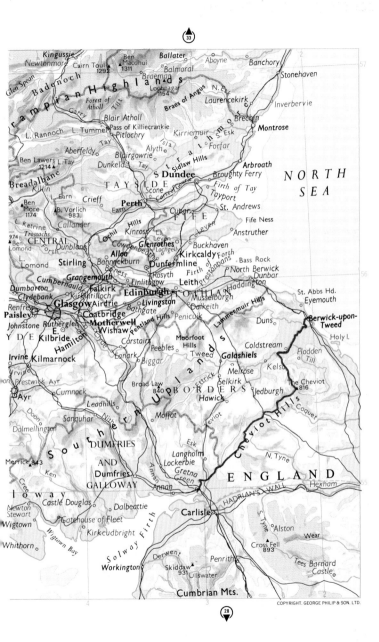

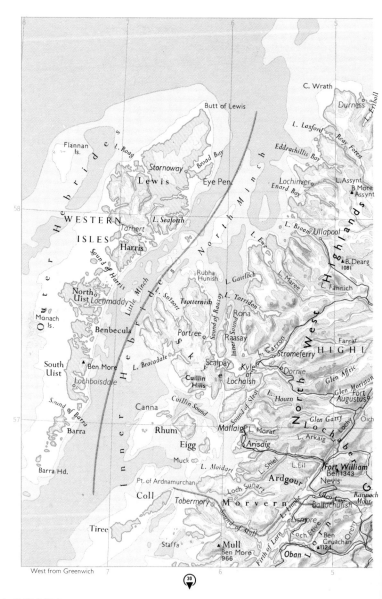

C. Wrath

Durness

L. Laxford

Reay Forest

Eddrachillis Bay

Butt of Lewis

Lochinver

L. Assynt

Enard Bay

B More

Assynt

Flannan
Is.

L. Roag

Broad Bay

Stornoway

Lewis

Eye Pen.

North Minch

L. Broom Ullapool

WESTERN

Tarbert

L. Seaforth

L. Ewe

B. Dearg
1081

ISLES

Harris

Sound of Harris

Little Minch

Rubha
Hunish

L. Gairloch

L. Maree

L. Fannich

Outer Hebrides

North
Uist Lochmaddy

L. Snizort

Trotternish

L. Torridon

West Highlands

Monach
Is.

Benbecula

Sound of Raasay

Rona

Raasay

Inner Sound

Carron

Farrar

HIGHI

Portree

Stromeferry

South
Uist

Ben More

L. Bracadale

Skye

Scalpay

Kyle
of
Lochalsh

Dornie

Glen Affric

Lochboisdale

Cuillin
Hills

Inner Hebrides

Glen Moriston

Fort
Augustus

Canna

Cuillin Sound

L. Hourn

Sound of Sleat

L. Ness

Lochaber

Glen Garry

Oich

Sound of Barra

Rhum

Mallaig L. Morar

L. Arkaig

Loch

Lochy

Barra

Eigg

Arisaig

Muck

L. Moidart

L. Shiel

L.Eil

Fort William
Ben 1343
Nevis

Barra Hd.

Pt. of Ardnamurchan

Ardgour

Coll

Tobermory

Morvern

Loch Sunart

Sound of Mull

Rannoch
Moor

Ballachulish

Glen Coe

Tiree

L. Linnhe

Lismore

Loch Etive

Ben
Cruachan
1124

Orchy

Staffa

Mull
Ben More
966

Firth of Lorn

Oban

1 : 2 000 000

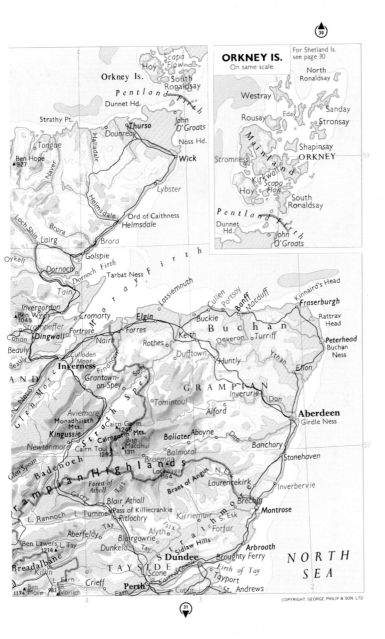

ORKNEY IS.
On same scale

For Shetland Is.
see page 30

Hoy · Scapa Flow
Orkney Is.
Pentland Firth
Dunnet Hd.
South Ronaldsay
Strathy Pt.
Thurso
Dounreay
John O'Groats
Noss Hd.
Tongue
Ben Hope ▲927
Wick
Naver
Lybster
Halladale
Loch Shin
Brora
Helmsdale
Ord of Caithness
Helmsdale
Lairg
Oykell
Brora
Golspie
Dornoch
Dornoch Firth
Tarbat Ness
Tain

North Ronaldsay
Westray
Rousay
Eday
Sanday
Stronsay
Stromness
Mainland
Shapinsay
ORKNEY
Kirkwall
Hoy
Scapa Flow
South Ronaldsay
Pentland Firth
Dunnet Hd.
John O'Groats

Moray Firth
Invergordon
Ben Wyvis ▲1045
Strathpeffer
Conon
Dingwall
Beauly
Beauly
Cromarty
Fortrose
Nairn
Forres
Elgin
Lossiemouth
Cullen
Portsoy
Banff
Macduff
Kinnaird's Head
Fraserburgh
Rattray Head
Buchan
Peterhead
Buchan Ness
Buckie
Keith
Rothes
Dufftown
Deveron
Turriff
Ythan
Ellon
Culloden Moor
Inverness
Grantown-on-Spey
Findhorn
Spey
Huntly
GRAMPIAN
Inverurie
Don
Aberdeen
Girdle Ness
Aviemore
Monadhliath Mts.
Strath Spey
Cairn Gorm 1245
Tomintoul
Alford
Kingussie
Cairngorm Mts.
Newtonmore
Cairn Toul 1292
Ben Macdhui 1311
Ballater
Aboyne
Dee
Banchory
Glen Spean
Badenoch
Grampian Highlands
Braemar
Balmoral
Lochnagar 1154
Stonehaven
Glen More
Garry
Forest of Atholl
Tilt
Braes of Angus
N.Esk
Laurencekirk
Inverbervie
Blair Atholl
Pass of Killiecrankie
Pitlochry
Isla
Kirriemuir
S.Esk
Brechin
Montrose
L. Rannoch
L. Tummel
Tummel
Aberfeldy
Tay
Forfar
Ben Lawers ▲1214
Tay
Blairgowrie
Alyth
Strathmore
Dunkeld
Tay
Sidlaw Hills
Arbroath
Breadalbane
Killin
Earn
Dundee
Broughty Ferry
Firth of Tay
NORTH SEA
Ben More ▲1174
783
Vorlich
Crieff
Scone
Tayport
Perth
Earn
Cupar
St. Andrews
Breadalbane
TAYSIDE

COPYRIGHT GEORGE PHILIP & SON LTD

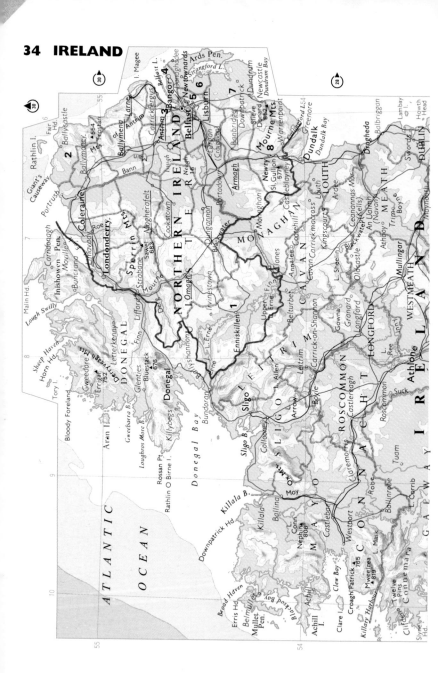

1 : 2 000 000

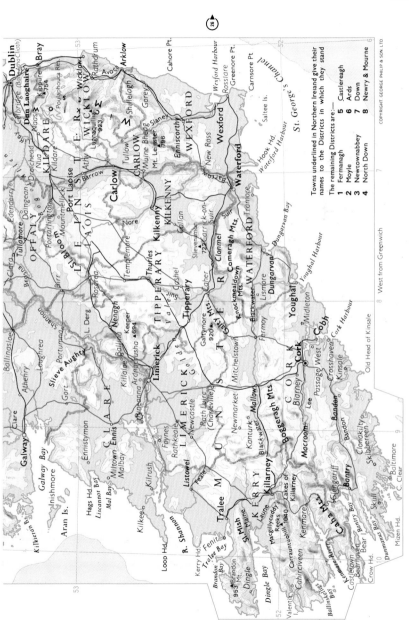

21

ENGLISH CHANNEL

Ile d'Ouessant

Cap Gris-Nez
Boulogne-sur-Mer
Étaples
Berck-Plage

Le Tréport
Dieppe
Neufchâtel-en-Bray
50

Alderney
Cap de la Hague Pointe de Barfleur
Cherbourg
Valognes
Carentan
Bayeux
St-Lô
Caen
Lisieux
Bernay
Fécamp
Bolbec
Le Havre
Deauville Trouville
Elbeuf
Louviers
Vernon
Evreux
Rouen
Seine
Mantes-la-Jolie
Dreux
Verneuil-sur-Avre

Guernsey
St. Peter Port
Channel Is. (Br.)
Jersey
St. Helier

Lannion
Morlaix
Guingamp
St-Malo
St-Brieuc
St-Servan-sur-Mer
Avranches
Granville
Vire
Flers
Argentan
Falaise
417
Alençon
Nogent-le-Rotrou
Chartres
PERCHE
BEAUCE
Châteaudun

Brest
Landerneau
B
391
Châteaulin
Crozon
Douarnenez
326
Pointe du Raz
Quimper
Concarneau
Quimperlé
Hennebont
Lorient
Ile de Groix
Belle-Ile
St-Nazaire
La Baule
Pointe de Penmarch

R E T A G N E
Loudéac
Pontivy
Ploërmel
Redon
Rennes
Vitré
Laval
Châteaubriant
Sarthe
La Flèche
Le Mans
Vendôme
Blois
ORL
Loir
Château-Renault
Amboise
Tours
Cher
Indre
TOURAINE
MAINE
ANJOU

Pointe du Raz
48
Auray
Vannes
Fougères

Ile de Noirmoutier
Ile d'Yeu
Les-Sables-d'Olonne
La Roche-sur-Yon
Chantonnay
Fontenay-le-Comte
Les Herbiers
Cholet
Angers
Nantes
Loire
Saumur
Chinon
Vienne
Bressuire
Parthenay
Châtellerault
Le Blanc
Creuse
Argen
Poitiers
FRANCE
POITOU
MAR

Ile de Ré
La Rochelle
AUNIS
Ile d'Oleron
Rochefort
Niort
Confolens
Bellac
St-Junien
Vienne
Limoges
LIMOUS
46

Royan
Pointe de Grave
Le Verdon-sur-Mer
Saintes
Cognac
Angoulême
St-Cieix-la-Perche
SAINTONGE
ANGOUMOIS
Bay of Biscay

C. Corse
Bastia
Calvi
Mt. Cinto
2710
Haute-Corse
Mte Rotondo
2625
Corse
Ajaccio
Corse du Sud
Bonifacio
Porto Vecchio
Bouches de Bonifacio

Pauillac
Le Verdon-sur-Mer
Dronne
Ribérac
Périgueux
Brive-la-Ga
42
Médoc
Coutras
Libourne
Dordogne
Gourdon
Bordeaux
Bergerac
Cap Ferret
Arcachon
La Teste
GUYENNE
Langon
Garonne
Marmande
Lot
Cahors
Tonneins
Villeneuve-sur-Lot
Agen
Moissac
Castelsarrasin
Aveyron
Montaub

Mimizan
Morcenx
Mont-de-Marsan
Nérac
44
Castets
GASCOGNE
Auch
Toul

Santander
Santoña
Torrelavega
Portugalete
Sestao
Bilbao
Guecho
Portugalete
Algorta
Elbar
Irún
Guernica
San Sebastián
St-Jean-de-Luz
Biarritz
Bayonne
Orthez
Mourenx-Ville-Nouvelle
Pau
Tarbes
Adour
Dax
Landes
Castets

BEARN
Oloron-Ste-Marie
Lourdes
Tarmezan
St-Gaudens
Muret
Auch
Pamiers
Toul

1 : 5 000 000

West from Greenwich

51

SPAIN
Jaca
250
3298
Pic d'Aneto
3404
Mt Perdu
Vielha
PYRÉNÉES
ANDO
FOI

BELGIUM
BRUSSEL
Kortrijk Ronse Liège Aachen
Lille Roubaix
Bruay Béthune Namur Marche- Verviers
en-Artois Bully-les-Mines Mons en-Famenne
Douai Valenciennes Charleroi 697
Arras Denain Maubeuge Dinant
Cambrai Le Cateau Fourmies Hirson A r d e n n e s Ettelbrück
Abbeville Somme Péronne Fumay LUXEM- Idar-Oberstein
Amiens St-Quentin Charleville- BOURG 816 GERMANY
PICARDIE Noyon Oise Mézières Luxembourg Arlon Esch Kaiserslautern
Beauvais Compiègne Chauny Laon Villerupt Neunkirchen
Nogent- Creil Senlis Soissons Aisne Hayange Thionville Völklingen Zweibrücken Pirmasens
sur-Seine Chantilly Reims Briey Hagondange Saarbrücken Homburg
Pontarcy Aube Château- Marne Verdun Metz Saargemünd Rastatt
PARIS Thierry Ménéhould Pont- Sarrebourg Baden
ILE Meaux Châlons- Mousson Hagenau Offenburg
Corbeil- sur-Marne Commercy Nancy Strasbourg
Essonnes Provins Bar-le-Duc Toul Lunéville Kehl
Etampes Melun Romilly- Vittel St-Dié Emmendingen
Fontainebleau Montereau- sur-Seine Neufchâteau Epinal Colmar Freiburg
Fault-Yonne Troyes Chaumont Gérardmer Günbweiler 1493
Montargis Sens St-Florentin Remiremont 1423 Löwach Rheinfelden
Auxerre Langres Vittel Mulhouse Rheinfelden
Gien Plateau de Langes Vesoul Belfort Basel Liestal
Salbris Vézelay Armançon 598 Dijon Besançon Montbéliard Olten
Vierzon Sancerre Côte d'Or Saône La Chaux- Längenthal
Bourges Nevers Autun Beaune Dôle de-Fonds Biel Bern
Issoudun Le Creusot Chalon-sur-Saône Neuchâtel Solothurn Fribourg Thun
St-Amand- Montceau-les-Mines St-Vallier Yverdon SWITZERLAND
Mont-Rond Moulins Paray- Loire Lausanne 4158
BOURBONNAIS le-Monial Mâcon Bourg- St-Claude Jungfrau
Montluçon Commentry Villefranche- Bresse 1718 Genève Berner Alpen
Guéret Vichy Cusset Roanne sur-Saône Bellegarde-sur- Rhône
Aubusson Riom Thiers Tarare Annecy Mont-Blanc Pennine
Clermont Ferrand Puy de Dôme Bellev Chambéry Aosta
1463 LYON Bourgoin- Jallieu ITALY
1534 Rive-de-Gier Vienne St-Chamond Voiron TORINO
1885 St-Etienne Firminy Grenoble Carmagnola
Puy de Sancy Annonay Massif du Susa
Massif Le Puy 1753 Romans- Pelvoux Pinerolo Cuneo Fossano
sur-Isère Mt Viso
1855 Valence 3841 L'Argentera
Central Aurillac Mende 1469 Privas Montélimar Orange Mt Ventoux 3297
Aubenas 1699 1909 Cune
Figeac Decazeville Bollène-Cèze Carpentras 3051 Maritime Alpes
Rodez Mende Pierrelatte Valréas
Villefranche- Orange MONACO
de-Rouergue 1585 Avignon Sorgues Grasse Nice
Carmaux Millau Nîmes Manosque Cannes
Albi 1267 Beaucaire Arles Salon-de- Aix-en- Draguignan
Castres Lodève Camargue Provence
Mazamet Montpellier Istres Etang de Berre St-Raphaël
Béziers Frontignan Port-St-Louis Martigues Hyères
Carcassonne Agde Sète Rhône MARSEILLE Toulon
Delta La Ciotat La Seyne Iles d'Hyères
Narbonne Golfe du Lion
Limoux
Rivesaltes
ROUSSILLON Perpignan Elne
Port-Vendres

East from Greenwich 6

COPYRIGHT
GEORGE PHILIP
& SON. LTD

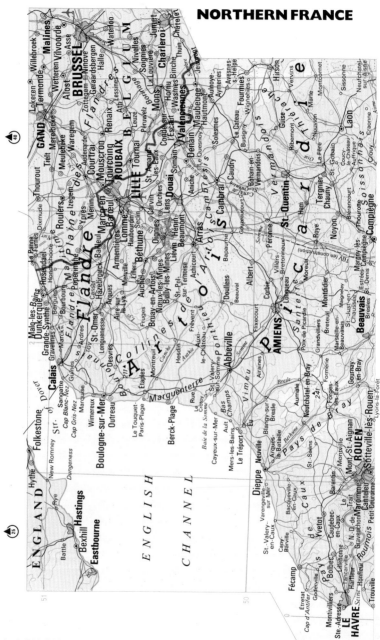

1 : 2 000 000

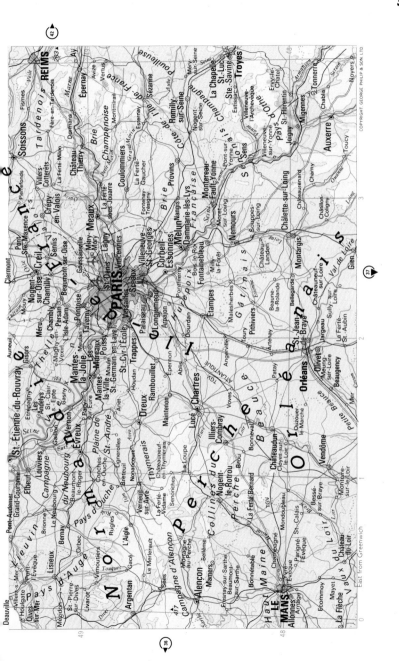

East from Greenwich

NORTH

SEA

WESTFRIESCHE Terschelli
Vlieland
Waddenz
Texel
Den Burgo
Den Helder   Den Oever
Staveren
Middenmeer   IJssel
Enkhuizen
Bergen-Binnen   Hoorn
Alkmaar
Heiloo   HOLLAND
Castricum   Edam
Wormer   Purmerend   Volendam
Beverwijk   Marken
IJmuiden   Zaanstad
Velsen
Haarlem   AMSTERDAM
Zandvoort   Weesp   Huizen
Heemstede   Bussum   Laren
Hillegom   Aalsmeer   Hilversum   Baarn
Noordwijk-aan-Zee   Lisse   Soest
Katwijk-aan-Zee   Leiden   UTRECHT
Wassenaar   Oude   Alphen   Rijn   Zeist
Scheveningen   Voorburg   Waddinx   Utrecht
s'GRAVENHAGE   Veen   IJsselstein
(The Hague)   Rijswijk   Gouda
Hoek van Holland   Delft   Lek
Europoort   Naaldwijk   Tiel
Maassluis   ZUID   Gorinchem   molser
Vlaardingen   Schiedam   ROTTERDAM   Hardinx   Maa
Goeree   Hellevoetsluis   Sliedrecht   Veld
Ouddorp   Overflakkee   Dordrecht   Waalwijk   'Her
Brouwershaven   Middelharnis   Madeo   Dongen   Vught
Schouwen   Zierikzee   DN   Oosterhout   Boxtel
Noord Beveland   Oudenbosch   Breda   Tilburg
Oosterschelde   Roosendaal   Goir
Walcheren   Bergen-op   Baarle
Middelburg   Goes   Zoom   Nassau   E
Vlissingen   Esen
(Flushing)   Westerschelde   Kalmthout   Rijkevorsel
Knokke   Brasschaat   Turnhout   Arendonk
Blankenberge   Zeeb Heist   Z   Pellen   ANTWERPEN   Lommel
Oostende   Brugge   Maldegem   Beveren   Schoten   Geel   Leopoldsbu
(Ostend)   (Bruges)   Eeklo   St-   Antwerpen   Hei   Beclaar   tessenderlo
Nieuwpoort   Eernegem   Zelzo   Niklaas   Hoboken   Eer   Nethe   G
Veurne   Torhout   Lokeren   Boom   Duffel   Nete   I
Diksmuide   St-Amandsberg   Willebroek   Mechelen   Kessel-Lo   Demer
Lo   Ruiselede   Ledeberg   Gent(Gand)   B   E   Aarschot   Diest   Hasselt
Poperinge   Hoogkede   Tielt   Deinze   Lebbeke   Vilvoorde   Leuven   Diepenbeek
Roeselare   Ingelmunster   Asse   Kessel-La
Izegem   Hazel   Zottegem   Aalst   Mere   BRUSSEL
Menen   Oudenaarde   Ninove   (Bruxelles)
Kortrijk

East from Greenwich   4   5

(38)

1 : 2 000 000

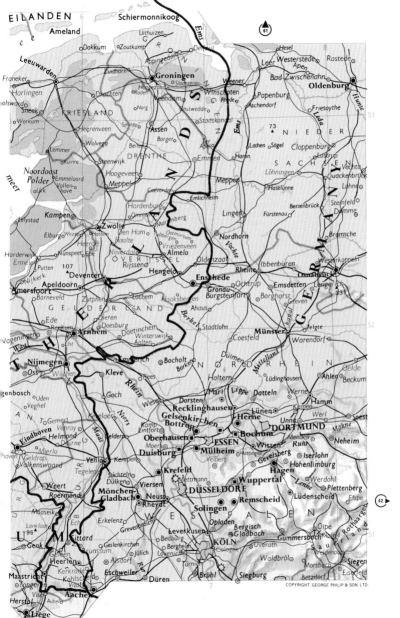

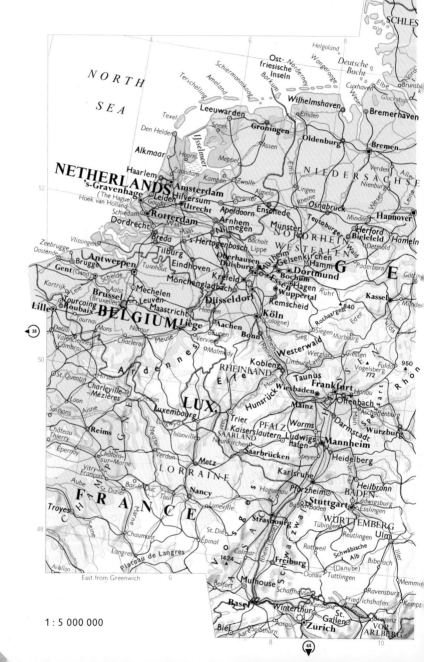

NORTH

SEA

SCHLES

Helgoland

Ost- Norderney *Deutsche*
friesische *Bucht*
Inseln

Schiermonnikoog Borkum Wangerooge Cuxhaven Elbe Brunsb

Ameland Glückstadt

Terschelling

Wilhelmshaven Bremerhaven

Texel Leeuwarden Emden Weser

Den Helder Sneek Groningen Oldenburg Bremen

Alkmaar Hoorn Assen Ems Verden Aller

Haarlem Zaandam Meppel NIEDERSACHSE Nienburg Leine

NETHERLANDS Kampen Zwolle Almelo Lingen Osnabrück Minden Hannover

's-Gravenhage Amsterdam Rhine

(The Hague) Leiden Hilversum Deventer Enschede

Hoek van Holland Gouda Utrecht Apeldoorn Teutoburger Herford Hameln

Schiedam Rotterdam Arnhem Münster NORDRHEIN Bielefeld Detmold

Dordrecht Waal Nijmegen Lippe WESTFALEN Paderborn G Göttin

Breda Maas 's-Hertogenbosch Bocholt

Vlissingen Tilburg Oberhausen Mülheim Gelsenkirchen Hamm

Zeebrugge **Antwerpen** Eindhoven Duisburg Essen **Dortmund**

Oostende Brugge Turnhout Krefeld Bochum Hagen Ruhr

Gent(Gand) Schelde Mönchengladbach Essen Wuppertal Kassel

Kortrijk Leie Mechelen **Düsseldorf** Remscheid Münden

Tourcoing Brussel Leuven Rothaargeb.840

Roubaix (Bruxelles) Maastricht **Köln** Eder Fulda

Lille Tournai **BELGIUM** Liège Aachen (Cologne) Siegen Marburg

Douai Mons Namur Eupen Bonn Rhine

Valenciennes Charleroi Verviers Sieg Westerwald

Cambrai Meuse Malmédy Wetzlar Giessen

St.Quentin **A r d e n n e s** RHEINLAND Koblenz Limburg Lahn Fulda 950

Laon Charleville- Eifel Mosel Taunus Vogelsberg 772 Rhön

Soissons -Mézières Sedan **Frankfurt** Hanau

Aisne Hunsrück Wiesbaden Offenbach Aschaffenburg

Château **LUX.** Mainz Würzburg

Thierry **Reims** Luxembourg Trier PFALZ Worms Darmstadt Main

Épernay Longwy Kaiserslautern Ludwigs- **Mannheim**

Châlons- Thionville SAARLAND hafen Sp

sur-Marne Neunkirchen Speyer Heidelberg

Vitry-le- Verdun **Saarbrücken**

François Metz Karlsruhe

Aube Bar-le-Duc Toul **L O R R A I N E** Heilbronn

St.Dizier **Nancy** Haguenau Pforzheim **BADEN**

Troyes **F R A N C E** Lunéville Baden-Baden **Stuttgart** Ludwigsburg

Seine **Strasbourg** Esslingen

Chaumont St.Dié **WÜRTTEMBERG** Ulm

Épinal Tübingen Reutlingen

Langres Colmar 1424 Rottweil Schwäbische (Danube) Biberach

Plateau de Langres **Freiburg** Alb

Avallon Donau Tuttlingen Memmi

East from Greenwich Mulhouse Schaffhausen Ravensburg

Belfort Friedrichshafen Kempt

Basel Winterthur Konstanz **VOR-**

Biel Aarau St. Bregenz **ARLBERG**

Aare Solothurn **Zürich** Gallen

1 : 5 000 000

38

44

Flensburg
WIG-
Schleswig
Puttgarden
Fehmarn
Mecklenburger
Bucht
Warnemünde
Kiel
Neumünster
HOLSTEIN
Lübeck
Altona
Hamburg
Harburg
Schwerin
Lauenburg
Lüneburg
Elbe
Müritz
See
Uelzen
Heide
Celle
Wittenberge
Stendal
Rathenow
Hildesheim
Braunschweig
Salzgitter
Magdeburg
Goslar
Halberstadt
Brocken
H42
Harz
Bernburg
Dessau
Nordhausen
Halle
Mühlhausen
Merseburg
Naumburg
Leipzig
Werra
Eisenach
Erfurt
Jena
Gera
Zeitz
Meissen
Gotha
Weimar
Thüringer Wald
Coburg
Hof
Schweinfurt
Bamberg
Erlangen
Fürth
Nürnberg
Amberg
Regensburg
B A Y E R N
Ingolstadt
Augsburg
Lech
Freising
München
(Munich)
Rosenheim

BALTIC SEA
Sassnitz
Rügen
Darłowo
Słupsk
Stralsund
Greifswald
Usedom
Swinoujście
Kołobrzeg
Koszalin
Rostock
Güstrow
Wismar
Wollin
Oder Haff
Szczecinek
Neu Brandenburg
Goleniów
Parchim
Szczecin (Stettin)
Dąbie
Stargard
Neustrelitz
Prenzlau
Choszczno
Piła
Neuruppin
Eberswalde
Gorzów
Noteć (Netze)
Oranienburg
Spandau
Skwierzyna
Warta (Warthe)
Charlottenburg
BERLIN
Kostrzyn
Międzychód
Poznań
Brandenburg
Potsdam
Frankfurt
Nowy Tomyśl
Lückenwalde
Świebodzin
Grodzisk
Zerbst
Wittenberg
Spree
Kościan
Gubin
Zielona
Cottbus
Góra
Leszno
Mulde
Torgau
Forst
Żagań
Głogów
Spremberg
Żary
Lauchhammer
Grossenhain
Bolesławiec
Wrocław
Bautzen
Görlitz
Legnica
Dresden
Świdnica
Liberec
Jelenia Góra
Riesengebirge
Chemnitz
1605
Wałbrzych
Karl-Marx-Stadt
Usti
Jablonec
Zwickau
nad Labem
Śnieżka
Trutnov
Reichenbach
Teplice
Litoměřice
Plauen
Erzgebirge
Ohre
Most
Mladá
Kłodzko
Boleslav
1492
Chomutov
Fichtel
geb
Karlovy
Kladno
Hradec
1051
Vary
Kralove
Bayreuth
Praha
Labe (Elbe)
Pardubice
Rhein Donau
Cheb
(Prague)
Kolín
Sumperk
Beroun
CZECH
Plzeň
Příbram
Sázava
Vrchovina
Olomouc
(Pilsen)
Hulíčkuv Brod
Naab
REPUBLIC
Prostějov
Klatovy
Písek
Tábor
Jihlava
Třebíč
Brno
Böhmerwald
1457
České
Třeboň
(Brünn)
Slavkov
Deggendorf
Budějovice
(Austerlitz)
Hodonín
1378
Znojmo
Landshut
Isar
Passau
Gmünd
Zwettl
Horn
Morava
Malé Karpaty
OBER-
Freistadt
Urfahr
NIEDER-
Wels
Linz
ÖSTERREICH
Stockerau
Ried
Steyr
COPYRIGHT GEORGE PHILIP & SON LTD
Gmunden
Salzburg
Bad Ischl
Ö S T E R R E I C H
Kufstein
A U S T R I A

POLAND
GERMANY

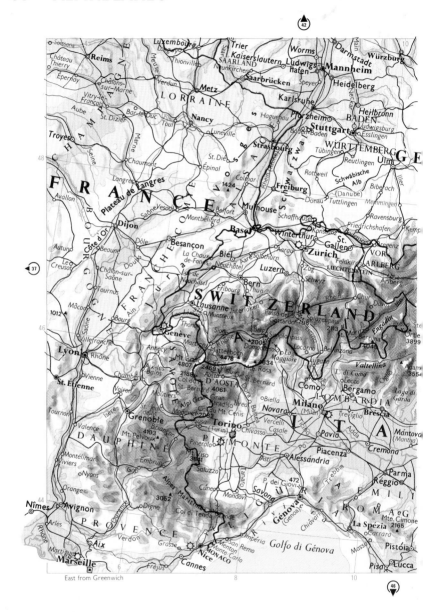

1 : 5 000 000

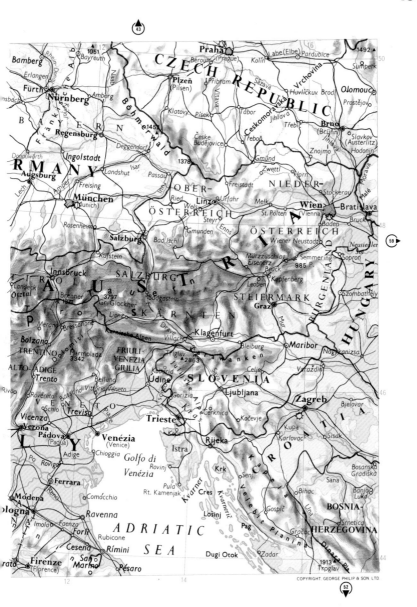

Bamberg
Erlangen
Fürth
Nürnberg
nsbach
Amberg
Regensburg
Ingolstadt
Augsburg
Donauwörth
Lech
BAYERN
Freising
München
(Munich)
Rosenheim

Rhein-Donau
Bayreuth
1051
Naab
Böhmerwald
1451
1378
Landshut
Isar
Ried
Inn

CZECH
Praha
(Prague)
Plzeň
(Pilsen)
Pribram
Klatovy
Písek
České
Budějovice
Deggendorf
Passau
OBER-
Linz

REPUBLIC
Beroun
Kolín
Labe (Elbe)
Pardubice
Sazava
Vltava
Tábor
Jihlava
Třeboň
Gmünd
Zwettl
Freistadt
Urfahr
Welser
Steyr
Enns
1492
Vrchovina
Havlíčkuv Brod
Třebíč
Horn
Melk
St. Pölten
Gmunden

50
Šumperk
Olomouc
Prostějov
Brno
(Brünn)
Slavkov
(Austerlitz)
Hodonin
Znojmo
Morava
Stockerau
Wien
(Vienna)
Bratislava
Baden
Bruck
Mělk
48

Münich
ÖSTERREICH
Salzburg
Bad Ischl
Innsbruck
Landeck
Ötztal
Brenner
1931
3797
ot Glockner
Merano
Bressanone
Bolzano
TRENTINO
Marmolada
3342
ALTO-ADIGE
Trento
Rovereto
Schio
Vicenza
Verona
Pádova
(Padua)
Adige
Rovigo
Ferrara
Módena
ologna
Imola
Faenza
Forlì
Cesena
Rubicone
Firenze
(Florence)
rato
San
Marino

TIROL
SALZBURG
Kufstein
Badgastein
Lienz
Kitzbühel
SKÄRNTEN
Karnische Alpen
Drava
Villach
Klagenfurt
FRIULI-
VENEZIA
GIULIA
Triglav
2863
Udine
Belluno
Vittorio Veneto
Conegliano
Treviso
VENETO
Po
Chioggia
Golfo di
Venézia
Venézia
(Venice)
Rt. Kamenjak
Comácchio
Ravenna
Rímini
Pésaro

Mürzzuschlag
Eisenerz
Bruck
Leoben
Kapfenberg
STEIERMARK
Graz
ÖSTERREICH
Wiener Neustadt
985 P.
Semmering
Mur
Bleiburg
Maribor
Karawanken
Celje
SLOVENIA
Ljubljana
Gorizia
Soča
Cerknica
Kočevje
Trieste
Istra
Pula
Kvarner
Cres
Lošinj
Krk
Rijeka
Kupa
Karlovac
Senj
Kvarnerić
Pag
ADRIATIC
SEA
Dugi Otok
Zadar

Wiener Neustadt
Neusiedler
Sopron
Szombathely
BURGENLAND
Nagykanizsa
Varaždin
HUNGARY
Zagreb
Bjelovar
Sisak
CROATIA
Bosanski
Gradiška
Sana
Banja
Luka
Bihać
Gospič
BOSNIA-
HERZEGOVINA
Srnetica
Gročac
Dinara Pl.
1913
Troglav
Velebit Planina
Una
59
46
44

COPYRIGHT GEORGE PHILIP & SON LTD

1 : 5 000 000

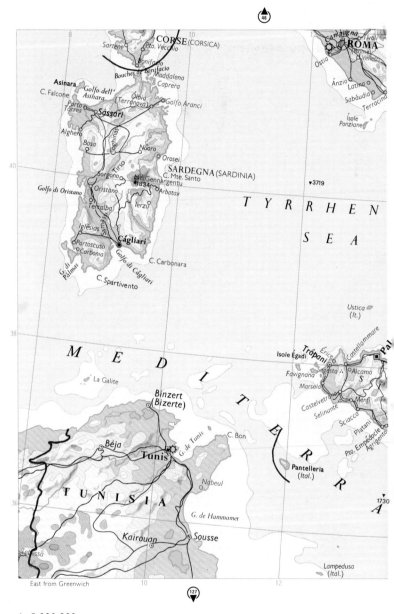

CORSE (CORSICA)
Sartene
Pto. Vecchio
Bonifacio
Bouches de Bonifacio
Maddalena
Caprera
Asinara
Golfo dell' Asinara
C. Falcone
Olbia (Terranova)
Golfo Aranci
Parto Torres
Sássari
Alghero
Oghinas
Bosa
Núoro
Orosei
SARDEGNA (SARDINIA)
Tirso
Sorgono
M. Gennargentu
C. Mte. Santo
▼3719
1834
Oristano
Árbatax
Golfo di Oristano
Terralba
Ierzu
Iglésias
Portoscuso
Cágliari
Carbonia
Golfo di Cágliari
G. di Pálmas
C. Carbonara
C. Spartivento

T Y R R H E N

S E A

ROMA (Rome)
Campagna
Tivoli
Velletri
Ostia
Ánzio
Latina
Sabáudia
Terracina
Ísole Ponziane

Ustica (It.)

Érice
Trápani
Isole Égadi
Castellammare
Pa
Segesta
Alcamo
S
Favignana
Marsala
Menfi
Castelvetrano
Selinunte
Sciacca
Platani
Pto. Empédocle
Agrigento

M E D I T E R R A N E

La Galite

Binzert (Bizerte)
C. Bon
Béja
Tunis
G. de Tunis
Pantelleria (Ital.)
Nábeul

T U N I S I A
▼1730

G. de Hammamet

Kairouan
Sousse
Tébessa

Lampedusa (Ital.)

1 : 5 000 000

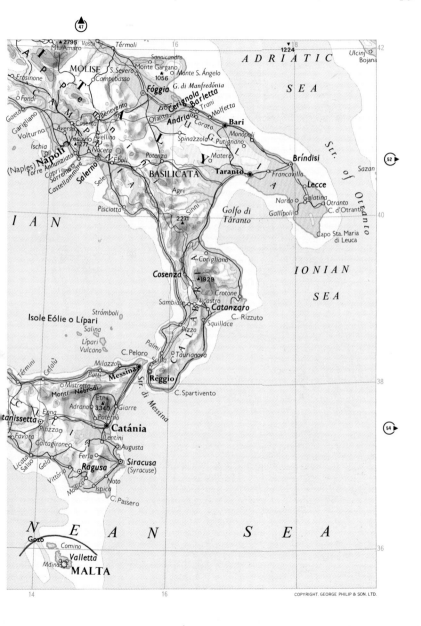

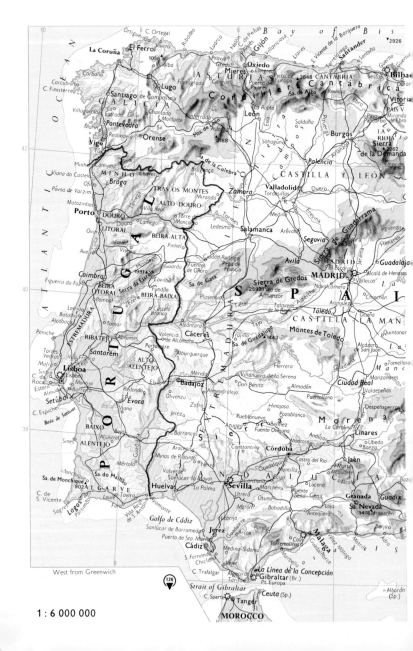

West from Greenwich

1 : 6 000 000

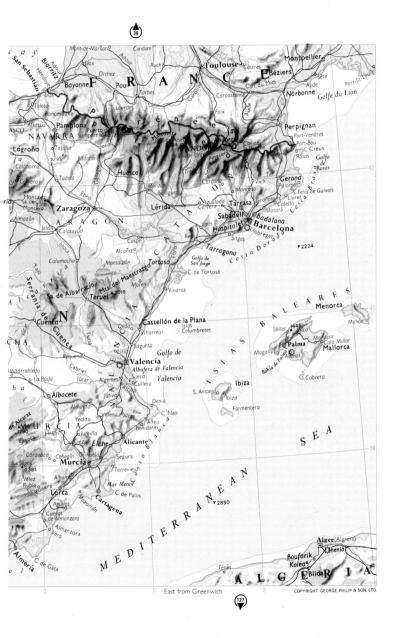

East from Greenwich

COPYRIGHT GEORGE PHILIP & SON. LTD.

East from Greenwich

1 : 6 000 000

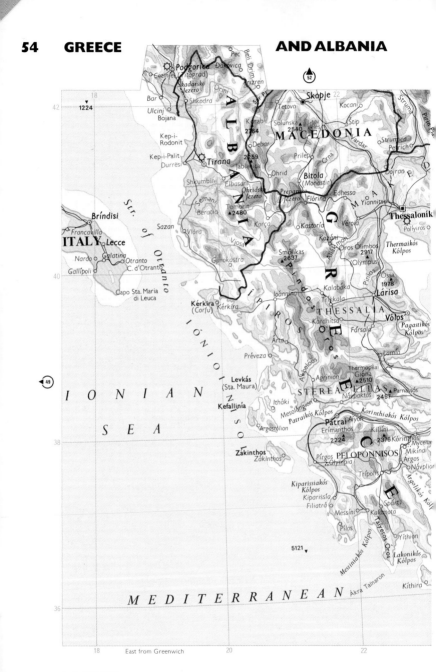

1 : 5 000 000

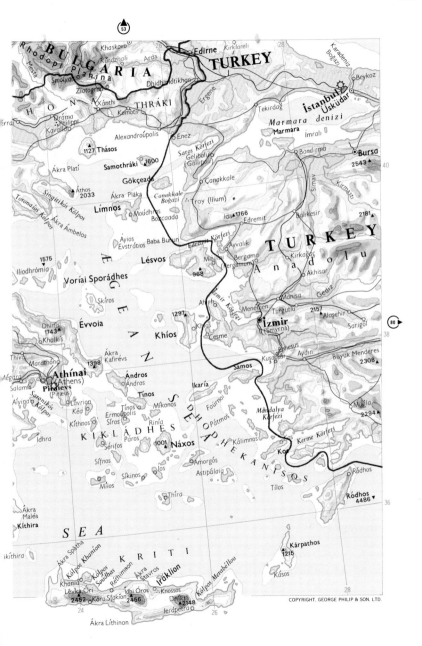

BULGARIA

Rhodopi Planina

Mesta
Smólyan
Zlatograd
Kŭrdzhali
Khaskovo
Arda
Dhidhimótikhon
Edirne
Kırklareli
TURKEY
Karadeniz Boğazı
Beykoz

HON
RÓDOPI Planina
Xánthi
THRÁKI
Ergene
Tekirdağ
İstanbul
Üsküdar

Dráma
Philippi
Kavalla
Komotiní
Marmara denizi
Marmara
İmralı I
Bandırma
Bursa

Alexandroúpolis
Énez
Sáros Körfezi
Gelibolu (Gallipoli)
2543▲
40

1127 Thásos
Samothráki ▲1600
Gökçeada
Çanakkale
2181▲

Ákra Platí
Áthos 2033
Ákra Pláka
Canakkale Boğazı
Troy (Ilium)
Ida▲1766
Edremit
Balıkesir

Toronaíos Kólpos
Singitikós Kólpos
Ákra Ámbelos
Limnos
Moúdhros
Boscaada
Edremit Körfezi
Ayvalık
Bergama
Pergamum
TURKEY
Anadolu
Kırkağaç
Akhisar

Áyios Evstrátios
Baba Burun
Mitilíni
968
Manisa
Gediz

Ilíodhrómia
1575
Vóriai Sporádhes
Skíros
Ahmetli
İzmir Körfezi
Menemen
Turgutlu
2157
Alaşehir
Sarıgöl
80
38

Dhírfis 1743▲
Khalkís
Évvoia
Khíos
1297▲
Khíos
Çeşme
İzmir (Smyrna)
Ephesus

Thívai
Marathón
Ákra Kafirévs
1398▲
Aydın
Büyük Menderes
2308▲

Mégara
Athínai (Athens)
Piraíévs (Piraeus)
Salamís
Saronikós Kólpos
Aíyina
Lávrion
Kéa
Ándros
Tínos
Míkonos
Ikaría
Fournoí
Sámos
Kuşadası

Idhra
Kíthnos
Ermoúpolis
Síros
Tínos
Ríniá
Pátmos
Mandalya Körfezi
2294▲

KIKLÁDHES
Páros
1001
Náxos
Kálimnos
Kerme Körfezi
Kos
Ródhos

Sérifos
Sífnos
Sikinos
Íos
Amorgós
Astipálaia
Tílos
DHODHEKÁNISOS

Mílos
Thíra
Ródhos 4486▲
36

Ákra Maléa
Kíthira
SEA
Kárpathos 1215

ikíthira
Kásos

Ákra Spátha
KRITI
Khaniá
Kólpos Khaníon
Kólpos Soúdhas
Réthimnon
Ákra Stavrós
Iráklion
Knossós
Kólpos Merabéllou

Lévka Óri 2452▲
Kóru Sfakíon
Ídhi Óros 2456▲
Dhíkti ▲2148
Ierápetra

Ákra Líthinon

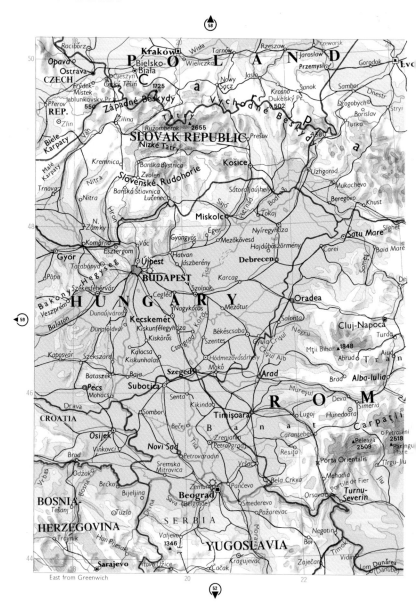

1 : 5 000 000

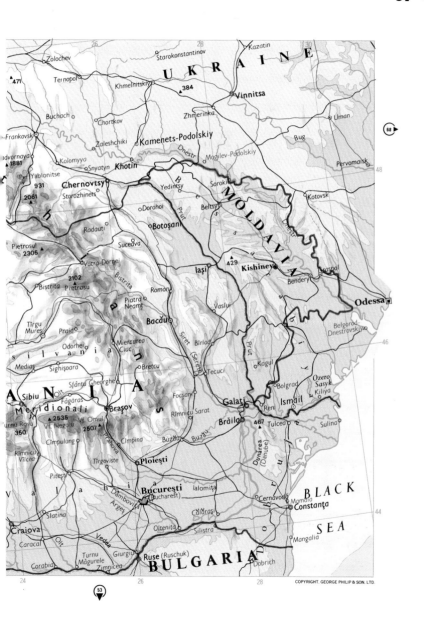

Zolochev

▲471

Ternopol

Buchach o

—Frankovsk o

Zaleshchiki

dvornaya o
▲1881

o Kolomyya

Per Yablonitse
▲931
2061 ▲

Snyatyn

Khotin

Starozhinets

Chernovtsy

h

Radauti

Suceava

Pietrosul
2306 ▲

o Vatra-Dornei

Bistrita

Bistrita o
2102
Pietrosu ▲

Tirgu
Mures

Praid o

Odorhei o

Medias o

Sighişoara

Sfântu Gheorghe o

A N I A

S i l v a n i a

A Sibiu

M e r i d i o n a l i

Fàgàras

urnu Roşu
350

Vf Omu
▲2535
Vf. Negoiu
2507 ▲

Cîmpulung

Rimnicu
Vîlcea

Piteşti o

Slatina o

Craiova

Caracal

Corabia o

Piatra
Neamt o

Bacău o

Braşov

Cîmpina

Tîrgovişte o

Starokonstantinov

U K R A I N E

Khmelnitsky

Kamenets-Podolskiy

Mogilev-Podolskiy

Yedintsy

Dorohoi o

o Botoşani

Roman o

Vaslui o

Bîrlad o

Bretcu o

Focşani o

Rîmnicu Sarat

Buzău o

Buzău

Vedea

Ploieşti

Bucureşti
(Bucharest)

Dâmboviţa

Arges

Oltenita o

Olt

Turnu
Măgurele

Giurgiu

o Zimnicea

Kazatin

▲384

Vinnitsa

Zhmerinka

Dnestr

Sorok

Beltsy

Iaşi

▲429 Kishinev

Bendery

s

Siret

Siret (Sereth)

Tecuci

Galati

Brăila

Bug

o Uman

o Pervomaisk

Kotovsk

M O L D A V I A

Odessa ■

Belgorod-
Dnestrovskiy

Kagul

Bolgrad

Reni

Ismail

Ozero
Sasyk
Kiliya

Tulcea o

467 ▲

Sulina o

Dunărea
(Danube)

Cernavodă o

Călăraşi

Silistra

Mamaia
Constanţa

B L A C K

S E A

o Mangalia

B U L G A R I A

Ruse (Ruschuk)

o Dobrich

68 ►

53

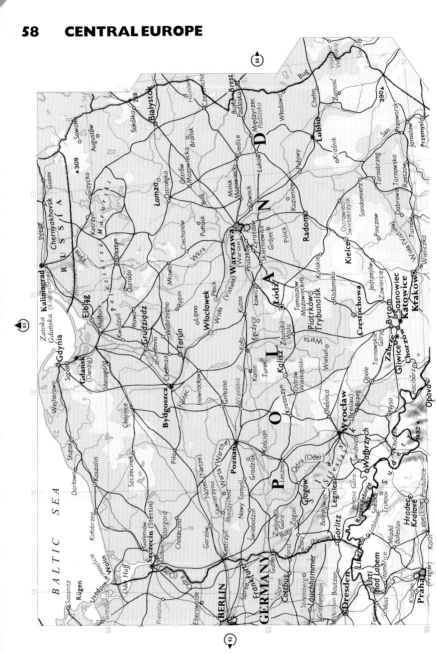

1 : 5 000 000

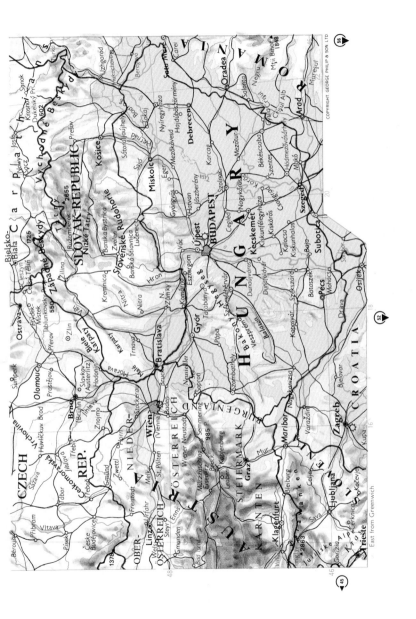

East from Greenwich

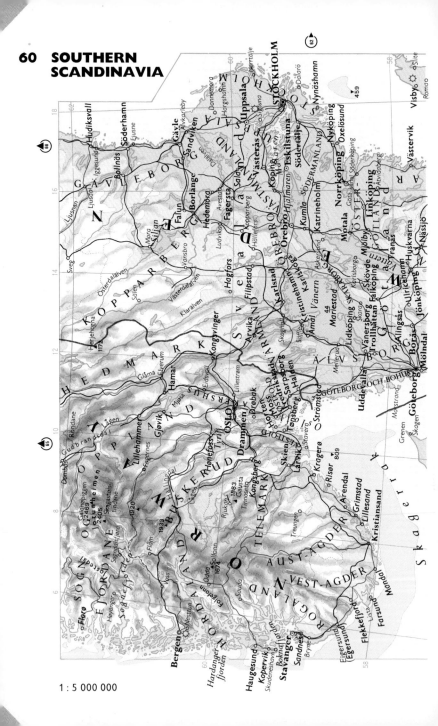

1 : 5 000 000

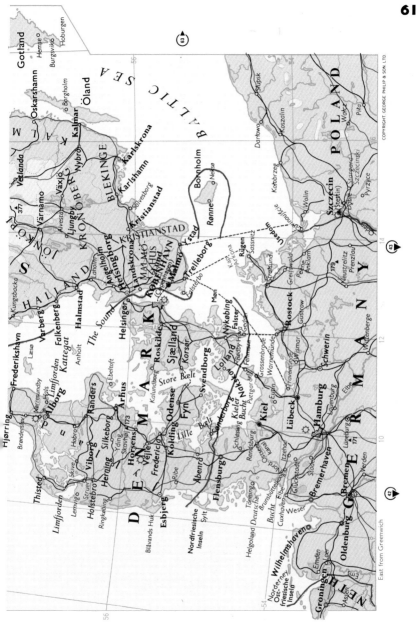

61

Gotland
Hemse ○
Burgsviko ○ Hoburgen

BALTIC SEA

Oskarshamn
Vetlanda
KALMAR
Borgholm
Öland
Kalmar
Nybro
Oskarshamn

Växjö
Ljungby
Värnamo
KRONOBERG
BLEKINGE
Karlskrona
Karlshamn
Alvesta
Sölvesborg
Kristianstad

Kungsbacka
HALLAND
Varberg
Falkenberg
Halmstad
Laholm
Ängelholm
Helsingborg
Landskrona
MALMÖHUS
MALMÖ
København
(Copenhagen)
Trelleborg
Ystad

Bornholm
Nekso ○
Rønne

Gedser
Darłowo
Koszalin
Słupsk

POLAND

Szczecin
(Stettin)
Swinoujscie
Wolin
Kołobrzeg
Wolin
Police
Goleniów
Pyrzyce
Gryfino
Szczecinek
Wałcz
Piła

Usedom
Rügen
Kap Arkona
Stralsund
Sassnitz
Bergen
Greifswald
Wolgast
Anklam
Peene
Usedom

GERMANY
Neustrelitz
Prenzlau
Neubrandenburg
179 ▲
Güstrow
Rostock
Warnemünde
Wismar
Schwerin
Wittenberge

KRISTIANSTAD

Gedser
Falster
Nykøbing
Lolland
Rødby
Fehmarn
Grossenbrode
Puttgarden
Travemünde

The Sound
Helsingør
Roskilde
Sjælland
Korsør
Store Bælt
Kalundborg
Svendborg
Lille Bælt
Fyn
Odense
Store Bælt
Nakskov
Nyborg

Frederikshavn
Læsø
Hjørring
Brønderslev
Nørresundby
Aalborg
Limfjorden
Nibe
Hobro
Randers
Århus
Ebeltoft
Anholt

Thisted
Skive
Struer
Lemvig
Holstebro
Ringkøbing
Viborg
Herning
Silkeborg
Yding Skovhøj 173
Horsens
Vejle
DENMARK
Kolding
Fredericia
Ribe
Esbjerg
Blåvands Huk

Sønderborg
Åbenrå
Flensburg
Sylt
Tønder
Nordfriesische Inseln
Husum
Schleswig
Rendsburg
Kiel
Kieler Bucht
Nord-Ostsee-Kanal
Neumünster
Itzehoe

Helgoland
Nordseebad
Deutsche Bucht
Büsum
Brunsbüttelkoog
Cuxhaven
Glückstadt
Elbe
Stade

Norderney
Ost-friesische Inseln
Emden
Leer
Ems
NETHERLANDS
Groningen
Assen
Oldenburg
Bremerhaven
Weser
Verden
Bremen
Lüneburg 171
Lauenburg
Lübeck
Hamburg
Eutin

East from Greenwich

COPYRIGHT GEORGE PHILIP & SON LTD

56
56
54
37
10
12
14

42 43 63

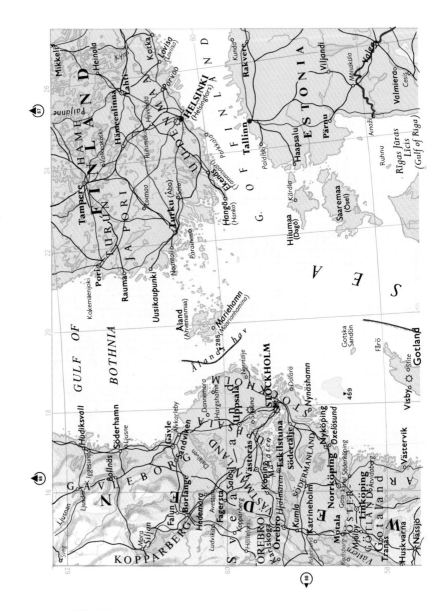

1 : 5 000 000

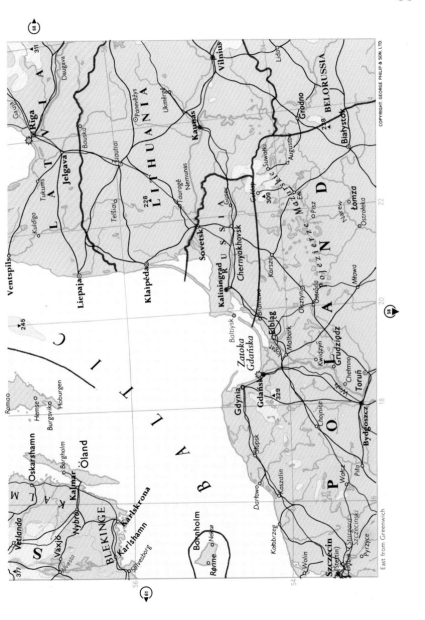

63

East from Greenwich

Ventspils○

Kuldīga○

○Roma○
Hemse○
Burgsviko○
Hoburgen○

L A T V I A

Gaija

○Riga
311

Daugava

Tukums○

Jelgava
Bouska○

Liepāja○

Telšiai○

Šiauliai

L I T H U A N I A
228

○Panevėžys

Ukmergė○

Vilnius

54

Lido

B E L O R U S S I A

Grodno○

Białystok○
218

Augusto○

Łomża○

○Ostrołeka

Narew○

P O L A N D

22

Kaunas○

Tauragė○
Nemunas

Suwałki○

○Gołdap
309
M a z u r y

○Ełk
○Pisz

Osterode○

Pojezierze

Mława○

○Olsztyno

Korsze○

○Ostróda

Klaipėda○

Sovetsk○
R U S S I A

Chernyakhovsk○
○Gusev

Kaliningrad○

Baltiysk○

Zatoka Gdańska

○Braniewo
Elblag

Malbork○

Kwidzyn○

○Chełmno
Grudziądz○

○Chełmno
Toruń○

20

18

37

VELANDA
S
Växjö○
○Nässjö

K A L M A R

Oskarshamn○

Bergholm○
Öland○

Kalmar
Nybro○
BLEKINGE
Karlskrona
Karlshamn
○Olvesborg

B   A   L   T   I   C

245

Bornholm
Rønne○ ○Neksø

Gdynia○

Gdańsk○
329

○Chojnice

Bydgoszcz○

Piła○

Wałcz○

Słupsk○

Darłowo○

Koszalin○

Kołobrzeg○

Wolin○

Szczecin
(Stettin)

Dąbie○
Gryfino○
○Szczeciński

○Pyrzyce

16

56

54

58

68

61

19

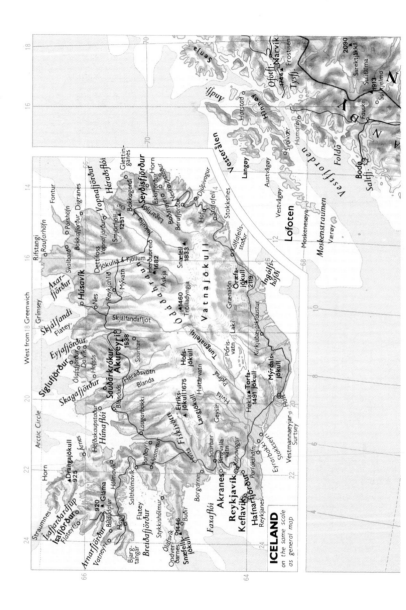

ICELAND
on the same scale
as general map

1 : 5 000 000

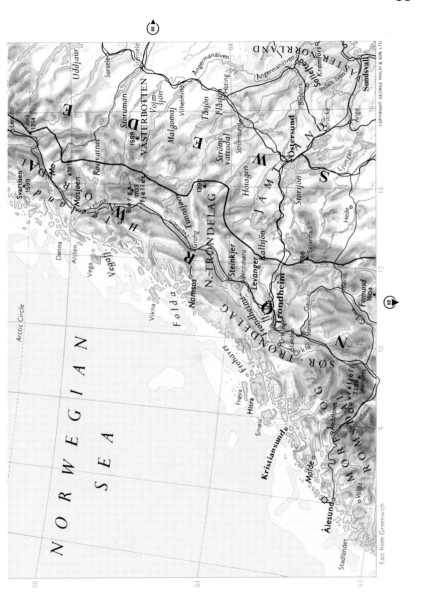

NORWEGIAN SEA

Arctic Circle

Svartisen 1599

Mo

Mosjøen

Vefsna

Donna

Alsten

Vega

Vegafj.

Vikna

Folda

Namsos

N-TRONDELAG

Steinkjer

Verdalsøra

Levanger

Kallsjön

Grong

Namsen

Tunnsjo

Bjørga 1703

Hattfjelldal

Uddjaur

Sorsele

Storuman

Stensele

Storman

Storavan

VÄSTERBOTTEN

Vojm. sjön

Malgomaj

Vilhelmina

Angermanälven

Hoting

Tåsjön

Flåsjön

Ströms vatudal

 Strömsund

Hotagen

Storsjön

Östersund

JÄMTLAND

Ljungan

Hede

Sylarna 1766

JÄMTLAND

Brācke

Ånge

Bispfors

Indals älven

Kramfors

Sollefteå

ÅNGERMANLAND

VÄSTERNORRLAND

Sundsvall

Trondheim

Trondheim

S-TRONDELAG

Orkla

Lokken

Orkanger

Storen

Gaula

Røros

Femund 1604

N

MORE OG ROMSDAL

Ålesund

Molde

Volda

Andalsnes

Snohetta 2286

Dovrefjell

Romsdalen

Stadlandet

Smola

Hitra

Froya

Frohavet

Kristiansund

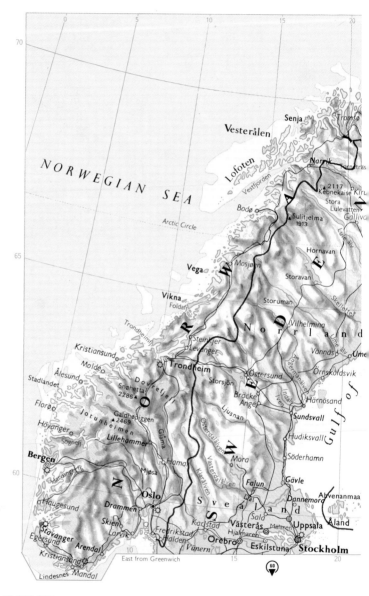

0 5 10 15 20

70

NORWEGIAN SEA

Senja Tromsø

Vesterålen

Lofoten Narvik Forneträs

Vestfjorden 2117 Kiru
Kebnekaise
Stora
Lulevatten
Galliva

Bodø

Sulitjelma
1913

Arctic Circle

65

Hornavan

Vega Mosjøen Storavan

Vikna Storuman Skellefte

Foldafj

N o r r l a n d

Trondheimfj Vilhelmina

Steinkjer Vännäs Ume

Levanger

Kristiansund Östersund Örnsköldsvik

Molde Storsjön
Ångermanälven
Ålesund Dovrefjell Bräcke Härnösand

Stadlandet Snøhetta Ange
2286 Indalsälven
Florø Galdhøpiggen Ljusnan Sundsvall

Jotunheimen 2469 Hudiksvall

Høyanger Österdalälven
Sognefj Lillehammer Glåma

Bergen Hamar Mora Söderhamn

Mjøsa Västerdalälven

Hardangerfj Falun Gävle

60 Oslo Klarälven Åhvenanmaa
S v e a Dannemora
Haugesund Drammen l a n d Åland

Skien Sala
Karlstad Västerås Uppsala
Stavanger Larvik Hjalmaren
Egersund Arendal Fredrikstad Örebro Eskilstuna Stockholm
Kristiansund Halden Vänern

Lindesnes Mandal East from Greenwich 15 20

60

1 : 10 000 000

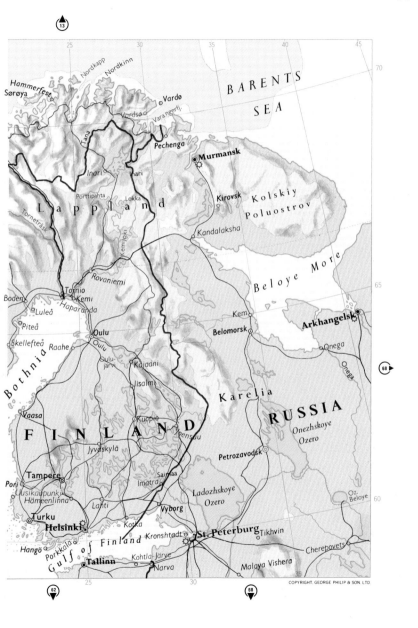

BARENTS

SEA

Nordkapp
Nordkinn

Hammerfest
Sørøya

Vardø
Vardsø
Vara ngerfj.

Pechenga

Murmansk

Inari
Inari

Kirovsk
Kolskiy
Poluostrov

Porttipahta
Lokka

L a p p l a n d

Tornetrask

Kandalaksha

Kemijoki

B e l o y e   M o r e

Rovaniemi

Boden
Torhio
Kemi
Haparanda

Luleå

Kem

Arkhangelsk

Piteå

Belomorsk

Skellefteå
Raahe

Oulu
Oulu

Onega

Onega

Oulu-
järvi

Kajaani

B o t h n i a

Iisalmi

K a r e l i a

RUSSIA

Vaasa

Kuopio

F I N L A N D

Onezhskoye
Ozero

Jyväskylä

Joensuu

Petrozavodsk

Tampere

Saimaa

Pori
Uusikaupunki
Hämeenlinna

Imatra

Lahti

Ladozhskoye
Ozero

Oz.
Beloye

Turku

Vyborg

Helsinki

Kotka

Kronstadt
St. Peterburg
Tikhvin

Hangö
Porkkalg

Gulf of Finland

Kohtla-Järve

Cherepovets

Tallinn

Narva

Malaya Vishera

COPYRIGHT GEORGE PHILIP & SON LTD

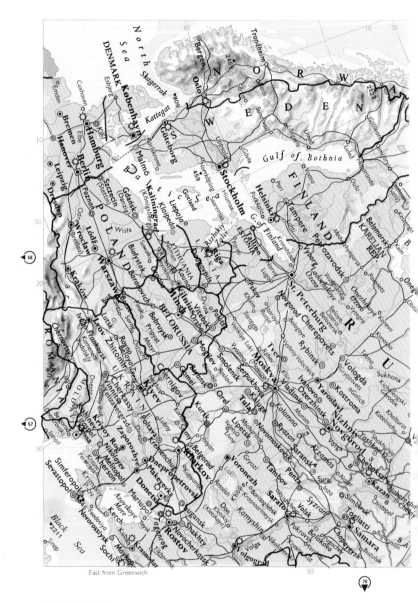

1 : 20 000 000

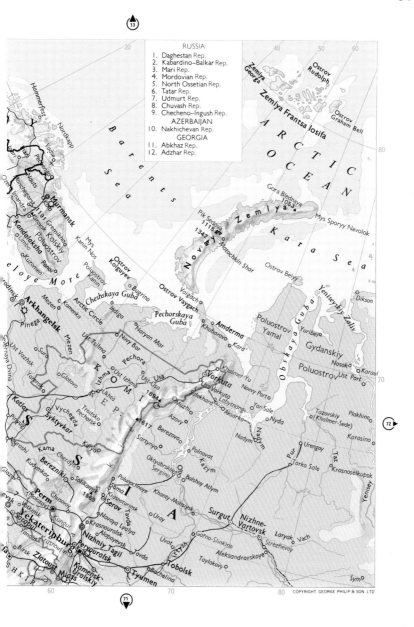

RUSSIA
1. Daghestan Rep.
2. Kabardino–Balkar Rep.
3. Mari Rep.
4. Mordovian Rep.
5. North Ossetian Rep.
6. Tatar Rep.
7. Udmurt Rep.
8. Chuvash Rep.
9. Checheno–Ingush Rep.
AZERBAIJAN
10. Nakhichevan Rep.
GEORGIA
11. Abkhaz Rep.
12. Adzhar Rep.

ARCTIC OCEAN

Barents Sea

Kara Sea

COPYRIGHT GEORGE PHILIP & SON, LTD

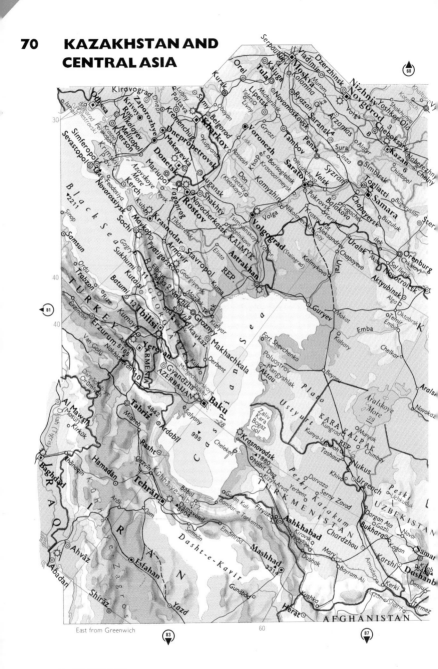

East from Greenwich

1 : 20 000 000

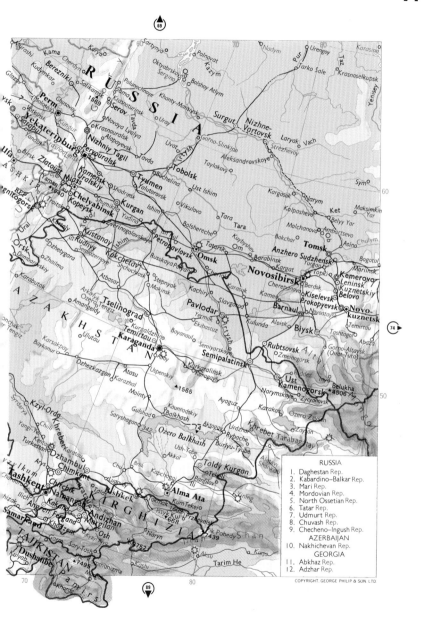

COPYRIGHT. GEORGE PHILIP & SON. LTD.

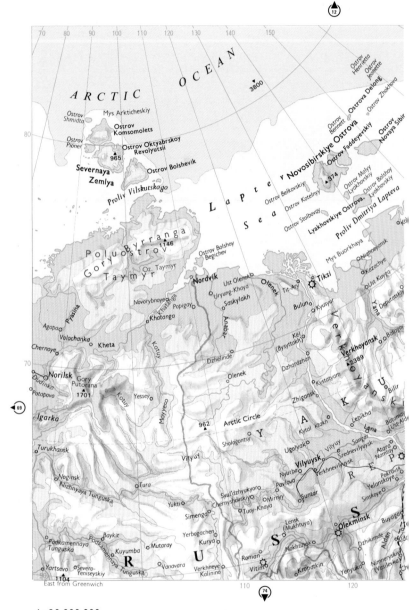

ARCTIC OCEAN

3800

Ostrov Henrietta
Ostrov Jeanette

Mys Arkticheskiy
Ostrov Shmidta
Ostrov Komsomolets
Ostrov Pioner
Ostrov Oktyabrskoy Revolyutsii
965
Severnaya Zemlya
Ostrov Bolshevik
Proliv Vilkutskogo

Ostrov Bennett
Ostrova Delong
Ostrov Zhokhova

Ostrov Belkovskiy
Novosibirskiye Ostrova
Ostrov Faddeyevskiy
Novaya Sibir

Laptev Sea

Ostrov Molyy Lyakhovskiy
Ostrov Bolshoy Lyakhovskiy
Lyakhovskiye Ostrova
Ostrov Kotelny
Ostrov Stolbovay
Ostrov Belkovskiy

Proliv Dmitriya Lapteva

Poluostrov Taymyr
Goryu Byrranga
1146
Oz. Taymyr

Mys Buorkhaya
Nizhneyansk
Kazachye
Ust Kuyga

Ostrov Bolshoy Begichev
Nordvik
Ust Olenek
Uryung-Khaya
Saskylakh
Olenek
Tit-Ary
Tiksi
Bulun
Kyusyur
Yana
Deputatskiy

Novorybnoye
Khatanga
Popigay
Anabar

Verkhoyansk
Batamay
(Ust-Aldan)

Agapa
Pyasina
Volochanka
Kheta
Kotuy
Dzhelinde
Kel (Bysyttakh)
Dzhardzhan

Chernoye
Verkhoyansk
2389
Bilir

Norilsk
Gory Putorana
1701
Dudinka
Potapovo
Kotuy
Yessey
Olenek
Zhigansk
Kytal Ktakh
Lepikha
Igna

Igarka
Moyyero
962
Arctic Circle
Kystatyam
Ugolyakh
Srednevilyuysk
Vilyuysk
Atara
Namskiy

Turukhansk
Vilyuy
Shologontsy
Kytal Ktakh
Vilyuy
Verkhnevilyuysk
Sangat
Pokrovsk
Yelanskoye
Sinskoyo

Noginsk
Nizhnyaya Tunguska
Tura
Yukti
Syul'dzhyukyoro
Chernyshevskiy
Pavlova
Nyurba
Mirnyy
Suntar
Lensk (Mukhtuya)
Olekminsk
Buyagos
Dzhikimde
Aldan

Podkamennaya Tunguska
Baykit
Podkamennaya Tunguska
Kuyumba
Mutaray
Simenga
Tuoy-Khaya
Yerbogachen
Kurya
Mokhtuyso
Yemukan
Nimnyerska (Vasilyevka)

Yartsevo
1104
East from Greenwich
Severo-Yeniseyskiy
Vanavara
Verkhneye Kalinino
Roman
Vitim
Kropatkin

R U S S

1 : 20 000 000

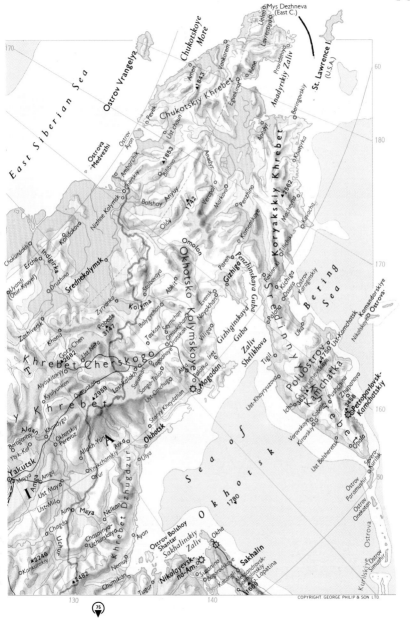

East Siberian Sea

Chukotskoye More

Ostrov Vrangelya

Mys Dezhneva
(East C.)

Uelen

Lavrentiya

St. Lawrence I.
(U.S.A.)

60

Chukotskiy Khrebet

Amen

▲1843

Vankarem

Inchoun

Rene

Egvekinot

Lorino

Providenya

Anadyrskiy Zaliv

Beringovskiy

170

Perek

Chaun

Ust-Chaun

Ostrova
Medvezhi

Ostrov
Ayon

Amborchik

▲1853

Pilltino

Anadyr

180

Ust-Chaun

Nizhne Kolymsk

Anyuy

1742

Veropol

Penzhino

Michterel

Kavacha

▲2562

Chunundokho

Erchoy

Bolshoy

Oloy

Markovo

Oftuchie

Khachyka

Uyandi
Otur-Kyuyd

Kondakova

Srednekolymsk

Anyuy

Veropol

Penzhino

Korshkovo

Parati

Kamenskoye

Rekinni

Kichiga

Indigirka

Zyryanka

Kolyma

Omolon

Gizhiga

Penzhinskaya Guba

Polona

Osoro

Kuchiga

Karaginskiy

170

Bering
Sea

Zashiversk

Khonu

Balyganchuk

Stolbovaya

Abkit

Evensk

Gizhiginskaya

Ukao

Ossora

Komandorskiye Ostrova

Pobeda
3147

Gora Chen
2662

Uss Nera

Takan

Seymchan

Omsukchan

Noyabchan

Guba

Zaliv
Shelikhova

Tigil

Nikolskoye

Ust-Kamchatsk

Khrebet Cherskogo

Alyaskitovyy

Kyulyunken

Omaakon

▲2959

Seymchan

Susuman

Yagodnoye

Palatka

Atka

Ust-Omchugo

Iret

Magadan

Khrebet

Staryy Kheydzhan

Songo Toion

Ust-Khoryuzovaya

Vorovskoye

Kirovskiy

Sobolevo

Klyuchevskaya
▲4750

Milkovo

 Key
3621

Pushtino

Yelizovo

Zhupanovo

▲3456

Polu ostrov

Kamchatka

160

Petropavlovsk-
Kamchatskiy

Ozernoy

Aldan

Khandygo

Nelkan Yurya

Ichoro

Ust Bolsheretsk

Opala

Borogontsy

Okhotskiy
Perevoz

Arkao

Okhotsk

Ozernaya

Severo-
Kurilsk

50

Yakutsk

Maya

Amga

Ust-Maya

Ulya

Sea of

Ostrov
Paramushir

Ust-Milo

Aimo

Maya

Nelkan

Okhotsk

1790

Ostrova
Onekotan

Ustj

Chasovnya-
Uchurskaya

Khrebet Dzhugdzur

Ayan

Ostrova

Chogdo

▲2246

Okonkurskiy

Nemuy

Tugur

Ostrov Bolshoy
Shantar

Sakhalinskiy
Zaliv

Okha

Sakhalin

Kurilskiye

Ostrov
Simushir

▲1482

Chumikan

Nikolayevsk-
na-Am.

Suanrino

Bogorodskoye

Katangli

Aleksandrovsk-
▲1609 Lopatina

130

140

COPYRIGHT GEORGE PHILIP & SON LTD

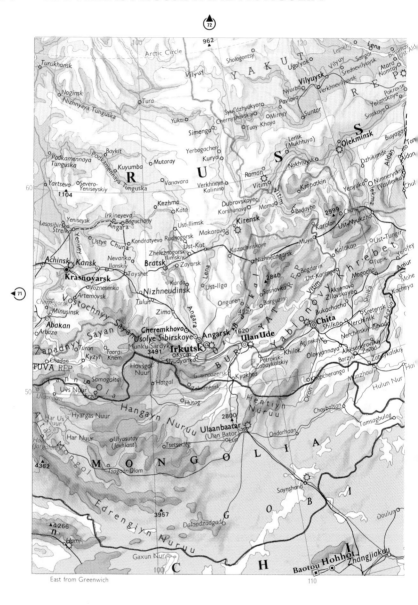

1 : 20 000 000

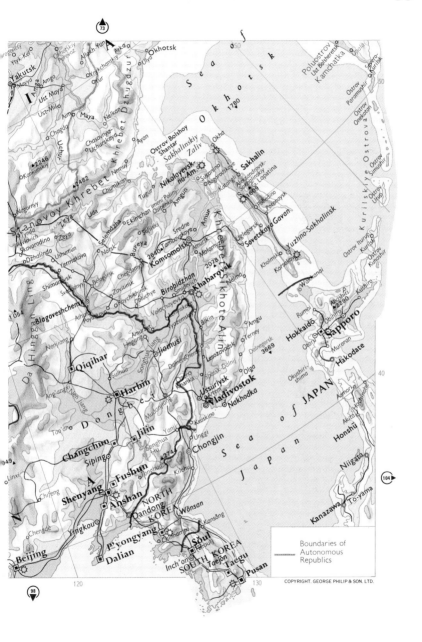

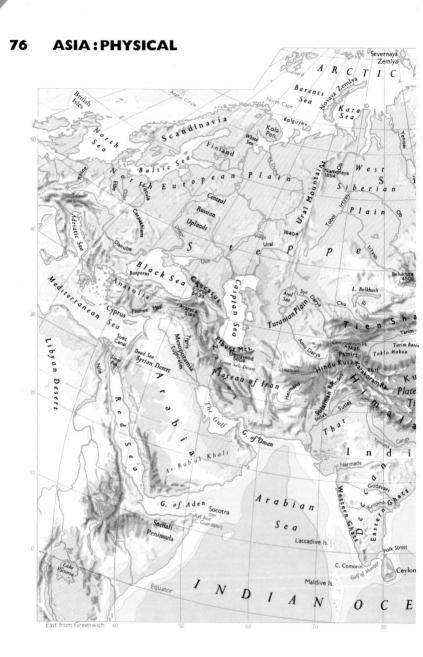

Svalbard
Severnaya Zemlya
A R C T I C
Barents Sea
Novaya Zemlya
Kara Sea
North Cape
Kolguyev I.
Yenisei

British Isles
Arctic Circle
North Sea
Scandinavia
Finland
White Sea
Kola Pen.
West Siberian
Narodnaya 1894
Ob
50

Rhine
Baltic Sea
North European Plain
Ural Mountains
S i b e r i a n
Tobol
Irtysh
Ob

Elbe
Oder
Vistula
Central Russian Uplands
Volga
1640
Plain
Irtysh
40

Adriatic Sea
Carpathians
Dniepr
Don
Ural
P   e
Belukha 4506

Danube
S
t   e   p   p   e
Aral Sea
Syr Darya
Chu
L. Balkhash
Ili

Black Sea
Bosporus
Caucasus
Elbruz 5633
Caspian Sea
Turanian Plain
T i e n S h a
30

Mediterranean
Anatolia
Taurus Mts.
Cyprus
Ararat 5165
Elburz Mts.
Demavend 5604
Amu Darya
Communism Pk. 7495
Pamirs
Tarim
Tarim Basin
Takla Makan

Suez Canal
Dead Sea
Tigris
Mesopotamia
Euphrates
Great Salt Desert
Plateau of Iran
Z a g r o s
Hindu Kush
Karakoram Ra.
Himala
Ku
20

Libyan Desert
Sinai Pen.
Syrian Desert
Nile
A
r
a
b
i
a
The Gulf
G. of Oman
Helmand
Harirud
Suleiman Ra.
Indus
Sutlej
8611
Thar
Plate
Ti

Red Sea
Ar Rub'al Khali
Narmada
Yamuna
Ganga
I n d i
10

G. of Aden
Socotra
Ras Asir (C. Guardafui)
Arabian Sea
Godavari
Krishna
Western Ghats
D e c c a n
Eastern Ghats

Somali Peninsula
Laccadive Is.
Palk Strait
0

Lake Victoria
C. Comorin
Gulf of Manaar
Ceylon
Maldive Is.

Equator
I N D I A N   O C E

East from Greenwich   40   50   60   70   80

1 : 60 000 000

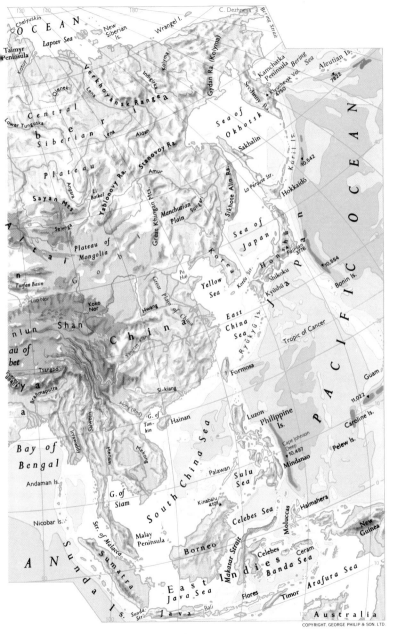

East from Greenwich 40

1 : 60 000 000

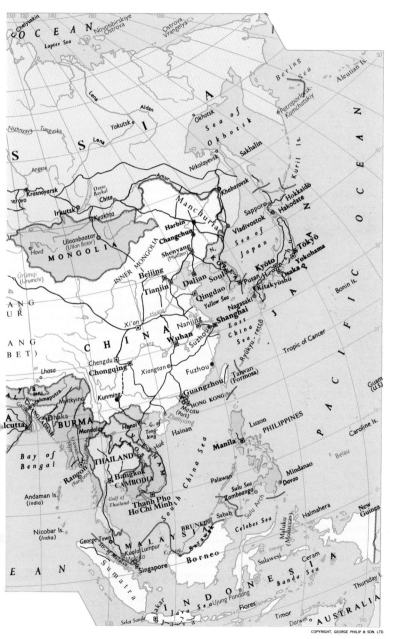

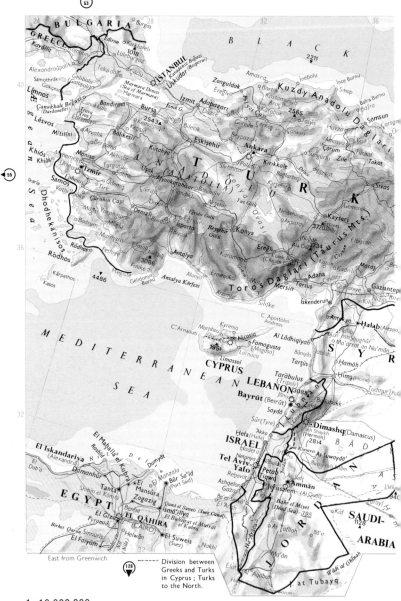

1 : 10 000 000

East from Greenwich

Division between
Greeks and Turks
in Cyprus ; Turks
to the North.

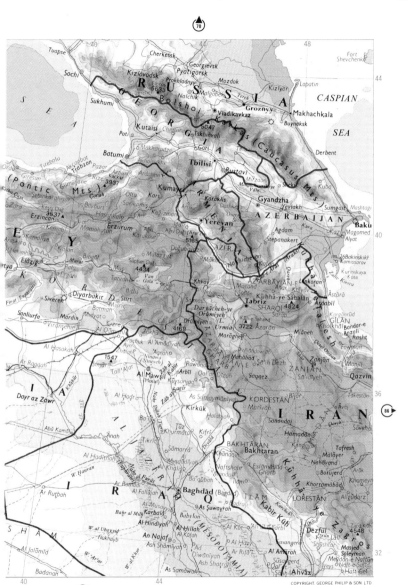

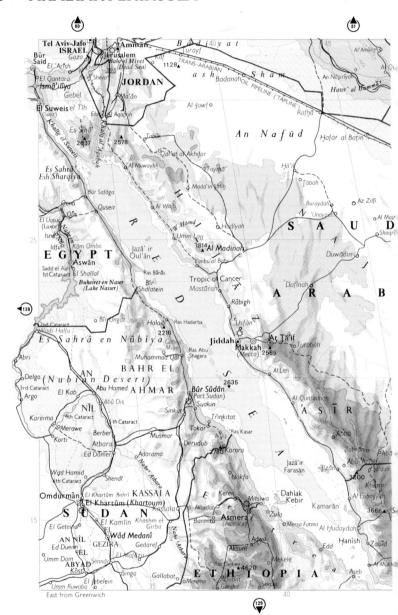

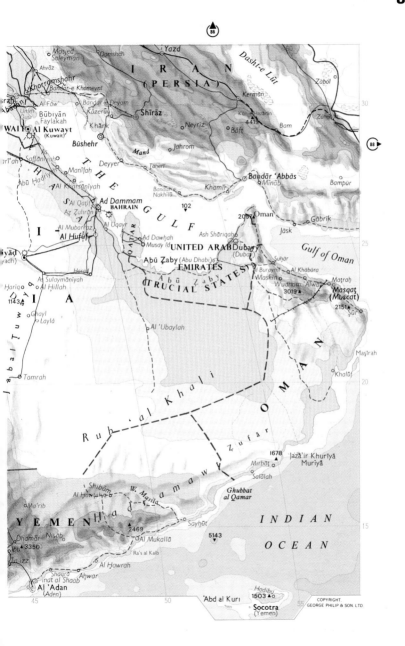

86

88 ►

Masjed
Soleyman
Domsheh
Ahvāz
Bandar-e Khomeynī
Khorramshahr
I R A N
(PERSIA)
Yazd
Dasht-e Lūt
Zābol
Kermān
Kūh-e Hazārān
4419
Bam
Zāhedān
30

Al Fāw
Umm
Qaşr
Būbīyān
Faylakah
WAIT Al Kuwayt
(Kuwait)
Bandar-e Deylam
Kāzerūn
Khārk
Shīrāz
Neyrīz
Būshehr
Bāft
Deyyer
Manīfah
Jahrom
Mand
Tāherī
Bandar 'Abbās
Mināb
Bampūr

'ār'ah
Aş Şaffānīyah
Abū Ḥadrīya
Al Khārsānīyah
T H E
Bandar
Nakhīlū
Khamīr
102
200?
Oman
Jāsk
Gābrīk
Gulf of Oman

S Al Qaţīf Ad Dammam
BAHRAIN
Aż Żuhrān
Al Mubarraz
Al Hufūf
Al 'Uqayr
Musay'īd
Ad Dawḥah
Ash Shāriqah
UNITED ARAB
Abū Ẓaby (Abu Dhabi)
EMIRATES
Şuḥār
Al Khābūra
Maşqaţ
(Muscat)
Maţraḥ

iyād
yadh)
Aş Sulaymānīyah
Al Hillah
Harad
Dukhān
QATAR
A b ū   Ż a b y
(TRUCIAL STATES)
Al Buraymī
Maskin
Wudhrum 'Alwa
3019
2151
Şūr

Hariq
1143
Ghayl
Laylā
D I A
Al 'Ubaylah
O M A N
Maşīrah
Khalūf
20

Tamrah
Jabal Ţuwayq
R u b '   a l   K h a l i
Z u f ā r
1678
Jazā'ir Khurīyā
Murīyā
Masīrah

H a d r a m a w t
Shibām
Al Ḥawṭaha
W. Maṣīla
Mirbāţ
Salālah
Ghubbat
al Qamar
INDIAN

Ma'rib
YEMEN
2469
Al Mukallā
Sayḥūt
5143
OCEAN
15

Dhamār
Nişāb
3350
Ra's al Kalb
'Izz
Shaqrā
'inat al Shaab
Aḥwar
Ras al Hawrah
Al 'Adan
(Aden)
Ḥadibu
1503
'Abd al Kurī
Socotra
(Yemen)

45   50   55

25

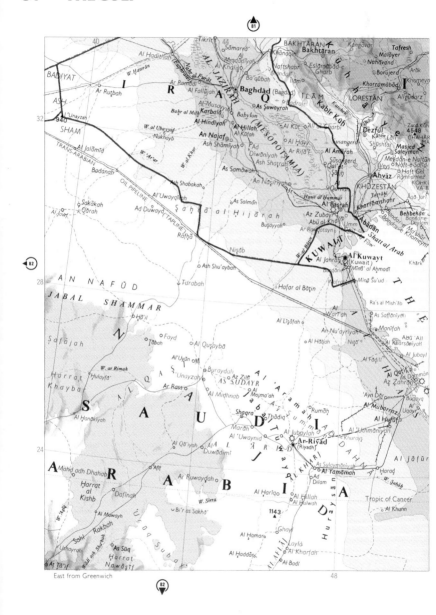

1 : 10 000 000

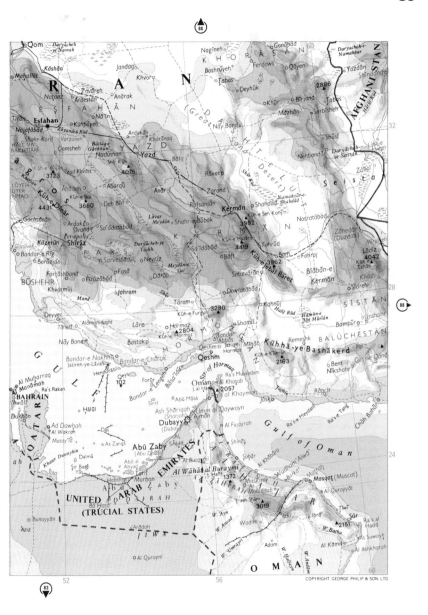

Qom
Daryācheh-ye Damak
Nāgineh-e
Gonābād
60
Daryācheh-ye-Namakzār
K H O R A S A N
Kāshān
Jandaqō
Boshrūyeh
Ferdows
Qāyen
Shindānd
Maḥallāt
Khvor
Deyhūk
Khūr
Tabas
Bīrjand
Tabas
Sarbīsheh
Natanz
Zavāreh
Anārak
R
Ardestān
Nā'īn
2886
AFGHANISTAN
Hari Rud
E S F A H Ā N
Māzhān
Hirīmand
32
Tīron
Esfahan
Kūhpāyeh
Nāy Band
Shūsf
Lūt
Najafābād
Zāyandeh Rud
Ardakān
Kharānaq
Nehbandān
Daryācheh-ye Seistān
Shahr-e Kord
Varzaneh
Y A Z D
Zābol
Qomsheh
Nadūshan
Shīr Kūh
Bāfq
S e i s t a
HĀLĪ VA
BAKHTĪĀRĪ
Zāhedān (Duzdāb)
a
Kūh-e ʿAlijuq
Gord Kūvāst
4075
Yazd
Rāvar
Namakzār-e-Shahdād
Mīrjā...
3723
Ābādeh
Zarand
Shahdād
Kūh-e Bol
Deh Bīd
Abarqū
Anār
Rafsanjān
Nosratābād
Zāhedān (Duzdāb)
4431
3660
Kūh-e Dīnār
Kermān
Lādīz
4042
Gachsārān
Ardakān
Saʿādatābād
3992
Seh Konj
Kūh-e Taftan
Sīvand
Persepolis
K E R M A N
Bam
Kāzerūn
Shīrāz
Daryācheh-ye Tashk
Sa'īdābād
4419
Tahrūd
Fahraj
Khāsh
Qanāvéh
F A R S
Sarvestān
Neyrīz
Bāft
Kūh-e eṣṭ Bārez
3962
Biābān-e
Bandar-e Rīg
Borāzjān
Meydān-e Gel
Dārāb
Fasā
Sabzvārān
Kermān
Sīāreh
BŪSHEHR
Farrāshband
Fīrūzābād
Dowlatābād
Khvormūj
Mand
Jahrom
Tārom
Kahnūj
Halīl Rūd
Hāmūn-e-Jāz Mūrīān
SISTAN
28
Deyyer
Kūh-e Furgun
3280
Shamīl
Bampūr
Īrānshahr
88
Tāherī
ʿAlāmarvdasht
Lāro
Hormoz
2804
Bandar-e ʿAbbās
Remeshk
BALŪCHESTĀN
Nāy Band
Bastako
Qeshm
Jaz.-ye Mīnāb
Kūhhā-ye Bashākerd
Rīp
Bent
G U L F
Jazireh-ye-Lāvān
Bandar-e Chārak
Qeshm
Kūh-e Kūhrān
2163
Nīkshahr
Bandar-e Nakhīlu
Hendōrābi
Forūr
Sīr-ye Hormoz
Ra's Musadam
Qesr-e Qand
Al Muharraq
Qeys
102
Bandar-e Lengeh
Bāsīdū
Oman
Juhīn
Manāmah
Ra's Rakan
Sirrī
Abū Mūsā
Jal Hāmun
2057
Jāsk
Rānch
Ra's-e Meydani
BAHRAIN
ʿAwālī
Hālūl
Ash Shāriqah
Jal al Khaymat
Ra's-e Tang
Chāh Bahār
QATAR
Dukhān
Ad Dawhah
(Sharjah)
Ajmān
Gulf of Oman
24
Al Wakrah
Dās
Umm al Qaywayn
Musay'īd
As Zarqā
Dubayy
Al Fujayrah
Dalmā
(Dubay)
Khawr Duwayhin
Abū Zaby
AL
Shinās
Masqat (Muscat)
Shīr Banī
Yās
(Abu Dhaby)
Al Buraymī
Suḥār
Wādhām 'Alwā
Mayhah
Al Qurayyāt
Habshān
Tarīf
Al Wāhāt al Buraymī
Maskīn
Malakādī
Murbān
1372
ash Shām
A b u
Z a b y
United
D H A F R A H
3019
Izkī
Ibrā
Tīwi
2151
Bunayyān
ARAB
EMIRATES
SĀHIL
Ra's al Hadd
Aziz
Arādah
(TRUCIAL STATES)
W. 'Ayn
Wadīm
W. Amad
Adam
W. Halfayn
Al Kāmil
Ra's Suwayh
Al Qurayni
J I W A
W. Umayrī
W. Andam
Al Ashkharah
O M A N
60

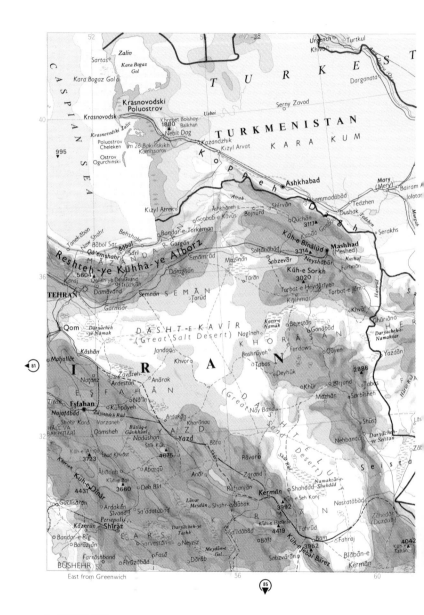

1 : 10 000 000

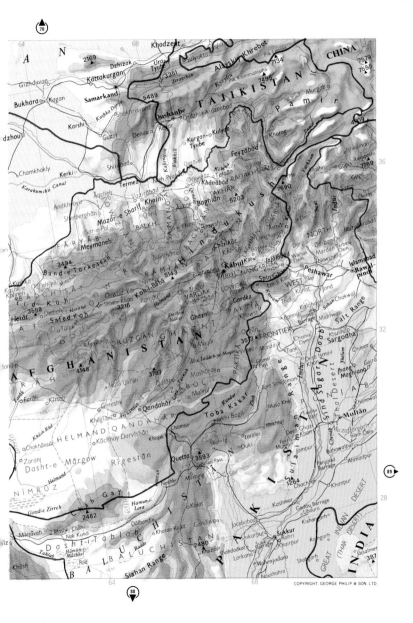

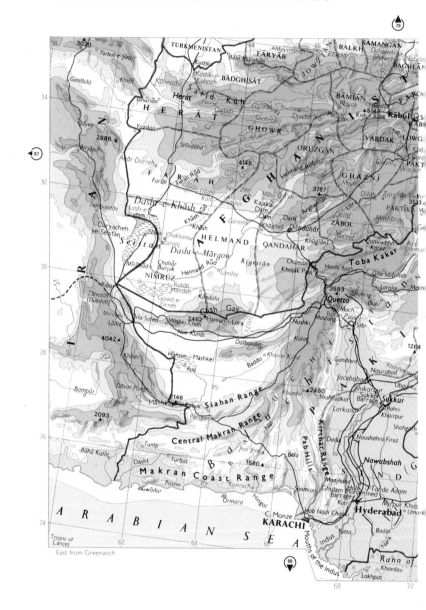

East from Greenwich

1 : 10 000 000

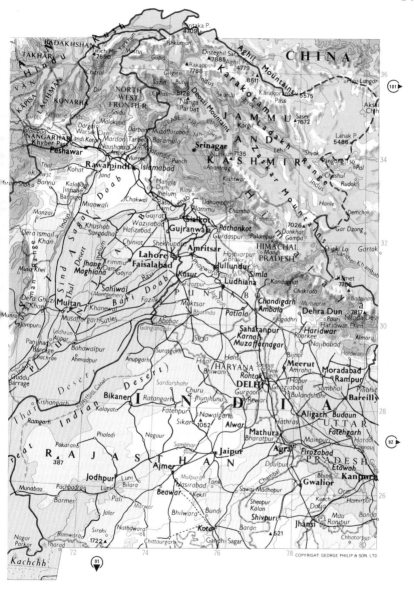

Antaka P. 4709

HINDU KUSH

BADAKHSHAN

TAKHAR

Ishkuman

Gupis

Disteghil Sar 7885

Aghil Pass

CHINA

Urich Mir 7680

Mastuj

Aghil Mountains

76

Rakaposhi 7788

7779

Karakoram

Chitral

Gilgit

Bunji

8611

Karakoram Pass 5575

Plari Langar

36

Dir

Cilas

8126

Deosai Mountains

Skardu

Aksai Chin

NORTH WEST FRONTIER

Nanga Parbat

Ladakh Range

Saser 7672

Dargai

Malakand

Darband

Muzaffarabad

Yan

Kargil

Leh

Lanak P. 5486

Mardan Tarbela Dam

Baramula

Srinagar

Shyok

Gangong Tso

34

Naushahra Dam

Murree

Nanhun 7135

Anantnag

Pangong Tso

Pal

Rudok

Punch

Kishtwar

Hanle

Demchok

Mangla Dam

Jhelum

Chamba

7026

Palampur

Dankhar Gompa

Gar Dzong

Gartok

32

Gujrat

Chakwal

Chenab

Udhampur

HIMACHAL PRADESH

Shipki Lo

Lanchen Khamba

Gartok

Gujranwala

Sialkot

Pathankot

Mandi

Gurdaspur

Amritsar

Hoshiarpur

Bhakra Dam

Kmet 7756

Lahore

Jullundur

Simla

Chakrata

Badrinath

Nanda Devi

Kasur

Ludhiana

Kandaghat

Mussoorie

Firozpur

Chandigarh

Dehra Dun 7817

PUNJAB

Ambala

Jagadhri

Pauri

Muktsar

Patiala

30

Bhatinda

Sirsa

Saharanpur

Roorkee

Haridwar

Haridwar Dam

Karnal

Najibabad

Almora

Muzaffarnagar

Haldwani

Hisar

HARYANA

Bijnor

Hansi

Bhiwani

Rohtak

Meerut

Moradabad

Amroha

Rampur

Pilibhit

28

DELHI

Ghaziabad

Sambhal

Gurgaon

Bulandshahr

Bareilly

Rewari

Aligarh

Budaun

INDIA

UTTAR

Alwar

Hathras

Fatehgarh

Mathura

Mainpuri

Hardoi

Bharatpur

Agra

Firozabad

PRADESH

Jaipur

Dholpur

Etawah

Ajmer

Gwalior

Kanpur

26

RAJASTHAN

Bhind

Hamirpur

COPYRIGHT GEORGE PHILIP & SON LTD

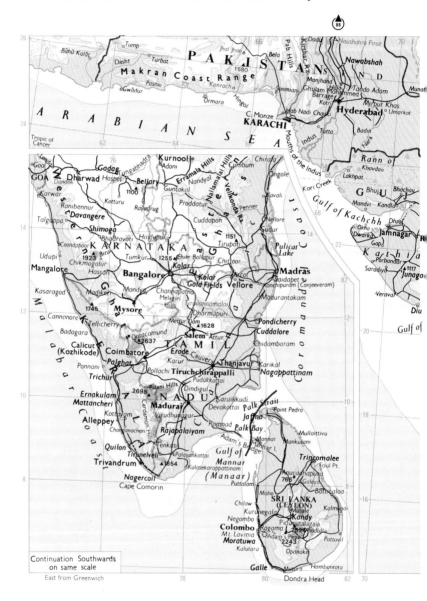

Continuation Southwards
on same scale

East from Greenwich

1 : 10 000 000

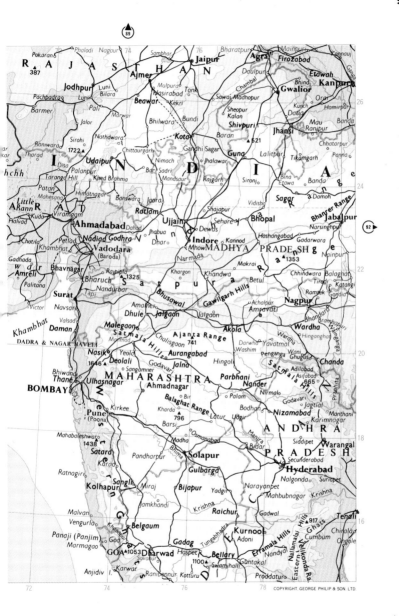

EASTERN INDIA, BANGLADESH AND BURMA

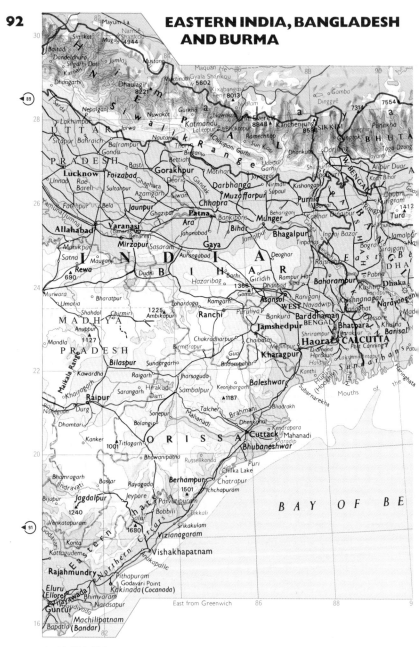

1 : 10 000 000

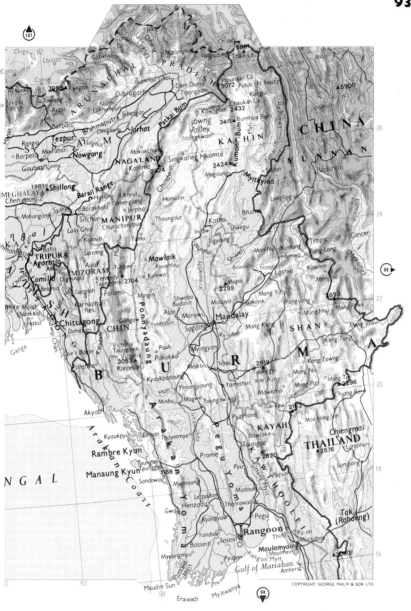

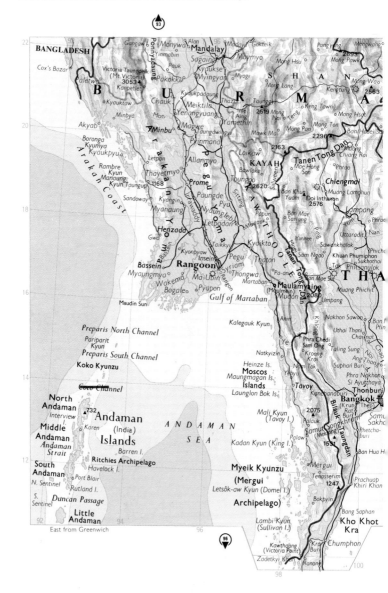

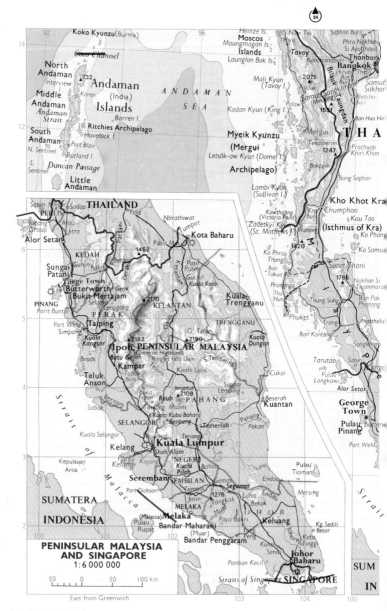

**PENINSULAR MALAYSIA
AND SINGAPORE**
1:6 000 000

50   0   50   100 km

East from Greenwich

1 : 10 000 000

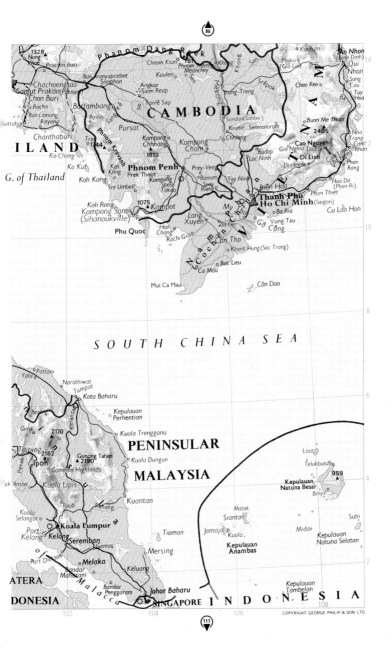

1328
Nong
Khae
Prachin Buri
Chachoengsao
Samut Prakan (Paknam)
Chon Buri
Si Racha
Ban Lamung
Rayong
sattahip
Chanthaburi
ILAND
Ko Chang
Trat
Ko Kut

Phanom Dang Rek
Cheom Ksan
Koulen
Ban Aranyaprathet
Sisophon
Angkor
Siem Reap
Battambang
Pailin
Phnom Kravanh
1744

Tonlé Sap
CAMBODIA
Pursat
1813
Kompong
Chhnang
Kompong
Cham
Chhlong

Phnom Tbeng
Meanchey
Sen
Stung-Treng
Srepok

Kontum
Pleiku
(Gia Lai)
Cheo Reo

An Nhon
Binh Dinh
Qui
Nhon
Song
Cau
Quy
Ho'a

14

Mekong
Kratie Senmonorom
Buon Me Thuot
2405
Cao Nguyen
Gia Nghia Da Lat

Nha
Trang
Cam
Rhan

12

Sandan (Sambor)
Budop
Loc Ninh
Di Linh
Djirlapne

Phan
Rang

Kas
Kong
Ko Chang
Ko Kut
Koh Kong
Sre Umbell
Phnom Penh
Prek Thnot
Kompong
Speu
Takeo

Prey-Veng
Banam
Sysy
Rieng
Tay Ninh
Bien Hoa

Hoa Da
(Phan Ri)
Phan Rang

G. of Thailand

Koh Rong
Kompong Som
(Sihanoukville)
1075
Kampot

Hon
Chong

Phu Quoc

Long
Xuyen
Sa Dec
Can Tho
My Tho
**Thanh Pho
Ho Chi Minh** (Saigon)
Go
Cong
Ba Ria
Vung Tau

Phon Thiet

Cu Lao Hon

10

Rach Gio
Khanh Hung (Soc Trang)
Bac Lieu
Ca Mau

Mui Ca Mau
Côn Dao

8

S O U T H   C H I N A   S E A

Pattani
Yala
Narathiwat
Tumpat
Kota Baharu

6

Bet
Gerik
2170
Taiping
2182
Gunong Tahan
2190
Ipoh
Cameron Highlands
uk Anson
Kuala Lipis

Kepulauan
Perhentian

Kuala Trengganu

Kuala Dungun

PENINSULAR

Laut
Telukbutun
959

4

MALAYSIA

Kuantan

Kepulauan
Natuna Besar
Binjai

Subi

Kuala
Selangor
Raub
Pahang

Matak
Siantan

Port
Kelang
Kuala Lumpur
Kelong
Seremban
Gemas
Port Dickson

Tioman
Jemaja
Kuala
Mersing

Midai

Kepulauan
Natuna Selatan

Kepulauan
Anambas

2

ATERA
DONESIA

Bandar
Maharani
Bandar
Penggaram
Keluang

Johor Baharu
SINGAPORE

Melaka

Malacca

Kepulauan
Tambelan

I N D O N E S I A

108

102
104
106

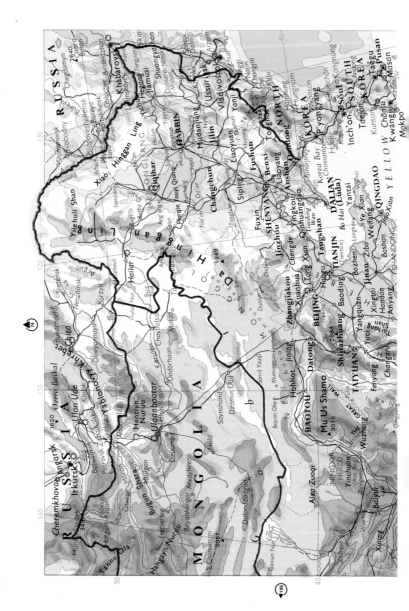

1 : 20 000 000

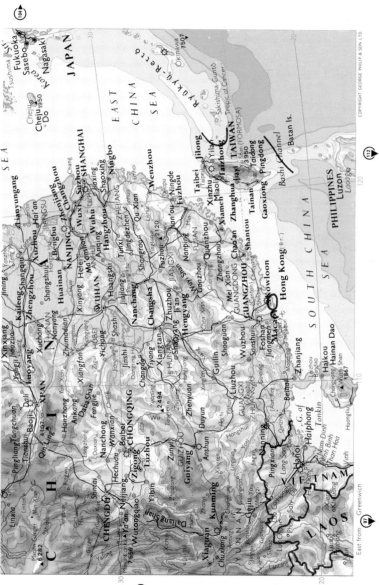

JAPAN

Tsushima
Fukuoka
Sasebo
Nagasaki
Korea

Cheju
Cheju 1950
Do

E A S T
C H I N A
S E A

Ryukyu-Retto

Okinawa 507
Sakishima Gunto
Tropic of Cancer.

Lianyungang
Xuzhou
Hai'an
Bengbu
JIANGSU
Changzhou
Zhenjiang
SHANGHAI
Wuxi
Suzhou
Jiaxing
Shaoxing
Ningbo
ZHEJIANG
Qu Xian
Wenzhou
Ningde
Fuzhou

Xinxiang
Jiaozuo
Kaifeng
Zhengzhou
Shangqiu
HENAN
Xuchang
Nanyang
Shanghui
Huainan
Xinyang
Hefei
ANHUI
Anqing
NANJING
Wuhu
Tunxi
Jingdezhen
Shangrao

Taibei
Xinzhu
TAIWAN
(FORMOSA)
Taizhong
Jiayi
Tainan
Gaoxiong
Pingdong
Bashi Channel
Batan Is.

XI'AN
Baoji
Hanzhong
Ankang
Daba Shan
Fengjie
Wanxian
CHONGQING
Zigong
Luzhou
Neijiang

Nanchong
Hechuan
Zunyi
GUIZHOU
Duyun
Guiyang
Anshun

WUHAN
HUBEI
Yichang
Shashi
HUNAN
Changde
Yiyang
Xiangtan
Changsha
Zhuzhou
Hengyang
JIANGXI
Nanchang
Ji'an
Ganzhou
Shaoguan

FUJIAN
Nanping
Quanzhou
Xiamen
Zhangzhou
Shantou
Chao'an
GUANGDONG
Mei Xian
Canton
GUANGZHOU
Foshan
Jiangmen
Macao
Kowloon
Hong Kong

S O U T H
C H I N A
S E A

CHENGDU
SICHUAN
Leshan
Xichang
Xiaguan
Chuxiong
Kunming
YUNNAN
Gejiu

Daliang Shan

Liuzhou
GUANGXI
Wuzhou
ZHUANG
Nanning
Pingxiang
Beihai
Zhanjiang
Haikou
Hainan Dao
Wuzhi Shan 1867

VIETNAM
Hanoi
Haiphong
G. of
Tonkin

LAOS

PHILIPPINES
Luzon

C H I N A

Lanzhou
Linxia

East from Greenwich

COPYRIGHT GEORGE PHILIP & SON LTD

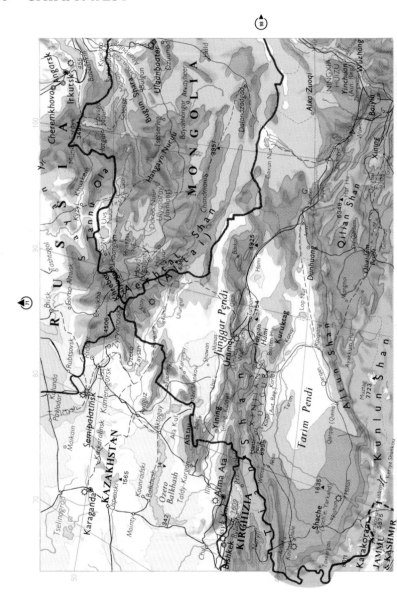

1 : 20 000 000

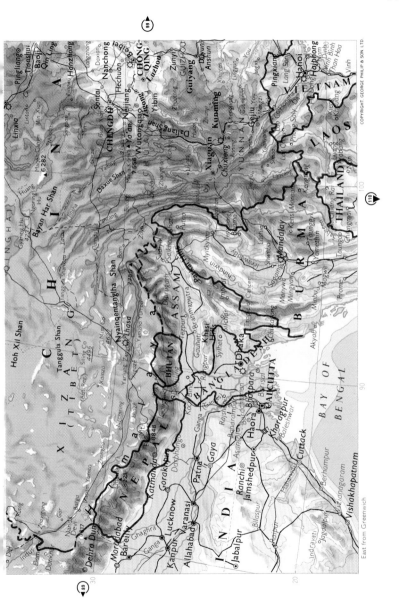

East from Greenwich

COPYRIGHT GEORGE PHILIP & SON, LTD

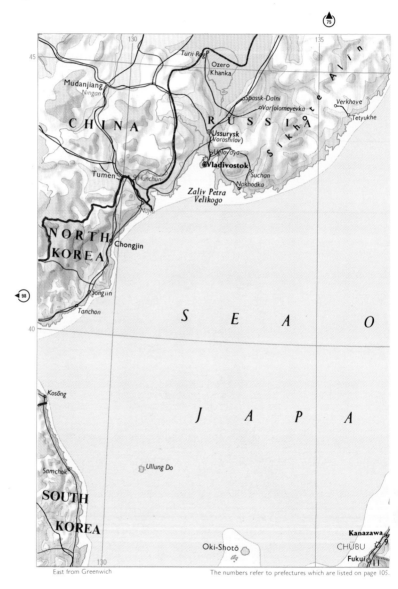

East from Greenwich

The numbers refer to prefectures which are listed on page 105.

1 : 7 500 000

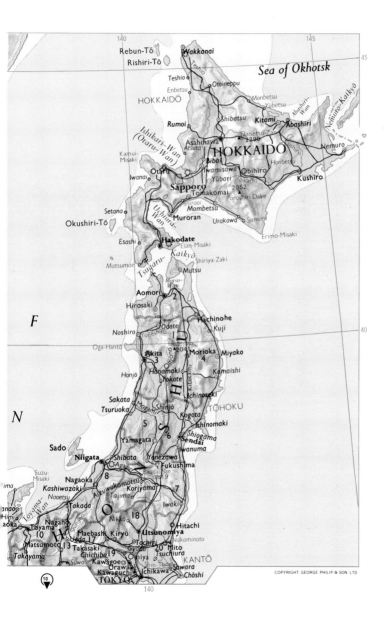

Rebun-Tō
Rishiri-Tō
Wakkanai
Teshio
Sea of Okhotsk
Otoineppu
Enbetsu
Monbetsu
HOKKAIDŌ
Yūbetsu
Abashiri-Wan
Rumoi
Shibatsu
Kitami
Abashiri
Nemuro-Kaikyō
Asahikawa
Daisetsu-Zan 2290
Kamui-
Misaki
Atsuta
HOKKAIDŌ
Nemuro
Bibai
Iwamisawa
Honbetsu
Otaru
Obihiro
Iwanai
Yūbari
Tokachi
Kushiro
Sapporo
Tomakomai
2052
Hiraoi
Mombetsu
Poroshiri Dake
Setana
Uchiura-Wan
Muroran
Urakawa
Samani
Okushiri-Tō
Erimo-Misaki
Esashi
Hakodate
Esan-Misaki
Matsumae
Kaikyō
Shiriya-Zaki
Tsugaru
Mutsu
Mutsu-
Wan
Aomori
2
Hirosaki
Towada
Hachinohe
Noshiro
Odate
Kuji
Yoneshiro
Oga-Hantō
2041
Iwate
Akita
Morioka
Miyako
3
Omono
Hanamaki
Kamaishi
Honjō
Yokote
Kitakami
Ichinoseki
Sakata
Mogami
Shinjō
TŌHOKU
Tsuruoka
5
Kogota
Ishinomaki
Yamagata
6
Shiogama
Sado
Sendai
Iwanuma
Niigata
Shibata
Yonezawa
Agano
Fukushima
Suzu-
Misaki
Nagaoka
Bandai-San
1819
Kashiwazaki
8
Aizuwakamatsu
Kōriyama
7
Naoetsu
Tajima
Iwaki
Takada
18
10
Nikkō
Hitachi
Nagano
Maebashi Kiryū
Utsunomiya
Nakaminato
Toyama
Ueda
17
Tochigi
Matsumoto
13
Takasaki
Gyōda
20
Mito
Takayama
Chichibu
19
Ōmiya
Tsuchiura
Suwa
Kawagoe
Urawa
Shin-Tone
Sawara
Kawaguchi
Ichikawa
Chōshi
TOKYO
KANTŌ

130
135

Samchŏk

○Ullung Do

S E A   O F   J A P A N

Kanazawa
CHŪBU
Fukui
Takefu
Tsuruga

Oki-Shotō

88

Kyō-ga-Saki Wakasa-
Wan
Hi-no-
Misaki Matsue   Tottori   Toyooka   25
Izumo ○Yonago 31 24 Maizuru 26
Pusan   CHŪGOKU   Ayabe 28   Hikone
35   32○Tsuyama   Ōtsu○ Ōkkaichi
KOREA STRAIT   Hamada○ 33   Hōkayama   Kyoto Ōsu
Tsushima Kaikyō   Masuda   Kurashiki Himeji○Amaga   Kōbe○ ○Ōsaka Tsu
Tsushima Kaikyō   Fukuyama Akashi   Sakai Nara 29 Mat
Hiroshima○ Onomichi○   Takamatsu○   Kishiwada Owase
Shimonoseki○ Hagi○ Tokuyama 35 Mihara○ Kure○ Marugame 27 ○Wakayama KINKI
Iki Ube○   Suō-Nada   Niihama ○Tokushima   30 ○Shingū
Fukuoka○ 40 Kitakyūshū   Matsuyama○ SHIKOKU 37 Shio-no-Misaki
Nakadori- Karatsu○41 Nakatsu○   38   39 Kōchi
Jima Sasebo○ Saga○ Beppu ○Iwatahama SHIKOKU
42 Kashima Ōmuta○ 44 Ōita○ Uwajima○ Muroto-Misaki
Isahaya○ 1592 Usuki○   Nakamura○
Nagasaki○ Kumamoto○ Saiki○ Ashizuri-zaki
Fukue Shimo- Shimabara○   P A C I F I C
Jima Jima Yatsushiro○ 43 45
Minamata○
Sendai○ 46 KYŪSHŪ Miyazaki○
Kagoshima○ Kobayashi○ O C E A N
KYŪSHŪ Kanoya Miyakonojō○
Makurazaki○ Shibushi-Wan
Kagoshima-Wan
Ōsumi-Kaikyō
Ōsumi-Shotō Nishinoomote○
Kuchinoerabu-Jima Tane-ga-Shima
Tokara-Kaikyō Yaku-Jima

Naka-no-Shima
Suwanose-Jima

130
East from Greenwich 135

1 : 7 500 000

HOKKAIDŌ	KINKI
1 Hokkaidō	24 Hyōgo
TOHŌKU	25 Kyōto
2 Aomori	26 Shiga
3 Akita	27 Ōsaka
4 Iwate	28 Nara
5 Yamagata	29 Mie
6 Miyagi	30 Wakayama
7 Fukushima	CHŪGOKU
CHŪBU	31 Tottori
8 Niigata	32 Okayama
9 Ishikawa	33 Shimane
10 Toyama	34 Hiroshima
11 Fukui	35 Yamaguchi
12 Gifu	SHIKOKU
13 Nagano	36 Kagawa
14 Yamanashi	37 Tokushima
15 Aichi	38 Ehime
16 Shizuoka	39 Kōchi
KANTŌ	KYŪSHŪ
17 Gumma	40 Fukuoka
18 Tochigi	41 Saga
19 Saitama	42 Nagasaki
20 Ibaraki	43 Kumamoto
21 Tōkyō	44 Ōita
22 Chiba	45 Miyazaki
23 Kanagawa	46 Kagoshima

136

CHŪBU-DISTRICT

Himi
Shinminato
Uozu
Takaoka
Oyabe
Namerikawa
Tsubata
Tonami
Toyama
Heiya
Kanazawa
Matsutā
Johana
Kamioka
Komatsu
Kaga
ISHIKAWA
Shirakawa
Furukawa
Takayama
Mikuni
Yamanaka
Haku San
Maruoka
Katsuyama
Fukui
Sabae
Ono
Echizen-Misaki
Ōta
Takefu
Kyō-ga-Saki
Tsuruga-Wan
Hachiman
Gero
Hokuriku Tunnel
Ibuki-Sanchi
Wakasa-Wan
Tsuruga
GIFU
Miyazu
Kakamigahara
Mino
Seki
Kiso-Gawa
Nakatsugawa
Maizuru
Obama
Nagahama
Ōgaki
Gifu
Mino-Kamo
Ena
Fukuchiyama
Biwa-
Ko
Hashima
Ichinomiya
Mizunami
Akechi
Ayabe
Hikone
Inazawa
Bisai
Komaki
Tajimi
Ōmi-
hachiman
Tsushima
Seto
Mino-Mikawa-Kōgen
Sasayama
Kameoka
KYŌTO
Ōtsu
Kuwana
NAGOYA
Toyota
Sonobe
Kusatsu
Hino
Tōkai
Kariya
Anjō
Okazaki
Takatsuki
Uji
Yokkaichi
Toyonaka
Ibaraki
Minakuchi
Suzuka
Tokoname
Hekinan
Shinshiro
Hirakarta
Kameyama
Handa
Toyokawa
KŌBE
Suita
Moriguchi
Ueno
Tsu
Chatta-
Hantō
Toyohashi
Hamamatsu
AMAGASAKI
Higashiōsaka
Nabari
Ise-Wan
Atsumi
ŌSAKA
Yao
Tenri
Matsusaka
Irako-Zaki
Sakai
Yamatotakada
Misugi
Matsubara
Sakurai
Ise
Enshū-
Izumiotsu
Kashihara
Shima-Hantō
Kishiwada
Izumi-
sano
Gose
Kawachi-Nagano
Gojō
Daiō-Misaki
Hashimoto
NARA
Wakayama
Hakken-Zan
Kainan
Arida
Kii-Hantō
KINKI-DISTRICT
Gobo
WAKAYAMA
Kumano
Tanabe
Kumano-Nada
Shirahama
Shingu
Nachikatsuura
Kushimoto
Shio-no-Misaki

East from Greenwich   136   137

1 : 2 500 000

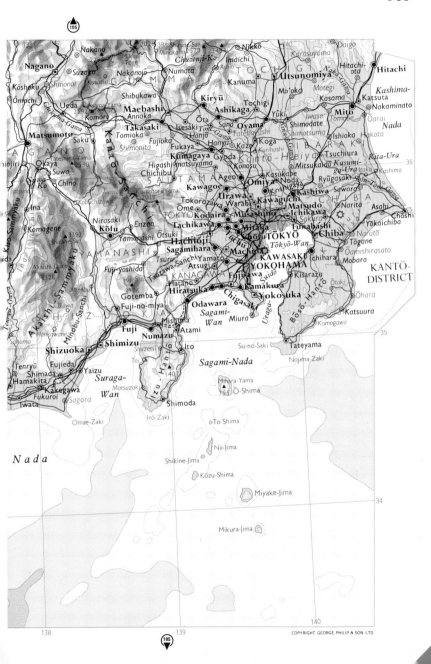

KANTŌ-
DISTRICT

Nada

Sagami-Nada

Nada

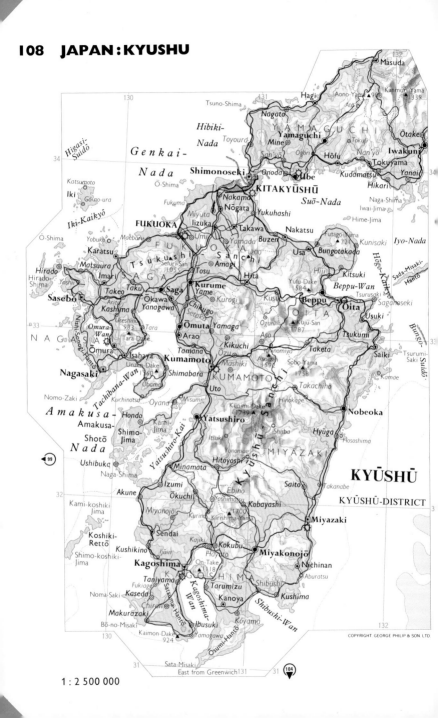

1 : 2 500 000

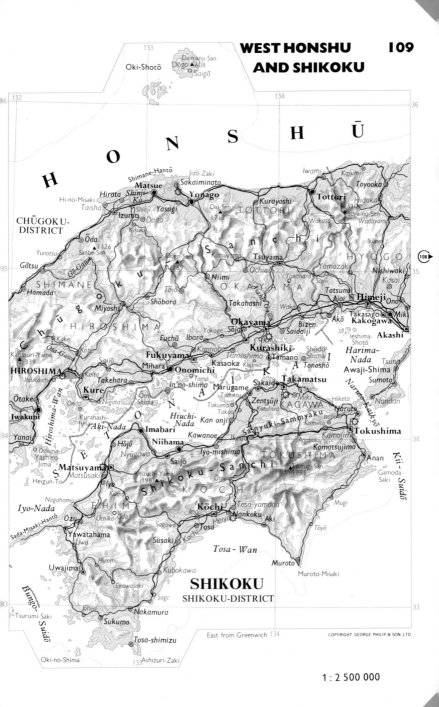

Oki-Shotō
Daimanji-San
Dōgo ▲608
Saigō

H O N S H Ū

Shimane-Hantō
Jizō-Zaki
Iwami
Kasumi
Toyooka

Matsue
Sakaiminato
Yonago
Kurayoshi
Tottori
Hidaka

Hi-no-Misaki
Hirata Shinji
Ka
Yasugi
Dai-Sen
Hidaka
Suga-no-Sen
Wadayama

Taisha
Izumo
Shinji
Daito
TOTTORI
Wakasa
Ikuno

CHŪGOKU-
DISTRICT
Ōda
Kisuki
Dōgo-San
Katsuyama
Tsuyama
Yamazaki
HYŌGO

Yunotsu
▲1126
Sanbe-San
S a n i n
Sayo
Nishiwaki
Kasai

Gōtsu
Gō-Gawa
▲1262
O K A Y A M A
Yonahara
Tatsuno
Aioi
Himeji
Ono

SHIMANE
Tōjō
Niimi
Ochiai
Wake
Akō
Takasago
Miki

Hamada
Miyoshi
Shōbara
Takahashi
Bizen
Saidaiji
Kakogawa

Köke
Sōja
Okayama
Shōdo-Shima
Ieshima-Shotō
Akashi

HIROSHIMA
Euchū
Ibara
Yakage
Kurashiki
Tonoshō
Harima-Nada

Kabe
Saijō
Kannabe
Tamashima
Tamano
I
Awaji-Shima
Tsuna

Kanmuri-Yama
▲1339
Ōta-Gawa
Kaita
Mihara
Fukuyama
Kasaoka
Kojima
Sumoto

HIROSHIMA
Itsukaichi
Takehara
Onomichi
Tomo
In'no-shima
Marugame
Sakaide
Takamatsu
Narto-Kaikyo
Nandan

Kure
Ōmi
Shima
Tadotsu
Miki
Hiketa
Naruto

Ōtake
Onda
Nigata
Hiuchi-Nada
Takuma
Kotohira
KAGAWA
Kamijima
Tokushima

Iwakuni
Kurahashi-Jima
Kan onji
Sanyuki Sammyaku
Kamiita
Komatsujima

Yanai
Aki-Nada
Imabari
Kawanoe
Ikeda
Anabuki
Anan

Ōshima
Yashiro-Jima
Hōjō
Niihama
Iyo-mishima
TOKUSHIMA
Tsurugi-San
Gamoda-Saki

Heigun-To
Nyūgawa
Saijo
▲1955
Kii
Suidō

Matsuyama
Shizuchi-Yama
Shikoku-Sanchi
Mugi

Matsusaki
▲1981
K O C H I
Ōtoyo

Iyo-Nada
Iyo
Kuma
EHIME
Ing
Tosa-yamada
Tōyō

Nagahama
Sagawa
Kōchi
Heiwa
Aki

Ōzu
Uchiko
Oda
Tosa
Nankoku
Muroto

Sada-Misaki-Hantō
Uwa
Susaki
Kochi
Muroto-Misaki

Yawatahama
Tosa-Wan

Uwajima
Hiromi
Kubokawa

Ekawasaki
Sage
SHIKOKU
SHIKOKU-DISTRICT

Bungo-Suidō
Tōhen
Nakamura

Tsurumi-Saki
Sukumo

Tosa-shimizu
East from Greenwich 134
COPYRIGHT GEORGE PHILIP & SON LTD

Oki-no-Shima
Ashizuri-Zaki

1 : 2 500 000

(106)

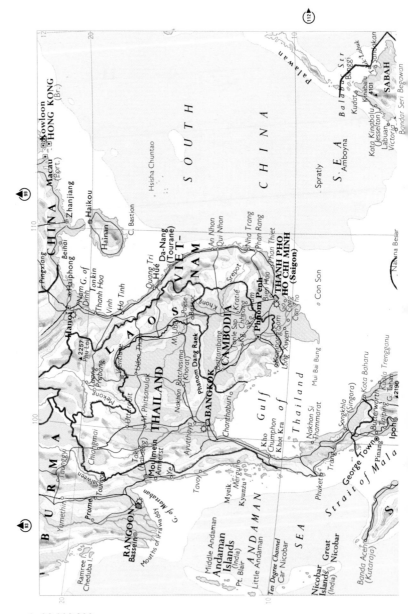

1 : 20 000 000

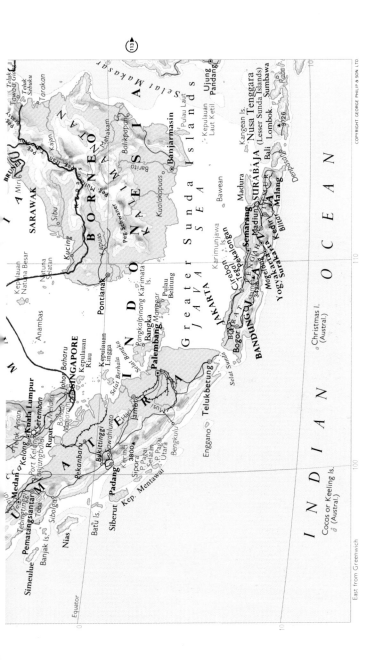

East from Greenwich

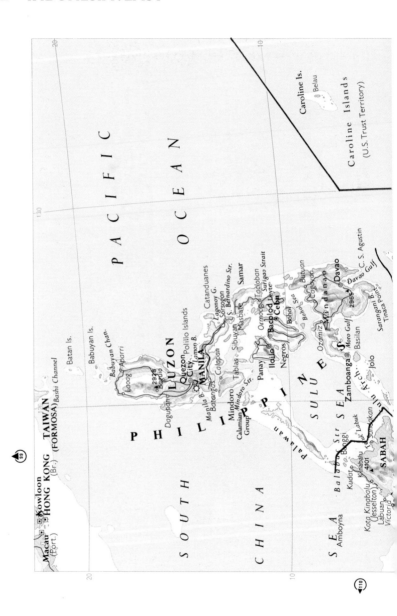

1 : 20 000 000

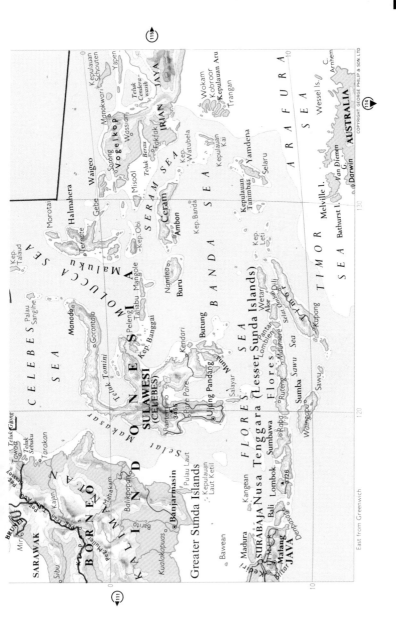

SARAWAK

BRUNEI

Miri

Sibu

BORNEO

KALIMANTAN

Kudalakapuas

Kajan

Tarakan

Balikpapan

Barito

Banjarmasin

Pegunungan

Teluk Apar

Teluk Sebuku

Teluk Tawau Cibang

Mahakam

Pulau Laut

Kepulauan Laut Ketil

Greater Sunda Islands

Bawean

Madura

Kangean

SURABAJA Bali

Kediri

Malang

Denpasar

JAVA

Lombok

3726

Sumbawa

Nusa Tenggara (Lesser Sunda Islands)

Raba

Bima

Ruteng

Sumba

Waingapu

F L O R E S   S E A

Flores

Labuanbajo

Sawu   Sea

Sawu

Salayar

Ujung Pandang

Rantepinto

3455

Bone Pare

S e l a t   M a k a s a r

SULAWESI (CELEBES)

C E L E B E S   S E A

Teluk Tomini

Gorontalo

Manado

Palau Sanghie

Kep. Talaud

M a l u k u

M O L U C C A   S E A

Morotai

Halmahera

Ternate

Gebe

Kep. Obi

Misool

Waigeo

Sorong   Vogelkop

Wassior

Manokwari

Kepulauan Schouten

Yapen

Teluk Cendera-wasih

IRIAN JAYA

Tidjok

Teluk Berau

S E R A M   S E A

Ceram

Ambon

Kep. Banda

Kep. Watubela

Kepulauan Kai

Wokam

Kobroor   Aru

Trangan

B A N D A   S E A

Namlea

Buru

Butung

Kendari

Tunw

Peleng

Talabu Mangole

Kep. Banggai

Kepulauan Tanimbar

Yamdena

Selaru

Kep. Leti

A R A F U R A   S E A

Wetar

Alor

Pantar

Lomblen

Selat Ombai

Dili

Maumere

Kupang

T I M O R

T I M O R   S E A

Melville I.

Bathurst I.

Van Diemen G.

Darwin

Wessel Is.

C. Arnhem

AUSTRALIA

10

120

130

East from Greenwich

COPYRIGHT GEORGE PHILIP & SON LTD

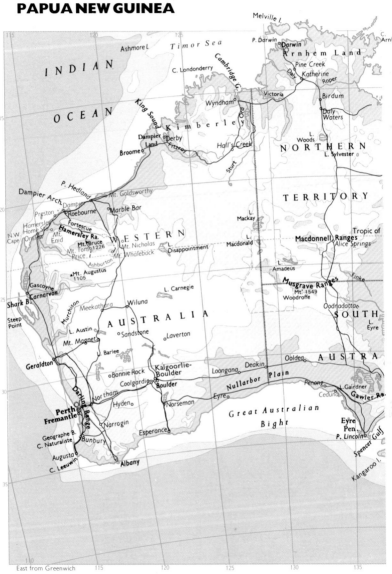

1 : 24 000 000

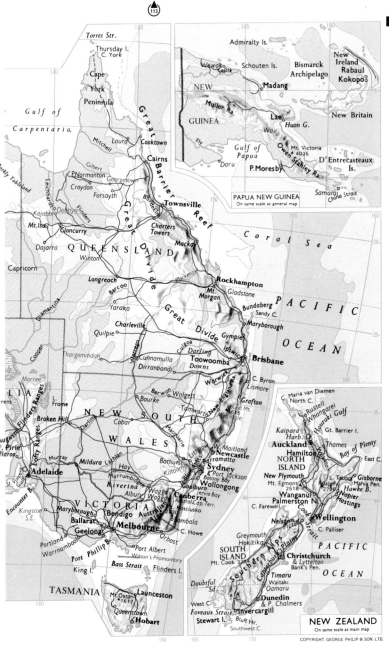

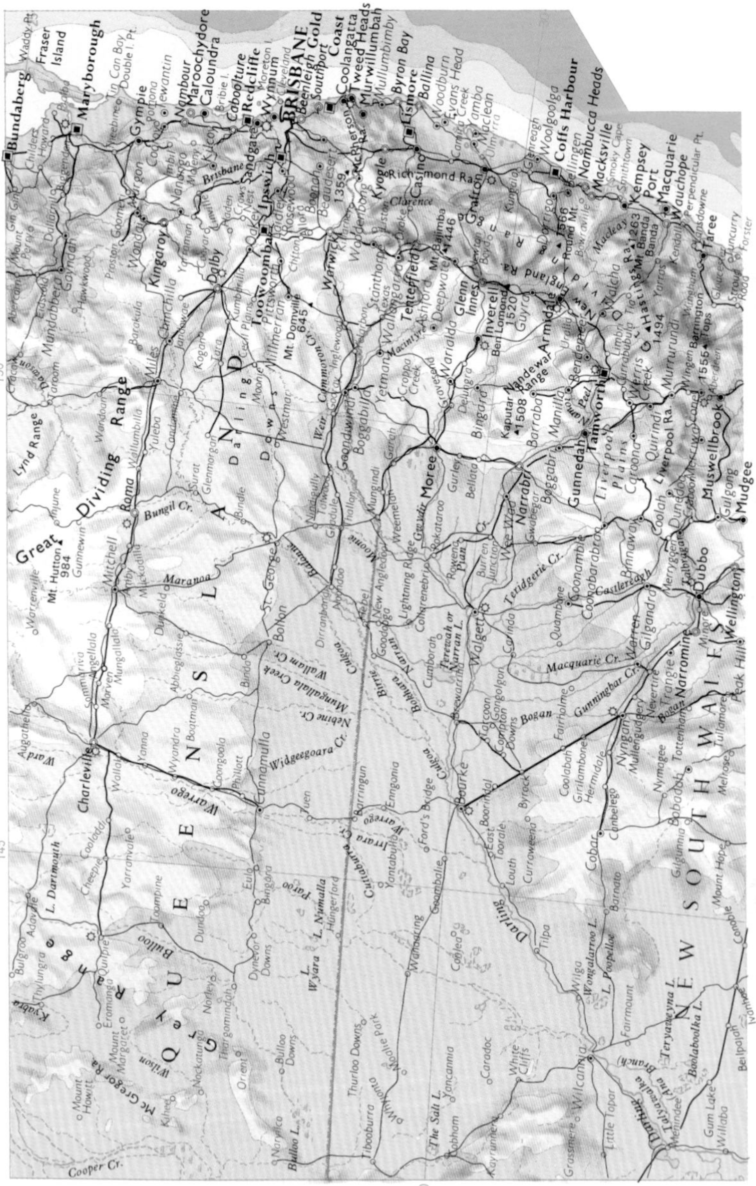

Bundaberg
Childers
Fraser Island
Waddy Pt.
Maryborough
Can Bay
Double I. Pt.
Gympie
Nambour
Caloundra
Cooroy
Newsantin
Caboolture
Redcliffe
Sandgate
Wynnum
BRISBANE
Ipswich
Coolangatta
Beenleigh
Southport
Gold Coast
Tweed Heads
Murwillumbah
Mullumbimby
Byron Bay
Woodburn
Ballina
Evans Head
Lismore
Kyogle
Richmond Ra.
Casino
Grafton
Clarence
Woolgoolga
Coffs Harbour
Nambucca Heads
Macksville
Kempsey
Port Macquarie
Wauchope
Taree
Forster

Kingaroy
Dalby
Toowoomba
Warwick
Stanthorpe
Tenterfield
Deepwater
Glen Innes
Inverell
Guyra
Armidale
Walcha
Nundle
Tamworth
Quirindi
Murrurundi
Muswellbrook
Scone
Singleton

Great Dividing Range
Mt Hutton 984
Mitchell
Maranoa
Roma
Miles
Condamine
Chinchilla
Dalby

Charleville
Augathella
Morven
Mitchell
Bollon
St George
Dirranbandi
Mungindi
Goondiwindi
Moree
Narrabri
Wee Waa
Walgett
Lightning Ridge
Coonamble
Gilgandra
Dubbo
Wellington
Mudgee

Quilpie
Eulo
Cunnamulla
Thargomindah
Hungerford
Bourke
Brewarrina
Nyngan
Warren
Narromine
Trangie
Nymagee
Cobar

Cooper Cr.
Thurlo Downs
The Salt L.
White Cliffs
Wilcannia
Darling
Menindee
Tibooburra

Great Dividing Range
QUEENSLAND
NEW SOUTH WALES
Grey Range

1 : 8 000 000

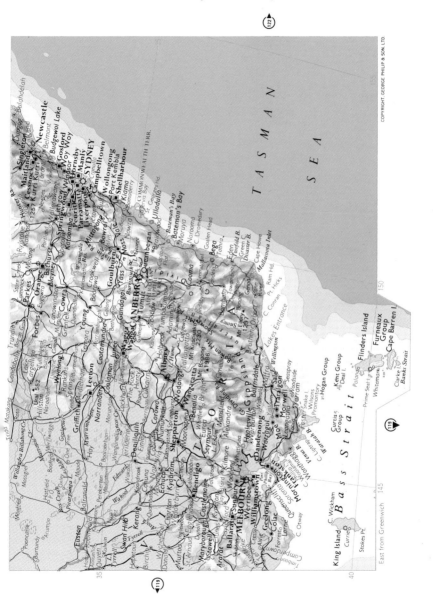

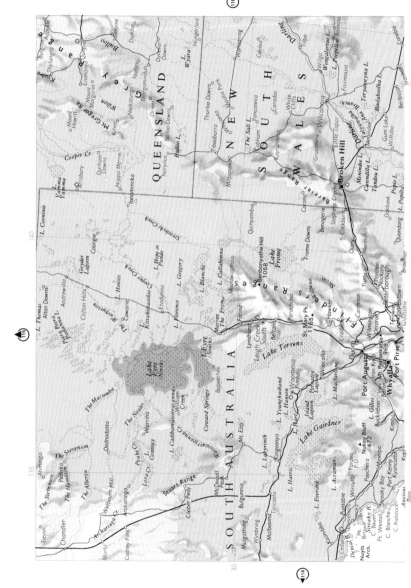

1 : 8 000 000

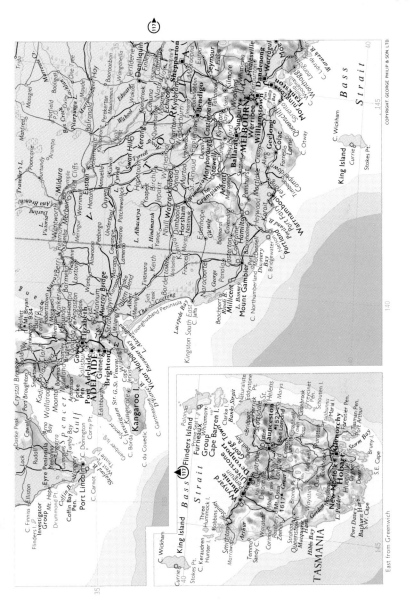

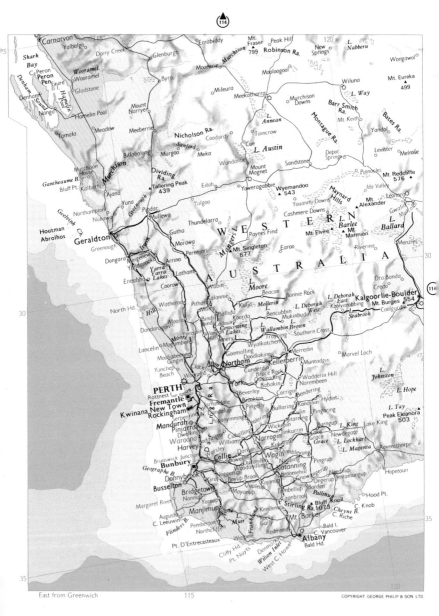

COPYRIGHT. GEORGE PHILIP & SON LTD

1 : 8 000 000

1 : 8 000 000

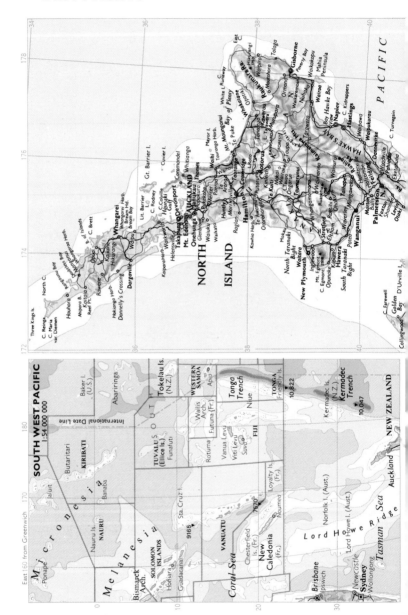

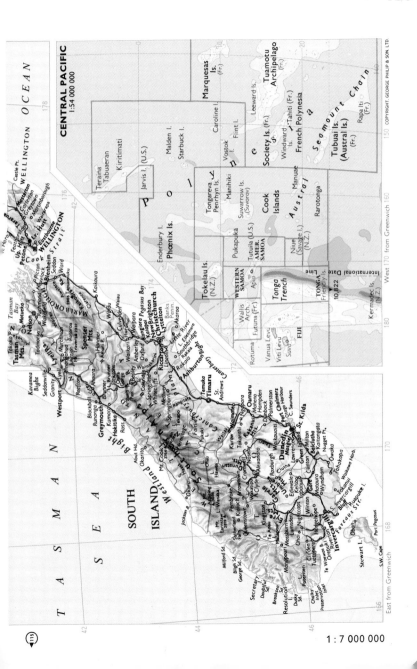

CENTRAL PACIFIC
1:54 000 000

OCEAN

TASMAN SEA

SOUTH ISLAND

WELLINGTON

CENTRAL PACIFIC

Marquesas Is. (Fr.)

Tuamotu Archipelago (Fr.)

Seamount Chain

Society Is. (Fr.)
Leeward Is.
Windward Is.
Tahiti (Fr.)
French Polynesia

Tubuai Is. (Austral Is.) (Fr.)

Rapa Iti (Fr.)

Teraina
Tabuaeran
Kiritimati

Jarvis I. (U.S.)

Malden I.
Starbuck I.

Caroline I.
Flint I.

Vostok
Is.

Polynesia

Tongareva
Penrhyn Is.
Manihiki
Suwarrow Is. (Suvorov)
Cook Islands

Austral

Rarotonga

Manuae

Enderbury I.
Phoenix Is.

Pukapuka
Tutuila (U.S.)
AMER. SAMOA

Niue (Savage I.) (N.Z.)

Tokelau Is. (N.Z.)
WESTERN SAMOA
Apia

Wallis Arch.
Futuna (Fr.)

Tonga Trench

TONGA (Friendly Is.)
10,822

International Date Line

Kermadec Is. (N.Z.)

Rotuma
Vanua Levu
Viti Levu
Suva
FIJI

178
176
174
172
170
168
166
180
West 170 from Greenwich
160
150
20

East from Greenwich
42
44
46

1 : 7 000 000

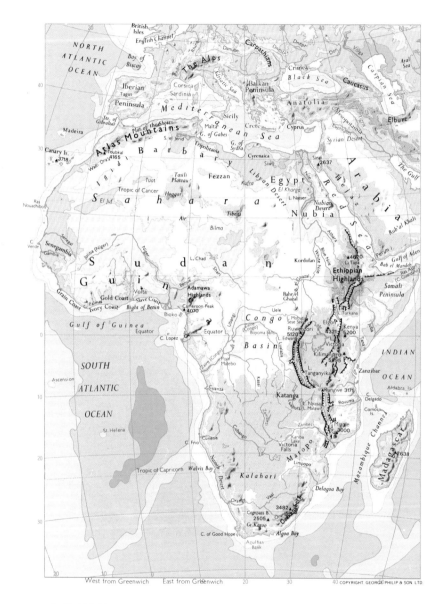

1 : 70 000 000

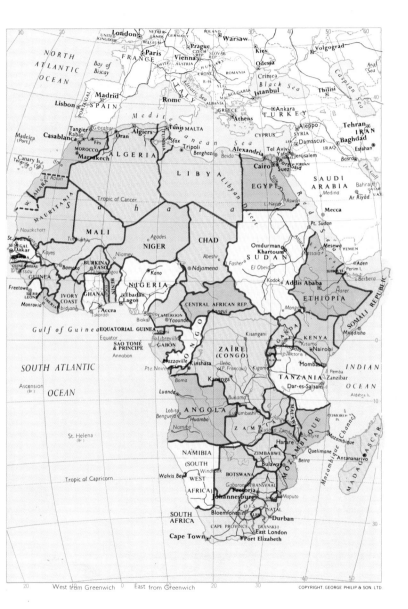

1 : 70 000 000

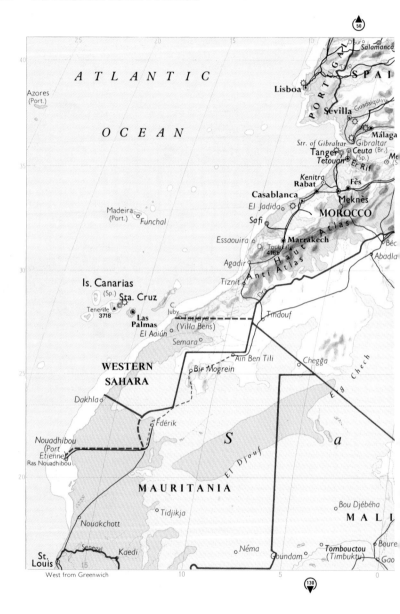

ATLANTIC

OCEAN

POR GA
Dour
Salamanca
SPAI

Azores
(Port.)

Lisboa

Sevilla
Guadalquivir

Málaga

Str. of Gibraltar
Gibraltar
Tanger
Ceuta (Br.)
Tetouan
(Sp.)
Me
Er Rif
S

Kenitra
Rabat
Fès

Casablanca
Meknès
El Jadida
MOROCCO
Safi

Madeira
(Port.)
Funchal

Essaouira
Marrákech
Béc
Dj. Toubkal
Abadla
4165
Haut Atlas

Agadir
Anti Atlas

Tiznit

Is. Canarias
(Sp.)
Sta. Cruz
Tenerife
3718
C.
Juby
Tarfaya
Tindouf
Las
(Villa Bens)
Palmas
El Aaiún
Semara

WESTERN
Aïn Ben Tili
Chegga
SAHARA
Bir Mogrein
Eg Chech

Dakhla

Fdérik

Nouadhibou
S
a
(Port
Etienne)
Ras Nouadhibou
El Djouf

MAURITANIA

Bou Djébéha

Tidjikja
MALI

Nouakchott

Tombouctou
St.
Néma
(Timbuktu)
Boure
Louis
Senegal
Kaedi
Goundam
Gao

1 : 20 000 000

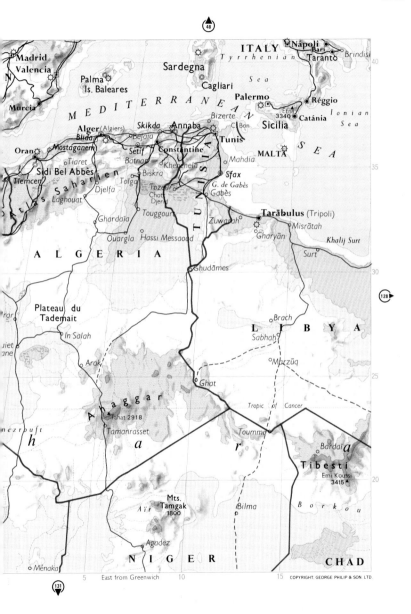

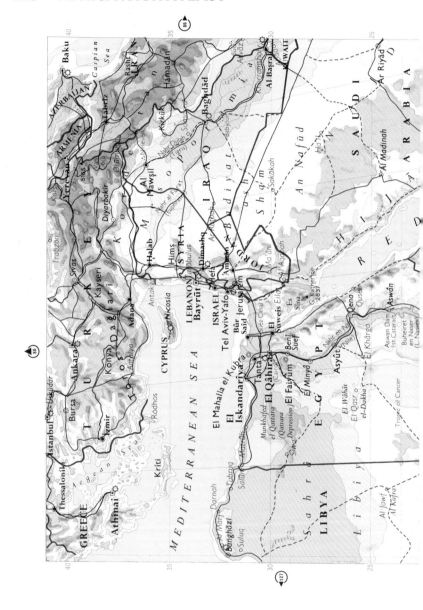

1 : 20 000 000

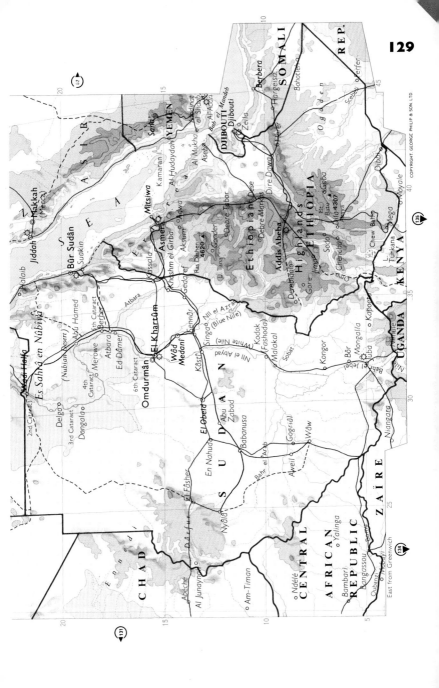

COPYRIGHT GEORGE PHILIP & SON LTD.

SOMALI REP.

Berbera

Berbera

Hargeisa

Bohotleh

O g a d e n

Scebeli Uefer

YEMEN

Sana

Madinat ash Sha'b
Al Agha

DJIBOUTI
Djibouti

Bab el Mandeb

Zeila

Dibbis

Moyale

Al Mukha

Aseb

Al Hudaydah

Asela

Dire Dawa

E T H I O P I A

Buya

Jijiga

Alu 4307

40

Kamaran

Ras Dashen
4620

Gondar

Debre Tabor

Jose

Debre Markos

Addis Abeba

Ethiopian Highlands

Sodo

Chencha

Chew Bahir

Mega

45

R E D   S E A

Makkah
(Mecca)

Jiddah

Bûr Sûdân

Sudkin

E R I T R E A

Mitsiwa

Asmera

Aksum

'Adwa

Kassala

Khashm el Girba

Gedaref

Tana

Denbidolo

Gore

Jima

Lake Turkana

KENYA

35

Talaib

Es Sahrâ en Nûbiya

Abû Hamed

Atbara

Atbara

Berber

Nil el Azraq
(Blue Nile)

Singga

Kodok
Foshoda

Malakal

Sobat

Kongor

Bôr

Mongalla

UGANDA

Wâdi Halfa

(Nubian Desert)

Merowe

Ed Dâmer

Sennâr

Wâd
Medani

Nil el Abyad
(White Nile)

Mongalla

Bahr el Jebel

Juba

Nile

30

2nd Cataract

Delgo

3rd Cataract

Dongola

4th Cataract

Atbara

6th Cataract

Omdurmân

El Khartûm

Kôstî

El Obeïd

Abu
Zabad

Babanusa

Gogrial

Wâw

Aweil

Bahr el Arab

Niangara

ZAÏRE

25

S U D A N

D â r f û r

En Nahud

Ed Fâsher

Nyâlâ

Ndélé

Yalinga

Bambari

Bangassou

CENTRAL
AFRICAN
REPUBLIC

20

CHAD

Ennedi

Abéché

Al Junaynah

Am-Timan

Oubangi

East from Greenwich

5

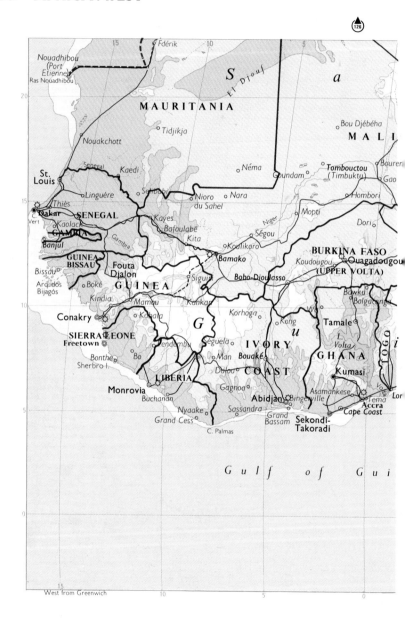

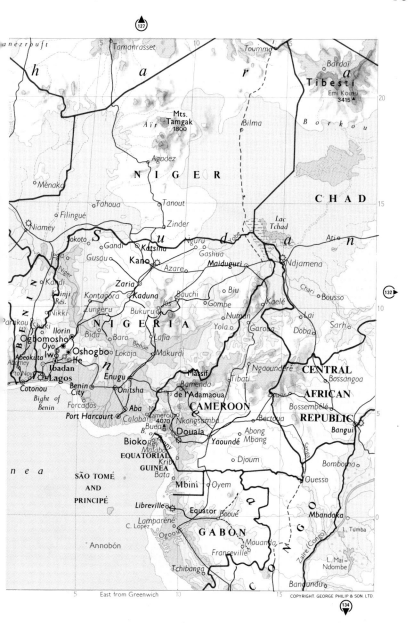

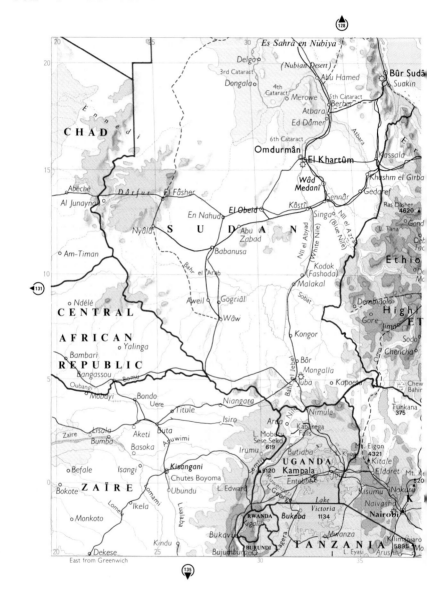

East from Greenwich

1 : 20 000 000

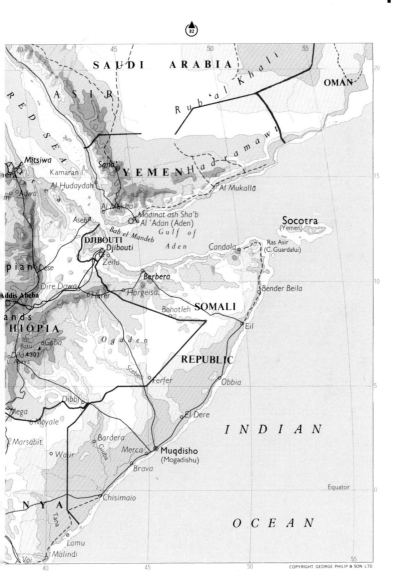

SAUDI   ARABIA

OMAN

Rub' al Khali

A S I R

R E D   S E A

Mitsiwa

Kamaran I.

Al Hudaydah

Sana'

Y E M E N   H *a d r a m a w t*

Al Mukalla

Al Mukha

Adwa

Aseb

Madinat ash Sha'b
Al 'Adan (Aden)

Bab el Mandeb   *Gulf of*

Socotra
(Yemen)

DJIBOUTI
Djibouti

A d e n

Candala

Ras Asir
(C. Guardafui)

Dese

Zeila

Dire Dawa

Berbera

Bender Beila

pian

Addis Abeba

Harer

Hargeisa

Bohotleh

SOMALI

ands

HIOPIA

O g a d e n

Goba

Batu
Dilo 4307
Awasa

Eil

REPUBLIC

Scebeli   Ferfer

Obbia

Dibbi

Mega

El Dere

Moyale

Marsabit

Bardera

Guba

Merca

Muqdisho
(Mogadishu)

I N D I A N

Wajir

Brava

N Y A

Chisimaio

Equator

Tana

Lamu

O C E A N

Voi

Malindi

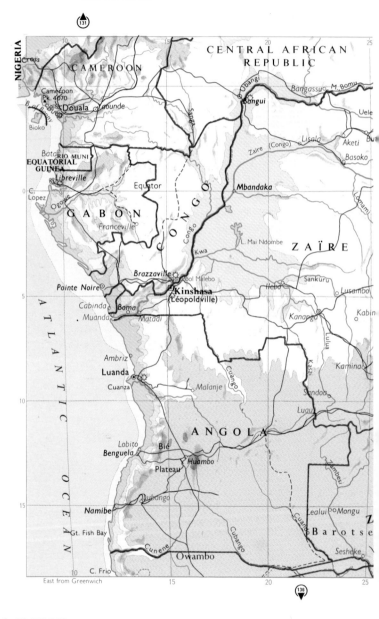

1 : 20 000 000

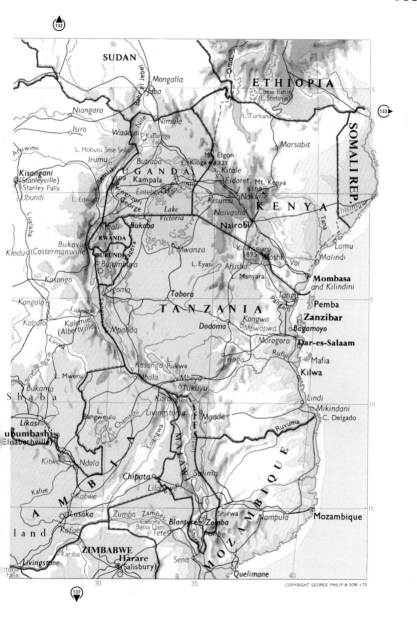

COPYRIGHT GEORGE PHILIP & SON LTD

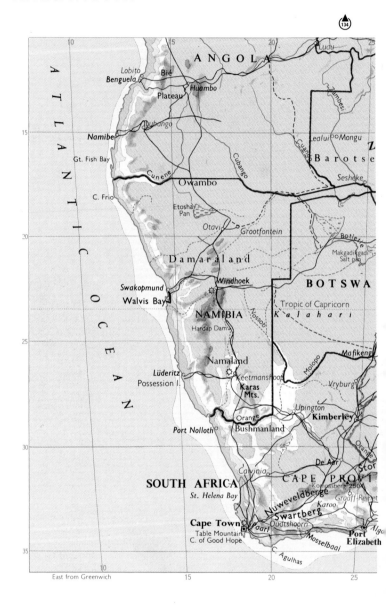

1 : 20 000 000

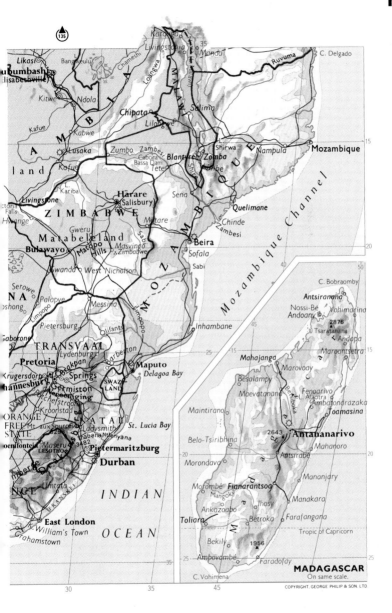

135

Likasi
Bangweulu
ubumbashi
(Elisabethville)
Kitwe
Ndola
Chambeshi
Manda
Ruvuma
C. Delgado
Karonga
Livingstonia
Luangwa
Loangwa
MALAWI
Kafue
Kabwe
Salima
Chipata
Lilongwe
Z A M B I A
Lusaka
Zumbo
Zambesi
Shirwa
Nampula
Mozambique
land
Kafue
Cabora
Bassa Dam
Tete
Blantyre
Zomba
15
L. Kariba
Zambesi
Livingstone
Harare
Salisbury
Sena
Quelimane
Victoria
Falls
Z I M B A B W E
Mutare
Chinde
Zambesi
Hwange
Gweru
Matabeleland
Beira
Bulawayo
Matopo
Hills
Masvingo
Zimbabwe
Sofala
20
Plumtree
West Nicholson
Sabi
40
50
Serowe
Palapye
Inhambane
C. Bobraomby
A N A
Gaborone
Messina
Limpopo
Antsiranana
Nossi-Bé
Vohimarina
Moshong
Pietersburg
Olifants
Andoany
2876
Tsaratanana
Andapa
T R A N S V A A L
Lydenburg
Inhambane
45
Mahajanga
Maroantsetra
15
Pretoria
Barberton
Maputo
Marovoay
Krugersdorp
Springs
Delagoa Bay
Besalampy
Fenoarivo
Ambatondrazaka
hannesburg
Germiston
SWAZI-
LAND
Maevatanana
L. Alaotra
Vereeniging
Kroonstad
Maintirano
Toamasina
ORANGE
FREE
STATE
Mt. aux Sources
Ladysmith
St. Lucia Bay
Belo-Tsiribihina
2643
Antananarivo
Maseru
Pietermaritzburg
Mahanoro
oenfontein
LESOTHO
Antsirabe
Morondava
20
N G E
Durban
Mananjary
Umtata
I N D I A N
Mofombé
Fianarantsoa
Mangoki
Ihosy
Manakara
Ankazoabo
East London
Toliara
Betroka
Farafangana
Grahamstown
O C E A N
Tropic of Capricorn
Bekily
1956
35
Ambovombé
Faradofay
C. Vohimena
MADAGASCAR
On same scale.

Mozambique Channel

M O Z A M B I Q U E

30
35
45

1 : 60 000 000

West from Greenwich 100 90

COPYRIGHT. GEORGE PHILIP & SON. LTD.

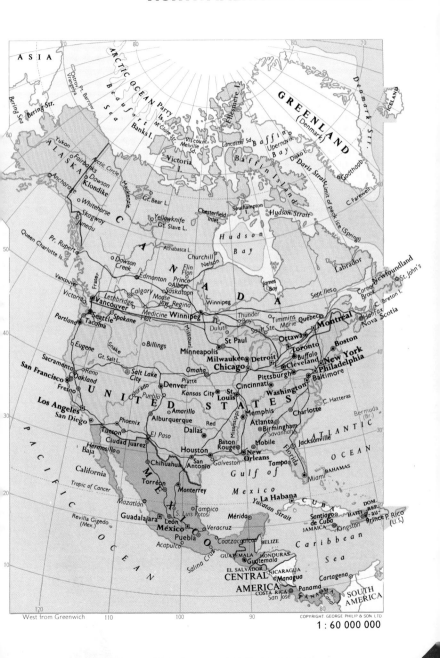

ASIA

ARCTIC OCEAN

Ostrov Vrangelya

Bering Sea

Bering Str.

Pt. Barrow

Beaufort Sea

Parry Is.

M'Clure Str.

Banks I.

Viscount Melville Sd.

Victoria I.

Lancaster Sd.

Ellesmere I.

GREENLAND (Denmark)

Baffin Bay

Upernavik

Disko I.

Davis Strait

C. Farewell

ICELAND

Denmark Str.

limit of pack-ice (Spring)

Baffin Island

ALASKA

Yukon

Fairbanks

Arctic Circle

Anchorage

Dawson

Klondike

Whitehorse

Skagway

Juneau

Pr. Rupert

Queen Charlotte Is.

Mackenzie

Gt. Bear L.

Yellowknife

Gt. Slave L.

Chesterfield Inlet

Southampton

Hudson Strait

C A N A D A

Vancouver I.

Victoria

Fraser

Dawson Creek

Edmonton

Prince Albert

Calgary

Lethbridge

Saskatoon

Regina

Medicine Hat

Athabasca L.

Churchill

Flin Flon

Nelson

Hudson Bay

James Bay

Labrador

Portland

Seattle

Tacoma

Spokane

Winnipeg

Winnipeg L.

Thunder Bay

Duluth

Sault Ste. Marie

Timmins

Sept Iles

Corner Brook

Newfoundland

St. John's

Eugene

Billings

Snake

Gt. Salt L.

Minneapolis

St Paul

Québec

Ottawa

Montréal

Toronto

Boston

C. Breton I.

Nova Scotia

Halifax

Sacramento

San Francisco

Oakland

Reno

Fresno

Salt Lake City

Colorado

Denver

Milwaukee

Chicago

Detroit

Cleveland

Buffalo

New York

Philadelphia

Baltimore

Washington

Pittsburgh

Cincinnati

Omaha

Platte

Kansas City

St. Louis

U N I T E D   S T A T E S

Los Angeles

San Diego

Phoenix

Tucson

Pueblo

Amarillo

Alburquerque

El Paso

Dallas

Red

Memphis

Atlanta

Birmingham

Charlotte

C. Hatteras

Bermuda (Br.)

Ciudad Juarez

Baja

California

Hermosillo

Chihuahua

Torreón

Houston

San Antonio

Galveston

Baton Rouge

New Orleans

Mobile

Mississippi

Jacksonville

Florida

Tampa

Gulf of Mexico

Miami

BAHAMAS

ATLANTIC OCEAN

PACIFIC OCEAN

Tropic of Cancer

Mazatlán

Revilla Gigedo (Mex.)

Guadalajara

León

S. Luis Potosí

Tampico

M E X I C O

Monterrey

Mexico

Mérida

Yucatan Strait

La Habana

CUBA

Santiago de Cuba

JAMAICA

Kingston

HAITI

DOM. REP.

Pt.-au-Prince

Puerto Rico (U.S.)

México

Puebla

Veracruz

Coatzacoalcos

BELIZE

Caribbean Sea

Acapulco

Salina Cruz

GUATEMALA

Guatemala

HONDURAS

EL SALVADOR

NICARAGUA

Managua

CENTRAL AMERICA

COSTA RICA

San José

PANAMA

Panama

Canal

Cartagena

SOUTH AMERICA

1 : 60 000 000

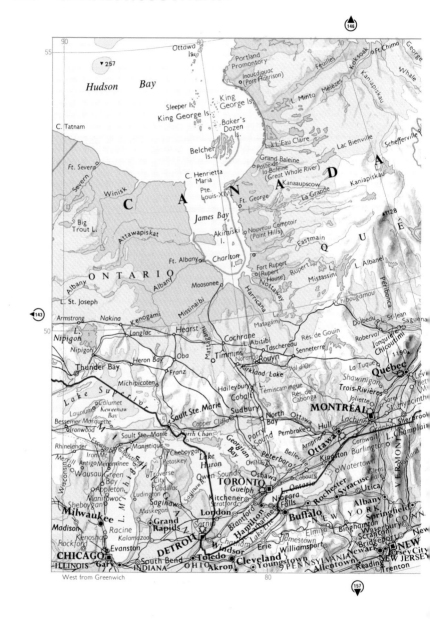

55

90

▼ 257

Hudson   Bay

Ottawa Is.

80

Portland Promontory

Inoucdjouac (Port Harrison)

Feuilles

Koksoak

Ft. Chimo

George

Whale

L. Minto

Mélèze

Kaniapiskau

Sleeper Is.

King George Is.

King George Is.

Baker's Dozen Is.

C. Tatnam

à L'Eau Claire

Lac Bienville

Schefferville

Belcher Is.

Ft. Severn

C. Henrietta Maria

Pte. Louis-XIV

Ft. George

Grand Baleine

Poste-de-la-Baleine (Great Whale River)

Kanaaupscow

La Grande

Kaniapiskau

▲1128

Winisk

Big Trout L.

Severn

Attawapiskat

James Bay

Akimiski I.

Nouveau Comptoir (Paint Hills)

Eastmain

C   A   N   A   D   A

É

U

B

E

Ft. Albany

Charlton I.

Fort Rupert (Rupert House)

Rupert

Nottaway

Mistassini

L. Albanel

Péribonca

O N T A R I O

Albany

Albany

Moosonee

Harricana

Chibougamau

L. St. Joseph

Nakina

Kenogami

Missinaibi

Matagami

Rés. de Gouin

Dolbeau

St-Jean

Saguenay

Armstrong

50

L. Nipigon

Longlac

Hearst

Cochrane

Tascherau

Roberval

Jonquière

Chicoutimi

Nipigon

Heron Bay

Oba

Timmins

L. Abitibi

Senneterre

La Tuque

1190

Thunder Bay

Franz

Kirkland Lake

Noranda

Rouyn

Val d'Or

Shawinigan

Québec

Michipicoten

Haileybury

Témiscamingue

Rés. de Cabonga

Trois-Rivières

Lév

Lake   Superior

Cobalt

Joliette

Sorel

St-Hyacinth

Calumet

Keweenaw Bay

Sault Ste. Marie

Copper Cliff

Sudbury

North Bay

Ottawa

MONTRÉAL

Lachine

Sherbrook

Laurium

Bessemer

Marquette

Sault Ste. Marie

North Chan.

Parry Sound

Pembroke

Hull

Cornwall

Cranb

L. Champlai

Ironwood

Georgian Bay

Arnprior

Ottawa

Kingston

Burlington

VERMONT

Rhinelander

Escanaba

Manistique

Cheboygan

Belle

Watertown

Menominee

Petoskey

Lake Huron

Orillia

Peterboro

Glens Falls

Waterbury

CONN.

Antigo

Iron Mt.

Traverse City

Owen Sound

Oshawa

Cobourg

L. Ontario

Rochester

Syracuse

Utica

Albany

Springfield

Wausau

Green Bay

Cadillac

Muskegon

Georgian

Guelph

TORONTO

Niagara

Binghamton

Elmira

Scranton

Bridgeport

NEW

Sheboygan

Manitowoc

Ludington

Saginaw

Kitchener

Stratford

Falls

Buffalo

N E W   Y O R K

Waterto

Newark

NEW JERSEY

Jersey City

Milwaukee

Grand Rapids

London

Brantford

Hamilton

St. Catharines

Erie

Jamestown

Williamsport

Allentown

Reading

Madison

Racine

Kalamazoo

Sarnia

L. Erie

PENNSYLVANIA

Trenton

Rockford

Kenosha

Evanston

DETROIT

Windsor

Cleveland

Youngstown

Akron

CHICAGO

Gary

South Bend

Toledo

INDIANA

OHIO

ILLINOIS

West from Greenwich

80

1 : 15 000 000

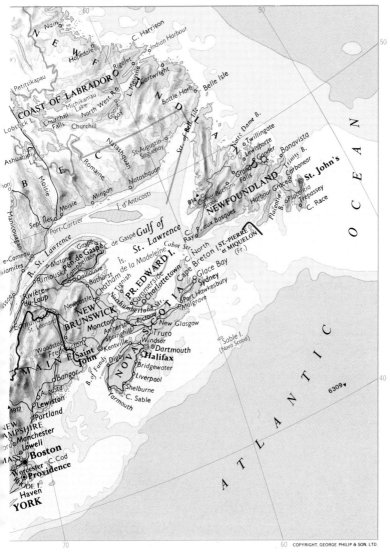

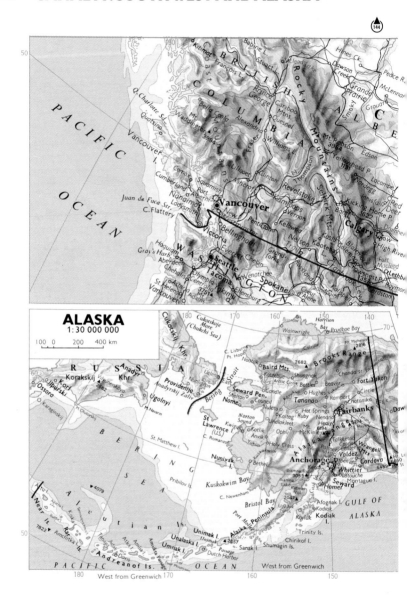

ALASKA
1:30 000 000

100 0   200   400 km

1 : 15 000 000

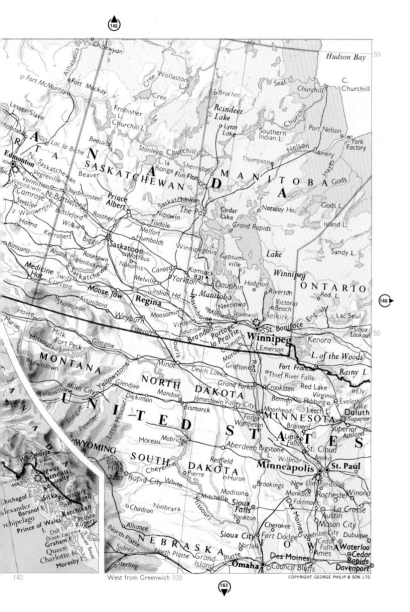

Hudson Bay

55

Chipewyan
Athabasca
Fort McMurray
Fort Mackay
Cree
Wollaston L.
Seal
C. Churchill
Churchill
Lesser Slave
Brochet
Frobisher L.
Reindeer Lake
Churchill L.
Lynn Lake
Southern Indian L.
Port Nelson
York Factory
Beauval
Stanley
Churchill
Thompson
Nelson
Amery
Gods
Edmonton
N. Saskatchewan
Vegreville
Lac la Biche
A
Beaver
Vermilion
Lloydminster
L. la Ronge
Flin Flon
Sherridon
Flon
Norway Ho.
Gods L.
Wetaskiwin
N. Battleford
Prince Albert
Saskatchewan
The Pas
Cedar Lake
Island L.
Camrose
Battleford
Nipawin
Grand Rapids
Stettler
Wilkie
Rosthern
Tisdale
Wainwright
Hanna
Humboldt
Winnipegosis
Gypsum-ville
Sandy L.
Kerrobert
Biggar
Saskatoon
Watrous
Nokomis
Bassano
Rosetown
Diefenbaker
Canora
Kamsack 831
Dauphin
Hodgson
Medicine Hat
Alsask
S. Saskatchewan
Melville
Yorkton
ONTARIO
Swift Current
Moose Jaw
Indian Hd.
L. Manitoba
Riverton
Red. L.
Havre
Shaunavon
Assiniboine
Regina
Assiniboine
Neepawa
Victoria Beach
Lac Seul
Milk
Weyburn
Moosomin
Minnedosa
Stonewall
Selkirk
English
Sioux Lookout
50
Missouri
Fort Peck
Glasgow
Estevan
Souris
Brandon
Portage la Prairie
St. Boniface
Winnipeg
Kenora
MONTANA
Lewistown
Yellowstone
Minot
Devils Lake
Moose
Carman
Emerson
L. of the Woods
Miles City
Glendive
NORTH DAKOTA
Grafton
Fort Frances
Thief River Falls
Rainy L.
Yellowstone
Dickinson
Mandan
Jamestown
Valley City
Grand Forks
Crookston
Red Lake
Bemidji
Virginia
Hibbing
Eveleth
Ely
Powder
Little Missouri
Bismarck
Moorhead
Fargo
MINNESOTA
Leech L.
Duluth
Superior
WYOMING
Moreau
Mobridge
Wahpeton
Brainerd
St. Cloud
Superior
Ashland
SOUTH DAKOTA
Aberdeen
Bigstone
Willmar
Anoka
Black Hills
Redfield
Cheyenne
White
Pierre
Huron
Brookings
New Ulm
Mankato
Faribault
Rochester
Winona
Rapid City
Madison
Fairmont
La Crosse
Niobrara
Mitchell
Sioux Falls
Austin
Chadron
Missouri
Yankton
Cherokee
Fort Dodge
Mason City
Dubuque
Alliance
Sioux City
Webster City
Cedar Falls
Waterloo
North Platte
NEBRASKA
Norfolk
Ames
Cedar Rapids
Sidney
North Platte
Grand Island
Platte
Des Moines
Davenport
Sterling
Omaha
Council Bluffs

Whitehorse
Skagway
Juneau
Admiralty
Chichagof I.
Sitka
Petersburg
Wrangell
Alexander
Baranof I.
Ketchikan
Archipelago
Prince of Wales
Prince Rupert
Dall I.
Dixon Entrance
Graham
Queen Charlotte Is.
Moresby
Hecate Strait

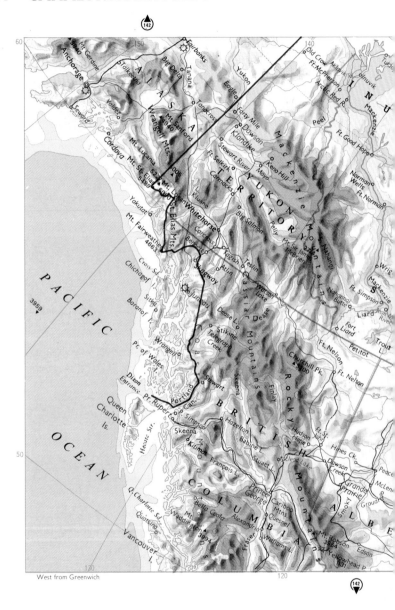

1 : 15 000 000

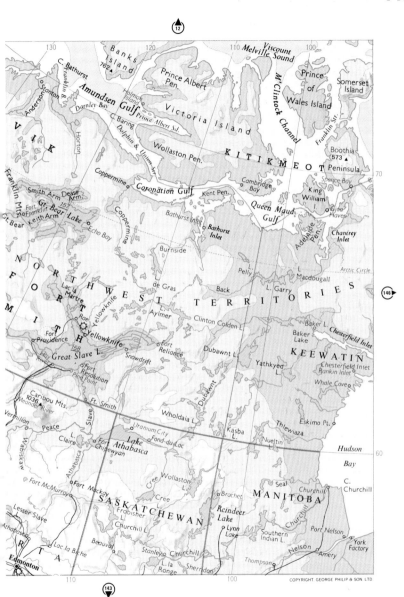

Banks Island
C. Bathurst
130
762▲
Prince Albert Pen.
120
110
Melville
Viscount Sound
100
Prince
C. Franklin B.
Stanton
Amundsen Gulf
Holmh Island
of
Wales Island
Somerset Island
Anderson
Darnley Bay
Prince Albert Sd.
M'Clintock Channel
V I K
Baring
Victoria Island
Horton
Dolphin & Union Str.
Wollaston Pen.
Franklin Strt.
Boothia
573 ▲
Peninsula
Franklin Mts
Coppermine
Coronation Gulf
Kent Pen.
K I T I K M E O T
70
Smith Arm Dease
Cambridge Bay
Spence Bay
157 Arm.
Fort Franklin
Gt. Bear Lake
Echo Bay
Coppermine
Queen Maud
Gulf
King William
Gjoa Haven
Gt. Bear
Keith Arm
Bathurst Inlet
Bathurst Inlet
Adelaide Pen.
Chantrey Inlet
N
Burnside
Arctic Circle
O
Pelly
L. Macdougall
146
R
L. de Gras
Back
L. Garry
T H W E S T
T E R R I T O R I E S
F
Lac la Martre
Yellowknife
L. Aylmer
Clinton Colden L.
Baker L. Chesterfield Inlet
M
Rae
Yellowknife
Baker Lake
I
Fort Providence
158
Fort Reliance
Dubawnt L.
K E E W A T I N
T
Great Slave L.
Snowdrift
Yathkyed L.
Chesterfield Inlet
Rankin Inlet
H
Hay River
Fort Resolution
Pine Point
Whale Cove
Caribou Mts.
1036
Ft. Smith
Dubawnt
Eskimo Pt.
Meander River
Slave
Wholdaia L.
Thlewiaza
Peace
Uranium City
Kasba L.
Vermilion
L. Claire
Fort Chipewyan
Fond-du-Lac
Nueltin L.
Hudson
60
Lake Athabasca
Bay
Mackenzie
Athabasca
Fort McMurray
Fort Mackay
Cree
Wollaston L.
Seal
Churchill
C. Churchill
Cree
la Broche
M A N I T O B A
Lesser Slave
S A S K A T C H E W A N
Reindeer Lake
Port Nelson
Athabasca
Frobisher L.
Lynn Lake
Southern Indian L.
Nelson
York Factory
R T A
Lac la Biche
Beauval
Churchill L.
Stanley Churchill
Thompson
Amery
Edmonton
110
L. la Ronge
Sherridon
100
COPYRIGHT GEORGE PHILIP & SON LTD

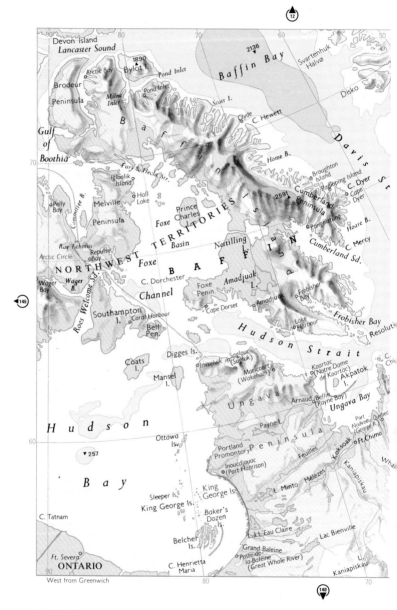

Devon Island
Lancaster Sound
1890
Arctic Bay
Bylot I.
Pond Inlet
Brodeur
Peninsula
Milne
Inlet
Pond Inlet
Scott I.
2136
Baffin Bay
Svartenhuk
Halvø
Disko
Gulf
of
Boothia
B a f f i n
Clyde
C. Hewett
Home B.
D a v i s   S t r.
Fury & Hecla Str.
Igloolik
Island
Hall
Lake
Pelly
Bay
Committee B.
Melville
Peninsula
Prince
Charles
I.
Broughton
Island
Pogloping Island
C. Dyer
Cape
Dyer
Cumberland
Peninsula
2591
Pangnirtung
Houre B.
C. Mercy
Cumberland Sd.
Rae Isthmus
Arctic Circle
Repulse
Bay
N O R T H W E S T   T E R R I T O R I E S
Foxe
Basin
Nettilling
L.
I s l a n d
Foxe
C. Dorchester
B A F F I N
Wager
Bay
Wager
B.
Channel
Foxe
Penin.
Amadjuak
L.
Frobisher
Bay
Rocs Welcome Sd.
Southampton
I.
Coral Harbour
Cape Dorset
Amadjuak
Lake
Harbour
Ft.
Frobisher Bay
Resoluti
Bell
Pen.
Digges Is.
H u d s o n   S t r a i t
Coats
I.
Mansel
I.
Invujivik
Sagluac
(Sugluk)
Maricourt
(Wakeham)
Koartac
Notre Dame
de Koartac)
Akpatok
I.
C. Chi
H u d s o n
Ungava
Arnaud
Bellin
(Payne Bay)
Ungava Bay
Port.
Nouveau Québec
(George R.)
Ft. Chimo
257
Ottawa
Is.
Payne L.
P e n i n s u l a
Portland
Promontory
Feuilles
Koksoak
Wha
B a y
Inoucdjouac
(Port Harrison)
Sleeper Is.
King
George Is.
L. Minto
Mélèzes
Kaniapiskau
King George Is.
C. Tatnam
Baker's
Dozen
Is.
L. à l'Eau Claire
Lac Bienville
Belcher
Is.
Grand Baleine
Poste-de-
la-Baleine
(Great Whale River)
L.
Kaniapiskau
Ft. Severn
ONTARIO
C. Henrietta
Maria

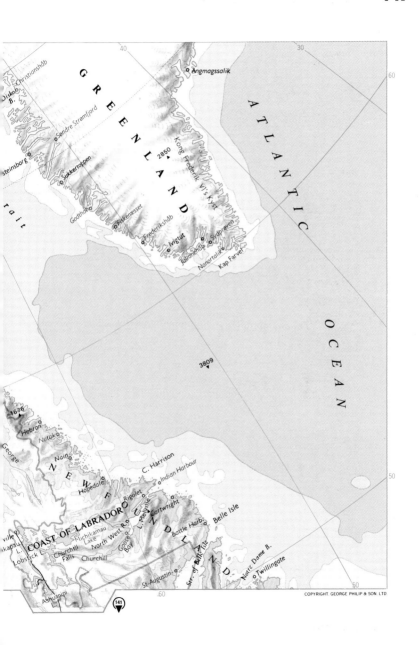

G R E E N L A N D

Christianshåb
Disko B.
Søndre Strømfjord
steinsborg
Sukkertoppen
2850 ▲
Gotthåb
Fiskenæsset
Frederikshåb
Ivigtut
Julianehåb
Sydprøven
Nanortalik
Kap Farvel

Angmagssalik

Kong Frederik VI's Kyst

A T L A N T I C

O C E A N

3809 ▼

1676
Hebron
Nutak
George
Nain
N E W
Hopedale
C. Harrison
Indian Harbour
Rigolet
F
COAST OF LABRADOR
L. Melville
Cartwright
U
Bottle Harb.
Belle Isle
Michikamau Lake
North West R.
N
Goose Bay
ville
L.
Lobstick L.
Churchill Falls
Churchill
D
L.
Str. of Belle Isle
Notre Dame B.
Twillingate
Ashuanipi
St-Augustin
141

COPYRIGHT GEORGE PHILIP & SON. LTD.

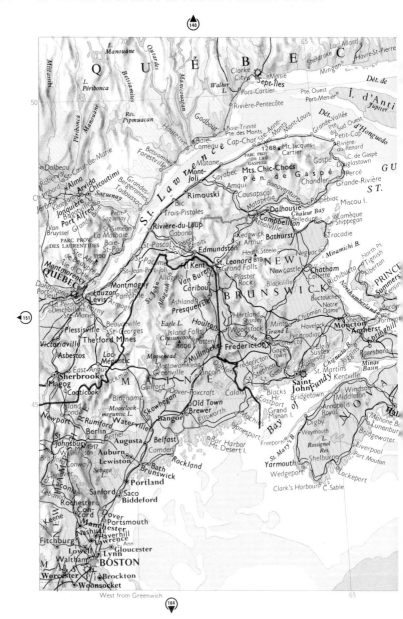

1 : 7 000 000

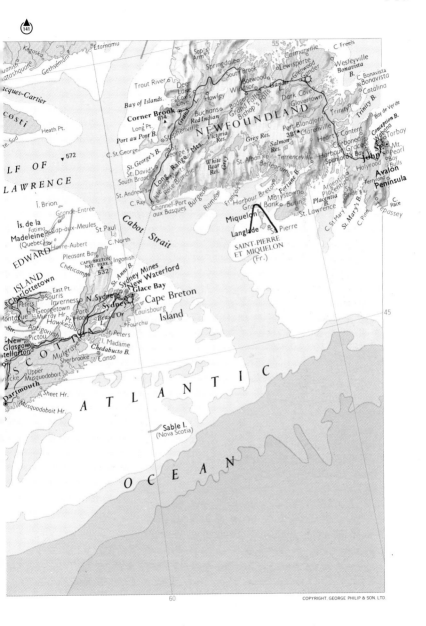

Etamamu

Kogaska
atashquane
Gethsemani
uanish

acques-Cartier

osti

Heath Pt.
te. Sud

Î. Brion

GULF OF

LAWRENCE

572

Îs. de la
Madeleine
(Quebec)
Cap-aux-Meules
Grande-Entrée
Fatima
Havre-Aubert

St. Paul

C. North

EDWARD

Pleasant Bay

ISLAND
Charlottetown
St. Peters
East Pt.
Souris
Inverness
Georgetown
Murray Hr.
Montague
Antigonish
Pictou
New
Glasgow
tellarton
licke
Upper
Musquodoboit
Dartmouth
Musquodoboit Hr.

Chéticamp

CAPE BRETON
NAT. PARK
532

Ingonish

St. Ann's B.

Sydney Mines
New Waterford
N. Sydney
Glace Bay
Sydney
Cape Breton
Bras d'Or
Port Hood
Louisbourg
Island
Fourchu

St. Peters
Î. Madame
Chedabucto B.
Canso

Mulgrave
Sherbrooke

SCOTIA

Sheet Hr.

Trout River
Bay of Islands
Corner Brook
814
Long Pt.
Port au Port B.

Deer
Lake
Cox's
Cove
Howley

Sop's
Arm
Springdale
South Brook
Botwood
Windsor
Grand Falls
Bishop's Falls
Buchans
Red Indian

Carmanville

Gander

Glenwood
Gander
Glovertown

Lewisporte

Wesleyville
Bonavista
B.
C. Bonavista
Bonavista
Catalina

C. Freels

Stephenville
St. George's B.
C. St. George

George's
Long
Range
Mts.
Victoria
Res.

NEWFOUNDLAND

Dark Cove
Port Blandford
Clarenville
381
Grey Res.

Trinity
Trinity B.
Heart's Content
Carbonear
Harbour Grace
Spaniard's Bay

Bay de Verde
Conception B.
Wabana

Torbay

St. Andrews
C. Ray.
South Branch
White
Bear
Res.
Victoria
Res.
Salmon
Res.
St. Alban's
Terrenceville
Belleoram
Harbour Breton

John's
Mt.
Pearl
Bay
Bulls
Ferryland
C.
Race
T'passey

Channel-Port
aux Basques
Burgeo
Ramea

Miquelon
Langlade
SAINT-PIERRE
ET MIQUELON
(Fr.)

Harbour Breton
Grand Bank
Fortune B.
Butin
St. Lawrence
Marystown
St. Pierre

Avalon
Peninsula
Argentia
Placentia
B.
Placentia
St.
Bride's
C. St. Mary's
St. Mary's B.
C. Pine

45

ATLANTIC

Sable I.
(Nova Scotia)

OCEAN

55

Cabot Strait

Rose Blanche

La Poile B.

60

COPYRIGHT. GEORGE PHILIP & SON. LTD.

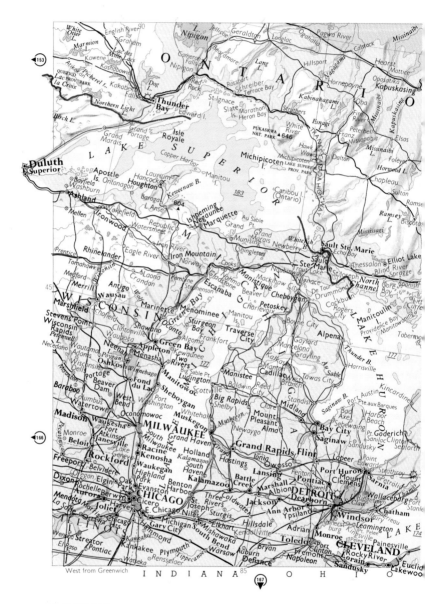

West from Greenwich

1 : 7 000 000

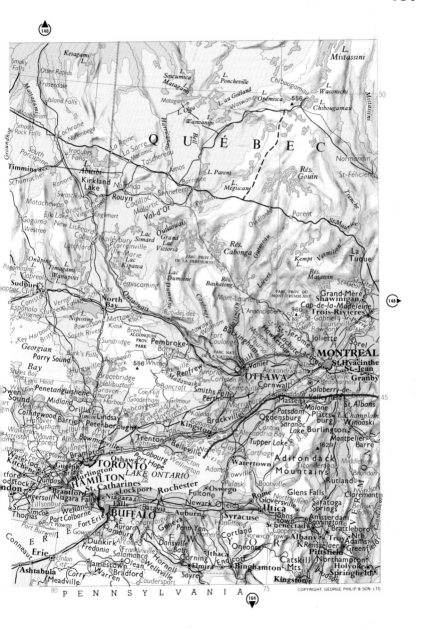

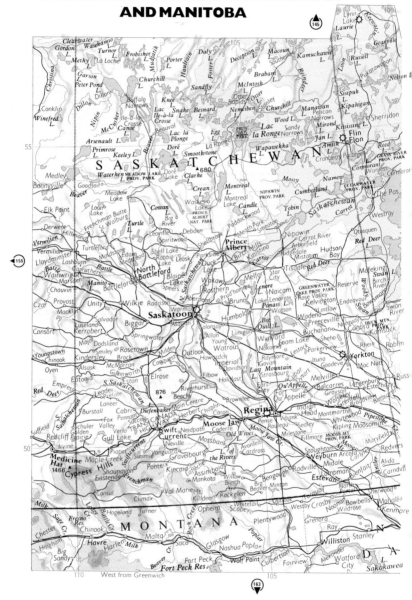

1 : 7 000 000

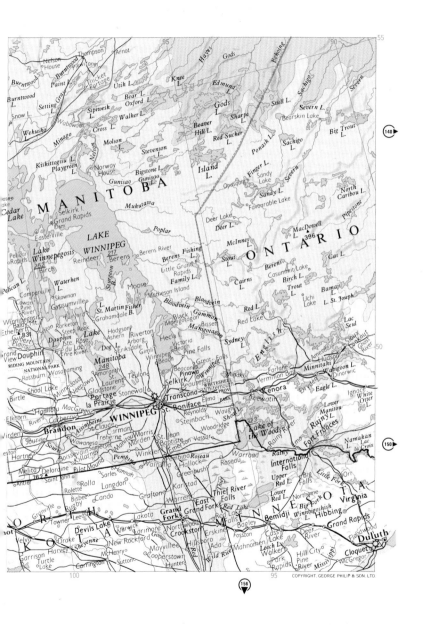

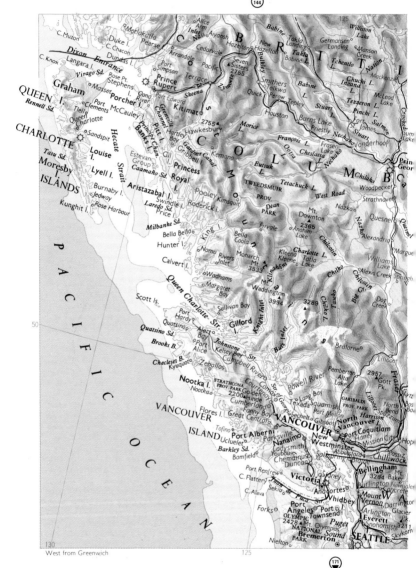

West from Greenwich

1 : 7 000 000

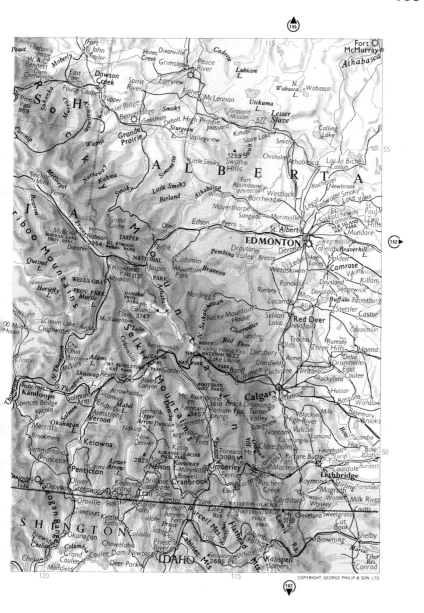

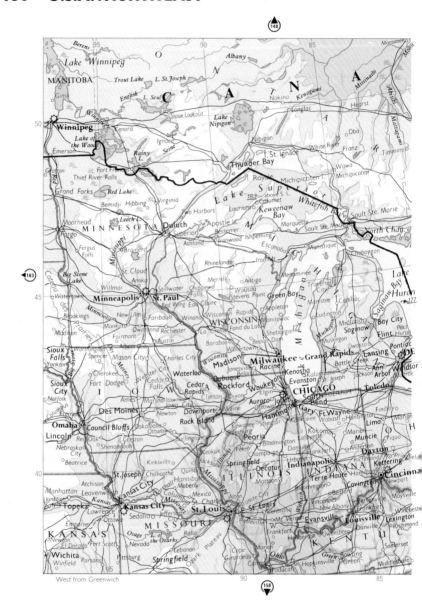

1 : 12 000 000

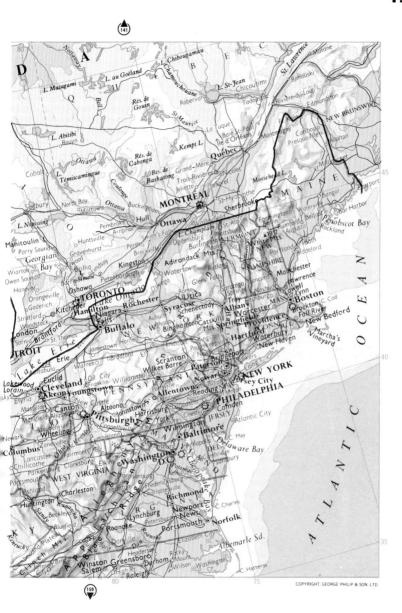

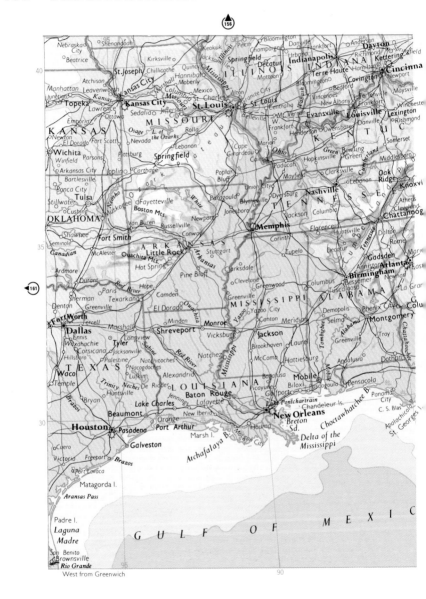

156
161

West from Greenwich

1 : 12 000 000

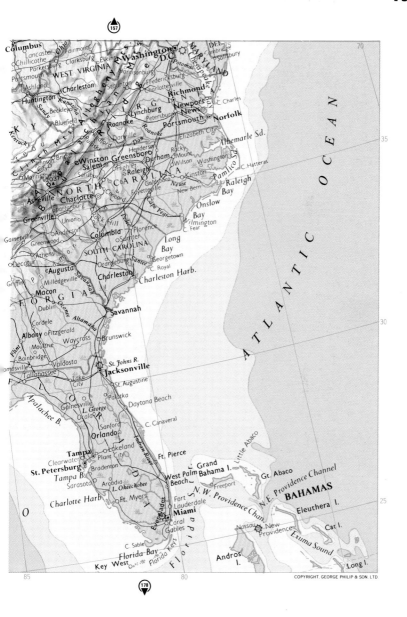

157

Columbus Lancaster Ohio Fairmont
Chillicothe Parkersburg Clarksburg Elkins MARYLAND
Portsmouth WEST VIRGINIA Washington D.C. Cambridge Salisbury
Ashland Charleston Harrisonburg Fredericksburg Potomac DEL.
Huntington Kanawha Staunton Charlottesville Richmond
Beckley Roanoke Lynchburg Petersburg Newport VIRGINIA C. Charles
Bluefield Danville Roanoke Portsmouth News Norfolk
Kentucky Bristol Dan Elizabeth City Albemarle Sd.
Johnson Henderson Rocky Mount Washington C. Hatteras
City Salem Winston Greensboro Durham Wilson Pamlico Sd.
Morristown Asheville High Pt. Raleigh Goldsboro Neuse Raleigh
NORTH CAROLINA Kinston Bay
Charlotte Concord Fayetteville New Bern
Greenville Spartanburg Cape Fear Onslow
Gainesville Union Rock Hill Pee Dee Wilmington Bay
Greenwood Anderson Columbia Florence C. Fear
Athens SOUTH CAROLINA Sumter Long
Decatur Orangeburg Santee Georgetown Bay
Augusta Milledgeville Charleston C. Royal
GEORGIA Charleston Harb.
Macon
Dublin Oconee Savannah
Cordele Altamaha
Albany Fitzgerald Brunswick
Moultrie Waycross
Bainbridge Flint
Thomasville Valdosta Lake St. Johns R.
Tallahassee City Jacksonville
Gainesville St. Augustine
Apalachee B. Palatka Daytona Beach
L. George Ocala
Sanford C. Canaveral
Orlando
Tampa Lakeland
Clearwater Plant City Ft. Pierce
St. Petersburg Bradenton West Palm Grand
Tampa Bay Sarasota Beach Bahama I. Little Abaco
Arcadia FLORIDA Fort Gt. Abaco
Charlotte Harb. L. Okeechobee Lauderdale Freeport N.E. Providence Channel
Ft. Myers N.W. Providence Chan. BAHAMAS
Everglades Miami Eleuthera I.
Coral Nassau New
C. Sable Gables Providence Exuma Sound Cat I.
Florida Bay Andros
Key West Florida Keys I. Long I.

ATLANTIC OCEAN

COPYRIGHT. GEORGE PHILIP & SON. LTD.

178

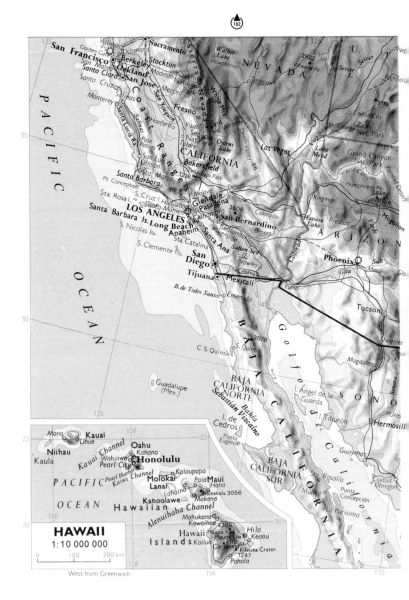

HAWAII
1:10 000 000
0   100   200 km

West from Greenwich

1 : 12 000 000

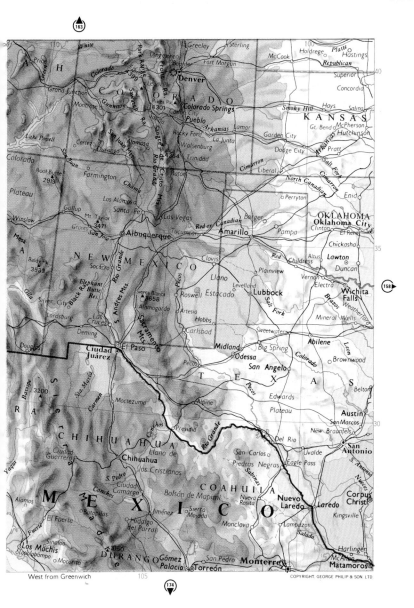

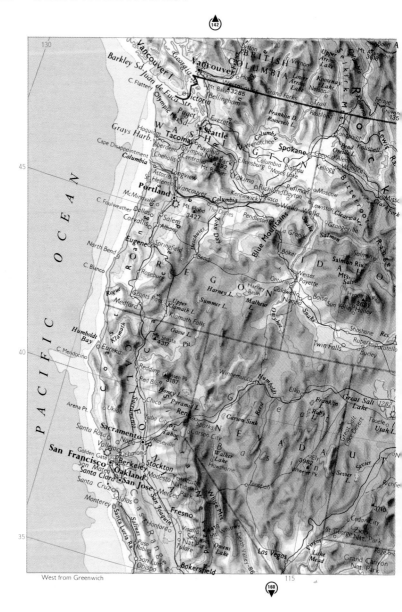

West from Greenwich

1 : 12 000 000

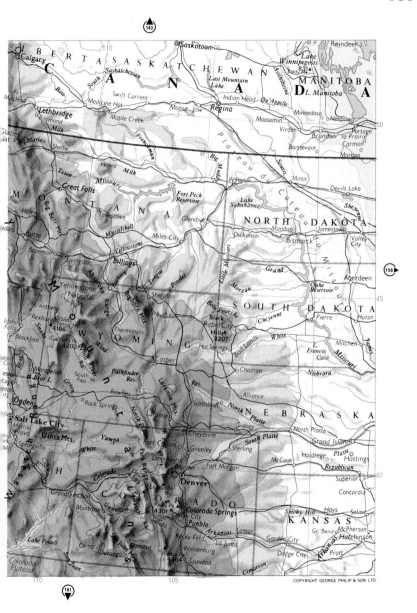

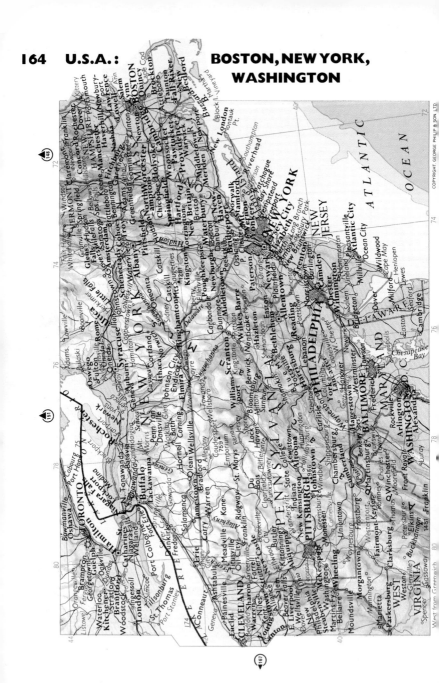

1 : 6 000 000

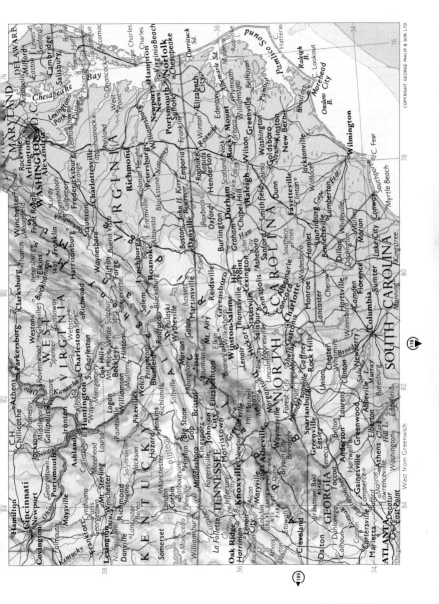

1 : 6 000 000

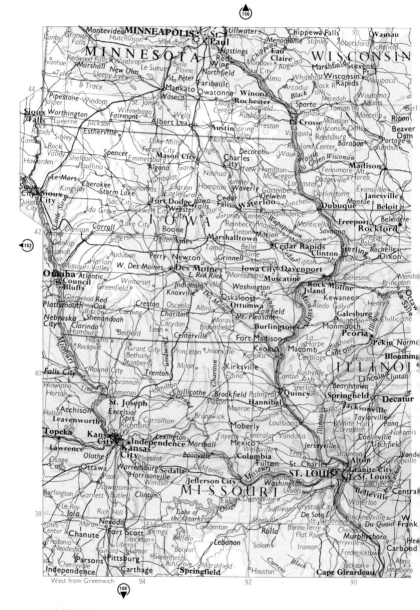

1 : 6 000 000

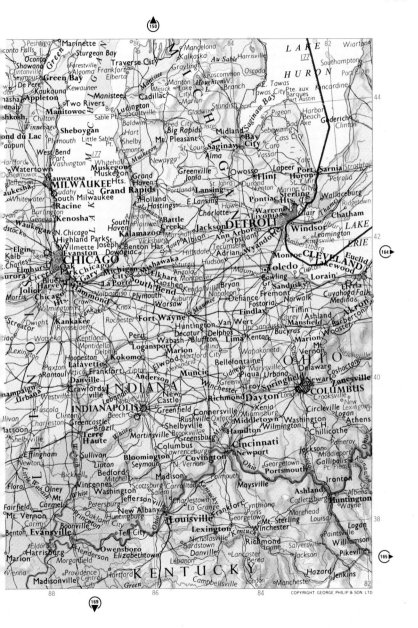

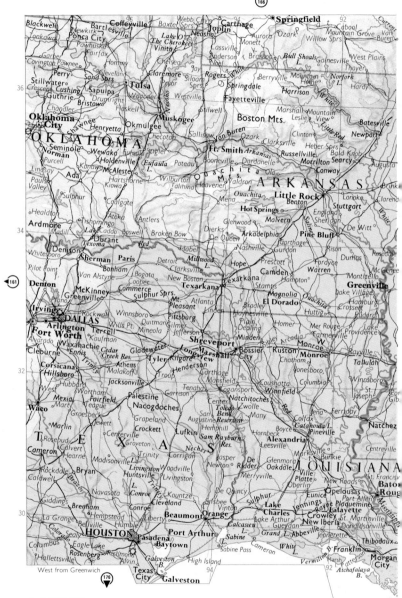

1 : 6 000 000

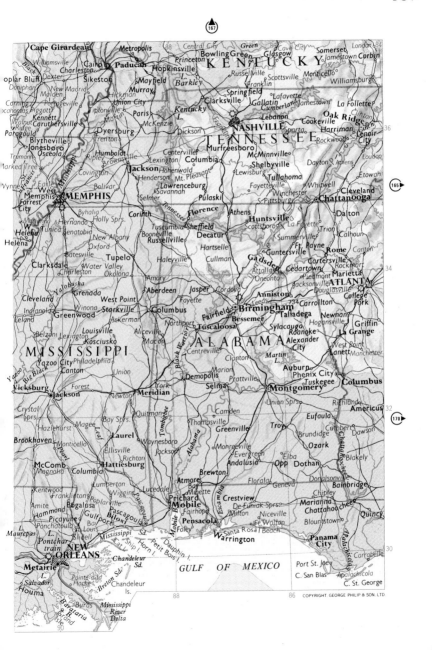

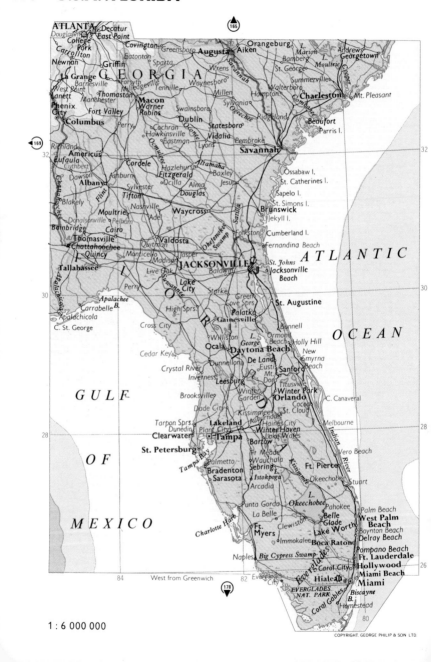

1 : 6 000 000

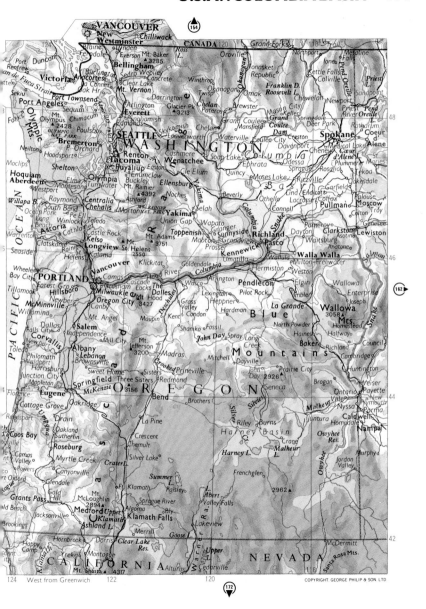

COPYRIGHT GEORGE PHILIP & SON. LTD.

1 : 6 000 000

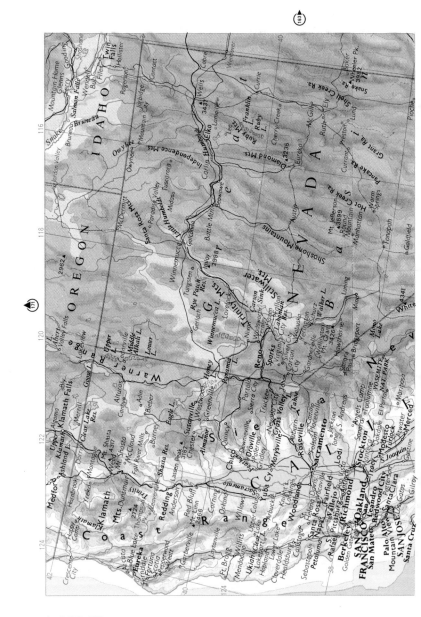

1 : 6 000 000

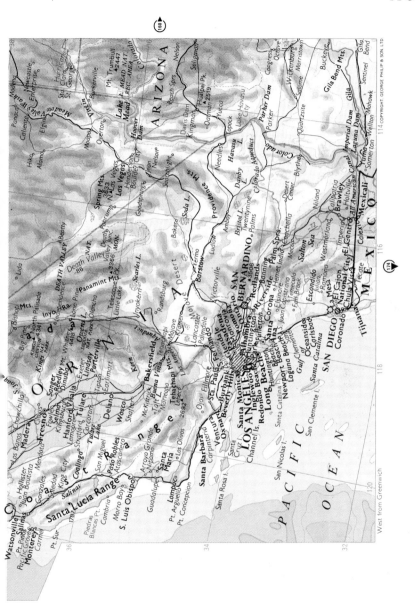

West from Greenwich

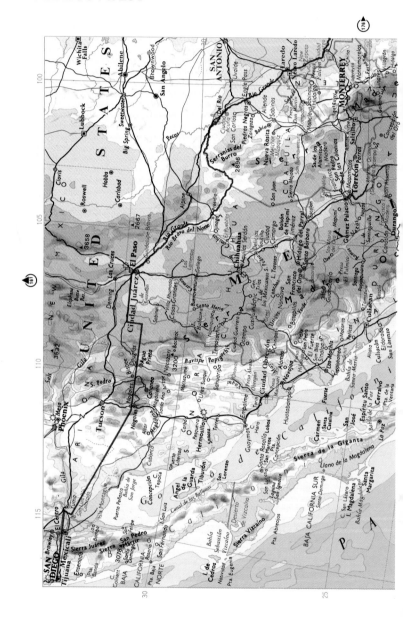

1 : 12 000 000

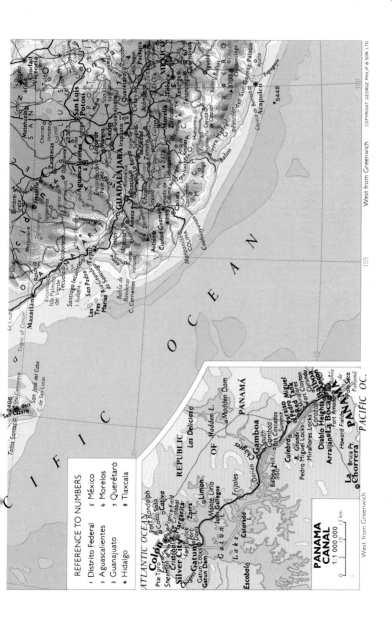

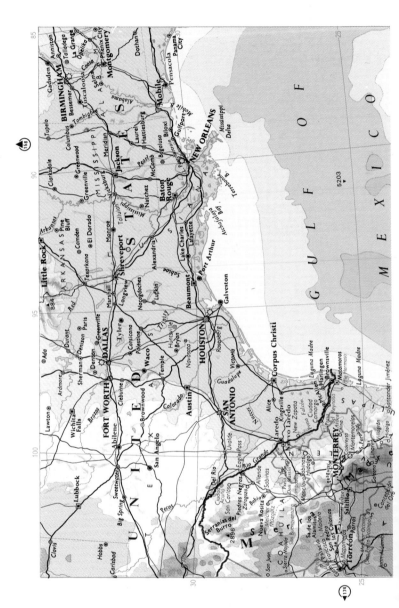

1 : 12 000 000

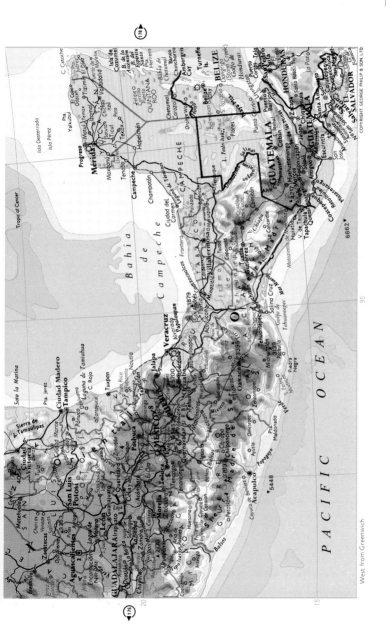

West from Greenwich

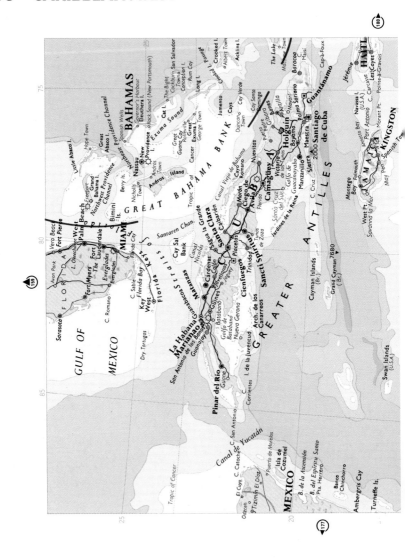

1 : 12 000 000

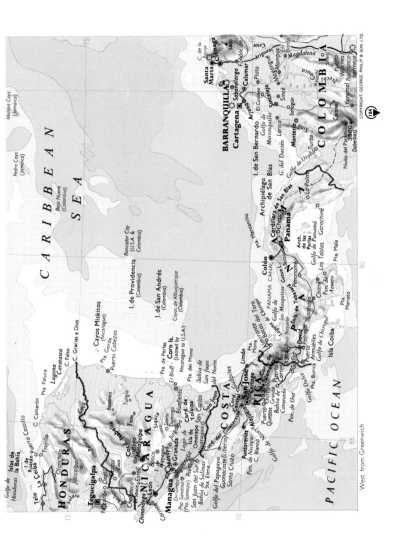

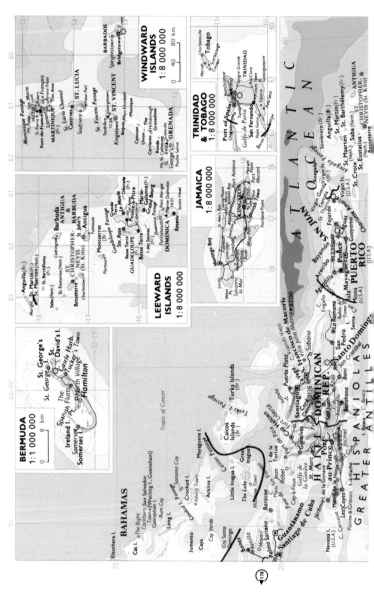

WINDWARD
ISLANDS
1:8 000 000

0   40   80 km

BARBADOS
Speightstown
Bridgetown

Martinique Passage
Mt. Pelée
St. Pierre
Fort-de-France
MARTINIQUE
(Fr.)
Castries
ST. LUCIA
Soufrière
St. Lucia Channel
St. Vincent Passage
ST. VINCENT
Kingstown
Georgetown
Bequia
Port Elizabeth
The Grenadines
Carriacou
Union I.
Mt. St. Catherine
1040 Grenville
St.
George's
GRENADA
Pointe Saline

TRINIDAD
& TOBAGO
1:8 000 000

Tobago
Scarborough
Charlotteville
Moruga
TRINIDAD
Port of Spain
San Fernando
Pointe Fortin
Galeota Point
Golfo de Paria
Guayaguayare
Bocas del Dragon

A T L A N T I C

O C E A N

LEEWARD
ISLANDS
1:8 000 000

Anguilla (Br.)
St. Martin (Fr.)
St. Maarten (Neth.)
St. Barthélemy (Fr.)
Saba (Neth.)
St. Eustatius (Neth.)
ST.
CHRISTOPHER-
NEVIS (St. Kitts)
Basseterre
Charlestown (St. Kitts)
Barbuda
ANTIGUA
&
BARBUDA
St. John's
Antigua
Falmouth
Montserrat
(Br.)
Plymouth
Guadeloupe Passage
Basse Terre
GUADELOUPE
(Fr.)
Basse Terre
Îles des Saintes
Marie-
Galante (Fr.)
Grande-
Terre
Pointe-à-Pitre
Le Moule
Ste. Rose
Portsmouth
DOMINICA
Roseau
Dominica Passage
Pointe Margot
Pte. Dishalion
Morne Diablotin
1447
Scotts Head

JAMAICA
1:8 000 000

KINGSTON
Montego Bay
Spanish Town
Portland Point
Morant
Port Antonio
Morant Point

PUERTO
RICO
(U.S.A.)
San Juan
Bayamón
Arecibo
1338
Ponce
Mayagüez
Fajardo
Virgin Is.

Anguilla (Br.)
Sombrero (Br.)
St. Martin (Fr.)
St. Barthélemy (Fr.)
ANTIGUA
ST.
CHRISTOPHER- &
NEVIS (St. Kitts)
Basseterre

BERMUDA
1:1 000 000

0   8 km

St. George's I.
St. George's
St.
David's I.
The
Spanish Flatts
Ireland I.
Castle Harb.
North Village
Hamilton
Flatts Village
Somerset I.

BAHAMAS

Eleuthera I.
Cat I.
The Bight
Cockburn Town
San Salvador
(Watling I., Guanahani)
Conception I.
Rum Cay
Long I.
Crooked I.
Albert Town
Acklins I.
Mayaguana I.
Little Inagua I.
The Lake
Great
Inagua I.
Matthew Town
Crooked I. Passage
Samana Cay
Jumento
Cays
Cay Santo
Cay Verde
Ragged I.

Tropic of Cancer

Turks Islands
Caicos
Islands
(Br.)
Turks I. Passage
Caicos Passage

HISPANIOLA

HAITI
Port-de-Paix
Cap Haïtien
Môle St.-Nicolas
I. de la Tortue
St. Marc
Gonaïves
Gonâve
Golfe de
la Gonâve
Port-
au-Prince
Jérémie
Les Cayes
I.-à-Vache
Pointe-à-Gravois
Fort Liberté
3175
Jacmel

DOMINICAN
REP.
Santiago
Monte Cristi
2030
La Vega
San
Cristóbal
Santo Domingo
San Pedro
de Macoris
La Romana
Bahía de
Yuma
Saona
Cabo Engaño
3200
Pico Duarte
Vallejuelo
Barahona
Villa Julia Molina
Cabo Francisco de Macoris
Cabo Isabela
Puerto Plata
Cabo Cabrón
Sabana

San
Juan

GREATER   ANTILLES

Santiago de Cuba
Guantánamo
C. Maisí
Navassa I.
(U.S.A.)
Baracoa

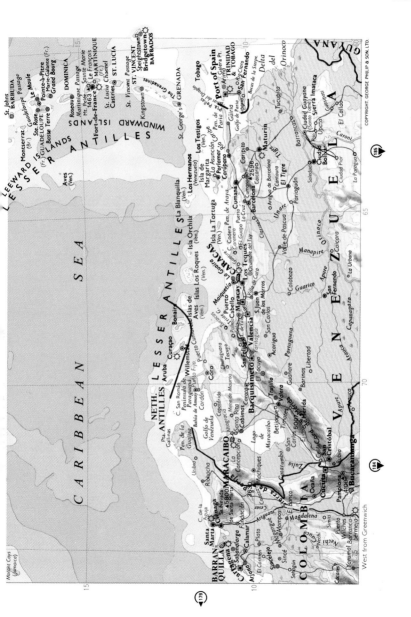

SOUTH AMERICA: PHYSICAL

Curaçao (Neth.)

Trinidad

G. of Darien

▲ 5800

10

Orinoco

Llanos

Cord. de Mérida

Magdalena

Kaieteur Falls

Demerara

Courantyne

Surinam

Roraima

▲ 2810

Sa. Pacaraima

G u i a n a

Orinoco

Corentyne

Esseguibo

Casiquiare

Sa. de Tumucumaque

Amazon

Marajó I.

Pará

Equator

Cotopaxi 5897

▲ Chimborazo 6267

Putumayo

Japurá

Negro

Amazon

Tocantins

Pta. Parinas

Marañón

S e l v a s

C. de São Roque

C. Branco

Ucayali

Purus

Madeira

Tapajós

Xingu

Araguaia

Tocantins

Parnaíba

A n d e s

▲ 6768

S. Antônio Falls

Aripuana

Guaporé

Plateau of Mato Grosso

São Francisco

B r a z i l i a n   H i g h l a n d s

L. Titicaca

Illampu Ancohuma ▲ 6550

Bolivian Plateau

Paraguay

Pilcomayo

Sa. da Mantiqueira

▲ 2890

C. Frio

20

Tropic of Capricorn

8050 ▼

Atacama Desert

P A C I F I C   O C E A N

G r a n   C h a c o

Paraguay

Paraná

Paraná

Iguaçu Falls

Sa. do Mar

Ojos del Salado ▲ 6863

Aconcagua ▲ 6960

P a m p a s

Entre Rios

Uruguay

Lagoa dos Patos

30

Juan Fernández

Colorado

Río de la Plata

Pta. Mogotes

A T L A N T I C

Negro

O C E A N

40

Chiloé

Patagonia

Chubut

G. of San Matías

Valdés Pen.

Chonos Arch.

G. of San Jorge

▲ 4058

A n d e s

6212 ▼

Falkland Is.

50

West from Greenwich

80

Magellan's Str.

Tierra del Fuego

Staten I.

C. Froward

70

C. Horn

60

50

40

COPYRIGHT. GEORGE PHILIP & SON. LTD.

1 : 50 000 000

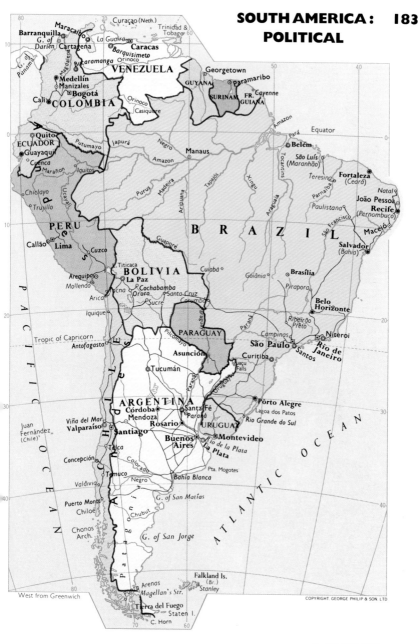

West from Greenwich

1 : 50 000 000

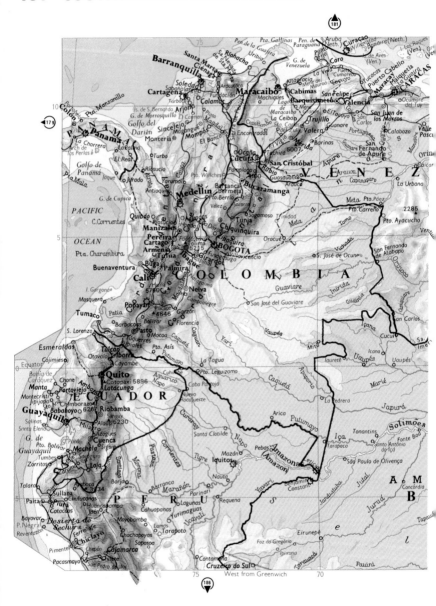

1 : 16 000 000

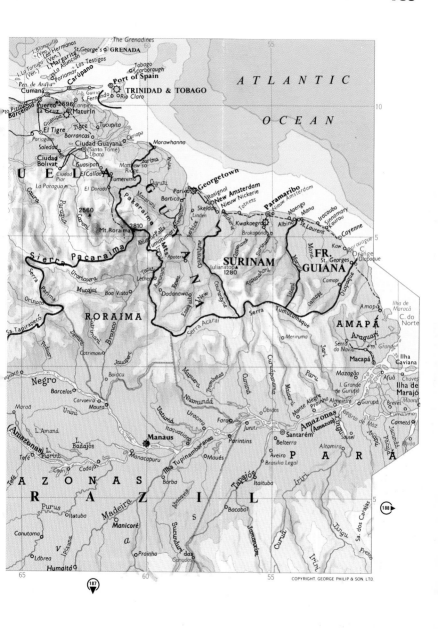

The Grenadines
I. Blanquilla (Ven.)
Los Hermanos (Ven.)
St.George's ⊙ GRENADA
I. La Tortuga (Ven.) I. Margarita
I.Margarita (Ven.) La Asunción
Porlamar Los Testigos
Pen. de Araya Carúpano
Cumaná
Tobago
Scarborough
Port of Spain
TRINIDAD & TOBAGO
S. Fernando
Rio Claro
Guiria
Pto. Piritu
Barcelona
Puerto 2696 Caripito
La Cruz Guanta
Maturín
El Tigre
Pariaguán
Barrancas
Soledad
Ciudad Guayana
(Santo Tomé)
Upata
Ciudad Bolívar
Ciudad Piar
Guasipati
Matthew s
Ridge
El Callao
La Paragua
Tumeremo
El Dorado
Morawhanna
Curiapo

ATLANTIC
OCEAN

10

Georgetown
Parika
New Amsterdam
Nieuw Amsterdam
Nieuw Nickerie
Totness
Paramaribo
Nieuw Amsterdam
Moengo
Mana
Iracoubo
Sinnamary
Kourou
Cayenne

Bartica
Rosignol
Skeldon
Linden
Kwakoegron
Albina
St.Laurent
Brokopondo

Kaw
Roraima
Apoera
Kaw
Orange
Oiapoque

2560
2810
Mt.Roraima
Kaieteur Falls
Tumutumari
Apoteri
SURINAM
Julianatop
1280
FR.
GUIANA
St. Georges
Orange
Oiapoque

Sierra Pacaraima
Urariçoera
Boa Vista
Camopi

Sa. Tapirapeco
Mucajaí
Lethem
Dadanawa
New
Courantyne
Tabaçamba
Camopi
Oiapoque

RORAIMA
Ilha de Maracá
C. do Norte

Serra Parima
Orinoco
Demini
Catrimani
Jauari
Serra Acarai
Meriruma
Serra do Navio
AMAPÁ
Araguari
Pto. Grande
Macapá
Ilha Caviana

Negro
Barcelos
Carvoeira
Moura
Maguari
Trombetas
Nhamundá
Cuminá
Curuapanema
Maicuru
Paru
Jari
Mazagão
I. Grande de Gurupá
Afuá
Ilha de Marajó
Breves
Gurupá

Maraã
Unini
L.Amaná
Uatumã
Itaquatiara
Urucará
Óbidos
Monte Alegre
Prainha
Almeirim
Porto de Móz
Anajás
Cametá
Curralinho

AZONAS
Manaus
Badajós
Manacapuru
Maués
Faro
Juruti
Parintins
Santarém
Belterra
Altamira
AMAZONAS
(Amazon)
Tucuruí
PARÁ
Baião

Tefé
Florini
Codajás
Ilha Tupinambaranas
Barba
Aveiro
Brasília Legal
Tapajós
Itaituba
Iriri
Xingu

BRAZIL
Purus
Madeira
Itatuba
Manicoré
Abacaxis
Bacabal
Jamanxim
Curuá
Sa. dos Carajás

Canutama
Lábrea
Humaitá
Prainha
Sucunduri
das
Canudos
Jamanxim
Fresco

65
60
55

187
188

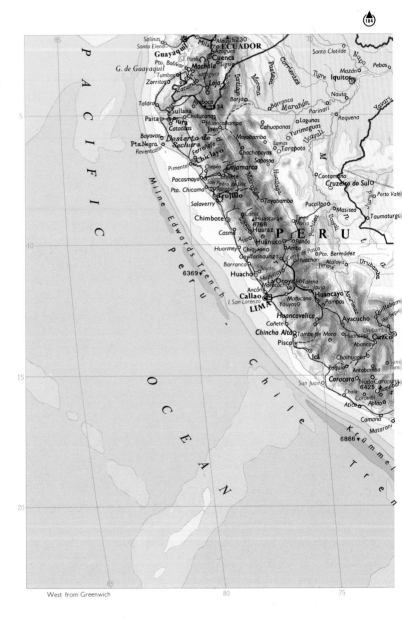

1 : 16 000 000

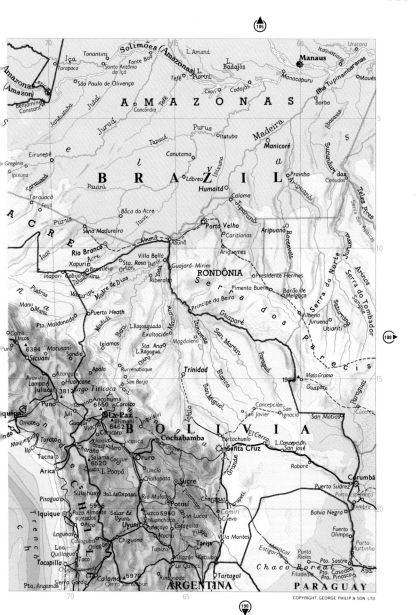

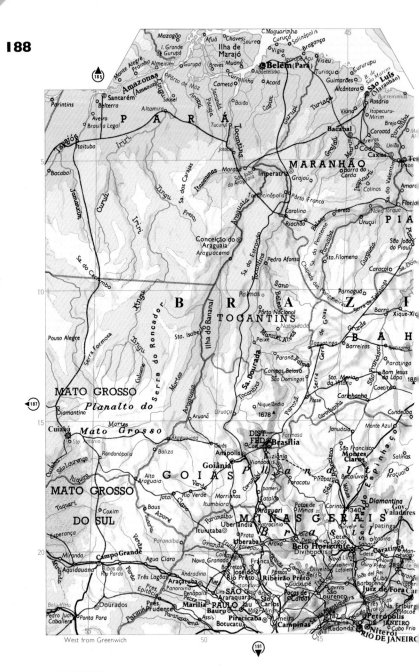

West from Greenwich

1 : 16 000 000

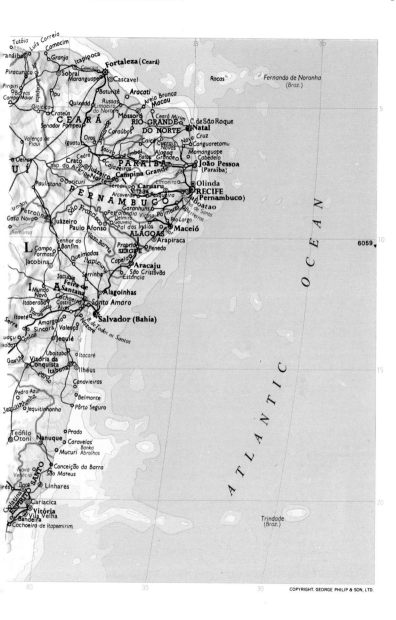

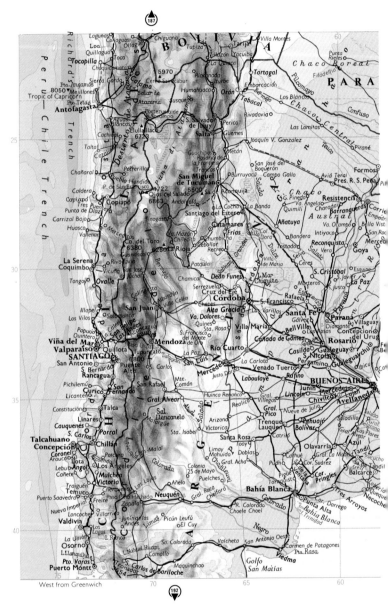

1 : 16 000 000

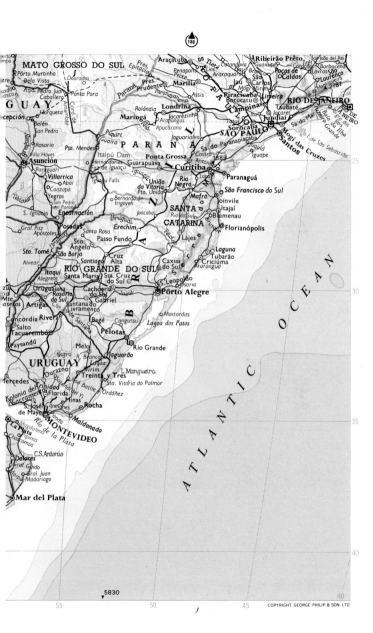

MATO GROSSO DO SUL

Araçatuba
Ribeirão Prêto
RIO DE JANEIRO

Pôrto Murtinho
Bela Vista
Dourados
Pres. Epitacio
Pres. Prudente
Marília
Assis
Araraquara
São Carlos
Jaú
Poços de Caldas
Barbacena
Lavras
Lourenço
2787

GUAY
cepción
Horqueta
Ponta Pora
Paranapanema
Paranaíba
Piracicaba
Limeira
Mogi das Cruzes

Pedro Juan Caballero
Rolândia
Londrina
Campinas
Taubaté
Jacareí
Santos

San Pedro
Maringá
Apucarana
Jacarèzinho
SÃO PAULO
Sorocaba
Jundiaí
São Sebastião

Rosario
Pto. Mendes
Puquiri
Guaíra
Jaguariaíva
PARANÁ
Castro
Iguape

Asunción
Itaipú Dam
Ponta Grossa
Sa. do Paranapiacaba
Iguaçu

Villarrica
Hernandarias
Foz de Iguaçu
Guarapuava
Curitiba
Paranaguá

Abaí
Caazapá
Iguaçu Falls
União da Vitoria
Rio Negro
São Francisco do Sul

Yegros
San Pedro del Paraná
Bernardo de Irigoyen
Pto. União
Mafra
Joinvile
Itajaí

Encarnación
Uruguai
Joaçaba
SANTA CATARINA
Blumenau

Gral. Paz
Apóstoles
Posadas
Santa Rosa
Erechim
Rio do Sul
Florianópolis

Sto. Tomé
São Borja
Sto. Ângelo
Passo Fundo
Lajes

Alvear
Itaqui
Santiago
Cruz Alta
Caxias do Sul
Laguna
Tubarão

Uruguaiana
Santa Maria
Sta. Cruz do Sul
São Leopoldo
Criciúma
Araranguá

Artigas
Quaraí
Rosario do Sul
Cachoeira do Sul
São Gabriel
Pôrto Alegre

Concordia
Rivera
Santana do Livramento
Bagé
Mostardas

Salto
Tacuarembó
Santa do Santa
Cangussú
Lagoa dos Patos

Paysandú
Melo
Rio Branco
Pelotas
Rio Grande

Mercedes
Durazno
Mirim
Jaguarão
L. Mangueira

URUGUAY
Treinta y Tres
Sta. Vitória do Palmar

Colonia del Sacramento
Trinidad
Florida
Minas
Rocha

S. José de Mayo
Canelones
Maldonado

La Plata
MONTEVIDEO

Dolores
C.S.Antonio

Gral. Guido
Gral. Juan Madariaga

Mar del Plata

ATLANTIC OCEAN

25
30
35
40

55
50
45

▼5830

COPYRIGHT GEORGE PHILIP & SON. LTD

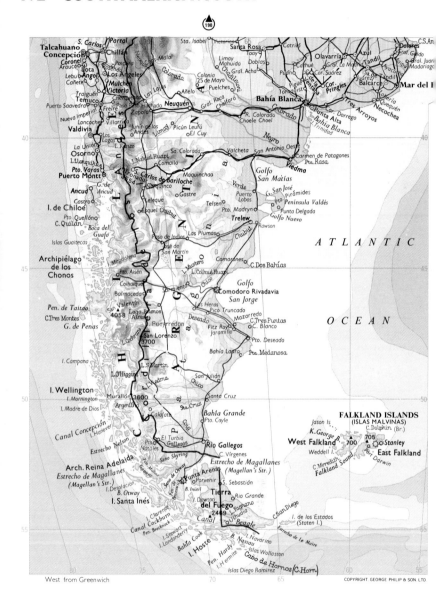

1 : 16 000 000

West from Greenwich

COPYRIGHT. GEORGE PHILIP & SON. LTD.

INDEX

Abbreviations used

Ala. – *Alabama*
Arch. – *Archipelago*
Ark. – *Arkansas*
Austral. – *Australia*
B. – *Baie, Bahia, Bay, Boca, Bucht, Bugt*
B.C. – *British Columbia*
Bangla. – *Bangladesh*
Br. – *British*
C. – *Cabo, Cap, Cape, Coast, Costa*
C. Rica – *Costa Rica*
Calif. – *California*
Cap. Terr. – *Capital Territory*
Cat. – *Cataract*
Cent. – *Central*
Chan. – *Channel*
Colo. – *Colorado*
Conn. – *Connecticut*
Cord. – *Cordillera*
D.C. – *District of Columbia*
Del. – *Delaware*
Dét. – *Détroit*
Dom. Rep. – *Dominican Republic*
Domin. – *Dominica*
E. – *East, Eastern*
Est. – *Estrecho*
Falk. Is. – *Falkland Islands*
Fla. – *Florida*
Fr. Gui. – *French Guiana*
G. – *Golfe, Golfo, Gulf, Guba, Gebel*
Ga. – *Georgia*
Gt. – *Great*
Guat. – *Guatemala*
Hants. – *Hampshire*
Hd. – *Head*
Hond. – *Honduras*
Hts. – *Heights*
I. (s) – *Ile, Ilha, Insel, Isla, Island(s)*
I. of W. – *Isle of Wight*
Ill. – *Illinois*
Ind. – *Indiana*
Ind. Oc. – *Indian Ocean*
J. – *Jabal, Jazira*
K. – *Kap, Kapp*
Kans. – *Kansas*
Ky. – *Kentucky*

L. – *Lac, Lacul, Lago, Lagoa, Lake, Limni, Loch, Lough*
La. – *Louisiana*
Lag. – *Laguna*
Lancs. – *Lancashire*
Man. – *Manitoba*
Mass. – *Massachusetts*
Md. – *Maryland*
Mich. – *Michigan*
Minn. – *Minnesota*
Miss. – *Mississippi*
Mo. – *Missouri*
Mont. – *Montana*
Mt.(s) – *Mont, Monta, Monti, Muntii, Montaña, Mount, Mountain(s)*
N. – *North, Northern*
N.B. – *New Brunswick*
M.C. – *North Carolina*
N. Dak. – *North Dakota*
N.H. – *New Hampshire*
N.J. – *New Jersey*
N. Mex. – *New Mexico*
N.S.W. – *New South Wales*
N.W.T. – *North West Territories*
N.Y. – *New York*
N.Z. – *New Zealand*
Nebr. – *Nebraska*
Neth. – *Netherlands*
Nev. – *Nevada*
Nfld. – *Newfoundland*
Nic. – *Nicaragua*
Okla. – *Oklahoma*
Ont. – *Ontario*
Oreg. – *Oregon*
Os. – *Ostrov*
Oz. – *Ozero*
P. – *Pass, Passo, Pasul, Pulau*
P.E.I. – *Prince Edward Island*
Pa. – *Pennsylvania*
Pac. Oc. – *Pacific Ocean*
Papua N.G. – *Papua New Guinea*
Pen. – *Peninsula*
Pk. – *Peak*
Plat. – *Plateau*

P-ov. – *Poluostrov*
Pt. – *Point*
Pta. – *Ponta, Punta*
Queens. – *Queensland*
R. – *Rio, River, Rivière*
R.I. – *Rhode Island*
Ra.(s) – *Range(s)*
Raj. – *Rajasthan*
Rep. – *Republic*
Res. – *Reserve, Reservoir*
S. – *South, Southern, Sea, Sur*
S.C. – *South Carolina*
S. Africa – *South Africa*
S. Dak. – *South Dakota*
Sa. – *Serra, Sierra*
Salop. – *Shropshire*
Sard. – *Sardinia*
Sask. – *Saskatchewan*
Sd. – *Sound*
Sev. – *Severnaya*
Si. Arabia – *Saudi Arabia*
St. – *Saint*
Sta. – *Santa*
Ste. – *Sainte*
Str. – *Strait, Stretto*
Switz. – *Switzerland*
Tas. – *Tasmania*
Tenn. – *Tennessee*
Terr. – *Territory*
Tex. – *Texas*
Tipp. – *Tipperary*
Trin. & Tob. – *Trinidad and Tobago*
U.K. – *United Kingdom*
U.S.A. – *United States of America*
Ut. P. – *Uttar Pradesh*
Va. – *Virginia*
Vic. – *Victoria*
Vol. – *Volcano*
Vt. – *Vermont*
Wash. – *Washington*
W. – *West, Western, Wadi*
W. Va. – *West Virginia*
Wis. – *Wisconsin*
Worcs. – *Worcestershire*
Yorks. – *Yorkshire*

Introduction to Index

The number printed in bold type against each entry indicates the map page where the feature can be found. This is followed by its geographical coordinates. The first coordinate indicates latitude, i.e. distance north or south of the Equator. The second coordinate indicates longitude, i.e. distance east or west of the meridian of Greenwich in England (shown as 0° longitude). Both latitude and longitude are measured in degrees and minutes (with 60 minutes in a degree), and appear on the map as horizontal and vertical gridlines respectively. Thus the entry for Paris in France reads:

Paris, France . . . . **39** 48 50N 2 20 E

This entry indicates that Paris is on page **39**, at latitude 48 degrees 50 minutes north (approximately five-sixths of the distance between horizontal gridlines 48 and 49, marked on either side of the page) and at longitude 2 degrees 20 minutes east (approximately one-third of the distance between vertical gridlines 2 and 3, marked at top and bottom of the page). Paris can be found where lines extended from these two points cross on the page. The geographical coordinates are sometimes only approximate but are close enough for the place to be located. Rivers have been indexed to their mouth or confluence.

An open square □ signifies that the name refers to an administrative subdivision of a country while a solid square ■ follows the name of a country. An arrow ⇀ follows the name of a river.

The alphabetical order of names composed of two or more words is governed primarily by the first word and then by the second. This rule applies even if the second word is a description or its abbreviation, R., L., I., for example:

> North Walsham
> Northallerton
> Northampton
> Northern Circars
> Northumberland Is.
> Northumberland Str.

Names composed of a proper name (Gibraltar) and a description (Strait of) are positioned alphabetically by the proper name. This is the case where the definite article follows a proper name (Mans, Le). If the same word occurs in the name of a town and a geographical feature, the town name is listed first followed by the name or names of the geographical features.

Names beginning with M', Mc are all indexed as if they were spelt Mac. All names beginning St. are alphabetised under Saint, but Sankt, Sint, Santa and San are all spelt in full and are alphabetised accordingly.

If the same place name occurs twice or more times in the index and all are in the same country, each is followed by the name of the administrative subdivision in which it is located. The names are placed in the alphabetical order of the subdivisions. If the same place name occurs twice or more in the index and the places are in different countries they will be followed by their country names, the latter governing the alphabetical order. In a mixture of these situations the primary order is fixed by the alphabetical sequence of the countries and the secondary order by that of the country subdivisions.

A

Aachen .... **42** 50 47N 6 4 E
Aalborg = Ålborg .... **61** 57 2N 9 54 E
Aalsmeer .... **40** 52 17N 4 43 E
Aalst .... **42** 50 56N 4 2 E
Aalten .... **41** 51 56N 6 35 E
Aarhus = Århus .... **61** 56 8N 10 11 E
Aba .... **131** 5 10N 7 19 E
Ābādān .... **84** 30 22N 48 20 E
Ābādeh .... **85** 31 8N 52 40 E
Abadla **126** 31 2N 2 45W
Abai **191** 25 58S 55 54W
Abakan .... **74** 53 40N 91 10 E
Abancay **186** 13 35S 72 55W
Abariringa I. **122** 2 50S 171 40W
Abashiri .... **103** 44 0N 144 15 E
Abashiri-Wan .... **103** 44 0N 144 30 E
Abaya, L. .... **133** 6 30N 37 50 E
Abbay = Nîl el Azraq ──► .. **129** 15 38N 32 31 E
Abbeville, France .... **38** 50 6N 1 49 E
Abbeville, U.S.A. **165** 34 12N 82 21W
Abéché .... **129** 13 50N 20 35 E
Abeokuta .... **131** 7 3N 3 19 E
Aberaeron **26** 52 15N 4 16W
Aberayron = Aberaeron **26** 52 15N 4 16W
Aberdare **27** 51 43N 3 27W
Aberdeen, U.K. **33** 57 9N 2 6W
Aberdeen, S. Dak., U.S.A. .. **163** 45 30N 98 30W
Aberdeen, Wash., U.S.A. .. **171** 47 0N 123 50W
Aberdovey **26** 52 33N 4 3W
Aberfeldy **33** 56 37N 3 50W
Abergavenny **26** 51 49N 3 1W
Aberystwyth **26** 52 25N 4 6W
Abha .... **82** 18 0N 42 34 E
Abidjan **130** 5 26N 3 58W
Abilene **161** 32 22N 99 40W
Abington **25** 55 30N 3 42W
Abkhaz Rep. □ .... **70** 43 0N 41 0 E
Abohar .... **89** 30 10N 74 10 E
Aboméy .... **131** 7 10N 2 5 E
Abong-Mbang .... **131** 4 0N 13 8 E
Abrud .... **56** 46 19N 23 5 E
Abruzzi □ .... **47** 42 15N 14 0 E
Absaroka Ra. **163** 44 40N 110 0W
Abū al Khaşīb .... **84** 30 25N 48 0 E
Abū 'Alī .... **84** 27 20N 49 27 E
Abū 'Arīsh .... **82** 16 58N 45 20 E
Abu Dhabi = Abū Zāby .. **85** 24 28N 54 22 E
Abu Hamed .... **129** 19 32N 33 13 E
Abū Zāby .... **85** 24 28N 54 22 E
Abunã **187** 9 40S 65 20W
Abunã ──► **187** 9 41S 65 20W
Abut Hd. .... **123** 43 7S 170 15 E
Acámbaro **177** 20 2N 100 44W
Acaponeta **175** 22 30N 105 22W
Acapulco **177** 16 51N 99 56W
Acatlán **177** 18 10N 98 3W
Acayucan **177** 17 57N 94 55W
Accra **130** 5 35N 0 6W
Accrington **28** 53 46N 2 22W
Achill I. **34** 53 58N 10 5W
Achinsk .... **74** 56 20N 90 20 E
Aconcagua, Cerro **190** 32 39S 70 0W
Aconquija, Mt. **190** 27 0S 66 0W
Açores, Is. dos = Azores .. **126** 38 44N 29 0W
Acre = 'Akko .... **80** 32 55N 35 4 E
Acre □ **187** 9 1S 71 0W
Ad Dawhah .... **85** 25 15N 51 35 E
Ada **168** 34 50N 96 45W
Adamaoua, Massif de l' .... **131** 7 20N 12 20 E
Adamawa Highlands =
  Adamaoua, Massif de l' .. **131** 7 20N 12 20 E
Adaminaby .... **117** 36 0S 148 45 E
Adams, Mt. **171** 46 10N 121 28W
Adam's Bridge .... **90** 9 15N 79 40 E
Adana .... **80** 37 0N 35 16 E
Adapazarı .... **80** 40 48N 30 25 E
Adare, C. .... **15** 71 0S 171 0 E
Addis Ababa = Addis Abeba **133** 9 2N 38 42 E

Addis Abeba .... **133** 9 2N 38 42 E
Adelaide .... **119** 34 52S 138 30 E
Adelaide Pen. **145** 68 15N 97 30W
Adélie, Terre .... **15** 68 0S 140 0 E
Aden = Al 'Adan .... **83** 12 45N 45 0 E
Aden, G. of .... **133** 13 0N 50 0 E
Adige ──► .... **47** 45 9N 12 20 E
Adirondack Mts. **151** 44 0N 74 15W
Admiralty Is. .... **115** 2 0S 147 0 E
Adoni **90** 15 33N 77 18W
Adrian **167** 41 55N 84 0W
Adriatic Sea .... **52** 43 0N 16 0 E
Adwa .... **132** 14 15N 38 52 E
Adzhar Rep. □ .... **70** 42 0N 42 0 E
Ægean Sea .... **55** 37 0N 25 0 E
Æolian Is. = Eólie, I. .... **49** 38 30N 14 50 E
Aerht'ai Shan .... **100** 46 40N 92 45 E
Afars & Issas, Terr. of =
  Djibouti ■ .... **133** 12 0N 43 0 E
Afghanistan ■ .... **87** 33 0N 65 0 E
Afuá **188** 0 15S 50 20W
Afyonkarahisar .... **80** 38 45N 30 33 E
Agadir **126** 30 28N 9 35W
Agano ──► .... **103** 37 57N 139 8 E
Agartala .... **93** 23 50N 91 23 E
Agen .... **36** 44 12N 0 38 E
Ageo .... **107** 35 58N 139 36 E
Aghil Pass .... **89** 36 15N 76 35 E
Agra .... **89** 27 17N 77 58 E
Ağri Daği .... **81** 39 50N 44 15 E
Água Clara **188** 20 25S 52 45W
Agua Prieta **174** 31 18N 109 34W
Aguadas **184** 5 40N 75 38W
Aguadilla **180** 18 27N 67 10W
Aguas Blancas **190** 24 15S 69 55W
Aguascalientes **175** 21 53N 102 18W
Aguascalientes □ **175** 22 0N 102 30W
Agulhas, Kaap .... **136** 34 52S 20 0 E
Ahaggar .... **127** 23 0N 6 30 E
Ahaura ──► .... **123** 42 21S 171 34 E
Ahmadabad .... **91** 23 0N 72 40 E
Ahmadnagar .... **91** 19 7N 74 46 E
Ahmedabad = Ahmadabad . **91** 23 0N 72 40 E
Ahmednagar = Ahmadnagar **91** 19 7N 74 46 E
Ahvāz .... **84** 31 20N 48 40 E
Ahvenanmaa = Åland .... **66** 60 15N 20 0 E
Ahwar .... **83** 13 30N 46 40 E
Aigle, L' .... **39** 48 46N 0 38 E
Aigues-Mortes .... **37** 43 35N 4 12 E
Aiken **170** 33 34N 81 50W
Ailsa Craig **30** 55 15N 5 7W
Aimorés **189** 19 30S 41 4W
Aïn Ben Tili **126** 25 59N 9 27W
Aioi .... **109** 34 48N 134 28 E
Aïr .... **127** 18 30N 8 0 E
Airdrie **31** 55 53N 3 57W
Aire ──► **29** 53 42N 0 55W
Airlie Beach .... **121** 20 16S 148 43 E
Aisne ──► .... **37** 49 26N 2 50 E
Aix-en-Provence .... **37** 43 32N 5 27 E
Aix-la-Chapelle = Aachen . **42** 50 47N 6 4 E
Aix-les-Bains .... **37** 45 41N 5 53 E
Aizuwakamatsu .... **105** 37 30N 139 56 E
Ajaccio .... **36** 41 55N 8 40 E
Ajanta Ra. .... **91** 20 28N 75 50 E
Ajmer .... **91** 26 28N 74 37 E
Akaishi-Dake .... **107** 35 27N 138 9 E
Akaishi-Sammyaku ...... **107** 35 25N 138 10 E
Akashi .... **109** 34 45N 135 0 E
Akershus fylke □ ...... **60** 60 0N 11 10 E
Akhelóös ──► .... **54** 38 36N 21 14 E
Akhisar .... **80** 38 56N 27 48 E
Aki .... **109** 33 30N 133 54 E
Aki-Nada .... **109** 34 5N 132 40 E
Akita .... **103** 39 45N 140 7 E
'Akko .... **80** 32 55N 35 4 E
Aklavik **144** 68 12N 135 0W
Akō .... **109** 34 45N 134 24 E
Akola .... **91** 20 42N 77 2 E
Akranes **64** 64 19N 21 58W
Akron **167** 41 7N 81 31W

Aksaray .... 80 38 25N 34 2 E
Aksarka .... 69 66 31N 67 50 E
Akşehir .... 80 38 18N 31 30 E
Aksum .... 132 14 5N 38 40 E
Aktyubinsk .... 70 50 17N 57 10 E
Akune .... 108 32 1N 130 12 E
Akureyri 64 65 40N 18 6W
Al 'Adan .... 83 12 45N 45 0 E
Al Amādīyah .... 81 37 5N 43 30 E
Al Amārah .... 84 31 55N 47 15 E
Al 'Aqabah .... 80 29 31N 35 0 E
Al Başrah .... 84 30 30N 47 50 E
Al Ḥadīthah .... 81 31 28N 37 8 E
Al Ḥamad .... 80 31 30N 39 30 E
Al Ḥasakah .... 81 36 35N 40 45 E
Al Ḥawrah .... 83 13 50N 47 35 E
Al Ḥayy .... 84 32 5N 46 5 E
Al Ḥillah, Iraq .... 84 32 30N 44 25 E
Al Ḥillah, Si. Arabia ...... 83 23 35N 46 50 E
Al Hindīyah .... 84 32 30N 44 10 E
Al Ḥudaydah .... 82 14 50N 43 0 E
Al Ḥūfuf .... 84 25 25N 49 45 E
Al Jāfūrah .... 84 25 0N 50 15 E
Al Jawf, Libya .... 128 24 10N 23 24 E
Al Jawf, Si. Arabia .... 82 29 55N 39 40 E
Al Jazirah .... 81 33 30N 44 0 E
Al Khafīl .... 80 31 32N 35 6 E
Al Kūt .... 84 32 30N 46 0 E
Al Kuwayt .... 84 29 30N 47 30 E
Al Lādhiqīyah .... 80 35 30N 35 45 E
Al Lidām .... 82 20 33N 44 45 E
Al Luḥayyah .... 82 15 45N 42 40 E
Al Madīnah .... 82 24 35N 39 52 E
Al Manāmah .... 85 26 10N 50 30 E
Al Marj .... 128 32 25N 20 30 E
Al Mawşil .... 81 36 15N 43 5 E
Al Mubarraz .... 84 25 30N 49 40 E
Al Muḥarraq .... 85 26 15N 50 40 E
Al Mukallā .... 83 14 33N 49 2 E
Al Qaṭīf .... 84 26 35N 50 0 E
Al Quds = Jerusalem ...... 80 31 47N 35 10 E
Al Qunfudhah .... 82 19 3N 41 4 E
Al Qurnah .... 84 31 1N 47 25 E
Al 'Ubaylah .... 83 21 59N 50 57 E
Al 'Uthmānīyah .... 84 25 5N 49 22 E
Al Wajh .... 82 26 10N 36 30 E
Alabama □ 169 33 0N 87 0W
Alabama → 169 31 8N 87 57W
Alagoas □ 189 9 0S 36 0W
Alagoinhas 189 12 7S 38 20W
Alajuela 179 10 2N 84 8W
Alamogordo 161 32 59N 106 0W
Alamos 174 27 1N 108 56W
Alamosa 163 37 30N 106 0W
Åland .... 66 60 15N 20 0 E
Alaska □ 142 65 0N 150 0W
Alaska, G. of 142 58 0N 145 0W
Alaska Pen. 142 56 0N 160 0W
Alaska Range 142 62 50N 151 0W
Alba Iulia .... 56 46 8N 23 39 E
Albacete 51 39 0N 1 50W
Albania ■ .... 52 41 0N 20 0 E
Albany, Australia .... 120 35 1S 117 58 E
Albany, Ga., U.S.A. 170 31 40N 84 10W
Albany, N.Y., U.S.A. 164 42 35N 73 47W
Albany, Oreg., U.S.A. 171 44 41N 123 0W
Albany → 140 52 17N 81 31W
Albemarle 165 35 27N 80 15W
Albemarle Sd. 165 36 0N 76 30W
Albert .... 38 50 0N 2 38 E
Albert, L. = Mobutu Sese
  Seko, L. .... 132 1 30N 31 0 E
Albert Lea 166 43 32N 93 20W
Alberta □ 155 54 40N 115 0W
Albertville = Kalemie ..... 135 5 55S 29 9 E
Albi .... 37 43 56N 2 9 E
Albion 167 42 15N 84 45W
Ålborg .... 61 57 2N 9 54 E
Alborz, Reshteh-ye Kühhä-ye 86 36 0N 52 0 E
Albuquerque 161 35 5N 106 47W
Alburquerque 50 39 15N 6 59W
Albury .... 117 36 3S 146 56 E
Alcántara 188 2 20S 44 30W
Alcázar de San Juan 50 39 24N 3 12W
Alcira 51 39 9N 0 30W
Aldan → .... 75 63 28N 129 35 E
Aldeburgh .... 25 52 9N 1 35 E
Alderney 36 49 42N 2 12W
Aldershot 25 51 15N 0 43W
Alençon .... 39 48 27N 0 4 E
Aleppo = Ḥalab .... 80 36 10N 37 15 E
Alès .... 37 44 9N 4 5 E
Alessándria .... 46 44 54N 8 37 E
Ålesund .... 65 62 28N 6 12 E
Aleutian Is. 142 52 0N 175 0W
Alexander Arch. 143 57 0N 135 0W
Alexander City 169 32 58N 85 57W
Alexandra, Australia ...... 117 37 8S 145 40 E
Alexandra, N.Z. .... 123 45 14S 169 25 E
Alexandretta = İskenderun . 80 36 32N 36 10 E
Alexandria = El Iskandarîya . 128 31 0N 30 0 E
Alexandria, La., U.S.A. 168 31 20N 92 30W
Alexandria, Va., U.S.A. 164 38 47N 77 1W
Alexandrina, L. .... 119 35 25S 139 10 E
Alexandroúpolis .... 55 40 50N 25 54 E
Alexis Creek 154 52 10N 123 20W
Alfreton 29 53 6N 1 22W
Algarve 50 36 58N 8 20W
Alger .... 127 36 42N 3 8 E
Algeria ■ .... 127 35 10N 3 11 E
Algiers = Alger .... 127 36 42N 3 8 E
Algoa B. .... 136 33 50S 25 45 E
Alhambra 173 34 2N 118 10W
Alicante 51 38 23N 0 30W
Alice Springs .... 114 23 40S 133 50 E
Aligarh .... 89 27 55N 78 10 E
Alipur Duar .... 92 26 30N 89 35 E
Aliquippa 164 40 38N 80 18W
Alkmaar .... 40 52 37N 4 45 E
Allahabad .... 92 25 25N 81 58 E
Allegheny Mts. 165 38 0N 80 0W
Allen, Bog of 35 53 15N 7 0W
Allende 174 28 20N 100 51W
Allentown 164 40 36N 75 30W
Alleppey .... 90 9 30N 76 28 E
Aller → .... 42 52 57N 9 10 E
Allier → .... 37 46 57N 3 4 E
Alloa 31 56 7N 3 49W
Alma, Canada 148 48 35N 71 40W
Alma, U.S.A. 167 43 25N 84 40W
Alma Ata .... 71 43 15N 76 57 E
Almada 50 38 40N 9 9W
Almelo .... 41 52 22N 6 42 E
Almería 51 36 52N 2 27W
Almirante 179 9 10N 82 30W
Alor .... 113 8 15S 124 30 E
Alor Setar .... 96 6 7N 100 22 E
Alpena 150 45 6N 83 24W
Alphen .... 40 51 29N 4 58 E
Alpine 161 30 25N 103 35W
Alps .... 16 47 0N 8 0 E
Alsace .... 37 48 15N 7 25 E
Alsask 152 51 21N 109 59W
Alston 28 54 48N 2 26W
Alta Gracia 190 31 40S 64 30W
Altagracia 184 10 45N 71 30W
Altai = Aerht'ai Shan ..... 100 46 40N 92 45 E
Altamaha → 170 31 19N 81 17W
Altamira 188 3 12S 52 10W
Alto Adige = Trentino-Alto
  Adige □ .... 47 46 30N 11 0 E
Alton 166 38 55N 90 5W
Altona .... 43 53 32N 9 56 E
Altoona 164 40 32N 78 24W
Altun Shan .... 100 38 30N 88 0 E
Alvarado 177 18 46N 95 46W
Älvsborgs län □ .... 60 58 30N 12 30 E
Alwar .... 89 27 38N 76 34 E
Alxa Zuoqi .... 98 38 50N 105 40 E
Am-Timan .... 129 11 0N 20 10 E
Amadjuak 146 64 0N 72 39W
Amadjuak L. 146 65 0N 71 8W

Name	Page	Lat	Lon
Amagasaki	106	34 42N	135 20 E
Amagi	108	33 25N	130 39 E
Amakusa-Nada	108	32 35N	130 5 E
Amalner	91	21 5N	75 5 E
Amapá	185	2 5N	50 50W
Amapá □	185	1 40N	52 0W
Amarillo	161	35 14N	101 46W
Amasya	80	40 40N	35 50 E
Amatitlán	177	14 29N	90 38W
Amazon = Amazonas →	185	0 5S	50 0W
Amazonas □	185	4 0S	62 0W
Amazonas →	185	0 5S	50 0W
Ambala	89	30 23N	76 56 E
Ambato	184	1 5S	78 42W
Ambikapur	92	23 15N	83 15 E
Ambleside	28	54 26N	2 58W
Ambo	186	10 5S	76 10W
Ambon	113	3 35S	128 20 E
Amboyna I.	112	7 50N	112 50 E
Amderma	69	69 45N	61 30 E
Ameca	175	20 33N	104 2W
Ameca, R. →	175	20 41N	105 18W
Ameland	41	53 27N	5 45 E
American Highland	14	73 0S	75 0 E
American Samoa ■	123	14 20S	170 40W
Americus	170	32 0N	84 10W
Amersfoort	40	52 9N	5 23 E
Amery	143	56 34N	94 3W
Ames	166	42 0N	93 40W
Amga →	75	62 38N	134 32 E
Amgu	75	45 45N	137 15 E
Amgun →	75	52 56N	139 38 E
Amherst	148	45 48N	64 8W
Amherstburg	150	42 6N	83 6W
Amiens	38	49 54N	2 16 E
Amlwch	26	53 24N	4 21W
'Ammān	80	31 57N	35 52 E
Amorgós	55	36 50N	25 57 E
Amos	151	48 35N	78 5W
Amoy = Xiamen	99	24 25N	118 4 E
Amravati	91	20 55N	77 45 E
Amreli	91	21 35N	71 17 E
Amritsar	89	31 35N	74 57 E
Amsterdam, Neths.	40	52 23N	4 54 E
Amsterdam, U.S.A.	164	42 58N	74 10W
Amudarya →	70	43 40N	59 0 E
Amundsen Gulf	145	71 0N	124 0W
Amundsen Sea	15	72 0S	115 0W
Amur →	75	52 56N	141 10 E
An Nafūd	82	28 15N	41 0 E
An Najaf	84	32 3N	44 15 E
An Nāşirīyah	84	31 0N	46 15 E
An Nhon	95	13 55N	109 7 E
An Nu'ayrīyah	84	27 30N	48 30 E
An Uaimh	34	53 39N	6 40W
Anabar →	72	73 8N	113 36 E
Anaconda	163	46 7N	113 0W
Anacortes	171	48 30N	122 40W
Anadolu	80	38 0N	30 0 E
Anadyr →	73	64 55N	176 5 E
Anadyrskiy Zaliv	73	64 0N	180 0 E
Anaheim	173	33 50N	118 0W
Anambas Is.	111	3 20N	106 30 E
Anamur	80	36 8N	32 58 E
Anan	109	33 54N	134 40 E
Anápolis	188	16 15S	48 50W
Anārak	85	33 25N	53 40 E
Anatolia = Anadolu	80	38 0N	30 0 E
Añatuya	190	28 20S	62 50W
Anchorage	142	61 10N	149 50W
Ancohuma, Nevada	187	16 0S	68 50W
Ancona	47	43 37N	13 30 E
Ancud	192	42 0S	73 50W
Ancud, G. de	192	42 0S	73 0W
Ándalsnes	65	62 35N	7 43 E
Andalucía □	50	37 35N	5 0W
Andalusia	169	31 19N	86 30W
Andalusia = Andalucía □	50	37 35N	5 0W
Andaman Is.	94	12 30N	92 30 E
Andaman Sea	94	13 0N	96 0 E
Andaman Str.	94	12 15N	92 20 E
Andelys, Les	39	49 15N	1 25 E
Anderson, Ind., U.S.A.	167	40 5N	85 40W
Anderson, S.C., U.S.A.	165	34 32N	82 40W
Andes, Cord. de los	182	20 0S	68 0W
Andhra Pradesh □	91	16 0N	79 0 E
Andikíthira	55	35 52N	23 15 E
Andizhan	71	41 10N	72 0 E
Andorra ■	36	42 30N	1 30 E
Andover	24	51 13N	1 29W
Andreanof Is.	142	52 0N	178 0W
Andrewilla	118	26 31S	139 17 E
Ándria	49	41 13N	16 17 E
Andropov = Rybinsk	68	58 5N	38 50 E
Ándros	55	37 50N	24 57 E
Andros I.	178	24 30N	78 0W
Angara →	74	58 30N	97 0 E
Angarsk	74	52 30N	104 0 E
Angaston	119	34 30S	139 8 E
Ånge	66	62 31N	15 35 E
Ängelholm	61	56 15N	12 58 E
Angels Camp	172	38 8N	120 30W
Ångerman →	66	64 0N	17 20 E
Angers	36	47 30N	0 35W
Angkor	95	13 22N	103 50 E
Anglesey	26	53 17N	4 20W
Angmagssalik	147	65 40N	37 20W
Angol	190	37 56S	72 45W
Angola ■	134	12 0S	18 0 E
Angoulême	36	45 39N	0 10 E
Angoumois	36	45 50N	0 25 E
Anguilla	180	18 14N	63 5W
Angus, Braes of	33	56 51N	3 10W
Anhui □	99	32 0N	117 0 E
Anhwei □ = Anhui □	99	32 0N	117 0 E
Anin	94	15 36N	97 50 E
Anjō	106	34 57N	137 5 E
Anjou	36	47 20N	0 15W
Anju	98	39 36N	125 40 E
Ankang	99	32 40N	109 1 E
Ankara	80	40 0N	32 54 E
Ann Arbor	167	42 17N	83 45W
Annaba	127	36 50N	7 46 E
Annam = Trung-Phan	95	16 0N	108 0 E
Annamitique, Chaîne	95	17 0N	106 0 E
Annan	31	55 0N	3 17W
Annapolis	164	39 0N	76 30W
Annecy	37	45 55N	6 8 E
Anniston	169	33 45N	85 50W
Annobón	131	1 25S	5 36 E
Annonay	37	45 15N	4 40 E
Annotto Bay	180	18 17N	77 3W
Anqing	99	30 30N	117 3 E
Anse, L'	150	46 47N	88 28W
Anshan	98	41 3N	122 58 E
Anshun	99	26 18N	105 57 E
Anstruther	31	56 14N	2 40W
Antabamba	186	14 40S	73 0W
Antakya	80	36 14N	36 10 E
Antalya	80	36 52N	30 45 E
Antalya Körfezi	80	36 15N	31 30 E
Antananarivo	137	18 55S	47 31 E
Antarctic Pen.	14	67 0S	60 0W
Antarctica	14	90 0S	0 0 E
Anti Atlas	126	30 0N	8 30W
Antibes	37	43 34N	7 6 E
Anticosti, Î. d'	148	49 30N	63 0W
Antigo	150	45 8N	89 5W
Antigua, Guatemala	177	14 34N	90 41W
Antigua, W. Indies	180	17 0N	61 50W
Antigua and Barbuda ■	180	17 20N	61 48W
Antilla	178	20 40N	75 50W
Antioch	172	38 7N	121 45W
Antioquia	184	6 40N	75 55W
Antipodes Is.	11	49 45S	178 40 E
Antofagasta	190	23 50S	70 30W
Antrim	34	54 43N	6 13W
Antrim, Mts. of	34	54 57N	6 8W
Antsiranana	137	12 25S	49 20 E
Antwerp = Antwerpen	42	51 13N	4 25 E
Antwerpen	42	51 13N	4 25 E
Anvers = Antwerpen	42	51 13N	4 25 E

Anvik **142** 62 37N 160 20W
Anxious B. . . . . **119** 33 24S 134 45 E
Anyang . . . . **98** 36 5N 114 21 E
Anzhero-Sudzhensk . . . . **71** 56 10N 86 0 E
Ánzio . . . . **46** 41′28N 12 37 E
Aoga-Shima . . . . **105** 32 28N 139 46 E
Aomori . . . . **103** 40 45N 140 45 E
Apalachee B. **170** 30 0N 84 0W
Apalachicola **170** 29 40N 85 0W
Apalachicola ~► **170** 29 40N 85 0W
Aparri . . . . **112** 18 22N 121 38 E
Apatzingan **175** 19 5N 102 21W
Apeldoorn . . . . **41** 52 13N 5 57 E
Apennines . . . . **16** 44 20N 10 20 E
Apizaco **177** 19 25N 98 9W
Aplao **186** 16 0S 72 40W
Apolo **187** 14 30S 68 30W
Apostle Is. **150** 47 0N 90 30W
Apostolos Andreas, C. . . . . . **80** 35 42N 34 35 E
Appalachian Mts. **138** 38 0N 80 0W
Appingedam . . . . **41** 53 19N 6 51 E
Appleby **28** 54 35N 2 29W
Appleton **167** 44 17N 88 25W
Apulia = Púglia □ . . . . **49** 41 0N 16 30 E
Apure ~► **184** 7 37N 66 25W
Aqabah = Al 'Aqabah . . . . . **80** 29 31N 35 0 E
Aquidauana **188** 20 30S 55 50W
Áquila, L' . . . . **47** 42 21N 13 24 E
Aquiles Serdán **174** 28 36N 105 53W
Ar Riyāḍ . . . . **83** 24 41N 46 42 E
Ar Ruṭbah . . . . **81** 33 0N 40 15 E
Ara . . . . **92** 25 35N 84 32 E
Arab, Bahr el ~► . . . . **129** 9 50N 29 0 E
Arab, Shatt al . . . . **84** 30 0N 48 31 E
Arabia . . . . **76** 25 0N 45 0 E
Arabian Gulf = Gulf, The . . . **85** 27 0N 50 0 E
Arabian Sea . . . . **76** 16 0N 65 0 E
Aracaju **189** 10 55S 37 4W
Aracati **189** 4 30S 37 44W
Araçatuba **188** 21 10S 50 30W
Arad . . . . **56** 46 10N 21 20 E
Arafura Sea . . . . **113** 9 0S 135 0 E
Aragón □ **51** 41 25N 1 0W
Araguacema **188** 8 50S 49 20W
Araguaia ~► **188** 5 21S 48 41W
Araguari **188** 18 38S 48 11W
Arāk . . . . **84** 34 0N 49 40 E
Arakan Coast . . . . **93** 19 0N 94 0 E
Arakan Yoma . . . . **93** 20 0N 94 40 E
Araks = Aras, Rūd-e ~► . . . **81** 39 10N 47 10 E
Aral Sea = Aralskoye More . **70** 44 30N 60 0 E
Aralsk . . . . **70** 46 50N 61 20 E
Aralskoye More . . . . **70** 44 30N 60 0 E
Aran I. **34** 55 0N 8 30W
Aran Is. **35** 53 5N 9 42W
Aranjuez **50** 40 1N 3 40W
Aransas Pass **158** 27 55N 97 9W
Arao . . . . **108** 32 59N 130 25 E
Araraquara **188** 21 50S 48 0W
Ararat . . . . **119** 37 16S 143 0 E
Ararat, Mt. = Ağri Daği . . . . **81** 39 50N 44 15 E
Aras, Rūd-e ~► . . . . **81** 39 10N 47 10 E
Araya, Pen. de **185** 10 40N 64 0W
Arbil . . . . **81** 36 15N 44 5 E
Arbroath **31** 56 34N 2 35W
Arcachon **36** 44 40N 1 10W
Arcadia **170** 27 20N 81 50W
Archangel = Arkhangelsk . . **69** 64 40N 41 0 E
Arcot . . . . **90** 12 53N 79 20 E
Arctic Bay **146** 73 1N 85 7W
Arctic Ocean **12** 78 0N 160 0W
Arctic Red River **144** 67 15N 134 0W
Ardabīl . . . . **81** 38 15N 48 18 E
Ardennes . . . . **42** 50 0N 5 10 E
Ardgour **32** 56 45N 5 25W
Ardlethan . . . . **117** 34 22S 146 53 E
Ardmore **168** 34 10N 97 5W
Ardnacrusha **35** 52 43N 8 38W
Ardnamurchan, Pt. of **32** 56 44N 6 14W
Ards Pen. **34** 54 30N 5 25W
Arecibo **180** 18 29N 66 42W

Arequipa **187** 16 20S 71 30W
Arezzo . . . . **46** 43 28N 11, 50 E
Argentan **39** 48 45N 0 1W
Argentário, Mte. . . . . **46** 42 23N 11 11 E
Argentina ■ **190** 35 0S 66 0W
Argentino, L. **192** 50 10S 73 0W
Árgos . . . . **54** 37 40N 22 43 E
Argostólion . . . . **54** 38 12N 20 33 E
Argun ~► . . . . **74** 53 20N 121 28 E
Århus . . . . **61** 56 8N 10 11 E
Arica, Chile **187** 18 32S 70 20W
Arica, Colombia **184** 2 0S 71 50W
Arida . . . . **106** 34 5N 135 8 E
Arima **180** 10 38N 61 17W
Ario de Rosales **175** 19 12N 101 43W
Aripuanã **187** 9 25S 60 30W
Aripuanã ~► **187** 5 7S 60 25W
Ariquemes **187** 9 55S 63 6W
Arisaig **32** 56 55N 5 50W
Aristazabal I. **154** 52 40N 129 10W
Arizona □ **160** 34 20N 111 30W
Arjona **184** 10 14N 75 22W
Arkadelphia **168** 34 5N 93 0W
Arkansas □ **168** 35 0N 92 30W
Arkansas ~► **168** 33 48N 91 4W
Arkansas City **158** 37 4N 97 3W
Arkhangelsk . . . . **69** 64 40N 41 0 E
Arklow **35** 52 48N 6 10W
Arkticheskiy, Mys . . . . **72** 81 10N 95 0 E
Arles . . . . **37** 43 41N 4 40 E
Arlington **164** 38 52N 77 5W
Armagh **34** 54 22N 6 40W
Armavir . . . . **70** 45 2N 41 7 E
Armenia **184** 4 35N 75 45W
Armenia ■ . . . . **70** 40 0N 41 0 E
Armentières . . . . **38** 50 40N 2 50 E
Armidale . . . . **116** 30 30S 151 40 E
Armstrong **155** 50 25N 119 10W
Arnaouti, C. . . . . **80** 35 6N 32 17 E
Arnaud ~► **146** 59 59N 69 46W
Arnhem . . . . **41** 51 58N 5 55 E
Arnhem, C. . . . . **115** 12 20S 137 30 E
Arnhem Land . . . . **114** 13 10S 134 30 E
Arnprior **151** 45 26N 76 21W
Arran **30** 55 34N 5 12W
Arras . . . . **38** 50 17N 2 46 E
Arriaga **177** 16 14N 93 54W
Árta . . . . **54** 39 8N 21 2 E
Artigas **191** 30 20S 56 30W
Artois . . . . **38** 50 20N 2 30 E
Aru, Kepulauan . . . . **113** 6 0S 134 30 E
Arua . . . . **132** 3 1N 30 58 E
Aruanã **188** 14 54S 51 10W
Aruba **181** 12 30N 70 0W
Arusha . . . . **135** 3 20S 36 40 E
Arvida **148** 48 25N 71 14W
Arys . . . . **71** 42 26N 68 48 E
'As Saffānīyah . . . . **84** 28 5N 48 50 E
As Samāwah . . . . **84** 31 15N 45 15 E
As Sulaymānīyah . . . . **83** 24 9N 47 18 E
As Sumaymānīyah . . . . **81** 35 35N 45 29 E
As Suwaydā' . . . . **80** 32 40N 36 30 E
As Ṣuwayrah . . . . **84** 32 55N 45 0 E
Asahi . . . . **107** 35 43N 140 39 E
Asahi-Gawa ~► . . . . **109** 34 36N 133 58 E
Asahigawa . . . . **103** 43 46N 142 22 E
Asama-Yama . . . . **107** 36 24N 138 31 E
Asamankese **130** 5 50N 0 40W
Asansol . . . . **92** 23 40N 87 1 E
Asbestos **148** 45 47N 71 58W
Ascension I. **125** 8 0S 14 15W
Áscoli Piceno . . . . **47** 42 51N 13 34 E
Aseb . . . . **133** 13 0N 42 40 E
Ash Shām, Bādiyat . . . . **80** 32 0N 40 0 E
Ash Shāmīyah . . . . **84** 31 55N 44 35 E
Ash Shāriqah . . . . **85** 25 23N 55 26 E
Ash Shaṭrah . . . . **84** 31 30N 46 10 E
Ashburton . . . . **123** 43 53S 171 48 E
Ashby-de-la-Zouch **28** 52 45N 1 29W
Ashcroft **155** 50 40N 121 20W
Asheboro **165** 35 43N 79 46W

Asheville **165** 35 39N 82 30W
Ashford, Australia .... **116** 29 15S 151 3 E
Ashford, U.K. .... **25** 51 8N   0 53 E
Ashikaga .... **107** 36 28N 139 29 E
Ashizuri-Zaki .... **109** 32 44N 133 0 E
Ashkhabad .... **70** 38 0N 57 50 E
Ashland, Kans., U.S.A. ... **156** 37 13N 99 43W
Ashland, Ky., U.S.A. **165** 38 25N 82 40W
Ashland, Oreg., U.S.A. ... **171** 42 10N 122 38W
Ashland, Wis., U.S.A. **150** 46 40N 90 52W
Ashq'elon .... **80** 31 42N 34 35 E
Ashtabula **164** 41 52N 80 50W
Ashton-under-Lyne **28** 53 30N   2 8W
Ashuanipi, L. **147** 52 45N 66 15W
Asinara I. .... **48** 41 5N   8 15 E
'Asīr □ .... **82** 18 40N 42 30 E
Asir, Ras .... **133** 11 55N 51 10 E
Asmara = Asmera .... **132** 15 19N 38 55 E
Asmera .... **132** 15 19N 38 55 E
Aso .... **108** 33 0N 131 5 E
Aso-Zan .... **108** 32 53N 131 6 E
Aspiring, Mt. .... **123** 44 23S 168 46 E
Assam □ .... **93** 26 0N 93 0 E
Assen .... **41** 53 0N   6 35 E
Assiniboia **152** 49 40N 105 59W
Assiniboine ➡ **153** 49 53N 97 8W
Assisi .... **46** 43 4N 12 36 E
Asti .... **46** 44 54N   8 11 E
Astipálaia .... **55** 36 32N 26 22 E
Astoria **171** 46 16N 123 50W
Astrakhan .... **70** 46 25N 48 5 E
Asturias □ **50** 43 15N   6 0W
Asunción **191** 25 10S 57 30W
Aswân .... **128** 24 4N 32 57 E
Asyûţ .... **128** 27 11N 31 4 E
At Ţafīlah .... **80** 30 45N 35 30 E
At Ta'if .... **82** 21 5N 40 27 E
Atacama, Desierto de **190** 24 0S 69 20W
Atacama, Salar de **190** 23 30S 68 20W
Atalaya **186** 10 45S 73 50W
Atami .... **107** 35 5N 139 4 E
Atbara .... **129** 17 42N 33 59 E
'Atbara ➡ .... **129** 17 40N 33 56 E
Atchafalaya B. **168** 29 30N 91 20W
Atchison **166** 39 40N 95 10W
Athabasca **155** 54 45N 113 20W
Athabasca ➡ **145** 58 40N 110 50W
Athabasca, L. **145** 59 15N 109 15W
Athenry **35** 53 18N   8 45W
Athens = Athínai .... **55** 37 58N 23 46 E
Athens, Ala., U.S.A. **169** 34 49N 86 58W
Athens, Ga., U.S.A. **165** 33 56N 83 24W
Athens, Ohio, U.S.A. **167** 39 25N 82 6W
Athens, Tenn., U.S.A. **169** 35 45N 84 38W
Athens, Tex., U.S.A. **168** 32 11N 95 48W
Atherton .... **121** 17 17S 145 30 E
Athínai .... **55** 37 58N 23 46 E
Athlone **34** 53 26N   7 57W
Atholl, Forest of **33** 56 51N   3 50W
Áthos .... **55** 40 9N 24 22 E
Athy **35** 53 0N   7 0W
Atico **186** 16 14S 73 40W
Atlanta **170** 33 50N 84 24W
Atlantic **166** 41 25N 95 0W
Atlantic City **164** 39 25N 74 25W
Atlantic Ocean **9** 0 0 20 0W
Atlas Mts. = Haut Atlas ... **126** 32 30N   5 0W
Atmore **169** 31 2N 87 30W
Atsugi .... **107** 35 25N 139 21 E
Atsumi .... **106** 34 35N 137 4 E
Atsumi-Wan .... **106** 34 44N 137 13 E
Attawapiskat ➡ **140** 52 57N 82 18W
Attleboro **164** 41 56N 71 18W
Aubagne .... **37** 43 17N   5 37 E
Aube ➡ .... **37** 48 34N   3 43 E
Aubenas .... **37** 44 37N   4 24 E
Auburn, Ala., U.S.A. **169** 32 37N 85 30W
Auburn, N.Y., U.S.A. **164** 42 57N 76 39W
Auckland .... **122** 36 52S 174 46 E
Auckland Is. .... **15** 50 40S 166 5 E
Aude ➡ .... **37** 43 13N   3 14 E

Augsburg .... **43** 48 22N 10 54 E
Augusta, Ga., U.S.A. **170** 33 29N 81 59W
Augusta, Maine, U.S.A. ... **148** 44 20N 69 46W
Aunis **36** 46 5N   0 50W
Aurangabad .... **91** 19 50N 75 23 E
Aurillac .... **37** 44 55N   2 26 E
Aurora **167** 41 42N 88 12W
Aust-Agder fylke □ ...... **60** 58 55N   7 40 E
Austin, Minn., U.S.A. **166** 43 37N 92 59W
Austin, Tex., U.S.A. **161** 30 20N 97 45W
Austral Is. = Tubuai Is. ... **123** 25 0S 150 0W
Australia ■ .... **114** 23 0S 135 0 E
Australian Alps .... **117** 36 30S 148 30 E
Australian Cap. Terr. □ ... **117** 35 30S 149 0 E
Austria ■ .... **45** 47 0N 14 0 E
Autlán **175** 19 40N 104 30W
Auvergne .... **37** 45 20N   3 15 E
Auxerre .... **39** 47 48N   3 32 E
Avalon Pen. **149** 47 30N 53 20W
Aveiro **185** 3 10S 55 5W
Avellaneda **190** 34 50S 58 10W
Aves, I. de **181** 15 45N 63 55W
Avesnes-sur-Helpe ...... **38** 50 8N   3 55 E
Aveyron ➡ .... **36** 44 7N   1 5 E
Aviemore **33** 57 11N   3 50W
Avignon .... **37** 43 57N   4 50 E
Ávila **50** 40 39N   4 43W
Avon □ **27** 51 30N   2 40W
Avon ➡, Avon, U.K. **24** 51 30N   2 43W
Avon ➡, Hants., U.K. ... **24** 50 44N   1 45W
Avonmouth **27** 51 30N   2 42W
Avranches **36** 48 40N   1 20W
Awaji-Shima .... **109** 34 30N 134 50 E
Aweil .... **129** 8 42N 27 20 E
Axel Heiberg I. **12** 80 0N 90 0W
Axminster **27** 50 47N   3 1W
Ayabe .... **106** 35 20N 135 20 E
Ayacucho **186** 13 0S 74 0W
Ayios Evstrátios .... **55** 39 34N 24 58 E
Ayon, Ostrov .... **73** 69 50N 169 0 E
Ayr, Australia .... **121** 19 35S 147 25 E
Ayr, U.K. **31** 55 28N   4 37W
Ayre, Pt. of **28** 54 27N   4 21W
Aytos .... **53** 42 42N 27 16 E
Ayutla **177** 16 58N 99 17W
Az Zahrān .... **84** 26 10N 50 7 E
Az Zubayr .... **84** 30 20N 47 50 E
Azamgarh .... **92** 26 5N 83 13 E
Azbine = Aïr .... **127** 18 30N   8 0 E
Azerbaijan ■ .... **70** 40 20N 48 0 E
Azores **126** 38 44N 29 0W
Azov Sea = Azovskoye More **68** 46 0N 36 30 E
Azovskoye More .... **68** 46 0N 36 30 E
Azúa de Compostela **180** 18 25N 70 44W
Azuero, Pen. de **179** 7 30N 80 30W
Azul **190** 36 42S 59 43W

B

Ba Ngoi = Cam Lam ..... **95** 11 54N 109 10 E
Baarn .... **40** 52 12N   5 17 E
Bāb el Mândeb .... **133** 12 35N 43 25 E
Babahoyo **184** 1 40S 79 30W
Babinda .... **121** 17 20S 145 56 E
Babine L. **154** 54 48N 126 0W
Bâbol .... **86** 36 40N 52 50 E
Babuyan Is. .... **112** 19 10N 121 40 E
Babylon .... **84** 32 40N 44 30 E
Bac Ninh .... **95** 21 13N 106 4 E
Bac Phan .... **95** 22 0N 105 0 E
Bac Quang .... **95** 22 30N 104 48 E
Bacabal **188** 4 15S 44 45W
Bacău .... **57** 46 35N 26 55 E
Back ➡ **145** 65 10N 104 0W
Bacolod .... **112** 10 40N 122 57 E
Bad Lands **163** 43 40N 102 10W
Badajoz **50** 38 50N   6 59W
Badakhshān □ .... **87** 36 30N 71 0 E

Name	Page	Lat °	′	N/S	Long °	′	E/W
Badalona	51	41	26N		2	15	E
Badanah	82	30	58N		41	30	E
Baden-Baden	42	48	45N		8	15	E
Baden-Württemberg □	42	48	40N		9	0	E
Bādghīsāt □	87	35	0N		63	0	E
Badin	88	24	38N		68	54	E
Baffin □	146	70	0N		80	0W	
Baffin B.	13	72	0N		64	0W	
Baffin I.	146	68	0N		75	0W	
Bafra	80	41	34N		35	54	E
Bāft	85	29	15N		56	38	E
Bagé	191	31	20S		54	15W	
Baghdād	84	33	20N		44	30	E
Baghlān	87	36	12N		69	0	E
Baghlān □	87	36	0N		68	30	E
Bahamas ■	178	24	0N		75	0W	
Baharampur	92	24	2N		88	27	E
Bahawalpur	89	29	24N		71	40	E
Bahia = Salvador	189	13	0S		38	30W	
Bahia □	189	12	0S		42	0W	
Bahía Blanca	190	38	35S		62	13W	
Bahr el Jebel →	129	7	30N		30	30	E
Bahraich	92	27	38N		81	37	E
Bahrain ■	85	26	0N		50	35	E
Baia Mare	56	47	40N		23	35	E
Baie Comeau	148	49	12N		68	10W	
Baie-St-Paul	148	47	28N		70	32W	
Ba'iji	81	35	0N		43	30	E
Baikal, L. = Baykal, Oz.	74	53	0N		108	0	E
Baile Atha Cliath = Dublin	35	53	20N		6	18W	
Bailleul	38	50	44N		2	41	E
Bainbridge	170	30	53N		84	34W	
Baird Mts.	142	67	10N		160	15W	
Bairnsdale	117	37	48S		147	36	E
Baiyin	98	36	45N		104	14	E
Baja	59	46	12N		18	59	E
Baja California	174	31	10N		115	12W	
Baja California Norte □	174	30	0N		115	0W	
Baja California Sur □	174	25	50N		111	50W	
Bajimba, Mt.	116	29	17S		152	6	E
Baker	171	44	50N		117	55W	
Baker I.	122	0	10N		176	35W	
Baker Lake	145	64	20N		96	3W	
Bakersfield	173	35	25N		119	0W	
Bākhtarān	84	34	23N		47	0	E
Bakony Forest = Bakony Hegység	59	47	10N		17	30	E
Bakony Hegység	59	47	10N		17	30	E
Baku	70	40	25N		49	45	E
Bala	26	52	54N		3	36W	
Balabac, Str.	112	7	53N		117	5	E
Balabakk	80	34	0N		36	10	E
Balaghat	91	21	49N		80	12	E
Balaghat Ra.	91	18	50N		76	30	E
Balaklava	119	34	7S		138	22	E
Balakovo	68	52	4N		47	55	E
Balaton	59	46	50N		17	40	E
Balboa	179	9	0N		79	30W	
Balbriggan	34	53	35N		6	10W	
Balcarce	190	38	0S		58	10W	
Balclutha	123	46	15S		169	45	E
Baldy Peak	161	33	50N		109	30W	
Baleares, Islas	51	39	30N		3	0	E
Balearic Is. = Baleares, Islas	51	39	30N		3	0	E
Bali	111	8	20S		115	0	E
Balikesir	80	39	35N		27	58	E
Balikpapan	111	1	10S		116	55	E
Balkan Mts. = Stara Planina	53	43	15N		23	0	E
Balkan Pen.	17	42	0N		22	0	E
Balkh □	87	36	30N		67	0	E
Balkhash	71	46	50N		74	50	E
Balkhash, Ozero	71	46	0N		74	50	E
Ballachulish	32	56	40N		5	10W	
Ballarat	117	37	33S		143	50	E
Ballard, L.	120	29	20S		120	10	E
Ballater	33	57	2N		3	2W	
Ballina, Australia	116	28	50S		153	31	E
Ballina, Mayo, Ireland	34	54	7N		9	10W	
Ballina, Tipp., Ireland	35	52	49N		8	27W	
Ballinasloe	35	53	20N		8	12W	
Ballinrobe	34	53	36N		9	13W	
Ballycastle	34	55	12N		6	15W	
Ballymena	34	54	53N		6	18W	
Ballymoney	34	55	5N		6	30W	
Ballyshannon	34	54	30N		8	10W	
Balmaceda	192	46	0S		71	50W	
Balmoral	33	57	3N		3	13W	
Balrampur	92	27	30N		82	20	E
Balranald	117	34	38S		143	33	E
Balsas, R. →	177	17	55N		102	10W	
Baltic Sea	16	56	0N		20	0	E
Baltimore	164	39	18N		76	37W	
Baluchistan □	88	27	30N		65	0	E
Bamako	130	12	34N		7	55W	
Bambari	129	5	40N		20	35	E
Bamberg	43	49	54N		10	53	E
Bāmīān □	87	35	0N		67	0	E
Ban Aranyaprathet	95	13	41N		102	30	E
Ban Don = Surat Thani	96	9	6N		99	20	E
Ban Houei Sai	95	20	22N		100	32	E
Ban Khe Bo	95	19	10N		104	39	E
Ban Khun Yuam	94	18	49N		97	57	E
Ban Nong Pling	94	15	40N		100	10	E
Ban Phai	95	16	4N		102	44	E
Banaras = Varanasi	92	25	22N		83	0	E
Banbridge	34	54	21N		6	17W	
Banbury	25	52	4N		1	21W	
Bancroft	151	45	3N		77	51W	
Banda	91	25	30N		80	26	E
Banda, Kepulauan	113	4	37S		129	50	E
Banda Aceh	111	5	35N		95	20	E
Banda Banda, Mt.	116	31	10S		152	28	E
Banda Sea	113	6	0S		130	0	E
Bandar = Machilipatnam	92	16	12N		81	8	E
Bandār 'Abbās	85	27	15N		56	15	E
Bandar-e Anzalī	81	37	30N		49	30	E
Bandar-e Khomeyni	84	30	30N		49	5	E
Bandar-e Lengeh	85	26	35N		54	58	E
Bandar-e Nakhīlū	85	26	58N		53	30	E
Bandar-e Torkeman	86	37	0N		54	10	E
Bandar Seri Begawan	112	4	52N		115	0	E
Bandeira, Pico da	188	20	26S		41	47W	
Bandirma	80	40	20N		28	0	E
Bandon	35	51	44N		8	45W	
Bandung	111	6	54S		107	36	E
Banes	178	21	0N		75	42W	
Banff, Canada	155	51	10N		115	34W	
Banff, U.K.	33	57	40N		2	32W	
Bangalore	90	12	59N		77	40	E
Bangassou	129	4	55N		23	7	E
Banggai	113	1	40S		123	30	E
Banghāzī	128	32	11N		20	3	E
Bangka, Selat	111	2	30S		105	30	E
Bangkok	94	13	45N		100	35	E
Bangladesh ■	92	24	0N		90	0	E
Bangor, N. Ireland, U.K.	34	54	40N		5	40W	
Bangor, Wales, U.K.	26	53	13N		4	9W	
Bangor, U.S.A.	148	44	48N		68	42W	
Bangui	131	4	23N		18	35	E
Bangweulu, L.	135	11	0S		30	0	E
Bani	180	18	16N		70	22W	
Banja Luka	52	44	49N		17	11	E
Banjarmasin	111	3	20S		114	35	E
Banjul	130	13	28N		16	40W	
Bankipore	92	25	35N		85	10	E
Banks I., B.C., Canada	154	53	20N		130	0W	
Banks I., N.W.T., Canada	145	73	15N		121	30W	
Banks Pen.	123	43	45S		173	15	E
Banks Str.	119	40	40S		148	10	E
Bann →	34	54	30N		6	31W	
Banning	173	33	58N		116	52W	
Bannockburn	31	56	5N		3	55W	
Bannu	89	33	0N		70	18	E
Bantry	35	51	40N		9	28W	
Baoding	98	38	50N		115	28	E
Baoji	99	34	20N		107	5	E
Baotou	98	40	32N		110	2	E
Ba'qūbah	81	33	45N		44	50	E
Bar	52	42	8N		19	8	E
Bar Harbor	148	44	15N		68	20W	
Baraboo	166	43	28N		89	46W	
Baracoa	178	20	20N		74	30W	

Name	Page	Lat		N/S	Long		E/W
Barahona	180	18	13N		71	7W
Barail Range	93	25	15N		93	20 E
Baramula	89	34	15N		74	20 E
Baran	91	25	9N		76	40 E
Baranof I.	143	57	0N		135	10W
Baranovichi	68	53	10N		26	0 E
Barbacoas	184	1	45N		78	0W
Barbados ■	180	13	0N		59	30W
Barbuda I.	180	17	30N		61	40W
Barca, La	175	20	17N		102	34W
Barcaldine	121	23	43S		145	6 E
Barcelona, Spain	51	41	21N		2	10 E
Barcelona, Venezuela	185	10	10N		64	40W
Barcelos	185	1	0S		63	0W
Barddhaman	92	23	14N		87	39 E
Bardera	133	2	20N		42	27 E
Bardsey I.	26	52	46N		4	47W
Bareilly	89	28	22N		79	27 E
Barentin	38	49	33N		0	58 E
Barents Sea	13	73	0N		39	0 E
Bargara	121	24	50S		152	25 E
Bari	49	41	6N		16	52 E
Bari Doab	89	30	20N		73	0 E
Barīm	82	12	39N		43	25 E
Barinas	184	8	36N		70	15W
Barisal	92	22	45N		90	20 E
Barito →	111	4	0S		114	50 E
Barlee, L.	120	29	15S		119	30 E
Barletta	49	41	20N		16	17 E
Barmer	91	25	45N		71	20 E
Barmera	119	34	15S		140	28 E
Barmouth	26	52	44N		4	3W
Barnard Castle	28	54	33N		1	55W
Barnaul	71	53	20N		83	40 E
Barneveld	41	52	7N		5	36 E
Barnsley	28	53	33N		1	29W
Barnstaple	27	51	5N		4	3W
Baro	131	8	35N		6	18 E
Baroda = Vadodara	91	22	20N		73	10 E
Barpeta	93	26	20N		91	10 E
Barquisimeto	184	10	4N		69	19W
Barra	32	57	0N		7	30W
Barra Hd.	32	56	47N		7	40W
Barraba	116	30	21S		150	35 E
Barranca	186	10	45S		77	50W
Barrancabermeja	184	7	0N		73	50W
Barrancas	185	8	55N		62	5W
Barranqueras	190	27	30S		59	0W
Barranquilla	184	11	0N		74	50W
Barre	151	44	15N		72	30W
Barreiros	188	8	49S		35	12W
Barrhead	155	54	10N		114	24W
Barrie	151	44	24N		79	40W
Barrier Ra.	118	31	0S		141	30 E
Barrington Tops	116	32	6S		151	28 E
Barrow →	35	52	10N		6	57W
Barrow, Pt.	138	71	22N		156	30W
Barrow-in-Furness	28	54	8N		3	15W
Barry	27	51	23N		3	19W
Barry's Bay	151	45	29N		77	41W
Barsi	91	18	10N		75	50 E
Barstow	173	34	58N		117	2W
Bartica	185	6	25N		58	40W
Bartow	170	27	53N		81	49W
Basel	44	47	35N		7	35 E
Bashi Channel	99	21	15N		122	0 E
Bashkir Rep. □	69	54	0N		57	0 E
Basilan	112	6	35N		122	0 E
Basildon	25	51	34N		0	29 E
Basilicata □	49	40	30N		16	0 E
Basim = Washim	91	20	3N		77	0 E
Basle = Basel	44	47	35N		7	35 E
Basoka	134	1	16N		23	40 E
Basque Provinces = Vascongadas	50	42	50N		2	45W
Basra = Al Başrah	84	30	30N		47	50 E
Bass Rock	31	56	5N		2	40W
Bass Str.	117	39	15S		146	30 E
Bassano	155	50	48N		112	20W
Basse-Terre	180	16	0N		61	40W
Bassein	93	16	45N		94	30 E
Basseterre	180	17	17N		62	43W
Basti	92	26	52N		82	55 E
Bastia	36	42	40N		˙9	30 E
Batabanó	178	22	40N		82	20W
Batamay	74	63	30N		129	15 E
Batan Is.	112	20	25N		121	59 E
Batang	101	30	1N		99	0 E
Batavia	164	43	0N		78	10W
Batemans Bay	117	35	44S		150	11 E
Batesville	168	35	48N		91	40W
Bath, U.K.	27	51	22N		2	22W
Bath, Maine, U.S.A.	148	43	50N		69	49W
Bath, N.Y., U.S.A.	164	42	20N		77	17W
Bathurst = Banjul	130	13	28N		16	40W
Bathurst, Australia	117	33	25S		149	31 E
Bathurst, Canada	148	47	37N		65	43W
Bathurst, C.	145	70	34N		128	0W
Bathurst Inlet	145	66	50N		108	1W
Batlow	117	35	31S		148	9 E
Batman	81	37	55N		41	5 E
Batna	127	35	34N		6	15 E
Baton Rouge	168	30	30N		91	5W
Batopilas	174	27	1N		107	44W
Battambang	95	13	7N		103	12 E
Batticaloa	90	7	43N		81	45 E
Battle	25	50	55N		0	30 E
Battle Creek	167	42	20N		85	6W
Battle Harbour	147	52	16N		55	35W
Battleford	152	52	45N		108	15W
Batu Gajah	96	4	28N		101	3 E
Batu Is.	111	0	30S		98	25 E
Batumi	70	41	30N		41	30 E
Bauchi	131	10	22N		9	48 E
Bauru	188	22	10S		49	0W
Bavaria = Bayern □	43	49	7N		11	30 E
Bawdwin	93	23	5N		97	20 E
Bawean	111	5	46S		112	35 E
Bawku	130	11	3N		0	19W
Bay City	167	43	35N		83	51W
Bay Shore	164	40	44N		73	15W
Bayamo	178	20	20N		76	40W
Bayamón	180	18	24N		66	10W
Bayan Har Shan	101	34	0N		98	0 E
Bayan Hot = Alxa Zuoqi	98	38	50N		105	40 E
Bayern □	43	49	7N		11	30 E
Bayeux	36	49	17N		0	42W
Bayfield	150	43	34N		81	42W
Baykal, Oz.	74	53	0N		108	0 E
Baykonur	71	47	48N		65	50 E
Bayonne	36	43	30N		1	28W
Bayreuth	43	49	56N		11	35 E
Bayrūt	80	33	53N		35	31 E
Baytown	168	29	42N		94	57W
Beachy Head	25	50	44N		0	16 E
Beagle, Canal	192	55	0S		68	30W
Béarn	36	43	8N		0	36W
Beauce, Plaine de la	37	48	10N		1	45 E
Beaudesert	116	27	59S		153	0 E
Beaufort	170	32	25N		80	40W
Beaufort Sea	12	72	0N		140	0W
Beaugency	39	47	47N		1	38 E
Beauharnois	151	45	20N		73	52W
Beauly	33	57	29N		4	27W
Beaumaris	26	53	16N		4	7W
Beaumont	168	30	5N		94	8W
Beaumont-sur-Oise	39	49	9N		2	17 E
Beauséjour	153	50	5N		96	35W
Beauvais	38	49	25N		2	8 E
Beauval	152	55	9N		107	37W
Beaver →	142	66	20N		147	30W
Beaver →	152	55	26N		107	45W
Beaver Falls	164	40	44N		80	20W
Beaverlodge	155	55	11N		119	29W
Beawar	91	26	3N		74	18 E
Bečej	52	45	36N		20	3 E
Béchar	127	31	38N		2	18W
Beckley	165	37	50N		81	8W
Bedford, U.K.	25	52	8N		0	29W
Bedford, U.S.A.	167	38	50N		86	30W
Bedford □	25	52	4N		0	28W
Beenleigh	116	27	43S		153	10 E

Name	Page	Lat	Long
Be'er Sheva'	**80**	31 15N	34 48 E
Beersheba = Be'er Sheva'	**80**	31 15N	34 48 E
Beeston	**29**	52 55N	1 11W
Bega	**117**	36 41S	149 51 E
Behbehān	**84**	30 30N	50 15 E
Beibei	**99**	29 47N	106 22 E
Beihai	**99**	21 28N	109 6 E
Beijing	**98**	39 55N	116 20 E
Beira	**137**	19 50S	34 52 E
Beira-Alta	**50**	40 35N	7 35W
Beira-Baixa	**50**	40 2N	7 30W
Beira-Litoral	**50**	40 5N	8 30W
Beirut = Bayrūt	**80**	33 53N	35 31 E
Bejaia	**127**	36 42N	5 2 E
Békéscsaba	**59**	46 40N	21 5 E
Bela	**92**	25 50N	82 0 E
Bela Crkva	**52**	44 55N	21 27 E
Belaya Tserkov	**68**	49 45N	30 10 E
Belcher Is.	**140**	56 15N	78 45W
Belém	**188**	1 20S	48 30W
Belfast, U.K.	**34**	54 35N	5 56W
Belfast, U.S.A.	**148**	44 30N	69 0W
Belfort	**37**	47 38N	6 50 E
Belgaum	**91**	15 55N	74 35 E
Belgium ■	**42**	50 30N	5 0 E
Belgorod	**68**	50 35N	36 35 E
Belgrade = Beograd	**52**	44 50N	20 37 E
Belitung	**111**	3 10S	107 50 E
Belize ■	**177**	17 0N	88 30W
Belize City	**177**	17 25N	88 0W
Bell Peninsula	**146**	63 50N	82 0W
Bell Ville	**190**	32 40S	62 40W
Bella Coola	**154**	52 25N	126 40W
Bellaire	**164**	40 1N	80 46W
Bellary	**90**	15 10N	76 56 E
Belle Fourche →	**163**	44 25N	102 19W
Belle Glade	**170**	26 43N	80 38W
Belle Isle	**147**	51 57N	55 25W
Belle Isle, Str. of	**141**	51 30N	56 30W
Bellefontaine	**167**	40 20N	83 45W
Belleville, Canada	**151**	44 10N	77 23W
Belleville, U.S.A.	**166**	38 30N	90 0W
Bellevue	**155**	49 35N	114 22W
Bellin	**146**	60 0N	70 0W
Bellingham	**171**	48 45N	122 27W
Bellingshausen Sea	**14**	66 0S	80 0W
Belmont	**117**	33 4S	151 42 E
Belmopan	**177**	17 18N	88 30W
Belo Horizonte	**188**	19 55S	43 56W
Belogorsk	**75**	51 0N	128 20 E
Beloit	**166**	42 35N	89 0W
Belomorsk	**68**	64 35N	34 30 E
Belorussia ■	**68**	53 30N	27 0 E
Belovo	**71**	54 30N	86 0 E
Beloye More	**69**	66 30N	38 0 E
Beloye Ozero	**68**	45 15N	46 50 E
Belper	**28**	53 2N	1 29W
Belukha	**71**	49 50N	86 50 E
Belyy, Ostrov	**69**	73 30N	71 0 E
Bemidji	**156**	47 30N	94 50W
Ben Lomond, N.S.W., Australia	**116**	30 1S	151 40 E
Ben Lomond, Tas., Australia	**119**	41 38S	147 42 E
Ben Macdhui	**33**	57 4N	3 40W
Ben More, Central, U.K.	**32**	56 23N	4 31W
Ben More, Strath., U.K.	**30**	56 26N	6 2W
Ben More Assynt	**32**	58 7N	4 51W
Ben Nevis	**32**	56 48N	5 0W
Benalla	**117**	36 30S	146 0 E
Benares = Varanasi	**92**	25 22N	83 0 E
Benbecula	**32**	57 26N	7 21W
Benbonyathe, Mt.	**118**	30 25S	139 11 E
Bencubbin	**120**	30 48S	117 52 E
Bend	**171**	44 2N	121 15W
Bendemeer	**116**	30 53S	151 8 E
Bender Beila	**133**	9 30N	50 48 E
Bendigo	**117**	36 40S	144 15 E
Benevento	**49**	41 7N	14 45 E
Bengal, Bay of	**92**	15 0N	90 0 E
Bengbu	**99**	32 58N	117 20 E
Benghazi = Banghāzī	**128**	32 11N	20 3 E
Benguela	**134**	12 37S	13 25 E
Beni →	**187**	10 23S	65 24W
Beni Suef	**128**	29 5N	31 6 E
Benidorm	**51**	38 33N	0 9W
Benin ■	**131**	10 0N	2 0 E
Benin, Bight of	**131**	5 0N	3 0 E
Benin City	**131**	6 20N	5 31 E
Benjamin Constant	**187**	4 40S	70 15W
Bennett	**144**	59 56N	134 53W
Bennettsville	**165**	34 38N	79 39W
Benton	**168**	34 30N	92 35W
Benue →	**131**	7 48N	6 46 E
Benxi	**98**	41 20N	123 48 E
Beograd	**52**	44 50N	20 37 E
Beppu	**108**	33 15N	131 30 E
Berau, Teluk	**113**	2 30S	132 30 E
Berber	**129**	18 0N	34 0 E
Berbera	**133**	10 30N	45 2 E
Berck-sur-Mer	**38**	50 25N	1 36 E
Berezniki	**69**	59 24N	56 46 E
Bérgamo	**46**	45 42N	9 40 E
Bergen, Neths.	**40**	52 40N	4 43 E
Bergen, Norway	**60**	60 23N	5 20 E
Bergen-op-Zoom	**40**	51 30N	4 18 E
Bergerac	**36**	44 51N	0 30 E
Berhala, Selat	**111**	1 0S	104 15 E
Berhampore = Baharampur	**92**	24 2N	88 27 E
Berhampur	**92**	19 15N	84 54 E
Bering Sea	**142**	58 0N	167 0 E
Bering Str.	**142**	66 0N	170 0W
Berkeley	**172**	37 52N	122 20W
Berkshire □	**25**	51 30N	1 20W
Berkshire Downs	**24**	51 30N	1 30W
Berlin, Germany	**43**	52 32N	13 24 E
Berlin, U.S.A.	**148**	44 29N	71 10W
Bermuda ■	**180**	32 45N	65 0W
Bern	**44**	46 57N	7 28 E
Bernay	**39**	49 5N	0 35 E
Berne = Bern	**44**	46 57N	7 28 E
Berri	**119**	34 14S	140 35 E
Berry	**37**	47 0N	2 0 E
Bertoua	**131**	4 30N	13 45 E
Berwick-upon-Tweed	**31**	55 47N	2 0W
Berwyn Mts.	**26**	52 54N	3 26W
Besançon	**37**	47 15N	6 0 E
Bessemer, Ala., U.S.A.	**169**	33 25N	86 57W
Bessemer, Mich., U.S.A.	**156**	46 27N	90 0W
Bethel	**142**	60 50N	161 50W
Bethlehem	**164**	40 39N	75 24W
Béthune	**38**	50 30N	2 38 E
Betsiboka →	**137**	16 3S	46 36 E
Beverley	**29**	53 52N	0 26W
Beverly Hills	**173**	34 4N	118 29W
Beverwijk	**40**	52 28N	4 38 E
Bexhill	**24**	50 51N	0 29 E
Beyneu	**70**	45 10N	55 3 E
Beyşehir Gölü	**80**	37 40N	31 45 E
Béziers	**37**	43 20N	3 12 E
Bezwada = Vijayawada	**92**	16 31N	80 39 E
Bhadravati	**90**	13 49N	75 40 E
Bhagalpur	**92**	25 10N	87 0 E
Bhakra Dam	**89**	31 30N	76 45 E
Bhandara	**91**	21 5N	79 42 E
Bhanrer Ra.	**91**	23 40N	79 45 E
Bharat = India ■	**78**	20 0N	78 0 E
Bharatpur	**89**	27 15N	77 30 E
Bharuch	**91**	21 47N	73 0 E
Bhatpara	**92**	22 50N	88 25 E
Bhaunagar = Bhavnagar	**91**	21 45N	72 10 E
Bhavnagar	**91**	21 45N	72 10 E
Bhilwara	**91**	25 25N	74 38 E
Bhima →	**91**	16 25N	77 17 E
Bhiwandi	**91**	19 20N	73 0 E
Bhiwani	**89**	28 50N	76 9 E
Bhopal	**91**	23 20N	77 30 E
Bhubaneshwar	**92**	20 15N	85 50 E
Bhusaval	**91**	21 3N	75 46 E
Bhutan ■	**92**	27 25N	90 30 E
Biafra, B. of = Bonny, Bight of	**131**	3 30N	9 20 E
Biała Podlaska	**58**	52 4N	23 6 E

Białystok ... 58 53 10N 23 10 E
Biarritz ... 36 43 29N 1 33W
Bibai ... 103 43 19N 141 52 E
Bicester ... 25 51 53N 1 9W
Biche, L. la ... 155 54 50N 112 3W
Bidar ... 91 17 55N 77 35 E
Biddeford ... 148 43 30N 70 28W
Bideford ... 27 51 1N 4 13W
Bié, Planalto de ... 136 12 0S 16 0 E
Bieber ... 172 41 4N 121 6W
Biel ... 44 47 8N 7 14 E
Bielé Karpaty ... 59 49 5N 18 0 E
Bielefeld ... 42 52 2N 8 31 E
Bielsko-Biała ... 59 49 50N 19 2 E
Bien Hoa ... 95 10 57N 106 49 E
Bienne = Biel ... 44 47 8N 7 14 E
Bienville, L. ... 146 55 5N 72 40W
Big Belt Mts. ... 163 46 50N 111 30W
Big Cypress Swamp ... 170 26 12N 81 10W
Big Horn Mts. = Bighorn Mts. ... 163 44 30N 107 30W
Big Rapids ... 167 43 42N 85 27W
Big Sioux → ... 156 42 30N 96 25W
Big Spring ... 161 32 10N 101 25W
Big Stone Gap ... 165 36 52N 82 45W
Big Trout L. ... 153 53 40N 90 0W
Biggar, Canada ... 152 52 4N 108 0W
Biggar, U.K. ... 31 55 38N 3 31W
Bighorn → ... 163 46 9N 107 28W
Bighorn Mts. ... 163 44 30N 107 30W
Bihar ... 92 25 5N 85 40 E
Bihar □ ... 92 25 0N 86 0 E
Bijagós, Arquipélago dos ... 130 11 15N 16 10W
Bijapur ... 91 16 50N 75 55 E
Bijeljina ... 52 44 46N 19 17 E
Bikaner ... 89 28 2N 73 18 E
Bikin ... 75 46 50N 134 20 E
Bilaspur ... 92 22 2N 82 15 E
Bilauk Taungdan ... 94 13 0N 99 0 E
Bilbao ... 50 43 16N 2 56W
Billingham ... 29 54 36N 1 18W
Billings ... 163 45 43N 108 29W
Billiton Is. = Belitung ... 111 3 10S 107 50 E
Bilma ... 127 18 50N 13 30 E
Biloela ... 121 24 24S 150 31 E
Biloxi ... 169 30 24N 88 53W
Bina-Etawah ... 91 24 13N 78 14 E
Bīnālūd, Kūh-e ... 86 36 30N 58 30 E
Bindi Bindi ... 120 30 37S 116 22 E
Bingara ... 116 29 52S 150 36 E
Bingerville ... 130 5 18N 3 49W
Bingham ... 148 45 5N 69 50W
Binghamton ... 164 42 9N 75 54W
Binh Dinh = An Nhon ... 95 13 55N 109 7 E
Binnaway ... 116 31 28S 149 24 E
Binzert = Bizerte ... 127 37 15N 9 50 E
Bioko ... 131 3 30N 8 40 E
Bir Mogrein ... 126 25 10N 11 25W
Birchip ... 119 35 56S 142 55 E
Bird I. = Aves, I. de ... 181 15 45N 63 55W
Birdum ... 114 15 39S 133 13 E
Birkenhead ... 28 53 24N 3 1W
Birmingham, U.K. ... 24 52 30N 1 55W
Birmingham, U.S.A. ... 169 33 31N 86 50W
Birobidzhan ... 75 48 50N 132 50 E
Birr ... 35 53 7N 7 55W
Bisai ... 106 35 16N 136 44 E
Biscay, B. of ... 36 45 0N 2 0W
Biscostasing ... 150 47 18N 82 9W
Bishkek ... 71 42 54N 74 46 E
Bishop Auckland ... 28 54 40N 1 40W
Bishop's Stortford ... 25 51 52N 0 11 E
Bismarck ... 163 46 49N 100 49W
Bismarck Arch. ... 115 2 30S 150 0 E
Bissagos = Bijagós,
Arquipélago dos ... 130 11 15N 16 10W
Bissau ... 130 11 45N 15 45W
Bitola ... 52 41 5N 21 10 E
Bitolj = Bitola ... 52 41 5N 21 10 E
Bitterroot Range ... 162 46 0N 114 20W
Biu ... 131 10 40N 12 3 E
Biwa-Ko ... 106 35 15N 136 10 E

Biysk ... 71 52 40N 85 0 E
Bizen ... 109 34 43N 134 8 E
Bizerte ... 127 37 15N 9 50 E
Bjørnøya ... 13 74 30N 19 0 E
Black → = Da → ... 95 21 15N 105 20 E
Black Diamond ... 155 50 45N 114 14W
Black Forest = Schwarzwald ... 42 48 0N 8 0 E
Black Hills ... 163 44 0N 103 50W
Black Mts. ... 26 51 52N 3 5W
Black Sea ... 17 43 30N 35 0 E
Blackall ... 121 24 25S 145 45 E
Blackburn ... 28 53 44N 2 30W
Blackpool ... 28 53 48N 3 3W
Blackwater ... 121 23 35S 148 53 E
Blackwater →, Meath, Ireland ... 34 53 46N 7 0W
Blackwater →, Munster, Ireland ... 35 51 55N 7 50W
Blackwater →, U.K. ... 34 54 31N 6 35W
Blackwell ... 168 36 55N 97 20W
Blaenau Ffestiniog ... 26 53 0N 3 57W
Blagoveshchensk ... 75 50 20N 127 30 E
Blair Atholl ... 33 56 46N 3 50W
Blairmore ... 155 49 40N 114 25W
Blanc, Mont ... 37 45 48N 6 50 E
Blanca Peak ... 163 37 35N 105 29W
Blanche L. ... 118 29 15S 139 40 E
Blanco, C. ... 171 42 50N 124 40W
Blandford Forum ... 24 50 52N 2 10W
Blantyre ... 137 15 45S 35 0 E
Blarney ... 35 51 57N 8 35W
Blaydon ... 28 54 56N 1 47W
Blayney ... 117 33 32S 149 14 E
Blekinge län □ ... 61 56 20N 15 20 E
Blenheim ... 123 41 38S 173 57 E
Bletchley ... 25 51 59N 0 44W
Blida ... 127 36 30N 2 49 E
Blind River ... 150 46 10N 82 58W
Blitar ... 111 8 5S 112 11 E
Bloemfontein ... 137 29 6S 26 14 E
Blois ... 36 47 35N 1 20 E
Bloody Foreland ... 34 55 10N 8 18W
Bloomington, Ill., U.S.A. ... 166 40 27N 89 0W
Bloomington, Ind., U.S.A. ... 167 39 10N 86 30W
Bloomsburg ... 164 41 0N 76 30W
Blue Mts., Oreg., U.S.A. ... 171 45 15N 119 0W
Blue Mts., Pa., U.S.A. ... 164 40 30N 76 30W
Blue Nile = Nîl el Azraq → ... 129 15 38N 32 31 E
Blue Ridge Mts. ... 165 36 30N 80 15W
Bluefield ... 165 37 18N 81 14W
Bluefields ... 179 12 20N 83 50W
Bluestack, mt. ... 34 54 46N 8 5W
Bluff ... 123 46 37S 168 20 E
Blumenau ... 191 27 0S 49 0W
Blyth ... 28 55 8N 1 32W
Bo ... 130 7 55N 11 50W
Bo Hai ... 98 39 0N 120 0 E
Boa Vista ... 185 2 48N 60 30W
Boaco ... 179 12 29N 85 35W
Bobadah ... 116 32 19S 146 41 E
Bobcaygeon ... 151 44 33N 78 33W
Bobo-Dioulasso ... 130 11 8N 4 13W
Bobraomby, Tanjon' i ... 137 12 40S 49 10 E
Bobruysk ... 68 53 10N 29 15 E
Bôca do Acre ... 187 8 50S 67 27W
Boca Raton ... 170 26 21N 80 5W
Bocas del Toro ... 179 9 15N 82 20W
Bocholt ... 42 51 50N 6 35 E
Bochum ... 42 51 28N 7 12 E
Boden ... 67 65 50N 21 42 E
Bodensee ... 44 47 35N 9 25 E
Bodhan ... 91 18 40N 77 44 E
Bodmin ... 27 50 28N 4 44W
Bodmin Moor ... 27 50 33N 4 36W
Bodø ... 64 67 17N 14 24 E
Bogalusa ... 169 30 50N 89 55W
Boggabilla ... 116 28 36S 150 24 E
Boggabri ... 116 30 45S 150 0 E
Boggeragh Mts. ... 35 52 2N 8 55W
Bognor Regis ... 25 50 47N 0 40W
Bogong, Mt. ... 117 36 47S 147 17 E

Place	Page	Lat	N/S	Long	E/W
Bogor	111	6 36	S	106 48	E
Bogota	184	4 34	N	74 0	W
Boguchany	74	58 40	N	97 30	E
Bohain	38	49 59	N	3 28	E
Bohemian Forest = Böhmerwald	43	49 30	N	12 40	E
Böhmerwald	43	49 30	N	12 40	E
Bohol	112	9 50	N	124 10	E
Bohol Sea	112	9 0	N	124 0	E
Bohotleh	133	8 20	N	46 25	E
Boise	162	43 43	N	116 9	W
Boissevain	153	49 15	N	100 5	W
Boké	130	10 56	N	14 17	W
Bolan Pass	88	29 50	N	67 20	E
Bolaños, R. →•	175	21 12	N	104 5	W
Bolbec	38	49 30	N	0 30	E
Bolgatanga	130	10 44	N	0 53	W
Bolívar	190	36 15	S	60 53	W
Bolivia ■	187	17 6	S	64 0	W
Bollnäs	60	61 21	N	16 24	E
Bollon	116	28 2	S	147 29	E
Bologna	47	44 30	N	11 20	E
Boloven, Cao Nguyen	95	15 10	N	106 30	E
Bolsena, L. di	46	42 35	N	11 55	E
Bolshevik, Ostrov	72	78 30	N	102 0	E
Bolshoi Kavkas	70	42 50	N	44 0	E
Bolshoy Begichev, Ostrov	72	74 20	N	112 30	E
Bolsward	41	53 3	N	5 32	E
Bolton	28	53 35	N	2 26	W
Bolzano	47	46 30	N	11 20	E
Boma	134	5 50	S	13 4	E
Bombala	117	36 56	S	149 15	E
Bombay	91	18 55	N	72 50	E
Bomu →•	129	4 40	N	23 30	E
Bon, C.	127	37 1	N	11 2	E
Bonaire	181	12 10	N	68 15	W
Bonavista	149	48 40	N	53 5	W
Bonifacio, Bouches de	48	41 12	N	9 15	E
Bonn	42	50 43	N	7 6	E
Bonneval	39	48 11	N	1 24	E
Bonnie Rock	120	30 29	S	118 22	E
Bonny, Bight of	131	3 30	N	9 20	E
Bonnyville	152	54 20	N	110 45	W
Bonthe	130	7 30	N	12 33	W
Boonah	116	27 58	S	152 41	E
Boone	166	42 5	N	93 53	W
Boonville	167	38 3	N	87 13	W
Boorowa	117	34 28	S	148 44	E
Boothia, Gulf of	146	71 0	N	90 0	W
Boothia Pen.	145	71 0	N	94 0	W
Bootle	28	53 28	N	3 1	W
Bôr	129	6 10	N	31 40	E
Borås	60	57 43	N	12 56	E
Borāzjān	85	29 22	N	51 10	E
Bordeaux	36	44 50	N	0 36	W
Borders □	31	55 35	N	2 50	W
Bordertown	119	36 19	S	140 45	E
Bordj Omar Driss	127	28 10	N	6 40	E
Borger	161	35 40	N	101 20	W
Borja	186	4 20	S	77 40	W
Borlänge	60	60 29	N	15 26	E
Borneo	111	1 0	N	115 0	E
Bornholm	61	55 10	N	15 0	E
Borujerd	84	33 55	N	48 50	E
Borzya	74	50 24	N	116 31	E
Boscastle	27	50 42	N	4 42	W
Boshan	98	36 28	N	117 49	E
Bosna →•	52	45 4	N	18 29	E
Bosnia-Herzegovina ■	52	44 0	N	18 0	E
Bōsō-Hantō	107	35 20	N	140 20	E
Bosporus = Karadeniz Boğazı	80	41 10	N	29 10	E
Bossangoa	131	6 35	N	17 30	E
Bossembélé	131	5 25	N	17 40	E
Bossier City	168	32 28	N	93 48	W
Bosten Hu	100	41 55	N	87 40	E
Boston, U.K.	29	52 59	N	0 2	W
Boston, U.S.A.	164	42 20	N	71 0	W
Bothnia, G. of	67	63 0	N	20 0	E
Botletle →•	136	20 10	S	23 15	E
Botoşani	57	47 42	N	26 41	E
Botswana ■	136	22 0	S	24 0	E
Botucatu	188	22 55	S	48 30	W
Bou Djébéha	126	18 25	N	2 45	W
Bouaké	130	7 40	N	5 2	W
Bougie = Bejaia	127	36 42	N	5 2	E
Boulogne-sur-Mer	38	50 42	N	1 36	E
Bourbonnais	37	46 28	N	3 0	E
Bourem	130	17 0	N	0 24	W
Bourg-en-Bresse	37	46 13	N	5 12	E
Bourges	37	47 9	N	2 25	E
Bourgogne	37	47 0	N	4 30	E
Bourke	116	30 8	S	145 55	E
Bournemouth	24	50 43	N	1 53	W
Bousso	131	10 34	N	16 52	E
Bouvet I. = Bouvetøya	14	54 26	S	3 24	E
Bouvetøya	14	54 26	S	3 24	E
Bowen	121	20 0	S	148 16	E
Bowland, Forest of	28	54 0	N	2 30	W
Bowling Green, Ky., U.S.A.	169	37 0	N	86 25	W
Bowling Green, Ohio, U.S.A.	167	41 22	N	83 40	W
Bowling Green, C.	121	19 19	S	147 25	E
Bowmanville	151	43 55	N	78 41	W
Bowral	117	34 26	S	150 27	E
Boyle	34	53 58	N	8 19	W
Boyne →•	34	53 43	N	6 15	W
Boyne City	150	45 13	N	85 1	W
Boyup Brook	120	33 50	S	116 23	E
Bozeman	163	45 40	N	111 0	W
Bozen = Bolzano	47	46 30	N	11 20	E
Brač	52	43 20	N	16 40	E
Bracciano, L. di	46	42 8	N	12 11	E
Bracebridge	151	45 2	N	79 19	W
Bräcke	66	62 45	N	15 26	E
Brad	56	46 10	N	22 50	E
Bradenton	170	27 25	N	82 35	W
Bradford, U.K.	28	53 47	N	1 45	W
Bradford, U.S.A.	164	41 58	N	78 41	W
Braemar	33	57 2	N	3 20	W
Braga	50	41 35	N	8 25	W
Bragança, Brazil	188	1 0	S	47 2	W
Bragança, Portugal	50	41 48	N	6 50	W
Brahmanbaria	93	23 58	N	91 15	E
Brahmani →•	92	20 39	N	86 46	E
Brahmaputra →•	93	24 2	N	90 59	E
Braidwood	117	35 27	S	149 49	E
Brăila	57	45 19	N	27 59	E
Brainerd	156	46 20	N	94 10	W
Braintree	25	51 53	N	0 34	E
Brampton	151	43 45	N	79 45	W
Branco →•	185	1 20	S	61 50	W
Branco, Cabo	182	7 9	S	34 47	W
Brandenburg	43	52 24	N	12 33	E
Brandon	153	49 50	N	99 57	W
Brantford	151	43 10	N	80 15	W
Brasil, Planalto	188	18 0	S	46 30	W
Brasília	188	15 47	S	47 55	E
Braşov	57	45 38	N	25 35	E
Brassey, Banjaran	111	5 0	N	117 15	E
Brasstown Bald, Mt.	165	34 54	N	83 45	W
Bratislava	59	48 10	N	17 7	E
Bratsk	74	56 10	N	101 30	E
Brattleboro	164	42 53	N	72 37	W
Braunschweig	43	52 17	N	10 28	E
Brava	133	1 20	N	44 8	E
Bravo del Norte →•	174	25 57	N	97 9	W
Brawley	173	32 58	N	115 30	W
Bray	35	53 12	N	6 6	W
Brazil	167	39 32	N	87 8	W
Brazil ■	188	10 0	S	50 0	W
Brazilian Highlands = Brasil, Planalto	188	18 0	S	46 30	W
Brazos →•	168	28 53	N	95 23	W
Brazzaville	134	4 9	S	15 12	E
Brčko	52	44 54	N	18 46	E
Breadalbane	31	56 30	N	4 15	W
Bream Bay	122	35 56	S	174 28	E
Brecon	26	51 57	N	3 23	W
Brecon Beacons	26	51 53	N	3 27	W
Breda	40	51 35	N	4 45	E
Breiðafjörður	64	65 15	N	23 15	W
Bremen	42	53 4	N	8 47	E

Bremerhaven	**42**	53	34N	8	35 E
Bremerton	**171**	47	30N	122	38W
Brenham	**168**	30	5N	96	27W
Brentwood	**25**	51	37N	0	19 E
Bréscia	**46**	45	33N	10	13 E
Breslau = Wrocław	**58**	51	5N	17	5 E
Brest, France	**36**	48	24N	4	31W
Brest, U.S.S.R.	**68**	52	10N	23	40 E
Bretagne	**36**	48	0N	3	0W
Bretçu	**57**	46	7N	26	18 E
Breton Sd.	**169**	29	40N	89	12W
Brett, C.	**122**	35	10S	174	20 E
Brewer	**148**	44	43N	68	50W
Brewster	**171**	48	10N	119	51W
Brewton	**169**	31	9N	87	2W
Brezhnev = Naberezhnyye					
Chelny	**68**	55	42N	52	19 E
Briançon	**37**	44	54N	6	39 E
Bridgend	**27**	51	30N	3	35W
Bridgeport	**164**	41	12N	73	12W
Bridgeton	**164**	39	29N	75	10W
Bridgetown, Australia	**120**	33	58S	116	7 E
Bridgetown, Barbados	**180**	13	0N	59	30W
Bridgnorth	**24**	52	33N	2	25W
Bridgwater	**27**	51	7N	3	0W
Bridlington	**29**	54	6N	0	11W
Bridport	**27**	50	43N	2	45W
Brigham City	**163**	41	30N	112	1W
Bright	**117**	36	42S	146	56 E
Brighton, Australia	**119**	42	42S	147	16 E
Brighton, U.K.	**25**	50	50N	0	9W
Bríndisi	**49**	40	39N	17	55 E
Brisbane	**116**	27	25S	153	2 E
Bristol, U.K.	**27**	51	26N	2	35W
Bristol, Conn., U.S.A.	**164**	41	44N	72	57W
Bristol, Tenn., U.S.A.	**165**	36	36N	82	11W
Bristol B.	**142**	58	0N	160	0W
Bristol Channel	**27**	51	18N	4	30W
Bristow	**168**	35	55N	96	28W
British Columbia □	**154**	55	0N	125	15W
British Guiana = Guyana ■	**185**	5	0N	59	0W
British Honduras = Belize ■	**177**	17	0N	88	30W
British Isles	**18**	55	0N	4	0W
Brittany = Bretagne	**36**	48	0N	3	0W
Brive-la-Gaillarde	**36**	45	10N	1	32 E
Brlik	**71**	44	0N	74	5 E
Brno	**59**	49	10N	16	35 E
Broach = Bharuch	**91**	21	47N	73	0 E
Broad Law	**31**	55	30N	3	22W
Broad Sd.	**121**	22	0S	149	45 E
Broads, The	**29**	52	45N	1	30 E
Brochet	**145**	57	53N	101	40W
Brockton	**164**	42	8N	71	2W
Brockville	**151**	44	35N	75	41W
Brod	**52**	41	35N	21	17 E
Brodeur Pen.	**146**	72	30N	88	10W
Broken Hill = Kabwe	**135**	14	30S	28	29 E
Broken Hill	**118**	31	58S	141	29 E
Bromley	**25**	51	20N	0	5 E
Brookhaven	**169**	31	40N	90	25W
Brooks	**155**	50	35N	111	55W
Brooks Ra.	**142**	68	40N	147	0W
Brosna ⟶	**35**	53	8N	8	0W
Brough	**28**	54	32N	2	19W
Broughty Ferry	**31**	56	29N	2	50W
Brouwershaven	**40**	51	45N	3	55 E
Brownsville	**158**	25	56N	97	25W
Brownwood	**161**	31	45N	99	0W
Bruay-en-Artois	**38**	50	29N	2	33 E
Bruce, Mt.	**114**	22	37S	118	8 E
Bruce Rock	**120**	31	52S	118	8 E
Bruck an der Leitha	**45**	48	1N	16	47 E
Bruges = Brugge	**42**	51	13N	3	13 E
Brugge	**42**	51	13N	3	13 E
Brunei = Bandar Seri					
Begawan	**112**	4	52N	115	0 E
Brunei ■	**111**	4	50N	115	0 E
Bruno	**152**	52	20N	105	30W
Brunswick = Braunschweig	**43**	52	17N	10	28 E
Brunswick, Ga., U.S.A.	**170**	31	10N	81	30W
Brunswick, Maine, U.S.A.	**148**	43	53N	69	50W

Bruny I.	**119**	43	20S	147	15 E
Brussel	**42**	50	51N	4	21 E
Bruthen	**117**	37	42S	147	50 E
Bruton	**27**	51	6N	2	28W
Bryan, Ohio, U.S.A.	**167**	41	30N	84	30W
Bryan, Tex., U.S.A.	**168**	30	40N	96	27W
Bryan, Mt.	**119**	33	30S	139	0 E
Bryansk	**68**	53	13N	34	25 E
Brzeg	**58**	50	52N	17	30 E
Bucaramanga	**184**	7	0N	73	0W
Buchan	**33**	57	32N	2	8W
Buchan Ness	**33**	57	29N	1	48W
Buchanan	**130**	5	57N	10	2W
Buchans	**149**	48	50N	56	52W
Bucharest = Bucureşti	**57**	44	27N	26	10 E
Buckhannon	**165**	39	2N	80	10W
Buckhaven	**31**	56	10N	3	2W
Buckingham, Canada	**151**	45	37N	75	24W
Buckingham, U.K.	**25**	52	0N	0	59W
Buckingham □	**25**	51	50N	0	55W
Buckleboo	**118**	32	54S	136	12 E
Bucureşti	**57**	44	27N	26	10 E
Bucyrus	**167**	40	48N	83	0W
Budalin	**93**	22	20N	95	10 E
Budapest	**59**	47	29N	19	5 E
Budaun	**89**	28	5N	79	10 E
Bude	**27**	50	49N	4	33W
Budgewoi Lake	**117**	33	13S	151	34 E
Buenaventura, Colombia	**184**	3	53N	77	4W
Buenaventura, Mexico	**174**	29	51N	107	29W
Buenos Aires	**190**	34	30S	58	20W
Buffalo	**164**	42	55N	78	50W
Bug ⟶	**58**	52	31N	21	5 E
Buga	**184**	4	0N	76	15W
Bugun Shara	**100**	49	0N	104	0 E
Builth Wells	**26**	52	10N	3	26W
Buir Nur	**98**	47	50N	117	42 E
Bujumbura	**135**	3	16S	29	18 E
Bukachacha	**74**	52	55N	116	50 E
Bukavu	**23**	2	20S	28	52 E
Bukhara	**70**	39	48N	64	25 E
Bukit Mertajam	**96**	5	22N	100	28 E
Bukittinggi	**111**	0	20S	100	20 E
Bukoba	**135**	1	20S	31	49 E
Bukuru	**131**	9	42N	8	48 E
Bulahdelah	**117**	32	23S	152	13 E
Bulandshahr	**89**	28	28N	77	51 E
Bulawayo	**137**	20	7S	28	32 E
Bulgaria ■	**53**	42	35N	25	30 E
Bull Shoals L.	**168**	36	40N	93	5W
Bully-les-Mines	**38**	50	27N	2	44 E
Bulsar = Valsad	**91**	20	40N	72	58 E
Bulun	**72**	70	37N	127	30 E
Bunbury	**120**	33	20S	115	35 E
Buncrana	**34**	55	8N	7	28W
Bundaberg	**116**	24	54S	152	22 E
Bundi	**91**	25	30N	75	35 E
Bundoran	**34**	54	24N	8	17W
Bungo-Suidō	**109**	33	0N	132	15 E
Buorkhaya, Mys	**72**	71	50N	132	40 E
Bûr Sa'îd	**128**	31	16N	32	18 E
Bûr Sûdân	**129**	19	32N	37	9 E
Buraymî, Al Wāhāt al	**83**	24	10N	55	43 E
Burbank	**173**	34	9N	118	23W
Burdur	**80**	37	45N	30	22 E
Burdwan = Barddhaman	**92**	23	14N	87	39 E
Burgas	**53**	42	33N	27	29 E
Burgenland □	**45**	47	20N	16	20 E
Burgos	**50**	42	21N	3	41W
Burgundy = Bourgogne	**37**	47	0N	4	30 E
Burin	**149**	47	1N	55	14W
Burkina Faso ■	**130**	12	0N	1	0W
Burlington, Canada	**151**	43	18N	79	45W
Burlington, Iowa, U.S.A.	**166**	40	50N	91	5W
Burlington, N.C., U.S.A.	**165**	36	7N	79	27W
Burlington, N.J., U.S.A.	**164**	40	5N	74	50W
Burlington, Vt., U.S.A.	**151**	44	27N	73	14W
Burma ■	**93**	21	0N	96	30 E
Burnie	**119**	41	4S	145	56 E
Burnley	**28**	53	47N	2	15W
Burns	**171**	43	40N	119	4W

Name			
Burns Lake	154	54 20N	125 45W
Burra	119	33 40S	138 55 E
Bursa	80	40 15N	29 5 E
Burton-upon-Trent	28	52 48N	1 39W
Buru	113	3 30S	126 30 E
Burundi ■	135	3 15S	30 0 E
Bury	28	53 36N	2 19W
Bury St. Edmunds	25	52 15N	0 42 E
Buryat Rep. □	74	53 0N	110 0 E
Buskerud fylke □	60	60 13N	9 0 E
Busselton	120	33 42S	115 15 E
Bussum	40	52 16N	5 10 E
Bute	30	55 48N	5 2W
Butiaba	132	1 50N	31 20 E
Butler	164	40 52N	79 52W
Butte	163	46 0N	112 31W
Butterworth	96	5 24N	100 23 E
Butuan	112	8 57N	125 33 E
Butung	113	5 0S	122 45 E
Buxton	28	53 16N	1 54W
Buyaga	74	59 50N	127 0 E
Buzău	57	45 10N	26 50 E
Buzen	108	33 35N	131 5 E
Buzzards Bay	164	41 45N	70 38W
Bydgoszcz	58	53 10N	18 0 E
Byelorussia = Belorussia ■	68	53 30N	27 0 E
Bylot I.	146	73 13N	78 34W
Byrd Land	15	79 30S	125 0W
Byron Bay	116	28 43S	153 37 E
Byrranga, Gory	72	75 0N	100 0 E
Bytom	58	50 25N	18 54 E

C

Name			
Cabimas	184	10 23N	71 25W
Cabinda	134	5 33S	12 11 E
Cabinda □	134	5 0S	12 30 E
Cabo Pantoja	184	1 0S	75 10W
Cabonga, Réservoir	151	47 20N	76 40W
Caboolture	116	27 5S	152 58 E
Cabora Bassa Dam	137	15 20S	32 50 E
Caborca	174	30 40N	112 10W
Cabot Strait	149	47 15N	59 40W
Cabrera, I.	51	39 8N	2 57 E
Cabri	152	50 35N	108 25W
Čačak	52	43 54N	20 20 E
Cáceres	50	39 26N	6 23W
Cache Bay	151	46 22N	80 0W
Cachoeira	189	12 30S	39 0W
Cachoeira de Itapemirim	189	20 51S	41 7W
Cachoeira do Sul	191	30 3S	52 53W
Cader Idris	26	52 43N	3 56W
Cadibarrawirracanna, L.	118	28 52S	135 27 E
Cadillac, Canada	151	48 14N	78 23W
Cadillac, U.S.A.	167	44 16N	85 25W
Cádiz	50	36 30N	6 20W
Cádiz, G. de	50	36 40N	7 0W
Caen	36	49 10N	0 22W
Caernarfon	26	53 8N	4 17W
Caernarfon B.	26	53 4N	4 40W
Caernarvon = Caernarfon	26	53 8N	4 17W
Caerphilly	27	51 34N	3 13W
Cagayan de Oro	112	8 30N	124 40 E
Cágliari	48	39 15N	9 6 E
Caguas	180	18 14N	66 4W
Caha Mts.	35	51 45N	9 40W
Caher	35	52 23N	7 56W
Cahors	36	44 27N	1 27 E
Cahuapanas	186	5 15S	77 0W
Caibarién	178	22 30N	79 30W
Caicos Is.	180	21 40N	71 40W
Cairngorm Mts.	33	57 6N	3 42W
Cairns	121	16 57S	145 45 E
Cairo = El Qâhira	128	30 1N	31 14 E
Cairo	169	37 0N	89 10W
Cajamarca	186	7 5S	78 28W
Calabar	131	4 57N	8 20 E
Calabozo	184	9 0N	67 28W
Calábria □	49	39 24N	16 30 E
Calais, France	38	50 57N	1 56 E
Calais, U.S.A.	148	45 11N	67 20W
Calama, Brazil	187	8 0S	62 50W
Calama, Chile	190	22 30S	68 55W
Calamar	184	10 15N	74 55W
Calamian Group	112	11 50N	119 55 E
Calca	187	13 22S	72 0W
Calcutta	92	22 36N	88 24 E
Caldwell	171	43 45N	116 42W
Calgary	155	51 0N	114 10W
Cali	184	3 25N	76 35W
Calicut	90	11 15N	75 43 E
California □	172	37 25N	120 0W
California, Golfo de	174	28 0N	112 0W
Callander	31	56 15N	4 14W
Callao	186	12 0S	77 0W
Caloundra	116	26 45S	153 10 E
Caltanissetta	49	37 30N	14 3 E
Cam Lam	95	11 54N	109 10 E
Cam Ranh	95	11 54N	109 12 E
Camagüey	178	21 20N	78 0W
Camaná	186	16 30S	72 50W
Camargue	37	43 34N	4 34 E
Camarones	192	44 50S	65 40W
Cambay = Khambhat	91	22 23N	72 33 E
Cambodia ■	95	12 15N	105 0 E
Camborne	27	50 13N	5 18W
Cambrai	38	50 11N	3 14 E
Cambrian Mts.	26	52 25N	3 52W
Cambridge, Canada	151	43 23N	80 15W
Cambridge, N.Z.	122	37 54S	175 29 E
Cambridge, U.K.	25	52 13N	0 8 E
Cambridge, Mass., U.S.A.	164	42 20N	71 8W
Cambridge, Md., U.S.A.	164	38 33N	76 2W
Cambridge, Ohio, U.S.A.	167	40 1N	81 35W
Cambridge Bay	145	69 10N	105 0W
Cambridge Gulf	114	14 55S	128 15 E
Cambridgeshire □	25	52 12N	0 7 E
Camden, Ark., U.S.A.	168	33 40N	92 50W
Camden, N.J., U.S.A.	164	39 57N	75 7W
Camden, S.C., U.S.A.	165	34 17N	80 34W
Cameroon ■	131	6 0N	12 30 E
Cameroun, Mt.	131	4 13N	9 10 E
Cametá	188	2 12S	49 30W
Camiri	187	20 3S	63 31W
Camocim	189	2 55S	40 50W
Campagna	46	40 40N	15 5 E
Campania □	49	40 50N	14 45 E
Campbell I.	15	52 30S	169 0 E
Campbell River	154	50 5N	125 20W
Campbellton	148	47 57N	66 43W
Campbelltown, Australia	117	34 4S	150 49 E
Campbeltown, U.K.	30	57 34N	4 2W
Campeche	177	19 51N	90 32W
Campeche □	177	19 0N	90 30W
Campeche, B. de	177	20 0N	94 0W
Camperdown	119	38 14S	143 9 E
Camperville	153	51 59N	100 9W
Campina Grande	189	7 20S	35 47W
Campinas	188	22 50S	47 0W
Campo Grande	188	20 25S	54 40W
Campos	188	21 50S	41 20W
Camrose	155	53 0N	112 50W
Can Tho	95	10 2N	105 46 E
Canada ■	139	60 0N	100 0W
Cañada de Gómez	190	32 40S	61 30W
Canadian ➤	158	35 27N	95 3W
Çanakkale Boğazi	80	40 0N	26 0 E
Cananea	174	30 57N	110 18W
Canarias, Is.	126	28 30N	16 0W
Canary Is. = Canarias, Islas	126	28 30N	16 0W
Canaveral, C.	170	28 28N	80 31W
Canberra	117	35 15S	149 8 E
Candala	133	11 30N	49 58 E
Candia = Iráklion	55	35 20N	25 12 E
Canea = Khaniá	55	35 30N	24 4 E
Çankırı	80	40 40N	33 37 E
Canmore	155	51 7N	115 18W
Canna	32	57 3N	6 33W
Cannanore	90	11 53N	75 27 E

Cannes	37	43	32N	7	0 E
Cannock	28	52	42N	2	2W
Canora	152	51	40N	102	30W
Canowindra	117	33	35S	148	38 E
Canso	149	45	20N	61	0W
Cantabrian Mts. =					
Cantábrica, Cordillera	50	43	0N	5	10W
Cantábrica, Cordillera	50	43	0N	5	10W
Canterbury	25	51	17N	1	5 E
Canterbury □	123	43	45S	171	19 E
Canterbury Bight	123	44	16S	171	55 E
Canterbury Plains	123	43	55S	171	22 E
Canton = Guangzhou	99	23	5N	113	10 E
Canton, Ill., U.S.A.	166	40	32N	90	0W
Canton, Miss., U.S.A.	169	32	40N	90	1W
Canton, Ohio, U.S.A.	167	40	47N	81	22W
Canutama	185	6	30S	64	20W
Cap-Chat	148	49	6N	66	40W
Cap-de-la-Madeleine	151	46	22N	72	31W
Cap-Haïtien	180	19	40N	72	20W
Cape Barren I.	119	40	25S	148	15 E
Cape Breton I.	149	46	0N	60	30W
Cape Coast	130	5	5N	1	15W
Cape Dorset	146	64	14N	76	32W
Cape Fear →	165	34	30N	78	25W
Cape Girardeau	169	37	20N	89	30W
Cape May	164	39	1N	74	53W
Cape Montague	149	46	5N	62	25W
Cape Province □	136	32	0S	23	0 E
Cape Town	136	33	55S	18	22 E
Cape Verde Is. ■	9	17	10N	25	20W
Cape York Peninsula	115	12	0S	142	30 E
Caquetá →	184	1	15S	69	15W
Caracal	57	44	8N	24	22 E
Caracas	184	10	30N	66	55W
Caratinga	188	19	50S	42	10W
Carberry	153	49	50N	99	25W
Carbonara, C.	48	39	8N	9	30 E
Carbondale	166	37	45N	89	10W
Carbonear	149	47	42N	53	13W
Carcassonne	37	43	13N	2	20 E
Carcross	144	60	13N	134	45W
Cárdenas, Cuba	178	23	0N	81	30W
Cárdenas, Mexico	177	21	0N	99	40W
Cardiff	27	51	28N	3	11W
Cardigan	26	52	6N	4	41W
Cardigan B.	26	52	30N	4	30W
Cardston	155	49	15N	113	20W
Cardwell	121	18	14S	146	2 E
Caribbean Sea	181	15	0N	75	0W
Cariboo Mts.	155	53	0N	121	0W
Caribou	148	46	55N	68	0W
Caribou Mts.	145	59	12N	115	40W
Carinhanha	188	14	15S	44	46W
Carinthia = Kärnten □	45	46	52N	13	30 E
Carlisle, U.K.	28	54	54N	2	55W
Carlisle, U.S.A.	164	40	12N	77	10W
Carlow	35	52	50N	6	58W
Carlow □	35	52	43N	6	50W
Carlsbad, Calif., U.S.A.	173	33	11N	117	25W
Carlsbad, N. Mex., U.S.A.	161	32	20N	104	14W
Carlyle	152	49	40N	102	20W
Carmacks	144	62	5N	136	16W
Carman	153	49	30N	98	0W
Carmarthen	26	51	52N	4	20W
Carmarthen B.	27	51	40N	4	30W
Carnarvon	120	24	51S	113	42 E
Carnegie, L.	114	26	5S	122	30 E
Carniche, Alpi	47	46	36N	13	0 E
Carnsore Pt.	35	52	10N	6	20W
Caroline Is.	122	8	0N	150	0 E
Caroona	116	31	24S	150	26 E
Carpathians, Mts.	17	49	50N	21	0 E
Carpaţii Meridionali	57	45	30N	25	0 E
Carpentaria, G. of	115	14	0S	139	0 E
Carrara	46	44	5N	10	7 E
Carrick-on-Shannon	34	53	57N	8	7W
Carrick-on-Suir	35	52	22N	7	30W
Carrickfergus	34	54	43N	5	50W
Carrickmacross	34	54	0N	6	43W
Carroll	166	42	2N	94	55W
Carrollton	170	33	36N	85	5W
Carse of Gowrie	31	56	30N	3	10W
Carson City	172	39	12N	119	46W
Carstairs	31	55	42N	3	41W
Cartagena, Colombia	184	10	25N	75	33W
Cartagena, Spain	51	37	38N	0	59W
Cartago, Colombia	184	4	45N	75	55W
Cartago, Costa Rica	179	9	50N	85	52W
Cartersville	169	34	11N	84	48W
Carthage	168	37	10N	94	20W
Cartwright	147	53	41N	56	58W
Caruaru	189	8	15S	35	55W
Carúpano	185	10	39N	63	15W
Caruthersville	169	36	10N	89	40W
Carvin	38	50	30N	2	57 E
Casablanca	126	33	36N	7	36W
Casas Grandes	174	30	22N	107	57W
Cascade Ra.	171	47	0N	121	30W
Casilda	190	33	10S	61	10W
Casino	116	28	52S	153	3 E
Casiquiare →	184	2	1N	67	7W
Casma	186	9	30S	78	20W
Casper	163	42	52N	106	20W
Caspian Sea	70	43	0N	50	0 E
Cassiar Mts.	144	59	30N	130	30W
Castellón de la Plana	51	39	58N	0	3W
Castelsarrasin	36	44	2N	1	7 E
Casterton	119	37	30S	141	30 E
Castilla La Nueva	50	39	45N	3	20W
Castilla La Vieja	50	41	55N	4	0W
Castle Douglas	31	54	57N	3	57W
Castlebar	34	53	52N	9	17W
Castleblaney	34	54	7N	6	44W
Castlegar	155	49	20N	117	40W
Castlemaine	117	37	2S	144	12 E
Castlereagh	34	53	47N	8	30W
Castletown	28	58	35N	3	22W
Castletown Bearhaven	35	51	40N	9	54W
Castor	155	52	15N	111	50W
Castres	37	43	37N	2	13 E
Castricum	40	52	33N	4	40 E
Castries	180	14	0N	60	50W
Castro	192	42	30S	73	50W
Cat I.	178	24	30N	75	30W
Catacáos	186	5	20S	80	45W
Catalonia = Cataluña □	51	41	40N	1	15 E
Cataluña □	51	41	40N	1	15 E
Catamarca	190	28	30S	65	50W
Catanduanes	112	13	50N	124	20 E
Catánia	49	37	31N	15	4 E
Catanzaro	49	38	54N	16	38 E
Catoche, C.	177	21	35N	87	5W
Catskill Mts.	164	42	15N	74	15W
Cauca →	184	8	54N	74	28W
Caucasus Mts. = Bolshoi					
Kavkas	70	42	50N	44	0 E
Caudry	38	50	7N	3	22 E
Cauquenes	190	36	0S	72	22W
Cavaillon	37	43	50N	5	2 E
Cavan	34	54	0N	7	22W
Cawnpore = Kanpur	91	26	28N	80	20 E
Caxias	188	4	55S	43	20W
Caxias do Sul	191	29	10S	51	10W
Cayenne	185	5	0N	52	18W
Cayes, Les	180	18	15S	73	46W
Cayman Is.	178	19	40N	80	30W
Ceanannus Mor	34	53	42N	6	53W
Ceará = Fortaleza	189	3	45S	38	35W
Ceará □	189	5	0S	40	0W
Cebu	112	10	18N	123	54 E
Cedar →	166	41	17N	91	21W
Cedar City	162	37	41N	113	3W
Cedar Falls	166	42	39N	92	29W
Cedar L.	152	53	10N	100	0W
Cedar Rapids	166	42	0N	91	38W
Cedartown	169	34	1N	85	15W
Ceduna	118	32	7S	133	46 E
Cegléd	59	47	11N	19	47 E
Ceiba, La	179	15	40N	86	50W
Celaya	177	20	31N	100	37W
Celebes = Sulawesi □	113	2	0S	120	0 E

Name	Page	Lat	Long
Celebes Sea	113	3 0N	123 0 E
Center	168	31 50N	94 10W
Centerville	166	40 45N	92 57W
Central □	31	56 10N	4 30W
Central, Cordillera	184	5 0N	75 0W
Central African Republic ■	129	7 0N	20 0 E
Central Makran Range	88	26 30N	64 15 E
Central Russian Uplands	17	54 0N	36 0 E
Central Siberian Plateau	77	65 0N	105 0 E
Centralia	166	38 32N	89 5W
Cephalonia = Kefallinía	54	38 20N	20 30 E
Ceram = Seram	113	3 10S	129 0 E
Ceram Sea = Seram Sea	113	2 30S	128 30 E
Cerignola	49	41 17N	15 53 E
Cerigo = Kíthira	55	36 9N	23 0 E
Cerritos	177	22 26N	100 17W
Cesena	47	44 9N	12 14 E
Českomoravská Vrchovina	59	49 30N	15 40 E
Český Těšín	59	49 45N	18 39 E
Cessnock	117	32 50S	151 21 E
Cetinje	52	42 23N	18 59 E
Ceuta	126	35 52N	5 18W
Cévennes	37	44 10N	3 50 E
Ceylon = Sri Lanka ■	90	7 30N	80 50 E
Chachapoyas	186	6 15S	77 50W
Chachoengsao	95	13 42N	101 5 E
Chad ■	131	15 0N	17 15 E
Chad, L. = Tchad, L.	131	13 30N	14 30 E
Chadron	163	42 50N	103 0W
Chagos Arch.	76	6 0S	72 0 E
Chāh Bahār	85	25 20N	60 40 E
Chakradharpur	92	22 45N	85 40 E
Chala	186	15 48S	74 20W
Chalcis = Khalkís	55	38 27N	23 42 E
Chalhuanca	186	14 15S	73 15W
Chalisgaon	91	20 30N	75 10 E
Challapata	187	18 53S	66 50W
Chalon-sur-Saône	37	46 48N	4 50 E
Châlons-sur-Marne	37	46 58N	4 20 E
Chambal →	91	26 29N	79 15 E
Chambersburg	164	39 53N	77 41W
Chambéry	37	45 34N	5 55 E
Chamonix	37	45 55N	6 51 E
Champagne	37	49 0N	4 40 E
Champaign	167	40 8N	88 14W
Champlain, L.	151	44 30N	73 20W
Chañaral	190	26 23S	70 40W
Chandigarh	89	30 43N	76 47 E
Chandler	118	27 0S	133 19 E
Chang Jiang →	99	31 48N	121 10 E
Changchiak'ou = Zhangjiakou	98	40 48N	114 55 E
Changchun	98	43 57N	125 17 E
Changde	99	29 4N	111 35 E
Changhai = Shanghai	99	31 15N	121 26 E
Changsha	99	28 12N	113 0 E
Changzhi	98	36 10N	113 6 E
Changzhou	99	31 47N	119 58 E
Channel Is.	36	49 30N	2 40W
Channel-Port aux Basques	149	47 30N	59 9W
Chanthaburi	95	12 38N	102 12 E
Chantilly	39	49 12N	2 29 E
Chanute	166	37 45N	95 25W
Chao Phraya →	94	13 32N	100 36 E
Ch'aoan	99	23 41N	116 33 E
Chapala, L. de	175	20 15N	103 0W
Chapayevsk	68	53 0N	49 40 E
Chapel Hill	165	35 53N	79 3W
Chapleau	150	47 50N	83 24W
Charagua	187	19 45S	63 10W
Charaña	187	17 30S	69 25W
Chard	27	50 52N	2 59W
Chardzhou	70	39 6N	63 34 E
Chari →	131	12 58N	14 31 E
Chārīkār	87	35 0N	69 10 E
Charleroi	42	50 24N	4 27 E
Charles, C.	165	37 10N	75 59W
Charles City	166	43 2N	92 41W
Charleston, S.C., U.S.A.	170	32 47N	79 56W
Charleston, W. Va., U.S.A.	165	38 24N	81 36W
Charleville = Rath Luirc	35	52 21N	8 40W
Charleville	116	26 24S	146 15 E
Charleville-Mézières	37	49 44N	4 40 E
Charlotte, Mich., U.S.A.	167	42 36N	84 48W
Charlotte, N.C., U.S.A.	165	35 16N	80 46W
Charlotte Amalie	180	18 22N	64 56W
Charlotte Harbor	170	26 58N	82 4W
Charlottenburg	43	52 31N	13 15 E
Charlottesville	165	38 1N	78 30W
Charlottetown	149	46 14N	63 8W
Charlton, Australia	117	36 16S	143 24 E
Charlton, Ont., U.S.A.	166	40 59N	93 20W
Charters Towers	121	20 5S	146 13 E
Chartres	39	48 29N	1 30 E
Chascomús	191	35 30S	58 0W
Château-du-Loir	39	47 40N	0 25 E
Château-Thierry	39	49 3N	3 20 E
Châteaubriant	36	47 43N	1 23W
Châteaudun	39	48 3N	1 20 E
Châteauroux	37	46 50N	1 40 E
Châtellerault	36	46 50N	0 30 E
Chatham, N.B., Canada	148	47 2N	65 28W
Chatham, Ont., Canada	141	42 24N	82 11W
Chatham, U.K.	25	51 22N	0 32 E
Chatta-Hantō	106	34 45N	136 55 E
Chattahoochee →	170	30 43N	84 51W
Chattanooga	169	35 2N	85 17W
Chaumont	37	48 7N	5 8 E
Chauny	38	49 37N	3 12 E
Cheboksary	68	56 8N	47 12 E
Cheboygan	150	45 38N	84 29W
Checheno-Ingush Rep. □	70	43 30N	45 29 E
Chegdomyn	75	51 7N	133 1 E
Chegga	126	25 27N	5 40W
Chehalis	171	46 44N	122 59W
Cheju Do	99	33 29N	126 34 E
Chekiang = Zhejiang □	99	29 0N	120 0 E
Chelforó	190	39 0S	66 33W
Chelkar Tengiz, Solonchak	70	48 0N	62 30 E
Chełm	58	51 8N	23 30 E
Chełmża	58	53 10N	18 39 E
Cheltenham	24	51 55N	2 5W
Chelyabinsk	71	55 10N	61 24 E
Chemainus	154	48 55N	123 42W
Chemnitz	43	50 50N	12 55 E
Chemult	171	43 14N	121 47W
Chen, Gora	73	65 16N	141 50 E
Chencha	132	6 15N	37 32 E
Chenchiang = Zhenjiang	99	32 11N	119 26 E
Chengchou = Zhengzhou	99	34 45N	113 34 E
Chengde	98	40 59N	117 58 E
Chengdu	99	30 38N	104 2 E
Ch'engtu = Chengdu	99	30 38N	104 2 E
Cheo Reo	95	13 25N	108 28 E
Chepstow	27	51 38N	2 40W
Cher →	36	47 21N	0 29 E
Cherbourg	36	49 39N	1 40W
Cheremkhovo	74	53 8N	103 1 E
Cherepovets	68	59 5N	37 55 E
Cherkassy	68	49 27N	32 4 E
Chernigov	68	51 28N	31 20 E
Chernovtsy	68	48 15N	25 52 E
Chernoye	72	70 30N	89 10 E
Cherokee	166	42 40N	95 30W
Cherrapunji	93	25 17N	91 47 E
Cherskiy	73	68 45N	161 18 E
Cherskogo Khrebet	73	65 0N	143 0 E
Cherwell →	25	51 46N	1 18W
Chesapeake	165	36 43N	76 15W
Chesapeake Bay	165	38 0N	76 12W
Cheshire □	28	53 14N	2 30W
Cheshskaya Guba	69	67 20N	47 0 E
Chester, U.K.	28	53 12N	2 53W
Chester, Pa., U.S.A.	164	39 54N	75 20W
Chester, S.C., U.S.A.	165	34 44N	81 13W
Chesterfield	28	53 14N	1 26W
Chesterfield Inlet	145	63 30N	90 45W
Chetumal	177	18 30N	88 18W
Cheviot, The	31	55 29N	2 8W
Cheviot Hills	31	55 20N	2 30W
Chew Bahir	132	4 40N	36 50 E

Name	Page	Lat	N/S	Long	E/W
Cheyenne	163	41	9N	104	49W
Cheyenne ~►	163	44	40N	101	15W
Chhapra	92	25	48N	84	44 E
Chiamussu = Jiamusi	98	46	40N	130	26 E
Chiang Mai	94	18	47N	98	59 E
Chiapa ~►	177	16	42N	93	0W
Chiapas □	177	16	30N	92	30W
Chiba	107	35	30N	140	7 E
Chibougamau	151	49	56N	74	24W
Chicago	167	41	53N	87	40W
Chicago Heights	167	41	29N	87	37W
Chicagof I.	143	58	0N	136	0W
Chichester	25	50	50N	0	47W
Chichibu	107	36	5N	139	10 E
Ch'ich'ihaerh = Qiqihar	98	47	26N	124	0 E
Chiclayo	186	6	42S	79	50W
Chico	172	39	45N	121	54W
Chicopee	164	42	6N	72	37W
Chicoutimi	148	48	28N	71	5W
Chidambaram	90	11	20N	79	45 E
Chidley C.	146	60	23N	64	26W
Chigasaki	107	35	19N	139	24 E
Chihli, G. of = Bo Hai	98	39	0N	120	0 E
Chihuahua	174	28	38N	106	5W
Chihuahua □	174	28	30N	106	0W
Chikugo	108	33	14N	130	28 E
Chilapa	177	17	40N	99	11W
Childress	161	34	30N	100	15W
Chile ■	190	35	0S	72	0W
Chilin = Jilin	98	43	44N	126	30 E
Chilka L.	92	19	40N	85	25 E
Chillán	190	36	40S	72	10W
Chillicothe, Mo., U.S.A.	166	39	45N	93	30W
Chillicothe, Ohio, U.S.A.	167	39	20N	82	58W
Chilliwack	154	49	10N	121	54W
Chiloé, I. de	192	42	30S	73	50W
Chilpancingo	177	17	30N	99	30W
Chiltern Hills	25	51	44N	0	42W
Chimborazo	184	1	29S	78	55W
Chimbote	186	9	0S	78	35W
Chimkent	71	42	18N	69	36 E
Chin □	93	22	0N	93	0 E
China ■	79	30	0N	110	0 E
Chinan = Jinan	98	36	38N	117	1 E
Chinandega	179	12	35N	87	12W
Chincha Alta	186	13	25S	76	7W
Chinchilla	116	26	45S	150	38 E
Chinchou = Jinzhou	98	41	5N	121	3 E
Chindwin ~►	93	21	26N	95	15 E
Ch'ingtao = Qingdao	98	36	5N	120	20 E
Chinju	98	35	12N	128	2 E
Chinnampo	98	38	52N	125	10 E
Chino	107	35	59N	138	9 E
Chinon	36	47	10N	0	15 E
Chippenham	24	51	27N	2	7W
Chippewa Falls	166	44	55N	91	22W
Chiquián	186	10	10S	77	0W
Chiquimula	177	14	51N	89	37W
Chiquinquira	184	5	37N	73	50W
Chirala	90	15	50N	80	26 E
Chirchik	71	41	29N	69	35 E
Chita	74	52	0N	113	35 E
Chitral	89	35	50N	71	56 E
Chitré	179	7	59N	80	27W
Chittagong	93	22	19N	91	48 E
Chittagong □	93	24	5N	91	0 E
Chivilcoy	190	34	55S	60	0W
Chkalov = Orenburg	70	51	45N	55	6 E
Chōfu	107	35	39N	120	33 E
Choix	174	26	43N	108	17W
Chojnice	58	53	42N	17	32 E
Cholet	36	47	4N	0	52W
Choluteca	179	13	20N	87	14W
Chon Buri	95	13	21N	101	1 E
Chongjin	98	41	47N	129	50 E
Chŏngju	98	36	39N	127	27 E
Chongqing	99	29	35N	106	25 E
Chŏnju	98	35	50N	127	4 E
Chonos, Arch. de los	192	45	0S	75	0W
Chorley	28	53	39N	2	39W
Chorzów	58	50	18N	18	57 E
Chōshi	107	35	45N	140	51 E
Christchurch, N.Z.	123	43	33S	172	47 E
Christchurch, U.K.	24	50	44N	1	33W
Christianshåb	147	68	50N	51	18W
Christmas I. = Kiritimati	123	1	58N	157	27W
Christmas I.	111	10	30S	105	40 E
Ch'uanchou = Quanzhou	99	24	55N	118	34 E
Chūbu □	106	36	45N	137	30 E
Chubut ~►	192	43	20S	65	5W
Chūgoku □	109	35	0N	133	0 E
Chūgoku-Sanchi	109	35	0N	133	0 E
Chukotskiy Khrebet	73	68	0N	175	0 E
Chukotskoye More	73	68	0N	175	0W
Chula Vista	173	32	39N	117	8W
Chulman	74	56	52N	124	52 E
Chulucanas	186	5	8S	80	10W
Chumikan	75	54	40N	135	10 E
Chumphon	94	10	35N	99	14 E
Chunchōn	98	37	58N	127	44 E
Chungking = Chongqing	99	29	35N	106	25 E
Chuquibamba	186	15	47S	72	44W
Chur	44	46	52N	9	32 E
Churchill ~►, Man., Canada	143	58	47N	94	12W
Churchill ~►, Nfld., Canada	147	53	19N	60	10W
Churchill, C.	143	58	46N	93	12W
Churchill Falls	147	53	36N	64	19W
Churchill Pk.	144	58	10N	125	10W
Churu	89	28	20N	74	50 E
Chuvash Rep.□	68	55	30N	47	0 E
Chuxiong	101	25	2N	101	28 E
Cicero	167	41	48N	87	48W
Ciego de Avila	178	21	50N	78	50W
Ciénaga	184	11	1N	74	15W
Cienfuegos	178	22	10N	80	30W
Cimarron ~►	161	36	10N	96	17W
Cincinnati	167	39	10N	84	26W
Cinto, Mt.	36	42	24N	8	54 E
Ciotat, La	37	43	12N	5	36 E
Circle	142	65	50N	144	10W
Circleville	167	39	35N	82	57W
Cirebon	111	6	45S	108	32 E
Cirencester	24	51	43N	1	59W
Citlaltépeti, Volcán	177	19	1N	97	16W
Ciudad Acuña	174	29	20N	100	58W
Ciudad Bolivar	185	8	5N	63	36W
Ciudad Camargo, Chihuahua, Mexico	174	27	40N	105	10W
Ciudad Camargo, Tamaulipas, Mexico	176	26	19N	98	50W
Ciudad de Valles	177	21	59N	99	1W
Ciudad del Carmen	177	18	38N	91	50W
Ciudad Guayana	185	8	0N	62	30W
Ciudad Guzmán	175	19	41N	103	29W
Ciudad Juárez	174	31	44N	106	29W
Ciudad Madero	177	22	16N	97	50W
Ciudad Mante	177	22	44N	98	57W
Ciudad Obregón	174	27	29N	109	56W
Ciudad Real	50	38	59N	3	55W
Ciudad Rodrigo	50	40	35N	6	32W
Ciudad Trujillo = Santo Domingo	180	18	30N	64	54W
Ciudad Victoria	177	23	44N	99	8W
Çivril	80	38	20N	29	43 E
Cizre	81	37	19N	42	10 E
Clare	119	33	50S	138	37 E
Clare □	35	52	20N	9	0W
Clare ~►	35	53	22N	9	5W
Clare I.	34	53	48N	10	0W
Claremont	164	43	23N	72	20W
Claremore	168	36	40N	95	37W
Claremorris	34	53	45N	9	0W
Claresholm	155	50	0N	113	33W
Clark Fork ~►	162	48	9N	116	15W
Clarksburg	164	39	18N	80	21W
Clarksdale	169	34	12N	90	33W
Clarkston	171	46	28N	117	2W
Clarksville	169	36	32N	87	20W
Clear, C.	20	51	26N	9	30W
Clearwater, Canada	155	51	38N	120	2W
Clearwater, U.S.A.	170	27	58N	82	45W
Cleburne	168	32	18N	97	25W

Clee Hills 24 52 26N 2 35W
Cleethorpes 29 53 33N 0 2W
Cleeve Hill 24 51 54N 2 0W
Clermont, Australia .... 121 22 49S 147 39 E
Clermont, France .... 39 49 23N 2 24 E
Clermont-Ferrand .... 37 45 46N 3 4 E
Clevedon 27 51 26N 2 52W
Cleveland, Miss., U.S.A. ... 169 33 43N 90 43W
Cleveland, Ohio, U.S.A. 167 41 28N 81 43W
Cleveland, Tenn., U.S.A. ... 169 35 9N 84 52W
Cleveland, Tex., U.S.A. 169 30 18N 95 0W
Cleveland □ .... 29 54 35N 1 8 E
Cleveleys 28 53 52N 3 3W
Clew B. 34 53 54N 9 50W
Clifton Beach .... 121 16 46S 145 39 E
Clifton Forge 165 37 49N 79 51W
Clinton, Canada 150 43 37N 81 32W
Clinton, Iowa, U.S.A. 166 41 50N 90 12W
Clinton, Mass., U.S.A. 164 42 26N 71 40W
Clinton, Mo., U.S.A. 166 38 20N 93 46W
Clinton, Okla., U.S.A. 161 35 30N 99 0W
Clinton, S.C., U.S.A. 165 34 30N 81 54W
Clinton Colden L. 145 63 58N 107 27W
Clonakilty 35 51 37N 8 53W
Cloncurry .... 115 20 40S 140 28 E
Clones 34 54 10N 7 13W
Clonmel 35 52 22N 7 42W
Clovis 161 34 20N 103 10W
Cluj-Napoca .... 56 46 47N 23 38 E
Clunes .... 117 37 20S 143 45 E
Clwyd □ 26 53 5N 3 20W
Clyde → 31 55 56N 4 29W
Clyde, Firth of 30 55 20N 5 0W
Clydebank 31 55 54N 4 25W
Coahuila □ 174 27 20N 102 0W
Coaldale 155 49 45N 112 35W
Coalinga 173 36 10N 120 21W
Coalville 29 52 43N 1 21W
Coast Mts. 144 55 0N 129 0W
Coast Ranges 173 41 0N 123 0W
Coatbridge 31 55 52N 4 2W
Coatepeque 177 14 46N 91 55W
Coats I. 146 62 30N 83 0W
Coats Land 14 77 0S 25 0W
Coatzacoalcos 177 18 9N 94 25W
Cobalt 151 47 25N 79 42W
Cobán 177 15 30N 90 21W
Cobar .... 116 31 27S 145 48 E
Cóbh 35 51 50N 8 18W
Cobham .... 118 30 18S 142 7 E
Cobourg 151 43 58N 78 10W
Cobram .... 117 35 54S 145 40 E
Cocanada = Kakinada ..... 92 16 57N 82 11 E
Cochabamba 187 17 26S 66 10W
Cochin China = Nam-Phan . 95 10 30N 106 0 E
Cochran 170 32 25N 83 23W
Cochrane 151 49 0N 81 0W
Cockburn, Canal 192 54 30S 72 0W
Coco → 179 15 0N 83 8W
Coco Chan. .... 94 13 50N 93 25 E
Cocos Is. .... 111 12 10S 96 55 E
Cod, C. 164 42 8N 70 10W
Codajás 185 3 55S 62 0W
Codó 185 4 30S 43 55W
Cœur d'Alene 171 47 45N 116 51W
Coffs Harbour .... 116 30 16S 153 5 E
Cohoes 164 42 47N 73 42W
Cohuna .... 117 35 45S 144 15 E
Coiba, I. 179 7 30N 81 40W
Coihaique 192 45 30S 71 45W
Coimbatore .... 90 11 2N 76 59 E
Coimbra 50 40 15N 8 27W
Cojimies 184 0 20N 80 0W
Cojutepeque 177 13 41N 88 54W
Colac .... 117 38 21S 143 35 E
Colchester .... 25 51 54N 0 55 E
Coldstream 31 55 39N 2 14W
Coleman 155 49 40N 114 30W
Coleraine, Australia ...... 119 37 36S 141 40 E
Coleraine, U.K. 34 55 8N 6 40W
Colima 175 19 14N 103 43W

Colima □ 175 19 10N 104 0W
Coll 30 56 40N 6 35W
College Park 170 33 42N 84 27W
Collie .... 120 33 22S 116 8 E
Collingwood 151 44 29N 80 13W
Collinsville .... 121 20 30S 147 56 E
Collooney 34 54 11N 8 28W
Colmar .... 37 48 5N 7 20 E
Colne 28 53 51N 2 11W
Cologne = Köln .... 42 50 56N 6 58 E
Colomb-Béchar = Béchar .. 127 31 38N 2 18W
Colômbia 188 20 10S 48 40W
Colombia ■ 184 3 45N 73 0W
Colombo .... 90 6 56N 79 58 E
Colón, Cuba 178 22 42N 80 54W
Colón, Panama 179 9 20N 79 54W
Colonia 191 34 25S 57 50W
Colonsay 30 56 4N 6 12W
Colorado □ 163 37 40N 106 0W
Colorado →, Argentina ... 190 39 50S 62 8W
Colorado →, Calif., U.S.A. 173 34 45N 114 40W
Colorado →, Tex., U.S.A. . 161 28 36N 95 58W
Colorado Desert 160 34 20N 116 0W
Colorado Plateau 161 36 40N 110 30W
Colorado Springs 163 38 55N 104 50W
Columbia, Miss., U.S.A. 169 31 16N 89 50W
Columbia, Mo., U.S.A. 166 38 58N 92 20W
Columbia, S.C., U.S.A. 165 34 0N 81 0W
Columbia, Tenn., U.S.A. 169 35 40N 87 0W
Columbia → 171 46 15N 124 5W
Columbia, District of □ 164 38 55N 77 0W
Columbia Basin 171 47 30N 118 30W
Columbretes, Is. .... 51 39 50N 0 50 E
Columbus, Ga., U.S.A. 170 32 30N 84 58W
Columbus, Ind., U.S.A. 167 39 14N 85 55W
Columbus, Miss., U.S.A. ... 169 33 30N 88 26W
Columbus, Ohio, U.S.A. 167 39 57N 83 1W
Colwyn Bay 26 53 17N 3 44W
Comeragh Mts. 35 52 17N 7 35W
Comilla .... 93 23 28N 91 10 E
Comitán 177 16 18N 92 9W
Committee B. 146 68 30N 86 30W
Communism Pk. =
 Kommunizma, Pik .... 71 39 0N 72 2 E
Como .... 46 45 48N 9 5 E
Como, L. di .... 46 46 5N 9 17 E
Comodoro Rivadavia 192 45 50S 67 40W
Comorin, C. .... 90 8 3N 77 40 E
Comoro Is. ■ .... 125 12 10S 44 15 E
Comox 154 49 42N 124 55W
Compiègne .... 38 49 24N 2 50 E
Côn Dao .... 95 8 45N 106 45 E
Conakry 130 9 29N 13 49W
Conceição da Barra 189 18 35S 39 45W
Concepción, Argentina ... 191 27 20S 65 35W
Concepción, Chile 190 36 50S 73 0W
Concepción, Est. de 192 50 30S 74 55W
Concepción del Oro 174 24 38N 101 25W
Concepción del Uruguay .. 190 32 35S 58 20W
Conchos, R. → 174 29 35N 104 25W
Concord, Calif., U.S.A. 172 37 59N 122 2W
Concord, N.C., U.S.A. 165 35 28N 80 35W
Concord, N.H., U.S.A. 164 43 12N 71 30W
Concordia, Argentina 190 31 20S 58 2W
Concordia, U.S.A. 161 39 35N 97 40W
Condamine .... 155 26 56S 150 9 E
Condé .... 38 50 26N 3 34 E
Condobolin .... 117 33 4S 147 6 E
Congleton 28 53 10N 2 12W
Congo = Zaïre → .... 134 6 4S 12 24 E
Congo (Kinshasa) = Zaïre ■ 134 3 0S 23 0 E
Congo ■ .... 134 1 0S 16 0 E
Congo Basin .... 124 0 10S 24 30 E
Conjeeveram = Kanchipuram 90 12 52N 79 45 E
Connacht 34 53 23N 8 40W
Conneaut 164 41 55N 80 32W
Connecticut □ 164 41 40N 72 40W
Connecticut → 157 41 17N 72 21W
Connemara 34 53 29N 9 45W
Connors Ra. .... 121 21 40S 149 10 E
Consett 28 54 52N 1 50W

212 Constance

Name	Page	Lat	N/S	Long	E/W
Constance = Konstanz	44	47 39	N	9 10	E
Constance, L. = Bodensee	44	47 35	N	9 25	E
Constanța	57	44 14	N	28 38	E
Constantine	127	36 25	N	6 42	E
Contamana	186	7 19	S	74 55	W
Conway = Conwy	26	53 17	N	3 50	W
Conway = Conwy →	26	53 18	N	3 50	W
Conway, N.H., U.S.A.	148	43 58	N	71 8	W
Conway, S.C., U.S.A.	165	33 49	N	79 2	W
Conwy	26	53 17	N	3 50	W
Conwy →	26	53 18	N	3 50	W
Cook, Mt.	123	43 36	S	170 9	E
Cook Inlet	142	59 0	N	151 0	W
Cook Is.	123	17 0	S	160 0	W
Cook Strait	123	41 15	S	174 29	E
Cookeville	169	36 12	N	85 30	W
Cookstown	34	54 40	N	6 43	W
Coolah	116	31 48	S	149 41	E
Coolamon	117	34 46	S	147 8	E
Coolangatta	116	28 11	S	153 29	E
Coolgardie	120	30 55	S	121 8	E
Cooma	117	36 12	S	149 8	E
Coonabarabran	116	31 14	S	149 18	E
Coonamble	116	30 56	S	148 27	E
Cooper Cr. →	118	12 7	S	132 41	E
Coorong, The	119	35 50	S	139 20	E
Coorow	120	29 53	S	116 2	E
Coos Bay	171	43 26	N	124 7	W
Cootamundra	117	34 36	S	148 1	E
Copenhagen = København	61	55 41	N	12 34	E
Copiapó	190	27 30	S	70 20	W
Copper Center	142	62 10	N	145 25	W
Coppermine	145	67 50	N	115 5	W
Coppermine →	145	67 49	N	116 4	W
Coquilhatville = Mbandaka	134	0 1	N	18 18	E
Coquimbo	190	30 0	S	71 20	W
Coracora	186	15 5	S	73 45	W
Coral Gables	170	25 45	N	80 16	W
Coral Harbour	146	64 8	N	83 10	W
Coral Sea	121	15 0	S	150 0	E
Corbeil-Essonnes	39	48 36	N	2 26	E
Corbin	165	37 0	N	84 3	W
Corby	25	52 29	N	0 41	W
Cordele	170	31 55	N	83 49	W
Córdoba, Argentina	190	31 20	S	64 10	W
Córdoba, Mexico	177	18 53	N	96 56	W
Córdoba, Spain	50	37 50	N	4 50	W
Córdoba, Sierra de	190	31 10	S	64 25	W
Cordova	142	60 36	N	145 45	W
Corfu = Kérkira	54	39 38	N	19 50	E
Corinth = Kórinthos	54	37 56	N	22 55	E
Corinth	169	34 54	N	88 30	W
Corinth, G. of = Korinthiakós Kólpos	54	38 16	N	22 30	E
Corinto, Brazil	188	18 20	S	44 30	W
Corinto, Nic.	179	12 30	N	87 10	W
Cork	35	51 54	N	8 30	W
Cork □	35	51 50	N	8 50	W
Çorlu	80	41 11	N	27 49	E
Corn Is. = Maíz, Islas del	179	12 15	N	83 4	W
Corner Brook	140	48 57	N	57 58	W
Cornwall	151	45 2	N	74 44	W
Cornwall □	27	50 26	N	4 40	W
Coro	184	11 25	N	69 41	W
Coroatá	188	4 8	S	44 0	W
Corocoro	187	17 15	S	68 28	W
Coroico	187	16 0	S	67 50	W
Coromandel Coast	90	12 30	N	81 0	E
Corona	173	33 49	N	117 36	W
Coronado	173	32 45	N	117 9	W
Coronation Gulf	145	68 25	N	110 0	W
Coronel	190	37 0	S	73 10	W
Coronel Pringles	190	38 0	S	61 30	W
Corowa	117	35 58	S	146 21	E
Corozal	177	9 19	N	75 18	W
Corpus Christi	161	27 50	N	97 28	W
Corrib, L.	34	53 5	N	9 10	W
Corrientes	190	27 30	S	58 45	W
Corrientes, C., Colombia	184	5 30	N	77 34	W
Corrientes, C., Cuba	178	21 43	N	84 30	W
Corrientes, C., Mexico	175	20 25	N	105 42	W
Corrigin	120	32 20	S	117 53	E
Corse	36	42 0	N	9 0	E
Corsica = Corse	36	42 0	N	9 0	E
Corsicana	168	32 5	N	96 30	W
Cortez	163	37 24	N	108 35	W
Cortland	164	42 35	N	76 11	W
Çorum	80	40 30	N	34 57	E
Corumbá	187	19 0	S	57 30	W
Coruña, La	50	43 20	N	8 25	W
Corunna = Coruña, La	50	43 20	N	8 25	W
Corvallis	171	44 36	N	123 15	W
Cosamaloapan	177	18 23	N	95 50	W
Cosenza	49	39 17	N	16 14	E
Coshocton	167	40 17	N	81 51	W
Costa Blanca	51	38 25	N	0 10	W
Costa Brava	51	41 30	N	3 0	E
Costa del Sol	50	36 30	N	4 30	W
Costa Dorada	51	40 45	N	1 15	E
Costa Rica ■	179	10 0	N	84 0	W
Cotagaita	187	20 45	S	65 40	W
Côte d'Or	37	47 10	N	4 50	E
Coteau des Prairies	156	44 30	N	97 0	W
Cotonou	131	6 20	N	2 25	E
Cotopaxi, Vol.	184	0 40	S	78 30	W
Cotswold Hills	24	51 42	N	2 10	W
Cottbus	43	51 44	N	14 20	E
Coulommiers	39	48 50	N	3 3	E
Council	142	64 55	N	163 45	W
Council Bluffs	166	41 20	N	95 50	W
Courantyne →	185	5 55	N	57 5	W
Courtrai = Kortrijk	42	50 50	N	3 17	E
Coventry	24	52 25	N	1 31	W
Covington, Ga., U.S.A.	170	33 36	N	83 50	W
Covington, Ky., U.S.A.	167	39 5	N	84 30	W
Cowdenbeath	31	56 7	N	3 20	W
Cowes	25	50 45	N	1 18	W
Cowra	117	33 49	S	148 42	E
Coxim	188	18 30	S	54 55	W
Cracow = Kraków	58	50 4	N	19 57	E
Craigavon = Lurgan	34	54 28	N	6 20	W
Craiova	57	44 21	N	23 48	E
Cranbrook, Australia	120	34 18	S	117 33	E
Cranbrook, Canada	155	49 30	N	115 46	W
Crateús	189	5 10	S	40 39	W
Crato	189	7 10	S	39 25	W
Crawfordsville	167	40 2	N	86 51	W
Crawley	24	51 7	N	0 10	W
Creil	39	49 15	N	2 34	E
Cremona	46	45 8	N	10 2	E
Crépy-en-Valois	39	49 14	N	2 54	E
Cres	52	44 58	N	14 25	E
Crescent City	172	41 45	N	124 12	W
Creston, Canada	155	49 10	N	116 31	W
Creston, U.S.A.	166	41 0	N	94 20	W
Crestview	169	30 45	N	86 35	W
Crete = Kríti	55	35 15	N	25 0	E
Creuse →	36	47 0	N	0 34	E
Creusot, Le	37	46 50	N	4 24	E
Crewe	28	53 6	N	2 28	W
Criciúma	191	28 40	S	49 23	W
Crieff	31	56 22	N	3 50	W
Crimea = Krymskiy P-ov.	68	45 0	N	34 0	E
Crișul Alb →	56	46 42	N	21 17	E
Crișul Negru →	56	46 38	N	22 26	E
Crna Gora = Montenegro □	52	42 40	N	19 20	E
Crna Gora	52	42 10	N	21 30	E
Croatia ■	52	45 20	N	18 0	E
Crockett	168	31 20	N	95 30	W
Cromarty	33	57 40	N	4 2	W
Cromer	29	52 56	N	1 18	E
Crooked I.	180	22 50	N	74 10	W
Crookwell	117	34 28	S	149 24	E
Cross Fell	28	54 44	N	2 29	W
Cross L.	153	54 45	N	97 30	W
Crosse, La	166	43 48	N	91 13	W
Crowley	168	30 15	N	92 20	W
Crowsnest Pass	155	49 40	N	114 40	W
Cruz, C.	178	19 50	N	77 50	W
Cruz Alta	191	28 45	S	53 40	W
Cruz del Eje	190	30 45	S	64 50	W
Cruzeiro do Sul	186	7 35	S	72 35	W

Name	Pg	Lat	Long
Crystal Brook	119	33 21S	138 12 E
Cu Lao Hon	95	10 54N	108 18 E
Cuando →	134	14 0S	19 30 E
Cuanza →	134	9 2S	13 30 E
Cuba ■	178	22 0N	79 0W
Cubango →	134	18 50S	22 25 E
Cucuí	184	1 12N	66 50W
Cúcuta	184	7 54N	72 31W
Cuddalore	90	11 46N	79 45 E
Cuddapah	90	14 30N	78 47 E
Cue	120	27 25S	117 54 E
Cuenca, Ecuador	184	2 50S	79 9W
Cuenca, Spain	51	40 5N	2 10W
Cuenca, Serranía de	51	39 55N	1 50W
Cuernavaca	177	18 55N	99 15W
Cuevo	187	20 15S	63 30W
Cuiabá	188	15 30S	56 0W
Cuillin Hills	32	57 14N	6 15W
Cuitzeo, L. de	175	19 55N	101 5W
Culcairn	117	35 41S	147 3 E
Culiacán	174	24 48N	107 24W
Cullarin Range	117	34 30S	149 30 E
Culloden Moor	33	57 29N	4 7W
Culverden	123	42 47S	172 49 E
Cumaná	185	10 30N	64 5W
Cumberland	164	39 40N	78 43W
Cumberland →	169	36 15N	87 0W
Cumberland Is.	121	20 35S	149 10 E
Cumberland Pen.	146	67 0N	64 0W
Cumberland Plat.	169	36 0N	84 30W
Cumberland Sd.	146	65 30N	66 0W
Cumbria □	28	54 35N	2 55W
Cumbrian Mts.	28	54 30N	3 0W
Cumbum	90	15 40N	79 10 E
Cummins	119	34 16S	135 43 E
Cumnock	31	55 27N	4 18W
Cunene →	134	17 20S	11 50 E
Cunnamulla	116	28 2S	145 38 E
Curaçao	181	12 10N	69 0W
Curaray →	184	2 20S	74 5W
Curiapo	185	8 33N	61 5W
Curicó	190	34 55S	71 20W
Curitiba	191	25 20S	49 10W
Curtis Group	117	39 30S	146 37 E
Curuá →	188	5 23S	54 22W
Curuçá	188	0 43S	47 50W
Curuzú Cuatiá	191	29 50S	58 5W
Cushing	168	35 59N	96 46W
Cusihuiriáchic	174	28 14N	106 50W
Cuthbert	170	31 47N	84 47W
Cuttack	92	20 25N	85 57 E
Cuxhaven	42	53 51N	8 41 E
Cuyahoga Falls	167	41 8N	81 30W
Cuzco, Bolivia	187	20 0S	66 50W
Cuzco, Peru	186	13 32S	72 0W
Cwmbran	27	51 39N	3 0W
Cypress Hills	152	49 40N	109 30W
Cyprus ■	80	35 0N	33 0 E
Cyrenaica	124	27 0N	23 0 E
Czech Republic ■	59	49 0N	15 0 E
Czeremcha	58	52 31N	23 21 E
Częstochowa	58	50 49N	19 7 E

D

Name	Pg	Lat	Long
Da →	95	21 15N	105 20 E
Da Hinggan Ling	98	48 0N	121 0 E
Da Nang	95	16 4N	108 13 E
Da Yunhe →	99	34 25N	120 5 E
Daba Shan	99	32 0N	109 0 E
Dacca = Dhaka	92	23 43N	90 26 E
Dacca □ = Dhaka □	93	24 25N	90 25 E
Dadanawa	185	2 50N	59 30W
Dadra and Nagar Haveli □	91	20 5N	73 0 E
Daghestan Rep. □	70	42 30N	47 0 E
Dahomey = Benin ■	131	10 0N	2 0 E
Dai-Sen	109	35 22N	133 32 E
Daiö-Misaki	106	34 15N	136 45 E
Daisetsu-Zan	103	43 30N	142 57 E
Daito	109	35 19N	132 58 E
Dajarra	115	21 42S	139 30 E
Dakar	130	14 34N	17 29W
Dakhla	126	23 50N	15 53W
Dakhla, El Wâhât el-	128	25 30N	28 50 E
Ðakovica	52	42 22N	20 26 E
Dalandzadgad	98	43 27N	104 30 E
Dalbeattie	31	54 55N	3 50W
Dalby	116	27 10S	151 17 E
Dalhousie	148	48 5N	66 26W
Dali	99	25 40N	100 10 E
Dalian	98	38 50N	121 40 E
Daliang Shan	99	28 0N	102 45 E
Dallas, Oreg., U.S.A.	171	45 0N	123 15W
Dallas, Tex., U.S.A.	168	32 50N	96 50W
Dalmacija	52	43 20N	17 0 E
Dalmatia = Dalmacija	52	43 20N	17 0 E
Daloa	130	7 0N	6 30W
Dalton	169	34 47N	84 58W
Daly Waters	114	16 15S	133 24 E
Daman	91	20 25N	72 57 E
Damaraland	136	21 0S	17 0 E
Damascus = Dimashq	80	33 30N	36 18 E
Damāvand	86	35 47N	52 0 E
Damāvand, Qolleh-ye	86	35 56N	52 10 E
Dampier	114	20 41S	116 42 E
Dampier Arch.	114	20 38S	116 32 E
Danbury	164	41 23N	73 29W
Dandenong	117	38 0S	145 15 E
Dandong	98	40 10N	124 20 E
Dangriga	177	17 0N	88 13W
Dannevirke	122	40 12S	176 8 E
Dansville	164	42 32N	77 41W
Danville, Ill., U.S.A.	167	40 10N	87 40W
Danville, Ky., U.S.A.	167	37 40N	84 45W
Danville, Va., U.S.A.	165	36 40N	79 20W
Danzig = Gdańsk	58	54 22N	18 40 E
Dar es Salaam	135	6 50S	39 12 E
Darbhanga	92	26 15N	85 55 E
Dardanelles = Çanakkale Boğazi	80	40 0N	26 0 E
Dârfûr	129	13 40N	24 0 E
Dargan Ata	70	40 29N	62 10 E
Dargaville	122	35 57S	173 52 E
Darién, G. del	184	9 0N	77 0W
Darjeeling = Darjiling	92	27 3N	88 18 E
Darjiling	92	27 3N	88 18 E
Darling →	119	34 4S	141 54 E
Darling Downs	116	27 30S	150 30 E
Darling Ra.	120	32 30S	116 0 E
Darlington	28	54 33N	1 33W
Darmstadt	42	49 51N	8 40 E
Darnley, C.	14	68 0S	69 0 E
Dart →	27	50 24N	3 36W
Dartmoor	27	50 36N	4 0W
Dartmouth, Canada	149	44 40N	63 30W
Dartmouth, U.K.	27	50 21N	3 35W
Darwin	114	12 25S	130 51 E
Dasht-e Kavīr	86	34 30N	55 0 E
Dasht-e Lūt	85	31 30N	58 0 E
Dasht-e Mārgow	87	30 40N	62 30 E
Datia	91	25 39N	78 27 E
Datong	98	40 6N	113 18 E
Daugavpils	68	55 53N	26 32 E
Dauphin	153	51 9N	100 5W
Dauphiné	37	45 15N	5 25 E
Davangere	90	14 25N	75 55 E
Davao	112	7 0N	125 40 E
Davenport	166	41 30N	90 40W
Daventry	24	52 16N	1 10W
David	179	8 30N	82 30W
Davis Sea	15	66 0S	92 0 E
Davis Str.	146	65 0N	58 0W
Davos	44	46 48N	9 49 E
Dawson	144	64 10N	139 30W
Dawson Creek	155	55 45N	120 15W
Dawson Range	121	24 30S	149 48 E
Daylesford	117	37 21S	144 9 E
Dayr az Zawr	81	35 20N	40 5 E
Dayton, Ohio, U.S.A.	167	39 45N	84 10W

Dayton, Wash., U.S.A.	171	46 20N	118	10W
Daytona Beach	170	29 14N	81	0W
De Aar	136	30 39S	24	0 E
De Land	170	29 1N	81	19W
De Ridder	168	30 48N	93	15W
De Soto	166	38 7N	90	33W
Deakin	114	30 46S	128	0 E
Deal	25	51 13N	1	25 E
Dean, Forest of	24	51 50N	2	35W
Deán Funes	190	30 20S	64	20W
Dease ⟶	144	59 56N	128	32W
Dease Lake	144	58 25N	130	6W
Death Valley	173	36 19N	116	52W
Deauville	38	49 23N	0	2 E
Debar	52	41 31N	20	30 E
Debre Markos	132	10 20N	37	40 E
Debre Tabor	132	11 50N	38	26 E
Debrecen	59	47 33N	21	42 E
Decatur, Ala., U.S.A.	169	34 35N	87	0W
Decatur, Ga., U.S.A.	170	33 47N	84	17W
Decatur, Ill., U.S.A.	166	39 50N	89	0W
Deccan	76	18 0N	79	0 E
Dedéagach = Alexandroúpolis	55	40 50N	25	54 E
Dee ⟶, Scotland, U.K.	33	57 4N	2	7W
Dee ⟶, Wales, U.K.	26	53 15N	3	7W
Deepwater	116	29 25S	151	51 E
Deer Lake	149	49 11N	57	27W
Defiance	167	41 20N	84	20W
Deh Bīd	85	30 39N	53	11 E
Dehra Dun	89	30 20N	78	4 E
Dej	56	47 10N	23	52 E
Del Rio	161	29 23N	100	50W
Delano	173	35 48N	119	13W
Delaware □	164	39 0N	75	40W
Delaware ⟶	164	39 20N	75	25W
Delaware B.	157	38 50N	75	0W
Delft	40	52 1N	4	22 E
Delfzijl	41	53 20N	6	55 E
Delgado, C.	137	10 45S	40	40 E
Delgo	129	20 6N	30	40 E
Delhi	89	28 38N	77	17 E
Delice ⟶	80	39 45N	34	15 E
Delicias	174	28 13N	105	28W
Delong, Ostrova	72	76 40N	149	20 E
Deloraine	119	41 30S	146	40 E
Delray Beach	170	26 27N	80	4W
Demanda, Sierra de la	50	42 15N	3	0W
Dembidolo	132	8 34N	34	50 E
Deming	161	32 10N	107	50W
Demopolis	169	32 30N	87	48W
Den Burg	40	53 3N	4	47 E
Den Haag = 's-Gravenhage	40	52 7N	4	17 E
Den Helder	40	52 57N	4	45 E
Den Oever	40	52 56N	5	2 E
Denain	38	50 20N	3	22 E
Denbigh	26	53 12N	3	26W
Denham	120	25 56S	113	31 E
Deniliquin	117	35 30S	144	58 E
Denison	168	33 50N	96	40W
Denizli	80	37 42N	29	2 E
Denmark ■	120	34 59S	117	25 E
Denmark ■	61	55 30N	9	0 E
Denmark Str.	13	66 0N	30	0W
Denton	168	33 12N	97	10W
D'Entrecasteaux Is.	115	9 0S	151	0 E
Denver	163	39 45N	105	0W
Deolali	91	19 58N	73	50 E
Deoria	92	26 31N	83	48 E
Deosai Mts.	89	35 40N	75	0 E
Dera Ghazi Khan	89	30 5N	70	43 E
Dera Ismail Khan	89	31 50N	70	50 E
Derby	28	52 55N	1	28W
Derby □	28	52 55N	1	28W
Derg, L.	35	53 0N	8	20W
Derry = Londonderry	34	55 0N	7	20W
Derryveagh Mts.	34	55 0N	8	40W
Derwent ⟶, Cumb., U.K.	28	54 42N	3	22W
Derwent ⟶, Derby, U.K.	29	52 53N	1	17W
Derwent ⟶, N. Yorks., U.K.	29	53 45N	0	57W
Derwent Water, L.	28	54 35N	3	9W
Des Moines	166	41 35N	93	37W
Des Moines ⟶	166	40 23N	91	25W
Deschutes ⟶	171	45 30N	121	0W
Dese	133	11 5N	39	40 E
Despeñaperros, Paso	50	38 24N	3	30W
Dessau	43	51 49N	12	15 E
Dessye = Dese	133	11 5N	39	40 E
Desvrès	38	50 40N	1	48 E
Detroit	167	42 23N	83	5W
Deurne	41	51 27N	5	49 E
Deutsche Bucht	42	54 10N	7	51 E
Devakottai	90	9 55N	78	45 E
Deventer	41	52 15N	6	10 E
Devizes	24	51 21N	2	0W
Devon I.	13	75 10N	85	0W
Devonport, Australia	119	41 10S	146	22 E
Devonport, N.Z.	122	36 49S	174	49 E
Devonport, U.K.	27	50 23N	4	11W
Devonshire □	27	50 50N	3	40W
Dewsbury	28	53 42N	1	38W
Dezfūl	84	32 20N	48	30 E
Dezhneva, Mys	73	66 5N	169	40W
Dhahran = Az Zahrān	84	26 10N	50	7 E
Dhaka	92	23 43N	90	26 E
Dhaka □	93	24 25N	90	25 E
Dhamar	83	14 30N	44	20 E
Dhar	91	22 35N	75	26 E
Dharmapuri	90	12 10N	78	10 E
Dharwad	90	15 22N	75	15 E
Dhidhimótikhon	55	41 22N	26	29 E
Dhikti	55	35 8N	25	22 E
Dhodhekánisos	55	36 35N	27	0 E
Dhuburi	92	26 2N	89	59 E
Dhule	91	20 58N	74	50 E
Di Linh, Cao Nguyen	95	11 30N	108	0 E
Diamantina	188	18 17S	43	40W
Diamantina ⟶	115	26 45S	139	10 E
Diamantino	188	14 30S	56	30W
Dibrugarh	93	27 29N	94	55 E
Dickinson	163	46 50N	102	48W
Didsbury	155	51 35N	114	10W
Diefenbaker L.	152	51 0N	106	55W
Dieppe	38	49 54N	1	4 E
Dieren	41	52 3N	6	6 E
Digby	148	44 38N	65	50W
Digne	37	44 5N	6	12 E
Dijlah, Nahr ⟶	81	31 0N	47	25 E
Dijon	37	47 20N	5	0 E
Dila	133	6 21N	38	22 E
Dillon	165	34 26N	79	20W
Dimashq	80	33 30N	36	18 E
Dimboola	119	36 28S	142	7 E
Dimbovita ⟶	57	44 14N	26	13 E
Dimitrovgrad	53	42 5N	25	35 E
Dimitrovo = Pernik	53	42 35N	23	2 E
Dinan	36	48 28N	2	2W
Dinara Planina	52	44 0N	16	30 E
Dinaric Alps = Dinara Planina	52	44 0N	16	30 E
Dindigul	90	10 25N	78	0 E
Dingle	35	52 9N	10	17W
Dingle B.	35	52 3N	10	20W
Dingwall	33	57 36N	4	26W
Dinuba	173	36 31N	119	22W
Dire Dawa	133	9 35N	41	45 E
Diriamba	179	11 51N	86	19W
Dirranbandi	116	28 33S	148	17 E
Disappointment L.	114	23 20S	122	40 E
Discovery B.	119	38 10S	140	40 E
Disko	146	69 45N	53	30W
Diss	25	52 23N	1	6 E
Diu	91	20 45N	70	58 E
Dives-sur-Mer	39	49 18N	0	8W
Dixon	166	41 50N	89	30W
Dixon Entrance	154	54 30N	132	0W
Diyarbakir	81	37 55N	40	18 E
Djakarta = Jakarta	111	6 9S	106	49 E
Djelfa	130	34 40N	3	15 E
Djerid, Chott	127	33 42N	8	30 E
Djibouti	133	11 30N	43	5 E
Djibouti ■	133	12 0N	43	0 E
Djoum	131	2 41N	12	35 E

Name	Page	Lat	N/S	Long	E/W
Dmitriya Lapteva, Proliv	72	73 0	N	140 0	E
Dnepr →	68	46 30	N	32 18	E
Dnepropetrovsk	68	48 30	N	35 0	E
Dnestr →	68	46 18	N	30 17	E
Dnestrovski = Belgorod	68	50 35	N	36 35	E
Dnieper = Dnepr →	68	46 30	N	32 18	E
Dniester = Dnestr →	68	46 18	N	30 17	E
Dobrich	53	43 37	N	27 49	E
Dobruja	57	44 30	N	28 15	E
Dodecanese = Dhodhekánisos	55	36 35	N	27 0	E
Dodge City	161	37 42	N	100 0	W
Dodoma	135	6 8	S	35 45	E
Doesburg	41	52 1	N	6 9	E
Doetinchem	41	51 59	N	6 18	E
Dogger Bank	124	54 50	N	2 0	E
Doi Luang	95	18 30	N	101 0	E
Dojran	54	41 10	N	22 45	E
Dokkum	41	53 20	N	5 59	E
Dolbeau	148	48 53	N	72 18	W
Dole	37	47 7	N	5 31	E
Dolgellau	26	52 44	N	3 53	W
Dolgelley = Dolgellau	26	52 44	N	3 53	W
Dolomites = Dolomiti	47	46 30	N	11 40	E
Dolomiti	47	46 30	N	11 40	E
Dolores	191	36 20	S	57 40	W
Dolphin and Union Str.	145	69 5	N	114 45	W
Domel I. = Letsôk-aw Kyun	94	11 30	N	98 25	E
Dominica ■	180	15 20	N	61 20	W
Dominican Rep. ■	180	19 0	N	70 30	W
Don →, Russia	68	47 4	N	39 18	E
Don →, U.K.	33	57 14	N	2 5	W
Donaghadee	34	54 38	N	5 32	W
Donau →	42	48 10	N	17 0	E
Doncaster	29	53 31	N	1 9	W
Dondra Head	90	5 55	N	80 40	E
Donegal	34	54 39	N	8 8	W
Donegal □	34	54 53	N	8 0	W
Donegal B.	34	54 30	N	8 35	W
Donetsk	68	48 0	N	37 45	E
Dongara	120	29 14	S	114 57	E
Dongen	40	51 38	N	4 56	E
Dongting Hu	99	29 18	N	112 45	E
Donnelly's Crossing	122	35 42	S	173 38	E
Donnybrook	120	33 34	S	115 48	E
Doon →	31	55 26	N	4 41	W
Dorada, La	184	5 30	N	74 40	W
Dorchester	27	50 42	N	2 28	W
Dorchester, C.	146	65 27	N	77 27	W
Dordogne □	36	45 5	N	0 40	E
Dordrecht	40	51 48	N	4 39	E
Dornoch	33	57 52	N	4 0	W
Dorrigo	116	30 20	S	152 44	E
Dorris	172	41 59	N	121 58	W
Dorset □	27	50 48	N	2 25	W
Dortmund	42	51 32	N	7 28	E
Dothan	169	31 10	N	85 25	W
Douai	38	50 21	N	3 4	E
Douala	131	4 0	N	9 45	E
Douarnenez	36	48 6	N	4 21	W
Douglas, U.K.	28	54 9	N	4 29	W
Douglas, U.S.A.	170	31 32	N	82 52	W
Doullens	38	50 10	N	2 20	E
Dounreay	33	58 34	N	3 44	W
Dourados	188	22 9	S	54 50	W
Douro →	50	41 8	N	8 40	W
Douro Litoral □	50	41 10	N	8 20	W
Dove →	28	52 51	N	1 36	W
Dover, U.K.	25	51 7	N	1 19	E
Dover, Del., U.S.A.	164	39 10	N	75 31	W
Dover, N.H., U.S.A.	164	43 12	N	70 51	W
Dover, Str. of	38	51 0	N	1 30	E
Dovey →	26	52 32	N	4 0	W
Downham Market	25	52 36	N	0 22	E
Downpatrick	34	54 20	N	5 43	W
Drachten	41	53 7	N	6 5	E
Dragoman, Prokhod	53	43 0	N	22 53	E
Draguignan	37	43 30	N	6 27	E
Drakensberg	137	31 0	S	28 0	E
Dráma	55	41 9	N	24 10	E
Drammen	60	59 42	N	10 12	E
Drau = Drava →	59	45 33	N	18 55	E
Drava →	59	45 33	N	18 55	E
Drayton Valley	155	53 12	N	114 58	W
Drenthe □	41	52 52	N	6 40	E
Dresden	43	51 2	N	13 45	E
Dreux	39	48 44	N	1 23	E
Driffield	29	54 0	N	0 25	W
Drin i zi →	52	41 37	N	20 28	E
Drina →	52	44 53	N	19 21	E
Drogheda	34	53 45	N	6 20	W
Droitwich	24	52 16	N	2 10	W
Dronne →	36	45 2	N	0 9	W
Dronning Maud Land	14	72 30	S	12 0	E
Drumheller	155	51 25	N	112 40	W
Drummond Ra.	121	23 45	S	147 10	E
Drummondville	151	45 55	N	72 25	W
Dryden	153	49 47	N	92 50	W
Du Bois	164	41 8	N	78 46	W
Du Quoin	166	38 0	N	89 10	W
Dubai = Dubayy	85	25 18	N	55 20	E
Dubawnt →	145	64 33	N	100 6	W
Dubawnt, L.	143	63 4	N	101 42	W
Dubayy	85	25 18	N	55 20	E
Dubbo	116	32 11	S	148 35	E
Dublin, Ireland	35	53 20	N	6 18	W
Dublin, U.S.A.	170	32 30	N	82 34	W
Dublin □	34	53 24	N	6 20	W
Dubrovnik	52	42 39	N	18 6	E
Dubuque	166	42 30	N	90 41	W
Dudley	24	52 30	N	2 5	W
Dugi Otok	52	44 0	N	15 0	E
Duisburg	42	51 27	N	6 42	E
Duluth	150	46 48	N	92 10	W
Dumbarton	31	55 58	N	4 35	W
Dumfries	31	55 4	N	3 37	W
Dumfries & Galloway □	31	55 0	N	4 0	W
Dun Laoghaire	35	53 17	N	6 9	W
Dunărea →	57	45 30	N	8 15	E
Dunaújváros	59	47 0	N	18 57	E
Dunbar	31	56 0	N	2 32	W
Dunblane	31	56 10	N	3 58	W
Duncan, Canada	154	48 45	N	123 40	W
Duncan, U.S.A.	161	34 25	N	98 0	W
Duncan Pass.	94	11 0	N	92 30	E
Dundalk	34	54 1	N	6 25	W
Dundas, Canada	151	43 17	N	79 59	W
Dundas, Greenland	13	77 0	N	69 0	W
Dundee	31	56 29	N	3 0	W
Dundrum	34	54 17	N	5 50	W
Dunedin	123	45 50	S	170 33	E
Dunedoo	116	32 0	S	149 25	E
Dunfermline	31	56 5	N	3 28	W
Dungannon	34	54 30	N	6 47	W
Dungarvan	35	52 6	N	7 40	W
Dungeness	25	50 54	N	0 59	E
Dungog	117	32 22	S	151 46	E
Dunhuang	100	40 8	N	94 36	E
Dunkeld	33	56 34	N	3 36	W
Dunkerque	38	51 2	N	2 20	E
Dunkery Beacon	27	51 15	N	3 37	W
Dunkirk = Dunkerque	38	51 2	N	2 20	E
Dunkirk	164	42 30	N	79 18	W
Dúnleary = Dun Laoghaire	35	53 17	N	6 9	W
Dunmore	164	41 27	N	75 38	W
Dunn	165	35 18	N	78 36	W
Dunnet Hd.	33	58 38	N	3 22	W
Duns	31	55 47	N	2 20	W
Dunsmuir	172	41 10	N	122 18	W
Dunstan Mts.	123	44 53	S	169 35	E
Durance →	37	43 55	N	4 45	E
Durango, Mexico	174	24 3	N	104 39	W
Durango, U.S.A.	163	37 16	N	107 50	W
Durango □	174	24 50	N	104 50	W
Durant	168	34 0	N	96 25	W
Durazno	191	33 25	S	56 31	W
Durban	137	29 49	S	31 1	E
Durg	92	21 15	N	81 22	E
Durham, U.K.	28	54 47	N	1 34	W
Durham, U.S.A.	165	36 0	N	78 55	W
Durham □	28	54 42	N	1 45	W
Durmitor	52	43 10	N	19 0	E

Name	Page	Lat	Long
Durness	**32**	58 34N	4 45W
D'Urville I.	**122**	40 50S	173 55 E
Dushanbe	**71**	38 33N	68 48 E
Düsseldorf	**42**	51 15N	6 46 E
Duwādimi	**82**	24 35N	44 15 E
Duyun	**99**	26 18N	107 29 E
Duzce	**80**	40 50N	31 10 E
Duzdab = Zähedān	**86**	29 30N	60 50 E
Dvina, Sev. →	**69**	64 32N	40 30 E
Dvinsk = Daugavpils	**68**	55 53N	26 32 E
Dyer, C.	**146**	66 40N	61 0W
Dyersburg	**169**	36 2N	89 20W
Dyfed □	**26**	52 0N	4 30W
Dysart	**121**	22 32S	148 23 E
Dzamin Üüd	**98**	43 50N	111 58 E
Dzerzhinsk	**68**	53 40N	27 1 E
Dzhalal-Abad	**71**	40 56N	73 0 E
Dzhalinda	**75**	53 26N	124 0 E
Dzhambul	**71**	42 54N	71 22 E
Dzhardzhan	**72**	68 10N	124 10 E
Dzhetygara	**71**	52 11N	61 12 E
Dzhezkazgan	**71**	47 44N	67 40 E
Dzhugdzur, Khrebet	**75**	57 30N	138 0 E
Dzuumod	**98**	47 45N	106 58 E

E

Name	Page	Lat	Long
Eagle	**142**	64 44N	141 7W
Eagle Pass	**161**	28 45N	100 35W
Eagle River	**150**	45 55N	89 17W
Ealing	**25**	51 30N	0 19W
Earn →	**31**	56 20N	3 19W
Easley	**165**	34 52N	82 35W
East Angus	**148**	45 30N	71 40W
East Bengal	**92**	24 0N	90 0 E
East Beskids = Vychodné Beskydy	**59**	49 30N	22 0 E
East C.	**122**	37 42S	178 35 E
East Chicago	**167**	41 40N	87 30W
East China Sea	**99**	30 5N	126 0 E
East Falkland	**192**	51 30S	58 30W
East Indies	**77**	0 0	120 0 E
East Kilbride	**31**	55 46N	4 10W
East Liverpool	**164**	40 39N	80 35W
East London	**137**	33 0S	27 55 E
East Main = Eastmain	**140**	52 10N	78 30W
East Pakistan = Bangladesh ■	**92**	24 0N	90 0 E
East Point	**170**	33 40N	84 28W
East St. Louis	**166**	38 37N	90 4W
East Schelde → = Oosterschelde	**40**	51 33N	4 0 E
East Siberian Sea	**73**	73 0N	160 0 E
East Sussex □	**25**	51 0N	0 20 E
Eastbourne, N.Z.	**123**	41 19S	174 55 E
Eastbourne, U.K.	**25**	50 46N	0 18 E
Eastern Ghats	**90**	14 0N	78 50 E
Eastleigh	**25**	50 58N	1 21W
Eastmain	**140**	52 10N	78 30W
Eastmain →	**140**	52 27N	78 26W
Easton	**164**	40 41N	75 15W
Eau Claire	**166**	44 46N	91 30W
Eau Claire, L. à l'	**146**	56 10N	74 25W
Ebbw Vale	**26**	51 47N	3 12W
Eboli	**49**	40 39N	15 2 E
Ebro →	**51**	40 43N	0 54 E
Echizen-Misaki	**106**	35 59N	135 57 E
Echo Bay	**145**	46 29N	84 4W
Echuca	**117**	36 10S	144 20 E
Ecuador ■	**184**	2 0S	78 0W
Ed Dâmer	**129**	17 27N	34 0 E
Edam	**40**	52 31N	5 3 E
Eddystone	**27**	50 11N	4 16W
Ede	**41**	52 4N	5 40 E
Eden →	**117**	37 3S	149 55 E
Eden →	**28**	54 57N	3 2W
Edenhope	**119**	37 4S	141 19 E
Edge Hill	**24**	52 7N	1 28W

Name	Page	Lat	Long
Edhessa	**54**	40 48N	22 5 E
Edinburgh	**31**	55 57N	3 12W
Edirne	**80**	41 40N	26 34 E
Edmonton, Australia	**121**	17 2S	145 46 E
Edmonton, Canada	**155**	53 30N	113 30W
Edmundston	**148**	47 23N	68 20W
Edson	**155**	53 35N	116 28W
Edward, L.	**132**	0 25S	29 40 E
Edward VII Land	**15**	80 0S	150 0W
Edwards Plat.	**161**	30 30N	101 5W
Effingham	**167**	39 8N	88 30W
Égadi, Ísole	**48**	37 55N	12 16 E
Eger	**59**	47 53N	20 27 E
Egmont, Mt.	**122**	39 17S	174 5 E
Eğridir Gölü	**80**	37 53N	30 50 E
Egypt ■	**128**	28 0N	31 0 E
Eifel	**42**	50 10N	6 45 E
Eigg	**32**	56 54N	6 10W
Eil	**133**	8 0N	49 50 E
Eindhoven	**41**	51 26N	5 30 E
Eirunepé	**187**	6 35S	69 53W
El Aaiún	**126**	27 9N	13 12W
El Cajon	**173**	32 49N	117 0W
El Callao	**185**	7 18N	61 50W
El Centro	**173**	32 50N	115 40W
El Cerro	**187**	17 30S	61 40W
El Dere	**133**	3 50N	47 8 E
El Djouf	**126**	20 0N	11 30 E
El Dorado	**168**	33 10N	92 40W
El Escorial	**50**	40 35N	4 7W
El Faiyûm	**128**	29 19N	30 50 E
El Fâsher	**129**	13 33N	25 26 E
El Ferrol	**50**	43 29N	8 15W
El Fuerte	**174**	26 25N	108 39W
El Geteina	**129**	14 50N	32 27 E
El Iskandarîya	**128**	31 0N	30 0 E
El Jadida	**126**	33 11N	8 17W
El Khârga	**128**	25 30N	30 33 E
El Khartûm	**129**	15 31N	32 35 E
El Mahalla el Kubra	**128**	31 0N	31 0 E
El Minyâ	**128**	28 7N	30 33 E
El Obeid	**129**	13 8N	30 10 E
El Oro	**177**	27 15N	103 30W
El Paso	**161**	31 50N	106 30W
El Progreso	**177**	15 26N	87 51W
El Qâhira	**128**	30 1N	31 14 E
El Qasr	**128**	25 44N	28 42 E
El Salvador ■	**177**	13 50N	89 0W
El Suweis	**128**	29 58N	32 31 E
El Tigre	**185**	8 44N	64 15W
El Turbio	**192**	51 45S	72 5W
Elat	**80**	29 30N	34 56 E
Elâziğ	**81**	38 37N	39 14 E
Elba	**46**	42 48N	10 15 E
Elbasani	**52**	41 9N	20 9 E
Elbe →	**42**	53 50N	9 0 E
Elbert, Mt.	**163**	39 5N	106 27W
Elberton	**165**	34 7N	82 51W
Elbeuf	**39**	49 17N	1 2 E
Elbing = Elbląg	**58**	54 10N	19 25 E
Elbląg	**58**	54 10N	19 25 E
Elbrus	**70**	43 21N	42 30 E
Elburg	**41**	52 26N	5 50 E
Elburz Mts. = Alborz, Reshteh-ye Kūhhā-ye	**86**	36 0N	52 0 E
Elche	**51**	38 15N	0 42W
Eldorado	**174**	24 20N	107 22W
Eldorado Springs	**166**	37 54N	93 59W
Eldoret	**132**	0 30N	35 17 E
Eleanora, Peak	**120**	32 57S	121 9 E
Electra	**161**	34 0N	99 0W
Elephant Butte Res.	**161**	33 45N	107 30W
Eleuthera	**178**	25 0N	76 20W
Elgin, U.K.	**33**	57 39N	3 20W
Elgin, Ill., U.S.A.	**167**	42 0N	88 20W
Elgin, Oreg., U.S.A.	**171**	45 37N	118 0W
Elgon, Mt.	**132**	1 10N	34 30 E
Elisabethville = Lubumbashi	**135**	11 40S	27 28 E
Elizabeth, Australia	**119**	34 42S	138 41 E
Elizabeth, U.S.A.	**164**	40 37N	74 12W
Elizabeth City	**165**	36 18N	76 16W

Elizabethton **165** 36 20N 82 13W
Elizabethtown **167** 37 40N 85 54W
Elk Point **152** 53 54N 110 55W
Elkhart **167** 41 42N 85 55W
Elkins **165** 38 53N 79 53W
Elko **172** 40 50N 115 50W
Ellensburg **171** 47 0N 120 30W
Ellery, Mt. .... **117** 37 28S 148 47 E
Ellesmere I. **13** 79 30N 80 0W
Ellesmere Port **28** 53 17N 2 55W
Ellice Is. = Tuvalu ■ ...... **122** 8 0S 178 0 E
Elliot Lake **150** 46 25N 82 35W
Ellore = Eluru .... **92** 16 48N 81 8 E
Ellsworth Land **14** 76 0S 89 0W
Ellsworth Mts. **14** 78 30S 85 0W
Elmhurst **167** 41 52N 87 58W
Elmira **164** 42 8N 76 49W
Elrose **152** 51 12N 108 0W
Eluru .... **92** 16 48N 81 8 E
Elvas **50** 38 50N 7 10W
Elwood **167** 40 20N 85 50W
Ely **172** 39 10N 114 50W
Elyria **167** 41 22N 82 8W
Emãmrūd .... **86** 36 30N 55 0 E
Emba ⟶ .... **70** 46 38N 53 14 E
Emden .... **42** 53 22N 7 12 E
Emerald .... **121** 23 32S 148 10 E
Emilia-Romagna □ .... **46** 44 33N 10 40 E
Emmeloord .... **41** 52 44N 5 46 E
Emmen .... **41** 52 48N 6 57 E
Empalme **174** 27 58N 110 51W
Emporia, Kans., U.S.A. .. **158** 38 25N 96 10W
Emporia, Va., U.S.A. **165** 36 41N 77 32W
Ems ⟶ .... **42** 52 37N 9 26 E
En Nahud .... **129** 12 45N 28 25 E
Ena .... **106** 35 25N 137 25 E
Ena-San .... **106** 35 26N 137 36 E
Encarnación **191** 27 15S 55 50W
Encarnación de Díaz **175** 21 31N 102 14W
Encontrados **184** 9 3N 72 14W
Enderby **155** 50 35N 119 10W
Enderby Land .... **14** 66 0S 53 0 E
Endicott **164** 42 6N 76 2W
Engaño, C. **180** 18 30N 68 20W
Engels = Pokrovsk .... **68** 51 28N 46 6 E
Enggano .... **111** 5 20S 102 40 E
England □ **21** 53 0N 2 0W
English Bazar = Ingraj Bazar **92** 24 58N 88 10 E
English Channel **16** 50 0N 2 0W
Enid **161** 36 26N 97 52W
Enkhuizen .... **40** 52 42N 5 17 E
Ennedi .... **129** 17 15N 22 0 E
Ennis **35** 52 51N 8 59W
Enniscorthy **35** 52 30N 6 35W
Enniskillen **34** 54 20N 7 40W
Enriquillo, L. **180** 18 20N 72 5W
Enschede .... **41** 52 13N 6 53 E
Ensenada **174** 31 52N 116 37W
Enshū-Nada .... **106** 34 27N 137 38 E
Entebbe .... **132** 0 4N 32 28 E
Enterprise **171** 45 30N 117 18W
Entre Ríos □ **190** 30 30S 58 30W
Enugu .... **131** 6 20N 7 30 E
Enzan .... **107** 35 42N 138 44 E
Eólie, I. .... **49** 38 30N 14 50 E
Epe .... **41** 52 21N 5 59 E
Épernay .... **39** 49 3N 3 56 E
Ephesus .... **80** 37 50N 27 33 E
Épinal .... **37** 48 10N 6 27 E
Epping .... **25** 51 42N 0 8 E
Equatorial Guinea ■ ...... **134** 2 0S 8 0 E
Er Rif **126** 35 1N 4 1W
Erãwadī Myit ⟶ =
  Irrawaddy ⟶ .... **93** 15 50N 95 6 E
Ercha .... **73** 69 45N 147 20 E
Erciyaş Daği .... **80** 38 30N 35 30 E
Erebus, Mt. .... **15** 77 35S 167 0 E
Erechim **191** 27 35S 52 15W
Ereğli .... **80** 41 15N 31 30 E
Erfurt .... **43** 50 58N 11 2 E
Erg Chech .... **126** 50 59N 11 0 E
Erie **164** 42 10N 80 7W
Erie, L. **151** 42 15N 81 0W
Erimanthos .... **54** 37 57N 21 50 E
Erimo-misaki .... **103** 41 50N 143 15 E
Eritrea □ .... **132** 14 0N 41 0 E
Ermoúpolis = Síros ...... **55** 37 28N 24 57 E
Erne, Lough **34** 54 26N 7 46W
Erode .... **90** 11 24N 77 45 E
Erramala Hills .... **90** 15 30N 78 15 E
Erris Hd. **34** 54 19N 10 0W
Erzgebirge .... **43** 50 25N 13 0 E
Erzincan .... **81** 39 46N 39 30 E
Erzurum .... **81** 39 57N 41 15 E
Es Sînâ' .... **128** 29 0N 34 0 E
Esan-Misaki .... **103** 41 40N 141 10 E
Esashi .... **103** 41 52N 140 7 E
Esbjerg .... **61** 55 29N 8 29 E
Escanaba **150** 45 44N 87 5W
Escondido **173** 33 9N 117 4W
Escuintla **177** 14 20N 90 48W
Eşfahān .... **85** 33 0N 53 0 E
Esh Sham = Dimashq .... **80** 33 30N 36 18 E
Esk ⟶ **29** 54 27N 0 36W
Eskilstuna .... **60** 59 22N 16 32 E
Eskimo Pt. **145** 61 10N 94 15W
Eskişehir .... **80** 39 50N 30 35 E
Eslāmābād-e Gharb ..... **84** 34 10N 46 30 E
Esmeraldas **184** 1 0N 79 40W
Espanola **151** 46 15N 81 46W
Esperance .... **114** 33 45S 121 55 E
Espinazo, Sierra del =
  Espinhaço, Serra do **188** 17 30S 43 30W
Espinhaço, Serra do **188** 17 30S 43 30W
Espírito Santo □ **189** 20 0S 40 45W
Essaouira **126** 31 32N 9 42W
Essen .... **42** 51 28N 6 59 E
Essequibo ⟶ **185** 6 50N 58 30W
Essex □ .... **25** 51 48N 0 30 E
Estados, I. de los **192** 54 40S 64 30W
Esteli **179** 13 9N 86 22W
Estevan **152** 49 10N 102 59W
Estherville **166** 43 25N 94 50W
Estonia ■ .... **68** 58 30N 25 30 E
Estoril **50** 38 42N 9 23W
Estrêla, Serra da **50** 40 10N 7 45W
Estremadura **50** 39 0N 9 0W
Étampes .... **39** 48 26N 2 10 E
Étaples .... **38** 50 30N 1 39 E
Etawah .... **91** 26 48N 79 6 E
Ethiopia ■ .... **133** 8 0N 40 0 E
Ethiopian Highlands ..... **132** 10 0N 37 0 E
Etna .... **49** 37 45N 15 0 E
Etosha Pan .... **136** 18 40S 16 30 E
Etzatlán **175** 20 46N 104 5W
Euboea = Évvoia .... **55** 38 30N 24 0 E
Euclid **167** 41 32N 81 31W
Eucumbene, L. .... **117** 36 2S 148 40 E
Eufaula **169** 35 20N 95 33W
Eugene **171** 44 0N 123 8W
Eupen .... **42** 50 37N 6 3 E
Euphrates = Furāt, Nahr
  al ⟶ .... **84** 31 0N 47 25 E
Eureka, Calif., U.S.A. ... **172** 40 50N 124 0W
Eureka, Nev., U.S.A. **172** 39 32N 116 2W
Euroa .... **117** 36 44S 145 35 E
Europa, Pta. de **50** 36 3N 5 21W
Europa Pt. = Europa, Pta. de **50** 36 3N 5 21W
Europoort .... **40** 51 57N 4 10 E
Euston .... **119** 34 30S 142 46 E
Eutsuk L. **154** 53 20N 126 45W
Evans Head .... **116** 29 7S 153 27 E
Evanston **167** 42 0N 87 40W
Evansville **167** 38 0N 87 35W
Everard, L. .... **118** 31 30S 135 0 E
Everest, Mt. .... **92** 28 5N 86 58 E
Everett **171** 48 0N 122 10W
Everglades **170** 26 0N 80 30W
Evesham **24** 52 6N 1 57W
Évora **50** 38 33N 7 57W
Évreux .... **39** 49 0N 1 8 E
Évvoia .... **55** 38 30N 24 0 E

Excelsior Springs 166 39 20N 94 10W
Exe ──▶ 27 50 38N 3 27W
Exeter 27 50 43N 3 31W
Exmoor 27 51 10N 3 59W
Exmouth 27 50 37N 3 26W
Extremadura □ 50 39 30N 6 5W
Eyasi, L. .... 135 3 30S 35 0 E
Eye Pen. 32 58 13N 6 10W
Eyre, L. .... 118 29 30S 137 26 E
Eyre Mts. .... 123 45 25S 168 25 E
Eyre Pen. .... 119 33 30S 137 17 E

F

Facatativá 184 4 49N 74 22W
Faddeyevskiy, Ostrov ..... 72 76 0N 150 0 E
Fair Hd. 34 55 14N 6 10W
Fairbanks 142 64 50N 147 50W
Fairfield, N.Z. .... 123 45 54S 170 24 E
Fairfield, Ala., U.S.A. 169 33 30N 87 0W
Fairfield, Calif., U.S.A. ... 172 38 14N 122 1W
Fairfield, Tex., U.S.A. 168 31 40N 96 0W
Fairmont, Minn., U.S.A. ... 166 43 37N 94 30W
Fairmont, W. Va., U.S.A. ... 164 39 29N 80 10W
Fairview 155 56 5N 118 25W
Fairweather, Mt. 143 58 55N 137 45W
Faisalabad .... 89 31 30N 73 5 E
Faizabad .... 92 26 45N 82 10 E
Fajardo 180 18 20N 65 39W
Fakenham .... 29 52 50N 0 51 E
Falam .... 93 23 0N 93 45 E
Falkirk 31 56 0N 3 47W
Falkland Is. 192 51 30S 59 0W
Falköping .... 60 58 12N 13 33 E
Fall River 164 41 45N 71 5W
Falls City 166 40 0N 95 40W
Falmouth, Jamaica 180 18 30N 77 40W
Falmouth, U.K. 27 50 9N 5 5W
Famagusta .... 80 35 8N 33 55 E
Farāh .... 87 32 20N 62 7 E
Farāh □ .... 87 32 25N 62 10 E
Fareham 25 50 52N 1 11W
Farewell, C. .... 122 40 29S 172 43 E
Farewell C. = Farvel, Kap .. 147 59 48N 43 55W
Fargo 156 46 52N 96 40W
Farmington, N.H., U.S.A. ... 157 43 25N 71 3W
Farmington, N. Mex., U.S.A. 161 36 45N 108 28W
Farnborough 25 51 17N 0 46W
Faro 50 37 2N 7 55W
Faroe Is. 16 62 0N 7 0W
Fars □ .... 85 29 30N 55 0 E
Fársala .... 54 39 17N 22 23 E
Farvel, Kap 147 59 48N 43 55W
Färyāb □ .... 87 36 0N 65 0 E
Fatehgarh .... 89 27 25N 79 35 E
Fatehpur, Raj., India ..... 92 28 0N 74 40 E
Fatehpur, Ut. P., India .... 89 25 56N 81 13 E
Faxaflói 64 64 29N 23 0W
Fayetteville, Ark., U.S.A. ... 168 36 0N 94 5W
Fayetteville, N.C., U.S.A. ... 165 35 0N 78 58W
Fazilka .... 89 30 27N 74 2 E
Fdérik 126 22 40N 12 45W
Fear, C. 165 33 51N 78 0W
Fécamp .... 38 49 45N 0 22 E
Feilding .... 122 40 13S 175 35 E
Feira de Santana 189 12 15S 38 57W
Felixstowe .... 25 51 58N 1 22 E
Fengjie .... 99 31 5N 109 36 E
Fens, The .... 29 52 45N 0 2 E
Fenyang .... 98 37 19N 111 46 E
Ferfer .... 133 5 4N 45 9 E
Fergana .... 71 40 23N 71 19 E
Fergus Falls 156 46 18N 96 7W
Fermoy 35 52 4N 8 18W
Fernando de Noronha 189 4 0S 33 10W
Fernando Póo = Bioko .... 131 3 30N 8 40 E
Fernie 155 49 30N 115 5W
Ferrara .... 47 44 50N 11 36 E

Ferté-Bernard, La .... 39 48 10N 0 40 E
Fès 126 34 0N 5 0W
Feuilles ──▶ 146 58 47N 70 4W
Feyzābād .... 87 37 7N 70 33 E
Fezzan .... 124 27 0N 15 0 E
Fianarantsoa .... 137 21 26S 47 5 E
Fichtelgebirge .... 43 50 10N 12 0 E
Fife □ 31 56 13N 3 2W
Fife Ness 31 56 17N 2 35W
Fiji ■ .... 122 17 20S 179 0 E
Filey 29 54 13N 0 18W
Findlay 167 41 0N 83 41W
Finisterre, C. 50 42 50N 9 19W
Finland ■ .... 67 63 0N 27 0 E
Finland, G. of .... 67 60 0N 26 0 E
Finlay ──▶ 144 57 0N 125 10W
Finley .... 117 35 38S 145 35 E
Firenze .... 47 43 47N 11 15 E
Firozabad .... 89 27 10N 78 25 E
Fishguard 26 51 59N 4 59W
Fishbury 164 42 35N 71 47W
Fiskenæsset 147 63 5N 50 45W
Fitchburg 164 42 35N 71 47W
Fitzgerald 170 31 45N 83 16W
Fitzroy ──▶ .... 121 23 32S 150 52 E
Fiume = Rijeka .... 52 45 20N 14 21 E
Flagstaff 160 35 10N 111 40W
Flamborough Hd. 29 54 8N 0 4W
Flannan Is. 32 58 9N 7 52W
Flattery, C. 171 48 21N 124 43W
Flèche, La 39 47 42N 0 4W
Fleetwood 28 53 55N 3 1W
Flekkefjord .... 60 58 18N 6 39 E
Flensburg .... 43 54 46N 9 28 E
Flers 36 48 47N 0 33W
Flin Flon 152 54 46N 101 53W
Flinders I. .... 117 40 0S 148 0 E
Flinders Ranges .... 118 31 30S 138 30 E
Flinders Reefs .... 121 17 37S 148 31 E
Flint, U.K. 26 53 15N 3 7W
Flint, U.S.A. 167 43 5N 83 40W
Flint ──▶ 170 30 52N 84 38W
Flodden 31 55 37N 2 8W
Flora 167 38 40N 88 30W
Florence = Firenze ...... 47 43 47N 11 15 E
Florence, Ala., U.S.A. 169 34 50N 87 40W
Florence, S.C., U.S.A. 165 34 12N 79 44W
Flores, Guatemala 177 16 59N 89 50W
Flores, Indonesia .... 113 8 35S 121 0 E
Flores Sea .... 113 6 30S 124 0 E
Floriano 188 6 50S 43 0W
Florianópolis 191 27 30S 48 30W
Florida 191 34 7S 56 10W
Florida □ 170 28 30N 82 0W
Florida, Straits of 159 25 0N 80 0W
Florida B. 159 25 0N 81 20W
Florida Keys 159 25 0N 80 40W
Flórina .... 54 40 48N 21 26 E
Flushing = Vlissingen .... 40 51 26N 3 34 E
Fly ──▶ .... 115 8 25S 143 0 E
Foam Lake 152 51 40N 103 32W
Fóggia .... 49 41 28N 15 31 E
Foix .... 36 42 58N 1 38 E
Folda .... 64 64 41N 10 50 E
Folkestone .... 25 51 5N 1 11 E
Follette, La 169 36 23N 84 9W
Fond-du-Lac, Canada 145 59 19N 107 12W
Fond du Lac, U.S.A. 167 43 46N 88 26W
Fontainebleau .... 39 48 24N 2 40 E
Fonte Boa 184 2 33S 66 0W
Foochow = Fuzhou .... 99 26 5N 119 16 E
Forbes .... 117 33 22S 148 0 E
Forestburg 155 52 35N 112 1W
Forestville 148 48 48N 69 2W
Forfar 33 56 40N 2 53W
Forlì .... 47 44 14N 12 2 E
Formby Pt. 28 53 33N 3 7W
Formentera .... 51 38 43N 1 27 E
Formosa = Taiwan ■ ..... 99 23 30N 121 0 E
Formosa 191 26 15S 58 10W
Forrest City 169 35 0N 90 50W
Fort Albany 140 52 15N 81 35W

Place	Map	Lat °	Lat ′	N/S	Long °	Long ′	E/W
Fort Augustus	32	57	9	N	4	40	W
Fort Chipewyan	145	58	42	N	111	8	W
Fort Collins	163	40	30	N	105	4	W
Fort-Coulonge	151	45	50	N	76	45	W
Fort-de-France	180	14	36	N	61	2	W
Fort Dodge	166	42	29	N	94	10	W
Fort Frances	153	48	36	N	93	24	W
Fort Franklin	145	65	10	N	123	30	W
Fort George	140	53	50	N	79	0	W
Fort Good-Hope	144	66	14	N	128	40	W
Fort Hertz = Putao	93	27	28	N	97	30	E
Fort Kent	148	47	12	N	68	30	W
Fort-Lamy = Ndjamena	131	12	10	N	14	59	E
Fort Lauderdale	170	26	10	N	80	5	W
Fort Liard	144	60	14	N	123	30	W
Fort Mackay	143	57	12	N	111	41	W
Fort Macleod	155	49	45	N	113	30	W
Fort McMurray	155	56	44	N	111	7	W
Fort McPherson	144	67	30	N	134	55	W
Fort Madison	166	40	39	N	91	20	W
Fort Morgan	163	40	10	N	103	50	W
Fort Myers	170	26	39	N	81	51	W
Fort Nelson	144	58	50	N	122	44	W
Fort Nelson →	144	59	32	N	124	0	W
Fort Payne	169	34	25	N	85	44	W
Fort Peck L.	163	47	40	N	107	0	W
Fort Pierce	170	27	29	N	80	19	W
Fort Providence	145	61	3	N	117	40	W
Fort Qu'Appelle	152	50	45	N	103	50	W
Fort Resolution	145	61	10	N	113	40	W
Fort Rupert	140	51	30	N	78	40	W
Fort St. James	154	54	30	N	124	10	W
Fort St. John	155	56	15	N	120	50	W
Fort Sandeman	88	31	20	N	69	31	E
Fort Saskatchewan	155	53	40	N	113	15	W
Fort Scott	166	37	50	N	94	40	W
Fort Severn	140	56	0	N	87	40	W
Fort Shevchenko	70	43	40	N	51	20	E
Fort Simpson	144	61	45	N	121	15	W
Fort Smith, Canada	145	60	0	N	111	51	W
Fort Smith, U.S.A.	168	35	25	N	94	25	W
Fort Smith Region □	145	63	0	N	120	0	W
Fort Trinquet = Bir Mogrein	126	25	10	N	11	25	W
Fort Valley	170	32	33	N	83	52	W
Fort Vermilion	145	58	24	N	116	0	W
Fort Wayne	167	41	5	N	85	10	W
Fort William	32	56	48	N	5	8	W
Fort Worth	168	32	45	N	97	25	W
Fort Yukon	142	66	35	N	145	20	W
Fortaleza	189	3	45	S	38	35	W
Forth →	31	56	9	N	4	18	W
Forth, Firth of	31	56	5	N	2	55	W
Fortuna	172	40	38	N	124	8	W
Foshan	99	23	4	N	113	5	E
Foster	117	38	40	S	146	15	E
Fougères	36	48	21	N	1	14	W
Foula, I.	30	60	10	N	2	5	W
Foulness I.	24	51	36	N	0	55	E
Fourmies	38	50	1	N	4	2	E
Foúrnoi	55	37	36	N	26	32	E
Fouta Djalon	130	11	20	N	12	10	W
Foveaux Str.	123	46	42	S	168	10	E
Fowey	27	50	20	N	4	39	W
Foxe Basin	146	66	0	N	77	0	W
Foxe Chan.	146	65	0	N	80	0	W
Foxe Pen.	146	65	0	N	76	0	W
Foxton	122	40	29	S	175	18	E
Foyle, Lough	34	55	6	N	7	8	W
Foynes	35	52	37	N	9	5	W
Franca	188	20	33	S	47	30	W
France ■	37	47	0	N	3	0	E
Franche-Comté	37	46	30	N	5	50	E
François	180	14	38	N	60	57	W
Franeker	41	53	12	N	5	33	E
Frankfort, Ind., U.S.A.	167	40	20	N	86	33	W
Frankfort, Ky., U.S.A.	165	38	12	N	84	52	W
Frankfurt am Main	42	50	7	N	8	40	E
Frankfurt an der Oder	43	52	50	N	14	31	E
Fränkische Alb	43	49	20	N	11	30	E
Franklin, La., U.S.A.	168	29	45	N	91	30	W
Franklin, N.H., U.S.A.	164	43	28	N	71	39	W
Franklin, W. Va., U.S.A.	165	38	38	N	79	21	W
Franklin D. Roosevelt L.	162	48	30	N	118	16	W
Franklin Mts.	145	65	0	N	125	0	W
Franklin Str.	145	72	0	N	96	0	W
Frankston	117	38	8	S	145	8	E
Franz	150	48	25	N	84	30	W
Fraser →	154	49	7	N	123	11	W
Fraser, Mt.	120	25	35	S	118	20	E
Fraser I.	116	25	15	S	153	10	E
Fraserburgh	33	57	41	N	2	0	W
Fray Bentos	190	33	10	S	58	15	W
Frederick	164	39	25	N	77	23	W
Fredericksburg	165	38	16	N	77	29	W
Fredericton	148	45	57	N	66	40	W
Frederikshavn	61	57	28	N	10	31	E
Fredrikstad	60	59	13	N	10	57	E
Freeport, Bahamas	178	26	30	N	78	47	W
Freeport, Ill., U.S.A.	166	42	18	N	89	40	W
Freeport, N.Y., U.S.A.	164	40	39	N	73	35	W
Freeport, Tex., U.S.A.	158	28	55	N	95	22	W
Freetown	130	8	30	N	13	17	W
Freiberg	42	50	55	N	13	20	E
Freibourg = Fribourg	44	46	49	N	7	9	E
Fréjus	37	43	25	N	6	44	E
Fremantle	120	32	7	S	115	47	E
Fremont, Calif., U.S.A.	172	37	32	N	122	1	W
Fremont, Nebr., U.S.A.	166	41	30	N	96	30	W
French Guiana ■	185	4	0	N	53	0	W
French Pass	123	40	55	S	173	55	E
French Terr. of Afars & Issas = Djibouti ■	133	12	0	N	43	0	E
Fresnillo	175	23	10	N	102	53	W
Fresno	173	36	47	N	119	50	W
Fria, C.	136	18	0	S	12	0	E
Frias	190	28	40	S	65	5	W
Fribourg	44	46	49	N	7	9	E
Friendly, Is. = Tonga ■	123	19	50	S	174	30	W
Friesland □	41	53	5	N	5	50	E
Frio, C.	182	22	50	S	41	50	W
Friuli-Venezia Giulia □	47	46	0	N	13	0	E
Frobisher B.	146	62	30	N	66	0	W
Frobisher Bay	146	63	44	N	68	31	W
Frobisher L.	152	56	20	N	108	15	W
Frome	27	51	16	N	2	17	W
Frome, L.	118	30	45	S	139	45	E
Frome Downs	118	31	13	S	139	45	E
Front Range	163	40	0	N	105	40	W
Front Royal	164	38	55	N	78	10	W
Frontera	177	18	32	N	92	38	W
Frostburg	164	39	43	N	78	57	W
Frunze = Bishkek	71	42	54	N	74	46	E
Frutal	188	20	0	S	49	0	W
Fuchou = Fuzhou	99	26	5	N	119	16	E
Fuchū, Hiroshima, Japan	109	34	34	N	133	14	E
Fūchū, Tōkyō, Japan	107	35	40	N	139	29	E
Fuerte, R. →	174	25	54	N	109	22	W
Fuji	107	35	9	N	138	39	E
Fuji-no-miya	107	35	10	N	138	40	E
Fuji-San	107	35	22	N	138	44	E
Fuji-yoshida	107	35	30	N	138	46	E
Fujian □	99	26	0	N	118	0	E
Fujieda	107	34	52	N	138	16	E
Fujisawa	107	35	22	N	139	29	E
Fukaya	107	36	12	N	139	12	E
Fukien = Fujian □	99	26	0	N	118	0	E
Fukuchiyama	106	35	19	N	135	9	E
Fukue-Shima	104	32	40	N	128	45	E
Fukui	106	36	0	N	136	10	E
Fukuoka	108	33	39	N	130	21	E
Fukushima	103	37	44	N	140	28	E
Fukuyama	109	34	35	N	133	20	E
Fulton, Mo., U.S.A.	166	38	50	N	91	55	W
Fulton, N.Y., U.S.A.	164	43	20	N	76	22	W
Funabashi	107	35	45	N	140	0	E
Funchal	126	32	38	N	16	54	W
Fundación	184	10	31	N	74	11	W
Fundy, B. of	148	45	0	N	66	0	W
Furāt, Nahr al →	84	31	0	N	47	25	E
Furneaux Group	119	40	10	S	147	50	E
Furness	28	54	14	N	3	8	W
Fürth	43	49	29	N	11	0	E

Fury and Hecla Str. 146 69 56N 84 0W
Fushun .... 98 41 50N 123 55 E
Fuxin .... 98 42 5N 121 48 E
Fuzhou .... 99 26 5N 119 16 E
Fylde 28 53 50N 2 58W
Fyn .... 61 55 20N 10 30 E
Fyne, L. 30 56 0N 5 20W

G

Gabès, Golfe de .... 127 34 0N 10 30 E
Gabon ■ .... 134 0 10S 10 0 E
Gaborone .... 137 24 45S 25 57 E
Gachsārān .... 85 30 15N 50 45 E
Gadag .... 90 15 30N 75 45 E
Gadsden 169 34 1N 86 0W
Gaeta .... 49 41 12N 13 35 E
Gaffney 165 35 3N 81 40W
Gagnon 141 51 50N 68 5W
Gainesville, Fla., U.S.A. 170 29 38N 82 20W
Gainesville, Ga., U.S.A. 165 34 17N 83 47W
Gainesville, Tex., U.S.A. 168 33 40N 97 10W
Gainsborough 29 53 23N 0 46W
Gairdner L. .... 118 31 30S 136 0 E
Galápagos 10 0 0 89 0W
Galas ─▶ .... 96 4 55N 101 57 E
Galashiels 31 55 37N 2 50W
Galați .... 57 45 27N 28 2 E
Galatina .... 49 40 10N 18 10 E
Galdhøpiggen .... 60 61 38N 8 18 E
Galesburg 166 40 57N 90 23W
Galicia □ 50 42 43N 7 45W
Galilee, L. .... 121 22 20S 145 50 E
Gallatin 169 36 24N 86 27W
Galle .... 90 6 5N 80 10 E
Gallinas, Pta. 184 12 28N 71 40W
Gallipoli = Gelibolu .... 80 40 28N 26 43 E
Gallipoli .... 49 40 8N 18 0 E
Gällivare .... 66 67 9N 20 40 E
Galloway 31 55 0N 4 25W
Galloway, Mull of 30 54 38N 4 50W
Gallup 161 35 30N 108 45W
Galty Mts. 35 52 22N 8 10W
Galveston 168 29 15N 94 48W
Galveston B. 168 29 30N 94 50W
Galway 35 53 16N 9 4W
Galway □ 34 53 16N 9 3W
Gamagori .... 106 34 50N 137 14 E
Gambia ■ 130 13 25N 16 0W
Gambia ─▶ 130 13 28N 16 34W
Gand = Gent .... 42 51 2N 3 42 E
Gander 149 48 58N 54 35W
Gandhi Sagar .... 91 24 40N 75 40 E
Gandi .... 131 12 55N 5 49 E
Ganga ─▶ .... 92 23 20N 90 30 E
Ganges = Ganga ─▶ ..... 92 23 20N 90 30 E
Gangtok .... 92 27 20N 88 37 E
Gannett Pk. 163 43 10N 109 38W
Gansu □ .... 98 36 0N 104 0 E
Ganzhou .... 99 25 51N 114 56 E
Gao 130 16 15N 0 5W
Gaoxiong .... 99 22 38N 120 18 E
Garachiné 179 8 0N 78 12W
Garanhuns 189 8 50S 36 30W
Garberville 172 40 11N 123 50W
Garda, L. di .... 46 45 40N 10 40 E
Garden City 161 38 0N 100 45W
Garden Grove 173 33 47N 117 55W
Gardēz .... 87 33 37N 69 9 E
Garmsār .... 86 35 20N 52 25 E
Garonne ─▶ 36 45 2N 0 36W
Garoua .... 131 9 19N 13 21 E
Garrison Res. = Sakakawea,
L. 163 47 30N 102 0W
Garry L. 145 65 58N 100 18W
Garvie Mts. .... 123 45 30S 168 50 E
Garwa = Garoua .... 131 9 19N 13 21 E
Gary 167 41 35N 87 20W

Garzón 184 2 10N 75 40W
Gascogne .... 36 43 45N 0 20 E
Gascony = Gascogne ..... 36 43 45N 0 20 E
Gaspé 148 48 52N 64 30W
Gaspé, C. de 148 48 48N 64 7W
Gaspé, Pén. de 148 48 45N 65 40W
Gastonia 165 35 17N 81 10W
Gastre 192 42 20S 69 15W
Gata, C. de 51 36 41N 2 13W
Gateshead 28 54 57N 1 37W
Gauhati .... 93 26 10N 91 45 E
Gävle .... 60 60 40N 17 9 E
Gävleborgs län □ .... 60 61 30N 16 15 E
Gawilgarh Hills .... 91 21 15N 76 45 E
Gawler .... 119 34 30S 138 42 E
Gawler Ranges .... 114 32 30S 135 45 E
Gaxun Nur .... 100 42 22N 100 30 E
Gaya .... 92 24 47N 85 4 E
Gaylord 150 45 1N 84 41W
Gayndah .... 116 25 35S 151 32 E
Gaza .... 80 31 30N 34 28 E
Gaziantep .... 80 37 6N 37 23 E
Gdańsk .... 58 54 22N 18 40 E
Gdańska, Zatoka .... 58 54 30N 19 20 E
Gdynia .... 58 54 35N 18 33 E
Gedaref .... 129 14 2N 35 28 E
Geelong .... 117 38 10S 144 22 E
Gejiu .... 99 23 20N 103 10 E
Gelderland □ .... 41 52 5N 6 10 E
Geldermalsen .... 40 51 53N 5 17 E
Geldrop .... 41 51 25N 5 32 E
Geleen .... 41 50 57N 5 49 E
Gelibolu .... 80 40 28N 26 43 E
Gelsenkirchen .... 42 51 30N 7 5 E
Gemert .... 41 51 33N 5 41 E
General Alvear 190 35 0S 67 40W
General Pico 190 35 45S 63 50W
Geneva = Genève .... 44 46 12N 6 9 E
Geneva 164 42 53N 77 0W
Geneva, L. = Léman, Lac .. 44 46 26N 6 30 E
Genève .... 44 46 12N 6 9 E
Genk .... 41 50 58N 5 32 E
Genkai-Nada .... 108 34 0N 130 0 E
Gennargentu, Mti. del .... 48 40 0N 9 10 E
Genoa = Génova .... 46 44 24N 8 56 E
Génova .... 46 44 24N 8 56 E
Génova, Golfo di .... 46 44 0N 9 0 E
Gent .... 42 51 2N 3 42 E
George, L. .... 132 0 5N 30 10 E
George River = Port
Nouveau-Québec 146 58 30N 65 59W
George Town .... 96 5 25N 100 15 E
Georgetown, Australia .... 119 18 17S 143 33 E
Georgetown, Canada 151 43 40N 79 56W
Georgetown, Guyana 185 6 50N 58 12W
Georgetown, U.S.A. 170 33 22N 79 15W
Georgia □ 170 32 0N 82 0W
Georgia ■ .... 70 42 0N 43 0 E
Georgian B. 151 45 15N 81 0W
Gera .... 43 50 53N 12 11 E
Geraldton, Australia ..... 120 28 48S 114 32 E
Geraldton, Canada 150 49 44N 86 59W
Gereshk .... 87 31 47N 64 35 E
Germany ■ .... 18 52 0N 12 0 E
Germiston .... 137 26 15S 28 10 E
Gerona .... 51 41 58N 2 46 E
Ghana ■ 130 6 0N 1 0W
Ghat .... 127 24 59N 10 11 E
Ghawdex = Gozo .... 49 36 0N 14 13 E
Ghaziabad .... 89 28 42N 77 26 E
Ghazipur .... 92 25 38N 83 35 E
Ghaznī .... 87 33 30N 68 28 E
Ghaznī □ .... 87 32 10N 68 20 E
Ghent = Gent .... 42 51 2N 3 42 E
Ghowr □ .... 87 34 0N 64 20 E
Ghulam Mohammad Barrage 88 25 30N 68 20 E
Giant's Causeway 34 55 15N 6 30W
Gibara 178 21 9N 76 11W
Gibraltar 50 36 7N 5 22W
Gibraltar, Str. of 50 35 55N 5 40W
Gien .... 39 47 40N 2 36 E

Gifu .... 106 35 30N 136 45 E
Gigha 30 55 42N 5 45W
Gijón 50 43 32N 5 42W
Gila → 173 32 43N 114 33W
Gīlān □ .... 81 37 0N 50 0 E
Gilbert Is. = Kiribati ■ .... 122 1 0N 176 0 E
Gilford I. 154 50 40N 126 30W
Gilgandra .... 116 31 43S 148 39 E
Gilgit .... 89 35 50N 74 15 E
Gillingham .... 25 51 23N 0 34 E
Gingin .... 120 31 22S 115 54 E
Gippsland .... 117 37 45S 147 15 E
Girardot 184 4 18N 74 48W
Giresun .... 81 40 55N 38 30 E
Gironde → 36 45 32N 1 7W
Girvan 30 55 15N 4 50W
Gisborne .... 122 38 39S 178 5 E
Gisors .... 39 49 15N 1 47 E
Gizhiga .... 73 62 3N 160 30 E
Gizhiginskaya, Guba ..... 73 61 0N 158 0 E
Giżycko .... 58 54 2N 21 48 E
Gjoa Haven 145 68 20N 96 8W
Glace Bay 149 46 11N 59 58W
Gladstone, Queens., Australia 121 23 52S 151 16 E
Gladstone, S. Austral.,
  Australia .... 118 33 15S 138 22 E
Gláma 64 65 48N 23 0W
Glasgow, U.K. 31 55 52N 4 14W
Glasgow, U.S.A. 169 37 2N 85 55W
Glastonbury 27 51 9N 2 42W
Gleiwitz = Gliwice .... 58 50 22N 18 41 E
Glen Coe 32 56 40N 5 0W
Glen Innes .... 116 29 44S 151 44 E
Glen Mor .... 33 57 12N 4 37 E
Glenburgh .... 120 25 26S 116 6 E
Glendale 173 34 7N 118 18W
Glendive 163 47 7N 104 40W
Glenelg .... 119 34 58S 138 31 E
Glenns Ferry 172 43 0N 115 15W
Glenorchy .... 119 42 49S 147 18 E
Glenrothes 31 56 12N 3 11W
Glens Falls 164 43 20N 73 40W
Gliwice .... 58 50 22N 18 41 E
Głogów .... 58 51 37N 16 5 E
Glossop 28 53 27N 1 56W
Gloucester 24 51 52N 2 15W
Gloucestershire □ 24 51 44N 2 10W
Gloversville 164 43 5N 74 18W
Gniezno .... 58 52 30N 17 35 E
Go Cong .... 95 10 22N 106 40 E
Goa .... 91 15 33N 73 59 E
Goa □ .... 90 15 33N 73 59 E
Goat Fell 30 55 37N 5 11W
Goba .... 133 7 1N 39 59 E
Gobi .... 98 44 0N 111 0 E
Gobō .... 106 33 53N 135 10 E
Godavari → .... 91 16 25N 82 18 E
Godbout 148 49 20N 67 38W
Goderich 150 43 45N 81 41W
Godhra .... 91 22 49N 73 40 E
Gods L. 153 54 40N 94 15W
Godthåb 147 64 10N 51 35W
Goeie Hoop, Kaap die ... 136 34 24S 18 30 E
Goeree .... 40 51 50N 4 0 E
Goes .... 40 51 30N 3 55 E
Gogama 151 47 35N 81 43W
Goiânia 188 16 43S 49 20W
Goiás □ 188 12 10S 48 0W
Goirle .... 40 51 31N 5 4 E
Gojō .... 106 34 21N 135 42 E
Gökçeada .... 55 40 10N 25 50 E
Gold Coast, Australia ... 116 28 0S 153 25 E
Gold Coast, W. Afr. 124 4 0N 1 40W
Golden Bay .... 122 40 40S 172 50 E
Golden Gate 172 37 54N 122 30W
Golden Hinde 154 49 40N 125 44W
Golden Vale 35 52 33N 8 17W
Goldfield 172 37 45N 117 13W
Goldsboro 165 35 24N 77 59W
Goldsworthy .... 114 20 21S 119 30 E
Golfo Aranci .... 48 41 0N 9 35 E

Gomel .... 68 52 28N 31 0 E
Gómez Palacio 174 25 34N 103 30W
Gonābād .... 86 34 15N 58 45 E
Gonaïves 180 19 20N 72 42W
Gonda .... 92 27 9N 81 58 E
Gonder .... 132 12 39N 37 30 E
Good Hope, C. of = Goeie
  Hoop, Kaap die .... 136 34 24S 18 30 E
Goole 29 53 42N 0 52W
Goondiwindi .... 116 28 30S 150 21 E
Goose Bay 147 53 15N 60 20W
Gorakhpur .... 92 26 47N 83 23 E
Gordonvale .... 121 17 5S 145 50 E
Gore, Ethiopia .... 132 8 12N 35 32 E
Gore, N.Z. .... 123 46 5S 168 58 E
Gorey 35 52 41N 6 18W
Gorinchem .... 40 51 50N 4 59 E
Gorkiy = Nizhniy Novgorod . 68 56 20N 44 0 E
Görlitz .... 43 51 10N 14 59 E
Gorna Oryakhovitsa ...... 53 43 7N 25 40 E
Gort 35 53 4N 8 50W
Gorzów Wielkopolski ..... 58 52 43N 15 15 E
Gosford .... 117 33 23S 151 18 E
Gospič .... 52 44 35N 15 23 E
Gosport 25 50 48N 1 8W
Göteborg .... 60 57 43N 11 59 E
Göteborgs och Bohus län □ . 60 58 30N 11 30 E
Gotemba .... 107 35 18N 138 56 E
Gotha .... 43 50 56N 10 42 E
Gotland .... 60 57 30N 18 33 E
Gōtsu .... 109 35 0N 132 14 E
Gottwaldov = Zlín .... 59 49 14N 17 40 E
Gouda .... 40 52 1N 4 42 E
Gouin, Rés. 151 48 35N 74 40W
Goulburn .... 117 34 44S 149 44 E
Goundam 130 16 25N 3 45W
Gournay-en-Bray .... 38 49 29N 1 44 E
Governador Valadares 188 18 15S 41 57W
Governor's Harbour 178 25 10N 76 14W
Gower, The 27 51 35N 4 10W
Goya 190 29 10S 59 10W
Gozo .... 49 36 0N 14 13 E
Graaff-Reinet .... 136 32 13S 24 32 E
Gracias a Dios, C. 179 15 0N 83 10W
Grafton .... 116 29 38S 152 58 E
Graham 165 36 5N 79 22W
Graham I. 154 53 40N 132 30W
Graham Land 14 65 0S 64 0W
Grahamstown .... 137 33 19S 26 31 E
Grain Coast 124 4 20N 10 0W
Grampian □ 33 57 0N 3 0W
Grampian Mts. 33 56 50N 4 0W
Grampians, The .... 119 37 0S 142 20 E
Gran Chaco 190 25 0S 61 0W
Gran Sasso d'Italia ...... 47 42 25N 13 30 E
Granada, Nic. 179 11 58N 86 0W
Granada, Spain 50 37 10N 3 35W
Granby 151 45 25N 72 45W
Grand Bank 149 47 6N 55 48W
Grand Bassam 130 5 10N 3 49W
Grand Canyon 160 36 3N 112 9W
Grand Cayman 178 19 20N 81 20W
Grand Cess 130 4 40N 8 12W
Grand Falls 149 48 56N 55 40W
Grand Forks, Canada 155 49 0N 118 30W
Grand Forks, U.S.A. 156 48 0N 97 3W
Grand Island 163 40 59N 98 25W
Grand Junction 163 39 0N 108 30W
Grand Mère 151 46 36N 72 40W
Grand Portage 150 47 58N 89 41W
Grand Rapids, Canada ... 153 53 12N 99 19W
Grand Rapids, U.S.A. ... 167 42 57N 86 40W
Grand St.-Bernard, Col. du . 44 45 53N 7 11 E
Grand Teton 163 43 54N 111 50W
Grand View 153 51 10N 100 42W
Grande →, Bolivia 187 15 51S 64 39W
Grande- →, Brazil 188 20 6S 51 4W
Grande, B. 192 50 30S 68 20W
Grande, La 171 45 15N 118 0W
Grande, La → 140 53 50N 79 0W
Grande Baleine, R. de la → . 140 55 16N 77 47W

Name	Page	Lat °	Lat '	N/S	Long °	Long '	E/W
Grande de Santiago, R. →	175	21	36N		105	26W	
Grande Prairie	155	55	10N		118	50W	
Grande-Rivière	148	48	26N		64	30W	
Grange, La	170	33	4N		85	0W	
Grangemouth	31	56	1N		3	43W	
Grangeville	162	45	57N		116	4W	
Granite City	166	38	45N		90	3W	
Grant, Mt.	172	38	34N		118	48W	
Grantham	29	52	55N		0	39W	
Grantown-on-Spey	33	57	19N		3	36W	
Grants Pass	171	42	30N		123	22W	
Grass Valley	172	39	18N		121	0W	
Grasse	37	43	38N		6	56 E	
Gravelbourg	152	49	50N		106	35W	
Gravelines	38	51	0N		2	10 E	
's-Gravenhage	40	52	7N		4	17 E	
Gravesend	25	51	25N		0	22 E	
Grayling	167	44	40N		84	42W	
Graz	45	47	4N		15	27 E	
Great Abaco I.	178	26	25N		77	10W	
Great Australian Bight	114	33	30S		130	0 E	
Great Bahama Bank	178	23	15N		78	0W	
Great Barrier I.	122	36	11S		175	25 E	
Great Barrier Reef	121	18	0S		146	50 E	
Great Basin	172	40	0N		116	30W	
Great Bear L.	145	65	30N		120	0W	
Great Britain	16	54	0N		2	15W	
Great Divide, The	117	35	0S		149	17 E	
Great Dividing Ra.	121	23	0S		146	0 E	
Great Exuma I.	178	23	30N		75	50W	
Great Falls	163	47	27N		111	12W	
Great Inagua I.	180	21	0N		73	20W	
Great Indian Desert = Thar Desert	89	28	0N		72	0 E	
Great Orme's Head	26	53	20N		3	52W	
Great Ouse →	29	52	47N		0	22 E	
Great Plains	138	47	0N		105	0W	
Great Salt Lake	162	41	0N		112	30W	
Great Salt Lake Desert	162	40	20N		113	50W	
Great Slave L.	145	61	23N		115	38W	
Great Wall	98	38	30N		109	30 E	
Great Whernside	28	54	9N		1	59W	
Great Yarmouth	29	52	40N		1	45 E	
Greater Antilles	181	17	40N		74	0W	
Greater Manchester □	28	53	30N		2	15W	
Greater Sunda Is.	111	2	30S		110	0 E	
Gredos, Sierra de	50	40	20N		5	0W	
Greece ■	54	40	0N		23	0 E	
Greeley	163	40	30N		104	40W	
Green →, Ky., U.S.A.	167	37	54N		87	30W	
Green →, Utah, U.S.A.	163	38	11N		109	53W	
Green Bay	167	44	30N		88	0W	
Greenfield	164	42	38N		72	38W	
Greenland □	147	66	0N		45	0W	
Greenland Sea	13	73	0N		10	0W	
Greenock	30	55	57N		4	46W	
Greensboro	165	36	7N		79	46W	
Greenville, Ala., U.S.A.	169	31	50N		86	37W	
Greenville, Mich., U.S.A.	167	43	12N		85	14W	
Greenville, Miss., U.S.A.	168	33	25N		91	0W	
Greenville, N.C., U.S.A.	165	35	37N		77	26W	
Greenville, S.C., U.S.A.	165	34	54N		82	24W	
Greenville, Tenn., U.S.A.	165	36	13N		82	51W	
Greenwood, Miss., U.S.A.	169	33	30N		90	4W	
Greenwood, S.C., U.S.A.	165	34	13N		82	13W	
Grenada	169	33	45N		89	50W	
Grenada ■	180	12	10N		61	40W	
Grenoble	37	45	12N		5	42 E	
Grenville	117	37	46S		143	52 E	
Gretna Green	31	55	0N		3	3W	
Grey Range	116	27	0S		143	30 E	
Grey Res.	149	48	20N		56	30W	
Greymouth	123	42	29S		171	13 E	
Griffin	170	33	17N		84	14W	
Griffith	117	34	18S		146	2 E	
Grimsby	29	53	35N		0	5W	
Grimshaw	155	56	10N		117	40W	
Grinnell	166	41	45N		92	43W	
Grodno	68	53	42N		23	52 E	
Groningen	41	53	15N		6	35 E	
Groningen □	41	53	16N		6	40 E	
Grootfontein	136	19	31S		18	6 E	
Groznyy	70	43	20N		45	45 E	
Grudziądz	58	53	30N		18	47 E	
Grytviken	14	53	50S		37	10W	
Gt. Stour = Stour →	25	51	15N		1	20 E	
Guadalajara, Mexico	175	20	40N		103	20W	
Guadalajara, Spain	50	40	37N		3	12W	
Guadalquivir →	50	36	47N		6	22W	
Guadalupe = Guadeloupe ■	180	16	20N		61	40W	
Guadalupe Bravos	174	31	23N		106	7W	
Guadarrama, Sierra de	50	41	0N		4	0W	
Guadeloupe ■	180	16	20N		61	40W	
Guadiana →	50	37	14N		7	22W	
Guadix	50	37	18N		3	11W	
Guaira	191	24	5S		54	10W	
Guajará-Mirim	187	10	50S		65	20W	
Gualeguay	190	33	10S		59	14W	
Gualeguaychú	190	33	3S		59	31W	
Guam	10	13	27N		144	45 E	
Guanabacoa	178	23	8N		82	18W	
Guanacaste, Cordillera del	179	10	40N		85	4W	
Guanahani = San Salvador	178	24	0N		74	40W	
Guanajay	178	22	56N		82	42W	
Guanajuato	177	21	1N		101	15W	
Guanajuato □	177	21	0N		101	0W	
Guanare	184	8	42N		69	12W	
Guangdong □	99	23	0N		113	0 E	
Guangxi Zhuangzu Zizhiqu □	99	24	0N		109	0 E	
Guangzhou	99	23	5N		113	10 E	
Guantánamo	178	20	10N		75	14W	
Guaporé →	187	11	55S		65	4W	
Guaqui	187	16	41S		68	54W	
Guarapuava	191	25	20S		51	30W	
Guarda	50	40	32N		7	20W	
Guardafui, C. = Asir, Ras	133	11	55N		51	10 E	
Guatemala	177	14	40N		90	22W	
Guatemala ■	177	15	40N		90	30W	
Guaviare →	184	4	3N		67	44W	
Guayama	180	17	59N		66	7W	
Guayaquil	184	2	15S		79	52W	
Guayaquil, G. de	186	3	10S		81	0W	
Guaymas	174	27	56N		110	54W	
Guddu Barrage	89	28	30N		69	50 E	
Gudur	90	14	12N		79	55 E	
Guelph	151	43	35N		80	20W	
Guernica	50	43	19N		2	40W	
Guernsey	36	49	30N		2	35W	
Guerrero □	177	17	40N		100	0W	
Guilin	99	25	18N		110	15 E	
Guimarães	188	2	9S		44	42W	
Guinea ■	130	10	20N		10	0W	
Guinea, Gulf of	130	3	0N		2	30 E	
Guinea-Bissau ■	130	12	0N		15	0W	
Güines	178	22	50N		82	0W	
Guiyang	99	26	32N		106	40 E	
Guizhou □	99	27	0N		107	0 E	
Gujarat □	91	23	20N		71	0 E	
Gujranwala	89	32	10N		74	12 E	
Gujrat	89	32	40N		74	2 E	
Gulbarga	91	17	20N		76	50 E	
Gulf, The	85	27	0N		50	0 E	
Gulfport	169	30	21N		89	3W	
Gulgong	116	32	20S		149	49 E	
Gull Lake	152	50	10N		108	29W	
Gümüsane	81	40	30N		39	30 E	
Guna	91	24	40N		77	19 E	
Gundagai	117	35	3S		148	6 E	
Gunnedah	116	30	59S		150	15 E	
Gunningbar Cr. →	116	31	14S		147	6 E	
Guntakal	90	15	11N		77	27 E	
Guntersville	169	34	18N		86	16W	
Guntur	92	16	23N		80	30 E	
Gurdaspur	89	32	5N		75	31 E	
Gurgaon	89	28	27N		77	1 E	
Gurkha	92	28	5N		84	40 E	
Gurupi →	188	1	13S		46	6W	
Guryev	70	47	5N		52	0 E	
Gusau	131	12	12N		6	40 E	
Guthrie	168	35	55N		97	30W	
Guyana ■	185	5	0N		59	0W	
Guyenne	36	44	30N		0	40 E	

Guyra	116	30	15S	151	40	E
Gwalior	91	26	12N	78	10	E
Gwent □	27	51	45N	2	55W	
Gweru	137	19	28S	29	45	E
Gwynedd □	26	53	0N	4	0W	
Gyandzha	70	40	45N	46	20	E
Gyaring Hu	101	34	50N	97	40	E
Gydanskiy P-ov.	69	70	0N	78	0	E
Gympie	116	26	11S	152	38	E
Gyoda	107	36	10N	139	30	E
Gyöngyös	59	47	48N	20	0	E
Györ	59	47	41N	17	40	E
Gypsumville	153	51	45N	98	40W	

H

Ha 'Arava	80	30	50N	35	20	E
Ha Giang	95	22	50N	104	59	E
Haarlem	40	52	23N	4	39	E
Habana, La	178	23	8N	82	22W	
Hachijō-Jima	105	33	5N	139	45	E
Hachinohe	103	40	30N	141	29	E
Hachiōji	107	35	40N	139	20	E
Hadera	80	32	27N	34	55	E
Hadhramaut = Ḥaḍramawt	83	15	30N	49	30	E
Hadiya	82	25	30N	36	56	E
Ḥaḍramawt	83	15	30N	49	30	E
Hadrians Wall	28	55	0N	2	30W	
Haeju	98	38	3N	125	45	E
Haerhpin = Harbin	98	45	48N	126	40	E
Hafar al Bāṭin	82	28	25N	46	0	E
Hafnarfjörður	64	64	4N	21	57W	
Haft-Gel	84	31	30N	49	32	E
Hagen	42	51	21N	7	29	E
Hagerstown	164	39	39N	77	46W	
Hagi	108	34	30N	131	22	E
Hags Hd.	35	52	57N	9	30W	
Hague, The = 's-Gravenhage	40	52	7N	4	17	E
Hai'an	99	32	37N	120	27	E
Haifa = Ḥefa	80	32	46N	35	0	E
Haikou	99	20	1N	110	16	E
Ḥā'il	82	27	28N	41	45	E
Hailar	98	49	10N	119	38	E
Hailey	162	43	30N	114	15W	
Haileybury	151	47	30N	79	38W	
Hainan	99	19	0N	110	0	E
Hainan Dao	99	19	0N	109	30	E
Haiphong	95	20	47N	106	41	E
Haiti ■	180	19	0N	72	30W	
Hakken-Zan	106	34	10N	135	54	E
Hakodate	103	41	45N	140	44	E
Ḥalab	80	36	10N	37	15	E
Halaib	129	22	12N	36	30	E
Halberstadt	43	51	53N	11	2	E
Halfmoon Bay	123	46	50S	168	5	E
Halifax, Canada	148	44	38N	63	35W	
Halifax, U.K.	28	53	43N	1	51W	
Halifax B.	121	18	50S	147	0	E
Hallands län □	61	56	50N	12	50	E
Halle	43	51	29N	12	0	E
Halls Creek	114	18	16S	127	38	E
Halmahera	113	0	40N	128	0	E
Halmstad	61	56	41N	12	52	E
Hälsingborg = Helsingborg	61	56	3N	12	42	E
Hamada	109	34	56N	132	4	E
Hamadān	81	34	52N	48	32	E
Hamadān □	81	35	0N	49	0	E
Hamāh	80	35	5N	36	40	E
Hamakita	107	34	45N	137	47	E
Hamamatsu	106	34	45N	137	45	E
Hamar	60	60	48N	11	7	E
Hamburg	43	53	32N	9	59	E
Hämeenlinna	67	61	0N	24	28	E
Hamelin Pool	120	26	22S	114	20	E
Hameln	42	52	7N	9	24	E
Hamhung	98	39	54N	127	30	E
Hamilton, Australia	119	37	45S	142	2	E
Hamilton, Bermuda	180	32	15N	64	45W	
Hamilton, Canada	151	43	15N	79	50W	
Hamilton, N.Z.	122	37	47S	175	19	E
Hamilton, U.K.	31	55	47N	4	2W	
Hamilton, U.S.A.	167	39	20N	84	35W	
Hamm	42	51	40N	7	49	E
Hammerfest	67	70	39N	23	41	E
Hammond, Ind., U.S.A.	167	41	40N	87	30W	
Hammond, La., U.S.A.	169	30	32N	90	30W	
Hampshire □	25	51	3N	1	20W	
Hampshire Downs	25	51	10N	1	10W	
Hampton	165	37	4N	76	18W	
Hanamaki	103	39	23N	141	7	E
Hancock	150	47	10N	88	40W	
Handa	106	34	53N	137	0	E
Handan	98	36	35N	114	28	E
Haney	154	49	12N	122	40W	
Hanford	173	36	23N	119	39W	
Hangayn Nuruu	100	47	30N	100	0	E
Hangchou = Hangzhou	99	30	18N	120	11	E
Hangö	67	59	50N	22	57	E
Hangu	98	39	18N	117	53	E
Hangzhou	99	30	18N	120	11	E
Hanna	155	51	40N	111	54W	
Hannibal	166	39	42N	91	22W	
Hannover	42	52	23N	9	43	E
Hanoi	95	21	5N	105	55	E
Hanover = Hannover	42	52	23N	9	43	E
Hanover, N.H., U.S.A.	148	43	43N	72	17W	
Hanover, Pa., U.S.A.	164	39	46N	76	59W	
Hansi	89	29	10N	75	57	E
Hanyū	107	36	10N	139	32	E
Hanzhong	99	33	10N	107	1	E
Haora	92	22	37N	88	20	E
Haparanda	67	65	52N	24	8	E
Ḥaraḍ, Si. Arabia	83	24	22N	49	0	E
Ḥaraḍ, Yemen	83	16	26N	43	5	E
Harare	137	17	43S	31	2	E
Harbin	98	45	48N	126	40	E
Harbour Breton	149	47	29N	55	50W	
Harbour Grace	149	47	40N	53	22W	
Hardap Dam	136	24	32S	17	50	E
Hardenberg	41	52	34N	6	37	E
Harderwijk	41	52	21N	5	38	E
Hardinxveld	40	51	49N	4	53	E
Hardwar = Haridwar	89	29	58N	78	9	E
Harer	133	9	20N	42	8	E
Harfleur	38	49	30N	0	10	E
Hargeisa	133	9	30N	44	2	E
Hari →	111	1	16S	104	5	E
Haridwar	89	29	58N	78	9	E
Harima-Nada	109	34	30N	134	35	E
Harīrūd →	86	34	20N	62	30	E
Harlech	26	52	52N	4	7W	
Harlingen, Neths.	41	53	11N	5	25	E
Harlingen, U.S.A.	161	26	20N	97	50W	
Harlow	25	51	47N	0	9	E
Harney Basin	171	43	30N	119	0W	
Härnösand	66	62	38N	18	0	E
Harriman	169	36	0N	84	35W	
Harris	32	57	50N	6	55W	
Harris L.	118	31	10S	135	10	E
Harrisburg, Ill., U.S.A.	167	37	42N	88	30W	
Harrisburg, Pa., U.S.A.	164	40	18N	76	52W	
Harrison	168	36	10N	93	4W	
Harrison, C.	147	54	55N	57	55W	
Harrison B.	142	70	25N	151	30W	
Harrisonburg	165	38	28N	78	52W	
Harrogate	28	53	59N	1	32W	
Harrow	25	51	35N	0	15W	
Hartford	164	41	47N	72	41W	
Hartland Pt.	27	51	2N	4	32W	
Hartlepool	29	54	42N	1	11W	
Hartsville	165	34	23N	80	2W	
Harvey, Australia	120	33	5S	115	54	E
Harvey, U.S.A.	167	41	40N	87	40W	
Harwich	25	51	56N	1	18	E
Haryana □	89	29	0N	76	10	E
Hashima	106	35	20N	136	40	E
Hashimoto	106	34	19N	135	37	E
Hastings, N.Z.	122	39	39S	176	52	E
Hastings, U.K.	25	50	51N	0	36	E

Hastings, U.S.A.	163	40 34N	98 22W
Hastings Ra.	116	31 15S	152 14 E
Hatano	107	35 22N	139 14 E
Hathras	89	27 36N	78 6 E
Hatteras, C.	165	35 10N	75 30W
Hattiesburg	169	31 20N	89 20W
Hatvan	59	47 40N	19 45 E
Hau Bon = Cheo Reo	95	13 25N	108 28 E
Hauraki Gulf	122	36 35S	175 5 E
Haut Atlas	126	32 30N	5 0W
Havana = Habana, La	178	23 8N	82 22W
Havant	25	50 51N	0 59W
Havelock	151	44 26N	77 53W
Haverfordwest	26	51 48N	4 59W
Haverhill	164	42 50N	71 2W
Havre	163	48 34N	109 40W
Havre, Le	38	49 30N	0 5 E
Hawaii □	160	20 30N	157 0W
Hawaiian Is.	160	20 30N	156 0W
Hawea Lake	123	44 28S	169 19 E
Hawera	122	39 35S	174 19 E
Hawick	31	55 25N	2 48W
Hawke B.	122	39 25S	177 20 E
Hawkesbury	151	45 37N	74 37W
Hawthorne	172	38 31N	118 37W
Hay, Australia	117	34 30S	144 51 E
Hay, U.K.	26	52 4N	3 9W
Hay River	145	60 51N	115 44W
Hayward's Heath	25	51 0N	0 5W
Hazard	165	37 18N	83 10W
Hazaribag	92	23 58N	85 26 E
Hazebrouck	38	50 42N	2 31 E
Hazelton	154	55 20N	127 42W
Hazleton	164	40 58N	76 0W
Healdsburg	172	38 33N	122 51W
Healesville	117	37 35S	145 30 E
Heanor	29	53 1N	1 20W
Hearst	150	49 40N	83 41W
Hebei □	98	39 0N	116 0 E
Hebel	116	28 58S	147 47 E
Hebrides	16	57 30N	7 0W
Hebron = Al Khalīl	80	31 32N	35 6 E
Hebron	147	58 5N	62 30W
Hecate Str.	154	53 10N	130 30W
Hechuan	99	30 2N	106 12 E
Hedmark fylke □	60	61 17N	11 40 E
Heemstede	40	52 22N	4 37 E
Heerenveen	41	52 57N	5 55 E
Heerlen	41	50 55N	6 0 E
Hefa	80	32 46N	35 0 E
Hefei	99	31 52N	117 18 E
Hegang	98	47 20N	130 19 E
Heidelberg	42	49 23N	8 41 E
Heilbronn	42	49 8N	9 13 E
Heilongjiang □	98	48 0N	126 0 E
Heilunkiang = Heilongjiang □	98	48 0N	126 0 E
Heinze Is.	94	14 25N	97 45 E
Hekimhan	81	38 50N	38 0 E
Hekinan	106	34 52N	137 0 E
Hekla	16	63 56N	19 35W
Helena, Ark., U.S.A.	169	34 30N	90 35W
Helena, Mont., U.S.A.	163	46 40N	112 0W
Helensburgh	30	56 0N	4 44W
Helmand ➔	87	31 12N	61 34 E
Helmond	41	51 29N	5 41 E
Helmsdale	33	58 7N	3 40W
Helsingborg	61	56 3N	12 42 E
Helsinki	67	60 15N	25 3 E
Helston	27	50 7N	5 17W
Helvellyn	28	54 31N	3 1W
Hemel Hempstead	25	51 45N	0 28W
Hempstead	164	30 5N	96 5W
Henan □	99	34 0N	114 0 E
Henderson	165	36 20N	78 25W
Hendersonville	165	35 21N	82 28W
Hengelo	41	52 16N	6 48 E
Hengyang	99	26 51N	112 30 E
Hénin-Beaumont	38	50 25N	2 58 E
Hennebont	36	47 49N	3 19W
Henrietta Maria C.	140	55 9N	82 20W
Henty	117	35 30S	147 0 E
Henzada	93	17 38N	95 26 E
Herât	87	34 20N	62 7 E
Herât □	87	35 0N	62 0 E
Herbert ➔	121	18 31S	146 17 E
Herbiers, Les	36	46 52N	1 0W
Hercegnovi	52	42 30N	18 33 E
Hercegovina = Bosnia & Herzegovina □	52	44 0N	18 0 E
Hereford	24	52 4N	2 42W
Hereford and Worcester □	24	52 10N	2 30W
Herford	42	52 7N	8 40 E
Hermosillo	174	29 4N	110 58W
Heroica = Caborca	174	30 40N	112 10W
Heroica Nogales = Nogales	174	31 20N	110 56W
Heron Bay	150	48 40N	86 25W
Herrin	166	37 50N	89 0W
Hertford □	25	51 51N	0 5W
's-Hertogenbosch	40	51 42N	5 17 E
Hesse = Hessen □	42	50 40N	9 20 E
Hessen □	42	50 40N	9 20 E
Hewett, C.	146	70 16N	67 45W
Hexham	28	54 58N	2 7W
Heysham	28	54 5N	2 53W
Heywood	119	38 8S	141 37 E
Hi-no-Misaki	109	35 26N	132 38 E
Hialeach	170	25 49N	80 17W
Hibiki-Nada	108	34 0N	130 0 E
Hickory	165	35 46N	81 17W
Hida-Gawa ➔	106	35 26N	137 3 E
Hida-Sammyaku	106	36 30N	137 40 E
Hida-Sanchi	106	36 10N	137 0 E
Hidaka	109	35 30N	134 44 E
Hidalgo □	177	20 30N	99 0W
Hidalgo del Parral	174	26 56N	105 40W
Higashi-matsuyama	107	36 2N	139 25 E
Higashiōsaka	106	34 40N	135 37 E
Higasi-Suidō	108	34 0N	129 30 E
High Atlas = Haut Atlas	126	32 30N	5 0W
High Point	165	35 57N	79 58W
High Prairie	155	55 30N	116 30W
Highland □	32	57 30N	5 0W
Highland Park	167	42 10N	87 50W
Ḥijārah, Ṣaḥrā' al	84	30 25N	44 30 E
Hikari	108	33 58N	131 58 E
Hikone	106	35 15N	136 10 E
Hildesheim	43	52 9N	9 55 E
Hillegom	40	52 18N	4 35 E
Hillsboro	171	45 31N	123 0W
Hillston	117	33 30S	145 31 E
Hilo	160	19 44N	155 5W
Hilversum	40	52 14N	5 10 E
Himachal Pradesh □	89	31 30N	77 0 E
Himalaya, Mts.	101	29 0N	84 0 E
Hime-Jima	108	33 43N	131 40 E
Himeji	109	34 50N	134 40 E
Himi	106	36 50N	137 0 E
Ḥimṣ	80	34 40N	36 45 E
Hinchinbrook I.	121	18 20S	146 15 E
Hinckley	25	52 33N	1 21W
Hindmarsh	119	34 54S	138 34 E
Hindu Kush	89	36 0N	71 0 E
Hindupur	90	13 49N	77 32 E
Hines Creek	155	56 20N	118 40W
Hingoli	91	19 41N	77 15 E
Hinton	165	37 40N	80 51W
Hirado	108	33 22N	129 33 E
Hirakarta	106	34 48N	135 40 E
Hirakud Dam	92	21 32N	83 45 E
Hirata	109	35 24N	132 49 E
Hiratsuka	107	35 19N	139 21 E
Hirosaki	103	40 34N	140 28 E
Hiroshima	109	34 24N	132 30 E
Hirson	38	49 55N	4 4 E
Hispaniola	180	19 0N	71 0W
Hita	108	33 20N	130 58 E
Hitachi	107	36 36N	140 39 E
Hitachiota	107	36 30N	140 30 E
Hitchin	25	51 57N	0 16W
Hitoyoshi	108	32 13N	130 45 E
Hitra	65	63 30N	8 45 E
Hiuchi-Nada	109	34 5N	133 20 E

Ho Chi Minh City = Thanh
Pho Ho Chi Minh .... 95 10 58N 106 40 E
Hoa Binh .... 95 20 50N 105 20 E
Hobart .... 119 42 50S 147 21 E
Hobbs 161 32 40N 103 3W
Hodaka-Dake .... 106 36 17N 137 39 E
Hódmezővásárhely .... 59 46 28N 20 22 E
Hoek van Holland .... 40 52 0N 4 7 E
Hofsjökull 64 64 49N 18 48W
Hōfu .... 108 34 3N 131 34 E
Hogan Group .... 117 39 13S 147 1 E
Hoh Xil Shan .... 101 35 0N 89 0 E
Hohhot .... 98 40 52N 111 40 E
Hōjō .... 109 33 58N 132 46 E
Hokitika .... 123 42 42S 171 0 E
Hokkaidō □ .... 103 43 30N 143 0 E
Holbrook .... 117 35 42S 147 18 E
Holderness 29 53 45N 0 5W
Holdrege 163 40 26N 99 22W
Holguín 178 20 50N 76 20W
Holland 167 42 47N 86 7W
Holly Springs 169 34 45N 89 25W
Hollywood, Calif., U.S.A. ... 173 34 7N 118 25W
Hollywood, Fla., U.S.A. 170 26 0N 80 9W
Holsteinsborg 147 66 40N 53 30W
Holsworthy 27 50 48N 4 21W
Holt 64 63 33N 19 48W
Holy I., Scotland, U.K. 31 55 31N 5 4W
Holy I., Wales, U.K. 26 53 17N 4 37W
Holyhead 26 53 18N 4 38W
Holyoke 164 42 14N 72 37W
Hombori 130 15 20N 1 38W
Home Hill .... 121 19 43S 147 25 E
Homer 142 59 40N 151 35W
Homs = Ḥimṣ .... 80 34 40N 36 45 E
Honan = Henan □ .... 99 34 0N 114 0 E
Hondo .... 108 32 27N 130 12 E
Honduras ■ 179 14 40N 86 30W
Honduras, Golfo de 177 16 50N 87 0W
Hong Kong ■ .... 99 22 11N 114 14 E
Hongha → .... 95 22 0N 104 0 E
Hongshui He → .... 99 23 48N 109 30 E
Honiton 27 50 48N 3 11W
Honolulu 160 21 19N 157 52W
Honshū .... 106 36 0N 138 0 E
Hoogeveen .... 41 52 44N 6 30 E
Hook Hd. 35 52 8N 6 57W
Hook of Holland = Hoek van
Holland .... 40 52 0N 4 7 E
Hoorn .... 40 52 38N 5 4 E
Hope, Canada .... 154 49 25N 121 25 E
Hope, U.S.A. 168 33 40N 93 36W
Hope Town 178 26 35N 76 57W
Hopedale 147 55 28N 60 13W
Hopei = Hebei □ .... 98 39 0N 116 0 E
Hopelchén 177 19 46N 89 51W
Hopetoun, Vic., Australia ... 119 35 42S 142 22 E
Hopetoun, W. Austral.,
Australia .... 120 33 57S 120 7 E
Hopkinsville 169 36 52N 87 26W
Hoquiam 171 46 50N 123 55W
Hordaland fylke □ .... 60 60 25N 6 15 E
Hormoz .... 85 27 35N 55 0 E
Hormuz Str. .... 85 26 30N 56 30 E
Horn, Cape = Hornos, Cabo
de 192 55 50S 67 30W
Hornavan .... 66 66 15N 17 30 E
Hornell 164 42 23N 77 41W
Hornos, Cabo de 192 55 50S 67 30W
Hornsby .... 117 33 42S 151 2 E
Hornsea 29 53 55N 0 10W
Horqin Youyi Qianqi .... 98 46 5N 122 3 E
Horsens .... 61 55 52N 9 51 E
Horsham .... 119 36 44S 142 13 E
Horton → 145 69 56N 126 52W
Hoshiarpur .... 89 31 30N 75 58 E
Hospet .... 90 15 15N 76 20 E
Hospitalet de Llobregat .... 51 41 21N 2 6 E
Hoste, I. 192 55 0S 69 0W
Hot Springs 168 34 30N 93 0W
Houghton 150 47 9N 88 39W

Houghton-le-Spring 28 54 51N 1 28W
Houhora .... 122 34 49S 173 9 E
Houlton 148 46 5N 67 50W
Houma 169 29 35N 90 44W
Houston, Canada 154 54 25N 126 39W
Houston, U.S.A. 168 29 50N 95 20W
Houtman Abrolhos .... 120 28 43S 113 48 E
Hovd .... 100 48 2N 91 37 E
Hove 25 50 50N 0 10W
Howe, C. .... 117 37 30S 150 0 E
Howrah = Haora .... 92 22 37N 88 20 E
Hoy I. 33 58 50N 3 15W
Hrádec Králové .... 58 50 15N 15 50 E
Hrvatska = Croatia ■ ..... 52 45 20N 18 0 E
Hsiamen = Xiamen .... 99 24 25N 118 4 E
Hsian = Xi'an .... 99 34 15N 109 0 E
Hsinhailien = Lianyungang . 99 34 40N 119 11 E
Hsüchou = Xuzhou .... 99 34 18N 117 10 E
Hua Hin .... 94 12 34N 99 58 E
Huacho 186 11 10S 77 35W
Huainan .... 99 32 38N 116 58 E
Huallaga → 186 5 0S 75 30W
Huambo .... 134 12 42S 15 54 E
Huancane 187 15 10S 69 44W
Huancavelica 186 12 50S 75 5W
Huancayo 186 12 5S 75 12W
Huanchaca 187 20 15S 66 40W
Huang Hai = Yellow Sea .. 99 35 0N 123 0 E
Huang Ho → .... 98 37 30N 118 50 E
Huangshi .... 99 30 10N 115 3 E
Huánuco 186 9 55S 76 15W
Huaraz 186 9 30S 77 32W
Huascarán 186 9 8S 77 36W
Huasco 190 28 30S 71 15W
Huatabampo 174 26 50N 109 38W
Huautla 177 17 51N 100 5W
Hubei □ .... 99 31 0N 112 0 E
Hubli-Dharwad = Dharwad . 90 15 22N 75 15 E
Huddersfield 28 53 38N 1 49W
Hudiksvall .... 66 61 43N 17 10 E
Hudson 164 42 15N 73 46W
Hudson → 164 40 42N 74 2W
Hudson Bay 146 52 51N 102 23W
Hudson Str. 146 62 0N 70 0W
Hudson's Hope 155 56 0N 121 54W
Hue .... 95 16 30N 107 35 E
Huehuetenango 177 15 20N 91 28W
Huelva 50 37 18N 6 57W
Huesca 51 42 8N 0 25W
Hughenden .... 121 20 52S 144 10 E
Huila, Nevado del 184 3 0N 76 0W
Huinca Renancó 190 34 51S 64 22W
Huixtla 177 15 9N 92 28W
Huizen .... 40 52 18N 5 14 E
Hukawng Valley .... 93 26 30N 96 30 E
Hull, Canada 151 45 25N 75 44W
Hull, U.K. 29 53 45N 0 20W
Hulst .... 40 51 17N 4 2 E
Hulun Nur .... 98 49 0N 117 30 E
Humaitá 187 27 2S 58 31W
Humber → 29 53 40N 0 10W
Humberside □ 29 53 50N 0 30W
Humboldt, Canada 152 52 15N 105 9W
Humboldt, U.S.A. 169 35 50N 88 55W
Humboldt → 172 40 2N 118 31W
Hume, L. .... 117 36 0S 147 0 E
Húnaflói 64 65 50N 20 50W
Hunan □ .... 99 27 30N 111 30 E
Hunedoara .... 56 45 40N 22 50 E
Hungary ■ .... 59 47 20N 19 20 E
Hungary, Plain of .... 17 47 0N 20 0 E
Hüngnam .... 98 39 49N 127 45 E
Hunsrück .... 42 49 30N 7 0 E
Hunstanton .... 29 52 57N 0 30 E
Hunter Ra. .... 117 32 45S 150 15 E
Huntingdon 25 52 20N 0 11W
Huntington, Ind., U.S.A. ... 167 40 52N 85 30W
Huntington, W. Va., U.S.A. . 165 38 20N 82 30W
Huntington Beach 173 33 40N 118 0W
Huntly .... 122 37 34S 175 11 E
Huntsville, Canada 151 45 20N 79 14W

Place	Page	Lat	Long
Huntsville, Ala., U.S.A.	169	34 45N	86 35W
Huntsville, Tex., U.S.A.	168	30 45N	95 35W
Huonville	119	43 0S	147 5 E
Hupeh = Hubei □	99	31 0N	112 0 E
Huron, L.	150	45 0N	83 0W
Hurricane	173	37 10N	113 12W
Húsavík	64	66 3N	17 21W
Hutchinson	161	38 3N	97 59W
Hvar	52	43 11N	16 28 E
Hwang Ho = Huang Ho ➤	98	37 30N	118 50 E
Hwange	137	18 18S	26 30 E
Hyden	120	32 24S	118 53 E
Hyderabad, India	91	17 22N	78 29 E
Hyderabad, Pakistan	88	25 23N	68 24 E
Hyères	37	43 8N	6 9 E
Hyndman Pk.	162	43 50N	114 10W
Hythe	24	51 4N	1 5 E
Hyūga	108	32 25N	131 35 E

I

Place	Page	Lat	Long
Iaşi	57	47 10N	27 40 E
Ibadan	131	7 22N	3 58 E
Ibagué	184	4 20N	75 20W
Ibara	109	34 36N	133 28 E
Ibaraki	106	34 49N	135 34 E
Ibarra	184	0 21N	78 7W
Iberian Peninsula	16	40 0N	5 0W
Ibiza	51	38 54N	1 26 E
Ibuki-Sanchi	106	35 25N	136 18 E
Ibusuki	108	31 12N	130 40 E
Icá	186	14 0S	75 48W
Iça ➤	184	2 55S	67 58W
Iceland ■	64	65 0N	19 0W
Icha	73	55 30N	156 0 E
Ich'ang = Yichang	99	30 40N	111 20 E
Ichchapuram	92	19 10N	84 40 E
Ichihara	107	35 28N	140 5 E
Ichikawa	107	35 44N	139 55 E
Ichinomiya	106	35 18N	136 48 E
Ichinoseki	103	38 55N	141 8 E
Idaho □	162	44 10N	114 0W
Idaho Falls	163	43 30N	112 1W
Idhi Óros	55	35 15N	24 45 E
Idhra	55	37 20N	23 28 E
Ierápetra	55	35 0N	25 44 E
Ife	131	7 30N	4 31 E
Igloolik	146	69 20N	81 49W
Iguaçu ➤	191	25 36S	54 36W
Iguaçu, Cat. del	191	25 41S	54 26W
Iguaçu Falls = Iguaçu, Cat. del	191	25 41S	54 26W
Iguala de la Independencia	177	18 21N	99 32W
Iguassu = Iguaçu ➤	191	25 36S	54 36W
Iida	107	35 35N	137 50 E
Iisalmi	67	63 32N	27 10 E
Iizuka	108	33 38N	130 42 E
IJmuiden	40	52 28N	4 35 E
IJsselmeer	40	52 45N	5 20 E
IJsselstein	40	52 1N	5 2 E
Ikaría	55	37 35N	26 10 E
Ikeda	109	34 1N	133 48 E
Iki	108	33 45N	129 42 E
Iki-Kaikyō	108	33 40N	129 45 E
Île-de-France	37	49 0N	2 20 E
Ilebo	134	4 17S	20 55 E
Ilfracombe	27	51 13N	4 8W
Ilhéus	189	14 49S	39 2W
Ili ➤	71	45 53N	77 10 E
Iliamna L.	142	59 35N	155 30W
Iliodhrómia	55	39 12N	23 50 E
Ilkeston	29	52 59N	1 19W
Illampu = Ancohuma, Nevada	187	16 0S	68 50W
Illinois □	166	40 15N	89 30W
Illinois ➤	166	38 55N	90 28W
Ilo	187	17 40S	71 20W
Iloilo	112	10 45N	122 33 E
Ilorin	131	8 30N	4 35 E

Place	Page	Lat	Long
Imabari	109	34 4N	133 0 E
Imari	108	33 15N	129 52 E
Imatra	67	61 12N	28 48 E
Immingham	29	53 37N	0 12W
Imperial	152	51 21N	105 28W
Imphal	92	24 48N	93 56 E
İmroz = Gökçeada	55	40 10N	25 50 E
Ina	107	35 50N	138 0 E
Iñapari	187	11 0S	69 40W
Inari	67	68 54N	27 5 E
Inarijärvi	67	69 0N	28 0 E
Inazawa	106	35 15N	136 47 E
Inchon	98	37 27N	126 40 E
Indalsälven ➤	66	62 36N	17 30 E
Independence, Kans., U.S.A.	166	37 10N	95 43W
Independence, Mo., U.S.A.	166	39 3N	94 25W
India ■	78	20 0N	78 0 E
Indian Head	152	50 30N	103 41W
Indiana	164	40 38N	79 9W
Indiana □	167	40 0N	86 0W
Indianapolis	167	39 42N	86 10W
Indigirka ➤	73	70 48N	148 54 E
Indonesia ■	111	5 0S	115 0 E
Indore	91	22 42N	75 53 E
Indre ➤	36	47 16N	0 19 E
Indus ➤	88	24 20N	67 47 E
Indus, Mouth of the	88	24 0N	68 0 E
İnebolu	80	41 55N	33 40 E
İnegöl	80	40 5N	29 31 E
Ingersoll	151	43 4N	80 55W
Ingham	121	18 43S	146 10 E
Ingleborough	28	54 11N	2 23W
Inglewood, N.Z.	122	39 9S	174 14 E
Inglewood, U.S.A.	173	33 58N	118 21W
Ingolstadt	43	48 45N	11 26 E
Ingraj Bazar	92	24 58N	88 10 E
Inhambane	137	23 54S	35 30 E
Ining = Yining	100	43 58N	81 10 E
Inishmore	35	53 8N	9 45W
Inishowen	34	55 14N	7 15W
Inn ➤	43	48 35N	13 28 E
Innamincka	118	27 44S	140 46 E
Inner Hebrides	32	57 0N	6 30W
Inner Mongolia = Nei Monggol Zizhiqu □	98	42 0N	112 0 E
Innisfail, Australia	121	17 33S	146 5 E
Innisfail, Canada	155	52 0N	113 57W
In'no-shima	109	34 19N	133 10 E
Innsbruck	45	47 16N	11 23 E
Inoucdjouac	146	58 25N	78 15W
Inowrocław	58	52 50N	18 12 E
Inquisivi	187	16 50S	67 10W
Insein	93	16 50N	96 5 E
Interlaken	44	46 41N	7 50 E
Inuvik	144	68 16N	133 40W
Inuvik □	144	70 0N	130 0W
Inuyama	106	35 23N	136 56 E
Inveraray	30	56 13N	5 5W
Invercargill	123	46 24S	168 24 E
Inverell	116	29 45S	151 8 E
Invergordon	33	57 41N	4 10W
Inverness	33	57 29N	4 12W
Investigator Group	119	34 45S	134 20 E
Investigator Str.	119	35 30S	137 0 E
Ioánnina	54	39 42N	20 47 E
Iola	166	38 0N	95 20W
Iona	30	56 20N	6 25W
Ionian Is. = Iónioi Nísoi	54	38 40N	20 0 E
Ionian Sea	54	37 30N	17 30 E
Iónioi Nísoi	54	38 40N	20 0 E
Íos	55	36 41N	25 20 E
Iowa □	166	42 18N	93 30W
Iowa City	166	41 40N	91 35W
Iowa Falls	166	42 30N	93 15W
Ipiales	184	0 50N	77 37W
Ipin = Yibin	99	28 45N	104 32 E
Ípiros □	54	39 30N	20 30 E
Ipoh	96	4 35N	101 5 E
Ipswich, Australia	116	27 35S	152 40 E
Ipswich, U.K.	25	52 4N	1 9 E
Iquique	187	20 19S	70 5W

Iquitos 186 3 45S 73 10W
Iracoubo 185 5 30N 53 10W
Iráklion . . . . 55 35 20N 25 12 E
Iran ■ . . . . 86 33 0N 53 0 E
Iran Ra. . . . . 111 2 20N 114 50 E
Irapuato 177 20 41N 101 28W
Iraq ■ . . . . 81 33 0N 44 0 E
Irbid . . . . 80 32 35N 35 48 E
Ireland ■ 34 53 0N   8 0W
Irian Jaya □ . . . . 113 4 0S 137 0 E
Iriri ⟶ 188 3 52S 52 37W
Irish Republic ■ 20 53 0N   8 0W
Irish Sea 20 54 0N   5 0W
Irkutsk . . . . 74 52 18N 104 20 E
Irō-Zaki . . . . 107 34 36N 138 51 E
Iron Gate = Portile de Fier . 56 44 42N 22 30 E
Iron Knob . . . . 118 32 46S 137 8 E
Iron Mountain 150 45 49N 88 4W
Ironbridge 24 52 38N   2 29W
Ironton 167 38 35N 82 40W
Ironwood 150 46 30N 90 10W
Iroquois Falls 151 48 46N 80 41W
Irrawaddy ⟶ . . . . 93 15 50N 95 6 E
Irtysh ⟶ . . . . 69 61 4N 68 52 E
Irumu . . . . 135 1 32N 29 53 E
Irún 51 43 20N   1 52W
Irvine 31 55 37N   4 40W
Irvinestown 34 54 28N   7 38W
Ísafjörður 64 66 5N 23 9W
Isahaya . . . . 108 32 52N 130 2 E
Ischia . . . . 49 40 45N 13 51 E
Ise . . . . 106 34 25N 136 45 E
Ise-Wan . . . . 106 34 43N 136 43 E
Isère ⟶ . . . . 37 44 59N   4 51 E
Isesaki . . . . 107 36 19N 139 12 E
Ishikari-Wan . . . . 103 43 25N 141 1 E
Ishinomaki . . . . 103 38 32N 141 20 E
Ishioka . . . . 107 36 11N 140 16 E
Ishkuman . . . . 89 36 30N 73 50 E
Ishpeming 150 46 30N 87 40W
İskenderun . . . . 80 36 32N 36 10 E
Islamabad . . . . 89 33 40N 73 10 E
Island L. 153 53 47N 94 25W
Island Pond 148 48 25N 56 23W
Islay 30 55 46N   6 10W
Isle-Adam, L' . . . . 39 49 6N   2 14 E
Isle Royale 150 48 0N 88 50W
İsparta . . . . 80 37 47N 30 30 E
Israel ■ . . . . 80 32 0N 34 50 E
Issoire . . . . 37 45 32N   3 15 E
Issyk-Kul, Ozero . . . . 71 42 25N 77 15 E
İstanbul . . . . 80 41 0N 29 0 E
Istra . . . . 52 45 10N 14 0 E
Istria = Istra . . . . 52 45 10N 14 0 E
Itabuna 189 14 48S 39 16W
Itaituba 185 4 10S 55 50W
Itajaí 191 27 50S 48 39W
Italy ■ . . . . 19 42 0N 13 0 E
Itaquatiara 185 2 58S 58 30W
Itaquí 191 29 8S 56 30W
Itchen ⟶ 24 50 57N   1 20W
Ithaca = Itháki . . . . 54 38 25N 20 40 E
Ithaca 164 42 25N 76 30W
Itháki . . . . 54 38 25N 20 40 E
Ito . . . . 107 34 58N 139 5 E
Ituaçu 189 13 50S 41 18W
Ituiutaba 188 19 0S 49 25W
Iturup, Ostrov . . . . 75 45 0N 148 0 E
Ivano-Frankovsk . . . . 68 48 40N 24 40 E
Ivanovo, Belorussia . . . . . . 68 52 7N 25 29 E
Ivanovo, Russia . . . . 68 57 5N 41 0 E
Ivigtut 147 61 14N 48 12W
Iviza = Ibiza . . . . 51 38 54N   1 26 E
Ivory Coast ■ 130 7 30N   5 0W
Iwai-Jima . . . . 108 33 47N 131 58 E
Iwaki . . . . 105 37 3N 140 55 E
Iwakuni . . . . 109 34 15N 132 8 E
Iwami . . . . 109 35 32N 134 15 E
Iwamizawa . . . . 103 43 12N 141 46 E
Iwanuma . . . . 103 38 7N 140 51 E
Iwata . . . . 107 34 42N 137 51 E

Iwo . . . . 131 7 39N   4 9 E
Ixiamas 187 13 50S 68 5W
Ixtepec 177 16 34N 95 6W
Ixtlán 175 20 11N 102 24W
Ixtlán de Juárez 177 17 23N 96 28W
Iyo . . . . 109 33 45N 132 45 E
Iyo-mishima . . . . 109 33 58N 133 30 E
Iyo-Nada . . . . 109 33 40N 132 20 E
Izamal 177 20 56N 89 1W
Izhevsk . . . . 69 56 51N 53 14 E
İzmir . . . . 80 38 25N 27 8 E
İzmit . . . . 80 40 45N 29 50 E
Izu-Hantō . . . . 107 34 45N 139 0 E
Izumi . . . . 108 32 5N 130 22 E
Izumi-sano . . . . 106 34 23N 135 18 E
Izumiotsu . . . . 106 34 30N 135 24 E
Izumo . . . . 109 35 20N 132 46 E

J

Jabalpur . . . . 91 23 9N 79 58 E
Jacarèzinho 191 23 5S 50 0W
Jackson, Mich., U.S.A. 167 42 18N 84 25W
Jackson, Miss., U.S.A. 169 32 20N 90 10W
Jackson, Tenn., U.S.A. 169 35 40N 88 50W
Jacksonville, Fla., U.S.A. . . 170 30 15N 81 38W
Jacksonville, Ill., U.S.A. . . . 166 39 42N 90 15W
Jacksonville, N.C., U.S.A. . . 165 34 50N 77 29W
Jacksonville, Tex., U.S.A. . . 168 31 58N 95 19W
Jacmel 180 18 14N 72 32W
Jacobabad . . . . 88 28 20N 68 29 E
Jacques Cartier, Dét. de . . 149 50 0N 63 30W
Jadotville = Likasi . . . . 135 10 55S 26 48 E
Jaén, Peru 186 5 25S 78 40W
Jaén, Spain 50 37 44N   3 43W
Jaffa = Tel Aviv-Yafo . . . . . 80 32 4N 34 48 E
Jaffna . . . . 90 9 45N 80 2 E
Jagdalpur . . . . 92 19 3N 82 0 E
Jaguariaíva 191 24 10S 49 50W
Jagüey Grande 178 22 35N 81 7W
Jahrom . . . . 85 28 30N 53 31 E
Jaipur . . . . 91 27 0N 75 50 E
Jakarta . . . . 111 6 9S 106 49 E
Jalalabad . . . . 87 34 30N 70 29 E
Jalapa, Guatemala 177 14 39N 89 59W
Jalapa, Mexico 177 17 43N 92 49W
Jalgaon . . . . 91 21 0N 75 42 E
Jalisco □ 175 20 20N 103 40W
Jalna . . . . 91 19 48N 75 38 E
Jalón ⟶ 51 41 47N   1 4W
Jalpaiguri . . . . 92 26 32N 88 46 E
Jamaica ■ 180 18 10N 77 30W
Jamalpur, Bangla. . . . . 92 24 52N 89 56 E
Jamalpur, India . . . . 92 25 18N 86 28 E
Jambi . . . . 111 1 38S 103 30 E
James ⟶ 163 42 52N 97 18W
James B. 140 51 30N 80 0W
Jamestown, Australia . . . . . 118 33 10S 138 32 E
Jamestown, N. Dak., U.S.A. 163 46 54N 98 42W
Jamestown, N.Y., U.S.A. . . 164 42 5N 79 18W
Jamkhandi . . . . 91 16 30N 75 15 E
Jammu . . . . 89 32 43N 74 54 E
Jammu & Kashmir □ . . . . . . 89 34 25N 77 0 E
Jamnagar . . . . 90 22 30N 70 6 E
Jamshedpur . . . . 92 22 44N 86 12 E
Jan Mayen Is. 13 71 0N   9 0W
Janesville 166 42 39N 89 1W
Januária 188 15 25S 44 25W
Jaora . . . . 91 23 40N 75 10 E
Japan ■ . . . . 79 36 0N 136 0 E
Japan, Sea of . . . . 102 40 0N 135 0 E
Japurá ⟶ 185 3 8S 64 46W
Jargalant = Hovd . . . . 100 48 2N 91 37 E
Jargeau . . . . 39 47 50N   2 1 E
Jarosław . . . . 58 50 2N 22 42 E
Jāsk . . . . 85 25 38N 57 45 E
Jasło . . . . 59 49 45N 21 30 E
Jasper, Canada 155 52 55N 118 5W

Name	Page	°	′		°	′	
Jasper, U.S.A.	169	33	48N		87	16W	
Jassy = Iaşi	57	47	10N		27	40 E	
Jataí	188	17	58S		51	48W	
Jaú	188	22	10S		48	30W	
Jaunpur	92	25	46N		82	44 E	
Java, I.	111	7	0S		110	0 E	
Java Sea	111	4	35S		107	15 E	
Javhlant = Ulyasutay	100	47	56N		97	28 E	
Jean Marie River	144	61	32N		120	38W	
Jean Rabel	180	19	50N		73	5W	
Jedburgh	31	55	28N		2	33W	
Jędrzejów	58	50	35N		20	15 E	
Jefferson, Mt.	171	44	45N		121	50W	
Jefferson City	166	38	34N		92	10W	
Jeffersonville	167	38	20N		85	42W	
Jelenia Góra	58	50	50N		15	45 E	
Jena	43	50	56N		11	33 E	
Jenkins	165	37	13N		82	41W	
Jennings	168	30	10N		92	45W	
Jeparit	119	36	8S		142	1 E	
Jequié	189	13	51S		40	5W	
Jequitinhonha	189	16	30S		41	0W	
Jérémie	180	18	40N		74	10W	
Jerez de García Salinas	175	22	39N		103	0W	
Jerez de la Frontera	50	36	41N		6	7W	
Jerez de los Caballeros	50	38	20N		6	45W	
Jericho	121	23	38S		146	6 E	
Jerilderie	117	35	20S		145	41 E	
Jerome	148	47	37N		82	14W	
Jersey, I.	36	49	13N		2	7W	
Jersey City	164	40	41N		74	8W	
Jerseyville	166	39	5N		90	20W	
Jerusalem	80	31	47N		35	10 E	
Jesselton = Kota Kinabalu	112	6	0N		116	4 E	
Jhang Maghiana	89	31	15N		72	22 E	
Jhansi	91	25	30N		78	36 E	
Jharsuguda	92	21	56N		84	5 E	
Jhelum →	89	31	20N		72	10 E	
Jhunjhunu	89	28	10N		75	30 E	
Jiamusi	98	46	40N		130	26 E	
Ji'an	99	27	6N		114	59 E	
Jiangmen	99	22	32N		113	0 E	
Jiangsu □	99	33	0N		120	0 E	
Jiangxi □	99	27	30N		116	0 E	
Jian'ou	99	27	3N		118	17 E	
Jiao Xian	98	36	18N		120	1 E	
Jiaozuo	99	35	16N		113	12 E	
Jiaxing	99	30	49N		120	45 E	
Jiayi	99	23	30N		120	24 E	
Jibuti = Djibouti ■	133	12	0N		43	0 E	
Jiddah	82	21	29N		39	10 E	
Jido	93	29	2N		94	58 E	
Jihlava	59	49	28N		15	35 E	
Jilin	98	43	44N		126	30 E	
Jilong	99	25	8N		121	42 E	
Jima	132	7	40N		36	47 E	
Jiménez	174	27	8N		104	54W	
Jinan	98	36	38N		117	1 E	
Jingdezhen	99	29	20N		117	11 E	
Jining, Nei Mongol Zizhiqu, China	98	41	5N		113	0 E	
Jining, Shandong, China	99	35	22N		116	34 E	
Jinja	132	0	25N		33	12 E	
Jinnah Barrage	89	32	58N		71	33 E	
Jinotega	179	13	6N		85	59W	
Jinotepe	179	11	50N		86	10W	
Jinshi	99	29	40N		111	50 E	
Jinzhou	98	41	5N		121	3 E	
Jipijapa	184	1	0S		80	40W	
Jiquilpan de Juárez	175	19	59N		102	43W	
Jisr ash Shughūr	80	35	49N		36	18 E	
Jiujiang	99	29	42N		115	58 E	
Jixi	98	45	20N		130	50 E	
João Pessoa	189	7	10S		34	52W	
Jodhpur	91	26	23N		73	8 E	
Joensuu	67	62	37N		29	49 E	
Jogjakarta = Yogyakarta	111	7	49S		110	22 E	
Jōhana	106	36	30N		136	57 E	
Johannesburg	137	26	10S		28	2 E	
John o' Groats	33	58	39N		3	3W	
Johnson City, N.Y., U.S.A.	164	42	7N		75	57W	
Johnson City, Tenn., U.S.A.	165	36	18N		82	21W	
Johnston	31	51	45N		5	5W	
Johnstown, N.Y., U.S.A.	164	43	1N		74	20W	
Johnstown, Pa., U.S.A.	164	40	19N		78	53W	
Johor □	96	2	5N		103	20 E	
Johor Baharu	96	1	28N		103	46 E	
Joigny	39	48	0N		3	20 E	
Joinvile	191	26	15S		48	55 E	
Joliet	167	41	30N		88	0W	
Joliette	151	46	3N		73	24W	
Jolo	112	6	0N		121	0 E	
Jonesboro	169	35	50N		90	45W	
Jönköping	60	57	45N		14	10 E	
Jönköpings län □	61	57	30N		14	30 E	
Jonquière	148	48	27N		71	14W	
Joplin	168	37	0N		94	31W	
Jordan ■	80	31	0N		36	0 E	
Jordan →	80	31	48N		35	32 E	
Jorhat	93	26	45N		94	12 E	
José de San Martín	192	44	4S		70	26W	
Jowzjān □	87	36	10N		66	0 E	
Juan de Fuca Str.	142	48	15N		124	0W	
Juan Fernández, Arch. de	183	33	50S		80	0W	
Juàzeiro	189	9	30S		40	30W	
Juàzeiro do Norte	189	7	10S		39	18W	
Jubbulpore = Jabalpur	91	23	9N		79	58 E	
Júcar →	51	39	5N		0	10W	
Juchitán de Zaragoza	177	16	26N		95	1W	
Jugoslavia = Yugoslavia ■	52	44	0N		21	0 E	
Juiz de Fora	188	21	43S		43	19W	
Julí	187	16	10S		69	25W	
Juliaca	187	15	25S		70	10W	
Julianehåb	147	60	43N		46	0W	
Jullundur	89	31	20N		75	40 E	
Jumla	92	29	15N		82	13 E	
Jumna = Yamuna →	92	25	30N		81	53 E	
Junagadh	91	21	30N		70	30 E	
Jundiaí	191	24	30S		47	0W	
Juneau	143	58	20N		134	20W	
Junee	117	34	53S		147	35 E	
Junggar Pendi	100	44	30N		86	0 E	
Junín	190	34	33S		60	57W	
Jura, Europe	37	46	35N		6	5 E	
Jura, U.K.	30	56	0N		5	50W	
Jurado	184	7	7N		77	46W	
Juruá →	184	2	37S		65	44W	
Juruena	187	13	0S		58	10W	
Juruena →	187	7	20S		58	3W	
Juticalpa	179	14	40N		86	12W	
Jutland = Jylland	61	56	25N		9	30 E	
Juventud, I. de la	178	21	40N		82	40W	
Jylland	61	56	25N		9	30 E	
Jyväskylä	67	62	14N		25	50 E	

K

Name	Page	°	′		°	′	
Kaapstad = Cape Town	136	33	55S		18	22 E	
Kabala	130	9	38N		11	37W	
Kabardino-Balkar Rep. □	70	43	30N		43	30 E	
Kabarega Falls	132	2	15N		31	30 E	
Kabīr Kūh	84	33	0N		47	30 E	
Kābul	87	34	28N		69	11 E	
Kābul □	87	34	30N		69	0 E	
Kabwe	135	14	30S		28	29 E	
Kachin □	93	26	0N		97	30 E	
Kadan Kyun	94	12	30N		98	20 E	
Kadina	119	34	0S		137	43 E	
Kaduna	131	10	30N		7	21 E	
Kaédi	126	16	9N		13	28W	
Käf	80	31	25N		37	29 E	
Kafirévs, Ákra	55	38	9N		24	38 E	
Kafue →	135	15	30S		26	0 E	
Kaga	106	36	16N		136	15 E	
Kagoshima	108	31	35N		130	33 E	
Kagoshima-Wan	108	31	25N		130	40 E	
Kai, Kepulauan	113	5	55S		132	45W	
Kaieteur Falls	185	5	1N		59	10W	
Kaifeng	99	34	49N		114	30 E	

Place	Page	Lat	Long
Kaikoura Ra.	123	41 59S	173 41 E
Kailua	160	19 39N	156 0W
Kaimanawa Mts.	122	39 15S	175 56 E
Kainan	106	34 9N	135 12 E
Kainji Res.	131	10 1N	4 40 E
Kaipara Harbour	122	36 25S	174 14 E
Kaiserslautern	42	49 30N	7 43 E
Kaitaia	122	35 8S	173 17 E
Kajaani	67	64 17N	27 46 E
Kajana = Kajaani	67	64 17N	27 46 E
Kakabeka Falls	150	48 24N	89 37W
Kakamigahara	106	35 28N	136 48 E
Kakanui Mts.	123	45 10S	170 30 E
Kakegawa	107	34 45N	138 1 E
Kakinada	92	16 57N	82 11 E
Kakogawa	109	34 46N	134 51 E
Kalabáka	54	39 42N	21 39 E
Kalahari	136	24 0S	21 30 E
Kalamata	54	37 3N	22 10 E
Kalamazoo	167	42 20N	85 35W
Kalamazoo →	167	42 40N	86 12W
Kalat	88	29 8N	66 31 E
Kalaupapa	160	21 12N	156 59W
Kalemie	135	5 55S	29 9 E
Kalgan = Zhangjiakou	98	40 48N	114 55 E
Kalgoorlie-Boulder	120	30 40S	121 22 E
Kálimnos	55	37 0N	27 0 E
Kalinin = Tver	68	56 55N	35 55 E
Kaliningrad	68	54 42N	20 32 E
Kalispell	162	48 10N	114 22W
Kalisz	58	51 45N	18 8 E
Kalmar	61	56 40N	16 20 E
Kalmar län □	61	57 25N	16 0 E
Kalmyk Rep. □	70	46 5N	46 1 E
Kalocsa	59	46 32N	19 0 E
Kaluga	68	54 35N	36 10 E
Kama →	68	55 45N	52 0 E
Kamaishi	103	39 16N	141 53 E
Kamakura	107	35 19N	139 33 E
Kamaran	82	15 21N	42 35 E
Kamchatka, P-ov.	73	57 0N	160 0 E
Kamenka	69	53 10N	44 5 E
Kamensk Uralskiy	69	56 25N	62 2 E
Kamenskoye	73	62 45N	165 30 E
Kameoka	106	35 0N	135 35 E
Kameyama	106	34 51N	136 27 E
Kami-koshiki-Jima	108	31 50N	129 52 E
Kamioka	106	36 25N	137 15 E
Kamloops	155	50 40N	120 20W
Kampala	132	0 20N	32 30 E
Kampar	96	4 18N	101 9 E
Kampen	41	52 33N	5 53 E
Kampot	95	10 36N	104 10 E
Kampuchea = Cambodia ■	95	12 15N	105 0 E
Kamsack	152	51 34N	101 54W
Kamui-Misaki	103	43 20N	140 21 E
Kamyshin	68	50 10N	45 24 E
Kananga	134	5 55S	22 18 E
Kanawha →	165	38 50N	82 8W
Kanazawa	106	36 30N	136 38 E
Kanchenjunga	92	27 50N	88 10 E
Kanchipuram	90	12 52N	79 45 E
Kandahar = Qandahār	87	31 32N	65 30 E
Kandalaksha	69	67 9N	32 30 E
Kandi	131	11 7N	2 55 E
Kandos	117	32 45S	149 58 E
Kandy	90	7 18N	80 43 E
Kangar	97	6 27N	100 12 E
Kangaroo I.	119	35 45S	137 0 E
Kangean Is.	113	6 55S	115 23 E
Kangnŭng	98	37 45N	128 54 E
Kangto	93	27 50N	92 35 E
Kaniapiskau →	146	56 40N	69 30W
Kanin, P-ov.	69	68 0N	45 0 E
Kaniva	119	36 22S	141 18 E
Kankakee	167	41 6N	87 50W
Kankakee →	167	41 23N	88 16W
Kankan	130	10 23N	9 15W
Kanmuri-Yama	109	34 30N	132 4 E
Kannapolis	165	35 32N	80 37W
Kano	131	12 2N	8 30 E
Kan'onji	109	34 7N	133 39 E
Kanoya	108	31 25N	130 50 E
Kanpur	91	26 28N	80 20 E
Kansas □	161	38 40N	98 0W
Kansas →	158	39 7N	94 36W
Kansas City, Kans., U.S.A.	166	39 0N	94 40W
Kansas City, Mo., U.S.A.	166	39 3N	94 30W
Kansk	74	56 20N	95 37 E
Kansu = Gansu □	98	36 0N	104 0 E
Kantō □	107	36 15N	139 30 E
Kantō-Sanchi	107	35 59N	138 50 E
Kanuma	107	36 34N	139 42 E
Kaohsiung = Gaoxiong	99	22 38N	120 18 E
Kaolack	130	14 5N	16 8W
Kāpīsā □	87	35 0N	69 20 E
Kapoeta	129	4 50N	33 35 E
Kapuas →	111	0 25S	109 20 E
Kapunda	119	34 20S	138 56 E
Kapuskasing	150	49 25N	82 30W
Kaputar, Mt.	116	30 15S	150 10 E
Kara Bogaz Gol, Zaliv	70	41 0N	53 30 E
Kara Kalpak Rep. □	70	43 0N	60 0 E
Kara Kum = Karakum, Peski	70	39 30N	60 0 E
Kara Sea	69	75 0N	70 0 E
Karabük	80	41 12N	32 37 E
Karachi	88	24 53N	67 0 E
Karad	91	17 15N	74 10 E
Karadeniz Boğazı	80	41 10N	29 10 E
Karaganda	71	49 50N	73 10 E
Karaj	86	35 48N	51 0 E
Karakoram Pass	89	35 33N	77 50 E
Karakoram Ra.	89	35 30N	77 0 E
Karakum, Peski	70	39 30N	60 0 E
Karaman	80	37 14N	33 13 E
Karamea Bight	123	41 22S	171 40 E
Karasuk	71	53 44N	78 2 E
Karatau, Khrebet	71	43 30N	69 30 E
Karbalā	84	32 36N	44 3 E
Karelian Rep. □	68	65 30N	32 30 E
Karen	94	12 49N	92 53 E
Kariba Lake	137	16 40S	28 25 E
Karimata I.	111	1 40S	109 0 E
Karimnagar	91	18 26N	79 10 E
Karimunjawa, Kepulauan	111	5 50S	110 30 E
Kariya	106	34 58N	137 1 E
Karl-Marx-Stadt = Chemnitz	43	50 50N	12 55 E
Karlskrona	61	56 10N	15 35 E
Karlsruhe	42	49 3N	8 23 E
Karlstad	60	59 23N	13 30 E
Karnal	89	29 42N	77 2 E
Karnaphuli Res.	93	22 40N	92 20 E
Karnataka □	90	13 15N	77 0 E
Kärnten □	45	46 52N	13 30 E
Kárpathos	55	35 37N	27 10 E
Kars	81	40 40N	43 5 E
Karshi	70	38 53N	65 48 E
Kasai →	134	3 30S	16 10 E
Kasaoka	109	34 30N	133 30 E
Kaseda	108	31 25N	130 19 E
Kāshān	86	34 5N	51 30 E
Kashi	100	39 30N	76 2 E
Kashihara	106	34 27N	135 46 E
Kashima	108	33 7N	130 6 E
Kashima-Nada	107	36 0N	140 45 E
Kashiwa	107	35 52N	139 59 E
Kāshmar	86	35 16N	58 26 E
Kashmir	78	34 0N	76 0 E
Kashun Noerh = Gaxun Nur	100	42 22N	100 30 E
Kásos	55	35 20N	26 55 E
Kassala	129	16 0N	36 0 E
Kassel	42	51 19N	9 32 E
Kastoria	54	40 30N	21 19 E
Kasugai	106	35 12N	136 59 E
Kasukabe	107	35 58N	139 49 E
Kasumiga-Ura	107	36 0N	140 25 E
Kasur	89	31 5N	74 25 E
Katanning	120	33 40S	117 33 E
Katha	93	24 10N	96 30 E
Katherîna, Gebel	128	28 30N	33 57 E
Katherine	114	14 27S	132 20 E
Kathiawar	91	22 20N	71 0 E

Katihar	92	25 34N	87	36 E
Katmandu	92	27 45N	85	20 E
Katoomba	117	33 41S	150	19 E
Katowice	58	50 17N	19	5 E
Katsuta	107	36 25N	140	31 E
Katsuura	107	35 10N	140	20 E
Katsuyama	106	36 3N	136	30 E
Kattegatt	61	57 0N	11	20 E
Katwijk-aan-Zee	40	52 12N	4	24 E
Kauai	160	22 0N	159	30W
Kaukauna	167	44 20N	88	13W
Kaunas	68	54 54N	23	54 E
Kawachi-Nagano	106	34 28N	135	31 E
Kawagoe	107	35 55N	139	29 E
Kawaguchi	107	35 52N	139	45 E
Kawanoe	109	34 1N	133	34 E
Kawarau	122	45 3S	168	45 E
Kawasaki	107	35 35N	139	42 E
Kayah □	93	19 15N	97	15 E
Kayes	130	14 25N	11	30W
Kayseri	80	38 45N	35	30 E
Kazachinskoye	74	56 16N	107	36 E
Kazachye	72	70 52N	135	58 E
Kazakhstan ■	71	50 0N	70	0 E
Kazan	68	55 48N	49	3 E
Kazanlúk	53	42 38N	25	20 E
Kázerün	85	29 38N	51	40 E
Kazo	107	36 7N	139	36 E
Kéa	55	37 35N	24	22 E
Keaau	160	19 37N	155	3W
Kebnekaise	66	67 53N	18	33 E
Kecskemét	59	46 57N	19	42 E
Kedah □	96	5 50N	100	40 E
Kediri	111	7 51S	112	1 E
Keeling Is. = Cocos Is.	111	12 10S	96	55 E
Keene	164	42 57N	72	17W
Keetmanshoop	136	26 35S	18	8 E
Keewatin	153	49 46N	94	34W
Keewatin □	145	63 20N	95	0W
Kefallinía	54	38 20N	20	30 E
Keflavik	64	64 2N	22	35W
Keighley	28	53 52N	1	54W
Keith, Australia	119	36 6S	140	20 E
Keith, U.K.	33	57 33N	2	58W
Kelang	96	3 2N	101	26 E
Kelantan □	96	5 10N	102	0 E
Kelantan →	96	6 13N	102	14 E
Kellerberrin	120	31 36S	117	38 E
Kellogg	162	47 30N	116	5W
Kells = Ceanannus Mor	34	53 42N	6	53W
Kelowna	155	49 50N	119	25W
Kelso, U.K.	31	55 36N	2	27W
Kelso, U.S.A.	171	46 10N	122	57W
Keluang	96	2 3N	103	18 E
Kelvington	152	52 10N	103	30W
Kemerovo	71	55 20N	86	5 E
Kemi	67	65 44N	24	34 E
Kemi →	67	67 30N	28	30 E
Kempsey	116	31 1S	152	50 E
Kendal	28	54 19N	2	44W
Keng Tung	93	21 0N	99	30 E
Kenitra	126	34 15N	6	40W
Kenmare	35	51 52N	9	35W
Kennewick	171	46 11N	119	2W
Keno Hill	144	63 57N	135	18W
Kenora	153	49 47N	94	29W
Kenosha	167	42 33N	87	48W
Kent	164	41 8N	81	20W
Kent □	25	51 12N	0	40 E
Kent Group	117	39 30S	147	20 E
Kent Pen.	145	68 30N	107	0W
Kentucky □	167	37 20N	85	0W
Kentucky →	167	38 41N	85	11W
Kenya ■	133	1 0N	38	0 E
Kenya, Mt.	132	0 10S	37	18 E
Keokuk	166	40 25N	91	24W
Kepsut	80	39 40N	28	9 E
Kerala □	90	11 0N	76	15 E
Kerang	117	35 40S	143	55 E
Kerch	68	45 20N	36	20 E
Kerki	70	37 50N	65	12 E
Kérkira	54	39 38N	19	50 E
Kerkrade	41	50 53N	6	4 E
Kermadec Is.	122	30 0S	178	15W
Kermán	85	30 15N	57	1 E
Kermán □	85	30 0N	57	0 E
Kermánsháh = Bákhtarán	84	34 23N	47	0 E
Kerrobert	152	52 0N	109	11W
Kerry □	35	52 7N	9	35W
Kerulen →	98	48 48N	117	0 E
Kestenga	68	66 0N	31	50 E
Keswick	28	54 35N	3	9W
Ketchikan	143	55 25N	131	40W
Kettering	156	39 41N	84	10W
Kewanee	166	41 18N	89	55W
Keweenaw B.	150	46 56N	88	23W
Key West	159	24 33N	82	0W
Keyser	164	39 26N	79	0W
Khabarovsk	75	48 30N	135	5 E
Khalkhál	81	37 37N	48	32 E
Khalkis	55	38 27N	23	42 E
Khalmer Yu	69	67 58N	65	1 E
Khambhat	91	22 23N	72	33 E
Khambhat, G. of	91	20 45N	72	30 E
Khamir	82	16 0N	44	0 E
Khánábád	87	36 45N	69	5 E
Khánaqín	81	34 23N	45	25 E
Khandwa	91	21 49N	76	22 E
Khanewal	89	30 20N	71	55 E
Khaniá	55	35 30N	24	4 E
Khanka, Ozero	75	45 0N	132	24 E
Kharagpur	92	22 20N	87	25 E
Kharkov	68	49 58N	36	20 E
Khartoum = El Khartûm	129	15 31N	32	35 E
Khashm el Girba	129	14 59N	35	58 E
Khaskovo	53	41 56N	25	30 E
Khatanga	72	72 0N	102	20 E
Khatanga →	72	72 55N	106	0 E
Khenchela	127	35 28N	7	11 E
Kherson	68	46 35N	32	35 E
Kheta →	72	71 54N	102	6 E
Khíos, I.	55	38 20N	26	0 E
Khmer Rep. = Cambodia ■	95	12 15N	105	0 E
Khodzhent	71	40 17N	69	37 E
Khojak P.	88	30 55N	66	30 E
Kholm	87	36 45N	67	40 E
Khon Kaen	95	16 30N	102	47 E
Khoper →	68	49 30N	42	20 E
Khorásán □	86	34 0N	58	0 E
Khorat = Nakhon Ratchasima	95	14 59N	102	12 E
Khorat, Cao Nguyen	95	15 30N	102	50 E
Khorog	71	37 30N	71	36 E
Khorramábád	84	33 30N	48	25 E
Khorrámshahr	84	30 29N	48	15 E
Khulna	92	22 45N	89	34 E
Khulna □	92	22 25N	89	35 E
Khushab	89	32 20N	72	20 E
Khúzestán □	84	31 0N	49	0 E
Khvor	86	33 45N	55	0 E
Khvoy	81	38 35N	45	0 E
Khyber Pass	89	34 10N	71	8 E
Kiama	117	34 40S	150	50 E
Kiangsi = Jiangxi □	99	27 30N	116	0 E
Kiangsu = Jiangsu □	99	33 0N	120	0 E
Kichiga	73	59 50N	163	5 E
Kicking Horse Pass	155	51 28N	116	16W
Kidderminster	24	52 24N	2	13W
Kidnappers, C.	122	39 38S	177	5 E
Kiel	43	54 16N	10	8 E
Kielce	58	50 52N	20	42 E
Kieler Bucht	42	54 30N	10	30 E
Kiev = Kiyev	68	50 30N	30	28 E
Kigali	135	1 59S	30	4 E
Kii-Hantō	106	34 0N	135	45 E
Kii-Sanchi	106	34 20N	136	0 E
Kii-Suidō	109	33 40N	135	0 E
Kikládhes □	55	37 0N	25	0 E
Kikuchi	108	32 59N	130	47 E
Kilcoy	116	26 59S	152	30 E
Kildare □	35	53 10N	6	50W
Kilimanjaro	132	3 7S	37	20 E
Kilis	80	36 50N	37	10 E

Name	Map	°	′		°	′	
Kilkenny	35	52	40N		7	17W	
Kilkenny □	35	52	35N		7	15W	
Killala B.	34	54	20N		9	12W	
Killarney, Canada	153	49	10N		99	40W	
Killarney, Ireland	35	52	2N		9	30W	
Killary Harbour	34	53	38N		9	52W	
Killiecrankie, Pass of	33	56	44N		3	46W	
Kilmarnock	31	55	36N		4	30W	
Kilmore	117	37	25S		144	53 E	
Kilrush	35	52	39N		9	30W	
Kimba	118	33	8S		136	23 E	
Kimberley, Australia	114	16	20S		127	0 E	
Kimberley, Canada	155	49	40N		115	59W	
Kimberley, S. Africa	136	28	43S		24	46 E	
Kinabalu	112	6	3N		116	14 E	
Kincardine	150	44	10N		81	40W	
Kindersley	152	51	30N		109	10W	
Kindia	130	10	0N		12	52W	
King Frederik VI Land =							
Kong Frederik VI.s Kyst	147	63	0N		43	0W	
King George Is.	140	57	20N		80	30W	
King I. = Kadan Kyun	94	12	30N		98	20 E	
King I., Australia	119	39	50S		144	0 E	
King I., Canada	154	52	10N		127	40W	
King Sd.	114	16	50S		123	20 E	
King William I.	145	69	10N		97	25W	
Kingaroy	116	26	32S		151	51 E	
Kingman	173	35	12N		114	2W	
King's Lynn	29	52	45N		0	25 E	
Kingscote	119	35	40S		137	38 E	
Kingsport	165	36	33N		82	36W	
Kingston, Canada	151	44	14N		76	30W	
Kingston, Jamaica	180	18	0N		76	50W	
Kingston, N.Z.	123	45	20S		168	43 E	
Kingston, U.S.A.	164	41	55N		74	0W	
Kingston South East	119	36	51S		139	55 E	
Kingstown	180	13	10N		61	10W	
Kingsville	150	42	2N		82	45W	
Kingussie	33	57	5N		4	2W	
Kinistino	152	52	57N		105	2W	
Kinki □	106	33	30N		136	0 E	
Kinnairds Hd.	33	57	40N		2	0W	
Kinsale, Old Hd. of	35	51	37N		8	32W	
Kinshasa	134	4	20S		15	15 E	
Kinston	165	35	18N		77	35W	
Kintyre	30	55	30N		5	35W	
Kintyre, Mull of	30	55	17N		5	55W	
Kinu-Gawa →	107	35	36N		139	57 E	
Kiparissia	54	37	15N		21	40 E	
Kirensk	74	57	50N		107	55 E	
Kirghizia ■	71	42	0N		75	0 E	
Kiribati ■	122	1	0N		176	0 E	
Kırıkkale	80	39	51N		33	32 E	
Kirin = Jilin	98	43	44N		126	30 E	
Kiritimati	123	1	58N		157	27W	
Kirkcaldy	31	56	7N		3	10W	
Kirkcudbright	31	54	50N		4	3W	
Kirkee	91	18	34N		73	56 E	
Kirkintilloch	31	55	57N		4	10W	
Kirkland Lake	151	48	9N		80	2W	
Kirksville	166	40	8N		92	35W	
Kirkūk	81	35	30N		44	21 E	
Kirkwall	33	58	59N		2	59W	
Kirov = Vyatka	69	58	35N		49	40 E	
Kirovabad = Gyandzha	70	40	45N		46	20 E	
Kirovograd = Yelizavetgrad	68	48	35N		32	20 E	
Kirthar Range	88	27	0N		67	0 E	
Kiruna	66	67	52N		20	15 E	
Kiryū	107	36	24N		139	20 E	
Kisangani	135	0	35N		25	15 E	
Kisarazu	107	35	23N		139	55 E	
Kiselevsk	71	54	5N		86	39 E	
Kishangarh	89	27	50N		70	30 E	
Kishinev	68	47	0N		28	50 E	
Kishiwada	106	34	28N		135	22 E	
Kiskunfélégyháza	59	46	42N		19	53 E	
Kiso-Gawa →	106	35	20N		136	45 E	
Kisumu	132	0	3S		34	45 E	
Kita	130	13	5N		9	25W	
Kita-Ura	107	36	0N		140	34 E	
Kitakami-Gawa →	103	38	25N		141	19 E	
Kitakyūshū	108	33	50N		130	50 E	
Kitale	132	1	0N		35	0 E	
Kitami	103	43	48N		143	54 E	
Kitchener	151	43	27N		80	29W	
Kithira	55	36	9N		23	0 E	
Kithnos	55	37	26N		24	27 E	
Kitikmeot □	145	70	0N		110	0W	
Kitimat	154	54	3N		128	38W	
Kitsuki	108	33	25N		131	37 E	
Kittakittaooloo, L.	118	28	3S		138	14 E	
Kitwe	135	12	54S		28	13 E	
Kiyev	68	50	30N		30	28 E	
Klagenfurt	45	46	38N		14	20 E	
Klaipeda	68	55	43N		21	10 E	
Klamath →	172	41	40N		124	4W	
Klamath Falls	171	42	20N		121	50W	
Klamath Mts.	172	41	20N		123	0W	
Kleena Kleene	154	52	0N		124	59W	
Klondike	144	64	0N		139	26W	
Kluane L.	144	61	15N		138	40W	
Klyuchevsk	73	55	50N		160	30 E	
Knaresborough	28	54	1N		1	29W	
Knockmealdown Mts.	35	52	16N		8	0W	
Knossos	55	35	16N		25	10 E	
Knoxville, Iowa, U.S.A.	166	41	20N		93	5W	
Knoxville, Tenn., U.S.A.	165	35	58N		83	57W	
Ko Chang	95	12	0N		102	20 E	
Ko Kut	95	11	40N		102	32 E	
Koartac	146	60	55N		69	40W	
Kobarid	52	46	15N		13	30 E	
Kobayashi	108	31	56N		130	59 E	
Kobdo = Hovd	100	48	2N		91	37 E	
Kōbe	106	34	45N		135	10 E	
København	61	55	41N		12	34 E	
Koblenz	42	50	21N		7	36 E	
Kobroor, Kepulauan	113	6	10S		134	30 E	
Kočani	53	41	55N		22	25 E	
Kōchi	109	33	30N		133	35 E	
Kochiu = Gejiu	99	23	20N		103	10 E	
Kodaira	107	35	44N		139	29 E	
Kodiak I.	142	57	30N		152	45W	
Kōfu	107	35	40N		138	30 E	
Koga	107	36	11N		139	43 E	
Kogota	103	38	33N		141	3 E	
Koh-i-Bābā	87	34	30N		67	0 E	
Kohat	89	33	40N		71	29 E	
Kokand	71	40	30N		70	57 E	
Kokchetav	71	53	20N		69	25 E	
Koko Kyunzu	94	14	10N		93	25 E	
Kokomo	167	40	30N		86	6W	
Kokopo	115	4	22S		152	19 E	
Koksoak →	146	58	30N		68	10W	
Kokubu	108	31	44N		130	46 E	
Kola Pen. = Kolskiy							
Poluostrov	69	67	30N		38	0 E	
Kolar	90	13	12N		78	15 E	
Kolar Gold Fields	90	12	58N		78	16 E	
Kolarovgrad	53	43	18N		26	55 E	
Kolding	61	55	30N		9	29 E	
Kolguyev, Ostrov	69	69	20N		48	30 E	
Kolhapur	91	16	43N		74	15 E	
Köln	42	50	56N		6	58 E	
Kolo	58	52	14N		18	40 E	
Kolomna	68	55	8N		38	45 E	
Kolskiy Poluostrov	69	67	30N		38	0 E	
Kolyma →	73	69	30N		161	0 E	
Komagene	107	35	44N		137	58 E	
Komaki	106	35	17N		136	55 E	
Komandorskiye, Is.	73	55	0N		167	0 E	
Komárno	59	47	49N		18	5 E	
Komatsu	106	36	25N		136	30 E	
Komatsujima	109	34	0N		134	35 E	
Komi Rep. □	69	64	0N		55	0 E	
Kommunizma, Pik	71	39	0N		72	2 E	
Komoro	107	36	19N		138	26 E	
Kompong Cham	95	12	0N		105	30 E	
Kompong Chhnang	95	12	20N		104	35 E	
Kompong Som	95	10	38N		103	30 E	
Komsomolets, Ostrov	72	80	30N		95	0 E	
Komsomolsk	75	50	30N		137	0 E	
Konarhá □	87	35	30N		71	3 E	

Name	Page	Lat	Long
Kong	130	8 54N	4 36W
Kong, Koh	95	11 20N	103 0 E
Kong Christian X.s Land	13	74 0N	29 0W
Kong Frederik Vl.s Kyst	147	63 0N	43 0W
Kong Frederik VIII.s Land	13	78 30N	26 0W
Kongor	129	7 1N	31 27 E
Königsberg = Kaliningrad	68	54 42N	20 32 E
Konin	58	52 12N	18 15 E
Konjic	52	43 42N	17 58 E
Konosha	68	61 0N	40 5 E
Konstanz	44	47 39N	9 10 E
Kontagora	131	10 23N	5 27 E
Konya	80	37 52N	32 35 E
Konya Ovasi	80	38 30N	33 0 E
Koolyanobbing	120	30 48S	119 36 E
Kopaonik Planina	52	43 10N	21 50 E
Kopeysk	71	55 7N	61 37 E
Kopparberg	60	59 52N	15 0 E
Koppeh Dāgh	86	38 0N	58 0 E
Korab	52	41 44N	20 40 E
Korça	52	40 37N	20 50 E
Korčula	52	42 57N	17 8 E
Kordestān □	81	36 0N	47 0 E
Korea Bay	98	39 0N	124 0 E
Korea Strait	104	34 0N	129 30 E
Korhogo	130	9 29N	5 28W
Korinthiakós Kólpos	54	38 16N	22 30 E
Kórinthos	54	37 56N	22 55 E
Kōriyama	105	37 24N	140 23 E
Koroit	119	38 18S	142 24 E
Kortrijk	42	50 50N	3 17 E
Koryakskiy Khrebet	73	61 0N	171 0 E
Kos	55	36 50N	27 15 E
Kosciusko	169	33 3N	89 34W
Kosciusko, Mt.	117	36 27S	148 16 E
Koshigaya	107	35 54N	139 48 E
K'oshih = Kashi	100	39 30N	76 2 E
Koshiki-Rettō	108	31 45N	129 49 E
Kōshoku	107	36 38N	138 6 E
Košice	59	48 42N	21 15 E
Kosovska-Mitrovica	52	42 54N	20 52 E
Kôstî	129	13 8N	32 43 E
Kostroma	68	57 50N	40 58 E
Koszalin	58	53 50N	16 8 E
Kota	91	25 14N	75 49 E
Kota Baharu	96	6 7N	102 14 E
Kota Kinabalu	112	6 0N	116 4 E
Kotelnich	68	58 20N	48 10 E
Kotka	67	60 28N	26 58 E
Kotlas	69	61 15N	47 0 E
Kotor	52	42 25N	18 47 E
Kotuy →	77	71 54N	102 6 E
Kotzebue	142	66 50N	162 40W
Kowloon	99	22 20N	114 15 E
Kōyama	108	31 20N	130 56 E
Koyukuk →	142	64 56N	157 30W
Kozáni	55	40 19N	21 47 E
Kozhikode = Calicut	90	11 15N	75 43 E
Kōzu-Shima	107	34 13N	139 10 E
Kra, Isthmus of = Kra, Kho Khot	94	10 15N	99 30 E
Kra, Kho Khot	94	10 15N	99 30 E
Kragujevac	52	44 2N	20 56 E
Kraków	58	50 4N	19 57 E
Kraljevo	52	43 44N	20 41 E
Krasnodar	68	45 5N	39 0 E
Krasnovodsk	70	40 0N	52 52 E
Krasnoyarsk	74	56 8N	93 0 E
Krasnyy Kut	68	50 50N	47 0 E
Kratie	95	12 32N	106 10 E
Kravanh, Chuor Phnum	95	12 0N	103 32 E
Krefeld	42	51 20N	6 32 E
Kremenchug	68	49 5N	33 25 E
Krishna →	91	15 57N	80 59 E
Krishnanagar	92	23 24N	88 33 E
Kristiansand	60	58 9N	8 1 E
Kristianstad	61	56 2N	14 9 E
Kristianstads län □	61	56 15N	14 0 E
Kristiansund	65	63 7N	7 45 E
Kriti	55	35 15N	25 0 E
Krivoy Rog	68	47 51N	33 20 E
Krk	52	45 8N	14 40 E
Kronobergs län □	61	56 45N	14 30 E
Kronshtadt	68	60 5N	29 45 E
Krotoszyn	58	51 42N	17 23 E
Krugersdorp	137	26 5S	27 46 E
Krung Thep = Bangkok	94	13 45N	100 35 E
Kruševac	52	43 35N	21 28 E
Krymskiy P-ov.	68	45 0N	34 0 E
Kuala Dungun	96	4 45N	103 25 E
Kuala Kangsar	96	4 46N	100 56 E
Kuala Lipis	96	4 10N	102 3 E
Kuala Lumpur	96	3 9N	101 41 E
Kuala Pilah	96	2 45N	102 15 E
Kuala Trengganu	96	5 20N	103 8 E
Kuangchou = Guangzhou	99	23 5N	113 10 E
Kuantan	96	3 49N	103 20 E
Kubak	88	27 10N	63 10 E
Kuban →	68	45 20N	37 30 E
Kubokawa	109	33 12N	133 8 E
Kuchinoerabu-Jima	104	30 28N	130 11 E
Kucing	111	1 33N	110 25 E
Kudamatsu	108	34 0N	131 52 E
Kueiyang = Guiyang	99	26 32N	106 40 E
Kūh-e-Jebāl Bārez	85	29 0N	58 0 E
Kūh-e Sorkh	86	35 30N	58 45 E
Kūhhā-ye-Bashākerd	85	26 45N	59 0 E
Kūhhā-ye Sabalān	81	38 15N	47 45 E
Kuji	103	40 11N	141 46 E
Kuldja = Yining	100	43 58N	81 10 E
Kulunda	71	52 35N	78 57 E
Kumagaya	107	36 9N	139 22 E
Kumamoto	108	32 45N	130 45 E
Kumano	106	33 54N	136 5 E
Kumano-Nada	106	33 47N	136 20 E
Kumasi	130	6 41N	1 38W
Kumayri	70	40 47N	43 50 E
Kumon Bum	93	26 30N	97 15 E
Kunashir, Ostrov	75	44 0N	146 0 E
Kunimi-Dake	109	32 33N	131 1 E
Kunlun Shan	100	36 0N	86 30 E
Kunming	101	25 1N	102 41 E
Kunsan	98	35 59N	126 45 E
Kuopio	67	62 53N	27 35 E
Kupang	113	10 19S	123 39 E
Kurashiki	109	34 40N	133 50 E
Kurayoshi	109	35 26N	133 50 E
Kure	109	34 14N	132 32 E
Kurgan	71	55 26N	65 18 E
Kuril Is. = Kurilskiye Ostrova	75	45 0N	150 0 E
Kurilskiye Ostrova	75	45 0N	150 0 E
Kurnool	90	15 45N	78 0 E
Kurobe-Gawe →	106	36 55N	137 25 E
Kurri Kurri	117	32 50S	151 28 E
Kursk	68	51 42N	36 11 E
Kuršumlija	52	43 9N	21 19 E
Kurume	108	33 15N	130 30 E
Kurunegala	90	7 30N	80 23 E
Kusatsu	106	34 58N	135 57 E
Kushikino	108	31 44N	130 16 E
Kushima	108	31 29N	131 14 E
Kushiro	103	43 0N	144 25 E
Kushka	70	35 20N	62 18 E
Kushtia	92	23 55N	89 5 E
Kuskokwim Bay	142	59 50N	162 56W
Kustanay	71	53 10N	63 35 E
Kusu	108	33 16N	131 9 E
Kütahya	80	39 30N	30 2 E
Kutaisi	70	42 19N	42 40 E
Kutaraja = Banda Aceh	111	5 35N	95 20 E
Kutno	58	52 15N	19 23 E
Kuujjuaq	146	58 6N	68 15W
Kuwait = Al Kuwayt	84	29 30N	47 30 E
Kuwait ■	84	29 30N	47 30 E
Kuwana	106	35 0N	136 43 E
Kuybyshev = Samara	68	53 8N	50 6 E
Kwakoegron	185	5 12N	55 25W
Kwangju	98	35 9N	126 54 E
Kwangsi-Chuang = Guangxi Zhuangzu Zizhiqu □	99	24 0N	109 0 E
Kwangtung = Guangdong □	99	23 0N	113 0 E

Kweichow = Guizhou □ ... 99 27 0N 107 0 E
Kwinana New Town ... 120 32 15S 115 47 E
Kyabram ... 117 36 19S 145 4 E
Kyaukpadaung ... 93 20 52N 95 8 E
Kyle of Lochalsh ... 32 57 17N 5 43W
Kyneton ... 117 37 10S 144 29 E
Kyō-ga-Saki ... 106 35 45N 135 15 E
Kyoga, L. ... 132 1 35N 33 0 E
Kyogle ... 116 28 40S 153 0 E
Kyōto ... 106 35 0N 135 45 E
Kyrenia ... 80 35 20N 33 20 E
Kyūshū ... 108 33 0N 131 0 E
Kyūshū □ ... 108 33 0N 131 0 E
Kyūshū-Sanchi ... 108 32 35N 131 17 E
Kyustendil ... 53 42 16N 22 41 E
Kyzyl ... 74 51 50N 94 30 E
Kyzylkum, Peski ... 70 42 30N 65 0 E
Kzyl-Orda ... 71 44 48N 65 28 E

L

Labe = Elbe → ... 42 53 50N 9 0 E
Laboulaye ... 190 34 10S 63 30W
Labrador, Coast of □ ... 147 53 20N 61 0W
Lábrea ... 187 7 15S 64 51W
Lac la Martre ... 145 63 8N 117 16W
Laccadive Is. =
Lakshadweep Is. ... 78 10 0N 72 30 E
Lachine ... 151 45 30N 73 40W
Lachute ... 151 45 39N 74 21W
Lackawanna ... 164 42 49N 78 50W
Lacombe ... 155 52 30N 113 44W
Laconia ... 148 43 32N 71 30W
Ladakh Ra. ... 89 34 0N 78 0 E
Ladoga, L. = Ladozhskoye
Ozero ... 68 61 15N 30 30 E
Ladozhskoye Ozero ... 68 61 15N 30 30 E
Ladysmith ... 154 49 0N 123 49W
Lae ... 115 6 40S 147 2 E
Lafayette, Ind., U.S.A. ... 167 40 25N 86 54W
Lafayette, La., U.S.A. ... 168 30 18N 92 0W
Laghmān □ ... 87 34 20N 70 0 E
Laghouat ... 127 33 50N 2 59 E
Lagny ... 39 48 52N 2 40 E
Lagos, Nigeria ... 131 6 25N 3 27 E
Lagos, Portugal ... 50 37 5N 8 41W
Lagos de Moreno ... 175 21 21N 101 55W
Laguna ... 191 28 30S 48 50W
Laguna Beach ... 173 33 31N 117 52W
Laguna Madre ... 158 27 0N 97 20W
Lagunas, Chile ... 187 21 0S 69 45W
Lagunas, Peru ... 186 5 10S 75 35W
Lahore ... 89 31 32N 74 22 E
Lahti ... 67 60 58N 25 40 E
Lahtis = Lahti ... 67 60 58N 25 40 E
Laï ... 131 9 25N 16 18 E
Laidley ... 116 27 39S 152 20 E
Lairg ... 33 58 1N 4 24W
Laja, R. de la → ... 177 20 55N 100 46W
Lajes ... 191 27 48S 50 20W
Lake Cargelligo ... 117 33 15S 146 22 E
Lake Charles ... 168 30 15N 93 10W
Lake City, Fla., U.S.A. ... 170 30 10N 82 40W
Lake City, S.C., U.S.A. ... 165 33 51N 79 44W
Lake Grace ... 120 33 7S 118 28 E
Lake Harbour ... 146 62 50N 69 50W
Lake Worth ... 170 26 36N 80 3W
Lakeland ... 170 28 0N 82 0W
Lakes Entrance ... 117 37 50S 148 0 E
Lakewood ... 167 41 28N 81 50W
Lakshadweep Is. ... 78 10 0N 72 30 E
Lala Ghat ... 93 24 30N 92 40 E
Lalitpur ... 91 24 42N 78 28 E
Lamar ... 163 38 9N 102 35W
Lambi Kyun ... 96 10 50N 98 20 E
Lameroo ... 119 35 19S 140 33 E
Lamia ... 54 38 55N 22 26 E
Lammermuir Hills ... 31 55 50N 2 40W

Lamon Bay ... 112 14 30N 122 20 E
Lampa ... 187 15 22S 70 22W
Lampang ... 94 18 16N 99 32 E
Lampeter ... 26 52 6N 4 6W
Lamu ... 133 2 16S 40 55 E
Lanark ... 31 55 40N 3 48W
Lancang Jiang → ... 101 21 40N 101 10 E
Lancashire □ ... 28 53 40N 2 30W
Lancaster, U.K. ... 28 54 3N 2 48W
Lancaster, U.S.A. ... 164 40 4N 76 19W
Lancaster Sd. ... 146 74 13N 84 0W
Lanchow = Lanzhou ... 99 36 1N 103 52 E
Landes, Les ... 36 44 20N 1 0W
Land's End ... 27 50 4N 5 43W
Landskrona ... 61 55 53N 12 50 E
Lanett ... 169 33 0N 85 15W
Langjökull ... 64 64 39N 20 12W
Langlade ... 149 46 50N 56 20W
Langøya ... 64 68 45N 14 50 E
Langres, Plateau de ... 37 47 45N 5 3 E
Languedoc ... 37 43 58N 4 0 E
Lannion ... 36 48 46N 3 29W
Lansing ... 167 42 47N 84 40W
Lanzhou ... 99 36 1N 103 52 E
Laois □ ... 35 53 0N 7 20W
Laon ... 38 49 33N 3 35 E
Laona ... 150 45 32N 88 41W
Laos ■ ... 95 17 45N 105 0 E
Lapeer ... 167 43 3N 83 20W
Lapland = Lappland ... 67 68 7N 24 0 E
Lappland ... 67 68 7N 24 0 E
Laptev Sea ... 72 76 0N 125 0 E
Laramie ... 163 41 20N 105 38W
Laramie Mts. ... 163 42 0N 105 30W
Laredo ... 161 27 34N 99 29W
Laren ... 40 52 16N 5 14 E
Largs ... 30 55 48N 4 51W
Lárisa ... 54 39 49N 22 28 E
Larkana ... 88 27 32N 68 18 E
Larnaca ... 80 35 0N 33 35 E
Larne ... 34 54 52N 5 50W
Laryak ... 69 61 15N 80 0 E
Las Cruces ... 161 32 18N 106 50W
Las Lajas ... 190 38 30S 70 25W
Las Palmas ... 126 28 7N 15 26W
Las Vegas, N. Mex., U.S.A. ... 161 35 35N 105 10W
Las Vegas, Nev., U.S.A. ... 173 36 10N 115 5W
Lashio ... 93 22 56N 97 45 E
Latacunga ... 184 0 50S 78 35W
Latakia = Al Lādhiqīyah ... 80 35 30N 35 45 E
Latium = Lazio □ ... 46 42 10N 12 30 E
Latrobe ... 119 41 14S 146 30 E
Latur ... 91 18 25N 76 40 E
Latvia ■ ... 68 56 50N 24 0 E
Lauchhammer ... 43 51 35N 13 48 E
Launceston, Australia ... 119 41 24S 147 8 E
Launceston, U.K. ... 27 50 38N 4 21W
Launglon Bok ... 94 13 50N 97 54 E
Laurel ... 169 31 41N 89 9W
Laurens ... 165 34 32N 82 2W
Laurentian Plat. ... 138 52 0N 70 0W
Laurinburg ... 165 34 50N 79 25W
Lausanne ... 44 46 32N 6 38 E
Laut, Pulau ... 111 3 40S 116 10 E
Laut Ketil, Kepulauan ... 113 4 45S 115 40 E
Lauzon ... 148 46 48N 71 10W
Laval ... 36 48 4N 0 48W
Lávrion ... 55 37 40N 24 4 E
Lawrence, Kans., U.S.A. ... 166 39 0N 95 10W
Lawrence, Mass., U.S.A. ... 164 42 40N 71 9W
Lawrenceburg ... 169 35 12N 87 19W
Lawton ... 161 34 33N 98 25W
Lazio □ ... 46 42 10N 12 30 E
Lea → ... 25 51 30N 0 10W
Leader ... 152 50 50N 109 30W
Leadhills ... 31 55 25N 3 47W
Leadville ... 163 39 17N 106 23W
Leamington, Canada ... 150 42 3N 82 36W
Leamington, U.K. ... 24 52 18N 1 32W
Leavenworth ... 166 39 25N 95 0W
Lebanon, Mo., U.S.A. ... 166 37 40N 92 40W

234 Lebanon

Name	Page	Lat °	'	N/S	Long °	'	E/W
Lebanon, Oreg., U.S.A.	171	44	31	N	122	57	W
Lebanon, Pa., U.S.A.	164	40	20	N	76	28	W
Lebanon, Tenn., U.S.A.	169	36	15	N	86	20	W
Lebanon ■	80	34	0	N	36	0	E
Lecce	49	40	20	N	18	10	E
Ledbury	24	52	3	N	2	25	W
Leduc	155	53	15	N	113	30	W
Leeds	28	53	48	N	1	34	W
Leek	28	53	7	N	2	2	W
Leerdam	40	51	54	N	5	6	E
Leesburg	170	28	47	N	81	52	W
Leeton	117	34	33	S	146	23	E
Leeuwarden	41	53	15	N	5	48	E
Leeuwin, C.	120	34	20	S	115	9	E
Leeward Is.	181	16	30	N	63	30	W
Leghorn = Livorno	46	43	32	N	10	18	E
Legnica	58	51	12	N	16	10	E
Leicester	25	52	39	N	1	9	W
Leicester □	25	52	40	N	1	10	W
Leichhardt	121	33	53	S	151	9	E
Leiden	40	52	9	N	4	30	E
Leigh Creek South	118	30	38	S	138	26	E
Leinster	120	27	51	S	120	36	E
Leinster □	35	53	0	N	7	10	W
Leinster, Mt.	35	52	38	N	6	47	W
Leipzig	43	51	20	N	12	23	E
Leith	31	55	59	N	3	10	W
Leith Hill	24	51	10	N	0	23	W
Leitrim	34	54	0	N	8	5	W
Lek →	40	51	54	N	4	35	E
Leleque	192	42	28	S	71	0	W
Léman, Lac	44	46	26	N	6	30	E
Lemmer	41	52	51	N	5	43	E
Lena →	72	72	52	N	126	40	E
Leninabad = Khodzhent	71	40	17	N	69	37	E
Leninakan = Kumayri	70	40	47	N	43	50	E
Leningrad = Sankt-Peterburg	68	59	55	N	30	20	E
Leninsk-Kuznetskiy	71	54	44	N	86	10	E
Leninskoye	75	47	56	N	132	38	E
Lenoir City	165	35	40	N	84	20	W
Lens, Belgium	38	50	33	N	3	54	E
Lens, France	37	50	26	N	2	50	E
Lensk	74	60	48	N	114	55	E
Leominster, U.K.	24	52	15	N	2	43	W
Leominster, U.S.A.	164	42	32	N	71	45	W
León, Mexico	177	21	7	N	101	40	W
León, Nic.	179	12	20	N	86	51	W
León, Spain	50	42	38	N	5	34	W
León □	50	42	40	N	5	55	W
Leongatha	117	38	30	S	145	58	E
Léopold II, Lac = Mai-Ndombe, L.	134	2	0	S	18	20	E
Léopoldville = Kinshasa	134	4	20	S	15	15	E
Lérida	51	41	37	N	0	39	E
Lerwick	30	60	10	N	1	10	W
Lesbos, I. = Lésvos	55	39	10	N	26	20	E
Lesotho ■	137	29	40	S	28	0	E
Lesozavodsk	75	45	30	N	133	29	E
Lesser Antilles	181	15	0	N	61	0	W
Lesser Slave L.	155	55	30	N	115	25	W
Lésvos	55	39	10	N	26	20	E
Letchworth	25	51	58	N	0	13	W
Lethbridge	155	49	45	N	112	45	W
Leti, Kepulauan	113	8	10	S	128	0	E
Leticia	184	4	9	S	70	0	W
Letsôk-aw Kyun	94	11	30	N	98	25	E
Letterkenny	34	54	57	N	7	42	W
Leuven	42	50	52	N	4	42	E
Levanger	65	63	45	N	11	19	E
Levin	122	40	37	S	175	18	E
Lévis	148	46	48	N	71	9	W
Levkás	54	38	40	N	20	43	E
Levkôsia = Nicosia	80	35	10	N	33	25	E
Lewes	25	50	53	N	0	2	E
Lewis	32	58	10	N	6	40	W
Lewis, Butt of	32	58	30	N	6	12	W
Lewis Ra.	162	48	0	N	113	15	W
Lewisporte	149	49	15	N	55	3	W
Lewiston	148	44	3	N	70	10	E
Lexington, Ky., U.S.A.	165	38	6	N	84	30	W
Lexington, Mo., U.S.A.	166	39	7	N	93	55	W
Lexington, N.C., U.S.A.	165	35	50	N	80	13	W
Lexington, Oreg., U.S.A.	171	45	29	N	119	46	W
Lexington Park	165	38	16	N	76	27	W
Leyte	112	11	0	N	125	0	E
Lhasa	101	29	50	N	91	3	E
Lhazê	101	29	5	N	87	38	E
Lianyungang	99	34	40	N	119	11	E
Liaoning □	98	41	40	N	122	30	E
Liaoyuan	98	42	58	N	125	2	E
Liard →	144	61	51	N	121	18	W
Libau = Liepaja	68	56	30	N	21	0	E
Liberec	58	50	47	N	15	7	E
Liberia ■	130	6	30	N	9	30	W
Lïbïya, Sahrâ'	128	27	35	N	25	0	E
Libreville	134	0	25	N	9	26	E
Libya ■	127	27	0	N	17	0	E
Lichfield	28	52	40	N	1	50	W
Liechtenstein ■	44	47	8	N	9	35	E
Liège	42	50	38	N	5	35	E
Liegnitz = Legnica	58	51	12	N	16	10	E
Lienyünchiangshih = Lianyungang	99	34	40	N	119	11	E
Liepaja	68	56	30	N	21	0	E
Liévin	38	50	24	N	2	47	E
Liffey →	35	53	21	N	6	20	W
Lifford	34	54	50	N	7	30	W
Liguria □	46	44	30	N	9	0	E
Ligurian Sea	46	43	20	N	9	0	E
Lihou Reefs and Cays	121	17	25	S	151	40	E
Lihue	160	21	59	N	159	24	W
Likasi	135	10	55	S	26	48	E
Lille, Belgium	38	51	15	N	4	50	E
Lille, France	37	50	38	N	3	3	E
Lille Bælt	61	55	20	N	9	45	E
Lillehammer	60	61	8	N	10	30	E
Lillers	38	50	35	N	2	28	E
Lillooet	154	50	44	N	121	57	W
Lilongwe	137	14	0	S	33	48	E
Lima, Peru	186	12	0	S	77	0	W
Lima, U.S.A.	167	40	42	N	84	5	W
Limassol	80	34	42	N	33	1	E
Limavady	34	55	3	N	6	58	W
Limbe	137	15	55	S	35	2	E
Limburg □	41	51	20	N	5	55	E
Limeira	188	22	35	S	47	28	W
Limerick	35	52	40	N	8	38	W
Limerick □	35	52	30	N	8	50	W
Limfjorden	61	56	55	N	9	0	E
Límnos	55	39	50	N	25	5	E
Limoges	36	45	50	N	1	15	E
Limón	179	10	0	N	83	2	W
Limousin	36	46	0	N	1	0	E
Limpopo →	137	25	15	S	33	30	E
Linares, Chile	190	35	50	S	71	40	W
Linares, Mexico	176	24	50	N	99	40	W
Linares, Spain	50	38	10	N	3	40	W
Lincoln, Argentina	190	34	55	S	61	30	W
Lincoln, U.K.	29	53	14	N	0	32	W
Lincoln, Ill., U.S.A.	166	40	10	N	89	20	W
Lincoln, Maine, U.S.A.	148	45	27	N	68	29	W
Lincoln, Nebr., U.S.A.	156	40	50	N	96	42	W
Lincoln □	29	53	14	N	0	32	W
Lincoln Sea	12	84	0	N	55	0	W
Lincoln Wolds	29	53	20	N	0	5	W
Lindsay, Canada	151	44	22	N	78	43	W
Lindsay, U.S.A.	173	36	14	N	119	6	W
Linea de la Concepción, La	50	36	15	N	5	23	W
Lingga, Kepulauan	111	0	10	S	104	30	E
Linguéré	130	15	25	N	15	5	W
Linköping	60	58	28	N	15	36	E
Linlithgow	31	55	58	N	3	38	W
Linxia	99	35	36	N	103	10	E
Linz	45	48	18	N	14	18	E
Lion, G. du	37	43	0	N	4	0	E
Lípari, Is.	49	38	30	N	14	50	E
Lipetsk	68	52	37	N	39	35	E
Lippe →	42	51	39	N	6	38	E
Lisboa	50	38	42	N	9	10	W
Lisbon = Lisboa	50	38	42	N	9	10	W
Lisburn	34	54	30	N	6	9	W
Lisburne, C.	142	68	50	N	166	0	W

Place	Map	Lat	Long
Lisieux	39	49 10N	0 12 E
Lismore	116	28 44S	153 21 E
Lister, Mt.	15	78 0S	162 0 E
Listowel	35	52 27N	9 30W
Litchfield	166	39 10N	89 40W
Lithgow	117	33 25S	150 8 E
Lithuania ■	68	55 30N	24 0 E
Little Andaman I.	94	10 40N	92 15 E
Little Barrier I.	122	36 12S	175 8 E
Little Current	150	45 55N	82 0W
Little Falls	164	43 3N	74 50W
Little Minch	32	57 35N	6 45W
Little Rann	91	23 25N	71 25 E
Little Rock	168	34 41N	92 10W
Littlehampton	25	50 48N	0 32W
Liuzhou	99	24 22N	109 22 E
Liverpool, Australia	117	33 54S	150 58 E
Liverpool, Canada	148	44 5N	64 41W
Liverpool, U.K.	28	53 25N	3 0W
Liverpool Plains	116	31 15S	150 15 E
Livingston, Guatemala	177	15 50N	88 50W
Livingston, U.K.	31	55 52N	3 33W
Livingston, Mont., U.S.A.	163	45 40N	110 40W
Livingston, Tex., U.S.A.	168	30 44N	94 54W
Livingstone	135	17 46S	25 52 E
Livonia	167	42 25N	83 23W
Livorno	46	43 32N	10 18 E
Lizard Pt.	27	49 57N	5 11W
Ljubljana	52	46 4N	14 33 E
Ljusnan →	66	61 12N	17 8 E
Llandeilo	26	51 53N	4 0W
Llandovery	26	51 59N	3 49W
Llandrindod Wells	26	52 15N	3 23W
Llandudno	26	53 19N	3 51W
Llanelli	27	51 41N	4 11W
Llanes	50	43 25N	4 50W
Llangollen	26	52 58N	3 10W
Llanidloes	26	52 28N	3 31W
Llano Estacado	161	34 0N	103 0W
Llanos	184	5 0N	71 35W
Lloydminster	152	53 17N	110 0W
Loc Ninh	95	11 50N	106 34 E
Lochaber	32	56 55N	5 0W
Lochboisdale	32	57 10N	7 20W
Lochem	41	52 9N	6 26 E
Lochgilphead	30	56 2N	5 37W
Lochinver	32	58 9N	5 15W
Lochmaddy	32	57 36N	7 10W
Lochy, L.	32	56 58N	4 55W
Lock Haven	164	41 7N	77 31W
Lockhart	117	35 14S	146 40 E
Lockport	164	43 12N	78 42W
Lodi	172	38 12N	121 16W
Łódź	58	51 45N	19 27 E
Lofoten	64	68 30N	15 0 E
Logan, Utah, U.S.A.	163	41 45N	111 50W
Logan, W. Va., U.S.A.	165	37 51N	81 59W
Logan, Mt	144	60 31N	140 22W
Logansport	167	40 45N	86 21W
Logroño	51	42 28N	2 27W
Loire →	36	47 16N	2 10W
Loja	184	3 59S	79 16W
Lokka	67	67 55N	27 35 E
Lolland	61	54 45N	11 30 E
Lom	53	43 48N	23 12 E
Lomami →	134	0 46N	24 16 E
Lombardia □	46	45 35N	9 45 E
Lombardy = Lombardia □	46	45 35N	9 45 E
Lombok	113	8 45S	116 30 E
Lomé	130	6 9N	1 20 E
Lomond, L.	31	56 8N	4 38W
Lompoc	173	34 41N	120 32W
Łomza	58	53 10N	22 2 E
London, Canada	150	42 59N	81 15W
London, U.K.	25	51 30N	0 5W
Londonderry	34	55 0N	7 20W
Londrina	191	23 18S	51 10W
Long Beach	173	33 46N	118 12W
Long I., Bahamas	178	23 20N	75 10W
Long I., U.S.A.	164	40 50N	73 20W
Long Range Mts.	149	49 30N	57 30W
Long Xuyen	95	10 19N	105 28 E
Longford, Australia	119	41 32S	147 3 E
Longford, Ireland	34	53 43N	7 50W
Longford □	34	53 42N	7 45W
Longlac	150	49 45N	86 25W
Longmont	163	40 10N	105 4W
Longreach	121	23 28S	144 14 E
Longview, Tex., U.S.A.	168	32 30N	94 45W
Longview, Wash., U.S.A.	171	46 9N	122 58W
Looe	27	50 24N	4 25W
Loop Hd.	35	52 34N	9 55W
Lop Nor	100	40 20N	90 10 E
Lopez, C.	134	0 47S	8 40 E
Lorain	167	41 28N	82 55W
Lorca	51	37 41N	1 42W
Lord Howe I.	122	31 33S	159 6 E
Lordsburg	161	32 22N	108 45W
Lorient	36	47 45N	3 23W
Lorn	30	56 26N	5 10W
Lorn, Firth of	30	56 20N	5 40W
Lorraine	37	49 0N	6 0 E
Los Alamos	161	35 57N	106 17W
Los Andes	190	32 50S	70 40W
Los Angeles, Chile	190	37 28S	72 23W
Los Angeles, U.S.A.	173	34 0N	118 10W
Los Angeles Aqueduct	173	35 25N	118 0W
Los Hermanos	181	11 45N	84 25W
Los Mochis	174	25 45N	108 57W
Los Testigos	181	11 23N	63 6W
Lošinj	52	44 30N	14 30 E
Lossiemouth	33	57 43N	3 17W
Lot →	36	44 18N	0 20 E
Lota	190	37 5S	73 10W
Lothian □	31	55 50N	3 0W
Loughborough	29	52 46N	1 11W
Loughrea	35	53 11N	8 33W
Louisburg	149	45 55N	60 0W
Louise I.	154	52 55N	131 50W
Louisiana □	168	30 50N	92 0W
Louisville, Ky., U.S.A.	167	38 15N	85 45W
Louisville, Miss., U.S.A.	169	33 7N	89 3W
Lourdes	36	43 6N	0 3W
Lourenço-Marques = Maputo	137	25 58S	32 32 E
Louth	29	53 23N	0 0 E
Louth □	34	53 55N	6 30W
Louvain = Leuven	42	50 52N	4 42 E
Louviers	39	49 12N	1 10 E
Lowell	164	42 38N	71 19W
Lower Austria = Niederösterreich □	45	48 25N	15 40 E
Lower California = Baja California	174	31 10N	115 12W
Lower Hutt	123	41 10S	174 55 E
Lower Saxony = Niedersachsen □	42	52 45N	9 0 E
Lowestoft	25	52 29N	1 44 E
Łowicz	58	52 6N	19 55 E
Loxton	119	34 28S	140 31 E
Loyalty Is. = Loyauté, Is.	122	21 0S	167 30 E
Loyang = Luoyang	99	34 40N	112 26 E
Loyauté, Is.	122	21 0S	167 30 E
Lualaba →	135	0 26N	25 20 E
Luan Chau	95	21 38N	103 24 E
Luanda	134	8 50S	13 15 E
Luang Prabang	95	19 52N	102 10 E
Luarca	50	43 32N	6 32W
Lubbock	161	33 40N	101 53W
Lübeck	43	53 52N	10 41 E
Lublin	58	51 12N	22 38 E
Lubnān, J.	80	33 50N	35 45 E
Lubumbashi	135	11 40S	27 28 E
Lucca	46	43 50N	10 30 E
Luce Bay	30	54 45N	4 48W
Lučenec	59	48 18N	19 42 E
Lucerne = Luzern	44	47 3N	8 18 E
Lucknow	92	26 50N	81 0 E
Lüda = Dalian	98	38 50N	121 40 E
Lüderitz	136	26 41S	15 8 E
Ludhiana	89	30 57N	75 56 E
Ludington	167	43 58N	86 27W
Ludlow	24	52 23N	2 42W

Name	Page	Lat °	Lat ′	N/S	Long °	Long ′	E/W
Ludwigshafen	42	49	27	N	8	27	E
Lufkin	168	31	25	N	94	40	W
Lugano	44	46	0	N	8	57	E
Lugansk	68	48	38	N	39	15	E
Lugo	50	43	2	N	7	35	W
Lugovoye	71	42	55	N	72	43	E
Luján	190	34	45	S	59	5	W
Łuków	58	51	55	N	22	23	E
Lule älv →	67	65	35	N	22	10	E
Luleå	67	65	35	N	22	10	E
Lüleburgaz	80	41	23	N	27	22	E
Lulua →	134	6	30	S	22	50	E
Luluabourg = Kananga	134	5	55	S	22	18	E
Lumberton	165	34	37	N	78	59	W
Lundy	27	51	10	N	4	41	W
Lune →	28	54	0	N	2	51	W
Lüneburg	43	53	15	N	10	23	E
Lüneburg Heath = Lüneburger Heide	43	53	0	N	10	0	E
Lüneburger Heide	43	53	0	N	10	0	E
Lüni →	91	24	41	N	71	14	E
Luoyang	99	34	40	N	112	26	E
Lurgan	34	54	28	N	6	20	W
Lusaka	135	15	28	S	28	16	E
Luta = Dalian	98	38	50	N	121	40	E
Luton	25	51	53	N	0	24	W
Lutsk	68	50	50	N	25	15	E
Luvua →	135	6	50	S	27	30	E
Luxembourg	42	49	37	N	6	9	E
Luxembourg ■	42	50	0	N	6	0	E
Luzern	44	47	3	N	8	18	E
Luzhou	99	28	52	N	105	20	E
Luziânia	188	16	20	S	48	0	W
Luzon	112	16	0	N	121	0	E
Lvov	68	49	50	N	24	0	E
Lyakhovskiye, Ostrova	72	73	40	N	141	0	E
Lyallpur = Faisalabad	89	31	30	N	73	5	E
Lyell I.	154	52	40	N	131	35	W
Lyell Range	123	41	38	S	172	20	E
Lyme Regis	27	50	44	N	2	57	W
Lymington	24	50	46	N	1	32	W
Lynchburg	165	37	23	N	79	10	W
Lynn	164	42	28	N	70	57	W
Lynn Lake	152	56	51	N	101	3	W
Lynton	27	51	14	N	3	50	W
Lyon	37	45	46	N	4	50	E
Lyons = Lyon	37	45	46	N	4	50	E
Lytham St. Anne's	28	53	45	N	2	58	W
Lyttelton	122	43	35	S	172	44	E

M

Name	Page	Lat °	Lat ′	N/S	Long °	Long ′	E/W
Ma'än	80	30	12	N	35	44	E
Ma'anshan	99	31	44	N	118	29	E
Ma'arrat an Nu'mān	80	35	43	N	36	43	E
Maas →	40	51	45	N	4	32	E
Maaseik	41	51	6	N	5	45	E
Maastricht	41	50	50	N	5	40	E
Mablethorpe	29	53	21	N	0	14	E
McAlester	168	34	57	N	95	46	W
Macao = Macau ■	99	22	16	N	113	35	E
Macapá	185	0	5	N	51	4	W
Macau	189	5	0	S	36	40	W
Macau ■	99	22	16	N	113	35	E
McBride	155	53	20	N	120	19	W
Macclesfield	28	53	16	N	2	9	W
McClure Str.	12	75	0	N	119	0	W
McComb	169	31	13	N	90	30	W
McCook	163	40	15	N	100	35	W
McDermitt	172	42	0	N	117	45	W
Macdonald L.	114	23	30	S	129	0	E
Macdonnell Ranges	114	23	40	S	133	0	E
McDouall Peak	118	29	51	S	134	55	E
Macduff	33	57	40	N	2	30	W
Macedonia ■	55	41	39	N	22	0	E
Maceió	189	9	40	S	35	41	W
Macfarlane, L.	118	32	0	S	136	40	E
Macgillycuddy's Reeks	35	52	2	N	9	45	W
Machala	184	3	20	S	79	57	W
Machida	107	35	28	N	139	23	E
Machilipatnam	92	16	12	N	81	8	E
Machiques	184	10	4	N	72	34	W
Machynlleth	26	52	36	N	3	51	W
Mackay	121	21	8	S	149	11	E
Mackay, L.	114	22	30	S	129	0	E
McKeesport	164	40	21	N	79	50	W
Mackenzie →	144	69	10	N	134	20	W
Mackenzie Bay	12	69	0	N	137	30	W
Mackenzie Mts.	144	64	0	N	130	0	W
McKinley, Mt.	142	63	2	N	151	0	W
McKinley Sea	13	84	0	N	10	0	W
McKinney	168	33	10	N	96	40	W
Macksville	116	30	40	S	152	56	E
Maclean	116	29	26	S	153	16	E
McLennan	155	55	42	N	116	50	W
MacLeod Lake	154	54	58	N	123	0	W
M'Clintock Chan.	145	72	0	N	102	0	W
McMinnville, Oreg., U.S.A.	171	45	16	N	123	11	W
McMinnville, Tenn., U.S.A.	169	35	43	N	85	45	W
McMurdo Sd.	15	77	0	S	170	0	E
McMurray = Fort McMurray	155	56	44	N	111	7	W
McNaughton L.	155	52	0	N	118	10	W
Macomb	166	40	25	N	90	40	W
Mâcon, France	37	46	19	N	4	50	E
Macon, U.S.A.	170	32	50	N	83	37	W
McPherson	161	38	25	N	97	40	W
Macpherson Ra.	116	28	15	S	153	15	E
Macquarie →	116	30	5	S	147	30	E
Macquarie Is.	15	54	36	S	158	55	E
MacRobertson Land	14	71	0	S	64	0	E
Macroom	35	51	54	N	8	57	W
Madagascar ■	137	20	0	S	47	0	E
Madang	115	5	12	S	145	49	E
Madaripur	93	23	19	N	90	15	E
Made	40	51	41	N	4	49	E
Madeira →	126	32	50	N	17	0	W
Madeira →	185	3	22	S	58	45	W
Madeleine, Îs. de la	149	47	30	N	61	40	W
Madera	173	37	0	N	120	1	W
Madhya Pradesh □	91	21	50	N	81	0	E
Madison, Fla., U.S.A.	170	30	29	N	83	39	W
Madison, Ind., U.S.A.	167	38	42	N	85	20	W
Madison, Wis., U.S.A.	166	43	5	N	89	25	W
Madisonville	167	37	20	N	87	30	W
Madiun	111	7	38	S	111	32	E
Madras = Tamil Nadu □	90	11	0	N	77	0	E
Madras, India	90	13	8	N	80	19	E
Madras, U.S.A.	171	44	40	N	121	10	W
Madre, Laguna	176	25	0	N	97	30	W
Madre de Dios →	187	10	59	S	66	8	W
Madre del Sur, Sa.	177	17	0	N	100	0	W
Madre Occidental, Sa.	174	25	0	N	105	0	W
Madre Oriental, Sa.	177	22	0	N	99	30	W
Madrid	50	40	25	N	3	45	W
Madura, Selat	111	7	30	S	113	20	E
Madurai	90	9	55	N	78	10	E
Madurantakam	90	12	30	N	79	50	E
Mae Rim	94	18	54	N	98	57	E
Maebashi	107	36	24	N	139	4	E
Maesteg	27	51	36	N	3	40	W
Maestra, Sierra	178	20	15	N	77	0	W
Mafeking	152	52	40	N	101	10	W
Maffra	117	37	53	S	146	58	E
Mafia	135	7	45	S	39	50	E
Mafikeng	136	25	50	S	25	38	E
Mafra	191	26	10	S	50	0	W
Magadan	73	59	38	N	150	50	E
Magallanes, Estrecho de	192	52	30	S	75	0	W
Magangué	184	9	14	N	74	45	W
Magdalena, Bolivia	187	13	13	S	63	57	W
Magdalena, Mexico	174	30	38	N	110	57	W
Magdalena →	184	11	6	N	74	51	W
Magdeburg	43	52	8	N	11	36	E
Magelang	111	7	29	S	110	13	E
Magellan's Str. = Magallanes, Estrecho de	192	52	30	S	75	0	W
Magherafelt	34	54	44	N	6	37	W
Magnitogorsk	71	53	27	N	59	4	E
Magog	148	45	18	N	72	9	W

Magosa = Famagusta	80	35	8N	33 55 E
Magrath	155	49	25N	112 50W
Mahābād	81	36	50N	45 45 E
Mahajanga □	137	17	0S	47 0 E
Mahakam ⁓►	111	0	35S	117 17 E
Maḥallāt	86	33	55N	50 30 E
Mahanadi ⁓►	92	20	20N	86 25 E
Maharashtra □	91	20	30N	75 30 E
Mahbubnagar	91	16	45N	77 59 E
Mahia Pen.	122	39	9S	177 55 E
Mahón	51	39	53N	4 16 E
Mahone Bay	148	44	30N	64 20W
Mahukona	160	20	11N	155 52W
Mai-Ndombe, L.	134	2	0S	18 20 E
Maidenhead	25	51	31N	0 42W
Maiduguri	131	12	0N	13 20 E
Maikala Ra.	92	22	0N	81 0 E
Main ⁓►	42	50	0N	8 18 E
Maine	36	48	0N	0 0 E
Maine □	148	45	20N	69 0W
Mainland, Orkney, U.K. ...	33	59	0N	3 10W
Mainland, Shet., U.K.	30	60	15N	1 22W
Mainpuri	89	27	18N	79 4 E
Mainz	42	50	0N	8 17 E
Maiquetía	184	10	36N	66 57W
Maisi, Pta. de	178	20	10N	74 10W
Maitland, N.S.W., Australia .	117	32	33S	151 36 E
Maitland, S. Austral., Australia	119	34	23S	137 40 E
Maiz, Islas del	179	12	15N	83 4W
Maizuru	106	35	25N	135 22 E
Majorca, I. = Mallorca	51	39	30N	3 0 E
Makarikari = Makgadikgadi				
Salt Pans	136	20	40S	25 45 E
Makasar = Ujung Pandang .	113	5	10S	119 20 E
Makasar, Selat	113	1	0S	118 20 E
Makedhonia = Macedonia □ ..	55	41	39N	22 0 E
Makena	160	20	39N	156 27W
Makeyevka	68	48	0N	38 0 E
Makgadikgadi Salt Pans ...	136	20	40S	25 45 E
Makhachkala	70	43	0N	47 30 E
Makkah	82	21	30N	39 54 E
Makó	59	46	14N	20 33 E
Makran Coast Range	88	25	40N	64 0 E
Makurazaki	108	31	15N	130 20 E
Makurdi	131	7	43N	8 35 E
Malabar Coast	90	11	0N	75 0 E
Malacca, Str. of	111	3	0N	101 0 E
Malad City	162	42	10N	112 20 E
Málaga	50	36	43N	4 23W
Malakal	129	9	33N	31 50 E
Malang	111	7	59S	112 45 E
Mälaren	60	59	30N	17 10 E
Malatya	81	38	25N	38 20 E
Malawi ■	137	13	0S	34 0 E
Malawi, L.	137	12	30S	34 30 E
Malay Pen.	97	7	25N	100 0 E
Malāyer	84	34	19N	48 51 E
Malaysia ■	111	5	0N	110 0 E
Malbaie, La	148	47	40N	70 10W
Malbork	58	54	3N	19 1 E
Malcolm	120	28	51S	121 25 E
Maldives ■	78	7	0N	73 0 E
Maldonado	191	35	0S	55 0W
Malebo, Pool	134	4	17S	15 20 E
Malegaon	91	20	30N	74 38 E
Mali ■	130	15	0N	2 0W
Mali Kyun	94	13	0N	98 20 E
Malin Hd.	34	55	18N	7 24W
Malindi	133	3	12S	40 5 E
Malines = Mechelen	42	51	2N	4 29 E
Mallaig	32	57	0N	5 50W
Mallorca	51	39	30N	3 0 E
Mallow	35	52	8N	8 40W
Malmédy	42	50	25N	6 2 E
Malmö	61	55	36N	12 59 E
Malmöhus län □	61	55	45N	13 30 E
Malone	151	44	50N	74 19W
Malta ■	49	35	50N	14 30 E
Malton	29	54	9N	0 48W
Maluku	113	1	0S	127 0 E
Malvern, U.K.	24	52	7N	2 19W
Malvern, U.S.A.	168	34	22N	92 50W
Malvern Hills	24	52	0N	2 19W
Malvinas, Is. = Falkland Is. .	192	51	30S	59 0W
Mamers	39	48	21N	0 22 E
Mamoré ⁓►	187	10	23S	65 53W
Mamou	130	10	15N	12 0W
Man	130	7	30N	7 40W
Man, I. of	28	54	15N	4 30W
Mana, Fr. Guiana	185	5	45N	53 55W
Mana, U.S.A.	160	22	3N	159 45W
Manaar, Gulf of = Mannar, G.				
of	90	8	30N	79 0 E
Manacapuru	185	3	16S	60 37W
Manado	113	1	29N	124 51 E
Managua	179	12	6N	86 20W
Manaos = Manaus	185	3	0S	60 0W
Manapouri	123	45	34S	167 39 E
Manaung	93	18	45N	93 40 E
Manaus	185	3	0S	60 0W
Mancha, La	50	39	10N	2 54W
Manchester, U.K.	28	53	30N	2 15W
Manchester, U.S.A.	164	42	58N	71 29W
Mandalay	93	22	0N	96 4 E
Mandale = Mandalay	93	22	0N	96 4 E
Mandurah	120	32	36S	115 48 E
Manfredónia, G. di	49	41	30N	16 10 E
Mangalore	90	12	55N	74 47 E
Mangla Dam	89	33	9N	73 44 E
Mangole	113	1	50S	125 55 E
Mangonui	122	35	1S	173 32 E
Mangyshlak P-ov.	70	44	30N	52 30 E
Manhattan	158	39	10N	96 40W
Manicoré	185	5	48S	61 16W
Manicouagan ⁓►	148	49	30N	68 30W
Manila	112	14	40N	121 3 E
Manilla	116	30	45S	150 43 E
Manipur □	93	25	0N	94 0 E
Manisa	80	38	38N	27 30 E
Manistee	167	44	15N	86 20W
Manistique	150	45	59N	86 18W
Manitoba □	153	55	30N	97 0W
Manitoba, L.	153	51	0N	98 45W
Manitoulin I.	150	45	40N	82 30W
Manitowoc	167	44	8N	87 40W
Manizales	184	5	5N	75 32W
Manjil	81	36	46N	49 30 E
Manjimup	120	34	15S	116 6 E
Mankato	166	44	8N	93 59W
Manly	117	33	48S	151 17 E
Mannar, G. of	90	8	30N	79 0 E
Mannar I.	90	9	5N	79 45 E
Mannheim	42	49	28N	8 29 E
Mannum	119	34	50S	139 20 E
Manosque	37	43	49N	5 47 E
Manouane, L.	148	50	45N	70 45W
Mans, Le	39	48	0N	0 10 E
Mansel I.	146	62	0N	80 0W
Mansfield, Australia	117	37	4S	146 6 E
Mansfield, U.K.	29	53	8N	1 12W
Mansfield, U.S.A.	167	40	45N	82 30W
Manta	184	1	0S	80 40W
Mantes-la-Jolie	39	49	0N	1 41 E
Mantiqueira, Serra da	188	22	0S	44 0W
Mántova	46	45	20N	10 42 E
Mantua = Mántova	46	45	20N	10 42 E
Manu	187	12	10S	70 51W
Manukau	122	35	14S	173 13 E
Manyara, L.	135	3	40S	35 50 E
Manzanillo, Cuba	178	20	20N	77 31W
Manzanillo, Mexico	175	19	3N	104 20W
Manzhouli	98	49	35N	117 25 E
Mapimí	174	25	49N	103 51W
Maple	152	43	51N	79 31W
Maputo	137	25	58S	32 32 E
Maquinchao	192	41	15S	68 50W
Mar, Serra do	191	25	30S	49 0W
Mar Chiquita, L.	190	30	40S	62 50W
Mar del Plata	191	38	0S	57 30W
Mar Menor, L.	51	37	40N	0 45W
Marabá	188	5	20S	49 5W
Maracaibo	184	10	40N	71 37W

Maracaibo, Lago de 184 9 40N 71 30W
Maracay 184 10 15N 67 28W
Marajó, Ilha de 188 1 0S 49 30W
Maranhão = São Luís 188 2 39S 44 15W
Maranhão □ 188 5 0S 46 0W
Marañón —► 186 4 30S 73 35W
Maraş .... 80 37 37N 36 53 E
Marathón .... 55 38 11N 23 58 E
Marbella 50 36 30N 4 57W
Marble Bar .... 114 21 9S 119 44 E
March .... 25 52 33N 0 5 E
Marché .... 36 46 0N 1 20 E
Marche □ .... 47 43 22N 13 10 E
Marchena 50 37 18N 5 23W
Marches = Marche □ ..... 47 43 22N 13 10 E
Mardan .... 89 34 20N 72 0 E
Mardin .... 81 37 20N 40 43 E
Mareeba .... 121 16 59S 145 28 E
Margarita 175 9 20N 79 55W
Margarita I. 185 11 0N 64 0W
Margate .... 25 51 23N 1 24 E
Mari Rep. □ .... 68 56 30N 48 0 E
Maria van Diemen, C. ..... 122 34 29S 172 40 E
Marianao 178 23 8N 82 24W
Marianna 169 30 45N 85 15W
Maribor .... 52 46 36N 15 40 E
Maricourt 146 61 30N 72 0W
Marie-Galante 180 15 56N 61 16W
Marienberg .... 41 52 30N 6 35 E
Marietta, Ga., U.S.A. 169 34 0N 84 30W
Marietta, Ohio, U.S.A. 164 39 27N 81 27W
Marília 188 22 13S 50 0W
Marín 50 42 23N 8 42W
Marinette 167 45 4N 87 40W
Maringá 191 23 26S 52 2W
Marion, Ill., U.S.A. 166 37 45N 88 55W
Marion, Ind., U.S.A. 167 40 35N 85 40W
Marion, Ohio, U.S.A. 167 40 38N 83 8W
Mariupol .... 68 47 5N 37 31 E
Marken .... 40 52 26N 5 12 E
Market Drayton 28 52 55N 2 30W
Market Harborough 25 52 29N 0 55W
Market Rasen 29 53 24N 0 20W
Markham, Mt. .... 15 83 0S 164 0 E
Marlborough 24 51 26N 1 44W
Marlborough □ .... 123 41 45S 173 33 E
Marlborough Downs 24 51 25N 1 55W
Marlin 168 31 25N 96 50W
Marmagao .... 91 15 25N 73 56 E
Marmara, Sea of = Marmara
  Denizi .... 80 40 45N 28 15 E
Marmara Denizi .... 80 40 45N 28 15 E
Marmaris .... 80 36 50N 28 14 E
Marne —► .... 39 8 23N 18 36 E
Maroochydore .... 116 26 29S 153 5 E
Marquesas Is. 123 9 30S 140 0W
Marquette 150 46 30N 87 21W
Marrakech 126 31 9N 8 0W
Marree .... 118 29 39S 138 1 E
Marsabit .... 133 2 18N 38 0 E
Marseille – .... 37 43 18N 5 23 E
Marseilles = Marseille .... 37 43 18N 5 23 E
Marshall, Minn., U.S.A. 166 44 25N 95 45W
Marshall, Mo., U.S.A. 166 39 8N 93 15W
Marshall, Tex., U.S.A. 168 32 29N 94 20W
Marshalltown 166 42 5N 92 56W
Marshfield 166 44 42N 90 10W
Martaban, G. of .... 93 16 5N 96 30 E
Martha's Vineyard 164 41 25N 70 35W
Martigues .... 37 43 24N 5 4 E
Martinique 180 14 40N 61 0W
Martinsburg 164 39 30N 77 57W
Martinsville, Ind., U.S.A. ... 167 39 29N 86 23W
Martinsville, Va., U.S.A. ... 165 36 41N 79 52W
Marton .... 122 40 4S 175 23 E
Marugame .... 109 34 15N 133 40 E
Maruoka .... 106 36 9N 136 16 E
Marwar .... 91 25 43N 73 45 E
Mary .... 70 37 40N 61 50 E
Maryborough = Port Laoise 35 53 2N 7 20W
Maryborough, Queens.,
  Australia .... 116 25 31S 152 37 E

Maryborough, Vic., Australia 117 37 0S 143 44 E
Maryland □ 164 39 10N 76 40W
Maryport 28 54 43N 3 30W
Marysville 172 39 14N 121 40W
Maryville 165 35 50N 84 0W
Marzūq .... 127 25 53N 13 57 E
Masan .... 98 35 11N 128 32 E
Masaya 179 12 0N 86 7W
Masbate, I. .... 112 12 21N 123 36 E
Mascota 175 20 32N 104 49W
Maseru .... 137 29 18S 27 30 E
Mashhad .... 86 36 20N 59 35 E
Masisea 186 8 35S 74 22W
Masjed Soleyman .... 84 31 55N 49 18 E
Mask, L. 34 53 36N 9 24W
Mason City 166 43 9N 93 12W
Masqat .... 83 23 37N 58 36 E
Massachusetts □ 164 42 25N 72 0W
Massawa = Mitsiwa ..... 132 15 35N 39 25 E
Massena 151 44 52N 74 55W
Massif Central .... 37 45 30N 2 21 E
Massillon 167 40 47N 81 30W
Mastanli = Momchilgrad .. 53 41 33N 25 23 E
Masterton .... 123 40 56S 175 39 E
Mastūrah .... 82 23 7N 38 52 E
Masuda .... 108 34 40N 131 51 E
Matachewan 151 47 56N 80 39W
Matadi .... 134 5 52S 13 31 E
Matagalpa 179 13 0N 85 58W
Matamoros, Coahuila, Mexico 174 25 32N 103 15W
Matamoros, Puebla, Mexico 177 18 2N 98 17W
Matane 148 48 50N 67 33W
Matanzas 178 23 0N 81 40W
Matapan, C. = Tainaron, Ákra 54 36 22N 22 27 E
Matarani 186 77 0S 72 10W
Matehuala 177 23 39N 100 39W
Mathura .... 89 27 30N 77 40 E
Matlock 28 53 8N 1 32W
Mato Grosso □ 188 14 0S 55 0W
Mato Grosso, Planalto do . 188 15 0S 59 57W
Matopo Hills .... 137 20 36S 28 20 E
Matrah .... 83 23 37N 58 30 E
Matsubara .... 106 34 33N 135 34 E
Matsudo .... 107 35 47N 139 54 E
Matsue .... 109 35 25N 133 10 E
Matsumoto .... 107 36 15N 138 0 E
Matsusaka .... 106 34 34N 136 32 E
Matsutō .... 106 36 31N 136 34 E
Matsuura .... 108 33 20N 129 49 E
Matsuyama .... 109 33 45N 132 45 E
Mattancheri .... 90 9 50N 76 15 E
Mattawa 151 46 20N 78 45W
Matterhorn .... 44 45 58N 7 39 E
Matucana 186 11 55S 76 25W
Maturín 185 9 45N 63 11W
Mau Ranipur .... 91 25 16N 79 8 E
Maubeuge .... 38 50 17N 3 57 E
Maudin Sun .... 93 16 0N 94 30 E
Maui .... 160 20 45N 156 20 E
Maulamyaing .... 93 16 30N 97 40 E
Mauna Kea 160 19 50N 155 28W
Mauna Loa 160 21 8N 157 10W
Maungmagan Kyunzu .... 94 14 0N 97 48 E
Mauritania ■ 126 20 50N 10 0W
Mauritius ■ .... 9 20 0S 57 0 E
Mawlaik .... 93 23 40N 94 26 E
May Pen 180 17 58N 77 15W
Maya —► .... 75 54 31N 134 41 E
Mayagüez 180 18 12N 67 9W
Mayerthorpe 155 53 57N 115 8W
Mayfield 169 36 45N 88 40W
Maykop .... 70 44 35N 40 25 E
Maynooth 34 53 22N 6 38W
Mayo 144 63 38N 135 57W
Mayo □ 34 53 47N 9 7W
Mayor I. .... 122 37 16S 176 17 E
Maysville 167 38 39N 83 46W
Mazagán = El Jadida 126 33 11N 8 17W
Mazán 186 3 30S 73 0W
Mazar-e Sharīf .... 87 36 41N 67 0 E
Mazarredo 192 47 10S 66 50W

Place	Page	Lat			Long		
Mazatenango	177	14	35N		91	30W	
Mazatlán	175	23	13N		106	25W	
Mbandaka	134	0	1N		18	18 E	
Mdina	49	35	51N		14	25 E	
Mead, L.	173	36	1N		114	44W	
Meadville	164	41	39N		80	9W	
Meander River	145	59	2N		117	42W	
Meath □	34	53	32N		6	40W	
Meaux	39	48	58N		2	50 E	
Mecca = Makkah	82	21	30N		39	54 E	
Mechelen	42	51	2N		4	29 E	
Mecklenburger Bucht	42	54	20N		11	40 E	
Medan	111	3	40N		98	38 E	
Medellin	184	6	15N		75	35W	
Medford	171	42	20N		122	52W	
Mediaş	57	46	9N		24	22 E	
Medicine Hat	152	50	0N		110	45W	
Medina = Al Madīnah	82	24	35N		39	52 E	
Medina	167	41	9N		81	50W	
Medina del Campo	50	41	18N		4	55W	
Mediterranean Sea	124	35	0N		15	0 E	
Medley	152	54	25N		110	16W	
Médoc	36	45	10N		0	56W	
Medvezhi, Ostrava	73	71	0N		161	0 E	
Medway →	25	51	28N		0	45 E	
Meekatharra	120	26	32S		118	29 E	
Meerut	89	29	1N		77	42 E	
Mega	133	3	57N		38	19 E	
Mégantic, L.	148	45	32N		70	53W	
Mégara	55	37	58N		23	22 E	
Meghalaya □	93	25	50N		91	0 E	
Mei Xian	99	24	16N		116	6 E	
Meknès	126	33	57N		5	33W	
Mekong →	95	9	30N		106	15 E	
Melaka	96	2	15N		102	15 E	
Melaka □	96	2	15N		102	15 E	
Melanesia	122	4	0S		155	0 E	
Melbourne	117	37	50S		145	0 E	
Melchor Muzquiz	174	27	53N		101	31W	
Melfort	152	52	50N		104	37W	
Melilla	126	35	21N		2	57W	
Melitopol	68	46	50N		35	22 E	
Melo	191	32	20S		54	10W	
Melrose	31	53	35N		2	44W	
Melton Mowbray	29	52	46N		0	52W	
Melun	39	48	32N		2	39 E	
Melville	152	50	55N		102	50W	
Melville, L.	147	53	30N		60	0W	
Melville I., Australia	114	11	30S		131	0 E	
Melville I., Canada	12	75	30N		112	0W	
Melville Pen.	146	68	0N		84	0W	
Memel = Klaipeda	68	55	43N		21	10 E	
Memphis	169	35	7N		90	0W	
Menai Strait	26	53	14N		4	10W	
Ménaka	131	15	59N		2	18 E	
Menan = Chao Phraya →	94	13	32N		100	36 E	
Menasha	167	44	13N		88	27W	
Mende	37	44	31N		3	30 E	
Mendip Hills	27	51	17N		2	40W	
Mendocino	172	39	26N		123	50W	
Mendoza	190	32	50S		68	52W	
Menindee	118	32	20S		142	25 E	
Menindee, L.	118	32	20S		142	25 E	
Menominee	150	45	9N		87	39W	
Menorca	51	40	0N		4	0 E	
Mentawai, Kepulauan	111	2	0S		99	0 E	
Menzies	120	29	40S		120	58 E	
Meppel	41	52	42N		6	12 E	
Merbein	119	34	10S		142	2 E	
Merca	133	1	48N		44	50 E	
Merced	172	37	18N		120	30W	
Mercedes, Buenos Aires, Argentina	190	34	40S		59	30W	
Mercedes, Corrientes, Argentina	191	29	10S		58	5W	
Mercedes, San Luis, Argentina	190	33	40S		65	21W	
Mercedes, Uruguay	191	33	12S		58	0W	
Mere	24	51	5N		2	16W	
Mergui Arch. = Myeik Kyunzu	94	11	30N		97	30 E	
Mérida, Mexico	177	20	58N		89	37W	
Mérida, Spain	50	38	55N		6	25W	
Mérida, Venezuela	184	8	24N		71	8W	
Mérida, Cord. de	182	9	0N		71	0W	
Meriden	164	41	33N		72	47W	
Meridian	169	32	20N		88	42W	
Merowe	129	18	29N		31	46 E	
Merredin	120	31	28S		118	18 E	
Merrill	156	45	11N		89	41W	
Merritt	155	50	10N		120	45W	
Merriwa	116	32	6S		150	22 E	
Mersey →	28	53	20N		2	56W	
Merseyside □	28	53	25N		2	55W	
Mersin	80	36	51N		34	36 E	
Merthyr Tydfil	27	51	45N		3	23W	
Méru	39	49	13N		2	8 E	
Merville	38	50	38N		2	38 E	
Mesa	160	33	20N		111	56W	
Mesa, La	173	32	48N		117	5W	
Meshed = Mashhad	86	36	20N		59	35 E	
Mesolóngion	54	38	21N		21	28 E	
Mesopotamia = Al Jazirah	81	33	30N		44	0 E	
Mesquite	173	36	47N		114	6W	
Messina, Italy	49	38	10N		15	32 E	
Messina, S. Africa	137	22	20S		30	0 E	
Messina, Str. di	49	38	5N		15	35 E	
Messini	54	37	4N		22	1 E	
Meta →	184	6	12N		67	28W	
Metairie	169	29	59N		90	9W	
Metán	190	25	30S		65	0W	
Metropolis	169	37	10N		88	47W	
Metz	37	49	8N		6	10 E	
Meuse →	42	50	45N		5	41 E	
Mexia	168	31	38N		96	32W	
Mexicali	174	32	40N		115	29W	
México, Mexico	177	19	20N		99	10W	
Mexico, U.S.A.	166	39	10N		91	55W	
México □	177	19	20N		99	30W	
Mexico ■	174	20	0N		100	0W	
Mexico, G. of	138	25	0N		90	0W	
Mezen →	69	66	11N		43	59 E	
Mhow	91	22	33N		75	50 E	
Miahuatlán	177	16	21N		96	36W	
Miami	170	25	45N		80	15W	
Miami Beach	170	25	49N		80	6W	
Mīāneh	81	37	30N		47	40 E	
Mianwali	89	32	38N		71	28 E	
Miaoli	99	24	37N		120	49 E	
Miass	69	54	59N		60	6 E	
Michigan □	167	44	40N		85	40W	
Michigan, L.	150	44	0N		87	0W	
Michigan City	167	41	42N		86	56W	
Michikamau L.	147	54	20N		63	10W	
Michipicoten	150	47	55N		84	55W	
Michoacán □	175	19	10N		101	50W	
Michurinsk	68	52	58N		40	27 E	
Micronesia	122	11	0N		160	0 E	
Mid Glamorgan □	27	51	40N		3	25W	
Middelburg	40	51	30N		3	36 E	
Middle Andaman I.	94	12	30N		92	30 E	
Middlesboro	165	36	36N		83	43W	
Middlesbrough	29	54	35N		1	14W	
Middleton	148	44	57N		65	4W	
Middletown, Conn., U.S.A.	164	41	37N		72	40W	
Middletown, N.Y., U.S.A.	164	41	28N		74	28W	
Middletown, Ohio, U.S.A.	167	39	29N		84	25W	
Midland, Canada	151	44	45N		79	50W	
Midland, Mich., U.S.A.	167	43	37N		84	17W	
Midland, Tex., U.S.A.	161	32	0N		102	3W	
Międzyrzec Podlaski	58	51	58N		22	45 E	
Miercurea Ciuc	57	46	21N		25	48 E	
Mieres	50	43	18N		5	48W	
Migennes	39	47	58N		3	31 E	
Mihara	109	34	24N		133	5 E	
Miki	109	34	48N		134	59 E	
Mikonos	55	37	30N		25	25 E	
Mikuni-Tōge	107	36	50N		138	50 E	
Mikura-Jima	107	33	52N		139	36 E	
Milagro	184	2	11S		79	36W	
Milan = Milano	46	45	28N		9	10 E	
Milano	46	45	28N		9	10 E	
Milâs	80	37	20N		27	50 E	

Name	Map	Lat °	Lat ′	N/S	Lon °	Lon ′	E/W
Mildura	119	34	13	S	142	9	E
Miles	116	26	40	S	150	9	E
Miles City	163	46	24	N	105	50	W
Milford	164	38	52	N	75	27	W
Milford Haven	27	51	43	N	5	2	W
Milk →	163	48	5	N	106	15	W
Millau	37	44	8	N	3	4	E
Millicent	119	37	34	S	140	21	E
Millinocket	148	45	45	N	68	45	W
Millmerran	116	27	53	S	151	16	E
Millom	28	54	13	N	3	16	W
Millville	164	39	22	N	75	0	W
Milne Inlet	146	72	30	N	80	0	W
Milos	55	36	44	N	24	25	E
Milton Keynes	25	52	3	N	0	42	W
Milwaukee	167	43	9	N	87	58	W
Milwaukie	171	45	27	N	122	39	W
Minamata	108	32	10	N	130	30	E
Minas	191	34	20	S	55	10	W
Minas Gerais □	188	18	50	S	46	0	W
Minatitlán	177	17	59	N	94	31	W
Mindanao	112	8	0	N	125	0	E
Mindanao Sea = Bohol Sea	112	9	0	N	124	0	E
Minden	168	32	40	N	93	20	W
Mindoro	112	13	0	N	121	0	E
Mindoro Strait	112	12	30	N	120	30	E
Mine	108	34	12	N	131	7	E
Minehead	27	51	12	N	3	29	W
Mineral Wells	161	32	50	N	98	5	W
Mingan	148	50	20	N	64	0	W
Mingenew	120	29	12	S	115	21	E
Minho □	50	41	25	N	8	20	W
Minneapolis	166	44	58	N	93	20	W
Minnedosa	153	50	14	N	99	50	W
Minnesota □	156	46	40	N	94	0	W
Mino	106	35	32	N	136	55	E
Mino-Kamo	106	35	23	N	137	2	E
Mino-Mikawa-Kōgen	106	35	10	N	137	23	E
Minorca = Menorca	51	40	0	N	4	0	E
Minot	163	48	10	N	101	15	W
Minsk	68	53	52	N	27	30	E
Mintaka Pass	89	37	0	N	74	58	E
Miquelon, I.	149	47	2	N	56	20	W
Miraj	91	16	50	N	74	45	E
Miranda do Douro	50	41	30	N	6	16	W
Mirpur Khas	88	25	30	N	69	0	E
Mirzapur	92	25	10	N	82	34	E
Mirzapur-cum-Vindhyachal = Mirzapur	92	25	10	N	82	34	E
Miscou I.	148	47	57	N	64	31	W
Mishawaka	167	41	40	N	86	8	W
Mishima	107	35	10	N	138	52	E
Miskitos, Cayos	179	14	26	N	82	50	W
Miskolc	59	48	7	N	20	50	E
Misool	113	1	52	S	130	10	E
Misrātah	127	32	24	N	15	3	E
Mission City	154	49	10	N	122	15	W
Mississippi □	169	33	0	N	90	0	W
Mississippi →	169	29	0	N	89	15	W
Mississippi, Delta of the	169	29	15	N	90	30	W
Missoula	162	46	52	N	114	0	W
Missouri □	166	38	25	N	92	30	W
Missouri →	166	38	50	N	90	8	W
Mistassini L.	151	51	0	N	73	30	W
Mitaka	107	35	40	N	139	33	E
Mitchell, Australia	116	26	29	S	147	58	E
Mitchell, U.S.A.	163	43	40	N	98	0	W
Mitchell →	115	15	12	S	141	35	E
Mitilini	55	39	6	N	26	35	E
Mito	107	36	20	N	140	30	E
Mitsiwa	132	15	35	N	39	25	E
Mitsukaidō	107	36	1	N	139	59	E
Mittagong	117	34	28	S	150	29	E
Mitú	184	1	8	N	70	3	W
Miura	107	35	12	N	139	40	E
Miyake-Jima	107	34	0	N	139	30	E
Miyako	103	39	40	N	141	59	E
Miyakonojō	108	31	40	N	131	5	E
Miyanojō	108	31	54	N	130	27	E
Miyazaki	108	31	56	N	131	30	E
Miyazu	106	35	35	N	135	10	E
Miyoshi	109	34	48	N	132	51	E
Mizamis = Ozamis	112	8	15	N	123	50	E
Mizen Hd.	35	51	27	N	9	50	W
Mizoram □	93	23	30	N	92	40	E
Mizunami	106	35	22	N	137	15	E
Mława	58	53	9	N	20	25	E
Mobara	107	35	25	N	140	18	E
Moberley	166	39	25	N	92	25	W
Mobile	169	30	41	N	88	3	W
Mobutu Sese Seko, L.	132	1	30	N	31	0	E
Moçâmedes = Namibe	134	15	7	S	12	11	E
Moctezuma, R. →	177	21	59	N	98	34	W
Módena	46	44	39	N	10	55	E
Modesto	172	37	43	N	121	0	W
Moe	117	38	12	S	146	19	E
Moei →	94	17	25	N	98	10	E
Moengo	185	5	45	N	54	20	W
Moffat	31	55	20	N	3	27	W
Mogadishu = Muqdisho	133	2	2	N	45	25	E
Mogador = Essaouira	126	31	32	N	9	42	W
Mogami →	103	38	45	N	140	0	E
Mogi das Cruzes	191	23	31	S	46	11	W
Mogilev	68	53	55	N	30	18	E
Mointy	71	47	10	N	73	18	E
Moisie	148	50	12	N	66	1	W
Mojave Desert	173	35	0	N	116	30	W
Mold	26	53	10	N	3	10	W
Moldavia ■	68	47	0	N	28	0	E
Molde	65	62	45	N	7	9	E
Molfetta	49	41	12	N	16	35	E
Moline	166	41	30	N	90	30	W
Molise □	49	41	45	N	14	30	E
Mollendo	187	17	0	S	72	0	W
Mölndal	60	57	40	N	12	3	E
Molong	117	33	5	S	148	54	E
Molopo →	136	28	30	S	20	13	E
Molotov = Perm	69	58	0	N	57	10	E
Molucca Sea	113	4	0	S	124	0	E
Moluccas = Maluku	113	1	0	S	127	0	E
Mombasa	135	4	2	S	39	43	E
Mombetsu	103	42	27	N	142	4	E
Momchilgrad	53	41	33	N	25	23	E
Mompós	184	9	14	N	74	26	W
Møn	61	54	57	N	12	15	E
Mona, Canal de la	180	18	30	N	67	45	W
Monach Is.	32	57	32	N	7	40	W
Monaco ■	37	43	46	N	7	23	E
Monaghan	34	54	15	N	6	58	W
Monaghan □	34	54	10	N	7	0	W
Monastir = Bitola	52	41	5	N	21	10	E
Mönchengladbach	42	51	12	N	6	23	E
Monchique	50	37	19	N	8	38	W
Monclova	174	26	50	N	101	30	W
Moncton	148	46	7	N	64	51	W
Monessen	164	40	9	N	79	50	W
Monforte	50	39	6	N	7	25	W
Mongalla	129	5	8	N	31	42	E
Monghyr = Munger	92	25	23	N	86	30	E
Mongolia ■	98	47	0	N	103	0	E
Monmouth, U.K.	26	51	48	N	2	43	W
Monmouth, U.S.A.	166	40	50	N	90	40	W
Monroe, La., U.S.A.	168	32	32	N	92	4	W
Monroe, Mich., U.S.A.	167	41	55	N	83	26	W
Monroe, N.C., U.S.A.	165	35	2	N	80	37	W
Monrovia, Liberia	130	6	18	N	10	47	W
Monrovia, U.S.A.	173	34	7	N	118	1	W
Mons	42	50	27	N	3	58	E
Mont-de-Marsan	36	43	54	N	0	31	W
Mont Laurier	151	46	35	N	75	30	W
Montague	172	41	47	N	122	30	W
Montana □	163	47	0	N	110	0	W
Montargis	39	48	0	N	2	43	E
Montauban	36	44	0	N	1	21	E
Montbéliard	37	47	31	N	6	48	E
Montceau-les-Mines	37	46	40	N	4	23	E
Montdidier	38	49	38	N	2	35	E
Monte-Carlo	37	43	46	N	7	23	E
Monte Caseros	191	30	10	S	57	50	W
Montego Bay	180	18	30	N	78	0	W
Montélimar	37	44	33	N	4	45	E
Montemorelos	176	25	11	N	99	42	W

Name	Page	Lat °	′	N/S	Long °	′	E/W
Montenegro □	52	42	40	N	19	20	E
Monterey	173	36	35	N	121	57	W
Monteria	184	8	46	N	75	53	W
Monterrey	176	25	40	N	100	30	W
Montes Claros	188	16	30	S	43	50	W
Montevideo, Uruguay	191	34	50	S	56	11	W
Montevideo, U.S.A.	166	44	55	N	95	40	W
Montgomery = Sahiwal	89	30	45	N	73	8	E
Montgomery, U.K.	26	52	34	N	3	9	W
Montgomery, U.S.A.	169	32	20	N	86	20	W
Montluçon	37	46	22	N	2	36	E
Montmagny	148	46	58	N	70	34	W
Montmorency	148	46	53	N	71	11	W
Montpelier, Idaho, U.S.A.	163	42	15	N	111	20	W
Montpelier, Vt., U.S.A.	151	44	15	N	72	38	W
Montpellier	37	43	37	N	3	52	E
Montréal	151	45	31	N	73	34	W
Montrose, U.K.	33	56	43	N	2	28	W
Montrose, U.S.A.	163	38	30	N	107	52	W
Montserrat	180	16	40	N	62	10	W
Monywa	93	22	7	N	95	11	E
Monze, C.	88	24	47	N	66	37	E
Mo'oka	107	36	26	N	140	1	E
Moonta	119	34	6	S	137	32	E
Moora	120	30	37	S	115	58	E
Moorfoot Hills	31	55	44	N	3	8	W
Moorhead	156	46	51	N	96	44	W
Mooroopna	117	36	25	S	145	22	E
Moose Jaw	152	50	24	N	105	30	W
Moosehead L.	148	45	34	N	69	40	W
Moosomin	152	50	9	N	101	40	W
Moosonee	140	51	17	N	80	39	W
Mopti	130	14	30	N	4	0	W
Moradabad	89	28	50	N	78	50	E
Moranbah	121	22	1	S	148	6	E
Moratuwa	90	6	45	N	79	55	E
Morava → =	59	48	10	N	16	59	E
Moravian Hts. = Ceskomoravská Vrchovina	59	49	30	N	15	40	E
Morawa	120	29	13	S	116	0	E
Morawhanna	185	8	30	N	59	40	W
Moray Firth	33	57	50	N	3	30	W
Morden	153	49	15	N	98	10	W
Mordovian Rep.□	68	54	20	N	44	30	E
Møre og Romsdal fylke □	65	62	30	N	8	0	E
Morecambe	28	54	5	N	2	52	W
Morecambe B.	28	54	7	N	3	0	W
Moree	116	29	28	S	149	54	E
Morehead City	165	34	46	N	76	44	W
Morelia	175	19	42	N	101	7	W
Morelos □	177	18	45	N	99	0	W
Morena, Sierra	50	38	20	N	4	0	W
Moresby I.	154	52	30	N	131	40	W
Morgan City	168	29	40	N	91	15	W
Morganton	165	35	46	N	81	48	W
Morgantown	164	39	39	N	79	58	W
Moriguchi	106	34	44	N	135	34	E
Morlaix	36	48	36	N	3	52	W
Mornington	117	38	15	S	145	5	E
Moro G.	112	6	30	N	123	0	E
Morocco ■	126	32	0	N	5	50	W
Moroleón	177	20	8	N	101	12	W
Morón	178	22	8	N	78	39	W
Morotai	113	2	10	N	128	30	E
Morrilton	168	35	10	N	92	45	W
Morrinhos	188	17	45	S	49	10	W
Morris	153	49	25	N	97	22	W
Morristown	165	36	18	N	83	20	W
Mortes, R. das →	188	11	45	S	50	44	W
Mortlake	119	38	5	S	142	50	E
Moruya	117	35	58	S	150	3	E
Morvern	30	56	38	N	5	44	W
Morwell	117	38	10	S	146	22	E
Moscos Is.	94	14	0	N	97	30	E
Moscow = Moskva	68	55	45	N	37	35	E
Moscow	171	46	45	N	116	59	W
Mosel →	42	50	22	N	7	36	E
Moselle = Mosel →	42	50	22	N	7	36	E
Mosgiel	123	45	53	S	170	21	E
Mosjøen	65	65	51	N	13	12	E
Moskva	68	55	45	N	37	35	E
Mosquera	184	2	35	N	78	24	W
Mosquitos, Golfo de los	179	9	15	N	81	10	W
Moss Vale	117	34	32	S	150	25	E
Mosselbaai	136	34	11	S	22	8	E
Mossman	121	16	21	S	145	15	E
Mossoró	189	5	10	S	37	15	W
Mostaganem	127	35	54	N	0	5	E
Mostar	52	43	22	N	17	50	E
Mosul = Al Mawşil	81	36	15	N	43	5	E
Motala	60	58	32	N	15	1	E
Motherwell	31	55	48	N	4	0	W
Motihari	92	26	30	N	84	55	E
Motueka	123	41	7	S	173	1	E
Motul	177	21	6	N	89	17	W
Moúdhros	55	39	50	N	25	18	E
Moule	180	16	20	N	61	22	W
Moulins	37	46	35	N	3	19	E
Moultrie	170	31	11	N	83	47	W
Moundsville	164	39	53	N	80	43	W
Mount Airy	165	36	31	N	80	37	W
Mount Barker, S. Austral., Australia	119	35	5	S	138	52	E
Mount Barker, W. Austral., Australia	120	34	38	S	117	40	E
Mount Carmel	167	38	20	N	87	48	W
Mount Forest	151	43	59	N	80	43	W
Mount Gambier	119	37	50	S	140	46	E
Mount Isa	115	20	42	S	139	26	E
Mount Lofty Ra.	119	34	35	S	139	5	E
Mount Magnet	120	28	2	S	117	47	E
Mount Maunganui	122	37	40	S	176	14	E
Mount Morgan	121	23	40	S	150	25	E
Mount Pearl	149	47	31	N	52	47	W
Mount Pleasant, Mich., U.S.A.	167	43	35	N	84	47	W
Mount Pleasant, Tex., U.S.A.	168	33	5	N	95	0	W
Mount Sterling	165	38	0	N	84	0	W
Mount Vernon, Ill., U.S.A.	166	38	17	N	88	57	W
Mount Vernon, N.Y., U.S.A.	164	40	57	N	73	49	W
Mount Vernon, Wash., U.S.A.	171	48	25	N	122	20	W
Mount Whaleback	114	23	18	S	119	44	E
Mountain City	172	41	54	N	116	0	W
Mountain View	172	37	26	N	122	5	W
Moura, Australia	121	24	35	S	149	58	E
Moura, Brazil	185	1	32	S	61	38	W
Mourne →	34	54	45	N	7	39	W
Mourne Mts.	34	54	10	N	6	0	W
Moyale	133	3	30	N	39	0	E
Mozambique ■	137	19	0	S	35	0	E
Mozambique Chan.	137	20	0	S	39	0	E
Mu Us Shamo	98	39	0	N	109	0	E
Muaná	188	1	25	S	49	15	W
Muang Chiang Rai	94	19	52	N	99	50	E
Muck	32	56	50	N	6	15	W
Mucuri	189	18	0	S	39	36	W
Mudanjiang	98	44	38	N	129	30	E
Mudgee	117	32	32	S	149	31	E
Muğla	80	37	15	N	28	22	E
Mukden = Shenyang	98	41	50	N	123	25	E
Mukhtuya = Lensk	74	60	48	N	114	55	E
Mukinbudin	120	30	55	S	118	5	E
Muktsar	89	30	30	N	74	30	E
Mulchén	190	37	45	S	72	20	W
Mulgrave	149	45	38	N	61	31	W
Mulhacén	50	37	4	N	3	20	W
Mülheim	42	51	26	N	6	53	E
Mulhouse	37	47	40	N	7	20	E
Mull	30	56	27	N	6	0	W
Muller, Pegunungan	111	0	30	N	113	30	E
Mullet Pen.	34	54	10	N	10	2	W
Mullewa	120	28	29	S	115	30	E
Mullingar	34	53	31	N	7	20	W
Mullumbimby	116	28	30	S	153	30	E
Multan	89	30	15	N	71	36	E
Muna	113	5	0	S	122	30	E
München	43	48	8	N	11	33	E
Munchen-Gladbach = Mönchengladbach	42	51	12	N	6	23	E
Muncie	167	40	10	N	85	20	W
Mundo Novo	189	11	50	S	40	29	W
Mungana	121	17	8	S	144	27	E
Munger	92	25	23	N	86	30	E

Munich = München ...... 43 48 8N 11 33 E
Munising 150 46 25N 86 39W
Munku-Sardyk .... 74 51 45N 100 20 E
Münster .... 42 51 58N 7 37 E
Munster □ 35 52 20N 8 40W
Muqdisho .... 133 2 2N 45 25 E
Murallón, Cuerro 192 49 48S 73 30W
Murchison —► .... 120 27 45S 114 0 E
Murchison Falls = Kabarega
  Falls .... 132 2 15N 31 30 E
Murcia 51 38 20N 1 10W
Murcia □ 51 37 50N 1 30W
Mureş —► .... 56 46 15N 20 13 E
Mureşul = Mureş —► ... 56 46 15N 20 13 E
Murfreesboro 169 35 50N 86 21W
Murgon .... 116 26 15S 151 54 E
Müritz See .... 43 53 25N 12 40 E
Murmansk .... 69 68 57N 33 10 E
Muroran .... 103 42 25N 141 0 E
Muroto .... 109 33 18N 134 9 E
Muroto-Misaki .... 109 33 15N 134 10 E
Murphysboro 166 37 50N 89 20W
Murray 169 36 40N 88 20W
Murray —► .... 119 35 20S 139 22 E
Murray Bridge .... 119 35 6S 139 14 E
Murrumbidgee —► .... 117 34 43S 143 12 E
Murrurundi .... 116 31 42S 150 51 E
Murtoa .... 119 36 35S 142 28 E
Murupara .... 122 38 28S 176 42 E
Murwillumbah .... 116 28 18S 153 27 E
Muş .... 81 38 45N 41 30 E
Musashino .... 107 35 42N 139 34 E
Muscat = Masqat ..... 83 23 37N 58 36 E
Muscat & Oman = Oman ■ 83 23 0N 58 0 E
Muscatine 166 41 25N 91 5W
Musgrave Ras. .... 114 26 0S 132 0 E
Musi —► .... 111 2 20S 104 56 E
Muskegon 167 43 15N 86 17W
Muskegon —► 167 43 25N 86 0W
Muskegon Hts. 167 43 12N 86 17W
Muskogee 168 35 50N 95 25W
Musselburgh 31 55 57N 3 3W
Muswellbrook .... 116 32 16S 150 56 E
Mutare .... 137 18 58S 32 38 E
Mutsu .... 103 41 5N 140 55 E
Mutsu-Wan .... 103 41 5N 140 55 E
Muzaffargarh .... 89 30 5N 71 14 E
Muzaffarnagar ...... 89 29 26N 77 40 E
Muzaffarpur .... 92 26 7N 85 23 E
Mwanza .... 135 2 30S 32 58 E
Mweru, L. .... 135 9 0S 28 40 E
My Tho .... 95 10 29N 106 23 E
Myanaung .... 93 18 18N 95 22 E
Myeik Kyunzu .... 94 11 30N 97 30 E
Myingyan .... 93 21 30N 95 20 E
Myitkyina .... 93 25 24N 97 26 E
Mýrdalsjökull 64 63 40N 19 6W
Myrtle Point 171 43 0N 124 4W
Mysore = Karnataka □ .... 90 13 15N 77 0 E
Mysore .... 90 12 17N 76 41 E

N

Naaldwijk .... 40 51 59N 4 13 E
Nabari .... 106 34 37N 136 5 E
Naberezhnyye Chelny ... 68 55 42N 52 19 E
Nablus = Nābulus ..... 80 32 14N 35 15 E
Nābulus .... 80 32 14N 35 15 E
Nacogdoches 168 31 33N 94 39W
Nacozari 174 30 24N 109 39W
Nadiad .... 91 22 41N 72 56 E
Nadym .... 69 65 35N 72 42 E
Nagahama .... 106 35 23N 136 16 E
Nagaland □ .... 93 26 0N 94 30 E
Nagano .... 107 36 40N 138 10 E
Nagaoka .... 105 37 27N 138 51 E
Nagappattinam .... 90 10 46N 79 51 E
Nagasaki .... 108 32 47N 129 50 E

Nagato .... 108 34 19N 131 5 E
Nagercoil .... 90 8 12N 77 26 E
Nagornyy .... 75 55 58N 124 57 E
Nagoya .... 106 35 10N 136 50 E
Nagpur .... 91 21 8N 79 10 E
Nahanni Butte 144 61 2N 123 31W
Nahāvand .... 84 34 10N 48 22 E
Naicam 152 52 30N 104 30W
Nain 147 56 34N 61 40W
Nainpur .... 91 22 30N 80 10 E
Nairn 33 57 35N 3 54W
Nairobi .... 132 1 17S 36 48 E
Naivasha .... 132 0 40S 36 30 E
Najafābād .... 85 32 40N 51 15 E
Najibabad .... 89 29 40N 78 20 E
Naka —► .... 107 36 20N 140 36 E
Naka-no-Shima .... 104 29 51N 129 46 E
Nakama .... 108 33 56N 130 43 E
Nakamura .... 109 33 0N 133 0 E
Nakano .... 107 36 45N 138 22 E
Nakanojō .... 107 36 35N 138 51 E
Nakatsu .... 108 33 34N 131 15 E
Nakatsugawa .... 106 35 29N 137 30 E
Nakhichevan Rep. □ ... 70 39 14N 45 30 E
Nakhodka .... 75 42 53N 132 54 E
Nakhon Phanom .... 95 17 23N 104 43 E
Nakhon Ratchasima ... 95 14 59N 102 12 E
Nakhon Sawan .... 94 15 35N 100 10 E
Nakhon Si Thammarat . 96 8 29N 100 0 E
Nakina 140 50 10N 86 40W
Nakskov .... 61 54 50N 11 8 E
Nakuru .... 132 0 15S 36 4 E
Nalchik .... 70 43 30N 43 33 E
Nalgonda .... 91 17 6N 79 15 E
Nam Co .... 101 30 30N 90 45 E
Nam Dinh .... 95 20 25N 106 5 E
Nam-Phan .... 95 10 30N 106 0 E
Nam Tha .... 95 20 58N 101 30 E
Nam Tok .... 94 14 21N 99 4 E
Namaland .... 136 24 30S 17 0 E
Namangan .... 71 41 0N 71 40 E
Nambour .... 116 26 32S 152 58 E
Nambucca Heads ...... 116 30 37S 153 0 E
Namerikawa .... 106 36 46N 137 20 E
Namib Desert = Namib-
  Woestyn .... 124 22 30S 15 0 E
Namib-Woestyn .... 124 22 30S 15 0 E
Namibe .... 134 15 7S 12 11 E
Namibia ■ .... 136 22 0S 18 9 E
Nampa 171 43 34N 116 34W
Namsos .... 65 64 29N 11 30 E
Namur .... 42 50 27N 4 52 E
Nanaimo 154 49 10N 124 0W
Nanango .... 116 26 40S 152 0 E
Nanao .... 105 37 0N 137 0 E
Nanchang .... 99 28 42N 115 55 E
Nanching = Nanjing ... 99 32 2N 118 47 E
Nanching .... 99 32 3N 118 47 E
Nancy .... 37 48 42N 6 12 E
Nanda Devi .... 101 30 23N 79 59 E
Nandan .... 109 34 10N 134 42 E
Nanded .... 91 19 10N 77 20 E
Nandurbar .... 91 21 20N 74 15 E
Nanga Parbat .... 89 35 10N 74 35 E
Nangarhár □ .... 87 34 20N 70 0 E
Nanjing .... 99 32 2N 118 47 E
Nanking = Nanching ... 99 32 3N 118 47 E
Nanking = Nanjing ... 99 32 2N 118 47 E
Nankoku .... 109 33 39N 133 44 E
Nanning .... 99 22 48N 108 20 E
Nanping .... 99 26 38N 118 10 E
Nantes 36 47 12N 1 33W
Nanticoke 164 41 12N 76 1W
Nanton 155 50 21N 113 46W
Nanuque 189 17 50S 40 21W
Napa 172 38 18N 122 17W
Napier .... 122 39 30S 176 56 E
Naples = Nápoli ..... 49 40 50N 14 17 E
Napo —► 186 3 20S 72 40W
Nápoli .... 49 40 50N 14 17 E
Nara, Japan .... 106 34 40N 135 49 E

Name		Lat		Long	
Nara, Mali	130	15 10N		7 20W	
Naracoorte	119	36 58S		140 45 E	
Narasapur	92	16 26N		81 40 E	
Narayanganj	92	23 40N		90 33 E	
Narayanpet	91	16 45N		77 30 E	
Narbonne	37	43 11N		3 0 E	
Narita	107	35 47N		140 19 E	
Narmada →	91	21 38N		72 36 E	
Narooma	117	36 14S		150 4 E	
Narrabri	116	30 19S		149 46 E	
Narrandera	117	34 42S		146 31 E	
Narrogin	120	32 58S		117 14 E	
Narromine	116	32 12S		148 12 E	
Naruto	109	34 11N		134 37 E	
Narvik	64	68 28N		17 26 E	
Narym	71	59 0N		81 30 E	
Naser, Buheirat en	128	23 0N		32 30 E	
Nashua	164	42 50N		71 25W	
Nashville	169	36 12N		86 46W	
Nasik	91	19 58N		73 50 E	
Nasirabad	91	26 15N		74 45 E	
Nassau	178	25 0N		77 20W	
Nasser, L. = Naser, Buheirat en	128	23 0N		32 30 E	
Nässjö	60	57 39N		14 42 E	
Natal	189	5 47S		35 13W	
Natal □	137	28 30S		30 30 E	
Natashquan	149	50 14N		61 46W	
Natchez	168	31 35N		91 25W	
Natchitoches	168	31 47N		93 4W	
Nathalia	117	36 1S		145 13 E	
National City	173	32 39N		117 7W	
Natuna Besar, Kepulauan	111	4 0N		108 15 E	
Natuna Selatan, Kepulauan	111	2 45N		109 0 E	
Nauru ■	122	1 0S		166 0 E	
Nauta	186	4 31S		73 35W	
Nautanwa	92	27 20N		83 25 E	
Nautla	177	20 20N		96 50W	
Navarra □	51	42 40N		1 40W	
Navojoa	174	27 0N		109 30W	
Navsari	91	20 57N		72 59 E	
Nawabshah	88	26 15N		68 25 E	
Nawalgarh	89	27 50N		75 15 E	
Náxos	55	37 8N		25 25 E	
Nāy Band	87	27 20N		52 40 E	
Nayakhan	73	61 56N		159 0 E	
Nayarit □	175	22 0N		105 0W	
Ndélé	129	8 25N		20 36 E	
Ndjamena	131	12 10N		14 59 E	
Ndola	135	13 0S		28 34 E	
Neagh, Lough	34	54 35N		6 25W	
Near Is.	142	53 0N		172 0 E	
Neath	27	51 39N		3 49W	
Nebraska □	163	41 30N		100 0W	
Nebraska City	166	40 40N		95 52W	
Nebrodi Mts.	49	37 55N		14 45 E	
Neches →	168	29 55N		93 52W	
Neckar →	42	49 31N		8 26 E	
Necochea	190	38 30S		58 50W	
Needles, The	24	50 39N		1 35W	
Neenah	167	44 10N		88 30W	
Neepawa	153	50 15N		99 30W	
Negapatam = Nagappattinam	90	10 46N		79 51 E	
Negeri Sembilan □	96	2 45N		102 10 E	
Negotin	53	44 16N		22 37 E	
Negra, Pta.	186	6 6S		81 10W	
Negro →, Argentina	190	41 2S		62 47W	
Negro →, Brazil	185	3 0S		60 0W	
Negros	112	9 30N		122 40 E	
Nehbandān	85	31 35N		60 5 E	
Nei Monggol Zizhiqu □	98	42 0N		112 0 E	
Neijiang	99	29 35N		104 55 E	
Neiva	184	2 56N		75 18W	
Nellore	90	14 27N		79 59 E	
Nelson, Canada	155	49 30N		117 20W	
Nelson, N.Z.	123	41 18S		173 16 E	
Nelson, U.K.	28	53 50N		2 14W	
Nelson →	153	54 33N		98 2W	
Néma	126	16 40N		7 15W	
Neman →	68	55 25N		21 10 E	
Nemours	39	48 16N		2 40 E	
Nemunas = Neman →	68	55 25N		21 10 E	
Nemuro	103	43 20N		145 35 E	
Nemuro-Kaikyō	103	43 30N		145 30 E	
Nenagh	35	52 52N		8 11W	
Nenana	142	64 30N		149 20W	
Nene →	29	52 38N		0 13 E	
Neosho	168	36 56N		94 28W	
Neosho →	168	35 59N		95 10W	
Nepal ■	92	28 0N		84 30 E	
Nephi	162	39 43N		111 52W	
Ness, Loch	33	57 15N		4 30W	
Netanya	80	32 20N		34 51 E	
Netherlands ■	41	52 0N		5 30 E	
Netherlands Antilles ■	181	12 15N		69 0W	
Netherlands Guiana = Surinam ■	185	4 0N		56 0W	
Nettilling L.	146	66 30N		71 0W	
Netzahualcoyotl, Presa	177	17 10N		93 30W	
Neuchâtel	44	47 0N		6 55 E	
Neuchâtel, Lac de	44	46 53N		6 50 E	
Neuquén	190	38 55S		68 0 E	
Neuse →	165	35 5N		76 30W	
Neusiedler See	45	47 50N		16 47 E	
Nevada	166	37 51N		94 22W	
Nevada □	172	39 20N		117 0W	
Nevada, Sierra, Spain	50	37 3N		3 15W	
Nevada, Sierra, U.S.A.	172	39 0N		120 30W	
Nevada City	172	39 20N		121 0W	
Nevada de Sta. Marta, Sa.	184	10 55N		73 50W	
Nevers	37	47 0N		3 9 E	
New Albany	167	38 20N		85 50W	
New Amsterdam	185	6 15N		57 36W	
New Bedford	164	41 40N		70 52W	
New Bern	165	35 8N		77 3W	
New Braunfels	161	29 43N		98 9W	
New Brighton	123	43 29S		172 43 E	
New Britain, Papua N. G.	115	5 50S		150 20 E	
New Britain, U.S.A.	164	41 41N		72 47W	
New Brunswick	164	40 30N		74 28W	
New Brunswick □	148	46 50N		66 30W	
New Caledonia = Nouvelle Calédonie	122	21 0S		165 0 E	
New Castile = Castilla La Nueva	50	39 45N		3 20W	
New Castle, Ind., U.S.A.	164	39 55N		85 23W	
New Castle, Pa., U.S.A.	164	41 0N		80 20W	
New England Ra.	116	30 20S		151 45 E	
New Forest	24	50 53N		1 40W	
New Glasgow	149	45 35N		62 36W	
New Hampshire □	164	43 40N		71 40W	
New Haven	164	41 20N		72 54W	
New Hebrides = Vanuatu ■	122	15 0S		168 0 E	
New Iberia	168	30 2N		91 54W	
New Ireland	115	3 20S		151 50 E	
New Jersey □	164	40 30N		74 10W	
New Kensington	164	40 36N		79 43W	
New London	164	41 23N		72 8W	
New Mexico □	161	34 30N		106 0W	
New Norfolk	119	42 46S		147 2 E	
New Orleans	169	30 0N		90 5W	
New Philadelphia	164	40 29N		81 25W	
New Plymouth	122	39 4S		174 5 E	
New Providence	178	25 25N		78 35W	
New Radnor	26	52 15N		3 10W	
New Siberian Is. = Novosibirskiye Ostrova	72	75 0N		142 0 E	
New South Wales □	116	33 0S		146 0 E	
New Ulm	166	44 15N		94 30W	
New Waterford	149	46 13N		60 4W	
New Westminster	154	49 13N		122 55W	
New York □	164	42 40N		76 0W	
New York City	164	40 45N		74 0W	
New Zealand ■	122	40 0S		176 0 E	
Newark, N.J., U.S.A.	164	40 41N		74 12W	
Newark, N.Y., U.S.A.	164	43 2N		77 10W	
Newark, Ohio, U.S.A.	167	40 5N		82 24W	
Newark-on-Trent	29	53 6N		0 48W	
Newberry, Mich., U.S.A.	150	46 20N		85 32W	
Newberry, S.C., U.S.A.	165	34 17N		81 37W	
Newburgh	164	41 30N		74 1W	
Newburyport	164	42 48N		70 50W	

Place	No.	Latitude	Longitude
Newcastle, Australia	117	33 0S	151 46 E
Newcastle, Canada	148	47 1N	65 38W
Newcastle, U.K.	34	54 13N	5 54W
Newcastle Emlyn	26	52 2N	4 29W
Newcastle-under-Lyme	28	53 2N	2 15W
Newcastle-upon-Tyne	28	54 59N	1 37W
Newfoundland □	149	53 0N	58 0W
Newhaven	25	50 47N	0 4 E
Newmarket	25	52 15N	0 23 E
Newnan	170	33 22N	84 48W
Newport, Gwent, U.K.	27	51 35N	3 0W
Newport, I. of W., U.K.	25	50 42N	1 18W
Newport, Ark., U.S.A.	168	35 38N	91 15W
Newport, Ky., U.S.A.	167	39 5N	84 23W
Newport, Oreg., U.S.A.	171	44 41N	124 2W
Newport, R.I., U.S.A.	164	41 13N	71 19W
Newport, Vt., U.S.A.	148	44 57N	72 17W
Newport Beach	173	33 40N	117 58W
Newport News	165	37 2N	76 30W
Newquay	27	50 24N	5 6W
Newry	34	54 10N	6 20W
Newton, Iowa, U.S.A.	166	41 40N	93 3W
Newton, Mass., U.S.A.	164	42 21N	71 10W
Newton Abbot	27	50 32N	3 37W
Newton Stewart	31	54 57N	4 30W
Newtonmore	33	57 4N	4 7W
Newtown	26	52 31N	3 19W
Newtownards	34	54 37N	5 40W
Ngaoundéré	131	7 15N	13 35 E
Ngoring Hu	101	34 55N	97 5 E
Nguru	131	12 56N	10 29 E
Nha Trang	95	12 16N	109 10 E
Nhill	119	36 18S	141 40 E
Niagara Falls, Canada	151	43 7N	79 5W
Niagara Falls, U.S.A.	164	43 5N	79 0W
Niamey	131	13 27N	2 6 E
Nias	111	1 0N	97 30 E
Nicaragua ■	179	11 40N	85 30W
Nicaragua, Lago de	179	12 0N	85 30W
Nice	37	43 42N	7 14 E
Nichinan	108	31 38N	131 23 E
Nicobar Is.	8	9 0N	93 0 E
Nicosia	80	35 10N	33 25 E
Nicoya, Pen. de	179	9 45N	85 40W
Nidd →	28	54 1N	1 32W
Niederösterreich □	45	48 25N	15 40 E
Niedersachsen □	42	52 45N	9 0 E
Nieuw Nickerie	185	6 0N	56 59W
Niger ■	131	13 30N	10 0 E
Niger →	131	5 33N	6 33 E
Nigeria ■	131	8 30N	8 0 E
Nii-Jima	107	34 20N	139 15 E
Niigata	103	37 58N	139 0 E
Niihama	109	33 55N	133 16 E
Niimi	109	34 59N	133 28 E
Nijkerk	41	52 13N	5 30 E
Nijmegen	41	51 50N	5 52 E
Nikki	131	9 58N	3 12 E
Nikkō	107	36 45N	139 35 E
Nikolayev	68	46 58N	32 0 E
Nikolayevsk-na-Amur	75	53 8N	140 44 E
Nikolskoye	73	55 12N	166 0 E
Nikšić	52	42 50N	18 57 E
Nîl, Nahr en →	128	30 10N	31 6 E
Nîl el Abyad →	129	15 38N	32 31 E
Nîl el Azraq →	129	15 38N	32 31 E
Nile = Nîl, Nahr en →	128	30 10N	31 6 E
Niles	164	41 8N	80 40W
Nîmes	37	43 50N	4 23 E
Nimule	129	3 32N	32 3 E
Nīnawá	81	36 25N	43 10 E
Nineveh = Nīnawá	81	36 25N	43 10 E
Ningbo	99	29 51N	121 28 E
Ningde	99	26 38N	119 23 E
Ningpo = Ningbo	99	29 51N	121 28 E
Ningsia Hui A.R. = Ningxia Huizu Zizhiqu □	98	38 0N	106 0 E
Ningxia Huizu Zizhiqu □	98	38 0N	106 0 E
Niobrara →	163	42 45N	98 0W
Nioro du Sahel	130	15 15N	9 30W
Niort	36	46 19N	0 29W
Nipawin	152	53 20N	104 0W
Nipigon	150	49 0N	88 17W
Nipigon, L.	150	49 50N	88 30W
Niš	53	43 19N	21 58 E
Niṣāb	83	14 25N	46 29 E
Nishinomiya	106	34 45N	135 20 E
Nishio	106	34 52N	137 3 E
Nishiwaki	109	34 59N	134 58 E
Niterói	188	22 52S	43 0W
Nith →	31	55 20N	3 5W
Nitra	59	48 19N	18 4 E
Nivernais	37	47 0N	3 40 E
Nizamabad	91	18 45N	78 7 E
Nizhne Kolymsk	73	68 34N	160 55 E
Nizhneudinsk	74	54 54N	99 3 E
Nizhnevartovsk	69	60 56N	76 38 E
Nizhniy Novgorod	68	56 20N	44 0 E
Nizhniy Tagil	69	57 55N	59 57 E
Nizhnyaya Tunguska →	74	64 20N	93 0 E
Nizké Tatry	59	48 55N	20 0 E
Nkongsamba	131	4 55N	9 55 E
Noatak	142	67 32N	162 59W
Nobeoka	108	32 36N	131 41 E
Noda	107	35 56N	139 52 E
Nogales	174	31 20N	110 56W
Nōgata	108	33 48N	130 44 E
Nogent-le-Rotrou	39	48 20N	0 50 E
Noi →	94	14 50N	100 15 E
Noirmoutier, Î. de	36	46 58N	2 10W
Nojima-Zaki	107	34 54N	139 53 E
Nok Kundi	88	28 50N	62 45 E
Nome	142	64 30N	165 24W
Nong Khae	95	14 29N	100 53 E
Nong Khai	95	17 50N	102 46 E
Nonoava	174	27 28N	106 44W
Noord Brabant □	40	51 40N	5 0 E
Noord Holland □	40	52 30N	4 45 E
Noordbeveland	40	51 35N	3 50 E
Noordoostpolder	41	52 45N	5 45 E
Noordwijk aan Zee	40	52 14N	4 26 E
Nootka I.	154	49 32N	126 42W
Nord-Trøndelag fylke □	65	64 20N	12 0 E
Nordaustlandet	13	79 14N	23 0 E
Nordegg	155	52 29N	116 5W
Nordkapp	67	71 10N	25 44 E
Nordkinn	67	71 8N	27 40 E
Nordland fylke □	65	65 40N	13 0 E
Nordrhein-Westfalen □	42	51 45N	7 30 E
Nordvik	72	74 2N	111 32 E
Nore →	35	52 40N	7 20W
Norfolk	165	36 40N	76 15W
Norfolk □	29	52 39N	1 0 E
Norfolk I.	122	28 58S	168 3 E
Norilsk	72	69 20N	88 6 E
Norman	168	35 12N	97 30W
Norman Wells	144	65 17N	126 51W
Normandie	39	48 45N	0 10 E
Normandin	151	48 49N	72 31W
Normandy = Normandie	39	48 45N	0 10 E
Normanton	115	17 40S	141 10 E
Norquinco	192	41 51S	70 55W
Norristown	164	40 9N	75 21W
Norrköping	60	58 37N	16 11 E
Norrland □	66	66 50N	18 0 E
Norseman	114	32 8S	121 43 E
Norsk	75	52 30N	130 0 E
North Andaman I.	94	13 15N	92 40 E
North Battleford	152	52 50N	108 17W
North Bay	151	46 20N	79 30W
North Bend	171	43 28N	124 14W
North Berwick	31	56 4N	2 44W
North C.	122	34 23S	173 4 E
North Carolina □	165	35 30N	80 0W
North Channel, Br. Is.	30	55 0N	5 30W
North Channel, Canada	150	46 0N	83 0W
North Dakota □	163	47 30N	100 0W
North Downs	25	51 17N	0 30 E
North European Plain	17	55 0N	20 0 E
North I.	122	38 0S	175 0 E
North Korea ■	98	40 0N	127 0 E
North Minch	32	58 5N	5 55W

North Ossetian Rep. □ .... **70** 43 30N 44 30 E
North Platte **163** 41 10N 100 50W
North Platte ~→ **163** 41 15N 100 45W
North Pole .... **12** 90 0N   0 0 E
North Ronaldsay **33** 59 20N   2 30W
North Saskatchewan ~→ .. **143** 53 15N 105 5W
North Sea .... **16** 56 0N   4 0 E
North Sentinel I. .... **94** 11 35N 92 15 E
North Sporades = Vóriai
  Sporádhes .... **55** 39 15N 23 30 E
North Sydney **149** 46 12N 60 15W
North Tonawanda **164** 43 5N 78 50W
North Uist **32** 57 40N   7 15W
North Vancouver **154** 49 25N 123 3W
North Walsham .... **29** 52 49N   1 22 E
North West Frontier □ .... **89** 34 0N 71 0 E
North West Highlands **32** 57 35N   5 2W
North West River **147** 53 30N 60 10W
North West Territories □ ... **145** 67 0N 110 0W
North York Moors **29** 54 25N   0 50W
North Yorkshire □ **28** 54 15N   1 25W
Northallerton **28** 54 20N   1 26W
Northam .... **120** 31 35S 116 42 E
Northampton, Australia .... **120** 28 27S 114 33 E
Northampton, U.K. **25** 52 14N   0 54W
Northampton, U.S.A. **164** 42 22N 72 31W
Northampton □ **25** 52 16N   0 55W
Northcliffe .... **120** 34 39S 116 7 E
Northern Circars .... **92** 17 30N 82 30 E
Northern Ireland □ **34** 54 45N   7 0W
Northern Territory □ ...... **114** 16 0S 133 0 E
Northfield **166** 44 30N 93 10W
Northumberland □ **28** 55 12N   2 0W
Northumberland Is. ...... **121** 21 30S 149 50 E
Northumberland Str. **148** 46 20N 64 0W
Northwich **28** 53 16N   2 30W
Norton Sd. **142** 64 0N 164 0W
Norwalk **164** 41 9N 73 25W
Norway ■ .... **18** 63 0N 11 0 E
Norwegian Sea .... **16** 66 0N   1 0 E
Norwich .... **29** 52 38N   1 17 E
Nos Kaliakra .... **53** 43 21N 28 30 E
Noshiro .... **103** 40 12N 140 0 E
Noss Hd. **33** 58 29N   3 4W
Nossob ~→ .... **136** 26 55S 20 37 E
Noteć ~→ .... **58** 52 44N 15 26 E
Notre Dame de Koartac =
  Koartac **146** 60 55N 69 40W
Nottaway ~→ **140** 51 22N 78 55W
Nottingham **29** 52 57N   1 10W
Nottingham □ **29** 53 10N   1 0W
Nouâdhibou **126** 20 54N 17 0W
Nouâdhibou, Ras **126** 20 50N 17 0W
Nouakchott **126** 18 9N 15 58W
Noumea .... **122** 22 17S 166 30 E
Nouveau Comptoir **140** 53 0N 78 49W
Nouvelle Calédonie ...... **122** 21 0S 165 0 E
Nova Friburgo **188** 22 16S 42 30W
Nova Granada **188** 20 30S 49 20W
Nova Lisboa = Huambo ... **134** 12 42S 15 54 E
Nova Scotia □ **149** 45 10N 63 0W
Novara .... **46** 45 27N   8 36 E
Novaya Sibir, Ostrov ..... **72** 75 10N 150 0 E
Novaya Zemlya .... **69** 75 0N 56 0 E
Novgorod .... **68** 58 30N 31 25 E
Novi Pazar .... **52** 43 12N 20 28 E
Novi Sad .... **52** 45 18N 19 52 E
Novocherkassk .... **68** 47 27N 40 5 E
Novokuznetsk .... **71** 53 45N 87 10 E
Novomoskovsk .... **68** 54 5N 38 15 E
Novorossiysk .... **68** 44 43N 37 46 E
Novosibirsk .... **71** 55 0N 83 5 E
Novosibirskiye Ostrova .... **72** 75 0N 142 0 E
Nowgong .... **93** 26 20N 92 50 E
Nowra .... **117** 34 53S 150 35 E
Nowy Sącz .... **59** 49 40N 20 41 E
Noyon .... **38** 49 34N   3 0 E
Nûbîya, Es Sahrâ En ...... **129** 21 30N 33 30 E
Nueces ~→ **161** 27 50N 97 30W
Nueltin L. **145** 60 30N 99 30W
Nueva Gerona **178** 21 53N 82 49W

Nueva Rosita **174** 27 57N 101 13W
Nuevitas **178** 21 30N 77 20W
Nuevo Laredo **176** 27 30N 99 30W
Nuevo Leon □ **176** 25 40N 100 0W
Nuhaka .... **122** 39 3S 177 45 E
Nukey Bluff, Mt. .... **118** 32 26S 135 29 E
Nukus .... **70** 42 20N 59 7 E
Nulato **142** 64 40N 158 10W
Nullarbor Plain .... **114** 30 45S 129 0 E
Numan .... **131** 9 29N 12 3 E
Numazu .... **107** 35 7N 138 51 E
Numurkah .... **117** 36 5S 145 26 E
Nuneaton **25** 52 32N   1 29W
Nunivak **142** 60 0N 166 0W
Nunspeet .... **41** 52 21N   5 45 E
Nuoro .... **48** 40 20N   9 20 E
Nuremburg = Nürnberg ... **43** 49 26N 11 5 E
Nuriootpa .... **119** 34 27S 139 0 E
Nürnberg .... **43** 49 26N 11 5 E
Nurran, L. = Terewah, L. .. **116** 29 52S 147 35 E
Nutak **147** 57 28N 61 59W
Nuweveldberge .... **136** 32 10S 21 45 E
Nuyts Arch. .... **118** 32 35S 133 20 E
Nyaake **130** 4 52N   7 37W
Nyaingentanglha Shan .... **101** 30 0N 90 0 E
Nyasa, L. = Malawi, L. .... **137** 12 30S 34 30 E
Nyiregyháza .... **59** 47 58N 21 47 E
Nyngan .... **116** 31 30S 147 8 E
Nysa .... **58** 50 30N 17 22 E

O

Oahe L. **163** 45 30N 100 25W
Oahu **160** 21 30N 158 0W
Oak Hill **165** 38 0N 81 7W
Oak Park **167** 41 55N 87 45W
Oak Ridge **169** 36 1N 84 12W
Oakengates **28** 52 42N   2 29W
Oakey .... **116** 27 25S 151 43 E
Oakham **29** 52 40N   0 43W
Oakland **172** 37 50N 122 18W
Oakridge **171** 43 47N 122 31W
Oamaru .... **123** 45 5S 170 59 E
Oaxaca **177** 17 2N 96 40W
Oaxaca □ **177** 17 0N 96 30W
Ob ~→ .... **69** 66 45N 69 30 E
Oba **150** 49 4N 84 7W
Obama .... **106** 35 30N 135 45 E
Oban **30** 56 25N   5 30W
Obbia .... **133** 5 25N 48 30 E
Oberhausen .... **42** 51 28N   6 50 E
Oberon .... **117** 33 45S 149 52 E
Oberösterreich □ .... **45** 48 10N 14 0 E
Obi, Is. .... **113** 1 30S 127 30 E
Obihiro .... **103** 42 56N 143 12 E
Obskaya Guba .... **69** 69 0N 73 0 E
Ocala **170** 29 11N 82 8W
Ocampo **174** 28 11N 108 23W
Ocaña **184** 8 15N 73 20W
Occidental, Cordillera **184** 5 0N 76 0W
Ocean City **164** 39 18N 74 34W
Oceanside **173** 33 13N 117 26W
Ochil Hills **31** 56 14N   3 40W
Oconee ~→ **170** 31 58N 82 32W
Oconto **167** 44 52N 87 53W
Ocotlán **175** 20 21N 102 46W
Ōda .... **109** 35 11N 132 30 E
Ódáðahraun **64** 65 5N 17 0W
Odate .... **103** 40 16N 140 34 E
Odawara .... **107** 35 20N 139 6 E
Ödemiş .... **80** 38 15N 28 0 E
Odense .... **61** 55 22N 10 23 E
Oder ~→ .... **58** 53 33N 14 38 E
Odessa, Ukraine .... **68** 46 30N 30 45 E
Odessa, U.S.A. **161** 31 51N 102 23W
Odra ~→ .... **58** 53 33N 14 38 E
Odžak .... **52** 45 3N 18 18 E
Offaly □ **35** 53 15N   7 30W

Offenbach	42	50	6N	8	46 E
Oga-Hantō	103	39	58N	139	47 E
Ogaden	133	7	30N	45	30 E
Ōgaki	106	35	21N	136	37 E
Ogbomosho	131	8	1N	4	11 E
Ogden	163	41	13N	112	1W
Ogdensburg	151	44	40N	75	27W
Ohio □	167	40	20N	14	10 E
Ohio ➝	167	38	0N	86	0W
Ohrid	52	41	8N	20	52 E
Ohridsko, Jezero	52	41	8N	20	52 E
Oil City	164	41	26N	79	40W
Oise ➝	38	49	0N	2	4 E
Oisterwijk	40	51	35N	5	12 E
Ōita	108	33	14N	131	36 E
Ojos del Salado, Cerro	190	27	0S	68	40W
Oka ➝	68	56	20N	43	59 E
Okawa	108	33	9N	130	21 E
Okaya	107	36	0N	138	10 E
Okayama	109	34	40N	133	54 E
Okazaki	106	34	57N	137	10 E
Okeechobee, L.	170	27	0N	80	50W
Okehampton	27	50	44N	4	1W
Okha	75	53	40N	143	0 E
Okhotsk	75	59	20N	143	10 E
Okhotsk, Sea of	77	55	0N	145	0 E
Okhotsko Kolymskoye	73	63	0N	157	0 E
Oki-no-Shima	109	32	44N	132	33 E
Oki-Shotō	109	36	5N	133	15 E
Okinawa-Jima	99	26	32N	128	0 E
Oklahoma □	161	35	20N	97	30W
Oklahoma City	161	35	25N	97	30W
Okmulgee	168	35	38N	96	0W
Oktabrsk	70	49	28N	57	25 E
Oktyabrskoy Revolyutsii, Os.	72	79	30N	97	0 E
Oktyabrskoye	69	62	28N	66	3 E
Ōkuchi	108	32	4N	130	37 E
Okuru	123	43	55S	168	55 E
Okushiri-Tō	103	42	15N	139	30 E
Olanchito	179	15	30N	86	30W
Öland	61	56	45N	16	38 E
Olary	118	32	18S	140	19 E
Olavarría	190	36	55S	60	20W
Old Castile = Castilla La Vieja	50	41	55N	4	0W
Old Town	148	45	0N	68	41W
Oldenburg	42	53	10N	8	10 E
Oldenzaal	41	52	19N	6	53 E
Oldham	28	53	33N	2	8W
Olds	155	51	50N	114	10W
Olekma ➝	74	60	22N	120	42 E
Olekminsk	74	60	25N	120	30 E
Olenek	72	68	28N	112	18 E
Olenek ➝	72	73	0N	120	10 E
Oléron, Île d'	36	45	55N	1	15W
Oleśnica	58	51	13N	17	22 E
Olifants ➝	137	24	5S	31	20 E
Ólimbos, Óros	54	40	6N	22	23 E
Oliveira	188	20	39S	44	50W
Oliver	155	49	13N	119	37W
Ollagüe	187	21	15S	68	10W
Olney	167	38	40N	88	0W
Olomouc	59	49	38N	17	12 E
Olsztyn	57	53	48N	20	29 E
Olt ➝	57	43	50N	24	40 E
Olympia, Greece	54	37	39N	21	39 E
Olympia, U.S.A.	171	47	0N	122	58W
Olympic Mts.	171	47	50N	123	45W
Olympus, Mt. = Ólimbos, Óros	54	40	6N	22	23 E
Olympus, Mt.	171	47	52N	123	40W
Ōmachi	107	36	30N	137	50 E
Omae-Zaki	107	34	36N	138	14 E
Omagh	34	54	36N	7	20W
Omaha	166	41	15N	96	0W
Omak	171	48	24N	119	31W
Oman ■	83	23	0N	58	0 E
Oman, G. of	83	24	30N	58	30 E
Omdurmân	129	15	40N	32	28 E
Ōme	107	35	47N	139	15 E
Omeo	117	37	6S	147	36 E
Omihachiman	106	35	7N	136	3 E
Ōmiya	107	35	54N	139	38 E
Omo ➝	132	6	25N	36	10 E
Omolon ➝	73	68	42N	158	36 E
Omono-Gawa ➝	103	39	46N	140	3 E
Omsk	71	55	0N	73	12 E
Ōmura	108	32	56N	130	0 E
Ōmuta	108	33	0N	130	26 E
Onega	68	64	0N	38	10 E
Onega, L. = Onezhskoye Ozero	68	62	0N	35	30 E
Onehunga	122	36	55S	174	48 E
Oneida	164	43	5N	75	40W
Onekotan, Ostrov	75	49	25N	154	45 E
Onezhskoye Ozero	68	62	0N	35	30 E
Ongerup	120	33	58S	118	28 E
Ongole	90	15	33N	80	2 E
Onguren	74	53	38N	107	36 E
Onitsha	131	6	6N	6	42 E
Ono, Fukui, Japan	106	35	59N	136	29 E
Ono, Hyōgo, Japan	109	34	51N	134	56 E
Onoda	108	34	2N	131	25 E
Onomichi	109	34	25N	133	12 E
Onslow	114	21	40S	115	12 E
Onslow B.	165	34	20N	77	20W
Ontake-San	106	35	53N	137	29 E
Ontario	173	34	2N	117	40W
Ontario □	140	52	0N	88	10W
Ontario, L.	151	43	40N	78	0W
Oodnadatta	118	27	33S	135	30 E
Ooldea	114	30	27S	131	50 E
Oostende	42	51	15N	2	50 E
Oosterhout	40	51	39N	4	47 E
Oosterschelde	40	51	33N	4	0 E
Opala	73	51	58N	156	30 E
Opava	58	49	57N	17	58 E
Opelousas	168	30	35N	92	7W
Ophir	142	63	10N	156	40W
Opole	58	50	42N	17	58 E
Oporto = Porto	50	41	8N	8	40W
Opp	169	31	19N	86	13W
Oppland fylke □	60	61	15N	9	40 E
Opua	122	35	19S	174	9 E
Oradea	56	47	2N	21	58 E
Öræfajökull	64	64	2N	16	39W
Orai	91	25	58N	79	30 E
Oran, Algeria	127	35	45N	0	39W
Oran, Argentina	190	23	10S	64	20W
Orange, Australia	117	33	15S	149	7 E
Orange, France	37	44	8N	4	47 E
Orange, U.S.A.	168	30	10N	93	50W
Orange ➝ = Oranje ➝	136	28	41S	16	28 E
Orange, C.	185	4	20N	51	30W
Orangeburg	170	33	35N	80	53W
Oranje ➝	136	28	41S	16	28 E
Oraşul Stalin = Braşov	57	45	38N	25	35 E
Orbost	117	37	40S	148	29 E
Orchies	38	50	28N	3	14 E
Ordos = Mu Us Shamo	98	39	0N	109	0 E
Ordu	81	40	55N	37	53 E
Ordzhonikidze = Vladikavkaz	70	43	0N	44	35 E
Ore Mts. = Erzgebirge	43	50	25N	13	0 E
Örebro	60	59	20N	15	18 E
Oregon □	171	44	0N	121	0W
Oregon City	171	45	21N	122	35W
Orel	68	52	57N	36	3 E
Orenburg	70	51	45N	55	6 E
Orense	50	42	19N	7	55W
Orepuki	123	46	19S	167	46 E
Orford Ness	24	52	6N	1	31 E
Oriental, Cordillera	184	6	0N	73	0W
Orillia	151	44	40N	79	24W
Orinoco ➝	185	9	15N	61	30W
Orissa □	92	20	0N	84	0 E
Oristano	48	39	54N	8	35 E
Oristano, Golfo di	48	39	50N	8	22 E
Orizaba	177	18	51N	97	6W
Orkney Is.	33	59	0N	3	0W
Orland	172	39	46N	122	12W
Orlando	170	28	30N	81	25W
Orléanais	39	48	0N	2	0 E
Orléans	39	47	54N	1	52 E

Place	Pg	Lat	Long
Ormara	88	25 16N	64 33 E
Ormskirk	28	53 35N	2 53W
Örnsköldsvik	66	63 17N	18 40 E
Orocué	184	4 48N	71 20W
Oroville	172	39 31N	121 30W
Orsha	68	54 30N	30 25 E
Orsk	70	51 12N	58 34 E
Ortegal, C.	50	43 43N	7 52W
Orūmīyeh	81	37 40N	45 0 E
Orūmīyeh, Daryācheh-ye	81	37 50N	45 30 E
Oruro	187	18 0S	67 9W
Oruzgān □	87	33 30N	66 0 E
Oryakhovo	53	43 40N	23 57 E
Osage ~►	166	38 35N	91 57W
Ōsaka	106	34 40N	135 30 E
Osceola	169	35 40N	90 0W
Ösel = Saaremaa	68	58 30N	22 30 E
Osh	71	40 37N	72 49 E
Oshawa	151	43 50N	78 50W
Oshima	107	33 55N	132 14 E
Oshkosh	167	44 3N	88 35W
Oshogbo	131	7 48N	4 37 E
Osijek	52	45 34N	18 41 E
Oskaloosa	166	41 18N	92 40W
Oslo	60	59 55N	10 45 E
Osmaniye	80	37 5N	36 10 E
Osnabrück	42	52 16N	8 2 E
Osorno	190	40 25S	73 0W
Oss	41	51 46N	5 32 E
Ossa, Mt.	119	41 52S	146 3 E
Ostend = Oostende	42	51 15N	2 50 E
Östergötlands län □	60	58 35N	15 45 E
Östersund	66	63 10N	14 38 E
Østfold fylke □	60	59 25N	11 25 E
Ostfriesische Inseln	42	53 45N	7 15 E
Ostia	46	41 40N	12 20 E
Ostrava	59	49 51N	18 18 E
Ostróda	58	53 42N	19 58 E
Ostrołeka	58	53 4N	21 32 E
Ostrów Mazowiecka	58	52 50N	21 51 E
Ostrów Wielkopolski	58	51 36N	17 44 E
Ōsumi-Kaikyō	104	30 55N	131 0 E
Ōsumi-Shotō	104	30 30N	130 0 E
Oswego	164	43 29N	76 30W
Oswestry	28	52 52N	3 3W
Ōta	107	36 18N	139 22 E
Otago □	123	44 44S	169 10 E
Ōtake	109	34 12N	132 13 E
Otaki	122	40 45S	175 10 E
Otaru	103	43 10N	141 0 E
Otaru-Wan = Ishikari-Wan	103	43 25N	141 1 E
Otira Gorge	123	42 53S	171 33 E
Otoineppu	103	44 44N	142 16 E
Otranto	49	40 9N	18 28 E
Otranto, C. d'	49	40 7N	18 30 E
Otranto, Str. of	52	40 15N	18 40 E
Ōtsu	106	35 0N	135 50 E
Ottawa, Canada	151	45 27N	75 42W
Ottawa, U.S.A.	166	38 40N	95 6W
Ottawa ~► = Outaouais ~►	146	45 27N	74 8W
Ottawa Is.	146	59 35N	80 10W
Otter Rapids, Ont., Canada	151	50 11N	81 39W
Otter Rapids, Sask., Canada	152	55 38N	104 44W
Ottumwa	166	41 0N	92 25W
Otwock	58	52 5N	21 20 E
Ouachita ~►	168	31 38N	91 49W
Ouachita Mts.	168	34 50N	94 30W
Ouagadougou	130	12 25N	1 30W
Ouahran = Oran	127	35 45N	0 39W
Ouargla	127	31 59N	5 16 E
Oubangi ~►	131	1 0N	17 50 E
Oudenbosch	40	51 35N	4 32 E
Oudtshoorn	136	33 35S	22 14 E
Ouessant, Île d'	36	48 28N	5 6W
Oujda	127	34 41N	1 55W
Oulu	67	65 1N	25 29 E
Oulujärvi	67	64 25N	27 15 E
Oulujoki ~►	67	65 1N	25 30 E
Ouse ~►	29	54 3N	0 7 E
Outaouais ~►	140	45 27N	74 8W
Outer Hebrides	32	57 30N	7 40W
Outlook	152	51 30N	107 0W
Outreau	38	50 40N	1 36 E
Ouyen	119	35 1S	142 22 E
Ovalle	190	30 33S	71 18W
Overflakkee	40	51 44N	4 10 E
Overijssel □	41	52 25N	6 35 E
Oviedo	50	43 25N	5 50W
Owaka	123	46 27S	169 40 E
Owase	106	34 7N	136 12 E
Owatonna	166	44 3N	93 10W
Owen Sound	151	44 35N	80 55W
Owen Stanley Range	115	8 30S	147 0 E
Owensboro	167	37 40N	87 5W
Owosso	167	43 0N	84 10W
Owyhee ~►	171	43 46N	117 2W
Oxford, U.K.	25	51 45N	1 15W
Oxford, U.S.A.	165	36 19N	78 36W
Oxford □	25	51 45N	1 15W
Oxford L.	153	54 51N	95 37W
Oxnard	173	34 10N	119 14W
Oyabe	106	36 47N	136 56 E
Oyama	107	36 18N	139 48 E
Oyana	108	32 32N	130 30 E
Oyo	131	7 46N	3 56 E
Oyonnax	37	46 16N	5 40 E
Ozamis	112	8 15N	123 50 E
Ozark	169	31 29N	85 39W
Ozark Plateau	168	37 20N	91 40W
Ozarks, L. of	166	38 10N	92 40W
Ozu, Ehime, Japan	109	33 30N	132 33 E
Ozu, Kumamoto, Japan	108	32 52N	130 52 E

P

Place	Pg	Lat	Long
Paarl	136	33 45S	18 56 E
Pabna	92	24 1N	89 18 E
Pacaraima, Sierra	185	4 0N	62 30W
Pacasmayo	186	7 20S	79 35W
Pachuca	177	20 10N	98 40W
Padang	111	1 0S	100 20 E
Pádova	47	45 24N	11 52 E
Padstow	27	50 33N	4 57W
Padua = Pádova	47	45 24N	11 52 E
Paducah	169	37 0N	88 40W
Pag	52	44 30N	14 50 E
Pagalu = Annobón	131	1 25S	5 36 E
Pagastikós Kólpos	54	39 15N	23 0 E
Page	160	36 57N	111 27W
Pahala	160	19 12N	155 25W
Pahang □	96	3 30N	102 45 E
Pahiatua	122	40 27S	175 50 E
Paignton	27	50 26N	3 33W
Painesville	167	41 42N	81 18W
Paint Hills = Nouveau Comptoir	140	53 0N	78 49W
Painted Desert	160	36 0N	111 30W
Paisley	31	55 51N	4 27W
Paita	186	5 11S	81 9W
Pak Sane	95	18 22N	103 39 E
Pakistan ■	78	30 0N	70 0 E
Pakistan, East = Bangladesh ■	92	24 0N	90 0 E
Pakokku	93	21 20N	95 0 E
Pakse	95	15 5N	105 52 E
Paktīā □	87	33 0N	69 15 E
Palanpur	91	24 10N	72 25 E
Palatka	170	29 40N	81 40W
Palawan	112	9 30N	118 30 E
Palembang	111	3 0S	104 50 E
Palencia	50	42 1N	4 34W
Palermo	48	38 8N	13 20 E
Palestine	168	31 42N	95 35W
Palghat	90	10 46N	76 42 E
Pali	91	25 50N	73 20 E
Palizada	177	18 15N	92 5W
Palk Bay	90	9 30N	79 15 E
Palk Strait	90	10 0N	79 45 E
Palm Is.	121	18 40S	146 35 E
Palm Springs	173	33 51N	116 35W

Palma, La **179** 8 15N 78 0W
Palma de Mallorca .... **51** 39 35N 2 39 E
Palma Soriano **178** 20 15N 76 0W
Palmas, C. **130** 4 27N 7 46W
Palmer Land **14** 73 0S 60 0W
Palmerston North .... **122** 40 21S 175 39 E
Palmi .... **49** 38 21N 15 51 E
Palmira **184** 3 32N 76 16W
Palmyra = Tudmur .... **80** 34 36N 38 15 E
Palo Alto **172** 37 25N 122 8W
Pamirs .... **71** 37 40N 73 0 E
Pamlico Sd. **165** 35 20N 76 0W
Pampa **161** 35 35N 100 58W
Pampas **190** 35 0S 63 0W
Pamplona **51** 42 48N 1 38W
Panaca **173** 37 51N 114 23W
Panaji .... **91** 15 25N 73 50 E
Panamá **179** 9 0N 79 25W
Panama ■ **179** 8 48N 79 55W
Panamá, Golfo de **179** 8 4N 79 20W
Panama Canal **175** 9 10N 79 37W
Panama City **169** 30 10N 85 41W
Panay .... **112** 11 10N 122 30 E
Pančevo .... **52** 44 52N 20 41 E
Pandharpur .... **91** 17 41N 75 20 E
Pangfou = Bengbu ...... **99** 32 58N 117 20 E
Pangkalpinang .... **111** 2 0S 106 0 E
Pangnirtung **146** 66 8N 65 54W
Panjim = Panaji .... **91** 15 25N 73 50 E
Panjinad Barrage ...... **89** 29 22N 71 15 E
Pantelleria .... **48** 36 52N 12 0 E
Pánuco **177** 22 3N 98 10W
Paoting = Baoding ..... **98** 38 50N 115 28 E
Paot'ou = Baotou ...... **98** 40 32N 110 2 E
Papien Chiang = Da → .. **95** 21 15N 105 20 E
Papua, Gulf of .... **115** 9 0S 144 50 E
Papua New Guinea ■ .... **115** 8 0S 145 0 E
Pará = Belém **188** 1 20S 48 30W
Pará □ **188** 3 20S 52 0W
Paracatu **188** 17 10S 46 50W
Paragua, La **185** 6 50N 63 20W
Paraguay ■ **191** 23 0S 57 0W
Paraguay → **191** 27 18S 58 38W
Paraíba = João Pessoa . **189** 7 10S 34 52W
Paraíba □ **189** 7 0S 36 0W
Parakou .... **131** 9 25N 2 40 E
Paramaribo **185** 5 50N 55 10W
Paraná **190** 31 45S 60 30W
Paraná □ **191** 24 30S 51 0W
Paraná → **190** 33 43S 59 15W
Paranaguá **191** 25 30S 48 30W
Paranaíba → **188** 20 6S 51 4W
Parbhani .... **91** 19 8N 76 52 E
Parecis, Serra dos **187** 13 0S 60 0W
Parent **151** 47 55N 74 35W
Paria, Golfo de **180** 10 20N 62 0W
Parika **185** 6 50N 58 20W
Parintins **185** 2 40S 56 50W
Pariparit Kyun .... **94** 14 55S 93 45 E
Paris, France .... **39** 48 50N 2 20 E
Paris, Tenn., U.S.A. ... **169** 36 20N 88 20W
Paris, Tex., U.S.A. ... **168** 33 40N 95 30W
Park Range **163** 40 0N 106 30W
Parker **173** 34 8N 114 16W
Parkersburg **164** 39 18N 81 31W
Parkes .... **117** 33 9S 148 11 E
Parma .... **46** 44 50N 10 20 E
Parnaguá **188** 10 10S 44 38W
Parnaíba **189** 2 54S 41 47W
Parnaíba → **188** 3 0S 41 50W
Parnassós .... **54** 38 35N 22 30 E
Pärnu .... **68** 58 28N 24 33 E
Páros .... **55** 37 5N 25 12 E
Parral **190** 36 10S 71 52W
Parramatta .... **117** 33 48S 151 1 E
Parras **174** 25 30N 102 20W
Parrett → **27** 51 7N 2 58W
Parry Is. **12** 77 0N 110 0W
Parry Sound **151** 45 20N 80 0W
Parsons **166** 37 20N 95 17W
Paruro **187** 13 45S 71 50W
Parvān □ .... **87** 35 0N 69 0 E

Pasadena, Calif., U.S.A. **173** 34 5N 118 9W
Pasadena, Tex., U.S.A. **168** 29 45N 95 14W
Pasaje **184** 3 23S 79 50W
Pascagoula **169** 30 21N 88 30W
Pasco **171** 46 10N 119 0W
Pasco, Cerro de **186** 10 45S 76 10W
Paso Robles **173** 35 40N 120 45W
Passero, C. .... **49** 36 42N 15 8 E
Passo Fundo **191** 28 10S 52 20W
Pasto **184** 1 13N 77 17W
Patagonia **192** 45 0S 69 0W
Patan .... **91** 23 54N 72 14 E
Patchogue **164** 40 46N 73 1W
Paterson **164** 40 55N 74 10W
Pathankot .... **89** 32 18N 75 45 E
Patiala .... **89** 30 23N 76 26 E
Patkai Bum .... **93** 27 0N 95 30 E
Pátmos .... **55** 37 21N 26 36 E
Patna .... **92** 25 35N 85 12 E
Patos, Lag. dos .... **191** 31 20S 51 0 E
Patos de Minas **188** 18 35S 46 32W
Pátrai .... **54** 38 14N 21 47 E
Patuca → **179** 15 50N 84 18W
Pátzcuaro **175** 19 32N 101 36W
Pau **36** 43 19N 0 25W
Paulistana **189** 8 9S 41 9W
Paulo Afonso **189** 9 21S 38 15W
Pavia .... **46** 45 10N 9 10 E
Pavlodar .... **71** 52 33N 77 0 E
Pavlovo .... **74** 63 5N 115 25 E
Pawtucket **164** 41 51N 71 22W
Payette **171** 44 0N 117 0W
Payne Bay = Bellin **146** 60 0N 70 0W
Payne L. **146** 59 30N 74 30W
Paynes Find .... **120** 29 15S 117 42 E
Paysandú **191** 32 19S 58 8W
Paz, La, Argentina **190** 30 50S 59 45W
Paz, La, Bolivia **187** 16 20S 68 10W
Paz, La, Mexico **174** 24 10N 110 18W
Pazardzhik .... **53** 42 12N 24 20 E
Peace → **145** 59 0N 111 25W
Peace River **155** 56 15N 117 18W
Peak, The **28** 53 24N 1 53W
Peak Hill .... **116** 32 47S 148 11 E
Pearl City **160** 21 24N 158 0W
Pearl Harbor **160** 21 20N 158 0W
Peary Land **13** 82 40N 33 0W
Pebas **186** 3 10S 71 46W
Pechenga .... **69** 69 30N 31 25 E
Pechora → .... **69** 68 13N 54 15 E
Pechorskaya Guba .... **69** 68 40N 54 0 E
Pecos **161** 31 25N 103 35W
Pecos → **161** 29 42N 102 30W
Pécs .... **59** 46 5N 18 15 E
Pedro Afonso **188** 9 0S 48 10W
Pedro Juan Caballero **191** 22 30S 55 40W
Peebles **31** 55 40N 3 12W
Peekskill **164** 41 18N 73 57W
Peel **28** 54 14N 4 40W
Peel → **144** 67 0N 135 0W
Pegasus Bay .... **123** 43 20S 173 10 E
Pegu .... **93** 17 20N 96 29 E
Pegu Yoma .... **93** 19 0N 96 0 E
Pehuajó **190** 35 45S 62 0W
Peip'ing = Beijing ...... **98** 39 55N 116 20 E
Pekalongan .... **111** 6 53S 109 40 E
Pekan .... **96** 3 30N 103 25 E
Pekanbaru .... **111** 0 30N 101 15 E
Pekin **166** 40 35N 89 40W
Peking = Beijing .... **98** 39 55N 116 20 E
Peleng .... **113** 1 20S 123 30 E
Pelly → **144** 62 47N 137 19W
Pelly Bay **146** 68 38N 89 50W
Peloponnes =
  Pelopónnisos □ .... **54** 37 10N 22 0 E
Pelopónnisos □ .... **54** 37 10N 22 0 E
Peloro, C. .... **49** 38 15N 15 40 E
Pelorus Sound .... **123** 40 59S 173 59 E
Pelotas **191** 31 42S 52 23W
Pelvoux, Massif de ...... **37** 44 52N 6 20 E
Pematangsiantar .... **111** 2 57N 99 5 E
Pemba .... **135** 5 0S 39 45 E

Name	Page	Lat		Long	
Pembroke, Canada	151	45 50N		77	7W
Pembroke, U.K.	27	51 41N		4	57W
Pen-y-Ghent	28	54 10N		2	15W
Penas, G. de	192	47 0S		75	0W
Pench'i = Benxi	98	41 20N		123	48 E
Pendembu	130	9 7N		12	14W
Pendleton	171	45 35N		118	50W
Penetanguishene	151	44 50N		79	55W
Penguin	119	41 8S		146	6 E
Penicuik	31	55 50N		3	14W
Peninsular Malaysia □	96	4 0N		102	0 E
Pennines	28	54 50N		2	20W
Pennsylvania □	164	40 50N		78	0W
Penola	119	37 25S		140	21 E
Penonomé	179	8 31N		80	21W
Penrith, Australia	117	33 43S		150	38 E
Penrith, U.K.	28	54 40N		2	45W
Pensacola	169	30 30N		87	10W
Pensacola Mts.	14	84 0S		40	0W
Penshurst	119	37 49S		142	20 E
Penticton	155	49 30N		119	38W
Pentland Firth	33	58 43N		3	10W
Pentland Hills	31	55 48N		3	25W
Penza	68	53 15N		45	5 E
Penzance	27	50 7N		5	32W
Penzhinskaya Guba	73	61 30N		163	0 E
Peoria	166	40 40N		89	40W
Perak □	96	5 0N		101	0 E
Perche	36	48 31N		1	1 E
Pereira	184	4 49N		75	43W
Perenjori	120	29 26S		116	16 E
Pergamino	190	33 52S		60	30W
Périgueux	36	45 10N		0	42 E
Perlis □	96	6 30N		100	15 E
Perm	69	58 0N		57	10 E
Pernambuco = Recife	189	8 0S		35	0W
Pernambuco □	189	8 0S		37	0W
Pernatty Lagoon	118	31 30S		137	12 E
Pernik	53	42 35N		23	2 E
Peron Pen.	120	26 0S		113	10 E
Péronne	38	49 55N		2	57 E
Perouse Str., La	77	45 40N		142	0 E
Perpignan	37	42 42N		2	53 E
Perry, Iowa, U.S.A.	166	41 48N		94	5W
Perry, Okla., U.S.A.	168	36 20N		97	20W
Persepolis	85	29 55N		52	50 E
Persia = Iran ■	86	33 0N		53	0 E
Persian Gulf = Gulf, The	85	27 0N		50	0 E
Perth, Australia	120	31 57S		115	52 E
Perth, Canada	151	44 55N		76	15W
Perth, U.K.	31	56 24N		3	27W
Perth Amboy	164	40 31N		74	16W
Peru	167	40 42N		86	0W
Peru ■	186	8 0S		75	0W
Perúgia	46	43 6N		12	24 E
Pervouralsk	69	56 55N		60	0 E
Pésaro	47	43 55N		12	53 E
Pescara	47	42 28N		14	13 E
Peshawar	89	34 2N		71	37 E
Pesqueria →	176	25 54N		99	11W
Petah Tiqwa	80	32 6N		34	53 E
Petaling Jaya	96	3 4N		101	42 E
Petaluma	172	38 13N		122	39W
Petatlán	177	17 31N		101	16W
Peterborough, Australia	118	32 58S		138	51 E
Peterborough, Canada	151	44 20N		78	20W
Peterborough, U.K.	25	52 35N		0	14W
Peterhead	33	57 30N		1	49W
Peterlee	29	54 45N		1	18W
Petersburg, Alaska, U.S.A.	143	56 50N		133	0W
Petersburg, Va., U.S.A.	164	37 17N		77	26W
Petit Goâve	180	18 27N		72	51W
Petitsikapau, L.	147	54 37N		66	25W
Petlad	91	22 30N		72	45 E
Petone	123	41 13S		174	53 E
Petoskey	150	45 22N		84	57W
Petrich	53	41 24N		23	13 E
Petrolia	150	42 54N		82	9W
Petrolina	189	9 24S		40	30W
Petropavlovsk	71	54 53N		69	13 E
Petropavlovsk-Kamchatskiy	73	53 3N		158	43 E
Petrópolis	188	22 33S		43	9W
Petrovaradin	52	45 16N		19	55 E
Petrozavodsk	68	61 41N		34	20 E
Pevek	73	69 41N		171	19 E
Pforzheim	42	48 53N		8	43 E
Phan Rang	95	11 34N		109	0 E
Phangan, Ko	96	9 45N		100	0 E
Phenix City	169	32 30N		85	0W
Philadelphia	164	40 0N		75	10W
Philippi	55	41 1N		24	16 E
Philippines ■	112	12 0N		123	0 E
Philippopolis = Plovdiv	53	42 8N		24	44 E
Phitsanulok	94	16 50N		100	12 E
Phnom Penh	95	11 33N		104	55 E
Phoenix	160	33 30N		112	10W
Phoenix Is.	123	3 30S		172	0W
Phra Chedi Sam Ong	94	15 16N		98	23 E
Phuket	96	7 52N		98	22 E
Piacenza	46	45 2N		9	42 E
Piauí □	188	7 0S		43	0W
Picardie	38	50 0N		2	15 E
Picardie, Plaine de	37	50 0N		2	0 E
Picardy = Picardie	38	50 0N		2	15 E
Picayune	169	30 31N		89	40W
Pickering	29	54 15N		0	46W
Picton, Australia	117	34 12S		150	34 E
Picton, N.Z.	123	41 18S		174	3 E
Pictou	149	45 41N		62	42W
Pidurutalagala	90	7 10N		80	50 E
Piedad, La	175	20 20N		102	1W
Piedmont = Piemonte □	46	45 0N		7	30 E
Piedmont Plat.	165	34 0N		81	30W
Piedras Negras	174	28 42N		100	31W
Piemonte □	46	45 0N		7	30 E
Pierre	163	44 23N		100	20W
Pietermaritzburg	137	29 35S		30	25 E
Pietrosul	57	47 35N		24	43 E
Pikeville	165	37 30N		82	30W
Pilcomayo →	190	25 21S		57	42W
Pilsen = Plzen	43	49 45N		13	22 E
Pimenta Bueno	187	11 35S		61	10W
Pinang □	96	5 20N		100	20 E
Pinar del Río	178	22 26N		83	40W
Pinaroo	119	35 17S		140	53 E
Pinawa	153	50 9N		95	50W
Pincher Creek	155	49 30N		113	57W
Pinczów	58	50 30N		20	35 E
Pindos Óros	54	40 0N		21	0 E
Pindus Mts. = Pindos Óros	54	40 0N		21	0 E
Pine Bluff	168	34 10N		92	0W
Pine Pass	155	55 25N		122	42W
Pineville	168	31 22N		92	30W
Ping →	94	15 42N		100	9 E
Pingdong	99	22 39N		120	30 E
Pingliang	99	35 35N		106	31 E
Pingxiang	99	22 6N		106	46 E
Piniós →	54	37 48N		21	20 E
Pinjarra	120	32 37S		115	52 E
Piombino	46	42 54N		10	30 E
Piotrków Trybunalski	58	51 23N		19	43 E
Piqua	167	40 10N		84	10W
Piracicaba	188	22 45S		47	40W
Piræus = Piraiévs	55	37 57N		23	42 E
Piraiévs	55	37 57N		23	42 E
Pirapora	188	17 20S		44	56W
Pírgos	54	37 40N		21	27 E
Pirin Planina	53	41 40N		23	30 E
Pirineos	51	42 40N		1	0 E
Pisa	46	43 43N		10	23 E
Pisagua	187	19 40S		70	15W
Pisco	186	13 50S		76	12W
Pistóia	46	43 57N		10	53 E
Pitcairn I.	10	25 5S		130	5W
Piteå	67	65 20N		21	25 E
Piteşti	57	44 52N		24	54 E
Pithiviers	39	48 10N		2	13 E
Pitlochry	33	56 43N		3	43W
Pitt I.	154	53 30N		129	50W
Pittsburg, Kans., U.S.A.	166	37 21N		94	43W
Pittsburg, Tex., U.S.A.	168	32 59N		94	58W
Pittsburgh	164	40 25N		79	55W
Pittsfield	164	42 28N		73	17W
Pittsworth	116	27 41S		151	37 E

Name	Page	Lat °	'	N/S	Long °	'	E/W
Piura	186	5	15	S	80	38	W
Placentia	149	47	20	N	54	0	W
Placerville	172	38	47	N	120	51	W
Placetas	178	22	15	N	79	44	W
Plainfield	164	40	37	N	74	28	W
Plainview	161	34	10	N	101	40	W
Plaster Rock	148	46	53	N	67	22	W
Plata, La	191	35	0	S	57	55	W
Plata, Rio de la	191	34	45	S	57	30	W
Platte →	163	39	16	N	94	50	W
Plattsburg	151	44	41	N	73	30	W
Plauen	43	50	29	N	12	9	E
Pleasantville	164	39	25	N	74	30	W
Plenty, Bay of	122	37	45	S	177	0	E
Plessisville	148	46	14	N	71	47	W
Pleven	53	43	26	N	24	37	E
Płock	58	52	32	N	19	40	E
Ploiești	57	44	57	N	26	5	E
Plovdiv	53	42	8	N	24	44	E
Plymouth	27	50	23	N	4	9	W
Plzen	43	49	45	N	13	22	E
Po →	47	44	57	N	12	4	E
Po Hai = Bo Hai	98	39	0	N	120	0	E
Pobeda	73	65	12	N	146	12	E
Pobedy Pik	71	40	45	N	79	58	E
Pocatello	163	42	50	N	112	25	W
Pochutla	177	15	50	N	96	31	W
Poços de Caldas	188	21	50	S	46	33	W
Podgorica	52	42	30	N	19	19	E
Podkamennaya Tunguska →	74	61	50	N	90	13	E
Point Edward	150	43	0	N	82	30	W
Pointe-à-Pitre	180	16	10	N	61	30	W
Pointe Noire	134	4	48	S	11	53	E
Poissy	39	48	55	N	2	0	E
Poitiers	36	46	35	N	0	20	E
Poitou, Plaines et Seuil du .	36	46	30	N	0	1	W
Pokaran	91	27	0	N	71	50	E
Pokrovsk	68	51	28	N	46	6	E
Pola = Pula	52	44	54	N	13	57	E
Poland ■	58	52	0	N	20	0	E
Polden Hills	27	51	7	N	2	50	W
Polesye	17	52	0	N	28	10	E
Polillo Is.	112	14	56	N	122	0	E
Polïyiros	55	40	23	N	23	25	E
Pollachi	90	10	35	N	77	0	E
Polotsk	68	55	30	N	28	50	E
Poltava	68	49	35	N	34	35	E
Polynesia	123	10	0	S	162	0	W
Pomona	173	34	2	N	117	49	W
Pompano Beach	170	26	12	N	80	6	W
Ponca City	168	36	40	N	97	5	W
Ponce	180	18	1	N	66	37	W
Pond Inlet	146	72	40	N	77	0	W
Pondicherry	90	11	59	N	79	50	E
Ponnyadaung	93	22	0	N	94	10	E
Ponoka	155	52	42	N	113	40	W
Pont-Audemer	39	49	21	N	0	30	E
Ponta Grossa	191	25	7	S	50	10	W
Ponta Pora	188	22	20	S	55	35	W
Pontchartrain, L.	169	30	12	N	90	0	W
Pontefract	29	53	42	N	1	19	W
Pontevedra	50	42	26	N	8	40	W
Pontiac	167	42	40	N	83	20	W
Pontianak	111	0	3	S	109	15	E
Pontine Is. = Ponziane, Isole	55	40	55	N	13	0	E
Pontoise	39	49	3	N	2	5	E
Pontypool	27	51	42	N	3	1	W
Pontypridd	27	51	36	N	3	21	W
Ponziane, Isole	48	40	55	N	13	0	E
Poochera	118	32	43	S	134	51	E
Poole	24	50	42	N	1	58	W
Pooley I.	154	52	45	N	128	15	W
Poona = Pune	91	18	29	N	73	57	E
Poopó, Lago de	187	18	30	S	67	35	W
Popayán	184	2	27	N	76	36	W
Poplar Bluff	169	36	45	N	90	22	W
Popocatépetl, Volcán	177	19	2	N	98	38	W
Porcher I.	154	53	50	N	130	30	W
Porcupine →	142	66	35	N	145	15	W
Pori	67	61	29	N	21	48	E
Porkkala	67	59	59	N	24	26	E
Port Adelaide	119	34	46	S	138	30	E
Port Alberni	154	49	40	N	124	50	W
Port Albert	115	38	42	S	146	42	E
Port Alfred	148	48	18	N	70	53	W
Port Angeles	171	48	7	N	123	30	W
Port Antonio	180	18	10	N	76	30	W
Port Arthur	168	30	0	N	94	0	W
Port-au-Prince	180	18	40	N	72	20	W
Port Augusta	118	32	30	S	137	50	E
Port Blair	94	11	40	N	92	30	E
Port-Cartier	148	50	2	N	66	50	W
Port Chalmers	123	45	49	S	170	30	E
Port Colborne	151	42	50	N	79	10	W
Port Coquitlam	154	49	15	N	122	45	W
Port Darwin	192	51	50	S	59	0	W
Port-de-Paix	180	19	50	N	72	50	W
Port Elgin	150	44	25	N	81	25	W
Port Elizabeth	136	33	58	S	25	40	E
Port Erin	28	54	5	N	4	45	W
Port Etienne = Nouâdhibou .	126	20	54	N	17	0	W
Port Fairy	119	38	22	S	142	12	E
Port Glasgow	30	55	57	N	4	40	W
Port Harcourt	131	4	40	N	7	10	E
Port Harrison = Inoucdjouac	146	58	25	N	78	15	W
Port Hawkesbury	149	45	36	N	61	22	W
Port Hope	151	43	56	N	78	20	W
Port Huron	167	43	0	N	82	28	W
Port Kembla	117	34	52	S	150	49	E
Port Laoise	35	53	2	N	7	20	W
Port Lavaca	158	28	38	N	96	38	W
Port Lincoln	119	34	42	S	135	52	E
Port Lyautey = Kenitra	126	34	15	N	6	40	W
Port Macquarie	116	31	25	S	152	25	E
Port Morant	180	17	54	N	76	19	W
Port Moresby	115	9	24	S	147	8	E
Port Nelson	143	57	3	N	92	36	W
Port Nolloth	136	29	17	S	16	52	E
Port Nouveau-Québec	146	58	30	N	65	59	W
Port of Spain	180	10	40	N	61	31	W
Port Phillip B.	117	38	10	S	144	50	E
Port Pirie	118	33	10	S	138	1	E
Port Said = Bûr Sa'îd	128	31	16	N	32	18	E
Port Simpson	154	54	30	N	130	20	W
Port Stanley	150	42	40	N	81	10	W
Port Sudan = Bûr Sûdân	129	19	32	N	37	9	E
Port Talbot	27	51	35	N	3	48	W
Port Townsend	171	48	7	N	122	50	W
Portadown	34	54	27	N	6	26	W
Portage La Prairie	153	49	58	N	98	18	W
Portarlington	35	53	10	N	7	10	W
Porte, La	167	41	36	N	86	43	W
Porterville	173	36	5	N	119	0	W
Porthcawl	27	51	28	N	3	42	W
Porthmadog	26	52	55	N	4	13	W
Portile de Fier	56	44	42	N	22	30	E
Portland, Australia	119	38	20	S	141	35	E
Portland, Maine, U.S.A.	148	43	40	N	70	15	W
Portland, Oreg., U.S.A.	171	45	35	N	122	40	W
Portland, Bill of	24	50	31	N	2	27	W
Portland Prom.	146	58	40	N	78	33	W
Porto	50	41	8	N	8	40	W
Pôrto Alegre	191	30	5	S	51	10	W
Porto Empédocle	48	37	18	N	13	30	E
Porto Mendes	191	24	30	S	54	15	W
Porto Novo	131	6	23	N	2	42	E
Pôrto Seguro	189	16	26	S	39	5	W
Pôrto Velho	187	8	46	S	63	54	W
Portoferráio	46	42	50	N	10	20	E
Portoscuso	48	39	12	N	8	22	E
Portoviejo	184	1	7	S	80	28	W
Portpatrick	30	54	50	N	5	7	W
Portree	32	57	25	N	6	11	W
Portrush	34	55	13	N	6	40	W
Portsmouth, Domin.	180	15	34	N	61	27	W
Portsmouth, U.K.	25	50	48	N	1	6	W
Portsmouth, N.H., U.S.A.	148	43	5	N	70	45	W
Portsmouth, Ohio, U.S.A.	167	38	45	N	83	0	W
Portsmouth, Va., U.S.A.	165	36	50	N	76	20	W
Porttipahta	67	68	5	N	26	40	E
Portugal ■	50	40	0	N	7	0	W
Portuguese-Guinea = Guinea-Bissau ■	130	12	0	N	15	0	W

Portuguese Timor ■ = Timor	113	9	0S	125	0 E
Portumna	35	53	5N	8	12W
Porvenir	192	53	10S	70	16W
Posadas	191	27	30S	55	50W
Poshan = Boshan	98	36	28N	117	49 E
Poste-de-la-Baleine	140	55	17N	77	45W
Potchefstroom	137	26	41S	27	7 E
Potenza	49	40	40N	15	50 E
Potomac ➤	165	38	0N	76	23W
Potosí	187	19	38S	65	50W
Potsdam, Germany	43	52	23N	13	4 E
Potsdam, U.S.A.	151	44	40N	74	59W
Pottsville	164	40	39N	76	12W
Pouce Coupé	155	55	40N	120	10W
Poughkeepsie	164	41	40N	73	57W
Poulaphouca Res.	35	53	8N	6	30W
Póvoa de Varzim	50	41	25N	8	46W
Powell, L.	163	37	25N	110	45W
Powell River	154	49	50N	124	35W
Powys □	26	52	20N	3	20W
Poyang Hu	99	29	10N	116	10 E
Poyarkovo	75	49	36N	128	41 E
Poznań	58	52	25N	16	55 E
Prachuap Khiri Khan	94	11	49N	99	48 E
Prague = Praha	58	50	5N	14	22 E
Praha	58	50	5N	14	22 E
Prainha, Amazonas, Brazil	187	7	10S	60	30W
Prainha, Pará, Brazil	185	1	45S	53	30W
Prairie du Chien	166	43	1N	91	9W
Prato	46	43	53N	11	5 E
Pratt	161	37	40N	98	45W
Prepansko Jezero	52	40	55N	21	0 E
Preparis North Channel	94	15	12N	93	40 E
Preparis South Channel	94	14	36N	93	40 E
Prescott	160	34	35N	112	30W
Preservation Inlet	123	46	8S	166	35 E
Presidencia Roque Saenz Peña	190	26	45S	60	30W
Presidente Prudente	188	22	5S	51	25W
Presidio	161	29	30N	104	20W
Prespa, L. = Prepansko Jezero	52	40	55N	21	0 E
Presque Isle	148	46	40N	68	0W
Preston, Borders, U.K.	28	55	48N	2	18W
Preston, Lancs., U.K.	21	53	46N	2	42W
Prestonpans	31	55	58N	3	0W
Prestwick	31	55	30N	4	38W
Pretoria	137	25	44S	28	12 E
Préveza	55	38	57N	20	47 E
Prichard	169	30	47N	88	5W
Prilep	52	41	21N	21	37 E
Prince Albert	152	53	15N	105	50W
Prince Albert Pen.	145	72	30N	116	0W
Prince Albert Sd.	145	70	25N	115	0W
Prince Charles I.	146	67	47N	76	12W
Prince Edward I. □	148	46	20N	63	20W
Prince George	154	53	55N	122	50W
Prince of Wales I., Canada	145	73	0N	99	0W
Prince of Wales I., U.S.A.	143	55	30N	133	0W
Prince Patrick I.	12	77	0N	120	0W
Prince Rupert	154	54	20N	130	20W
Princess Royal I.	154	53	0N	128	40W
Princeton	155	49	27N	120	30W
Principe, I. de	131	1	37N	7	27 E
Principe da Beira	187	12	20S	64	30W
Pripet = Pripyat ➤	68	51	20N	30	9 E
Pripet Marshes = Polesye	17	52	0N	28	10 E
Pripyat ➤	68	51	20N	30	9 E
Pripyat Marshes = Polesye	17	52	0N	28	10 E
Priština	52	42	40N	21	13 E
Privolzhskaya Vozvyshennost	17	51	0N	46	0 E
Prizren	52	42	13N	20	45 E
Proddatur	90	14	45N	78	30 E
Progreso	177	21	17N	89	40W
Prokopyevsk	71	54	0N	86	45 E
Proserpine	121	20	21S	148	36 E
Provence	37	43	40N	5	46 E
Providence	164	41	50N	71	28W
Provo	163	40	16N	111	37W
Prudhoe Bay	142	70	20N	148	20W
Pruszków	58	52	9N	20	49 E
Prut ➤	57	46	3N	28	10 E
Przemyśl	58	49	50N	22	45 E
Przeworsk	58	50	6N	22	32 E
Pskov	68	57	50N	28	25 E
Pucallpa	186	8	25S	74	30W
Puebla	177	19	3N	98	12W
Puebla □	177	18	50N	98	0W
Pueblo	163	38	20N	104	40W
Puelches	190	38	5S	65	51W
Puente Alto	190	33	32S	70	35W
Puerto Armuelles	179	8	20N	82	51W
Puerto Ayacucho	184	5	40N	67	35W
Puerto Barrios	177	15	40N	88	32W
Puerto Cabello	184	10	28N	68	1W
Puerto Cabezas	179	14	0N	83	30W
Puerto Castilla	179	16	0N	86	0W
Puerto Cortes, Costa Rica	179	8	55N	84	0W
Puerto Cortés, Honduras	177	15	51N	88	0W
Puerto Heath	187	12	34S	68	39W
Puerto La Cruz	185	10	13N	64	38W
Puerto Libertad	174	29	55N	112	41W
Puerto Lobos	192	42	0S	65	3W
Puerto Maldonado	187	12	30S	69	10W
Puerto Montt	190	41	28S	73	0W
Puerto Padre	178	21	13N	76	35W
Puerto Pinasco	191	22	36S	57	50W
Puerto Plata	180	19	48N	70	45W
Puerto Quepos	179	9	29N	84	6W
Puerto Rico ■	180	18	15N	66	45W
Puerto Vallarta	175	20	37N	105	15W
Puertollano	50	38	43N	4	7W
Puget Sd.	171	47	15N	122	30W
Púglia □	49	41	0N	16	30 E
Pula	52	44	54N	13	57 E
Pulaski, Tenn., U.S.A.	169	35	10N	87	0W
Pulaski, Va., U.S.A.	165	37	4N	80	49W
Pulicat, L.	90	13	40N	80	15 E
Pullman	171	46	49N	117	10W
Punakha	92	27	42N	89	52 E
Punata	187	17	32S	65	50W
Pune	91	18	29N	73	57 E
Punjab □, India	89	31	0N	76	0 E
Punjab □, Pakistan	89	30	0N	72	0 E
Puno	187	15	55S	70	3W
Punta Alta	190	38	53S	62	4W
Punta Arenas	192	53	10S	71	0W
Punta Gorda	177	16	10N	88	45W
Puntabie	118	32	12S	134	13 E
Puntarenas	179	10	0N	84	50W
Punto Fijo	184	11	50N	70	13W
Puquio	186	14	45S	74	10W
Pur ➤	69	67	31N	77	55 E
Purbeck, Isle of	24	50	40N	2	5W
Purmerend	40	52	30N	4	58 E
Purnia	92	25	45N	87	31 E
Pursat	95	12	34N	103	50 E
Purus ➤	185	3	42S	61	28W
Pusan	98	35	5N	129	0 E
Putao	93	27	28N	97	30 E
Putorana, Gory	72	69	0N	95	0 E
Putumayo ➤	184	3	7S	67	58W
Puy, Le	37	45	2N	3	53 E
Puy-de-Dôme	37	45	46N	2	57 E
Puyallup	171	47	10N	122	22W
Pwllheli	26	52	54N	4	26W
Pyasina ➤	72	73	30N	87	0 E
Pyatigorsk	70	44	2N	43	6 E
Pyinmana	93	19	45N	96	12 E
P'yŏngyang	98	39	0N	125	30 E
Pyramid L.	172	40	0N	119	30W
Pyrénées	124	42	45N	0	18 E

Q

Qā'emshahr	86	36	30N	52	55 E
Qahremānshahr = Bākhtarān	84	34	23N	47	0 E
Qaidam Pendi	100	37	0N	95	0 E
Qal'at al Akhḑar	82	28	0N	37	10 E
Qamar, Ghubbat al	83	16	20N	52	30 E
Qamdo	101	31	15N	97	6 E

Name	Page	Lat	Long
Qandahār	87	31 32N	65 30 E
Qaṣr-e Qand	85	26 15N	60 45 E
Qatar ■	85	25 30N	51 15 E
Qāyen	86	33 40N	59 10 E
Qazvin	81	36 15N	50 0 E
Qena	128	26 10N	32 43 E
Qeshm	85	26 55N	56 10 E
Qilian Shan	100	38 30N	96 0 E
Qingdao	98	36 5N	120 20 E
Qinghai □	101	36 0N	98 0 E
Qinghai Hu	100	36 40N	100 10 E
Qinhuangdao	98	39 56N	119 30 E
Qiqihar	98	47 26N	124 0 E
Qom	86	34 40N	51 0 E
Qomsheh	85	32 0N	51 55 E
Qondūz □	87	36 50N	68 50 E
Qu Xian	99	30 48N	106 58 E
Quang Ngai	95	15 13N	108 58 E
Quantock Hills	27	51 8N	3 10W
Quanzhou	99	24 55N	118 34 E
Quatsino	154	50 30N	127 40W
Queanbeyan	117	35 17S	149 14 E
Québec	148	46 52N	71 13W
Québec □	140	50 0N	70 0W
Queen Alexandra Ra.	15	85 0S	170 0 E
Queen Charlotte	154	53 15N	132 2W
Queen Charlotte Is.	154	53 20N	132 10W
Queen Charlotte Str.	154	51 0N	128 0W
Queen Elizabeth Is.	138	76 0N	95 0W
Queen Mary Land	15	70 0S	95 0 E
Queen Maud G.	145	68 15N	102 30W
Queen Maud Mts.	15	86 0S	160 0W
Queenscliff	117	38 16S	144 39 E
Queensland □	115	22 0S	142 0 E
Queenstown, Australia	119	42 4S	145 35 E
Queenstown, N.Z.	123	45 1S	168 40 E
Quelimane	137	17 53S	36 58 E
Quelpart = Cheju Do	99	33 29N	126 34 E
Querétaro	177	20 36N	100 23W
Querétaro □	177	21 0N	99 55W
Quesnel	154	53 0N	122 30W
Quetta	88	30 15N	66 55 E
Quezaltenango	177	14 50N	91 30W
Quezon City	112	14 38N	121 0 E
Qui Nhon	95	13 40N	109 13 E
Quibdo	184	5 42N	76 40W
Quillabamba	186	12 50S	72 50W
Quilon	90	8 50N	76 38 E
Quilpie	116	26 35S	144 11 E
Quimper	36	48 0N	4 9W
Quincy, Calif., U.S.A.	172	39 56N	121 0W
Quincy, Fla., U.S.A.	170	30 34N	84 34W
Quincy, Ill., U.S.A.	166	39 55N	91 20W
Quincy, Mass., U.S.A.	164	42 14N	71 0W
Quintana Roo □	177	19 40N	88 30W
Quirindi	116	31 28S	150 40 E
Quitman	170	30 49N	83 35W
Quito	184	0 15S	78 35W
Quixadá	189	4 55S	39 0W
Quorn	118	32 25S	138 0 E
Quseir	128	26 7N	34 16 E

R

Name	Page	Lat	Long
Raahe	67	64 40N	24 28 E
Raasay	32	57 25N	6 4W
Rabat	126	34 2N	6 48W
Rabaul	115	4 24S	152 18 E
Rābigh	82	22 50N	39 5 E
Race, C.	149	46 40N	53 5W
Rach Gia	95	10 5N	105 5 E
Racibórz	58	50 7N	18 18 E
Racine	167	42 41N	87 51W
Radium Hot Springs	155	50 35N	116 2W
Radnor Forest	26	52 17N	3 10W
Radom	58	51 23N	21 12 E
Radomir	53	42 37N	23 4 E
Radstock	27	51 17N	2 25W
Radville	152	49 30N	104 15W

Name	Page	Lat	Long
Rae	145	62 50N	116 3W
Rae Bareli	92	26 18N	81 20 E
Raetihi	122	39 25S	175 17 E
Rafaela	190	31 10S	61 30W
Rafḥā	82	29 35N	43 35 E
Rafsanjān	85	30 30N	56 5 E
Ragama	90	7 0N	79 50 E
Raglan	122	37 55S	174 55 E
Ragusa	49	36 56N	14 42 E
Rahaeng = Tak	94	16 52N	99 8 E
Raichur	91	16 10N	77 20 E
Rainier, Mt.	171	46 50N	121 50W
Rainy L.	153	48 42N	93 10W
Rainy River	153	48 43N	94 29W
Raipur	92	21 17N	81 45 E
Rajahmundry	92	17 1N	81 48 E
Rajapalaiyam	90	9 25N	77 35 E
Rajasthan □	91	26 45N	73 30 E
Rajasthan Canal	89	28 0N	72 0 E
Rajkot	91	22 15N	70 56 E
Rajshahi □	92	25 0N	89 0 E
Raleigh	165	35 47N	78 39W
Raleigh B.	165	34 50N	76 15W
Rambouillet	39	48 40N	1 48 E
Rampur	89	28 50N	79 5 E
Ramsey	28	54 20N	4 21W
Rancagua	190	34 10S	70 50W
Ranchi	92	23 19N	85 27 E
Rangiora	123	43 19S	172 36 E
Rangoon	93	16 45N	96 20 E
Rangpur	92	25 42N	89 22 E
Raniwara	91	24 50N	72 10 E
Rankin Inlet	145	62 30N	93 0W
Rankins Springs	117	33 49S	146 14 E
Rannoch, L.	33	56 41N	4 20W
Rannoch Moor	30	56 38N	4 48W
Rapid City	163	44 0N	103 0W
Ras Dashen	132	13 8N	38 26 E
Rasa, Punta	192	40 50S	62 15W
Rasht	81	37 20N	49 40 E
Rat Is.	142	51 50N	178 15 E
Ratangarh	89	28 5N	74 35 E
Rath Luirc	35	52 21N	8 40W
Rathlin I.	34	55 18N	6 14W
Ratibor = Racibórz	58	50 7N	18 18 E
Ratlam	91	23 20N	75 0 E
Ratnagiri	91	16 57N	73 18 E
Rattray Hd.	33	57 38N	1 50W
Raub	96	3 47N	101 52 E
Raukumara Ra.	122	38 5S	177 55 E
Ravenna	47	44 28N	12 15 E
Ravenshoe	121	17 37S	145 29 E
Ravensthorpe	120	33 35S	120 2 E
Rawalpindi	89	33 38N	73 8 E
Rawlins	163	41 50N	107 20W
Ray, C.	149	47 33N	59 15W
Raymond	155	49 30N	112 35W
Razgrad	53	43 33N	26 34 E
Ré, Île de	36	46 12N	1 30W
Reading, U.K.	25	51 27N	0 57W
Reading, U.S.A.	164	40 20N	75 53W
Reay Forest	32	58 20N	4 55W
Rebun-Tō	103	45 23N	141 2 E
Recife	189	8 0S	35 0W
Reconquista	190	29 10S	59 45W
Recreo	190	29 25S	65 10W
Red →	168	31 0N	91 40W
Red Bluff	172	40 11N	122 11W
Red Cliffs	119	34 19S	142 11 E
Red Deer	155	52 20N	113 50W
Red Lake	153	51 3N	93 49W
Red Oak	166	41 0N	95 10W
Red Sea	128	25 0N	36 0 E
Red Tower Pass = Turnu Rosu Pasul	57	45 33N	24 17 E
Red Wing	166	44 32N	92 35W
Redcar	29	54 37N	1 4W
Redcliff	152	50 10N	110 50W
Redcliffe	116	27 12S	153 0 E
Redding	172	40 30N	122 25W
Redditch	24	52 18N	1 57W
Redlands	173	34 0N	117 11W

Name	Page	Lat	Long
Redruth	27	50 14N	5 14W
Redwater	155	53 55N	113 6W
Redwood City	172	37 30N	122 15W
Ree, L.	34	53 35N	8 0W
Reedley	173	36 36N	119 27W
Regensburg	43	49 1N	12 7 E
Réggio di Calábria	49	38 7N	15 38 E
Réggio nell' Emilia	46	44 42N	10 38 E
Regina	152	50 27N	104 35W
Rehovot	80	31 54N	34 48 E
Reichenbach	43	50 36N	12 19 E
Reidsville	165	36 21N	79 40W
Reims	39	49 15N	4 0 E
Reina Adelaida, Arch.	192	52 20S	74 0W
Reindeer L.	143	57 15N	102 15W
Reliance	145	63 0N	109 20W
Remanso	189	9 41S	42 4W
Remarkable, Mt.	118	32 48S	138 10 E
Remscheid	42	51 11N	7 12 E
Rendsburg	42	54 18N	9 41 E
Renfrew, Canada	151	45 30N	76 40W
Renfrew, U.K.	31	55 52N	4 24W
Renkum	41	51 58N	5 43 E
Renmark	119	34 11S	140 43 E
Rennes	36	48 7N	1 41W
Reno	172	39 30N	119 50W
Republic	150	46 25N	87 59W
Republican →	163	39 3N	96 48W
Repulse Bay	146	66 30N	86 30W
Requena	186	5 5S	73 52W
Resht = Rasht	81	37 20N	49 40 E
Resistencia	190	27 30S	59 0W
Resolution I., Canada	146	61 30N	65 0W
Resolution I., N.Z.	123	45 40S	166 40 E
Retalhuleu	177	14 33N	91 46W
Réthímnon	55	35 18N	24 30 E
Réunion	9	22 0S	56 0 E
Reval = Tallinn	68	59 22N	24 48 E
Revelstoke	155	51 0N	118 10W
Revilla Gigedo, Is.	139	18 40N	112 0W
Rewa	92	24 33N	81 25 E
Rewari	89	28 15N	76 40 E
Rexburg	163	43 55N	111 50W
Rey Malabo	131	3 45N	8 50 E
Reykjavík	64	64 10N	21 57 E
Reynosa	176	26 5N	98 18W
Rhayader	26	52 19N	3 30W
Rhein →	42	51 52N	6 20 E
Rheinland-Pfalz □	42	50 0N	7 0 E
Rhin = Rhein →	42	51 52N	6 20 E
Rhine = Rhein →	42	51 52N	6 20 E
Rhineland-Palatinate = Rheinland-Pfalz □	42	50 0N	7 0 E
Rhinelander	150	45 38N	89 29W
Rhode Island □	164	41 38N	71 37W
Rhodes = Ródhos	55	36 15N	28 10 E
Rhodesia = Zimbabwe ■	137	20 0S	30 0 E
Rhodope Mts. = Rhodopi Planina	53	41 40N	24 20 E
Rhodopi Planina	53	41 40N	24 20 E
Rhön	42	50 24N	9 58 E
Rhondda	27	51 39N	3 30W
Rhône →	37	43 28N	4 42 E
Rhum	32	57 0N	6 20W
Rhyl	26	53 19N	3 29W
Rhymney	27	51 45N	3 17W
Riachão	188	7 20S	46 37W
Riau, Kepulauan	111	0 30N	104 20 E
Ribatejo □	50	39 15N	8 30W
Ribble →	28	54 13N	2 20W
Ribeirão Prêto	188	21 10S	47 50W
Riberalta	187	11 0S	66 0W
Riccarton	123	43 32S	172 37 E
Richland	171	46 15N	119 15W
Richmond, Australia	116	20 43S	143 8 E
Richmond, N.Z.	123	41 20S	173 12 E
Richmond, N. Yorks., U.K.	28	54 24N	1 43W
Richmond, Surrey, U.K.	25	51 28N	0 18W
Richmond, Calif., U.S.A.	172	37 58N	122 21W
Richmond, Ind., U.S.A.	167	39 50N	84 50W
Richmond, Ky., U.S.A.	165	37 40N	84 20W
Richmond, Va., U.S.A.	165	37 33N	77 27W
Richwood	165	38 17N	80 32W
Ridgeway	164	42 56S	147 16 E
Riga	68	56 53N	24 8 E
Rîgestãn □	87	30 15N	65 0 E
Rigolet	147	54 10N	58 23W
Rijeka	52	45 20N	14 21 E
Rijssen	41	52 19N	6 30 E
Rijswijk	40	52 4N	4 22 E
Rimini	47	44 3N	12 33 E
Rîmnicu Vîlcea	57	45 9N	24 21 E
Rimouski	148	48 27N	68 30W
Rinia	55	37 23N	25 13 E
Rio Branco	187	9 58S	67 49W
Rio Claro	180	10 20N	61 25W
Rio Cuarto	190	33 10S	64 25W
Rio de Janeiro	188	23 0S	43 12W
Rio de Janeiro □	188	22 50S	43 0W
Rio Gallegos	192	51 35S	69 15W
Rio Grande	191	32 0S	52 20W
Rio Grande →	161	25 57N	97 9W
Rio Grande do Norte □	189	5 40S	36 0W
Rio Grande do Sul □	191	30 0S	53 0W
Rio Mulatos	187	19 40S	66 50W
Rio Negro	191	26 0S	50 0W
Rio Verde	188	17 50S	51 0W
Riobamba	184	1 50S	78 45W
Riohacha	184	11 33N	72 55W
Rioja, La	190	29 20S	67 0W
Rioja, La □	50	42 20N	2 20W
Riosucio	184	7 27N	77 7W
Ripon	28	54 8N	1 31W
Rishiri-Tō	103	45 11N	141 15 E
Ritchies Archipelago	94	12 5N	94 0 E
Rivas	179	11 30N	85 50W
Riverhead	164	40 53N	72 40W
Riverside	173	34 0N	117 22W
Riverton	153	51 1N	97 0W
Riviera di Levante	46	44 23N	9 15 E
Riviera di Ponente	46	43 50N	7 58 E
Rivière-du-Loup	148	47 50N	69 30W
Riyadh = Ar Riyāḍ	83	24 41N	46 42 E
Roanne	37	46 3N	4 4 E
Roanoke, Ala., U.S.A.	169	33 9N	85 23W
Roanoke, Va., U.S.A.	165	37 19N	79 55W
Roanoke →	165	35 56N	76 43W
Roanoke Rapids	165	36 28N	77 42W
Robinvale	119	34 40S	142 45 E
Roblin	152	51 14N	101 21W
Roboré	187	18 10S	59 45W
Robson, Mt.	155	53 10N	119 10W
Roca, C. da	50	38 40N	9 31W
Rocha	191	34 30S	54 25W
Rochdale	28	53 36N	2 10W
Roche-sur-Yon, La	36	46 40N	1 25W
Rochefort	36	45 56N	0 57W
Rochelle, La	36	46 10N	1 9W
Rochester, Minn., U.S.A.	166	44 1N	92 28W
Rochester, N.H., U.S.A.	164	43 19N	70 57W
Rochester, N.Y., U.S.A.	164	43 10N	77 40W
Rock Hill	165	34 55N	81 2W
Rock Island	166	41 30N	90 35W
Rock Sprs.	163	41 40N	109 10W
Rockall	16	57 37N	13 42W
Rockford	166	42 20N	89 0W
Rockglen	152	49 11N	105 57W
Rockhampton	119	23 22S	150 32 E
Rockingham	120	32 15S	115 38 E
Rockland	148	44 6N	69 6W
Rocky Mount	165	35 55N	77 48W
Rocky Mountain House	155	52 22N	114 55W
Rocky Mts.	138	55 0N	121 0W
Ródhos	55	36 15N	28 10 E
Roebourne	114	20 44S	117 9 E
Roermond	41	51 12N	6 0 E
Roes Welcome Sd.	146	65 0N	87 0W
Rogaland fylke □	60	59 12N	6 20 E
Rogers	168	36 20N	94 5W
Rohri	88	27 45N	68 51 E
Rohtak	89	28 55N	76 43 E
Rojo, C.	177	21 33N	97 20W
Rolla	166	37 56N	91 42W
Roma, Australia	116	26 32S	148 49 E

Name	Page	Lat °	′	N/S	Long °	′	E/W
Roma, Italy	**46**	41	54N		12	30	E
Romaine →	**141**	50	18N		63	47W	
Roman	**57**	46	57N		26	55	E
Romana, La	**180**	18	27N		68	57W	
Romania ■	**57**	46	0N		25	0	E
Romans	**37**	45	3N		5	3	E
Romanzof, C.	**142**	62	0N		165	50W	
Rome = Roma	**46**	41	54N		12	30	E
Rome, Ga., U.S.A.	**169**	34	20N		85	0W	
Rome, N.Y., U.S.A.	**164**	43	14N		75	29W	
Romilly	**39**	48	31N		3	44	E
Romney Marsh	**25**	51	0N		1	0	E
Rona	**32**	57	33N		6	0W	
Rondônia □	**187**	11	0S		63	0W	
Rong, Koh	**95**	10	45N		103	15	E
Ronge, L. la	**152**	55	6N		105	17W	
Roosendaal	**40**	51	32N		4	29	E
Roraima □	**185**	2	0N		61	30W	
Roraima, Mt.	**185**	5	10N		60	40W	
Rosario, Argentina	**190**	33	0S		60	40W	
Rosário, Brazil	**188**	3	0S		44	15W	
Rosario, Mexico	**175**	22	58N		105	53W	
Rosario, Paraguay	**191**	24	30S		57	35W	
Rosário do Sul	**191**	30	15S		54	55W	
Roscommon	**34**	53	38N		8	11W	
Roscommon □	**34**	53	40N		8	15W	
Roscrea	**35**	52	58N		7	50W	
Roseau	**180**	15	20N		61	24W	
Roseburg	**171**	43	10N		123	20W	
Rosenberg	**168**	29	30N		95	48W	
Rosendaël	**38**	51	3N		2	24	E
Rosetown	**152**	51	35N		107	59W	
Roseville	**172**	38	46N		121	17W	
Rosewood	**116**	27	38S		152	36	E
Roskilde	**61**	55	38N		12	3	E
Ross on Wye	**24**	51	55N		2	34W	
Ross Sea	**15**	74	0S		178	0	E
Rossan Pt.	**34**	54	42N		8	47W	
Rossland	**155**	49	6N		117	50W	
Rosslare	**35**	52	17N		6	23W	
Røssvatnet	**65**	65	45N		14	5	E
Rosthern	**152**	52	40N		106	20W	
Rostock	**43**	54	4N		12	9	E
Rostov	**68**	47	15N		39	45	E
Roswell	**161**	33	26N		104	32W	
Rosyth	**31**	56	2N		3	26W	
Rother →	**25**	50	59N		0	40	E
Rotherham	**29**	53	26N		1	21W	
Rothesay	**30**	55	50N		5	3W	
Roto	**117**	33	0S		145	30	E
Rotorua	**122**	38	9S		176	16	E
Rotorua, L.	**122**	38	5S		176	18	E
Rotterdam	**40**	51	55N		4	30	E
Rotuma	**122**	12	25S		177	5	E
Roubaix	**37**	50	40N		3	10	E
Rouen	**38**	49	27N		1	4	E
Round Mt.	**116**	30	26S		152	16	E
Roussillon	**37**	42	30N		2	35	E
Rouyn	**151**	48	20N		79	0W	
Rovaniemi	**67**	66	29N		25	41	E
Rovno	**68**	50	40N		26	10	E
Ruahine Ra.	**122**	39	55S		176	2	E
Ruapehu	**122**	39	17S		175	35	E
Rub' al Khali	**83**	18	0N		48	0	E
Rubh a' Mhail	**30**	55	55N		6	10W	
Rubio	**184**	7	43N		72	22W	
Rubtsovsk	**71**	51	30N		81	10	E
Rudnyy	**71**	52	57N		63	7	E
Rudolf, Ostrov	**69**	81	45N		58	30	E
Rufiji →	**135**	7	50S		39	15	E
Rufino	**190**	34	20S		62	50W	
Rugby	**25**	52	23N		1	16W	
Rügen	**43**	54	22N		13	25	E
Ruhr →	**42**	51	25N		6	44	E
Rukwa L.	**135**	8	0S		32	20	E
Rumania = Romania ■	**57**	46	0N		25	0	E
Rumford	**148**	44	30N		70	30W	
Rumoi	**103**	43	56N		141	39W	
Runcorn	**28**	53	20N		2	44W	
Rupat	**111**	1	45N		101	40	E
Rupert →	**140**	51	29N		78	45W	
Rupert House = Fort Rupert	**140**	51	30N		78	40W	
Ruschuk = Ruse	**53**	43	48N		25	59	E
Ruse	**53**	43	48N		25	59	E
Russell	**152**	50	50N		101	20W	
Russellville, Ala., U.S.A.	**169**	34	30N		87	44W	
Russellville, Ark., U.S.A.	**168**	35	15N		93	8W	
Russia ■	**78**	60	0N		100	0	E
Ruston	**168**	32	30N		92	58W	
Rutherglen	**31**	55	50N		4	11W	
Rutland I.	**94**	11	25N		92	40	E
Ruwenzori	**132**	0	30N		29	55	E
Rwanda ■	**135**	2	0S		30	0	E
Ryan, L.	**30**	55	0N		5	2W	
Ryazan	**68**	54	40N		39	40	E
Rybache	**71**	46	40N		81	20	E
Rybinsk	**68**	58	5N		38	50	E
Ryde	**25**	50	44N		1	9W	
Rye	**25**	50	57N		0	46	E
Rylstone	**117**	32	46S		149	58	E
Ryōhaku-Sanchi	**106**	36	9N		136	49	E
Ryūgasaki	**107**	35	54N		140	11	E
Rzeszów	**58**	50	5N		21	58	E

S

Name	Page	Lat °	′	N/S	Long °	′	E/W
Sa Dec	**95**	10	20N		105	46	E
Saar →	**42**	49	41N		6	32	E
Saarbrücken	**42**	49	15N		6	58	E
Saaremaa	**68**	58	30N		22	30	E
Saarland □	**42**	49	15N		7	0	E
Sabadell	**51**	41	28N		2	7	E
Sabae	**106**	35	57N		136	11	E
Sabah □	**112**	6	0N		117	0	E
Sábana de la Mar	**180**	19	7N		69	24W	
Sabhah	**127**	27	9N		14	29	E
Sabi →	**137**	18	50S		31	40	E
Sabinas	**174**	27	51N		101	7W	
Sabinas Hidalgo, R. →	**176**	26	50N		99	35W	
Sabine →	**158**	30	0N		93	35W	
Sable, C., Canada	**148**	43	29N		65	38W	
Sable, C., U.S.A.	**159**	25	13N		81	0W	
Sable I.	**149**	44	0N		60	0W	
Sabrina Coast	**15**	68	0S		120	0	E
Sabzevār	**86**	36	15N		57	40	E
Saco	**148**	43	30N		70	27W	
Sacramento	**172**	38	33N		121	30	E
Sacramento →	**172**	38	3N		121	56W	
Sacramento Mts.	**161**	32	30N		105	30W	
Sado, Shima	**103**	38	15N		138	30	E
Safed Koh	**87**	34	0N		70	0	E
Saffron Walden	**25**	52	2N		0	15	E
Safi	**126**	32	18N		9	20W	
Saga	**108**	33	15N		130	16	E
Sagami-Nada	**107**	34	58N		139	30	E
Sagami-Wan	**107**	35	15N		139	25	E
Sagamihara	**107**	35	33N		139	25	E
Sagar	**91**	14	14N		75	6	E
Sagara	**107**	34	41N		138	12	E
Saginaw	**167**	43	26N		83	55W	
Saginaw B.	**167**	43	50N		83	40W	
Saglouc	**146**	62	14N		75	38W	
Sagres	**50**	37	0N		8	58W	
Sagua la Grande	**178**	22	50N		80	10W	
Saguenay →	**148**	48	22N		71	0W	
Sahara	**126**	23	0N		5	0	E
Saharanpur	**89**	29	58N		77	33	E
Saharien, Atlas	**127**	33	30N		1	0	E
Sahiwal	**89**	30	45N		73	8	E
Sahuaripa	**174**	29	3N		109	14W	
Saigō	**109**	36	12N		133	20	E
Saigon = Thanh Pho Ho Chi Minh	**95**	10	58N		106	40	E
Saijō, Ehime, Japan	**109**	33	55N		133	11	E
Saijō, Hiroshima, Japan	**109**	34	25N		132	45	E
Saikhoa Ghat	**93**	27	50N		95	40	E
Saiki	**108**	32	58N		131	51	E
Saimaa	**67**	61	15N		28	15	E
Şa'in Dezh	**81**	36	40N		46	25	E
St. Abb's Head	**31**	55	55N		2	10W	
St. Albans, U.K.	**25**	51	44N		0	19W	

Name	Page	Lat	N/S	Long	E/W
St. Albans, U.S.A.	151	44 49	N	73 7	W
St. Alban's Head	24	50 34	N	2 3	W
St. Albert	155	53 37	N	113 32	W
St. Andrews	31	56 20	N	2 48	W
St. Arnaud	119	36 40	S	143 16	E
St. Asaph	26	53 15	N	3 27	W
St-Augustin-Saguenay	141	51 13	N	58 38	W
St. Augustine	170	29 52	N	81 20	W
St. Austell	27	50 20	N	4 48	W
St. Bee's Hd.	28	54 30	N	3 38	E
St. Boniface	153	49 53	N	97 5	W
St. Bride's B.	26	51 48	N	5 15	W
St-Brieuc	36	48 30	N	2 46	W
St. Catharines	151	43 10	N	79 15	W
St. Charles	166	38 46	N	90 30	W
St. Christopher-Nevis ■	180	17 20	N	62 40	W
St. Cloud	156	45 30	N	94 11	W
St. Croix	180	17 45	N	64 45	W
St. David's	26	51 54	N	5 16	W
St. David's Head	26	51 55	N	5 16	W
St-Denis	39	48 56	N	2 22	E
St-Dizier	37	48 40	N	5 0	E
St. Elias, Mt.	144	60 14	N	140 50	W
St. Elias Mts.	144	60 33	N	139 28	W
St-Étienne	37	45 27	N	4 22	E
St-Félicien	151	48 40	N	72 25	W
St. Gallen	44	47 25	N	9 20	E
St. George, Australia	116	28 1	S	148 30	E
St. George, Bermuda	180	32 24	N	64 42	W
St. Georges, Fr. Guiana	185	4 0	N	52 0	W
St. George's, Grenada	180	12 5	N	61 43	W
St. George's Channel	20	52 0	N	6 0	W
St. Gotthard P. = San Gottardo, Paso del	44	46 33	N	8 33	E
St. Helena	125	15 55	S	5 44	W
St. Helena B.	136	32 40	S	18 10	E
St. Helens, Australia	119	41 20	S	148 15	E
St. Helens, U.K.	28	53 28	N	2 44	W
St. Helens, U.S.A.	171	45 55	N	122 50	W
St. Helier	36	49 11	N	2 6	W
St-Hyacinthe	151	45 40	N	72 58	W
St. Ives, Cambs., U.K.	25	52 20	N	0 5	W
St. Ives, Corn., U.K.	27	50 13	N	5 29	W
St-Jean	151	45 20	N	73 20	W
St-Jérôme	151	45 47	N	74 0	W
St. John	148	45 20	N	66 8	W
St. John's	149	47 35	N	52 40	W
St. John's →	170	30 20	N	81 30	W
St. Johnsbury	148	44 25	N	72 1	W
St. Joseph, Mich., U.S.A.	167	42 5	N	86 30	W
St. Joseph, Mo., U.S.A.	166	39 46	N	94 50	W
St. Kilda, N.Z.	123	45 53	S	170 31	E
St. Kilda, U.K.	22	57 9	N	8 34	W
St. Lawrence	149	46 54	N	55 23	W
St. Lawrence →	148	49 30	N	66 0	W
St. Lawrence, Gulf of	149	48 25	N	62 0	W
St. Lawrence I.	142	63 0	N	170 0	W
St. Leonard	148	47 12	N	67 58	W
St-Louis	130	16 8	N	16 27	W
St. Louis	166	38 40	N	90 12	W
St. Lucia ■	180	14 0	N	60 50	W
St. Maarten	180	18 0	N	63 5	W
St-Malo	36	48 39	N	2 1	W
St-Marc	180	19 10	N	72 41	W
St-Martin, I.	180	18 0	N	63 0	W
St. Mary Pk.	118	31 32	S	138 34	E
St. Marys	164	41 27	N	78 33	W
St. Matthews, I. = Zadetkyi Kyun	94	10 0	N	98 25	E
St. Michael's Mt.	27	50 7	N	5 30	W
St. Moritz	44	46 30	N	9 51	E
St-Nazaire	36	47 17	N	2 12	W
St. Neots	25	52 14	N	0 16	W
St-Omer	38	50 45	N	2 15	E
St. Pascal	148	47 32	N	69 48	W
St. Paul	166	44 54	N	93 5	W
St. Paul, I.	149	47 12	N	60 9	W
St-Petersburg = Sankt-Peterburg	68	59 55	N	30 20	E
St. Petersburg	170	27 45	N	82 40	W
St-Pierre et Miquelon □	149	46 55	N	56 10	W
St-Quentin	38	49 50	N	3 16	E
St-Raphaël	37	43 25	N	6 46	E
St-Servan-sur-Mer	36	48 38	N	2 0	W
St. Thomas, Canada	151	42 45	N	81 10	W
St. Thomas, W. Indies	180	18 21	N	64 55	W
St-Tropez	37	43 17	N	6 38	E
St. Vincent and the Grenadines ■	180	13 0	N	61 10	W
Ste-Adresse	38	49 31	N	0 5	E
Ste. Anne de Beaupré	148	47 2	N	70 58	W
Ste. Marie	180	14 48	N	61 1	W
Ste-Rose	180	16 20	N	61 45	W
Ste. Rose du lac	153	51 4	N	99 30	W
Saintes	36	45 45	N	0 37	W
Saintonge	36	45 40	N	0 50	W
Saito	108	32 3	N	131 24	E
Sajama	187	18 7	S	69 0	W
Sakai	106	34 30	N	135 30	E
Sakaide	109	34 15	N	133 50	E
Sakaiminato	109	35 38	N	133 11	E
Sakakawea, L.	163	47 30	N	102 0	W
Sakata	103	38 55	N	139 50	E
Sakhalin	79	51 0	N	143 0	E
Sakhalinskiy Zaliv	75	54 0	N	141 0	E
Saku	107	36 17	N	138 31	E
Sakura	107	35 43	N	140 14	E
Sakurai	106	34 30	N	135 51	E
Salaberry-de-Valleyfield	151	45 15	N	74 8	W
Salado →	190	31 40	S	60 41	W
Salado, R. →	176	26 52	N	99 19	W
Salamanca, Spain	50	40 58	N	5 39	W
Salamanca, U.S.A.	164	42 10	N	78 42	W
Salamis	55	37 56	N	23 30	E
Salcombe	27	50 14	N	3 47	W
Sale	117	38 6	S	147 6	E
Salem, India	90	11 40	N	78 11	E
Salem, Mass., U.S.A.	164	42 29	N	70 53	W
Salem, Oreg., U.S.A.	171	45 0	N	123 0	W
Salem, Va., U.S.A.	165	37 19	N	80 8	W
Salerno	49	40 40	N	14 44	E
Salford	28	53 30	N	2 17	W
Salida	163	38 35	N	106 0	W
Salina, Italy	49	38 35	N	14 50	E
Salina, U.S.A.	161	38 50	N	97 40	W
Salina Cruz	177	16 10	N	95 12	W
Salinas, Ecuador	184	2 10	S	80 58	W
Salinas, U.S.A.	173	36 40	N	121 41	W
Salinas →	173	36 45	N	121 48	W
Salinas Grandes	190	30 0	S	65 0	W
Salisbury = Harare	137	17 43	S	31 2	E
Salisbury, U.K.	24	51 4	N	1 48	W
Salisbury, Md., U.S.A.	165	38 20	N	75 38	W
Salisbury, N.C., U.S.A.	165	35 20	N	80 29	W
Salisbury Plain	24	51 13	N	1 50	W
Salle, La	166	41 20	N	89 6	W
Salmon	162	45 12	N	113 56	W
Salmon →	171	45 51	N	116 46	W
Salmon Arm	155	50 40	N	119 15	W
Salmon River Mts.	162	45 0	N	114 30	W
Salon-de-Provence	37	43 39	N	5 6	E
Salonica = Thessaloniki	54	40 38	N	22 58	E
Salop = Shropshire □	24	52 36	N	2 45	W
Salt Fork →	161	36 37	N	97 7	W
Salt Lake City	163	40 45	N	111 58	W
Salta	190	24 57	S	65 25	W
Saltcoats	30	55 38	N	4 47	W
Saltillo	174	25 25	N	101 0	W
Salto	191	31 27	S	57 50	W
Salton Sea	173	33 20	N	115 50	W
Salûm	128	31 31	N	25 7	E
Salvador	189	13 0	S	38 30	W
Salween →	93	16 31	N	97 37	E
Salzburg	45	47 48	N	13 2	E
Salzburg □	45	47 15	N	13 0	E
Salzgitter	43	52 13	N	10 22	E
Sam Neua	95	20 29	N	104 0	E
Sama	69	60 12	N	60 22	E
Samangán □	87	36 15	N	68 3	E
Samar	112	12 0	N	125 0	E
Samara	68	53 8	N	50 6	E
Samarkand	70	39 40	N	66 55	E
Sāmarrā	81	34 12	N	43 52	E
Sambalpur	92	21 28	N	84 4	E

Sambhal	89	28	35N	78	37 E
Sámos	55	37	45N	26	50 E
Samothráki	55	40	28N	25	28 E
Samsun	80	41	15N	36	22 E
Samut Prakan	95	13	32N	100	40 E
Samut Sakhon	94	13	31N	100	13 E
Samut Songkhram ⟶	94	13	24N	100	1 E
San Andreas	172	38	0N	120	39W
San Andres Mts.	161	33	0N	106	45W
San Andrés Tuxtla	177	18	27N	95	13W
San Angelo	161	31	30N	100	30W
San Antonio, Chile	190	33	40S	71	40W
San Antonio, U.S.A.	161	29	30N	98	30W
San Antonio, C., Argentina	191	36	15S	56	40W
San Antonio, C., Cuba	178	21	50N	84	57W
San Antonio de los Baños	178	22	54N	82	31W
San Antônio Falls	182	9	30S	65	0W
San Antonio Oeste	192	40	40S	65	0W
San Bernardino	173	34	7N	117	18W
San Bernardino Str.	112	13	0N	125	0 E
San Bernardo	190	33	40S	70	50W
San Blas, C.	169	29	40N	85	12W
San Carlos, Chile	190	36	10S	72	0W
San Carlos, Mexico	174	29	1N	100	51W
San Carlos, Nic.	179	11	12N	84	50W
San Carlos de Bariloche	192	41	10S	71	25W
San Clemente I.	173	32	53N	118	30W
San Cristóbal, Argentina	190	30	20S	61	10W
San Cristóbal, Dom. Rep.	180	18	25N	70	6W
San Cristóbal, Venezuela	184	16	50N	92	40W
San Cristóbal de las Casas	177	16	45N	92	38W
San Diego	173	32	43N	117	10W
San Felipe, Chile	190	32	43S	70	42W
San Felipe, Colombia	184	1	55N	67	6W
San Fernando, Chile	190	34	30S	71	0W
San Fernando, Mexico	174	30	0N	115	10W
San Fernando, Trin. & Tob.	180	10	20N	61	30W
San Fernando, U.S.A.	173	34	15N	118	29W
San Fernando de Apure	184	7	54N	67	15W
San Francisco	172	37	47N	122	30W
San Francisco de Macorís	180	19	19N	70	15W
San Francisco del Oro	174	26	52N	105	51W
San Gabriel	191	0	36N	77	49W
San Gottardo, Paso del	44	46	33N	8	33 E
San Ignacio	187	16	20S	60	55W
San Joaquin ⟶	172	37	4N	121	51W
San Jorge, Golfo	192	46	0S	66	0W
San Jorge, G. de	51	40	50N	0	55W
San José, Bolivia	187	17	53S	60	50W
San José, Costa Rica	179	10	0N	84	2W
San José, U.S.A.	172	37	20N	121	53W
San José de Mayo	191	34	27S	56	40W
San José del Cabo	175	23	3N	109	41W
San José del Guaviare	184	2	35N	72	38W
San Juan, Argentina	190	31	30S	68	30W
San Juan, Dom. Rep.	180	18	49N	71	12W
San Juan, Puerto Rico	180	18	28N	66	8W
San Juan ⟶	179	10	56N	83	42W
San Juan de los Morros	184	9	55N	67	21W
San Juan Mts.	163	38	30N	108	30W
San Julián	192	49	15S	67	45W
San Leandro	172	37	40N	122	6W
San Lorenzo	184	1	15N	78	50W
San Lucas, C. de	175	22	50N	110	0W
San Luis	190	33	20S	66	20W
San Luis de la Paz	177	21	18N	100	31W
San Luis Obispo	173	35	21N	120	38W
San Luis Potosí	177	22	9N	100	59W
San Luis Potosí □	177	22	30N	100	30W
San Marcos	177	14	59N	91	52W
San Marino ■	47	43	56N	12	25 E
San Mateo	172	37	32N	122	19W
San Matías	187	16	25S	58	20W
San Matías, Golfo	192	41	30S	64	0W
San Miguel	177	13	30N	88	12W
San Miguel de Tucumán	190	26	50S	65	20W
San Pedro ⟶	175	21	45N	105	30W
San Pedro de las Colonias	174	25	45N	102	59W
San Pedro de Macorís	180	18	30N	69	18W
San Pedro Sula	177	15	30N	88	0W
San Rafael, Argentina	190	34	40S	68	21W
San Rafael, U.S.A.	172	37	59N	122	32W

San Roque	190	28	25S	58	45W
San Salvador, Bahamas	178	24	0N	74	40W
San Salvador, El Salv.	177	13	40N	89	10W
San Salvador de Jujuy	190	24	10S	64	48W
San Sebastián	51	43	17N	1	58W
San Valentin, Mte.	192	46	30S	73	30W
Sana'	82	15	27N	44	12 E
Sanandaj	81	35	18N	47	1 E
Sancti-Spíritus	178	21	52N	79	33W
Sanda	106	34	53N	135	14 E
Sandgate	116	27	18S	153	3 E
Sandomierz	58	50	40N	21	43 E
Sandpoint	171	48	20N	116	34W
Sandringham	29	52	50N	0	30 E
Sandstone	120	27	59S	119	16 E
Sandusky	167	41	25N	82	40W
Sandwip Chan.	93	22	35N	91	35 E
Sandy C.	119	41	25S	144	45 E
Sandy Lake	153	53	0N	93	15W
Sanford, Fla., U.S.A.	170	28	45N	81	20W
Sanford, Maine, U.S.A.	148	43	28N	70	47W
Sanford, N.C., U.S.A.	165	35	30N	79	10W
Sangay	184	2	0S	78	20W
Sangihe, P.	113	3	45N	125	30 E
Sangli	91	16	55N	74	33 E
Sangre de Cristo Mts.	161	37	0N	105	0W
Sankt-Peterburg	68	59	55N	30	20 E
Sankuru ⟶	134	4	17S	20	25 E
Sanliurfa	81	37	12N	38	50 E
Sano	107	36	19N	139	35 E
Sanok	59	49	35N	22	10 E
Sanquhar	31	55	21N	3	56W
Sanshui	99	23	10N	112	56 E
Santa Ana, Bolivia	187	13	50S	65	40W
Santa Ana, Mexico	174	30	33N	111	7W
Santa Ana, U.S.A.	173	33	48N	117	55W
Santa Bárbara, Mexico	174	26	48N	105	49W
Santa Barbara, U.S.A.	173	34	25N	119	40W
Santa Barbara I.	160	33	29N	119	2W
Santa Catarina □	191	27	25S	48	30W
Santa Clara, Cuba	178	22	20N	80	0W
Santa Clara, U.S.A.	162	37	21N	122	0W
Santa Clotilde	186	2	33S	73	45W
Santa Cruz, Bolivia	187	17	43S	63	10W
Santa Cruz, U.S.A.	172	36	55N	122	1W
Santa Cruz, Is.	122	10	30S	166	0 E
Santa Cruz de Tenerife	126	28	28N	16	15W
Santa Cruz del Sur	178	20	44N	78	0W
Santa Cruz do Sul	191	29	42S	52	25W
Santa Fe, Argentina	190	31	35S	60	41W
Santa Fe, U.S.A.	161	35	40N	106	0W
Santa Inés, I.	192	54	0S	73	0W
Santa Isabel = Rey Malabo	131	3	45N	8	50 E
Santa Lucia Range	173	36	0N	121	20W
Santa Maria, Brazil	191	29	40S	53	48W
Santa Maria, U.S.A.	173	34	58N	120	29W
Santa Maria da Vitória	188	13	24S	44	12W
Santa Maria di Leuca, C.	49	39	48N	18	20 E
Santa Marta	184	11	15N	74	13W
Santa Maura = Levkás	54	38	40N	20	43 E
Santa Monica	173	34	0N	118	30W
Santa Rosa, Argentina	190	36	40S	64	17W
Santa Rosa, U.S.A.	172	38	26N	122	43W
Santa Rosa I., Calif., U.S.A.	173	34	0N	120	6W
Santa Rosa I., Fla., U.S.A.	169	30	23N	87	0W
Santa Rosalía	174	27	19N	112	17W
Santana do Livramento	191	30	55S	55	30W
Santander	50	43	27N	3	51W
Santander Jiménez	176	24	13N	98	28W
Santarém, Brazil	185	2	25S	54	42W
Santarém, Portugal	50	39	12N	8	42W
Santiago, Brazil	191	29	11S	54	52W
Santiago, Chile	190	33	24S	70	40W
Santiago, Panama	179	8	0N	81	0W
Santiago de Compostela	50	42	52N	8	37W
Santiago de Cuba	178	20	0N	75	49W
Santiago de los Cabelleros	180	19	30N	70	40W
Santiago del Estero	190	27	50S	64	15W
Santiago Ixcuintla	175	21	50N	105	11W
Santo Amaro	189	12	30S	38	43W
Santo Ângelo	191	28	15S	54	15W
Santo Domingo	180	18	30N	64	54W

Place	Ref	Lat	Lat	N/S	Long	Long	E/W
Santo Tomé	191	28	40S		56	5W	
Santoña	50	43	29N		3	27W	
Santos	191	24	0S		46	20W	
São Borja	191	28	39S		56	0W	
São Carlos	188	22	0S		47	50W	
São Francisco →	189	10	30S		36	24W	
São Francisco do Sul	191	26	15S		48	36W	
São João del Rei	188	21	8S		44	15W	
São José do Rio Prêto	188	20	50S		49	20W	
São Leopoldo	191	29	50S		51	10W	
São Lourenço	188	22	7S		45	3W	
São Luís	188	2	39S		44	15W	
São Paulo	191	23	32S		46	37W	
São Paulo □	188	22	0S		49	0W	
São Paulo de Olivença	184	3	27S		68	48W	
São Roque, C. de	189	5	30S		35	16W	
São Tomé	131	0	10N		6	39 E	
São Tomé & Principe ■	131	0	12N		6	39 E	
São Vicente, Cabo de	50	37	0N		9	0W	
Saône →	37	45	44N		4	50 E	
Sapporo	103	43	0N		141	21 E	
Sapulpa	168	36	0N		96	0W	
Saqqez	81	36	15N		46	20 E	
Sar Planina	52	42	10N		21	0 E	
Saragossa = Zaragoza	51	41	39N		0	53W	
Sarajevo	52	43	52N		18	26 E	
Saranac Lake	151	44	20N		74	10W	
Sarangani B.	112	6	0N		125	13 E	
Saransk	68	54	10N		45	10 E	
Sarapul	69	56	28N		53	48 E	
Sarasota	165	27	20N		82	30W	
Saratoga Springs	164	43	5N		73	47W	
Saratov	68	51	30N		46	2 E	
Sarawak □	111	2	0N		113	0 E	
Sardegna	48	39	57N		9	0 E	
Sardinia = Sardegna	48	39	57N		9	0 E	
Sargodha	89	32	10N		72	40 E	
Sarh	131	9	5N		18	23 E	
Sārī	86	36	30N		53	4 E	
Sarina	121	21	22S		149	13 E	
Sarmiento	192	45	35S		69	5W	
Sarnia	150	42	58N		82	23W	
Saronikós Kólpos	55	37	45N		23	45 E	
Sarre = Saar →	42	49	41N		6	32 E	
Sarre, La	151	48	45N		79	15W	
Sarthe →	36	47	33N		0	31W	
Sasaram	92	24	57N		84	5 E	
Sasebo	108	33	10N		129	43 E	
Saskatchewan □	152	54	40N		106	0W	
Saskatchewan →	152	53	37N		100	40W	
Saskatoon	152	52	10N		106	38W	
Sassandra	130	5	0N		6	8W	
Sássari	48	40	44N		8	33 E	
Sata-Misaki	108	30	59N		130	40 E	
Satara	91	17	44N		73	58 E	
Satmala Hills	91	20	15N		74	40 E	
Satna	92	24	35N		80	50 E	
Satpura Ra.	91	21	25N		76	10 E	
Sattahip	95	12	41N		100	54 E	
Satu Mare	56	47	46N		22	55 E	
Sauðarkrókur	64	65	45N		19	40W	
Saudi Arabia ■	82	26	0N		44	0 E	
Sault Ste. Marie, Canada	150	46	30N		84	20W	
Sault Ste. Marie, U.S.A.	150	46	27N		84	22W	
Saumur	36	47	15N		0	5W	
Sava →	52	44	50N		20	26 E	
Savanna la Mar	180	18	10N		78	10W	
Savannah	170	32	4N		81	4W	
Savannah →	170	32	2N		80	53W	
Savannakhet	95	16	30N		104	49 E	
Savoie □	37	45	26N		6	35 E	
Savona	46	44	19N		8	29 E	
Sawankhalok	94	17	19N		99	50 E	
Sawara	107	35	55N		140	30 E	
Sawatch Mts.	163	38	30N		106	30W	
Sawu, I.	113	10	35S		121	50 E	
Sawu Sea	113	9	30S		121	50 E	
Saxony, Lower = Niedersachsen □	42	52	45N		9	0 E	
Sayan, Zapadnyy	77	52	30N		94	0 E	
Saydā	80	33	35N		35	25 E	
Sayḥut	83	15	12N		51	10 E	
Sayula	175	19	52N		103	36W	
Sazan	52	40	30N		19	20 E	
Scafell Pikes	28	54	26N		3	14W	
Scalloway	30	60	9N		1	16W	
Scandinavia	16	64	0N		12	0 E	
Scapa Flow	33	58	52N		3	6W	
Scarborough	29	54	17N		0	24W	
Schaffhausen	44	47	42N		8	39 E	
Schefferville	146	54	48N		66	50W	
Schelde →	42	51	15N		4	16 E	
Schenectady	164	42	50N		73	58W	
Scheveningen	40	52	6N		4	16 E	
Schiedam	40	51	55N		4	25 E	
Schiermonnikoog	41	53	30N		6	15 E	
Schleswig-Holstein □	42	54	10N		9	40 E	
Schouten I.	119	42	20S		148	20 E	
Schouten Is.	113	1	0S		136	0 E	
Schouwen	40	51	43N		3	45 E	
Schreiber	150	48	45N		87	20W	
Schwäbische Alb	42	48	30N		9	30 E	
Schwarzwald	42	48	0N		8	0 E	
Schwerin	43	53	37N		11	22 E	
Schwyz	44	47	2N		8	39 E	
Scilly, Isles of	20	49	55N		6	15W	
Scone, Australia	116	32	5S		150	52 E	
Scone, U.K.	31	56	25N		3	26W	
Scoresbysund	13	70	20N		23	0W	
Scotia Sea	14	56	5S		56	0W	
Scotland □	23	57	0N		4	0W	
Scottsbluff	163	41	55N		103	35W	
Scottsdale	119	41	9S		147	31 E	
Scranton	164	41	22N		75	41W	
Scunthorpe	29	53	35N		0	38W	
Scutari = Üsküdar	80	41	0N		29	5 E	
Seaforth	150	43	35N		81	25W	
Searcy	168	35	15N		91	45W	
Seascale	28	54	24N		3	29W	
Seattle	171	47	41N		122	15W	
Sebastián Vizcaino, B.	174	28	0N		114	30W	
Sebastopol = Sevastopol	68	44	35N		33	30 E	
Sebring	170	27	30N		81	26W	
Sebta = Ceuta	126	35	52N		5	18W	
Sebuku, Teluk	111	4	0N		118	10 E	
Sechura, Desierto de	186	6	0S		80	30W	
Seclin	38	50	33N		3	2 E	
Sedalia	166	38	40N		93	18W	
Segamat	96	2	30N		102	50 E	
Ségou	130	13	30N		6	16W	
Segovia = Coco →	179	15	0N		83	8W	
Segovia	50	40	57N		4	10W	
Séguéla	130	7	55N		6	40W	
Segura →	51	38	6N		0	54W	
Seine →	38	49	26N		0	26 E	
Seistan	85	30	50N		61	0 E	
Seki	106	35	29N		136	55 E	
Sekondi-Takoradi	130	4	58N		1	45W	
Selangor □	96	3	10N		101	30 E	
Selby	29	53	47N		1	5W	
Sélibabi	130	15	10N		12	15W	
Selkirk, Canada	153	50	10N		96	55W	
Selkirk, U.K.	31	55	33N		2	50W	
Selkirk Mts.	155	51	15N		117	40W	
Selma, Ala., U.S.A.	169	32	30N		87	0W	
Selma, Calif., U.S.A.	173	36	39N		119	39W	
Selsey Bill	24	50	44N		0	47W	
Selvas	187	6	30S		67	0W	
Semarang	111	7	0S		110	26 E	
Seminole	168	35	15N		96	45W	
Semipalatinsk	71	50	30N		80	10 E	
Semnān	86	35	55N		53	25 E	
Semnān □	86	36	0N		54	0 E	
Sendai, Kagoshima, Japan	108	31	50N		130	20 E	
Sendai, Miyagi, Japan	103	38	15N		140	53 E	
Senegal ■	130	14	30N		14	30W	
Senegal →	126	15	48N		16	32W	
Senge Khambab = Indus →	88	24	20N		67	47 E	
Senhor-do-Bonfim	189	10	30S		40	10W	
Senja I.	64	69	15N		17	30 E	
Senlis	39	49	13N		2	35 E	
Sennâr	129	13	30N		33	35 E	
Senneterre	151	48	25N		77	15W	

Name	Map	Lat	Long
Sens	39	48 11N	3 15 E
Senta	52	45 55N	20 3 E
Seoul = Sŏul	98	37 31N	126 58 E
Sept-Îles	148	50 13N	66 22W
Seram	113	3 10S	129 0 E
Seram Sea	113	2 30S	128 30 E
Seremban	96	2 43N	101 53 E
Serena, La	190	29 55S	71 10W
Sereth = Siret ~►	57	47 58N	26 5 E
Sergipe □	189	10 30S	37 30W
Sérifos	55	37 9N	24 30 E
Serny Zavod	70	39 59N	58 50 E
Serov	69	59 29N	60 35 E
Serowe	137	22 25S	26 43 E
Serpukhov	68	54 55N	37 28 E
Serra do Navio	185	0 59N	52 3W
Sèrrai	55	41 5N	23 31 E
Sesheke	134	17 29S	24 13 E
Setana	103	42 26N	139 51 E
Sète	37	43 25N	3 42 E
Sétif	127	36 9N	5 26 E
Seto	106	35 14N	137 6 E
Setonaikai	109	34 20N	133 30 E
Settle	28	54 5N	2 18W
Setúbal	50	38 30N	8 58W
Sevastopol	68	44 35N	33 30 E
Seven Sisters	154	54 56N	128 10W
Severn ~►, Canada	140	56 2N	87 36W
Severn ~►, U.K.	24	51 35N	2 38W
Severnaya Zemlya	72	79 0N	100 0 E
Severodinsk	69	64 27N	39 58 E
Sevilla	50	37 23N	6 0W
Seville = Sevilla	50	37 23N	6 0W
Seward	142	60 6N	149 26W
Seward Pen.	142	65 0N	164 0W
Seychelles ■	78	5 0S	56 0 E
Seyðisfjörður	64	65 16N	14 0W
Seymour	117	37 0S	145 10 E
Seyne-sur-Mer, La	37	43 7N	5 52 E
Sézanne	39	48 40N	3 40 E
Sfax	127	34 49N	10 48 E
Sfintu Gheorghe	57	45 52N	25 48 E
Shaanxi □	99	35 0N	109 0 E
Shaba □	135	8 0S	25 0 E
Shache	100	38 20N	77 10 E
Shaftesbury	24	51 0N	2 12W
Shahdād	85	30 30N	57 40 E
Shakhty	68	47 40N	40 16 E
Shamo = Gobi	98	44 0N	111 0 E
Shamokin	164	40 47N	76 33W
Shan □	93	21 30N	98 30 E
Shandong □	99	36 0N	118 0 E
Shanghai	99	31 15N	121 26 E
Shangqiu	99	34 26N	115 36 E
Shangrao	99	28 25N	117 59 E
Shangshui	99	33 42N	114 35 E
Shannon ~►	35	52 35N	9 30W
Shansi = Shanxi □	98	37 0N	112 0 E
Shantou	99	23 18N	116 40 E
Shantung = Shandong □	99	36 0N	118 0 E
Shanxi □	98	37 0N	112 0 E
Shaoguan	99	24 48N	113 35 E
Shaoxing	99	30 0N	120 35 E
Shaoyang	99	27 14N	111 25 E
Shap	28	54 32N	2 40W
Sharjah = Ash Shāriqah	85	25 23N	55 26 E
Shark B.	120	25 55S	113 32 E
Sharon	164	41 18N	80 30W
Shashi	99	30 25N	112 14 E
Shasta, Mt.	172	41 30N	122 12W
Shasta L.	172	40 50N	122 15W
Shaunavon	152	49 35N	108 25W
Shawano	167	44 45N	88 38W
Shawinigan	151	46 35N	72 50W
Shawnee	168	35 15N	97 0W
Shcherbakov = Andropov	68	58 5N	38 50 E
Shebele, Wabi ~►	133	2 0N	44 0 E
Sheboygan	167	43 46N	87 45W
Sheerness	24	51 26N	0 47 E
Sheffield	28	53 23N	1 28W
Shekhupura	89	31 42N	73 58 E
Shelburne	148	43 47N	65 20W
Shelby, Mont., U.S.A.	163	48 30N	111 52W
Shelby, N.C., U.S.A.	165	35 18N	81 34W
Shelbyville, Ind., U.S.A.	167	39 30N	85 42W
Shelbyville, Tenn., U.S.A.	169	35 30N	86 25W
Shelikhova, Zaliv	73	59 30N	157 0 E
Shellharbour	117	34 31S	150 51 E
Shelton	171	47 15N	123 6W
Shenandoah	166	40 50N	95 25W
Shensi = Shaanxi □	99	35 0N	109 0 E
Shenyang	98	41 50N	123 25 E
Shepparton	117	36 23S	145 26 E
Sheppey, I. of	24	51 23N	0 50 E
Sherborne	27	50 56N	2 31W
Sherbrooke	148	45 28N	71 57W
Sheridan	163	44 50N	107 0W
Sherman	168	33 40N	96 35W
Sherridon	152	55 8N	101 5W
Sherwood Forest	29	53 5N	1 5W
Shetland Is.	30	60 30N	1 30W
Shibām	83	16 0N	48 36 E
Shibata	103	37 57N	139 20 E
Shibetsu	103	44 10N	142 23 E
Shibukawa	107	36 29N	139 0 E
Shibushi-Wan	108	31 24N	131 8 E
Shiel, L.	32	56 48N	5 32W
Shihchiachuangi = Shijiazhuang	98	38 2N	114 28 E
Shijiazhuang	98	38 2N	114 28 E
Shikarpur	88	27 57N	68 39 E
Shikine-Jima	107	34 19N	139 13 E
Shikoku	109	33 30N	133 30 E
Shikoku □	109	33 30N	133 30 E
Shikoku-Sanchi	109	33 30N	133 30 E
Shillong	93	25 35N	91 53 E
Shimabara	108	32 48N	130 20 E
Shimada	107	34 49N	138 10 E
Shimizu	107	35 0N	138 30 E
Shimo-Jima	108	32 15N	130 7 E
Shimo-Koshiki-Jima	108	31 40N	129 43 E
Shimoda	107	34 40N	138 57 E
Shimodate	107	36 20N	139 55 E
Shimoga	90	13 57N	75 32 E
Shimonoseki	108	33 58N	131 0 E
Shin, L.	33	58 7N	4 30W
Shin-Tone ~►	107	35 44N	140 51 E
Shinano ~►	105	36 50N	138 30 E
Shingū	106	33 40N	135 55 E
Shinji Ko	109	35 26N	132 57 E
Shinjō	103	38 46N	140 18 E
Shinminato	106	36 47N	137 4 E
Shinshiro	106	34 54N	137 30 E
Shio-no-Misaki	106	33 25N	135 45 E
Shiogama	103	38 19N	141 1 E
Shiojiri	107	36 6N	137 58 E
Shipka	53	42 46N	25 33 E
Shirane-San, Gumma, Japan	107	36 48N	139 22 E
Shirane-San, Yamanashi, Japan	107	35 42N	138 9 E
Shīrāz	85	29 42N	52 30 E
Shire ~►	137	17 42S	35 19 E
Shiriya-Zaki	103	41 25N	141 30 E
Shivpuri	91	25 26N	77 42 E
Shizuoka	107	35 0N	138 24 E
Shkoder = Shkodra	52	42 6N	19 20 E
Shkodra	52	42 6N	19 20 E
Shkumbini ~►	52	41 5N	19 50 E
Shō-Gawa ~►	106	36 47N	137 4 E
Shōbara	109	34 51N	133 1 E
Shoeburyness	24	51 31N	0 49 E
Sholapur = Solapur	91	17 43N	75 56 E
Shoshone	172	43 0N	114 27W
Shreveport	168	32 30N	93 50W
Shrewsbury	28	52 42N	2 45W
Shrirampur	92	22 44N	88 21 E
Shropshire □	24	52 36N	2 45W
Shuangyashan	98	46 37N	131 22 E
Siahan Range	88	27 30N	64 40 E
Sialkot	89	32 32N	74 30 E
Siam = Thailand ■	95	16 0N	102 0 E
Sian = Xi'an	99	34 15N	109 0 E

Name	Page	Latitude	Longitude
Siberia	77	60 0N	100 0 E
Siberut	111	1 30S	99 0 E
Sibi	88	29 30N	67 54 E
Sibiu	57	45 45N	24 9 E
Sichuan □	99	31 0N	104 0 E
Sicilia	49	37 30N	14 30 E
Sicily = Sicilia	49	37 30N	14 30 E
Sicuani	187	14 21S	71 10W
Sidi-bel-Abbès	127	35 13N	,0 39W
Sidlaw Hills	31	56 32N	3 10W
Sidley, Mt.	15	77 2S	126 2W
Sidmouth	27	50 40N	3 13W
Sidney	154	48 39N	123 24W
Sidon = Saydā	80	33 35N	35 25 E
Sidra, G. of = Surt, Khalīj	127	31 40N	18 30 E
Siedlce	58	52 10N	22 20 E
Siena	46	43 20N	11 20 E
Sierra Blanca Pk.	161	33 20N	105 54W
Sierra Leone ■	130	9 0N	12 0W
Sifnos	55	37 0N	24 45 E
Siglufjörður	64	66 12N	18 55W
Sihanoukville = Kompong			
Som	95	10 38N	103 30 E
Siirt	81	37 57N	41 55 E
Sikar	89	27 33N	75 10 E
Sikeston	169	36 52N	89 35W
Sikhote Alin, Khrebet	75	46 0N	136 0 E
Sikinos	55	36 40N	25 8 E
Sikkim □	92	27 50N	88 30 E
Silchar	93	24 49N	92 48 E
Silesia = Slask	58	51 0N	16 30 E
Siling Co	101	31 50N	89 20 E
Silloth	28	54 53N	3 25W
Simbirsk	68	54 20N	48 25 E
Simcoe	151	42 50N	80 20W
Simenga	74	62 42N	108 25 E
Simeulue	111	2 45N	95 45 E
Simferopol	68	44 55N	34 3 E
Simi Valley	173	34 16N	118 47W
Simla	89	31 2N	77 9 E
Simplon Pass	44	46 15N	8 0 E
Simushir, Ostrov	75	46 50N	152 30 E
Sinai = Es Sînâ'	128	29 0N	34 0 E
Sinaloa	174	25 50N	108 20W
Sinaloa □	174	25 0N	107 30W
Sincelejo	184	9 18N	75 24W
Sinclair Mills	155	54 5N	121 40W
Sind □	88	26 0N	69 0 E
Sind Sagar Doab	89	32 0N	71 30 E
Singa	129	13 10N	33 57 E
Singapore ■	96	1 17N	103 51 E
Singapore, Straits of	96	1 15N	104 0 E
Singkaling Hkamti	92	26 0N	95 39 E
Singleton	117	32 33S	151 0 E
Singora = Songkhla	97	7 13N	100 37 E
Sinkiang Uighur = Xinjiang			
Uygur Zizhiqu □	100	42 0N	86 0 E
Sioux City	166	42 32N	96 25W
Sioux Falls	166	43 35N	96 40W
Sioux Lookout	153	50 10N	91 50W
Siping	98	43 8N	124 21 E
Sipora	111	2 18S	99 40 E
Siracusa	49	37 4N	15 17 E
Sirajganj	92	24 25N	89 47 E
Siret →	57	47 58N	26 5 E
Síros	55	37 28N	24 57 E
Sitapur	92	27 38N	80 45 E
Sitka	143	57 9N	135 20W
Sittard	41	51 0N	5 52 E
Sivas	80	39 43N	36 58 E
Siverek	81	37 50N	39 19 E
Sivrihisar	80	39 30N	31 35 E
Sîwa	128	29 11N	25 31 E
Siwalik Range	92	28 0N	83 0 E
Sizewell	24	52 13N	1 38 E
Sjumen = Kolarovgrad	53	43 18N	26 55 E
Skadarsko Jezero	52	42 10N	19 20 E
Skagerrak	60	57 30N	9 0 E
Skagway	143	59 23N	135 20W
Skaraborgs län □	60	58 20N	13 30 E
Skeena →	154	54 9N	130 5W
Skegness	29	53 9N	0 20 E
Skellefte →	66	65 30N	18 30 E
Skellefteå	67	64 45N	20 58 E
Skerries, The	26	53 27N	4 40W
Skiddaw	28	54 39N	3 9W
Skien	60	59 12N	9 35 E
Skierniewice	58	51 58N	20 10 E
Skikda	127	36 50N	6 58 E
Skipton	28	53 57N	2 1W
Skíros	55	38 55N	24 34 E
Skopje	52	42 1N	21 32 E
Skowhegan	148	44 49N	69 40W
Skull	35	51 32N	9 40W
Skye	32	57 15N	6 10W
Skyros = Skíros	55	38 55N	24 34 E
Slaney →	35	52 52N	6 45W
Slask	58	51 0N	16 30 E
Slave →	145	61 18N	113 39W
Slave Coast	124	6 0N	2 30 E
Sleaford	29	53 0N	0 22W
Sliedrecht	40	51 50N	4 45 E
Slieve Aughty	35	53 4N	8 30W
Slieve Bloom	35	53 4N	7 40W
Slieve Donard	34	54 10N	5 57W
Slieve Mish	35	52 12N	9 50W
Slievenamon	35	52 25N	7 37W
Sligo	34	54 17N	8 28W
Sligo □	34	54 10N	8 35W
Slovak Republic ■	59	48 30N	20 0 E
Slovakian Ore Mts. =			
Slovenské Rudohorie	59	48 45N	20 0 E
Slovenia ■	52	45 58N	14 30 E
Slovenské Rudohorie	59	48 45N	20 0 E
Słupsk	58	54 30N	17 3 E
Slyne Hd.	34	53 25N	10 10W
Smara	126	32 9N	8 16W
Smithers	154	54 45N	127 10W
Smithfield	165	35 31N	78 10W
Smiths Falls	151	44 55N	76 0W
Smithton	119	40 53S	145 6 E
Smolensk	68	54 45N	32 0 E
Smolikas, Óros	54	40 9N	20 58 E
Smyrna = İzmir	80	38 25N	27 8 E
Snæfell, Iceland	64	64 48N	15 34W
Snaefell, U.K.	28	54 18N	4 26W
Snæfellsjökull	64	64 49N	23 46W
Snake →	171	46 12N	119 2W
Sneek	41	53 2N	5 40 E
Snowdon	26	53 4N	4 8W
Snowdrift	145	62 24N	110 44W
Snowy Mts.	117	36 30S	148 20 E
Sobat →	129	8 32N	32 40 E
Sobral	177	3 50S	40 20W
Soch'e = Shache	100	38 20N	77 10 E
Sochi	70	43 35N	39 40 E
Société, Is. de la	123	17 0S	151 0W
Society Is. = Société, Is. de			
la	123	17 0S	151 0W
Socorro	161	34 4N	106 54W
Socotra	78	12 30N	54 0 E
Söderhamn	60	61 18N	17 10 E
Södermanlands län □	60	59 10N	16 30 E
Södertälje	60	59 12N	17 39 E
Sodo	132	7 0N	37 41 E
Sofala	137	33 4S	149 43 E
Sofia = Sofiya	53	42 45N	23 20 E
Sofiya	53	42 45N	23 20 E
Sogn og Fjordane fylke □	60	61 40N	6 0 E
Soissons	39	49 25N	3 19 E
Sôja	109	34 40N	133 45 E
Söke	80	37 48N	27 28 E
Sol Iletsk	70	51 10N	55 0 E
Solapur	91	17 43N	75 56 E
Soledad, Colombia	184	10 55N	74 46W
Soledad, Venezuela	185	8 10N	63 34W
Solent, The	24	50 45N	1 25W
Solesmes	38	50 10N	3 30 E
Solikamsk	69	59 38N	56 50 E
Solimões = Amazonas →	185	0 5S	50 0W
Sóller	51	39 46N	2 43 E
Sololá	177	14 49N	91 10 E

Solomon Is. ■	122	6	0S	155	0 E
Solţānābād	86	36	29N	58	5 E
Solway Firth	31	54	45N	3	38W
Somali Rep. ■	133	7	0N	47	0 E
Sombor	52	45	46N	19	9 E
Sombrerete	175	23	38N	103	39W
Somerset, Bermuda	180	32	16N	64	55W
Somerset, U.S.A.	169	37	5N	84	40W
Somerset □	27	51	9N	3	0W
Somerset I.	145	73	30N	93	0W
Somme □	36	50	0N	2	20 E
Somport, Puerto de	51	42	48N	0	31W
Søndre Strømfjord	147	66	59N	50	40W
Songkhla	97	7	13N	100	37 E
Sonora □	174	29	20N	110	40W
Soochow = Suzhou	99	31	19N	120	38 E
Sop's Arm	149	49	46N	56	56W
Sør-Rondane	14	72	0S	25	0 E
Sør-Trøndelag fylke □	65	63	0N	10	0 E
Sorata	187	15	50S	68	40W
Sorel	151	46	0N	73	10W
Soria	51	41	43N	2	32W
Sorocaba	191	23	31S	47	27W
Sørøya	67	70	40N	22	30 E
Sorsogon	112	13	0N	124	0 E
Sosnowiec	58	50	20N	19	10 E
Sotteville-lès-Rouen	38	49	24N	1	5 E
Sŏul	98	37	31N	126	58 E
Souris, Man., Canada	153	49	40N	100	20W
Souris, P.E.I., Canada	149	46	21N	62	15W
South Africa, Rep. of ■	136	32	0S	17	0 E
South Australia □	118	32	0S	139	0 E
South Bend	167	41	38N	86	20W
South Carolina □	165	33	45N	81	0W
South Charleston	165	38	20N	81	40W
South China Sea	77	10	0N	113	0 E
South Dakota □	163	45	0N	100	0W
South Downs	25	50	53N	0	10W
South Georgia	183	54	30S	37	0W
South Glamorgan □	27	51	30N	3	20W
South Haven	167	42	22N	86	20W
South Island	123	44	0S	170	0 E
South Korea ■	98	36	0N	128	0 E
South Orkney Is.	14	63	0S	45	0W
South Platte →	163	41	7N	100	42W
South Pole	14	90	0S	0	0 E
South Porcupine	151	48	30N	81	12W
South Ronaldsay	33	58	46N	2	58W
South Sandwich Is.	14	57	0S	27	0W
South Sentinel I.	94	11	1N	92	16 E
South Shetland Is.	14	62	0S	59	0W
South Shields	28	54	59N	1	26W
South Taranaki Bight	122	39	40S	174	5 E
South Uist	32	57	20N	7	15W
South West Africa =					
Namibia ■	136	22	0S	18	9 E
South West Cape	123	47	16S	167	31 E
South Yorkshire □	29	53	30N	1	20W
Southampton	25	50	54N	1	23W
Southampton I.	146	64	30N	84	0W
Southend-on-Sea	25	51	32N	0	42 E
Southern Alps	123	43	41S	170	11 E
Southern Cross	120	31	12S	119	15 E
Southern Indian L.	143	57	10N	98	30W
Southern Uplands	31	55	30N	3	3W
Southland □	123	45	51S	168	13 E
Southport, Australia	116	27	58S	153	25 E
Southport, U.K.	28	53	38N	3	1W
Southwold	25	52	19N	1	41 E
Sovetskaya Gavan	75	48	50N	140	0 E
Sōya-Kaikyō = Perouse Str.,					
La	77	45	40N	142	0 E
Spain ■	50	40	0N	5	0W
Spalding	29	52	47N	0	9W
Spandau	43	52	35N	13	7 E
Spanish Fork	163	40	10N	111	37W
Spanish Town	180	18	0N	76	57W
Sparks	172	39	30N	119	45W
Sparta = Spárti	54	37	5N	22	25 E
Sparta	166	43	55N	90	47W
Spartanburg	165	35	0N	82	0W
Spárti	54	37	5N	22	25 E
Spartivento, C., Calabria, Italy	49	37	56N	16	4 E
Spartivento, C., Sard., Italy	48	38	52N	8	50 E
Spassk-Dalniy	75	44	40N	132	48 E
Speightstown	180	13	15N	59	39W
Spence Bay	145	69	32N	93	32W
Spencer	166	43	5N	95	19W
Spencer G.	119	34	0S	137	20 E
Spenser Mts.	123	42	15S	172	45 E
Sperrin Mts.	34	54	50N	7	0W
Spessart	42	50	10N	9	20 E
Spey →	33	57	26N	3	25W
Spézia, La	46	44	8N	9	50 E
Spinazzola	49	40	58N	16	5 E
Spithead	25	50	43N	1	5W
Spitzbergen = Svalbard	13	78	0N	17	0 E
Split	52	43	31N	16	26 E
Splügenpass	44	46	30N	9	20 E
Spokane	171	47	45N	117	25W
Sporyy Navolok, Mys	69	75	50N	68	40 E
Spratly, I.	112	8	20N	112	0 E
Spring Mts.	173	36	20N	115	43W
Springfield, Ill., U.S.A.	166	39	48N	89	40W
Springfield, Mass., U.S.A.	164	42	8N	72	37W
Springfield, Mo., U.S.A.	168	37	15N	93	20W
Springfield, Ohio, U.S.A.	167	39	58N	83	48W
Springfield, Oreg., U.S.A.	171	44	2N	123	0W
Springfield, Tenn., U.S.A.	169	36	35N	86	55W
Springfield, Vt., U.S.A.	164	43	20N	72	30W
Springhill	148	45	40N	64	4W
Springs	137	26	13S	28	25 E
Springwood	117	33	41S	150	33 E
Spurn Hd.	29	53	34N	0	8 E
Squamish	154	49	45N	123	10W
Sredinnyy Khrebet	73	57	0N	160	0 E
Srednekolymsk	73	67	27N	153	40 E
Sremska Mitrovica	52	44	59N	19	33 E
Srepok →	95	13	33N	106	16 E
Sretensk	74	52	10N	117	40 E
Sri Lanka ■	90	7	30N	80	50 E
Srinagar	89	34	5N	74	50 E
Stadskanaal	41	53	4N	6	55 E
Staffa	30	56	26N	6	21W
Stafford	28	52	49N	2	9W
Stafford □	28	52	53N	2	10W
Staines	25	51	26N	0	30W
Stalingrad = Volgograd	68	48	40N	44	25 E
Stalino = Donetsk	68	48	0N	37	45 E
Stalinogorsk =					
Novomoskovsk	68	54	5N	38	15 E
Stalybridge	28	53	29N	2	4W
Stamford, U.K.	25	52	39N	0	29W
Stamford, U.S.A.	164	41	5N	73	30W
Stanislav = Ivano-Frankovsk	68	48	40N	24	40 E
Stanley, Canada	152	55	24N	104	22W
Stanley, Falk. Is.	192	51	40S	59	51W
Stanovoy Khrebet	75	55	0N	130	0 E
Stanthorpe	116	28	36S	151	59 E
Stara Planina	53	43	15N	23	0 E
Stara Zagora	53	42	26N	25	39 E
Starkville	169	33	26N	88	48W
Start Pt.	27	50	13N	3	38W
State College	164	40	47N	77	49W
Staten, I. = Estados, I. de los	192	54	40S	64	30W
Statesboro	170	32	26N	81	46W
Statesville	165	35	48N	80	51W
Staunton	165	38	7N	79	4W
Stavanger	60	58	57N	5	40 E
Staveren	40	52	53N	5	22 E
Stavropol	70	45	5N	42	0 E
Stawell	119	37	5S	142	47 E
Steenwijk	41	52	47N	6	7 E
Stefanie L. = Chew Bahir	132	4	40N	36	50 E
Steiermark □	45	47	26N	15	0 E
Steinbach	153	49	32N	96	40W
Steinkjer	65	63	59N	11	31 E
Stellarton	149	45	32N	62	30W
Stephenville	149	48	31N	58	35W
Stereá Ellás □	54	38	50N	22	0 E
Sterling, Colo., U.S.A.	163	40	40N	103	15W
Sterling, Ill., U.S.A.	166	41	45N	89	45W

Name	Map	Lat°	Lat′	Long°	Long′
Sterlitamak	71	53	40N	56	0 E
Stettin = Szczecin	58	53	27N	14	27 E
Stettler	155	52	19N	112	40W
Steubenville	164	40	21N	80	39W
Stevens Port	166	44	32N	89	34W
Stewart	144	63	19N	139	26W
Stewart I.	123	46	58S	167	54 E
Stikine →	144	56	40N	132	30W
Stillwater, Minn., U.S.A.	166	45	3N	92	47W
Stillwater, Okla., U.S.A.	168	36	5N	97	3W
Stillwater Ra.	172	39	45N	118	6W
Štip	53	41	42N	22	10 E
Stirling	31	56	7N	3	57W
Stirling Ra.	120	34	23S	118	0 E
Stockholm	60	59	20N	18	3 E
Stockholms län □	60	59	30N	18	20 E
Stockport	28	53	25N	2	11W
Stockton	172	38	0N	121	20W
Stockton-on-Tees	29	54	34N	1	20W
Stoke-on-Trent	28	53	1N	2	11W
Stonehaven	33	56	58N	2	11W
Stonehenge	24	51	9N	1	45W
Stonewall	153	50	10N	97	19W
Stora Lulevatten	66	67	10N	19	30 E
Storavan	66	65	45N	18	10 E
Store Bælt	61	55	20N	11	0 E
Storm B.	119	43	10S	147	30 E
Storm Lake	166	42	35N	95	11W
Stornoway	32	58	12N	6	23W
Storsjön	66	63	12N	14	18 E
Storuman	66	65	5N	17	10 E
Stour →, Here. & Worcs., U.K.	24	52	25N	2	13W
Stour →, Kent, U.K.	25	51	15N	1	20 E
Stour →, Suffolk, U.K.	25	51	55N	1	5 E
Stourbridge	24	52	28N	2	8W
Stowmarket	25	52	11N	1	0 E
Strabane	34	54	50N	7	28W
Stralsund	43	54	17N	13	5 E
Strangford, L.	34	54	30N	5	37W
Stranraer	30	54	54N	5	0W
Strasbourg	37	48	35N	7	42 E
Stratford, Canada	151	43	23N	81	0W
Stratford, N.Z.	122	39	20S	174	19 E
Stratford-on-Avon	24	52	12N	1	42W
Strath Spey	33	57	15N	3	40W
Strathalbyn	119	35	13S	138	53 E
Strathclyde □	30	56	0N	4	50W
Strathmore	33	56	40N	3	4W
Strathy Pt.	33	58	35N	4	0W
Streaky B.	118	32	51S	134	18 E
Streator	167	41	9N	88	52W
Strómboli	49	38	48N	15	12 E
Stromeferry	32	57	20N	5	33W
Stromness	33	58	58N	3	18W
Stronsay	33	59	8N	2	38W
Stroud	24	51	44N	2	12W
Strumica	53	41	28N	22	41 E
Stuart L.	154	54	30N	124	30W
Stung Treng	95	13	31N	105	58 E
Sturgeon Bay	167	44	52N	87	20W
Sturgeon Falls	151	46	25N	79	57W
Stuttgart, Germany	42	48	46N	9	10 E
Stuttgart, U.S.A.	168	34	30N	91	33W
Styria = Steiermark □	45	47	26N	15	0 E
Suakin	129	19	8N	37	20 E
Subotica	52	46	6N	19	49 E
Suchitoto	177	13	56N	89	0W
Suchou = Suzhou	99	31	19N	120	38 E
Süchow = Xuzhou	99	34	18N	117	10 E
Sucre	187	19	0S	65	15W
Sudan ■	129	15	0N	30	0 E
Sudbury, Canada	151	46	30N	81	0W
Sudbury, U.K.	25	52	2N	0	44 E
Sudetan Mts. = Sudety	58	50	20N	16	45 E
Sudety	58	50	20N	16	45 E
Suez = El Suweis	128	29	58N	32	31 E
Suez Canal = Suweis, Qanâl es	128	31	0N	32	20 E
Suffolk	165	36	47N	76	33W
Suffolk □	25	52	16N	1	0 E
Sugluk = Saglouc	146	62	14N	75	38W
Suhbaatar	98	50	17N	106	10 E
Suir →	35	52	15N	7	10W
Suita	106	34	45N	135	32 E
Sukhona →	68	60	30N	45	0 E
Sukhumi	70	43	0N	41	0 E
Sukkertoppen	147	65	26N	52	55W
Sukkur	88	27	42N	68	54 E
Sukkur Barrage	88	27	40N	68	50 E
Sukumo	109	32	56N	132	44 E
Sulaiman Range	89	30	30N	69	50 E
Sulawesi □	113	2	0S	120	0 E
Sulina	57	45	10N	29	40 E
Sulitjelma	66	67	9N	16	3 E
Sullana	186	4	52S	80	39W
Sullivan	167	39	5N	87	26W
Sullivan I. = Lambi Kyun	96	10	50N	98	20 E
Sulphur Springs	168	33	5N	95	36W
Sulu Arch.	112	6	0N	121	0 E
Sulu Sea	112	8	0N	120	0 E
Suluq	128	31	44N	20	14 E
Sumatera □	111	0	40N	100	20 E
Sumatra = Sumatera □	111	0	40N	100	20 E
Sumba	113	9	45S	119	35 E
Sumbawa	113	8	26S	117	30 E
Sumburgh Hd.	30	59	52N	1	17W
Summerland	155	49	32N	119	41W
Summerside	148	46	24N	63	47W
Sumoto	109	34	21N	134	54 E
Sumter	165	33	55N	80	22W
Sumy	68	50	57N	34	50 E
Sunbury, Australia	117	37	35S	144	44 E
Sunbury, U.S.A.	164	40	50N	76	46W
Sunda, Selat	111	6	20S	105	30 E
Sundarbans, The	92	22	0N	89	0 E
Sunderland	28	54	54N	1	22W
Sundsvall	66	62	23N	17	17 E
Sungei Patani	96	5	38N	100	29 E
Sungei Siput	96	4	51N	101	6 E
Sungurlu	80	40	12N	34	21 E
Sunnyside	171	46	24N	120	2W
Sunnyvale	172	37	23N	122	2W
Suntar	74	62	15N	117	30 E
Suō-Nada	108	33	50N	131	30 E
Superior	150	46	45N	92	5W
Superior, L.	150	47	40N	87	0W
Suphan Daği	81	38	54N	42	48 E
Sūr	80	22	34N	59	32 E
Surabaja = Surabaya	111	7	17S	112	45 E
Surabaya	111	7	17S	112	45 E
Surakarta	111	7	35S	110	48 E
Surat	91	21	12N	72	55 E
Surat Thani	96	9	6N	99	20 E
Suratgarh	89	29	18N	73	55 E
Surgut	69	61	14N	73	20 E
Surin	95	14	50N	103	34 E
Surinam ■	185	4	0N	56	0W
Surrey □	25	51	16N	0	30W
Surt	127	31	11N	16	39 E
Surt, Khalij	127	31	40N	18	30 E
Suruga-Wan	107	34	45N	138	30 E
Susaki	109	33	22N	133	17 E
Susanville	172	40	28N	120	40W
Susquehanna →	164	39	33N	76	5W
Sutherland Falls	123	44	48S	167	46 E
Sutlej →	89	29	23N	71	3 E
Sutton-in-Ashfield	29	53	7N	1	20W
Suva	122	18	6S	178	30 E
Suwa	107	36	2N	138	8 E
Suwa-Ko	107	36	3N	138	5 E
Suwannee →	170	29	18N	83	9W
Suwanose-Jima	104	29	38N	129	43 E
Suweis, Qanâl es	128	31	0N	32	20 E
Suzaka	107	36	39N	138	19 E
Suzhou	99	31	19N	120	38 E
Suzu-Misaki	105	37	31N	137	21 E
Svalbard	13	78	0N	17	0 E
Svartenhuk Halvø	146	71	50N	54	30W
Svendborg	61	55	4N	10	35 E
Sverdlovsk = Yekaterinburg	69	56	50N	60	30 E
Sverdrup Is.	12	79	0N	97	0W

Svishtov	**53**	43 36N	25	23 E
Svobodnyy	**75**	51 20N	128	0 E
Swabian Alps = Schwäbische Alb	**42**	48 30N	9	30 E
Swakopmund	**136**	22 37S	14	30 E
Swale —►	**28**	54 5N	1	20W
Swan Hill	**117**	35 20S	143	33 E
Swan Hills	**155**	54 42N	115	24W
Swan Islands	**178**	17 22N	83	57W
Swan River	**152**	52 10N	101	16W
Swanage	**24**	50 36N	1	59W
Swansea	**27**	51 37N	3	57W
Swartberge	**136**	33 20S	22	0 E
Swatow = Shantou	**99**	23 18N	116	40 E
Swaziland ■	**137**	26 30S	31	30 E
Sweden ■	**66**	57 0N	15	0 E
Sweetwater	**161**	32 30N	100	28W
Swift Current	**152**	50 20N	107	45W
Swindon	**24**	51 33N	1	47W
Switzerland ■	**44**	46 30N	8	0 E
Swords	**34**	53 27N	6	15W
Sydney, Australia	**117**	33 53S	151	10 E
Sydney, Canada	**149**	46 7N	60	7W
Sydney Mines	**149**	46 18N	60	15W
Sydprøven	**147**	60 30N	45	35W
Sydra G. of = Surt, Khalīj	**127**	31 40N	18	30 E
Syktyvkar	**69**	61 45N	50	40 E
Sylacauga	**169**	33 10N	86	15W
Sylhet	**92**	24 54N	91	52 E
Sylvan Lake	**155**	52 20N	114	3W
Syracuse	**164**	43 4N	76	11W
Syrdarya —►	**71**	46 3N	61	0 E
Syria ■	**80**	35 0N	38	0 E
Syrian Desert	**76**	31 0N	40	0 E
Syzran	**68**	53 12N	48	30 E
Szczecin	**58**	53 27N	14	27 E
Szechwan = Sichuan □	**99**	31 0N	104	0 E
Szeged	**59**	46 16N	20	10 E
Székesfehérvár	**59**	47 15N	18	25 E
Szolnok	**59**	47 10N	20	15 E
Szombathely	**59**	47 14N	16	38 E

T

Tabacal	**190**	23 15S	64	15W
Ţābah	**82**	26 55N	42	38 E
Tabasco □	**177**	18 0N	92	40W
Taber	**155**	49 47N	112	8W
Tablas	**112**	12 25N	122	2 E
Table Mt.	**136**	34 0S	18	22 E
Table Top, Mt.	**121**	23 24S	147	11 E
Tabora	**135**	5 2S	32	50 E
Tabrīz	**81**	38 7N	46	20 E
Tabūk	**82**	28 23N	36	36 E
Tachibana-Wan	**108**	32 45N	130	7 E
Tachikawa	**107**	35 42N	139	25 E
Tacna	**187**	18 0S	70	20W
Tacoma	**171**	47 15N	122	30W
Tacuarembó	**191**	31 45S	56	0W
Tademaït, Plateau du	**127**	28 30N	2	30 E
Tadoussac	**148**	48 11N	69	42W
Taegu	**98**	35 50N	128	37 E
Taejŏn	**98**	36 20N	127	28 E
Taganrog	**68**	47 12N	38	50 E
Tagish	**144**	60 19N	134	16W
Tagua, La	**184**	0 3N	74	40W
Tagus = Tajo —►	**50**	38 40N	9	24W
Tahiti	**123**	17 37S	149	27W
Tahoua	**131**	14 57N	5	16 E
Taibei	**99**	25 4N	121	29 E
T'aichung = Taizhong	**99**	24 12N	120	35 E
Taidong	**99**	22 43N	121	9 E
Taihape	**122**	39 41S	175	48 E
Tailem Bend	**119**	35 12S	139	29 E
Taimyr = Taymyr, Poluostrov	**72**	75 0N	100	0 E
Tain	**33**	57 49N	4	4W
Tainan	**99**	23 17N	120	18 E
Taínaron, Ákra	**54**	36 22N	22	27 E

T'aipei = Taibei	**99**	25 4N	121	29 E
Taiping	**96**	4 51N	100	44 E
Taisha	**109**	35 24N	132	40 E
Taitao, Pen. de	**192**	46 30S	75	0W
Taiwan ■	**99**	23 30N	121	0 E
Taiyuan	**98**	37 52N	112	33 E
Taizhong	**99**	24 12N	120	35 E
Ta'izz	**83**	13 35N	44	2 E
Tajikistan ■	**71**	35 30N	70	0 E
Tajimi	**106**	35 19N	137	8 E
Tajo —►	**50**	38 40N	9	24W
Tak	**94**	16 52N	99	8 E
Takachiho	**108**	32 42N	131	18 E
Takada	**105**	37 7N	138	15 E
Takahashi	**109**	34 51N	133	39 E
Takamatsu	**109**	34 20N	134	5 E
Takaoka	**106**	36 47N	137	0 E
Takapuna	**122**	36 47S	174	47 E
Takasago	**109**	34 45N	134	48 E
Takasaki	**107**	36 20N	139	0 E
Takatsuki	**106**	34 51N	135	37 E
Takawa	**108**	33 38N	130	51 E
Takayama	**106**	36 18N	137	11 E
Takayama-Bonchi	**106**	36 0N	137	18 E
Takefu	**106**	35 50N	136	10 E
Takehara	**109**	34 21N	132	55 E
Taketa	**108**	32 58N	131	24 E
Takhār □	**87**	36 40N	70	0 E
Takla Landing	**154**	55 30N	125	50W
Takla Makan	**76**	39 0N	83	0 E
Taku	**108**	33 18N	130	3 E
Talara	**186**	4 38S	81	18 E
Talaud, Kepulauan	**113**	4 30N	127	10 E
Talca	**190**	35 28S	71	40W
Talcahuano	**190**	36 40S	73	10W
Ţalesh, Kūhhā-ye	**81**	39 0N	48	30 E
Talguppa	**90**	14 10N	74	45 E
Taliabu	**113**	1 45S	125	0 E
Talkeetna	**142**	62 20N	150	9W
Tall 'Afar	**81**	36 22N	42	27 E
Talladega	**169**	33 28N	86	2W
Tallahassee	**170**	30 25N	84	15W
Tallangatta	**117**	36 15S	147	19 E
Tallinn	**68**	59 22N	24	48 E
Tallulah	**168**	32 25N	91	12W
Tamale	**130**	9 22N	0	50W
Tamana	**108**	32 58N	130	32 E
Tamano	**109**	34 29N	133	59 E
Tamanrasset	**127**	22 50N	5	30 E
Tamar —►	**27**	50 33N	4	15W
Tamaulipas □	**176**	24 0N	98	45W
Tambellup	**120**	34 4S	117	37 E
Tambov	**68**	52 45N	41	28 E
Tamgak, Mts.	**127**	19 12N	8	35 E
Tamil Nadu □	**90**	11 0N	77	0 E
Tammerfors = Tampere	**67**	61 30N	23	50 E
Tamo Abu, Pegunungan	**111**	3 10N	115	0 E
Tampa	**170**	27 57N	82	38W
Tampa B.	**170**	27 40N	82	40W
Tampere	**67**	61 30N	23	50 E
Tampico	**177**	22 20N	97	50W
Tamrah	**83**	20 24N	45	25 E
Tamsagbulag	**98**	47 14N	117	21 E
Tamworth, Australia	**116**	31 7S	150	58 E
Tamworth, U.K.	**24**	52 38N	1	41W
Tana —►, Kenya	**133**	2 32S	40	31 E
Tana —►, Norway	**67**	70 30N	28	23 E
Tana, L.	**132**	13 5N	37	30 E
Tanabe	**106**	33 44N	135	22 E
Tanana	**142**	65 10N	152	15W
Tananarive = Antananarivo	**137**	18 55S	47	31 E
Tanba-Sanchi	**106**	35 7N	135	48 E
Tandil	**190**	37 15S	59	6W
Tando Adam	**88**	25 45N	68	40 E
Tane-ga-Shima	**104**	30 30N	131	0 E
Tanen Tong Dan	**93**	16 30N	98	30 E
Tanezrouft	**127**	23 9N	0	11 E
Tanga	**135**	5 5S	39	2 E
Tanganyika, L.	**135**	6 40S	30	0 E
Tanger	**126**	35 50N	5	49W
Tanggula Shan	**101**	32 40N	92	10 E

Place	Page	Lat °	Lat ′	N/S	Long °	Long ′	E/W
Tangier = Tanger	126	35	50	N	5	49	W
Tangshan	98	39	38	N	118	10	E
Tanimbar, Kepulauan	113	7	30	S	131	30	E
Taniyama	108	31	31	N	130	31	E
Tanjore = Thanjavur	90	10	48	N	79	12	E
Tannu Ola	74	51	0	N	94	0	E
Tanout	131	14	50	N	8	55	E
Tanta	128	30	45	N	30	57	E
Tantung = Dandong	98	40	10	N	124	20	E
Tanunda	119	34	30	S	139	0	E
Tanzania ■	135	6	40	S	34	0	E
Tapa Shan = Daba Shan	99	32	0	N	109	0	E
Tapachula	177	14	54	N	92	17	W
Tapajós →	185	2	24	S	54	41	W
Tapanui	123	45	56	S	169	18	E
Tapi →	91	21	8	N	72	41	E
Tara →	71	56	42	N	74	36	E
Tarabagatay, Khrebet	71	48	0	N	83	0	E
Tarābulus, Lebanon	80	34	31	N	35	50	E
Tarābulus, Libya	127	32	49	N	13	7	E
Taranaki □	122	39	5	S	174	51	E
Táranto	49	40	30	N	17	11	E
Táranto, G. di	49	40	0	N	17	15	E
Tarapoto	186	6	30	S	76	20	W
Tarare	37	45	54	N	4	26	E
Tararua Range	123	40	45	S	175	25	E
Tarauacá	187	8	6	S	70	48	W
Tarbela Dam	89	34	8	N	72	52	E
Tarbert	32	57	54	N	6	49	W
Tarbes	36	43	15	N	0	3	E
Tarcoola	118	30	44	S	134	36	E
Taree	116	31	50	S	152	30	E
Tarfaya	126	27	55	N	12	55	W
Tarifa	50	36	1	N	5	36	W
Tarija	187	21	30	S	64	40	W
Tarim →	100	41	5	N	86	40	E
Tarim Pendi	100	40	0	N	84	0	E
Tarko Sale	69	64	55	N	77	50	E
Tarn →	36	44	5	N	1	6	E
Tarnobrzeg	58	50	35	N	21	41	E
Tarnów	58	50	3	N	21	0	E
Tarragona	51	41	5	N	1	17	E
Tarrasa	51	41	34	N	2	1	E
Tarsus	80	36	58	N	34	55	E
Tartagal	190	22	30	S	63	50	W
Tarṭūs	80	34	55	N	35	55	E
Tarumizu	108	31	29	N	130	42	E
Tarutao, Ko	96	6	33	N	99	40	E
Taschereau	151	48	40	N	78	40	W
Tashi Chho Dzong = Thimphu	92	27	31	N	89	45	E
Tashkent	71	41	20	N	69	10	E
Tasman B.	123	40	59	S	173	25	E
Tasman Mts.	123	41	3	S	172	25	E
Tasman Sea	122	36	0	S	160	0	E
Tasmania □	119	42	0	S	146	30	E
Tatabánya	59	47	32	N	18	25	E
Tatarsk	71	55	14	N	76	0	E
Tateshina-Yama	107	36	8	N	138	11	E
Tateyama	107	35	0	N	139	50	E
Tatra = Tatry	59	49	20	N	20	0	E
Tatry	59	49	20	N	20	0	E
Tatsuno	109	34	52	N	134	33	E
Tat'ung = Datong	98	40	6	N	113	18	E
Taubaté	191	23	0	S	45	36	W
Tauern	45	47	15	N	12	40	E
Taumarunui	122	38	53	S	175	15	E
Taunggyi	93	20	50	N	97	0	E
Taungup Taunggya	93	18	20	N	93	40	E
Taunton, U.K.	27	51	1	N	3	7	W
Taunton, U.S.A.	164	41	54	N	71	6	W
Taunus	42	50	15	N	8	20	E
Taupo	122	38	41	S	176	7	E
Taupo, L.	122	38	46	S	175	55	E
Tauranga	122	37	42	S	176	11	E
Taurus Mts. = Toros Daglari	80	37	0	N	35	0	E
Taverny	39	49	2	N	2	13	E
Tavistock	27	50	33	N	4	9	W
Tavoy	94	14	2	N	98	12	E
Tawas City	167	44	16	N	83	31	W
Tay →	33	56	37	N	3	38	W
Tayabamba	186	8	15	S	77	16	W
Taylor Mt.	161	35	16	N	107	36	W
Taymā	82	27	35	N	38	45	E
Taymyr, Poluostrov	72	75	0	N	100	0	E
Tayshet	74	55	58	N	98	1	E
Tayside □	31	56	25	N	3	30	W
Taz →	69	67	32	N	78	40	E
Tbilisi	70	41	43	N	44	50	E
Tchad = Chad ■	131	15	0	N	17	15	E
Tchad, L.	131	13	30	N	14	30	E
Tch'eng-tou = Chengdu	99	30	38	N	104	2	E
Tch'ong-k'ing = Chongqing	99	29	35	N	106	25	E
Te Anau, L.	123	45	15	S	167	45	E
Te Kuiti	122	38	20	S	175	11	E
Tecuala	175	22	23	N	105	27	W
Tefé	185	3	25	S	64	50	W
Tegal	111	6	52	S	109	8	E
Tegucigalpa	179	14	5	N	87	14	W
Tehachapi Mts.	173	35	0	N	118	40	W
Tehrān	86	35	44	N	51	30	E
Tehuacán	177	18	27	N	97	23	E
Tehuantepec	177	16	21	N	95	13	W
Tehuantepec, G. de	177	16	0	N	94	50	W
Tehuantepec, Istmo de	177	17	0	N	94	30	W
Teifi →	26	52	4	N	4	14	W
Teignmouth	27	50	33	N	3	30	W
Tejo →	50	38	40	N	9	24	W
Tekax	177	20	12	N	89	17	W
Tekeli	71	44	50	N	79	0	E
Tekirdağ	80	40	58	N	27	30	E
Tel Aviv-Yafo	80	32	4	N	34	48	E
Tela	179	15	40	N	87	28	W
Telanaipura = Jambi	111	1	38	S	103	30	E
Telegraph Cr. →	144	58	0	N	131	10	W
Telemark fylke □	60	59	25	N	8	30	E
Teles Pires →	187	7	21	S	58	3	W
Telford	28	52	42	N	2	31	W
Tell City	167	38	0	N	86	44	W
Teme →	24	52	23	N	2	15	W
Temerloh	96	3	27	N	102	25	E
Temirtau	71	50	5	N	72	56	E
Temora	117	34	30	S	147	30	E
Temosachic	174	28	57	N	107	51	W
Temple	158	31	5	N	97	22	W
Temuco	190	38	45	S	72	40	W
Temuka	123	44	14	S	171	17	E
Tenali	91	16	15	N	80	35	E
Tenancingo	177	19	0	N	99	33	W
Tenango	177	19	7	N	99	33	W
Tenby	27	51	40	N	4	42	W
Tenerife	126	28	15	N	16	35	W
Teng Xian	99	35	5	N	117	10	E
Tennessee □	169	36	0	N	86	30	W
Tennessee →	169	37	4	N	88	34	W
Tenri	106	34	39	N	135	49	E
Tenryū	107	34	52	N	137	49	E
Tenryū-Gawa →	107	35	39	N	137	48	E
Tenterfield	116	29	0	S	152	0	E
Teófilo Otoni	189	17	50	S	41	30	W
Tepic	175	21	30	N	104	54	W
Terang	119	38	15	S	142	55	E
Terek →	70	44	0	N	47	30	E
Terengganu □	96	4	55	N	103	0	E
Teresina	188	5	9	S	42	45	W
Terewah, L.	116	29	52	S	147	35	E
Termez	70	37	15	N	67	15	E
Términos, L. de	177	18	37	N	91	33	W
Terneuzen	40	51	20	N	3	50	E
Terni	46	42	34	N	12	38	E
Terrace	154	54	30	N	128	35	W
Terre Haute	167	39	28	N	87	24	W
Terrell	168	32	44	N	96	19	W
Terschelling	40	53	25	N	5	20	E
Teruel	51	40	22	N	1	8	W
Teshio	103	44	53	N	141	44	E
Teslin	144	60	10	N	132	43	W
Test →	24	51	7	N	1	30	W
Tete	137	16	13	S	33	33	E
Teteven	53	42	58	N	24	17	E
Tétouan	126	35	35	N	5	21	W
Tetuán = Tétouan	126	35	35	N	5	21	W

Name	Page	Lat °	Lat ′		Lon °	Lon ′	
Teuco →	**190**	25	35	S	60	11	W
Teutoburger Wald	**42**	52	5	N	8	20	E
Tevere →	**46**	41	44	N	12	14	E
Tewkesbury	**24**	51	59	N	2	8	W
Texarkana, Ark., U.S.A.	**168**	33	25	N	94	0	W
Texarkana, Tex., U.S.A.	**168**	33	25	N	94	3	W
Texas □	**161**	31	40	N	98	30	W
Texel	**40**	53	5	N	4	50	E
Teziutlán	**177**	19	49	N	97	21	W
Tezpur	**93**	26	40	N	92	45	E
Thabana Ntlenyana	**137**	29	30	S	29	16	E
Thailand ■	**95**	16	0	N	102	0	E
Thailand, G. of	**95**	11	30	N	101	0	E
Thal Desert	**89**	31	10	N	71	30	E
Thame →	**24**	51	35	N	1	8	W
Thames	**122**	37	7	S	175	34	E
Thames →	**25**	51	30	N	0	35	E
Thane	**91**	19	12	N	72	59	E
Thanh Hoa	**95**	19	48	N	105	46	E
Thanh Pho Ho Chi Minh	**95**	10	58	N	106	40	E
Thanjavur	**90**	10	48	N	79	12	E
Thar Desert	**89**	28	0	N	72	0	E
Thásos	**55**	40	40	N	24	40	E
Thaungdut	**93**	24	30	N	94	40	E
Thazi	**93**	21	0	N	96	5	E
The Dalles	**171**	45	40	N	121	11	W
The Grenadines, Is.	**180**	12	40	N	61	20	W
The Hague = 's-Gravenhage	**40**	52	7	N	4	17	E
The Macumba →	**118**	27	52	S	137	12	E
The Neales →	**118**	28	8	S	136	47	E
The Pas	**152**	53	45	N	101	15	W
The Rock	**117**	35	15	S	147	2	E
The Warburton →	**118**	28	4	S	137	28	E
Thebes = Thívai	**55**	38	19	N	23	19	E
Thermaïkos Kólpos	**54**	40	15	N	22	45	E
Thermopolis	**163**	43	35	N	108	10	W
Thessalía □	**54**	39	30	N	22	0	E
Thessalon	**150**	46	20	N	83	30	W
Thessaloníki	**54**	40	38	N	22	58	E
Thessaly = Thessalía □	**54**	39	30	N	22	0	E
Thetford Mines	**148**	46	8	N	71	18	W
Thicket Portage	**153**	55	19	N	97	42	W
Thies	**130**	14	50	N	16	51	W
Thimphu	**92**	27	31	N	89	45	E
Thionville	**37**	49	20	N	6	10	E
Thíra	**55**	36	23	N	25	27	E
Thirsk	**29**	54	15	N	1	20	W
Thisted	**61**	56	58	N	8	40	E
Thívai	**55**	38	19	N	23	19	E
Thomaston	**170**	32	54	N	84	20	W
Thomasville, Ga., U.S.A.	**170**	30	50	N	84	0	W
Thomasville, N.C., U.S.A.	**165**	35	55	N	80	4	W
Thon Buri	**94**	13	43	N	100	29	E
Thornaby on Tees	**29**	54	36	N	1	19	W
Thrace = Thráki □	**55**	41	9	N	25	30	E
Thráki □	**55**	41	9	N	25	30	E
Three Hills	**155**	51	43	N	113	15	W
Three Hummock I.	**119**	40	25	S	144	55	E
Thule	**13**	77	40	N	69	0	W
Thundelarra	**120**	28	53	S	117	7	E
Thunder B.	**150**	45	0	N	83	20	W
Thunder Bay	**150**	48	20	N	89	15	W
Thüringer Wald	**43**	50	35	N	11	0	E
Thurles	**35**	52	40	N	7	53	W
Thursday I.	**115**	10	30	S	142	3	E
Thurso	**33**	58	34	N	3	31	W
Tian Shan	**100**	43	0	N	84	0	E
Tianjin	**98**	39	8	N	117	10	E
Tianshui	**99**	34	32	N	105	40	E
Tiber = Tevere →	**46**	41	44	N	12	14	E
Tibesti	**127**	21	0	N	17	30	E
Tibet = Xizang □	**101**	32	0	N	88	0	E
Tibooburra	**118**	29	26	S	142	1	E
Ticul	**177**	20	24	N	89	32	W
Tiel	**40**	51	53	N	5	26	E
Tien Shan	**76**	42	0	N	80	0	E
Tien-tsin = Tianjin	**98**	39	8	N	117	10	E
T'ienching = Tianjin	**98**	39	8	N	117	10	E
Tientsin = Tianjin	**98**	39	8	N	117	10	E
Tierra de Campos	**50**	42	10	N	4	50	W
Tierra del Fuego □	**192**	54	0	S	67	45	W
Tiffin	**167**	41	8	N	83	10	W
Tiflis = Tbilisi	**70**	41	43	N	44	50	E
Tifton	**170**	31	28	N	83	32	W
Tignish	**148**	46	58	N	64	2	W
Tigris = Dijlah, Nahr →	**81**	31	0	N	47	25	E
Tijuana	**174**	32	32	N	117	1	W
Tiksi	**72**	71	40	N	128	45	E
Tilburg	**40**	51	31	N	5	6	E
Tilbury	**25**	51	27	N	0	24	E
Tillsonburg	**151**	42	53	N	80	44	W
Tilos	**55**	36	27	N	27	27	E
Timaru	**123**	44	23	S	171	14	E
Timbuktu = Tombouctou	**130**	16	50	N	3	0	W
Timişoara	**56**	45	43	N	21	15	E
Timmins	**151**	48	28	N	81	25	W
Timor	**113**	9	0	S	125	0	E
Timor Sea	**113**	10	0	S	127	0	E
Tinaca Pt.	**112**	5	30	N	125	25	E
Tindouf	**126**	27	42	N	8	10	W
Tinnevelly = Tirunelveli	**90**	8	45	N	77	45	E
Tinogasta	**190**	28	5	S	67	32	W
Tinos	**55**	37	33	N	25	8	E
Tioman, Pulau	**96**	2	50	N	104	10	E
Tipperary	**35**	52	28	N	8	10	W
Tipperary □	**35**	52	37	N	7	55	W
Tipton	**24**	52	32	N	2	4	W
Tirana	**52**	41	18	N	19	49	E
Tiraspol	**68**	46	55	N	29	35	E
Tire	**80**	38	5	N	27	50	E
Tirebolu	**81**	40	58	N	38	45	E
Tiree	**30**	56	31	N	6	55	W
Tîrgu Mureş	**57**	46	31	N	24	38	E
Tirol □	**45**	47	3	N	10	43	E
Tiruchirappalli	**90**	10	45	N	78	45	E
Tirunelveli	**90**	8	45	N	77	45	E
Tisa →	**59**	45	15	N	20	17	E
Tisdale	**152**	52	50	N	104	0	W
Titicaca, L.	**187**	15	30	S	69	30	W
Titograd = Podgorica	**52**	42	30	N	19	19	E
Titov Veles	**53**	41	46	N	21	47	E
Titovo Užice	**52**	43	55	N	19	50	E
Tiverton	**27**	50	54	N	3	30	W
Tívoli	**46**	41	58	N	12	45	E
Tizimín	**177**	21	9	N	88	9	W
Tjirebon = Cirebon	**111**	6	45	S	108	32	E
Tlaxcala □	**177**	19	25	N	98	10	W
Tlaxiaco	**177**	17	18	N	97	40	W
Tlemcen	**127**	34	52	N	1	21	W
To-Shima	**107**	34	31	N	139	17	E
Toamasina	**137**	18	10	S	49	25	E
Toba Kakar	**88**	31	30	N	69	0	E
Tobago	**180**	11	10	N	60	30	W
Tobermory	**30**	56	37	N	6	4	W
Tobolsk	**69**	58	15	N	68	10	E
Tobruk = Tubruq	**128**	32	7	N	23	55	E
Tocantins →	**188**	1	45	S	49	10	W
Toccoa	**165**	34	32	N	83	17	W
Tochigi	**107**	36	25	N	139	45	E
Tocopilla	**190**	22	5	S	70	10	W
Todos Santos	**175**	23	27	N	110	13	W
Tōgane	**107**	35	33	N	140	22	E
Togliatti	**68**	53	32	N	49	24	E
Togo ■	**130**	6	15	N	1	35	E
Tōhoku □	**103**	39	50	N	141	45	E
Tōjō	**109**	34	53	N	133	16	E
Tokai	**106**	35	2	N	136	55	E
Tokaj	**58**	48	8	N	21	27	E
Tokara Kaikyō	**104**	30	0	N	130	0	E
Tokat	**80**	40	22	N	36	35	E
Tokelau Is.	**123**	9	0	S	171	45	W
Toki	**106**	35	18	N	137	8	E
Tokoname	**106**	34	53	N	136	51	E
Tokorozawa	**107**	35	47	N	139	28	E
Tokushima	**109**	34	4	N	134	34	E
Tokuyama	**108**	34	3	N	131	50	E
Tōkyō	**107**	35	45	N	139	45	E
Tōkyō-Wan	**107**	35	25	N	139	47	E
Tolbukhin = Dobrich	**53**	43	37	N	27	49	E
Toledo, Spain	**50**	39	50	N	4	2	W
Toledo, U.S.A.	**167**	41	37	N	83	33	W
Tolga	**127**	34	40	N	5	22	E

Name	Page	Latitude	Longitude
Tolima, Vol.	184	4 40N	75 19W
Toluca	177	19 20N	99 40W
Tomakomai	103	42 38N	141 36 E
Tombigbee →	169	31 4N	87 58W
Tombouctou	130	16 50N	3 0W
Tomini, Teluk	113	0 10S	122 0 E
Tomsk	71	56 30N	85 5 E
Tonalá	177	16 4N	93 45W
Tonantins	184	2 45S	67 45W
Tonbridge	25	51 12N	0 18 E
Tong Xian	98	39 55N	116 35 E
Tonga ■	123	19 50S	174 30W
Tongchuan	99	35 6N	109 3 E
Tonghua	98	41 42N	125 58 E
Tongking, G. of	95	20 0N	108 0 E
Tongue	33	58 29N	4 25W
Tonk	91	26 6N	75 54 E
Tonkin = Bac Phan	95	22 0N	105 0 E
Tonlé Sap	95	13 0N	104 0 E
Tonopah	172	38 4N	117 12W
Tonoshō	109	34 29N	134 11 E
Tooele	162	40 30N	112 20W
Toowoomba	116	27 32S	151 56 E
Topeka	166	39 3N	95 40W
Toppenish	171	46 27N	120 16W
Torbay	27	50 26N	3 31W
Torino	46	45 4N	7 40 E
Tormes →	50	41 18N	6 29W
Torne älv →	67	65 50N	24 12 E
Torneå = Tornio	67	65 50N	24 12 E
Torneträsk	66	68 24N	19 15 E
Tornio	67	65 50N	24 12 E
Toro, Cerro del	190	29 10S	69 50W
Toronto, Australia	117	33 0S	151 30 E
Toronto, Canada	151	43 39N	79 20W
Toros Daglari	80	37 0N	35 0 E
Torquay	27	50 27N	3 31W
Torre Annunziata	49	40 45N	14 26 E
Tòrre de Moncorvo	50	41 12N	7 8W
Torremolinos	50	36 38N	4 30W
Torrens, L.	119	31 0S	137 50 E
Torreón	174	25 33N	103 26W
Torres Vedras	50	39 5N	9 15W
Torridge →	27	50 51N	4 10W
Torrington	164	41 50N	73 9W
Tortosa	51	40 49N	0 31 E
Tortosa, C.	51	40 41N	0 52 E
Toruń	58	53 0N	18 39 E
Tory I.	34	55 17N	8 12W
Tosa-Shimizu	109	32 52N	132 58 E
Tosa-Wan	109	33 15N	133 30 E
Toscana	46	43 30N	11 5 E
Tostado	190	29 15S	61 50W
Tosu	109	33 22N	130 31 E
Totnes	27	50 26N	3 41W
Totonicapán	177	14 58N	91 12W
Tottori	109	35 30N	134 15 E
Toubkal, Djebel	126	31 0N	8 0W
Touggourt	127	33 6N	6 4 E
Toulon	37	43 10N	5 55 E
Toulouse	36	43 37N	1 27 E
Toungoo	93	19 0N	96 30 E
Touraine	36	47 20N	0 30 E
Tourane = Da Nang	95	16 4N	108 13 E
Tourcoing	38	50 42N	3 10 E
Tournai	42	50 35N	3 25 E
Tours	36	47 22N	0 40 E
Townsville	121	19 15S	146 45 E
Towson	164	39 26N	76 34W
Toyama	106	36 40N	137 15 E
Toyama-Wan	105	37 0N	137 30 E
Toyohashi	106	34 45N	137 25 E
Toyokawa	106	34 48N	137 27 E
Toyonaka	106	34 50N	135 28 E
Toyooka	109	35 35N	134 48 E
Toyota	106	35 3N	137 7 E
Tozeur	127	33 56N	8 8 E
Trabzon	81	41 0N	39 45 E
Tracy	172	37 46N	121 27W
Trafalgar, C.	50	36 10N	6 2W
Trail	155	49 5N	117 40W
Tralee	35	52 16N	9 42W
Tralee B.	35	52 17N	9 55W
Tran Ninh, Cao Nguyen	95	19 30N	103 10 E
Trangan	113	6 40S	134 20 E
Trangie	116	32 4S	148 0 E
Transantarctic Mts.	15	85 0S	170 0W
Transcona	153	49 55N	97 0W
Transilvania	57	46 19N	25 0 E
Transkei	137	32 15S	28 15 E
Transvaal □	137	25 0S	29 0 E
Transylvania = Transilvania .	57	46 19N	25 0 E
Transylvanian Alps	17	45 30N	25 0 E
Trápani	48	38 1N	12 30 E
Traralgon	117	38 12S	146 34 E
Trasimeno, L.	46	43 10N	12 5 E
Travers, Mt.	123	42 1S	172 45 E
Traverse City	167	44 45N	85 39W
Travnik	52	44 17N	17 39 E
Tredegar	27	51 47N	3 16W
Tregaron	26	52 14N	3 56W
Treinta y Tres	191	33 16S	54 17W
Trelew	192	43 10S	65 20W
Trenque Lauquen	190	36 5S	62 45W
Trent →	29	53 33N	0 44W
Trentino-Alto Adige □	47	46 30N	11 0 E
Trento	47	46 5N	11 8 E
Trenton, Canada	151	44 10N	77 34W
Trenton, Mo., U.S.A.	166	40 5N	93 37W
Trenton, N.J., U.S.A.	164	40 15N	74 41W
Tréport, Le	38	50 3N	1 20 E
Tres Arroyos	190	38 26S	60 20W
Três Lagoas	188	20 50S	51 43W
Tres Montes, C.	192	46 50S	75 30W
Tres Puntas, C.	192	47 0S	66 0W
Treviso	47	45 40N	12 15 E
Trichinopoly = Tiruchchirappalli	90	10 45N	78 45 E
Trichur	90	10 30N	76 18 E
Trier	42	49 45N	6 37 E
Trieste	47	45 39N	13 45 E
Tríkkala	54	39 34N	21 47 E
Trincomalee	90	8 38N	81 15 E
Trinidad, Bolivia	187	14 46S	64 50W
Trinidad, Colombia	184	5 25N	71 40W
Trinidad, Cuba	178	21 48N	80 0W
Trinidad, Uruguay	191	33 30S	56 50W
Trinidad, U.S.A.	163	37 15N	104 30W
Trinidad & Tobago ■	180	10 30N	61 20W
Trinity →	168	30 30N	95 0W
Trinity Mts.	172	40 20N	118 50W
Tripoli = Tarābulus, Lebanon	80	34 31N	35 50 E
Tripoli = Tarābulus, Libya	127	32 49N	13 7 E
Tripolis	54	37 31N	22 25 E
Tripura □	93	24 0N	92 0 E
Trivandrum	90	8 41N	77 0 E
Trois-Rivières	151	46 25N	72 34W
Troitsk	71	54 10N	61 35 E
Trollhättan	60	58 17N	12 20 E
Tromsø	66	69 40N	18 56 E
Trondheim	65	63 36N	10 25 E
Trossachs, The	31	56 14N	4 24W
Trotternish	32	57 32N	6 15W
Trouville	38	49 21N	0 5 E
Trowbridge	24	51 18N	2 12W
Troy, Ala., U.S.A.	169	31 50N	85 58W
Troy, N.Y., U.S.A.	164	42 45N	73 39W
Troyes	39	48 19N	4 3 E
Trucial States = United Arab Emirates ■	85	23 50N	54 0 E
Trujillo, Honduras	179	16 0N	86 0W
Trujillo, Peru	186	8 6S	79 0W
Trujillo, Venezuela	184	9 22N	70 38W
Trundle	117	32 53S	147 35 E
Trung-Phan	95	16 0N	108 0 E
Truro, Canada	149	45 21N	63 14W
Truro, U.K.	27	50 17N	5 2W
Tselinograd	71	51 10N	71 30 E
Tsinan = Jinan	98	36 38N	117 1 E
Tsinghai = Qinghai □	101	36 0N	98 0 E
Tsingtao = Qingdao	98	36 5N	120 20 E
Tsu	106	34 45N	136 25 E

Name					
Tsuchiura	107	36	5N	140	15 E
Tsugaru-Kaikyō	103	41	35N	141	0 E
Tsukumi	108	33	4N	131	52 E
Tsukushi-Sanchi	108	33	25N	130	30 E
Tsuruga	106	35	45N	136	2 E
Tsurugi-San	109	33	51N	134	6 E
Tsuruoka	103	38	44N	139	50 E
Tsushima, Gifu, Japan	106	35	10N	136	43 E
Tsushima, Nagasaki, Japan	104	34	20N	129	20 E
Tuamotu Arch.	123	17	0S	144	0W
Tubarão	191	28	30S	49	0W
Tubruq	128	32	7N	23	55 E
Tubuai Is.	123	25	0S	150	0W
Tucacas	184	10	48N	68	19W
Tucson	160	32	14N	110	59W
Tucumcari	161	35	12N	103	45W
Tucupita	185	9	2N	62	3W
Tucuruí	188	3	42S	49	44W
Tudmur	80	34	36N	38	15 E
Tuktoyaktuk	144	69	27N	133	2W
Tula, Mexico	177	23	0N	99	43W
Tula, Russia	68	54	13N	37	38 E
Tulare	173	36	15N	119	26W
Tulcán	184	0	48N	77	43W
Tullahoma	169	35	23N	86	12W
Tullamore	35	53	17N	7	30W
Tully	121	17	56S	145	55 E
Tulsa	168	36	10N	96	0W
Tulua	184	4	6N	76	11W
Tuma →	179	13	6N	84	35W
Tumaco	184	1	50N	78	45W
Tumatumari	185	5	20N	58	55W
Tumbarumba	117	35	44S	148	0 E
Túmbes	186	3	37S	80	27W
Tumkur	90	13	18N	77	6 E
Tummel, L.	33	56	43N	3	55W
Tummo	127	22	45N	14	8 E
Tump	88	26	7N	62	16 E
Tumucumaque, Serra	188	2	0N	55	0W
Tumut	117	35	16S	148	13 E
Tunbridge Wells	25	51	7N	0	16 E
Tundzha →	53	41	40N	26	35 E
Tunis	127	36	50N	10	11 E
Tunisia ■	127	33	30N	9	10 E
Tunja	184	5	33N	73	25W
Tunxi	99	29	42N	118	25 E
Tupelo	169	34	15N	88	42W
Tupiza	187	21	30S	65	40W
Tupper L.	151	44	18N	74	30W
Tuque, La	151	47	30N	72	50W
Túquerres	184	1	5N	77	37W
Tura	92	25	30N	90	16 E
Turayf	82	31	41N	38	39 E
Turfan = Turpan	100	43	58N	89	10 E
Turfan Depression = Turpan Hami	100	42	40N	89	25 E
Tŭrgovishte	53	43	17N	26	38 E
Turgutlu	80	38	30N	27	48 E
Turin = Torino	46	45	4N	7	40 E
Turkana, L.	132	3	30N	36	5 E
Turkestan	71	43	17N	68	16 E
Turkey ■	80	39	0N	36	0 E
Turkmenistan ■	70	39	0N	59	0 E
Turks Is.	180	21	20N	71	20W
Turku	67	60	30N	22	19 E
Turlock	172	37	30N	120	55W
Turnagain, C.	122	40	28S	176	38 E
Turnhout	42	51	19N	4	57 E
Tŭrnovo	53	43	5N	25	41 E
Turnu Rosu Pasul	57	45	33N	24	17 E
Turnu-Severin	56	44	39N	22	41 E
Turpan	100	43	58N	89	10 E
Turpan Hami	100	42	40N	89	25 E
Turukhansk	74	65	21N	88	5 E
Tuscaloosa	169	33	13N	87	31W
Tuscany = Toscana	46	43	30N	11	5 E
Tuskegee	169	32	24N	85	39W
Tutrakan	53	44	2N	26	40 E
Tuvalu ■	122	8	0S	178	0 E
Tuxpan	177	20	57N	97	24W
Tuxtla Gutiérrez	177	16	45N	93	7W
Tuy Hoa	95	13	5N	109	10 E
Tuyen Hoa	95	17	50N	106	10 E
Tuz Gölü	80	38	45N	33	30 E
Ţūz Khurmātū	81	34	56N	44	38 E
Tuzla	52	44	34N	18	41 E
Tver	68	56	55N	35	55 E
Tweed →	31	55	42N	2	10W
Tweed Heads	116	28	10S	153	31 E
Twin Falls	172	42	30N	114	30W
Two Harbors	156	47	1N	91	40W
Tyler	168	32	18N	95	18W
Tyne →	28	54	58N	1	28W
Tyne & Wear □	28	54	55N	1	35W
Tynemouth	28	55	1N	1	27W
Tyrol = Tirol □	45	47	3N	10	43 E
Tyrrhenian Sea	48	40	0N	12	30 E
Tyumen	69	57	11N	65	29 E
Tzukong = Zigong	99	29	15N	104	48 E

U

Name					
Uaupés	184	0	8S	67	5W
Ubangi = Oubangi →	131	1	0N	17	50 E
Ube	108	33	56N	131	15 E
Uberaba	188	19	50S	47	55W
Uberlândia	188	19	0S	48	20W
Ubon Ratchathani	95	15	15N	104	50 E
Ucayali →	186	4	30S	73	30W
Uchi Lake	153	51	5N	92	35W
Uchiura-Wan	103	42	25N	140	40 E
Uchur →	75	58	48N	130	35 E
Udaipur	91	24	36N	73	44 E
Uddevalla	60	58	21N	11	55 E
Údine	47	46	5N	13	10 E
Udmurt Rep. □	69	57	30N	52	30 E
Udon Thani	95	17	29N	102	46 E
Ueda	107	36	24N	138	16 E
Uelen	73	66	10N	170	0W
Uelzen	43	53	0N	10	33 E
Ueno	106	34	45N	136	8 E
Ufa	69	54	45N	55	55 E
Uganda ■	132	2	0N	32	0 E
Uinta Mts.	163	40	45N	110	30W
Uithuizen	41	53	24N	6	41 E
Uji	106	34	53N	135	48 E
Ujjain	91	23	9N	75	43 E
Újpest	59	47	32N	19	6 E
Ujung Pandang	113	5	10S	119	20 E
Ukiah	172	39	10N	123	9W
Ukraine ■	68	49	0N	32	0 E
Ulaanbaatar	98	47	55N	106	53 E
Ulan Bator = Ulaanbaatar	98	47	55N	106	53 E
Ulan Ude	74	51	45N	107	40 E
Ulcinj	52	41	58N	19	10 E
Ulhasnagar	91	19	15N	73	10 E
Ulladulla	117	35	21S	150	29 E
Ullapool	32	57	54N	5	10W
Ullswater	28	54	35N	2	52W
Ulm	42	48	23N	10	0 E
Ulster □	34	54	35N	6	30W
Ulverston	28	54	13N	3	7W
Ulverstone	119	41	11S	146	11 E
Ulyanovsk = Simbirsk	68	54	20N	48	25 E
Ulyasutay	100	47	56N	97	28 E
Umbrella Mts.	123	45	35S	169	5 E
Umbria □	46	42	53N	12	30 E
Ume älv →	66	63	45N	20	20 E
Umeå	66	63	45N	20	20 E
Umm al Qaywayn	85	25	30N	55	35 E
Umm Lajj	82	25	0N	37	23 E
Umnak	142	53	20N	168	20W
Umpang	94	16	3N	98	54 E
Umtata	137	31	36S	28	49 E
Unalaska	142	53	40N	166	40W
Ungava B.	146	59	30N	67	30W
Ungava Pen.	146	60	0N	74	0W
União da Vitória	191	26	13S	51	5W
Unimak	142	55	0N	164	0W

Union City 169 36 25N 89 0W
Uniontown 164 39 54N 79 45W
United Arab Emirates ■ .... 85 23 50N 54 0 E
United Kingdom ■ 18 55 0N   3 0W
United States of America ■ . 139 37 0N 96 0W
Unity 152 52 30N 109 5W
Unnao .... 92 26 35N 80 30 E
Unst 30 60 50N   0 55W
Uozu .... 106 36 48N 137 24 E
Upata 185 8 1N 62 24W
Upper Austria =
  Oberösterreich □ .... 45 48 10N 14 0 E
Upper Hutt .... 123 41 8S 175 5 E
Upper Taimyr ~► .... 72 74 15N 99 48 E
Upper Volta = Burkina
  Faso ■ 130 12 0N   1 0W
Uppsala .... 60 59 53N 17 38 E
Uppsala län □ .... 60 60 0N 17 30 E
Ur .... 84 30 55N 46 25 E
Uracara 185 2 20S 57 50W
Urakawa .... 103 42 9N 142 47 E
Ural ~► .... 70 47 0N 51 48 E
Ural Mts. = Uralskie Gory .. 69 60 0N 59 0 E
Uralsk .... 70 51 20N 51 20 E
Uralskie Gory .... 69 60 0N 59 0 E
Uranium City 145 59 34N 108 37W
Urawa .... 107 35 50N 139 40 E
Urbana, Ill., U.S.A. 167 40 7N 88 12W
Urbana, Ohio, U.S.A. 167 40 9N 83 44W
Urbana, La 184 7 8N 66 56W
Urcos 187 13 40S 71 38W
Ures 174 29 26N 110 24W
Urfa = Sanliurfa .... 81 37 12N 38 50 E
Urgench .... 70 41 40N 60 41 E
Uribia 184 11 43N 72 16W
Urk .... 41 52 39N   5 36 E
Urmia = Orūmīyeh .... 81 37 40N 45 0 E
Urmia, L. = Orūmīyeh,
  Daryācheh-ye .... 81 37 50N 45 30 E
Uruapan 175 19 30N 102 0W
Uruçuí 188 7 20S 44 28W
Uruguaiana 191 29 50S 57 0W
Uruguay ■ 191 32 30S 56 30W
Uruguay ~► 191 34 12S 58 18W
Urumchi = Ürümqi ...... 100 43 45N 87 45 E
Ürümqi .... 100 43 45N 87 45 E
Urup, Os. .... 75 46 0N 151 0 E
Usa .... 108 33 31N 131 21 E
Uşak .... 80 38 43N 29 28 E
Usfan .... 82 21 58N 39 27 E
Ushant = Ouessant, Île d' .. 36 48 28N   5 6W
Ushibuka .... 108 32 11N 130 1 E
Ushuaia 192 54 50S 68 23W
Usk ~► 26 51 37N   2 56W
Üsküdar .... 80 41 0N 29 5 E
Usolye Sibirskoye .... 74 52 48N 103 40 E
Uspenskiy .... 71 48 41N 72 43 E
Ussuriysk .... 75 43 48N 131 59 E
Ust-Aldan = Batamay ..... 74 63 30N 129 15 E
Ust-Ilimsk .... 74 58 3N 102 39 E
Ust-Kamchatsk .... 73 56 10N 162 28 E
Ust-Kamenogorsk .... 71 50 0N 82 36 E
Ust Maya .... 75 60 30N 134 28 E
Ust Olenek .... 72 73 0N 119 48 E
Ust Port .... 69 69 40N 84 26 E
Ust Urt = Ustyurt, Plato ... 70 44 0N 55 0 E
Ust Vorkuta .... 69 67 24N 64 0 E
Ústí nad Labem .... 58 50 41N 14 3 E
Ustica .... 48 38 42N 13 10 E
Ustinov .... 69 56 51N 53 14 E
Ustyurt, Plato .... 70 44 0N 55 0 E
Usu .... 100 44 27N 84 40 E
Usuki .... 108 33 8N 131 49 E
Usumbura = Bujumbura ... 135 3 16S 29 18 E
Utah □ 163 39 30N 111 30W
Utah, L. 163 40 10N 111 58W
Uthai Thani .... 94 15 22N 100 3 E
Utica 164 43 5N 75 18W
Uto .... 108 32 41N 130 40 E
Utrecht .... 40 52 5N   5 8 E
Utrecht □ .... 40 52 6N   5 7 E

Utrera 50 37 12N   5 48W
Utsunomiya .... 107 36 30N 139 50 E
Uttar Pradesh □ .... 92 27 0N 80 0 E
Uttoxeter 28 52 53N   1 50W
Uusikaupunki .... 66 60 47N 21 25 E
Uvalde 161 29 15N 99 48W
Uvs Nuur .... 74 50 20N 92 30 E
Uwajima .... 109 33 10N 132 35 E
Uzbekistan ■ .... 70 41 30N 65 0 E

V

Vaal ~► .... 137 29 4S 23 38 E
Vaals .... 41 50 46N   6 1 E
Vaasa .... 67 63 6N 21 38 E
Vác .... 58 47 49N 19 10 E
Vach ~► .... 69 60 45N 76 45 E
Vadodara .... 91 22 20N 73 10 E
Vadsø .... 67 70 3N 29 50 E
Váh ~► .... 59 47 55N 18 0 E
Vaigach .... 69 70 10N 59 0 E
Val d'Or 151 48 7N 77 47W
Valahia .... 57 44 35N 25 0 E
Valcheta 192 40 40S 66 8W
Valdés, Pen. 192 42 30S 63 45W
Valdez 142 61 14N 146 17W
Valdivia 190 39 50S 73 14W
Valdosta 170 30 50N 83 20W
Valence .... 37 44 57N   4 54 E
Valencia, Spain 51 39 27N   0 23W
Valencia, Venezuela 184 10 11N 68 0W
Valencia □ 51 39 20N   0 40W
Valencia, Albufera de 51 39 20N   0 27W
Valencia, G. de .... 51 39 30N   0 20 E
Valencia de Alcántara 50 39 25N   7 14W
Valenciennes .... 38 50 20N   3 34 E
Valentia I. 35 51 54N 10 22W
Valera 184 9 19N 70 37W
Valkenswaard .... 41 51 21N   5 29 E
Valladolid, Mexico 177 20 41N 88 12W
Valladolid, Spain 50 41 38N   4 43W
Valle d'Aosta □ .... 46 45 45N   7 22 E
Valle de la Pascua 184 9 13N 66 0W
Valle de Santiago 177 20 23N 101 12W
Vallecas 50 40 23N   3 41W
Vallejo 172 38 12N 122 15W
Valletta .... 49 35 54N 14 30 E
Valley City 163 46 57N 98 0W
Valley View 155 40 39N 76 33W
Valona = Vlóra .... 52 40 32N 19 28 E
Valparaíso, Chile 190 33 2S 71 40W
Valparaíso, Mexico 175 22 46N 103 34W
Valsad .... 91 20 40N 72 58 E
Van .... 81 38 30N 43 20 E
Van, L. = Van Gölü .... 81 38 30N 43 0 E
Van Buren, Canada 148 47 10N 67 55W
Van Buren, U.S.A. 168 35 28N 94 18W
Van Gölü .... 81 38 30N 43 0 E
Van Wert 167 40 52N 84 31W
Vancouver, Canada 154 49 15N 123 10W
Vancouver, U.S.A. 171 45 44N 122 41W
Vancouver I. 154 49 50N 126 0W
Vandalia 166 38 57N 89 4W
Vanderhoof 154 54 0N 124 0W
Vänern .... 60 58 47N 13 30 E
Vanier 151 45 27N 75 40W
Vankarem .... 73 67 51N 175 50 E
Vännäs .... 66 63 58N 19 48 E
Vannes 36 47 40N   2 47W
Vanua Levu .... 122 16 33S 179 15 E
Vanuatu ■ .... 122 15 0S 168 0 E
Varanasi .... 92 25 22N 83 0 E
Varangerfjorden .... 67 70 3N 29 25 E
Varaždin .... 52 46 20N 16 20 E
Vardak □ .... 87 34 0N 68 0 E
Vardø .... 67 70 23N 31 5 E
Värmland .... 60 60 0N 13 30 E
Varna .... 53 43 13N 27 56 E

Vascongadas	50	42	50N	2	45W
Västerås	60	59	37N	16	38 E
Västmanlands län □	60	59	45N	16	20 E
Vatnajökull	64	64	30N	16	48W
Vatra-Dornei	57	47	22N	25	22 E
Vättern	60	58	25N	14	30 E
Vaygach, Ostrov	69	70	0N	60	0 E
Veendam	41	53	5N	6	52 E
Vega, La	180	19	20N	70	30W
Veghel	41	51	37N	5	32 E
Vegreville	155	53	30N	112	5W
Vela, La	184	11	27N	69	34W
Vellore	90	12	57N	79	10 E
Venado Tuerto	190	33	50S	62	0W
Vendôme	39	47	47N	1	3 E
Véneto □	47	45	40N	12	0 E
Venézia	47	45	27N	12	20 E
Venézia, Golfo di	47	45	20N	13	0 E
Venezuela ■	184	8	0N	65	0W
Venezuela, Golfo de	184	11	30N	71	0W
Vengurla	91	15	53N	73	45 E
Venice = Venézia	47	45	27N	12	20 E
Venlo	41	51	22N	6	11 E
Venraij	41	51	31N	6	0 E
Ventnor	24	50	35N	1	12W
Ventoux	37	44	10N	5	17 E
Ventura	173	34	16N	119	18W
Veracruz	177	19	10N	96	10W
Veracruz □	177	19	20N	96	40W
Verde, R. ~►	175	15	59N	97	50W
Verdun	37	49	12N	5	24 E
Vereeniging	137	26	38S	27	57 E
Verkhoyansk	72	67	35N	133	25 E
Verkhoyanskiy Khrebet	72	66	0N	129	0 E
Vermilion	152	53	20N	110	50W
Vermont □	164	43	40N	72	50W
Verneuil-sur-Avre	39	48	45N	0	55 E
Vernon, Canada	155	50	20N	119	15W
Vernon, France	39	49	5N	1	30 E
Vernon, U.S.A.	161	34	10N	99	20W
Verona	46	45	27N	11	0 E
Versailles	39	48	48N	2	8 E
Vert, C.	130	14	45N	17	30W
Verviers	42	50	37N	5	52 E
Vest-Agder fylke □	60	58	30N	7	15 E
Vesterålen	64	68	45N	15	0 E
Vestfjorden	64	67	55N	14	0 E
Vestfold fylke □	60	59	15N	10	0 E
Vestspitsbergen	13	78	40N	17	0 E
Vesuvio	49	40	50N	14	22 E
Vesuvius, Mt. = Vesuvio	49	40	50N	14	22 E
Viacha	187	16	39S	68	18W
Viborg	61	56	27N	9	23 E
Vicenza	47	45	32N	11	31 E
Vichy	37	46	9N	3	26 E
Vicksburg	169	32	22N	90	56W
Victor Harbor	119	35	30S	138	37 E
Victoria, Canada	154	48	30N	123	25W
Victoria, Chile	190	38	13S	72	20W
Victoria, U.S.A.	158	28	50N	97	0W
Victoria □	117	37	0S	144	0 E
Victoria, L.	132	1	0S	33	0 E
Victoria de las Tunas	178	20	58N	76	59W
Victoria Falls	137	17	58S	25	52 E
Victoria I.	145	71	0N	111	0W
Victoria Ld.	15	75	0S	160	0 E
Victoriaville	148	46	4N	71	56W
Vidalia	170	32	13N	82	25W
Vidin	53	43	59N	22	50 E
Viedma	192	40	50S	63	0W
Vienna = Wien	45	48	12N	16	22 E
Vienne	37	45	31N	4	53 E
Vienne ~►	36	47	13N	0	5 E
Vientiane	95	17	58N	102	36 E
Vientos, Paso de los	180	20	0N	74	0W
Vietnam ■	95	19	0N	106	0 E
Vigo	50	42	12N	8	41W
Vijayawada	92	16	31N	80	39 E
Vila Real de Santo António	50	37	10N	7	28W
Vilhelmina	66	64	35N	16	39 E
Vilhena	187	12	40S	60	5W
Villa Bella	187	10	25S	65	22W
Villa Bens = Tarfaya	126	27	55N	12	55W
Villa Cisneros = Dakhla	126	23	50N	15	53W
Villa Dolores	190	31	58S	65	15W
Villa María	190	32	20S	63	10W
Villa Montes	187	21	10S	63	30W
Villaguay	190	32	0S	59	0W
Villahermosa	177	17	59N	92	55W
Villanueva de la Serena	50	38	59N	5	50W
Villarreal	51	39	55N	0	3W
Villarrica	191	39	15S	72	15W
Villazón	187	22	0S	65	35W
Ville Platte	168	30	45N	92	17W
Villefranche-sur-Saône	37	45	59N	4	43 E
Villers-Cotterêts	39	49	15N	3	4 E
Vilnius	68	54	38N	25	19 E
Vilskutskogo, Proliv	72	78	0N	103	0 E
Vilyuy ~►	74	64	24N	126	26 E
Vilyuysk	74	63	40N	121	35 E
Viña del Mar	190	33	0S	71	30W
Vincennes	167	38	42N	87	29W
Vindhya Ra.	91	22	50N	77	0 E
Vinh	95	18	45N	105	38 E
Vinita	168	36	40N	95	12W
Vinkovci	52	45	19N	18	48 E
Vinnitsa	68	49	15N	28	30 E
Viramgam	91	23	5N	72	0 E
Virden	153	49	50N	100	56W
Vire	36	48	50N	0	53W
Vírgenes, C.	192	52	19S	68	21W
Virgin ~►	173	36	50N	114	10W
Virgin Is.	180	18	40N	64	30W
Virginia	156	47	30N	92	32W
Virginia □	165	37	45N	78	0W
Virginia Beach	165	36	54N	75	58W
Visalia	173	36	25N	119	18W
Visby	60	57	37N	18	18 E
Viscount Melville Sd.	145	74	10N	108	0W
Višegrad	52	43	47N	19	17 E
Vishakhapatnam	92	17	45N	83	20 E
Vistula = Wisła ~►	58	54	22N	18	55 E
Vitebsk	68	55	10N	30	15 E
Viti Levu	122	17	30S	177	30 E
Vitim ~►	74	59	26N	112	34 E
Vitória, Brazil	189	20	20S	40	22W
Vitoria, Spain	50	42	50N	2	41W
Vitória da Conquista	189	14	51S	40	51W
Vizianagaram	92	18	6N	83	30 E
Vlaardingen	40	51	55N	4	21 E
Vladikavkaz	70	43	0N	44	35 E
Vladimir	68	56	15N	40	30 E
Vladivostok	75	43	10N	131	53 E
Vlieland	40	53	16N	4	55 E
Vlissingen	40	51	26N	3	34 E
Vlóra	52	40	32N	19	28 E
Vltava ~►	59	50	21N	14	30 E
Vogelkop	113	1	25S	133	0 E
Vogels Berg	42	50	37N	9	30 E
Vohimena, Tanjon' i	137	25	36S	45	8 E
Voi	133	3	25S	38	32 E
Volendam	40	52	30N	5	4 E
Volga ~►	68	48	30N	46	0 E
Volga Hts. = Privolzhskaya Vozvyshennost	17	51	0N	46	0 E
Volgograd	68	48	40N	44	25 E
Vollenhove	41	52	40N	5	58 E
Vologda	68	59	10N	40	0 E
Vólos	54	39	24N	22	59 E
Volsk	68	52	5N	47	22 E
Volta ~►	130	5	46N	0	41 E
Volta, L.	130	7	30N	0	15 E
Volta Redonda	188	22	31S	44	5W
Voorburg	40	52	5N	4	24 E
Vopnafjörður	64	65	45N	14	40W
Voriai Sporádhes	55	39	15N	23	30 E
Voronezh	68	51	40N	39	10 E
Voroshilovgrad = Lugansk	68	48	38N	39	15 E
Vosges	37	48	20N	7	10 E
Vostochnyy Sayan	74	54	0N	96	0 E
Vrangelya, Ostrov	73	71	0N	180	0 E
Vranje	53	42	34N	21	54 E
Vratsa	53	43	13N	23	30 E

Vršac .... **52** 45 8N 21 18 E
Vught .... **40** 51 38N 5 20 E
Vulcan **155** 50 25N 113 15W
Vyatka .... **69** 58 35N 49 40 E
Vyborg .... **68** 60 43N 28 47 E
Vychegda ~► .... **69** 61 18N 46 36 E
Východné Beskydy .... **59** 49 30N 22 0 E

W

Wa **130** 10 7N 2 25W
Waal ~► .... **41** 51 59N 4 30 E
Waalwijk .... **40** 51 42N 5 4 E
Wabash **167** 40 48N 85 46W
Wabash ~► **167** 37 46N 88 2W
Wąbrzeźno .... **58** 53 16N 18 57 E
Waco **168** 31 33N 97 5W
Wād Medanī .... **129** 14 28N 33 30 E
Waddenzee .... **40** 53 6N 5 10 E
Waddington, Mt. **154** 51 23N 125 15W
Waddinxveen .... **40** 52 2N 4 40 E
Wadena **152** 51 57N 103 47W
Wadi Halfa .... **129** 21 53N 31 19 E
Wageningen .... **41** 51 58N 5 40 E
Wager Bay **146** 65 56N 90 49W
Wagga Wagga .... **117** 35 7S 147 24 E
Wagin .... **120** 33 17S 117 25 E
Waigeo .... **113** 0 20S 130 40 E
Waihi .... **122** 37 23S 175 52 E
Waikerie .... **119** 34 9S 140 0 E
Waikokopu .... **122** 39 3S 177 52 E
Waimate .... **123** 44 45S 171 3 E
Wainwright, Canada ... **152** 52 50N 110 50W
Wainwright, U.S.A. **142** 70 39N 160 1W
Waipara .... **123** 43 3S 172 46 E
Waipu .... **122** 35 59S 174 29 E
Waipukurau .... **122** 40 1S 176 33 E
Wairoa .... **122** 39 3S 177 25 E
Waitara .... **122** 38 59S 174 15 E
Wajima .... **105** 37 30N 137 0 E
Wajir .... **133** 1 42N 40 5 E
Wakasa-Wan .... **106** 35 40N 135 30 E
Wakatipu, L. .... **123** 45 5S 168 33 E
Wakayama .... **106** 34 15N 135 15 E
Wakefield, N.Z. .... **123** 41 24S 173 5 E
Wakefield, U.K. **28** 53 41N 1 31W
Wakkanai .... **103** 45 28N 141 35 E
Walbrzych .... **58** 50 45N 16 18 E
Walcha .... **116** 30 55S 151 31 E
Walcheren .... **40** 51 30N 3 35 E
Wales □ **26** 52 30N 3 30W
Walgett .... **116** 30 0S 148 5 E
Walkerton **151** 44 10N 81 10W
Walla Walla **171** 46 3N 118 25W
Wallaceburg **150** 42 34N 82 23W
Wallachia = Valahia .... **57** 44 35N 25 0 E
Wallangarra .... **116** 28 56S 151 58 E
Wallaroo .... **119** 33 56S 137 39 E
Wallasey **28** 53 26N 3 2W
Wallerawang .... **117** 33 25S 150 4 E
Wallis & Futuna **122** 13 18S 176 10W
Wallowa, Mts. **171** 45 20N 117 30W
Wallsend, Australia ... **117** 32 55S 151 40 E
Wallsend, U.K. **28** 54 59N 1 30W
Walney, Isle of **28** 54 5N 3 15W
Walpole .... **120** 34 58S 116 44 E
Walsall **24** 52 36N 1 59W
Walvis Bay .... **136** 23 0S 14 28 E
Wana .... **88** 32 20N 69 32 E
Wanaka L. .... **123** 44 33S 169 7 E
Wang Saphung .... **95** 17 18N 101 46 E
Wanganui .... **122** 39 56S 175 3 E
Wangaratta .... **117** 36 21S 146 19 E
Wanxian .... **99** 30 42N 108 20 E
Warabi .... **107** 35 49N 139 41 E
Warangal .... **91** 17 58N 79 35 E
Warburton .... **117** 37 47S 145 42 E
Wardha .... **91** 20 45N 78 39 E
Wardha ~► .... **91** 19 57N 79 11 E

Warialda .... **116** 29 29S 150 33 E
Warley **24** 52 30N 2 0W
Warner Mts. **172** 41 30N 120 20W
Waroona .... **120** 32 50S 115 58 E
Warracknabeal .... **119** 36 9S 142 26 E
Warragul .... **117** 38 10S 145 58 E
Warrego ~► .... **116** 30 24S 145 21 E
Warrego Ra. .... **121** 24 58S 146 0 E
Warren, Australia .... **116** 31 42S 147 51 E
Warren, Ark., U.S.A. **168** 33 35N 92 3W
Warren, Mich., U.S.A. ... **167** 42 31N 83 2W
Warren, Ohio, U.S.A. **164** 41 18N 80 52W
Warren, Pa., U.S.A. **164** 41 52N 79 10W
Warrenpoint **34** 54 7N 6 15W
Warrensburg **166** 38 45N 93 45W
Warrington, U.K. **28** 53 25N 2 38W
Warrington, U.S.A. **169** 30 22N 87 16W
Warrnambool .... **119** 38 25S 142 30 E
Warsaw = Warszawa ...... **58** 52 13N 21 0 E
Warszawa .... **58** 52 13N 21 0 E
Warta ~► .... **58** 52 35N 14 39 E
Warthe = Warta ~► ...... **58** 52 35N 14 39 E
Warwick, Australia .... **116** 28 10S 152 1 E
Warwick, U.K. **24** 52 17N 1 36W
Warwick, U.S.A. **164** 41 43N 71 25W
Warwick □ **24** 52 20N 1 30W
Wasatch Ra. **163** 40 30N 111 15W
Wasco **173** 35 37N 119 16W
Wash, The .... **29** 52 58N 0 20 E
Washim .... **91** 20 3N 77 0 E
Washington, D.C., U.S.A. ... **165** 38 52N 77 0W
Washington, Ind., U.S.A. ... **167** 38 40N 87 8W
Washington, Mo., U.S.A. ... **166** 38 35N 91 1W
Washington, Pa., U.S.A. ... **164** 40 10N 80 20W
Washington □ **171** 47 45N 120 30W
Wassenaar .... **40** 52 8N 4 24 E
Waterbury **164** 41 32N 73 0W
Waterford **35** 52 16N 7 8W
Waterford □ **35** 52 10N 7 40W
Waterloo, Canada **151** 43 30N 80 32W
Waterloo, U.S.A. **166** 42 27N 92 20W
Watertown, N.Y., U.S.A. **151** 43 58N 75 57W
Watertown, Wis., U.S.A. **167** 43 15N 88 45W
Waterville **148** 44 35N 69 40W
Watling I. = San Salvador .. **178** 24 0N 74 40W
Watrous **152** 51 40N 105 25W
Watson Lake **144** 60 6N 128 49W
Watsonville **173** 36 55N 121 49W
Watubela, Kepulauan ...... **113** 4 28S 131 35 E
Wauchope .... **116** 31 28S 152 45 E
Waukegan **167** 42 22N 87 54W
Waukesha **167** 43 0N 88 15W
Wausau **166** 44 57N 89 40W
Wauwatosa **167** 43 6N 87 59W
Waveney ~► .... **25** 52 24N 1 20 E
Wâw .... **129** 7 45N 28 1 E
Waxahachie **168** 32 22N 96 53W
Waycross **170** 31 12N 82 25W
Waynesboro, Pa., U.S.A. ... **164** 39 46N 77 32W
Waynesboro, Va., U.S.A. ... **165** 38 4N 78 57W
Waynesville **165** 35 31N 83 0W
Wazirabad .... **89** 32 30N 74 8 E
Weald, The .... **25** 51 7N 0 9 E
Webo = Nyaake **130** 4 52N 7 37W
Weddell Sea **14** 72 30S 40 0W
Wedderburn .... **117** 36 26S 143 33 E
Wee Waa .... **116** 30 11S 149 26 E
Weert .... **41** 51 15N 5 43 E
Weesp .... **40** 52 18N 5 2 E
Weifang .... **98** 36 47N 119 10 E
Weiser **171** 44 10N 117 0W
Welbourn Hill .... **118** 27 21S 134 6 E
Welch **165** 37 29N 81 36W
Welland **151** 43 0N 79 15W
Welland ~► **29** 52 43N 0 10W
Wellingborough **25** 52 18N 0 41W
Wellington, Australia .... **116** 32 35S 148 59 E
Wellington, N.Z. .... **123** 41 19S 174 46 E
Wellington, Shrops., U.K. .. **28** 52 42N 2 31W
Wellington, Somst., U.K. .. **27** 50 58N 3 13W
Wellington □ .... **123** 40 8S 175 36 E
Wellington, I. **192** 49 30S 75 0W

Wells, Norfolk, U.K. .... **29** 52 57N 0 51 E
Wells, Somst., U.K. **27** 51 12N 2 39W
Wells, U.S.A. **172** 41 8N 115 0W
Wellsville, N.Y., U.S.A. **164** 42 9N 77 53W
Wellsville, Ohio, U.S.A. **164** 40 36N 80 40W
Welshpool **26** 52 40N 3 9W
Wem **28** 52 52N 2 45W
Wenatchee **171** 47 30N 120 17W
Wenchow = Wenzhou ..... **99** 28 0N 120 38 E
Wensleydale **28** 54 18N 2 0W
Wentworth .... **119** 34 2S 141 54 E
Wenzhou .... **99** 28 0N 120 38 E
Werribee .... **117** 37 54S 144 40 E
Werris Creek .... **116** 31 18S 150 38 E
Weser ➤ .... **42** 53 33N 8 30 E
West Bengal □ .... **92** 23 0N 88 0 E
West Bromwich **24** 52 32N 2 1W
West Falkland **192** 51 40S 60 0W
West Frankfort **166** 37 56N 89 0W
West Glamorgan □ **27** 51 40N 3 55W
West Memphis **169** 35 5N 90 11W
West Midlands □ **24** 52 30N 1 55W
West Palm Beach **170** 26 44N 80 3W
West Schelde =
  Westerschelde ➤ ...... **40** 51 25N 3 25 E
West Siberian Plain ...... **76** 62 0N 75 0 E
West Sussex □ **25** 50 55N 0 30W
West Virginia □ **165** 39 0N 81 0W
West Yorkshire □ **28** 53 45N 1 40W
Western Australia □ ..... **114** 25 0S 118 0 E
Western Ghats .... **90** 14 0N 75 0 E
Western Isles □ **32** 57 30N 7 10W
Western Sahara ■ **126** 25 0N 13 0W
Western Samoa ■ **123** 14 0S 172 0W
Westerschelde ➤ .... **40** 51 25N 3 25 E
Westerwald .... **42** 50 39N 8 0 E
Westfriesche Eilanden .... **40** 53 20N 5 10 E
Westland □ .... **123** 43 33S 169 59 E
Westland Bight .... **123** 42 55S 170 5 E
Westlock **155** 54 9N 113 55W
Westmeath □ **34** 53 30N 7 30W
Westminster **164** 39 34N 77 1W
Weston **165** 39 3N 80 29W
Weston-super-Mare **27** 51 20N 2 59W
Westport .... **123** 41 46S 171 37 E
Westray **33** 59 18N 3 0W
Wetar .... **113** 7 30S 126 30 E
Wetaskiwin **155** 52 55N 113 24W
Wewaka **168** 35 10N 96 35W
Wexford **35** 52 20N 6 28W
Wexford □ **35** 52 20N 6 25W
Weyburn **152** 49 40N 103 50W
Weymouth **27** 50 36N 2 28W
Whakatane .... **122** 37 57S 177 1 E
Whale Cove **145** 62 11N 92 36W
Whalsay **30** 60 22N 1 0W
Whangamomona .... **122** 39 8S 174 44 E
Whangarei .... **122** 35 43S 174 21 E
Wharfe ➤ **29** 53 55N 1 30W
Wheeler Pk. **172** 38 57N 114 15W
Wheeling **164** 40 2N 80 41W
Whernside **28** 54 14N 2 24W
Whitby **29** 54 29N 0 37W
Whitchurch **28** 52 58N 2 42W
White ➤, Ark., U.S.A. **168** 33 53N 91 3W
White ➤, Ind., U.S.A. **167** 38 25N 87 45W
White ➤, S. Dak., U.S.A. . **163** 43 45N 99 30W
White Cliffs .... **118** 30 50S 143 10 E
White Mts. **157** 44 15N 71 15W
White Nile = Nîl el
  Abyad ➤ .... **129** 15 38N 32 31 E
White Russia = Belorussia ■ **68** 53 30N 27 0 E
White Sea = Beloye More .. **69** 66 30N 38 0 E
Whitecliffs .... **123** 43 26S 171 55 E
Whitehaven **28** 54 33N 3 35W
Whitehorse **144** 60 43N 135 3W
Whitney, Mt. **173** 36 35N 118 14W
Whitstable .... **25** 51 21N 1 2 E
Whitsunday I. .... **121** 20 15S 149 4 E
Whittier **142** 60 46N 148 48W
Whyalla .... **118** 33 2S 137 30 E
Wichita **158** 37 40N 97 20W

Wichita Falls **161** 33 57N 98 30W
Wick **33** 58 26N 3 5W
Wickepin .... **120** 32 50S 117 30 E
Wicklow **35** 53 0N 6 2W
Wicklow □ **35** 52 59N 6 25W
Wicklow Mts. **35** 53 0N 6 4W
Widnes **28** 53 22N 2 44W
Wieluń .... **58** 51 15N 18 34 E
Wien .... **45** 48 12N 16 22 E
Wiesbaden .... **42** 50 7N 8 17 E
Wigan **28** 53 33N 2 38W
Wight, I. of **25** 50 40N 1 20W
Wigtown **31** 54 52N 4 27W
Wigtown B. **31** 54 46N 4 15W
Wilcannia .... **118** 31 30S 143 26 E
Wildwood **164** 38 59N 74 46W
Wilhelmshaven .... **42** 53 30N 8 9 E
Wilkes Barre **164** 41 15N 75 52W
Wilkes Sub-Glacial Basin .. **15** 75 0S 130 0 E
Wilkie **152** 52 27N 108 42W
Willamina **171** 45 9N 123 32W
Willemstad **181** 12 5N 69 0W
Williams L. **154** 51 48N 90 45W
Williamsburg **165** 37 17N 76 44W
Williamson **165** 37 46N 82 17W
Williamsport **164** 41 18N 77 1W
Williamstown .... **117** 37 51S 144 52 E
Williston **163** 48 10N 103 35W
Willits **172** 39 28N 123 17W
Willmar **156** 45 5N 95 0W
Wilmette **167** 42 6N 87 44W
Wilmington, Del., U.S.A. ... **164** 39 45N 75 32W
Wilmington, N.C., U.S.A. ... **165** 34 14N 77 54W
Wilson **165** 35 44N 77 54W
Wilsons Promontory ...... **117** 38 55S 146 25 E
Wilton **24** 51 5N 1 52W
Wiltshire □ **24** 51 20N 2 0W
Wiluna .... **120** 26 36S 120 14 E
Wimereux .... **38** 50 45N 1 37 E
Winchester, U.K. **25** 51 4N 1 19W
Winchester, Ind., U.S.A. ... **167** 40 10N 84 56W
Winchester, Ky., U.S.A. ... **165** 38 0N 84 8W
Winchester, Va., U.S.A. ... **164** 39 14N 78 8W
Wind River Range **163** 43 0N 109 30W
Windermere **28** 54 24N 2 56W
Windermere, L. **28** 54 20N 2 57W
Windhoek .... **136** 22 35S 17 4 E
Windsor, Australia .... **117** 33 37S 150 50 E
Windsor, Nfld., Canada ... **149** 48 57N 55 40W
Windsor, Ont., Canada ... **150** 42 18N 83 0W
Windsor, U.K. **25** 51 28N 0 36W
Windward Is. **181** 13 0N 63 0W
Windward Passage =
  Vientos, Paso de los ... **180** 20 0N 74 0W
Winisk ➤ **140** 55 17N 85 5W
Winkler **153** 49 10N 97 56W
Winnemucca **172** 41 0N 117 45W
Winnfield **168** 31 57N 92 38W
Winnipeg **153** 49 54N 97 9W
Winnipeg, L. **153** 52 0N 97 0W
Winnipegosis L. **153** 52 30N 100 0W
Winona **166** 44 2N 91 39W
Winooski **151** 44 31N 73 11W
Winschoten .... **41** 53 9N 7 3 E
Winslow **161** 35 2N 110 41W
Winston-Salem **165** 36 7N 80 15W
Winter Haven **170** 28 0N 81 42W
Winter Park **170** 28 34N 81 19W
Winterswijk .... **41** 51 58N 6 43 E
Winterthur .... **44** 47 30N 8 44 E
Wirral **28** 53 25N 3 0W
Wisbech .... **29** 52 39N 0 10 E
Wisconsin □ **166** 44 30N 90 0W
Wisconsin ➤ **166** 43 0N 91 15W
Wisconsin Rapids **166** 44 25N 89 50W
Wishaw **31** 55 46N 3 55W
Wisła ➤ .... **58** 54 22N 18 55 E
Witham ➤ **29** 53 3N 0 8W
Withernsea .... **29** 53 43N 0 2 E
Witney **24** 51 47N 1 29W
Włocławek .... **58** 52 40N 19 3 E
Wodonga .... **117** 36 5S 146 50 E

Wokam	113	5	45S	134 28 E
Woking	25	51	18N	0 33W
Wolin	58	53	50N	14 37 E
Wollaston L.	145	58	7N	103 10W
Wollaston Pen.	145	69	30N	115 0W
Wollongong	117	34	25S	150 54 E
Wolverhampton	24	52	35N	2 6W
Wondai	116	26	20S	151 49 E
Wŏnsan	98	39	11N	127 27 E
Wonthaggi	117	38	37S	145 37 E
Woodburn	116	29	6S	153 23 E
Woodenbong	116	28	24S	152 39 E
Woodend	117	37	20S	144 33 E
Woodland	172	38	40N	121 50W
Woods, L. of the	153	49	15N	94 45W
Woodstock, N.B., Canada	148	46	11N	67 37W
Woodstock, Ont., Canada	151	43	10N	80 45W
Woolgoolga	116	30	6S	153 11 E
Woomera	118	31	30S	137 10 E
Woonsocket	164	42	0N	71 30W
Wooroloo	120	31	48S	116 18 E
Worcester, U.K.	24	52	12N	2 12W
Worcester, U.S.A.	164	42	14N	71 49W
Workington	28	54	39N	3 34W
Worksop	29	53	19N	1 9W
Wormerveer	40	52	30N	4 46 E
Worms	42	49	37N	8 21 E
Worthing	25	50	49N	0 21W
Worthington	166	43	35N	95 36W
Wou-han = Wuhan	99	30	31N	114 18 E
Woy Woy	117	33	30S	151 19 E
Wrangel I.	138	71	0N	180 0 E
Wrangell	143	56	30N	132 25W
Wrangell Mts.	142	61	40N	143 30W
Wrath, C.	32	58	38N	5 0W
Wrekin, The	28	52	41N	2 35W
Wrexham	26	53	5N	3 0W
Wrigley	144	63	16N	123 37W
Wrocław	58	51	5N	17 5 E
Września	58	52	21N	17 36 E
Wu Jiang →	99	29	40N	107 20 E
Wubin	120	30	6S	116 37 E
Wuhan	99	30	31N	114 18 E
Wuhsi = Wuxi	99	31	33N	120 18 E
Wuhu	99	31	22N	118 21 E
Wulumuchi = Ürümqi	100	43	45N	87 45 E
Wuppertal	42	51	15N	7 8 E
Würzburg	42	49	46N	9 55 E
Wutongqiao	99	29	22N	103 50 E
Wuxi	99	31	33N	120 18 E
Wuzhong	98	38	2N	106 12 E
Wuzhou	99	23	30N	111 18 E
Wyalkatchem	120	31	8S	117 22 E
Wyandotte	167	42	14N	83 13W
Wycheproof	119	36	0S	143 17 E
Wye →	27	51	36N	2 40W
Wyndham	114	15	33S	128 3 E
Wynnum	116	27	27S	153 9 E
Wynyard	152	51	45N	104 10W
Wyoming □	163	42	48N	109 0W
Wytheville	165	37	0N	81 3W

X

Xánthi	55	41	10N	24 58 E
Xapuri	187	10	35S	68 35W
Xenia	167	39	42N	83 57W
Xiamen	99	24	25N	118 4 E
Xi'an	99	34	15N	109 0 E
Xiangfan	99	32	2N	112 8 E
Xiangtan	99	27	51N	112 54 E
Xiao Hinggan Ling	98	49	0N	127 0 E
Xigazê	101	29	5N	88 45 E
Xingtai	98	37	3N	114 32 E
Xingu →	188	1	30S	51 53W
Xining	98	36	34N	101 40 E
Xinjiang Uygur Zizhiqu □ ..	100	42	0N	86 0 E
Xinxiang	99	35	18N	113 50 E

Xinyang	99	32	6N	114 3 E
Xinzhu	99	24	49N	120 57 E
Xique-Xique	188	10	50S	42 40W
Xizang □	101	32	0N	88 0 E
Xuanhua	98	40	40N	115 2 E
Xuchang	99	34	2N	113 48 E
Xuzhou	99	34	18N	117 10 E

Y

Ya'an	99	29	58N	103 5 E
Yablonovy Khrebet	74	53	0N	114 0 E
Yablonovy Ra. = Yablonovy Khrebet	74	53	0N	114 0 E
Yacuiba	187	22	0S	63 43W
Yaizu	107	34	52N	138 20 E
Yakima	171	46	42N	120 30W
Yaku-Jima	104	30	20N	130 30 E
Yakut Rep. □	72	62	0N	130 0 E
Yakutat	143	59	29N	139 44W
Yakutsk	75	62	5N	129 50 E
Yalgoo	120	28	16S	116 39 E
Yalinga	129	6	33N	23 10 E
Yamaga	108	33	1N	130 41 E
Yamagata	103	38	15N	140 15 E
Yamaguchi	108	34	10N	131 32 E
Yamal, Poluostrov	69	71	0N	70 0 E
Yamato	107	35	27N	139 25 E
Yamatotakada	106	34	31N	135 45 E
Yamazaki	109	35	0N	134 32 E
Yamba	116	29	26S	153 23 E
Yambol	53	42	30N	26 36 E
Yamdena	113	7	45S	131 20 E
Yame	108	33	13N	130 35 E
Yamma-Yamma, L.	118	26	16S	141 20 E
Yampa →	163	40	37N	108 59W
Yamuna →	92	25	30N	81 53 E
Yamzho Yumco	101	28	48N	90 35 E
Yana →	72	71	30N	136 0 E
Yanagawa	108	33	10N	130 24 E
Yanai	109	33	58N	132 7 E
Yanco	117	34	38S	146 27 E
Yangch'ü = Taiyuan	98	37	52N	112 33 E
Yangquan	98	37	58N	113 31 E
Yangtze Kiang = Chang Jiang →	99	31	48N	121 10 E
Yanji	98	42	59N	129 30 E
Yantai	98	37	34N	121 22 E
Yao	106	34	32N	135 36 E
Yaoundé	131	3	50N	11 35 E
Yaqui →	174	27	37N	110 39W
Yare →	25	52	36N	1 28 E
Yarensk	69	61	10N	49 8 E
Yarkand = Shache	100	38	20N	77 10 E
Yarmouth	148	43	50N	66 7W
Yaroslavl	68	57	35N	39 55 E
Yarram	117	38	29S	146 9 E
Yashiro-Jima	109	33	55N	132 15 E
Yass	117	34	49S	148 54 E
Yasugi	109	35	26N	133 15 E
Yatsushiro	108	32	30N	130 40 E
Yavari →	186	4	21S	70 2W
Yavatmal	91	20	20N	78 15 E
Yawatahama	109	33	27N	132 24 E
Yazd	85	31	55N	54 27 E
Yazoo →	169	32	35N	90 50W
Yazoo City	169	32	48N	90 28W
Ye Xian	98	37	8N	119 57 E
Yegros	191	26	20S	56 25W
Yekaterinburg	69	56	50N	60 30 E
Yelizavetgrad	68	48	35N	32 20 E
Yell	30	60	35N	1 5W
Yellow Sea	99	35	0N	123 0 E
Yellowhead P.	155	52	53N	118 25W
Yellowknife	145	62	27N	114 29W
Yellowstone →	163	47	58N	103 59W
Yellowstone National Park	163	44	35N	110 0W
Yemen ■	82	15	0N	44 0 E
Yenisey →	69	71	50N	82 40 E
Yeniseyskiy Zaliv	69	72	20N	81 0 E

Yeo → **27** 51 10N 3 0W
Yeola .... **91** 20 0N 74 30 E
Yeovil **27** 50 57N 2 38W
Yeppoon .... **121** 23 5S 150 47 E
Yerevan .... **70** 40 10N 44 31 E
Yes Tor **27** 50 41N 3 59W
Yetman .... **116** 28 56S 150 48 E
Yezd = Yazd .... **85** 31 55N 54 27 E
Yiannitsa .... **54** 40 46N 22 24 E
Yibin .... **99** 28 45N 104 32 E
Yichang .... **99** 30 40N 111 20 E
Yichun .... **98** 47 44N 128 52 E
Yilan .... **99** 24 51N 121 44 E
Yinchuan .... **98** 38 30N 106 15 E
Yingkou .... **98** 40 37N 122 18 E
Yingtan .... **99** 28 12N 117 0 E
Yining .... **100** 43 58N 81 10 E
Yithion .... **54** 36 46N 22 34 E
Yiyang .... **99** 28 45N 112 16 E
Yogyakarta .... **111** 7 49S 110 22 E
Yōkaichiba .... **107** 35 42N 140 33 E
Yokkaichi .... **106** 35 0N 136 38 E
Yokohama .... **107** 35 27N 139 28 E
Yokosuka .... **107** 35 20N 139 40 E
Yokote .... **103** 39 20N 140 30 E
Yonago .... **109** 35 25N 133 19 E
Yoneshiro → .... **103** 40 15N 140 15 E
Yonezawa .... **103** 37 57N 140 4 E
Yongji .... **99** 34 52N 110 28 E
Yonkers **164** 40 57N 73 51W
York, Australia .... **120** 31 52S 116 47 E
York, U.K. **29** 53 58N 1 7W
York, U.S.A. **164** 39 57N 76 43W
Yorke Pen. .... **119** 34 50S 137 40 E
Yorkshire Wolds **29** 54 0N 0 30W
Yorkton **152** 51 11N 102 28W
Yosemite National Park **172** 38 0N 119 30W
Youghal **35** 51 58N 7 51W
Young .... **117** 34 19S 148 18 E
Younghusband Pen. .... **119** 36 0S 139 25 E
Youngstown **164** 41 7N 80 41W
Yuba City **172** 39 12N 121 37W
Yūbari .... **103** 43 4N 141 59 E
Yūbetsu .... **103** 43 13N 144 5 E
Yucatán □ **177** 20 50N 89 0W
Yucatán, Canal de **178** 22 0N 86 30W
Yucatan Str. = Yucatán,
   Canal de **178** 22 0N 86 30W
Yuci .... **98** 37 42N 112 46 E
Yugoslavia ■ .... **52** 44 0N 21 0 E
Yukon → **142** 65 30N 150 0W
Yukon Territory □ **144** 63 0N 135 0W
Yuma **173** 32 45N 114 37W
Yunnan □ .... **101** 25 0N 102 30 E
Yuribei .... **69** 71 8N 76 58 E
Yurimaguas **186** 5 55S 76 7W
Yushu .... **101** 33 5N 96 55 E
Yuzhno-Sakhalinsk .... **75** 46 58N 142 45 E
Yvetot .... **38** 49 37N 0 44 E

Z

Zaandam .... **40** 52 26N 4 49 E
Zabaykalskiy .... **74** 49 40N 117 25 E
Zabid .... **82** 14 0N 43 10 E
Zābol .... **85** 31 0N 61 32 E
Zābol □ .... **87** 32 0N 67 0 E
Zabrze .... **58** 50 18N 18 50 E
Zacapa **177** 14 59N 89 31W
Zacatecas **175** 22 47N 102 35W
Zacatecas □ **175** 23 0N 103 0W
Zacatecoluca **177** 13 29N 88 51W
Zadar .... **52** 44 8N 15 14 E
Zadetkyi Kyun .... **94** 10 0N 98 25 E
Zagreb .... **52** 45 50N 16 0 E
Zāhedān .... **86** 29 30N 60 50 E
Zahlah .... **80** 33 52N 35 50 E
Zaïre ■ .... **134** 3 0S 23 0 E
Zaïre → .... **134** 6 4S 12 24 E
Zákinthos .... **54** 37 47N 20 57 E

Zambeze → .... **135** 18 55S 36 4 E
Zambezi = Zambeze → .. **135** 18 55S 36 4 E
Zambia ■ .... **135** 15 0S 28 0 E
Zamboanga .... **112** 6 59N 122 3 E
Zamora, Mexico **175** 20 0N 102 21W
Zamora, Spain **50** 41 30N 5 45W
Zandvoort .... **40** 52 22N 4 32 E
Zanesville **167** 39 56N 82 2W
Zanjan .... **81** 36 40N 48 35 E
Zante = Zákinthos ...... **54** 37 47N 20 57 E
Zanzibar .... **135** 6 12S 39 12 E
Zaouiet El-Kala = Bordj Omar
   Driss .... **127** 28 10N 6 40 E
Zaouiet Reggane .... **127** 26 32N 0 3 E
Zapadnaya Dvina → ...... **68** 57 4N 24 3 E
Západné Beskydy .... **59** 49 30N 19 0 E
Zapala **190** 39 0S 70 5W
Zaporozhye .... **68** 47 50N 35 10 E
Zaragoza, Mexico **174** 28 29N 100 55W
Zaragoza, Spain **51** 41 39N 0 53W
Zaranj .... **87** 30 55N 61 55 E
Zaria .... **131** 11 0N 7 40 E
Zaruma **184** 3 40S 79 38W
Zaskar Mountains .... **89** 33 15N 77 30 E
Zavitinsk .... **75** 50 10N 129 20 E
Zaysan, Oz. .... **71** 48 0N 83 0 E
Zayü .... **101** 28 48N 97 27 E
Zduńska Wola .... **58** 51 37N 18 59 E
Zeebrugge .... **42** 51 19N 3 12 E
Zeeland □ .... **40** 51 30N 3 50 E
Zeila .... **133** 11 21N 43 30 E
Zeist .... **40** 52 5N 5 15 E
Zemlya Frantsa Iosifa ..... **13** 81 0N 55 0 E
Zentsūji .... **109** 34 14N 133 47 E
Zeya .... **75** 53 48N 127 14 E
Zêzere → **50** 39 28N 8 20W
Zhanghua .... **99** 24 6N 120 29 E
Zhangjiakou .... **98** 40 48N 114 55 E
Zhangzhou .... **99** 24 30N 117 35 E
Zhanjiang .... **99** 21 15N 110 20 E
Zhdanov = Mariupol ..... **68** 47 5N 37 31 E
Zhejiang □ .... **99** 29 0N 120 0 E
Zhengzhou .... **99** 34 45N 113 34 E
Zhenjiang .... **99** 32 11N 119 26 E
Zhenyuan .... **99** 27 4N 108 21 E
Zhijiang .... **99** 27 27N 109 42 E
Zhitomir .... **68** 50 20N 28 40 E
Zhumadian .... **99** 32 59N 114 2 E
Zhupanovo .... **73** 53 40N 159 52 E
Zhuzhou .... **99** 27 49N 113 12 E
Zibo .... **98** 36 47N 118 3 E
Zielona Góra .... **58** 51 57N 15 31 E
Zierikzee .... **40** 51 40N 3 55 E
Zigong .... **99** 29 15N 104 48 E
Zile .... **80** 40 15N 35 52 E
Žilina .... **59** 49 12N 18 42 E
Zimbabwe .... **137** 20 16S 30 54 E
Zimbabwe ■ .... **137** 20 0S 30 0 E
Zinder .... **131** 13 48N 9 0 E
Zipaquirá **184** 5 0N 74 0W
Zitácuaro **175** 19 24N 100 22W
Zlatograd .... **53** 41 22N 25 7 E
Zlatoust .... **69** 55 10N 59 40 E
Zlin .... **59** 49 14N 17 40 E
Zomba .... **137** 15 22S 35 19 E
Zonguldak .... **80** 41 28N 31 50 E
Zorritos **186** 3 43S 80 40W
Zoutkamp .... **41** 53 20N 6 18 E
Zrenjanin .... **52** 45 22N 20 23 E
Zufar .... **83** 17 40N 54 0 E
Zug .... **44** 47 10N 8 31 E
Zuid-Holland □ .... **40** 52 0N 4 35 E
Zuidhorn .... **41** 53 15N 6 23 E
Zungeru .... **131** 9 48N 6 8 E
Zunyi .... **99** 27 42N 106 53 E
Zürich .... **44** 47 22N 8 32 E
Zutphen .... **41** 52 9N 6 12 E
Zuwārah .... **127** 32 58N 12 1 E
Zvolen .... **59** 48 33N 19 10 E
Zwickau .... **43** 50 43N 12 30 E
Zwolle .... **41** 52 31N 6 6 E
Zyryanovsk .... **71** 49 43N 84 20 E